Modelling Individual Choice

Modelling Individual Choice

The Econometrics of Corners, Kinks and Holes

Stephen Pudney

Basil Blackwell

First published 1989

Basil Blackwell Ltd
108 Cowley Road, Oxford, OX4 1JF, UK

Basil Blackwell Inc.
432 Park Avenue South, Suite 1503
New York, NY 10016, USA

British Library Cataloguing in Publication Data

Pudney, Stephen
Modelling individual choice: the
econometrics of corners, kinks and
holes.
1. Consumer behaviour. Economic models
I. Title
339.4′7′0724

ISBN 0-631-14589-3

Library of Congress Cataloging in Publication Data

Pudney, Stephen.
Modelling individual choice: the econometrics of corners, kinks, and holes/Stephen Pudney.
p. cm.
Includes bibliographical references and index.
ISBN 0-631-14589-3
1. Demand (Economic theory)—Econometric models. 2. Labour supply-Econometric models. I. Title.
HB801.P78 1989
338.5′212′0724—dc19

88-23356
CIP

Typeset in 10 on 12pt Times
by Colset Private Limited, Singapore
Printed in Great Britain by T.J. Press (Padstow) Ltd, Padstow, Cornwall.

Contents

Figures

A note on notation

Throughout this book, I have tried to use consistent notation as far as possible. With minor necessary exceptions, the following symbols retain their meanings in all chapters.

$C(.)$	the cost function
d	a dummy variable
$D(.)$	the distance function
$f(.)$, $F(.)$	the probability density function (p.d.f.) (or discrete frequency function) and cumulative distribution function (c.d.f.) of an observation in the sample
$g(.)$, $G(.)$	the p.d.f. and c.d.f. of a random variable in the population
$H(.)$	the indirect utility function
N	the sample size; individual observations are identified by a subscript n
$\mathbf{p}$	a vector of prices
u	utility
$V(.)$	the direct utility function
w	a wage rate
$\mathbf{x}$	a vector of quantities characterizing one member of the set of possible choices; $\tilde{\mathbf{x}}$ represents the individual's optimal choice; $\mathbf{x}$ is usually the dependent variable of a statistical model

y	the resource level constraining the individual's choice (for instance, income)
$\mathbf{z}$	a vector containing observable attributes of the individual (such as age, sex, educational attainment etc.)
β	a vector of (unobserved) variables that determine the individual's tastes
ϵ, v, ν	unobservable random disturbance terms
ζ, ξ	vectors of explanatory variables
θ	the full set of unknown parameters requiring estimation
$\varphi(.)$	the p.d.f. of the $N(0,1)$ distribution: $\varphi(s) = (2\pi)^{-1/2} \exp(-s^2/2)$
$\Phi(.)$	the c.d.f. of the $N(0,1)$ distribution: $\Phi(s)$ is the integral of $\varphi(.)$ over $(-\infty, s)$
$\varphi(.;\mu,\Sigma)$	the p.d.f. of the multivariate $N(\mu,\Sigma)$ distribution: $\varphi(s;\mu,\Sigma) = (2\pi)^{-q/2}\lvert\Sigma\rvert^{-1/2} \exp[-\frac{1}{2}(s-\mu)'\Sigma^{-1}(s-\mu)]$
$\Phi(.;\mu,\Sigma)$	the c.d.f. of the $N(\mu,\Sigma)$ distribution: $\Phi(s;\mu,\Sigma)$ is $\varphi(.;\mu,\Sigma)$ integrated over $(-\infty,s_1)\times(-\infty,s_2)\times\ldots\times(-\infty,s_q)$
LCN, UCN	shorthand for the lower and upper censored normal distributions: e.g. LCN(μ,σ^2,c) is the $N(\mu,\sigma^2)$ distribution censored from below at the point c
LTN, UTN	shorthand for the lower and upper truncated normal distributions: e.g. LTN(μ,σ^2,c) is the $N(\mu,\sigma^2)$ distribution truncated from below at c
$\succ, \succcurlyeq, \sim$	these represent preference relations: respectively – strictly preferred to, preferred or indifferent to, and indifferent between

Introduction

The econometrics of individual behaviour

Nevertheless, to speak paradoxically, the existence of insignificant people has very important consequences in the world. It can be shown to affect the price of bread and the rate of wages, to call forth many evil tempers from the selfish, and many heroisms from the sympathetic, and, in other ways, to play no small part in the tragedy of life.

George Eliot

I.1 The microeconometric approach

There are no universally accepted 'economic laws'. No-one has ever discovered an empirical relationship in economics that displays the apparent fit and stability of the laws of Newtonian mechanics. But not only has applied research in economics failed to establish any unassailable conclusions, there is not even any agreement on the best way to conduct such research: no agreed apparatus of investigation to compare with the experimental methods available to researchers in most of the physical sciences. There remains no 'right way' to do applied economics.

For most of the period since the 1920s, during which the development of modern econometrics took place, applied econometric research concentrated very heavily on macroeconomic analysis, using the time-series data provided by government statistical offices. Until recently, the analysis of data relating to individual decision-makers played only a minor role in economics, and applied work in most areas of pure microeconomics, such as industrial economics, income distribution, taxation and poverty, were predominantly non-econometric.

All this has now changed. In the last 15 years or so there has been an enormous growth in the use of micro data and in the use of econometric techniques for the study of microeconomic problems. The economics and econometrics journals are now full of applied and theoretical work in these fields, and the amount of literature is expanding very rapidly. This is partly a reaction to the availability of new forms of survey data, particularly the surveys associated with the income support experiments conducted in the USA in the 1970s, but there has also been a new interest among econometricians in microeconomic policy issues, and, among microeconomists, in the use of formal statistical methods. There now seems to be an acceptance that econometric analysis of micro data is often the best way to investigate a problem in applied economics.

The microeconometric approach has many important advantages over traditional macroeconometric modelling. It is often the natural, and even the only feasible, approach to take: if we are interested in the behaviour or welfare of very narrowly defined groups of people, there is frequently no alternative aggregate source of data available. For instance, aggregate statistics on the income and characteristics of the poor, the aged or those living in particular areas of the country are incomplete and often unreliable, and there is simply no alternative to individual-based analysis. If we are interested in the effects of government policy on the distribution of economic welfare in the population, there is no way of examining this, except in the crudest terms, using traditional time-series macroeconometrics.

Microeconometrics is also easier to understand: our unit of analysis is the individual decision-maker, and, being individuals ourselves, we find it easier to produce insights into the behaviour of these units than we do into the behaviour of economy-wide aggregates. Also, by working with data at the individual level, we avoid (for the most part, at least) the aggregation problems faced by the macroeconomist. The typical aggregative study is cast in terms of a 'representative individual', whose behaviour is assumed to conform to some microeconomic theory. However, it is known in most cases that perfect aggregation from a micro model to an analogous macro model is impossible without stringent assumptions about the cross-section distribution of the explanatory variables (see, for instance, Green, 1961). This introduces into the analysis aggregation errors whose consequences tend to be rather obscure.

The econometrician working with micro data has a further advantage: he or she usually has much more insight into the process by which the data are collected than does the macroeconometrician. Although observations on micro quantities are not necessarily any more accurate than their macro counterparts (and sometimes much less so), the design of the survey that yields those observations is usually well known, and its defects are easy to detect; thus the microeconometrician stands some chance of being able to understand and compensate for the effects of measurement errors. In contrast, macroeconomic statistics are usually constructed by government bodies who make compromises between conflicting data sources, without making public the detailed methods used to generate their data. In macroeconometric work, it is sometimes hard to escape the idea that one is modelling the behaviour of the government statistical office as much as the behaviour of individuals in the economy.

Against these, of course, must be set some disadvantages. Individual behaviour appears to be very random, and even the most successful cross-section models seldom 'explain' more than 30 per cent of the variability in the sample. This poor 'signal to noise' ratio offsets the beneficial effects of the very large sample sizes that are available, and one generally finds that cross-section estimates have no better statistical precision than comparable aggregate time-series estimates. The existence of all this randomness also implies that stochastic specification - the way we build randomness into our models - can be very important.

Orthodox microeconomic analysis is based on the very strong assumption that the economy is made up of completely independent individuals, each operating in its own interests without any direct influence from the activities of others. This is another potential weakness. Although we can allow for some interdependence of behaviour by defining individuals as small groups of people (the household and the firm, for instance), it is almost impossible to cope with the existence of phenomena such as altruism, imitative behaviour or other forms of externality within the framework of conventional microeconometrics except by the use of crude devices such as dummy variables reflecting differences in behaviour between the social classes. This is in sharp contrast with much of sociology, where social interdependence is often stressed very heavily.

A major problem associated with micro data is the need to use rather complicated statistical models to cope with the awkward features that such data usually display. It is these awkward features that are the subject matter of this book, and that motivate its title. Nearly every set of survey data provides examples. When we work with detailed data on demand, we usually observe some non-consumers of the good - people operating at a corner in the set of available consumption quantities; in the analysis of labour supply, we know that when someone's income exceeds a tax threshold his or her marginal tax rate increases, inducing a kink in the work–income tradeoff; when choosing which brand of a good to buy, each consumer is faced with a few discrete varieties, and the observed relation between price and quality is discontinuous, displaying gaps or holes. What these examples have in common is some discreteness in the behaviour we are trying to explain: the distribution of our dependent variables is not completely continuous. Except in very special cases, traditional regression-based econometric techniques are inappropriate to problems in which the dependent variables are discrete, and so a new body of econometric theory has had to be developed to deal with these difficulties.

However, this complexity cannot really be regarded as a particular disadvantage of microeconometrics. The macroeconomist is able to ignore such complications only because the process of aggregation conceals them behind an apparent continuity of variation, not because they are absent from macro data. One can argue that the use of micro data allows us to study real behaviour, rather than an over-simplified macro analogue, and that statistical complexity is a small price to pay for this opportunity.

I.2 About this book

This book is not intended as a textbook of microeconometric theory. Excellent accounts of the statistical theory used by econometricians in this field already exist, notably those by Maddala (1983) and Amemiya (1986), and I have avoided any very detailed or rigorous discussion of statistical inference or computational methods. Instead, I have tried to approach the subject from the viewpoint of the economic theorist who is interested in applying microeconomic models to direct observations of individual behaviour. I have resisted the temptation to survey the applied literature, because this is already enormous and is growing so fast that any account of it would be seriously out of date by the time it were published. Instead, the book is intended to occupy the middle ground between applied and theoretical econometrics; my intention is to discuss the various modelling approaches that an economist can adopt in implementing economic theories at this level. This is done with the aid of simple illustrative models that are often far removed from those to be found in the applied literature, but which serve to motivate the econometric approach.

However, even avoiding a full discussion of statistical theory and empirical findings, this is an ambitious undertaking, and I have further limited the coverage of the book quite severely. For the most part, it deals only with formal models based on the economic theory of rational choice. In part, this reflects my suspicion that econometric research will only ever generate conclusive results in cases where it has a secure foundation in economic theory; and the theory of choice is, after all, the fundamental idea of economics. In part, it simply reflects my own interests, and a desire to give the book a continuous thread linking otherwise disparate econometric techniques. The book can be read almost as a technical appendix to a text on choice theory, such as that by Deaton and Muellbauer (1980a).

I have restricted attention almost exclusively to static choice models under certainty, chiefly to avoid the extreme complexity that usually arises if intertemporal choice under uncertainty is treated at all seriously. I have also kept the presentation static in a statistical sense. Except for chapter 6, there is virtually no discussion of lagged variables, stochastic processes or the use of panel data, since this would have entailed an enormous increase in the length and statistical sophistication of the book. A very good account of many of the issues neglected here can be found in Hsaio's (1986) book on panel data.

Despite these omissions, there should be enough material here for it to be of use in graduate-level econometrics courses, and parts of it for specialist final-year undergraduates. I hope that researchers in applied economics will also find it a useful reference.

The technical background required of the reader is a good command of statistical and microeconomic theory, to the level of the final year of a specialist undergraduate degree in quantitative economics. Good background references for these are Cox and Hinkley (1974) and Deaton and Muellbauer (1980a). The necessary mathematical background includes elementary multivariate differential and integral calculus, and a little matrix algebra. I also assume some familiarity with the terminology and subject matter of an econometrics text such as those by Theil (1971) or Chow (1983).

The book is organized as follows. Chapter 1 gives a concise summary of the static theory of rational choice, and defines the economic background of the later chapters. Chapter 2 covers some of the statistical theory relevant to cross-section survey data. Chapters 3, 4 and 5 deal respectively with discrete choice ('holes'), zero expenditures ('corners') and non-linear budget frontiers ('kinks', but a few holes and corners too). Chapter 6 extends the theory of sequential discrete choice to continuous time, using the concept of the hazard function, and finally chapter 7 discusses the implications of barriers to the exercise of free choice. There are also three appendices, which contain technical material common to more than one chapter. Although these are bundled together at the end of the book, they are rather more necessary to an understanding of the main body of the book than is usually true of technical appendices. It is a good idea to skim through the appendices before starting the book itself.

I.3 Acknowledgements

This book has had a long and difficult gestation, and I have several people to thank for their help and encouragement. I am particularly grateful to Tony Atkinson, Richard Blundell, Ruth Hancock, Wiji Narendranathan, Bob Redpath, Peter Robinson, Christine Sharrock, Nick Stern, Mark Stewart and the members of the London School of Economics (LSE) econometrics workshop for comments on various drafts. The Economic and Social Research Council, the Leverhulme Trust and the Australian National University (ANU) have all supported my work on this book in various ways, and a large number of LSE and ANU students have allowed me to use them as guinea pigs during its development.

1

The theory of rational choice

Life's business being just the terrible choice

Robert Browning

The models of choice that we examine in this book are all of orthodox micro-economic type. Their most notable feature is the sharp distinction which is made between the psychology of the individual and the objective opportunities which are available to him or her. In other words, our typical individual, when asked to choose between smoked salmon and caviar will make the choice on the basis of the same system of preferences as when offered a choice between a crust of bread and a piece of cheese. As a psychological theory, this is perhaps a little naive, and some psychologists have indeed used models of choice based on a rather different view of behaviour. However, these alternative theories have seen no applied use in the economics literature, and we do not pursue them further apart from one example in chapter 3.

Our intention in this chapter is to outline the basic concepts involved in the modelling problems we examine in later chapters. Throughout, we shall refer to the economic agent whose behaviour we are attempting to analyse as the individual consumer, despite the fact that many of the examples we eventually consider will involve something other than a single person purchasing consumption goods. In fact, virtually all economic models of individual choice have the same logical structure, and our use of the term 'consumer' is simply as a shorthand for someone who is faced with the problem of choosing between competing alternatives, which may be simple quantities or more abstract entities such as organizations to join or markets in which to participate.

Less innocuous is our use of the term 'individual' in cases where the observations with which we work refer to collections of people, usually the household or family. To assume that a single independent person is rational is probably fairly innocent; to assume that a family behaves as if it were a rational individual is much less so. Arrow's (1951) impossibility theorem establishes that it is not generally possible to aggregate the preferences of a collection of individuals in this way without making restrictive assumptions. In particular, if, as seems plausible, families make important decisions collectively and leave less important decisions to the individual family member within whose sphere of interest it falls, then the family, when seen as a unit, will be observed to make choices which appear inconsistent or irrational. This is an extremely important problem which could undermine the foundations of the type of microeconometrics we consider in this book. Unfortunately, economists have devoted very little research effort to the study of decision-making within the household, and we therefore have little alternative but to ignore the problem and hope that departures from consistency are sufficiently small to be unimportant.

Sections 1.1 and 1.2 establish the theoretical basis of conventional choice models, and sections 1.3–1.6 describe some of the theoretical 'tricks' that are often useful in specifying an econometric model of choice. Finally, section 1.7 deals with the role of systematic demographic factors, and introduces the issues involved in the process of transforming a non-stochastic economic model into a stochastic econometric model.

1.1 Choice sets, preferences and utility functions

Preference theory is a collection of assertions about the psychology of individuals: about the way they respond when faced with the necessity of choosing between mutually exclusive alternatives. Initially, our discussion relates to an arbitrary individual at a particular instant of time. Applied work necessarily involves the comparison of individuals and the passage of time, and the problems raised by this will be discussed later, in section 1.7.

We begin with the idea of the *choice set* Ψ, which is the complete set of entities over which the individual's preferences are defined. In the familiar model of a consumer choosing the amounts to buy of q perfectly divisible commodities, Ψ is a subset of q-dimensional Euclidean space, with each dimension representing consumption of one of the goods. However, we shall also be concerned with examples in which the objects of desire are not the purchased goods themselves, but rather the characteristics they possess. For example, it is clearly more useful to view a consumer deciding which model of refrigerator to buy as having preferences defined over characteristics such as reliability, storage capacity, appearance etc. rather than over the competing goods themselves. In these cases the choice set is the set of all possible vectors of characteristics (although only a few such vectors will actually be available through market purchases at any time). This characteristics approach is widely used in applied work, since it allows us to assume a fundamental regularity of behaviour even in cases where different individuals are offered technically different goods, where the nature of goods may change, or where the available alternatives are abstract unmeasurable entities (the membership or non-membership of a trade union, for example).

In all the cases with which we deal, Ψ will be a subset of Euclidean space R^q, and usually this subset is the non-negative orthant. However, there may be restrictions: for instance, positive subsistence quantities of goods or characteristics below which the consumer cannot go. This is illustrated in figure 1.1(a), where Ψ is two dimensional and consists of all vectors $\mathbf{x}' = (x_1, x_2)$ satisfying $x_1 \geqslant x_1^*$ and $x_2 \geqslant 0$; x_1 might be food, for example, with x_1^* the minimum necessary food intake, and x_2 representing other consumption. Minimum or maximum consumption levels are often a feature of applied models. Sometimes these are physical limits, such as the number of hours in the week as a limit on weekly consumption of leisure, but often they arise as an incidental part of a flexible parametric representation of preferences, rather than as a consequence of physical necessity.

Figure 1.1(a) gives an example in which Ψ is a connected set: in other words, there are no breaks or divisions in the choice set. However, in some of the modelling problems we shall encounter, this is not the case. For example, consider the problem facing a couple planning the size of their family. There is usually a tradeoff between family size and the family's standard of living, so we could regard the problem as one of choosing between points in (x_1, x_2) space, with x_1 the number of children and x_2 the standard of living (which we assume to be measurable). Since it is not possible even to contemplate non-integral numbers of children, Ψ must be defined as the set of vectors (x_1, x_2) satisfying $x_1 \in I$ and $x_2 \geqslant 0$, where I is the set of non-negative integers. This is illustrated in figure 1.1(b), where Ψ consists only of the vertical lines drawn there.

At first sight, this seems a very pervasive phenomenon, particularly when we consider durable goods: it makes no more sense to consider half a refrigerator than it does to consider half a child. However, this indivisibility often disappears if we adopt the more fundamental approach of working with characteristics rather than particular goods. For example, consider a consumer choosing between two models of refrigerator. It is possible to contemplate only integer values for x_1 and x_2 if these are defined as the quantities purchased. Thus Ψ consists of the isolated points illustrated in figure 1.1(c). However, suppose the consumer is in fact interested in two characteristics of any refrigeration system: the capacities of the refrigerator and of the freezer compartments (denoted by r and f), say. It is then perfectly reasonable to assume that the consumer is in principle able to express preferences over any combination of those characteristics, even though it is only possible actually to purchase a limited range of models of refrigerator. Suppose that model 1 refrigerators have capacities r_1 and f_1, while model 2 refrigerators are characterized by r_2 and f_2. The choice set Ψ in this case contains all points (x_1, x_2) such that $x_1 \geqslant 0$, $x_2 \geqslant 0$, where x_1 and x_2 represent refrigerator and freezer

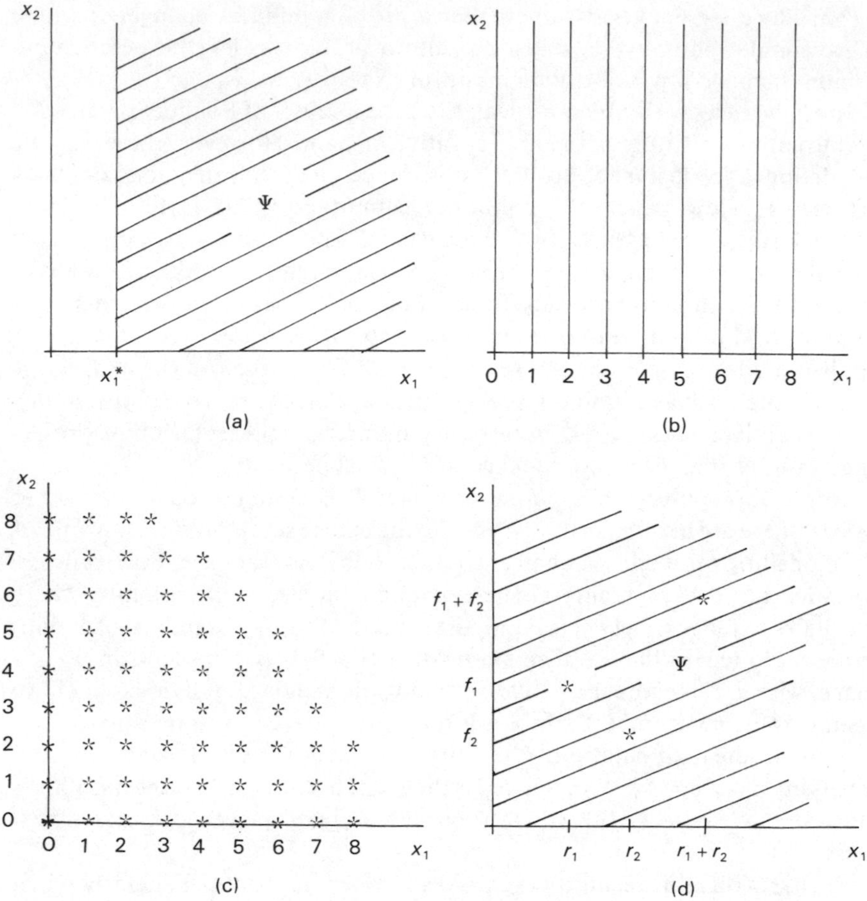

Figure 1.1 Choice sets with (a) a subsistence quantity, (b) one indivisible and one divisible good, (c) a pair of indivisible goods and (d) indivisible goods yielding divisible characteristics.

capacities. Ψ therefore corresponds to the shaded area in figure 1.1(d), and points are marked to indicate the combinations of characteristics yielded by one model 1 refrigerator, one model 2 refrigerator, and one of each. This example suggests that, even in the presence of indivisible goods, the problem can often be stated in such a way that the choice set is connected. The real difficulty raised by the indivisibility of goods is usually not that there are problems with the definition of consumer preferences, but rather that many elements of the choice set are unattainable by the individual, owing to the failure of the market to supply a complete range of goods. This leads to the problem of discrete choice examined in chapter 3.

We are now in a position to discuss the preference relation which is taken to underlie the individual's behaviour. Suppose that $\mathbf{x}^1$ and $\mathbf{x}^2$ are alternatives belonging to the set Ψ. If the individual strictly prefers $\mathbf{x}^1$ to $\mathbf{x}^2$, then we write $\mathbf{x}^1 \succ \mathbf{x}^2$; if he or she either prefers $\mathbf{x}^1$ to $\mathbf{x}^2$ or is indifferent between them, then we write $\mathbf{x}^1 \succsim \mathbf{x}^2$; in the case of indifference between the two alternatives, we write $\mathbf{x}^1 \sim \mathbf{x}^2$. It is clear that the relation $\succsim$ is reflexive: $\mathbf{x} \succsim \mathbf{x}$ for all $\mathbf{x} \in \Psi$. In addition, we assume that the following two axioms of choice hold:

(A1) *Completeness*: for every $\mathbf{x}^1, \mathbf{x}^2 \in \Psi$, either $\mathbf{x}^1 \succsim \mathbf{x}^2$ or $\mathbf{x}^2 \succsim \mathbf{x}^1$ or both.

(A2) *Transitivity*: for every $\mathbf{x}^1, \mathbf{x}^2, \mathbf{x}^3 \in \Psi$ such that $\mathbf{x}^1 \succsim \mathbf{x}^2$ and $\mathbf{x}^2 \succsim \mathbf{x}^3$, $\mathbf{x}^1 \succsim \mathbf{x}^3$.

Axiom (A1) states that the consumer is able to express preferences over the whole of the choice set; given our definition of the choice set, it is virtually tautological. Axiom (A2) is much more important, since it implies that the individual is rational in the sense that his or her preferences are not, even indirectly, self-contradictory. However, given that we are considering preferences at a single instant, while actual choices are necessarily made over time, (A2) is irrefutable: observed inconsistencies could always be explained away by asserting that preferences underwent some change in the intervals separating the three choices involved in the statement of (A2). It is not until we supply an assumption that preferences are either constant or change in some known way that transitivity becomes a testable proposition. Then it is the real content of the theory of choice.

If (A1) and (A2) are satisfied, there exists a preference ordering (or preordering) on the choice set Ψ. However, for the purposes of applied work using conventional statistical techniques, we need to be able to specify parametric models based on continuous utility functions. To justify this, we need a further assumption:

(A3) *Continuity*: for every $\mathbf{x}^1 \in \Psi$, the sets $\{\mathbf{x} \in \Psi | \mathbf{x}^1 \succsim \mathbf{x}\}$ and $\{\mathbf{x} \in \Psi | \mathbf{x} \succsim \mathbf{x}^1\}$ are closed.

The continuity axiom says in essence that if two alternatives are very close together in Ψ they should be near one another in the individual's preference ordering. This serves to rule out lexicographic preferences, where preference is based primarily on a subvector of $\mathbf{x}$, and the other elements of $\mathbf{x}$ are only considered at all in the event of indifference with respect to that subvector. Models based on preferences of this type will be encountered in chapter 3, but usually we feel able to exclude such pathological cases a priori.

If (A3) is satisfied, it is possible to work with indifference schedules which provide a convenient continuous representation of the individual's preference ordering. An indifference schedule is the locus, passing through a particular reference point in Ψ, of all vectors $\mathbf{x}$ between which the individual is indifferent. Figure 1.2 gives three two-dimensional examples.

The first is the traditional textbook diagram of a family of smooth

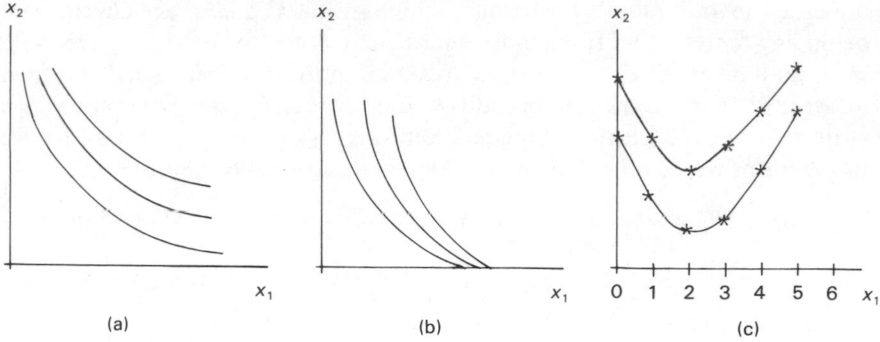

Figure 1.2 Examples of indifference schedules.

indifference curves which do not touch the axes: for such a case, if supplies of both x_1 and x_2 are available, both will be consumed in some non-zero quantities, however small. In the second example, the indifference curves are smooth, but intersect the x_1 axis: in this case, some of x_1 will always be chosen, whereas it may be optimal not to consume any of x_2. The third example shows preferences defined on a choice set which only permits integer values for x_1; as before, x_1 might represent the number of children in a family, and x_2 the standard of living. The effect of this is that the indifference schedule is merely an isolated set of points rather than a continuous indifference curve. However, there is nothing to prevent us thinking of these as points on some continuous curve in (x_1, x_2) space, provided we bear in mind that the curve only has meaning where x_1 is an integer.

The individual's indifference map is such that he or she is indifferent between any two alternatives on a single indifference schedule, and strictly prefers a point on a higher indifference schedule to any point on a lower schedule. If these schedules exist (as they do under axioms (A1)–(A2)), then it is possible to devise some scheme of attaching a numerical label to each member of the infinite family of indifference schedules in such a way that, as we move onto higher schedules, the labels increase in value. Such a labelling scheme is a utility indicator, defined as a function $V(.)$ which is continuous on Ψ and has the property that, for every $\mathbf{x}^1, \mathbf{x}^2 \in \Psi$, $V(\mathbf{x}^1) > V(\mathbf{x}^2)$ if and only if $\mathbf{x}^1 \succ \mathbf{x}^2$ and $V(\mathbf{x}^1) = V(\mathbf{x}^2)$ if and only if $\mathbf{x}^1 \sim \mathbf{x}^2$. The existence of a continuous utility function under (A1)–(A3) was proved by Debreu (1954). $V(.)$ is obviously not unique: its purpose is merely to document the order in which the elements of the choice set appear in the individual's scale of preferences, and this order will be preserved under any monotonically increasing transformation. Thus, if $V(.)$ is a valid utility function, then so is $\psi[V(.)]$, for any continuous increasing function $\psi(.)$. The utility function is therefore a purely ordinal concept: its value is arbitrary, and any statistical model based on the assumption of utility maximization should have the property that its observable implications are invariant to monotonic transformations of the function used as a utility indicator.

It is almost universal practice in applied work to go a little further than is justified by Debreu's existence theorem and to assume that $V(.)$ is not only continuous but also differentiable to any required order. Differentiability does not correspond to any simple property of the individual's preference relation, and so it cannot be regarded as a particularly natural assumption to make. However, for the practical purpose of constructing applied models, it is an assumption which is very convenient and occasionally indispensible, and it hard to see any compelling reason for avoiding it. Therefore, we generally assume utility functions to be differentiable.

Given this differentiability assumption, two important further concepts can be defined. The *marginal utility* of the ith good or characteristic at the point x is the partial derivative $\partial V(\mathbf{x})/\partial x_i$ and reflects the rate at which the individual moves up in his or her preference ordering when given an additional unit of x_i. Like the utility function itself, the marginal utilities are arbitrary: if we replace $V(\mathbf{x})$ by $\psi[V(\mathbf{x})]$, each marginal utility is multiplied by the factor $\psi'[V(\mathbf{x})]$. Thus it is important to avoid attaching any particular importance to the numerical values of the $\partial V(\mathbf{x})/\partial x_i$. However, their ratios are independent of the normalization used for the utility function, and these ratios are the *marginal rates of substitution*:

$$\text{MRS}_{ij}(\mathbf{x}) = \frac{\partial V(\mathbf{x})/\partial x_i}{\partial V(\mathbf{x})/\partial x_j} = -\left.\frac{\mathrm{d}x_j}{\mathrm{d}x_i}\right|_{V\text{ constant}} \qquad (1.1)$$

The marginal rates of substitution characterize the indifference surfaces in terms of their slopes: they describe the substitutions between goods or characteristics that the individual is able to make in the neighbourhood of $\mathbf{x}$ without becoming worse or better off. In the case of indivisible goods, of course, these concepts cannot be used in this marginal form, although discrete analogues can be defined. However, one can regard discrete indifference schedules as collections of points on underlying fictitious smooth indifference surfaces, and these surfaces can always be described in terms of marginal rates of substitution.

Axioms (A1)–(A3) are fundamental to utility-based choice theory; they are all that is required for us to be able to model consumer behaviour through the constrained maximization of a utility function. However, two further assumptions play an important role in the standard theory.

(A4) *Convexity*: for every $\mathbf{x}^1, \mathbf{x}^2 \in \Psi$ such that $\mathbf{x}^1 \succcurlyeq \mathbf{x}^2$, and every $\lambda \in [0, 1]$, $\lambda\mathbf{x}^1 + (1-\lambda)\mathbf{x}^2 \succcurlyeq \mathbf{x}^2$ provided that $\lambda\mathbf{x}^1 + (1-\lambda)\mathbf{x}^2 \in \Psi$.

The convexity assumption asserts that the set of points in Ψ which lie above any indifference schedule is convex: indifference schedules are therefore convex to the origin. Note that (A4) refers only to convexity of the preference relation; it does not require convexity of the choice set. This is particularly important if we are dealing with indivisible goods, since in that case Ψ is not a convex subset of R^q (see, for example, figure 1.1). Axiom (A4), when translated into utility function terms, says that $V(\mathbf{x})$ is a convex-contoured, or quasi-concave, function. It is important to make a distinction between convexity as defined in (A4) and strict convexity, where the symbol $\succcurlyeq$ is replaced by $\succ$.

The significance of this is that under convexity the indifference schedules are permitted to have flat sections or to be completely linear (corresponding to a linear utility function). Along such sections, the goods or characteristics concerned are viewed by the individual as perfect substitutes: the marginal rate of substitution between them is independent of the proportions in which they are consumed. Under strict convexity, preferences of this type are ruled out: there is always some curvature in the indifference schedule. Figure 1.3 gives examples of three cases. In the first, the indifference curves bulge outwards in one region and are therefore non-convex; it is very hard to find real examples of such behaviour, and we usually feel justified in excluding this possibility a priori.

Figure 1.3(b) illustrates the case where x_1 and x_2 are perfectly substitutable everywhere in Ψ. The third example also shows preferences which are convex but not strictly convex, and represents the other extreme of perfect complementarity: because the flat sections are parallel to the axes, the only combination of x_1 and x_2 we ever expect to observe is that corresponding to the kink in each indifference curve. Such cases usually arise from some strict technical relation between the goods or characteristics x_1 and x_2, e.g. if they figure in some recipe which involves fixed proportions. Fixed-coefficient relationships are much more common in production economics and will not play a significant part in this book. Generally, we shall assume that preferences are strictly convex.

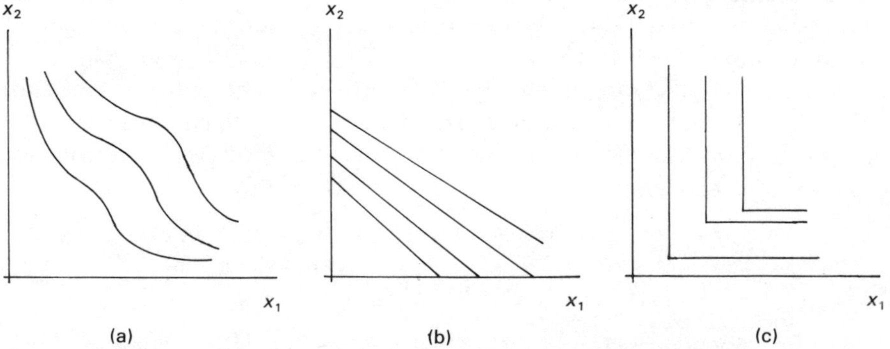

Figure 1.3 (a) Non-convex preferences; (b) perfect substitutability; (c) perfect complementarity.

A final assumption that is often made in the theory of choice is the monotonicity or non-satiation axiom. In its strictest form, this is as follows.

(A5) *Non-satiation*: for every $\mathbf{x}^1, \mathbf{x}^2 \in \Psi$ such that $\mathbf{x}^1 - \mathbf{x}^2$ is a non-negative vector with at least one element positive, $\mathbf{x}^1 \succ \mathbf{x}^2$.

Thus, more is always preferred to less, and this implies that the utility function $V(.)$ is increasing in all its arguments. Unlike (A1)–(A4), it is not difficult to think of perfectly sensible examples that fail to satisfy the non-satiation assumption, at least in this strong form. Counter-examples to (A5) involve indifference schedules that, over some region of Ψ, veer away from the axis. Figure 1.2(c) gives one such example, with additional children yielding disutility after a certain number. The same is clearly true of many goods or characteristics, and so we cannot regard (A5) as having any general validity. Thus we shall not always assume that $V(\mathbf{x})$ is monotonic. For most purposes it is sufficient to make the reasonable and much weaker assumption that $V(\mathbf{x})$ is always increasing in at least one of its arguments.

Many of the models examined in later chapters are concerned with individuals' labour supply decisions. These decisions can be viewed as choices between leisure and the consumption that can be financed by earnings. In this case it is particularly difficult to justify the strong assumption (A5), since it is easy to find examples of individuals satiated with leisure. A proper analysis would have to recognize that there are at least three dimensions present in any individual's labour supply problem. Let x_1 represent weekly consumption of a composite consumption good; x_2 is the number of hours per week of leisure and x_3 is the number of hours spent at work per week. These three are quite distinct in the way the individual views them. It is reasonable to assume $V(.)$ increasing in x_1, and predominantly also increasing in x_2. However, there may be exceptions: an extra hour of leisure, if it be spent in poverty or in isolation, may not be a desirable thing. One can think of this as an extreme form of complementarity. Since many leisure activities require the availability of consumption goods, x_1 can be regarded as complementary to x_2, and at low levels of consumption and high levels of leisure this complementarity may be so strong that $V(.)$ is locally decreasing in x_2.

Economists frequently assume that work yields only 'disutility', so that $V(.)$ is decreasing in x_3. However, this is hard to justify. Many people enjoy their work, and even if work itself is unenjoyable, having a job may yield other benefits: the opportunity to meet people, to have a more varied life etc. Thus for many people $V(.)$ is likely to be initially increasing in x_3 before it becomes decreasing.

If we follow conventional practice and regard all time spent away from work as leisure, then x_2 and x_3 are not independently variable: x_2 is identically equal to $T - x_3$, where T is the total number of hours available. This identity allows us to reduce the labour supply problem to a two-dimensional one in either of two ways: $V(x_1, x_2, x_3)$ can be reduced to a utility indicator defined on consumption and hours of leisure,

$$V^*(x_1, x_2) = V(x_1, x_2, T-x_2) \tag{1.2}$$

or on consumption and hours of work,

$$V^{**}(x_1, x_3) = V(x_1, T-x_3, x_3). \tag{1.3}$$

Frequently, in the latter formulation, utility is regarded as a function of $-x_3$, on the assumption that work yields disutility, so that a conventional monotonically increasing function of x_1 and $-x_3$ can be used to represent preferences. Our discussion of the possible behaviour of $V(.)$ makes it clear that this may be too restrictive an assumption.

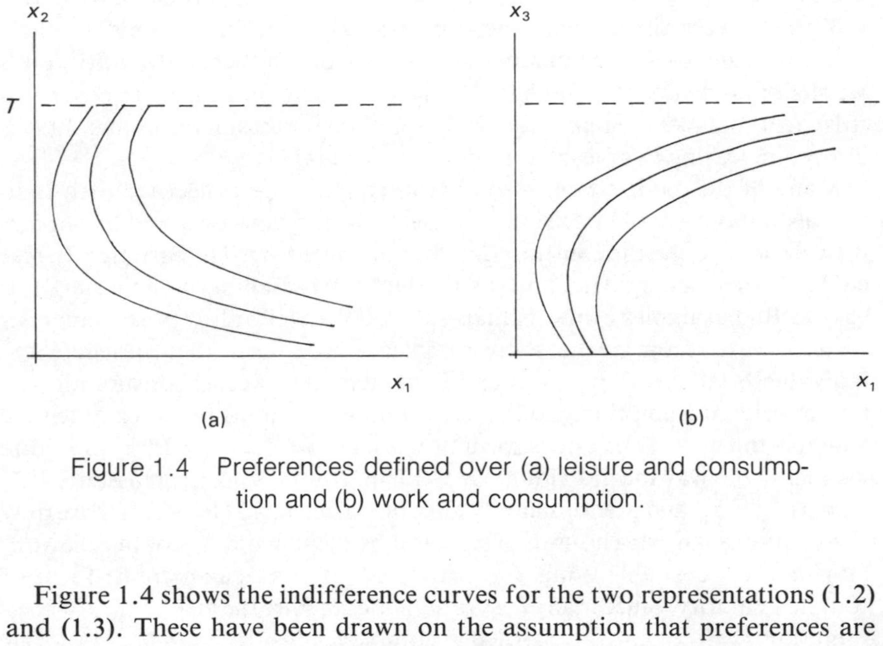

Figure 1.4 Preferences defined over (a) leisure and consumption and (b) work and consumption.

Figure 1.4 shows the indifference curves for the two representations (1.2) and (1.3). These have been drawn on the assumption that preferences are such that $V^{**}(.)$ is first increasing in x_3 and then decreasing. Since the two representations are equivalent, we shall henceforth use labour supply or leisure as the basic variable purely on grounds of notational convenience for the problem at hand.

1.2 The opportunity set

The previous section described the conventional economic model of consumers' psychology in rather abstract terms. No reference was made to the alternatives which might actually be available for the consumer to choose. Our task now is to introduce the notion of the opportunity set, and to examine the particular forms which it might take in various types of microeconometric problem.

The *opportunity set* is merely the complete set of alternatives that it would be feasible for the consumer to choose. We shall refer to this set as Ω. If the economic model is completely specified, it is clear that Ω must be a subset of Ψ, for otherwise the consumer would not be able to express preferences over some of the available alternatives. An economically rational consumer who is also an efficient decision-maker will make a choice from the members of the set Ω in such a way that the chosen $\mathbf{x}$ ($\tilde{\mathbf{x}}$, say) satisfies $\tilde{\mathbf{x}} \succcurlyeq \mathbf{x}$ for every $\mathbf{x}$ in Ω. Thus an efficient consumer always chooses the best that is available, and this can be expressed in utility terms by saying that the consumer chooses $\tilde{\mathbf{x}}$ to maximize $V(\mathbf{x})$ over Ω. However, without being more specific about the nature of the opportunity set, it is not possible for us to say very much about the nature of the optimal choice $\tilde{\mathbf{x}}$ (indeed, it is not even generally possible for us to show that $\tilde{\mathbf{x}}$ is unique). Therefore, in the remainder of this section, we attempt to identify the important features of the opportunity sets we encounter in applied microeconomics and to produce a typology of cases. The econometric problems raised by these various forms for Ω are the subjects of chapters 3–5, where they are discussed much more fully. In this section we shall simply introduce the important ideas, giving just a single example of each case. As in the previous section, we talk in terms of the opportunity set confronting an arbitrary individual. However, it should be borne in mind that, in practice, different people often have very different opportunities open to them, and so Ω will typically vary enormously, both in size and general character, across individuals. This variation is frequently of much greater importance in explaining observed behaviour than any variation in preferences. However, in general in applied work Ω either is observed directly or can be constructed without the need for statistical estimation, so this raises no great problems of model specification.

1.2.1 Classical linear budget constraints

The simplest problem in demand analysis involves a vector $\mathbf{x}$ whose elements $x_1, \ldots, x_q$ are the quantities in which each of q perfectly divisible consumption goods are purchased at fixed prices $\mathbf{p}' = (p_1, \ldots, p_q)$. If y is the maximum amount that the consumer has available to spend, then the opportunity set is the set of vectors $\mathbf{x}$ such that $\mathbf{p}'\mathbf{x} \leqslant y$. Ω thus takes the form of a simple convex polyhedron, as illustrated for the $q = 3$ case in figure 1.5. If we are dealing with a normal problem in which the consumer is non-satiated with respect to at least one good, optimal behaviour corresponds to a point on the frontier of this opportunity set, rather than a point in its interior. For this reason, the budget constraint is often taken to be the equality $\mathbf{p}'\mathbf{x} = y$ rather than the inequality it in fact is. Orthodox demand analysis using aggregate data also tends to be based on the further assumption that points on the boundary of this frontier (points at which one or more of the x_i is zero) can never be optimal. This is really an assumption about preferences rather than the opportunity set, since it requires that the indifference surfaces never meet the axes, thus ruling out corner solutions. This enormously simplifies the task

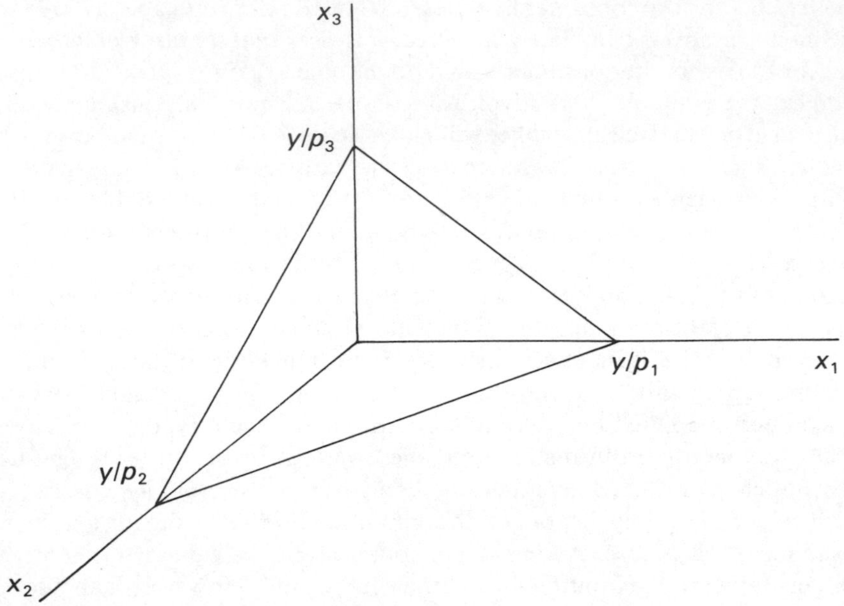

Figure 1.5 The classical opportunity set.

of constructing an applied demand model, since it permits the use of ordinary differential calculus. However, in microeconometrics it is frequently found that some individuals purchase only a subset of the goods available, a phenomenon which causes substantial difficulties, even for this simple type of opportunity set.

We shall not consider applied examples in which observed behaviour necessarily corresponds to a classical point of tangency in the interior of the budget plane, since there are few special difficulties to be encountered in such cases. Nevertheless, the theory of the interior optimum still finds some use even in less straightforward problems, and sections 1.3–1.6 are devoted to it. Chapter 4 is concerned with the econometric problems involved in coping with zero observed purchases.

1.2.2 Discrete alternatives

The standard models of consumer behaviour are all based on the assumption that it is possible for the consumer to make continuous substitutions of one good (or characteristic) for another through the medium of market transactions. In practice, this is very often not the case: even if markets exist for all the x_i, substitution is not always possible in a continuous fashion. Many examples of the discreteness of alternatives will be considered in chapter 3; for the present, we consider only the simplest case of indivisible commodities.

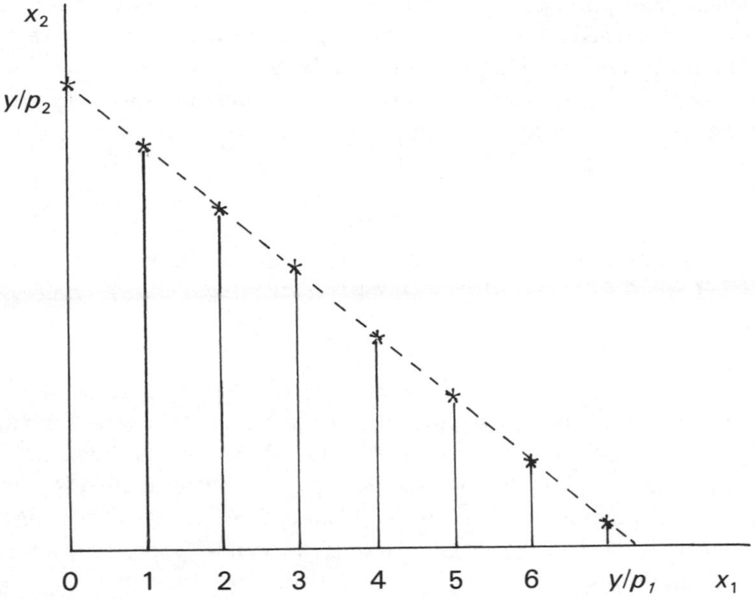

Figure 1.6 The opportunity set for choice between a divisible and an indivisible good at fixed prices.

Suppose that x_1 is a good that can be purchased only in integer quantities, while x_2 is perfectly divisible. Both goods can be traded at fixed prices p_1 and p_2, and the maximum amount that may be spent on these two goods is y. The opportunity set is the set of vectors $\mathbf{x}' = (x_1, x_2)$ such that $\mathbf{p}'\mathbf{x} \leqslant y$ and $x_1 \in I$, where I is the set of non-negative integers. This corresponds to the set of points lying on the vertical lines drawn in figure 1.6. Provided that the consumer is non-satiated with respect to x_2 and is efficient in making and executing decisions, only the eight starred points lying on the frontier of the opportunity set will ever be observed. For this reason, discrete choice problems are often thought of as involving choice between a number of isolated points in x space rather than choice from a set of the type illustrated here. In less simple cases, the alternatives may be very complex bundles of characteristics, some of which may themselves be opportunities to make further decisions.

1.2.3 Convex opportunity sets with kinked frontiers

The third major class of opportunity sets which we shall consider arises in many different areas of microeconomics, often as a result of government policy. This the case where the opportunity set Ω has a frontier made up of connected sections, each of which is part of a hyperplane in $\mathbf{x}$ space. By far the most common example of this is in labour supply analysis in the presence of income taxation. The simplest example involves choice between a single divisible consumption good x_2 and leisure x_1. The consumer's gross income is the sum of unearned income y^* and earned income $w(T-x_1)$, where w is the fixed hourly wage and T is the consumer's total time endowment, so that labour supply is $T-x_1$ hours. Suppose first that there is a single uniform rate of income taxation, τ, and that this applies to the whole of the consumer's income. Then the budget constraint is

$$p_2x_2 \leqslant (1-\tau)[y^* + w(T-x_1)]$$

which says that spending must not exceed post-tax income. This can be re-expressed as

$$w(1-\tau)x_1 + p_2x_2 \leqslant (1-\tau)(y^* + wT) \tag{1.4}$$

which is of the classical form $p_1x_1 + p_2x_2 \leqslant y$, where the price p_1 of leisure is $w(1-\tau)$ and the measure y of total resources includes the post-tax value of both unearned income and the market value of the time endowment T; y is known as (post-tax) full income. However, the problem differs from the classical case since, in addition to the usual non-negativity conditions on x_1 and x_2, there is a further constraint that leisure cannot exceed the amount of time available:

$$x_1 \leqslant T. \tag{1.5}$$

Condition (1.5) is responsible for an important change in the nature of the opportunity set, which is now bounded by a frontier consisting of two linear segments, one of which is vertical. Assuming non-satiation in x_2, only points on the sloping part of the frontier are optimal, and there are only two types of optimal choice which are likely to be observed. Point A in figure 1.7 is the standard interior optimum, and point B is a corner solution for a person who chooses not to participate in the labour market.

Corner solutions of this type present interesting econometric problems, which are discussed in chapter 4. However, the assumption that a uniform tax rate is applicable to the whole of income is clearly unrealistic; in practice there are tax allowances and also a progressive increase in the marginal rate of taxation as income increases. For the moment we shall not consider the latter feature but simply examine the form which Ω takes in the presence of tax allowances. More realistic examples will be discussed in chapter 5. Suppose that the consumer has an allowance of $\bar{y}$: only income above this level is taxed. Moreover, assume that unearned income is less than this amount, since otherwise the general nature of Ω is similar to that illustrated in figure 1.7. Under our assumptions, tax is only paid if $x_1 < T-(\bar{y}-y^*)/w$, after which point it is paid at the rate τ. There are therefore three sections of the budget constraint: a vertical part corresponding to the condition $x_1 \leqslant T$; a part applying to income below the tax threshold, defined by $p_2x_2 \leqslant y^* + w(T-x_1)$; and a part applying to taxable income, defined by $p_2x_2 \leqslant (1-\tau)[y^* + w(T-x_1)] + \tau\bar{y}$. This very simple picture of the working of the direct tax system clearly

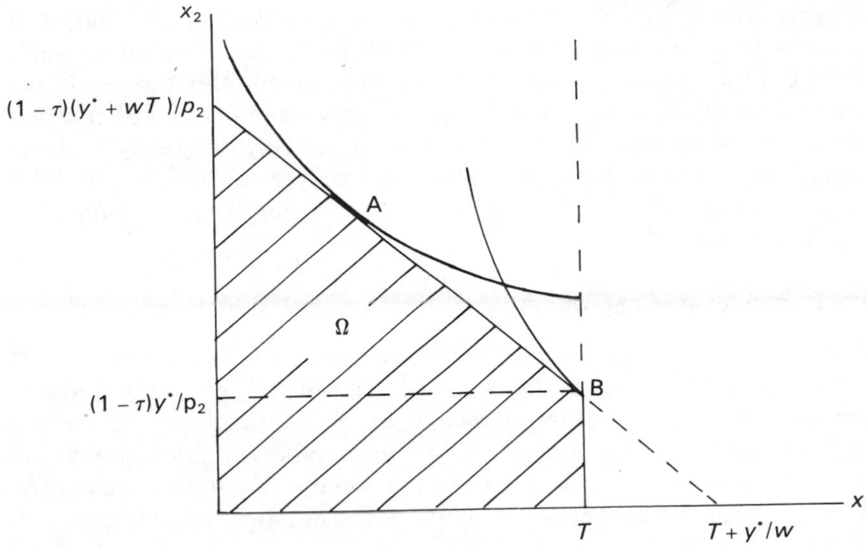

Figure 1.7 Labour supply under uniform income taxation.

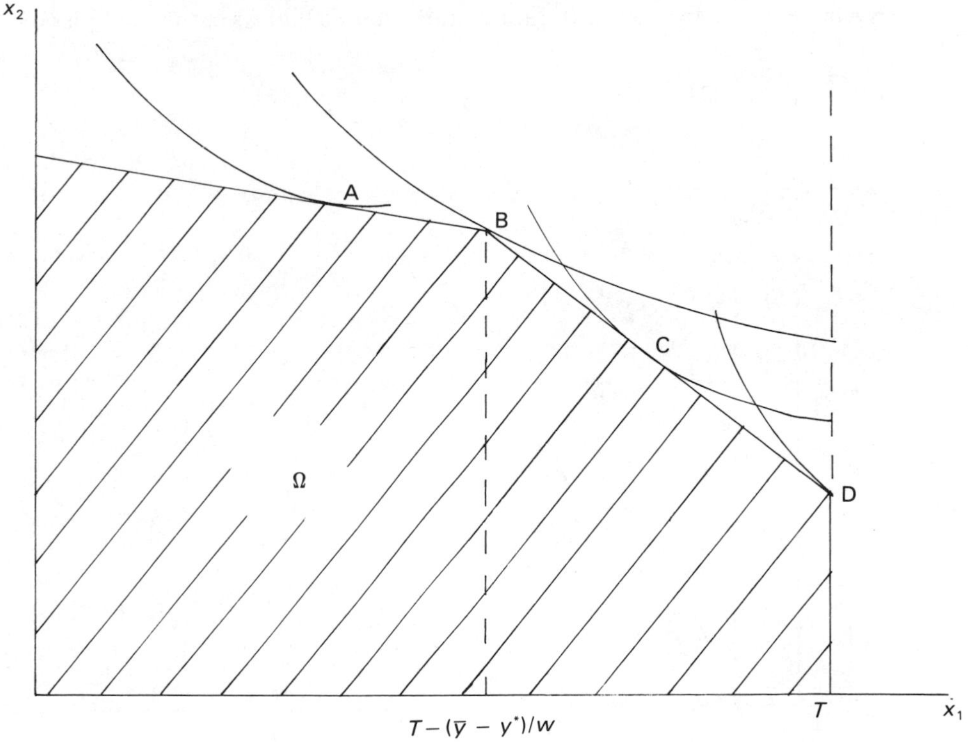

Figure 1.8 Labour supply in the presence of tax allowances.

presents quite substantial difficulties for the construction of a model of labour supply, since there are now four distinct types of optimum which might be observed: two corner solutions at points B and D in figure 1.8, and two tangencies, such as A and C. Opportunity sets with kinked frontiers similar to the one illustrated here are encountered very frequently in microeconometrics, and are not confined to labour supply models. Chapter 5 discusses a variety of examples and examines the econometric techniques to which they lead.

1.2.4 Non-convex opportunity sets

Consider the following pricing scheme, incorporating a discount for bulk buying: quantities of commodity x_1 smaller than an amount $\bar{x}_1$ are priced at p_1 per unit, while quantities larger than $\bar{x}_1$ are priced at p_1^* per unit, where $p_1 > p_1^*$. Such schemes are not uncommon in practice, although they are often accompanied by some form of indivisibility, which we exclude here. Assuming that choice is between a good priced in this way and another, x_2, which has a single fixed price, with total expenditure not to exceed a fixed amount y, the opportunity set takes the form illustrated in figure 1.9. The important feature of this type of opportunity set is that it is not convex: there is a break in the frontier of Ω, rather than a simple kink as in the examples of

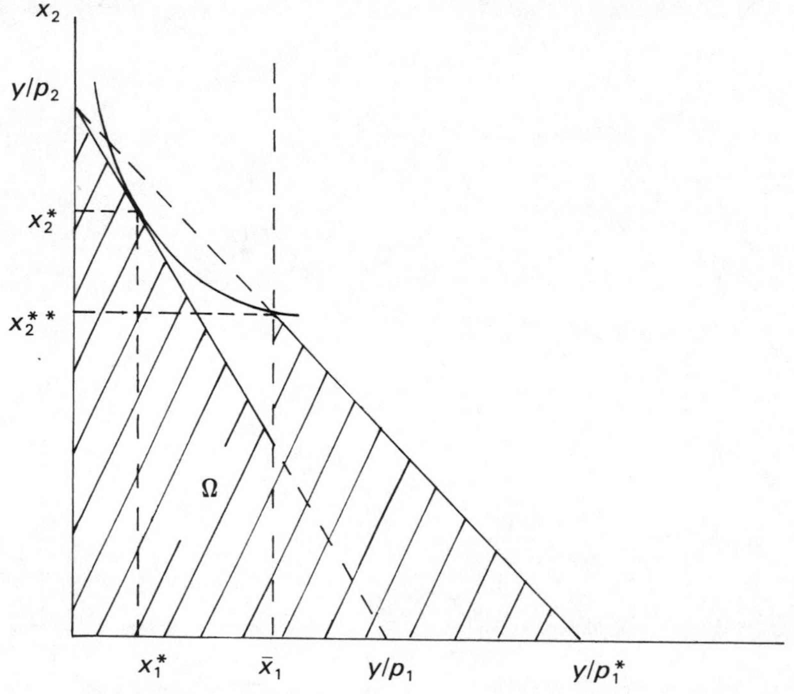

Figure 1.9 The opportunity set under discontinuous pricing.

the last subsection. The effect of this break is to render certain parts of the frontier suboptimal, so that there exist ranges of values for x_1 and x_2 which will never be observed for an efficient consumer with preferences of a particular form. In the example illustrated here, observations lying in the intervals $(x_1^*, \bar{x}_1)$ and (x_2^{**}, x_2^*) could only arise through some inefficiency on the part of the consumer. In fact, this feature is not confined to cases where the boundary of Ω is discontinuous: any local non-convexity can lead to similar gaps in the observable range of $\tilde{\mathbf{x}}$. This is of considerable importance for stochastic specification, and we return to this point in section 1.7, where another example is considered. The corresponding econometric problems are discussed in chapter 5.

1.3 Direct utility and the interior optimum

In this and the next three sections, the intention is to survey the classical theory of the consumer in order to establish some important concepts and theoretical results which will prove useful in later chapters. We make the following standard assumptions: the direct utility function $V(x_1, \ldots, x_q)$, is strictly increasing in at least one of the x_i; it is strictly quasi-concave and also continuously twice differentiable. Prices $p_1, \ldots, p_q$ and the limit on total expenditure y are fixed. Under these assumptions, the budget constraint can be treated as an equality and the consumer's problem takes the form

$$\max_{x_1, \ldots, x_q} \quad V(x_1, \ldots, x_q) \tag{1.6}$$

subject to

$$p_1 x_1 + \ldots + p_q x_q = y.$$

If we assume that preferences are such that there is no corner solution to this problem, the consumer's optimum consumption vector $\tilde{\mathbf{x}}$ is unique and satisfies the first-order conditions

$$\tilde{\lambda} p_i = \frac{\partial V(\tilde{\mathbf{x}})}{\partial \tilde{x}_i} \qquad i=1, \ldots, q \tag{1.7}$$

where $\tilde{\lambda}$ is the value, at the optimum, of the Lagrange multiplier associated with the budget constraint. Although we shall encounter some models that are based directly on these first-order conditions, and therefore involve $\tilde{\lambda}$, it is usual to express (1.7) in a different form. The reason for this is that $\tilde{\lambda}$ and the marginal utility on the right-hand side of (1.7) are essentially indeterminate, since they depend on the precise normalization that is used for the utility function. If (1.7) is multiplied by $\tilde{x}_i$ and the resulting equations are summed over $i=1, \ldots, q$, we have

$$\tilde{\lambda} y = \sum_i \tilde{x}_i \frac{\partial V}{\partial \tilde{x}_i}. \tag{1.8}$$

To eliminate $\tilde{\lambda}$, divide (1.7) by (1.8) to obtain an optimality condition which is now independent of the way we have chosen to normalize the utility function:

$$\frac{p_i}{y} = \frac{\partial V/\partial \tilde{x}_i}{\Sigma_j \, \tilde{x}_j (\partial V/\partial \tilde{x}_j)} \qquad i=1,\ldots,q. \tag{1.9}$$

The right-hand side of each of the equations in system (1.9) is a function of the optimal consumption vector $\tilde{\mathbf{x}}$. In principle, therefore, (1.9) can be inverted to give the system of Marshallian demand functions:

$$\tilde{x}_i = \tilde{x}_i(p_1/y, \ldots, p_q/y). \tag{1.10}$$

There are two major difficulties with this type of analysis. Firstly, it is generally very difficult to make the transition from (1.9) to (1.10) since it involves the solution of a very complicated system of non-linear functions. Only in the case of very simple forms for $V(\mathbf{x})$ is it possible to write down closed-form expressions for the Marshallian demand functions, and even these simple cases are often best analysed using other approaches. Secondly, even if we were to decide to work with (1.9) as our model, rather than (1.10), we are generally faced with the problem of estimating a system of non-linear equations with endogenous variables on the right-hand sides. Non-linear systems of simultaneous equations can be extremely difficult to estimate, and so this would be likely to raise as many problems as it solves.

For these reasons, it is often much more convenient to approach the problem through an indirect route, exploiting the theory of duality. Indeed, the only property of the consumer's optimum which is immediately apparent if we adopt this direct approach is the homogeneity of demand functions: $\tilde{\mathbf{x}}$ is a function of the normalized prices $p_1/y, \ldots, p_q/y$ rather than $p_1, \ldots, p_q$ and y separately. However, even this is really a property of the budget constraint rather than the consumer's behaviour, since the constraint can be written in the more revealing form

$$(p_1/y)x_1 + \ldots + (p_q/y)x_q = 1 \tag{1.11}$$

from which it is immediately apparent that any problem involving prices and income through the medium of the budget constraint alone must possess the homogeneity property.

1.4 Indirect utility and Roy's identity

Consider once again the consumer's optimization problem. The highest indifference curve that can be reached under the constraint (1.11) is labelled $\tilde{u}$, say, where $\tilde{u}$ is given by

$$\tilde{u} = \max_{\mathbf{x}} [V(\mathbf{x}) \,|\, \mathbf{p}'\mathbf{x} = y]$$

$$= V[\tilde{\mathbf{x}}(\mathbf{p}/y)]$$
$$= H(\mathbf{p}/y). \tag{1.12}$$

The function $H(.)$ is known as the indirect utility function; it serves to indicate the maximum utility (i.e. the label of the highest indifference curve) attainable when choice is constrained by a linear budget constraint involving normalized prices $\mathbf{p}/y$. Under our assumptions, $H(.)$ is decreasing and strictly quasi-concave. Its great advantage over the direct utility function for theoretical purposes is that the transition from $H(.)$ to the vector of Marshallian demand functions, $\tilde{\mathbf{x}}(\mathbf{p}/y)$, is particularly simple, and involves only partial differentiation. The derivatives of $H(.)$ are

$$\frac{\partial \tilde{u}}{\partial p_i} = \sum_j \frac{\partial V}{\partial \tilde{x}_j} \frac{\partial \tilde{x}_j}{\partial p_i} = \tilde{\lambda} \sum_j p_j \frac{\partial \tilde{x}_j}{\partial p_i} \qquad i=1,\ldots,q \tag{1.13}$$

and

$$\frac{\partial \tilde{u}}{\partial y} = \sum_j \frac{\partial V}{\partial \tilde{x}_j} \frac{\partial \tilde{x}_j}{\partial y} = \tilde{\lambda} \sum_j p_j \frac{\partial \tilde{x}_j}{\partial y}. \tag{1.14}$$

But partial differentiation of the budget constraint reveals that

$$\sum_j p_j \frac{\partial \tilde{x}_j}{\partial p_i} + \tilde{x}_i = 0 \tag{1.15}$$

and

$$\sum_j p_j \frac{\partial \tilde{x}_j}{\partial y} = 1 \tag{1.16}$$

which permit (1.13) and (1.14) to be expressed as

$$\frac{\partial \tilde{u}}{\partial p_i} = -\tilde{\lambda}\tilde{x}_i \tag{1.17}$$

and

$$\frac{\partial \tilde{u}}{\partial y} = \tilde{\lambda}. \tag{1.18}$$

Equation (1.18) allows us to interpret the value of the Lagrange multiplier $\tilde{\lambda}$ as the marginal utility of income, in other words the marginal benefit of a relaxation of the budget constraint. If (1.18) is substituted into (1.17) and the derivatives of $\tilde{u}$ are written as derivatives of $H(.)$

$$\tilde{x}_i = -\frac{\partial H/\partial p_i}{\partial H/\partial y} \tag{1.19}$$

which is Roy's identity. Note that (1.19) can be expressed in an equivalent budget share form, which is often more convenient:

$$\frac{p_i \tilde{x}_i}{y} = \frac{\partial \log H / \partial \log p_i}{\Sigma_{j=1}^{q} \partial \log H / \partial \log p_j}. \tag{1.20}$$

If we are faced with the problem of constructing a model of demand, it is usually very much easier to adopt a specific form for $H(\mathbf{p}/y)$ and to derive the demand functions using Roy's identity than it would be to adopt a functional form for $V(\mathbf{x})$ and to solve the corresponding first-order conditions. Very many applied models are derived in this way, and we shall therefore make frequent use of the indirect utility function and Roy's identity.

1.5 The cost function and Shephard's lemma

In recent years the cost function has come to play a very important role in consumer theory. The indirect utility function records the maximum utility attainable at given prices and income; it therefore represents the solution to the consumer's primal maximization problem. The cost function, on the other hand, gives the solution $C(\mathbf{p}, u)$ of the dual minimization problem

$$C(\mathbf{p}, u) = \min_{\mathbf{x}} \; [\mathbf{p}'\mathbf{x} \,|\, V(\mathbf{x}) \geqslant u]. \tag{1.21}$$

$C(\mathbf{p}, u)$ is linearly homogeneous in $\mathbf{p}$, increasing in $\mathbf{p}$ and u, and concave in $\mathbf{p}$. Under our assumptions, it is also differentiable everywhere. The choice of $\mathbf{x}$ which solves the problem (1.21) is $\tilde{\mathbf{x}}(\mathbf{p}, u)$, say, which is the vector of compensated or Hicksian demand functions. These differ from the conventional Marshallian demands in that utility is held constant; they therefore describe the responses of demand to changes in price if income is adjusted in such a way that the consumer remains on the original indifference curve. Such compensating changes do not, of course, occur in practice, so the Hicksian demand functions are not directly useful in modelling observed consumer behaviour; however, the fundamental implications of classical demand theory are more easily expressed in terms of the Hicksian demands, and so $\tilde{\mathbf{x}}(\mathbf{p}, u)$ is of considerable importance. To go from the cost function to the compensated demand functions is a simple matter. $C(\mathbf{p}, u)$ and $\tilde{\mathbf{x}}(\mathbf{p}, u)$ are related through the equation

$$\mathbf{p}'\tilde{\mathbf{x}}(\mathbf{p}, u) = C(\mathbf{p}, u). \tag{1.22}$$

If this is differentiated with respect to p_i, holding constant the other prices and utility, we find

$$\tilde{x}_i(\mathbf{p}, u) + \sum_j p_j \frac{\partial \tilde{x}_j}{\partial p_i} = \frac{\partial C(\mathbf{p}, u)}{\partial p_i}. \tag{1.23}$$

But consider the change in utility, which must be zero if the consumer is to remain on the same indifference curve:

$$d\tilde{u} = \sum_j \frac{\partial V(\tilde{\mathbf{x}})}{\partial \tilde{x}_j} \frac{\partial \tilde{x}_j}{\partial p_i} dp_i$$

$$= \tilde{\lambda} \sum_j p_j \frac{\partial \tilde{x}_j}{\partial p_i} dp_i \tag{1.24}$$

since $\tilde{\lambda} p_j = \partial V / \partial \tilde{x}_j$ in equilibrium. If utility is held constant, (1.24) implies that $\Sigma p_j (\partial \tilde{x}_j / \partial p_i)$ must be zero, and (1.23) then reduces to

$$\tilde{x}_i(\mathbf{p}, u) = \frac{\partial C(\mathbf{p}, u)}{\partial p_i} \tag{1.25}$$

which is Shephard's lemma: the compensated demand functions are the partial derivatives of the cost functions. One direct consequence of this simple relationship is Slutsky's integrability result, which follows from the symmetry of second derivatives. Since the order of differentiation is unimportant, we have

$$\frac{\partial \tilde{x}_i(\mathbf{p}, u)}{\partial p_j} = \frac{\partial^2 C(\mathbf{p}, u)}{\partial p_i \, \partial p_j} = \frac{\partial^2 C(\mathbf{p}, u)}{\partial p_j \, \partial p_i} = \frac{\partial \tilde{x}_j(\mathbf{p}, u)}{\partial p_i}. \tag{1.26}$$

Equation (1.26) is the most important result of classical demand theory; its practical significance is to almost halve the number of price responses that require estimation. The only difficulty is that the $q(q-1)/2$ restrictions (1.26) apply to the compensated demand functions rather than the directly observable Marshallian demand functions, and this rather complicates the problem of either testing or imposing them. For the most part, we shall work with models which automatically satisfy these symmetry restrictions, although the problem of testing their validity (which amounts to testing the correctness of specification of the model) remains important. A further, more awkward, property of the compensated demand responses follows from the concavity of the cost function. Concavity implies that the matrix of second derivatives of $C(\mathbf{p}, u)$ is negative semi-definite:

$$\sum_{i=1}^{q} \sum_{j=1}^{q} \xi_i \frac{\partial^2 C(\mathbf{p}, u)}{\partial p_i \, \partial p_j} \xi_j \leqslant 0$$

which implies

$$\sum_i \sum_j \xi_i \frac{\partial \tilde{x}_i}{\partial p_j} \xi_j \leqslant 0 \tag{1.27}$$

for every possible choice of the numbers $\xi_1, \ldots, \xi_q$. The linear homogeneity of $C(\mathbf{p}, u)$ in prices means that (1.27) holds with equality when the vector ξ is proportional to the price vector $\mathbf{p}$. Inequality restrictions such as this are difficult to test, and also rather difficult to impose: it is hard to find a simple flexible functional form for $C(\mathbf{p}, u)$ which is globally concave. For this reason, econometricians tend either to assume very simple functional forms which automatically satisfy the relevant concavity restrictions or to assume much more general forms which are not globally concave but which might provide a good approximation over a limited range of variation in prices and income. The latter approach is the more common in conventional aggregate demand analysis, but microeconometric models often involve highly restrictive functions which do have the appropriate theoretical properties. We shall see many examples of this in later chapters.

These very simple derivations of the fundamental properties (1.26) and (1.27) are made possible by the cost function and its derivative property (1.25). However, for these results to be of any operational significance, we still require a link between the compensated demand functions to which they relate and the uncompensated demand functions which we observe. This link is provided by the duality between the cost function and the indirect utility function. At the optimum, the following two equalities both hold:

$$y = C(\mathbf{p}, \tilde{u}) \tag{1.28}$$

and

$$\tilde{u} = H(\mathbf{p}/y). \tag{1.29}$$

These merely represent a single relationship between $\tilde{u}$ and y (for given $\mathbf{p}$) in different ways, so the indirect utility function $H(\mathbf{p}/y)$ can be regarded as the solution of (1.28) for $\tilde{u}$, while the cost function $C(\mathbf{p}, \tilde{u})$ can be regarded as the solution of (1.29) for y. The relative simplicity of the transition from (1.28) to (1.29) makes this dualistic approach particularly attractive; although we have to solve an equation, it is an equation in only a single variable: if we were to use the direct approach, beginning with $V(\mathbf{x})$, we would be faced with the problem of solving a whole set of first-order conditions. To complete the process of deriving the Marshallian demands, all that is necessary is to substitute the value $H(\mathbf{p}/y)$ for $\tilde{u}$ in $\tilde{\mathbf{x}}(\mathbf{p}, \tilde{u})$ to give the observable demands $\tilde{\mathbf{x}}(\mathbf{p}/y)$.

It remains in this section only to use the cost function to derive some further results concerning two very important special cases: homothetic and quasi-homothetic preferences. The former refers to the case in which preferences can be represented by a utility function expressible as an increasing transform of a linearly homogeneous function of $\mathbf{x}$. This means that it is possible to normalize utility so that $V(\mathbf{x})$ is itself linearly homogeneous; assume that this is done, so that $V(k\mathbf{x}) = kV(\mathbf{x})$ for any positive scalar k. Under these circumstances, we can reason as follows:

$$\begin{aligned} C(\mathbf{p}, u) &= \min_{\mathbf{x}} \, [\mathbf{p}'\mathbf{x} \mid V(\mathbf{x}) \geqslant u] \\ &= \min_{\mathbf{x}} \left\{ \frac{1}{k} \, \mathbf{p}'(k\mathbf{x}) \mid V\left[\frac{1}{k} \, (k\mathbf{x})\right] \geqslant u \right\} \end{aligned}$$

$$= \frac{1}{k} \min_{\mathbf{x}} \left[\mathbf{p}'(k\mathbf{x}) \,\middle|\, \frac{1}{k} V(k\mathbf{x}) \geqslant u \right]$$

$$\frac{1}{k} \min_{k\mathbf{x}} [\mathbf{p}'(k\mathbf{x}) \mid V(k\mathbf{x}) \geqslant ku]$$

$$\frac{1}{k} C(\mathbf{p}, ku).$$

Thus homotheticity of $V(\mathbf{x})$ implies that

$$C(\mathbf{p}, ku) = k\, C(\mathbf{p}, u) \tag{1.30}$$

which means that the cost function is linearly homogeneous in u. But a function of a single variable must be a direct proportionality if it is to be linearly homogeneous, so that under homothetic preferences the cost function must be expressible in the form

$$C(\mathbf{p}, u) = \alpha(\mathbf{p})u \tag{1.31}$$

where $\alpha(\mathbf{p})$ is a function linearly homogeneous in $\mathbf{p}$. Equating this to y and solving gives the corresponding form for the indirect utility function:

$$H(\mathbf{p}/y) = \frac{1}{\alpha(\mathbf{p})} y = \frac{1}{\alpha(\mathbf{p}/y)}. \tag{1.32}$$

Differentiation of (1.31) gives the Hicksian demands

$$\tilde{x}_i(\mathbf{p}, u) = \frac{\partial \alpha(\mathbf{p})}{\partial p_i} u \tag{1.33}$$

and, upon substitution of $H(\mathbf{p}/y)$ for u,

$$\tilde{x}_i(\mathbf{p}/y) = \frac{\partial \alpha(\mathbf{p})}{\partial p_i} \frac{y}{\alpha(\mathbf{p})} \tag{1.34}$$

as the corresponding Marshallian demands. This proportional form for the demand functions implies that the budget shares $p_i \tilde{x}_i / y$ are independent of income; in other words, if preferences were homothetic, the rich and the poor would be observed to consume goods in exactly the same proportions. In general, it is clear that this will be a very unreasonable assumption, so homotheticity must be confined to problems in which proportional expenditures are not unrealistic. Unfortunately, the great analytical simplicity of homothetic preferences leads to their being assumed much more frequently than is really justifiable; in general, it is probably wiser to make no such assumption.

It is possible to relax the homotheticity assumption without greatly complicating matters by adopting a more general linear form than (1.31):

$$C(\mathbf{p}, u) = \alpha_1(\mathbf{p}) + \alpha_2(\mathbf{p})\, u \tag{1.35}$$

where the functions $\alpha_1(\mathbf{p})$ and $\alpha_2(\mathbf{p})$ are both homogeneous of degree one. The form (1.35) is called the Gorman polar form (Gorman, 1961) and preferences which lead to cost functions of this type are referred to as *quasi-homothetic*. The corresponding indirect utility function is

$$H(\mathbf{p}/y) = \frac{y - \alpha_1(\mathbf{p})}{\alpha_2(\mathbf{p})} \tag{1.36}$$

and, using Shephard's lemma, the Hicksian demands are

$$\tilde{x}_i(\mathbf{p}, u) = \frac{\partial \alpha_1(\mathbf{p})}{\partial p_i} + \frac{\partial \alpha_2(\mathbf{p})}{\partial p_i} u. \tag{1.37}$$

Substitution of $H(\mathbf{p}/y)$ for u gives the following Marshallian demands:

$$\tilde{x}_i(\mathbf{p}/y) = \left[\frac{\partial \alpha_1(\mathbf{p})}{\partial p_i} - \frac{\alpha_1(\mathbf{p})}{\alpha_2(\mathbf{p})} \frac{\partial \alpha_2(\mathbf{p})}{\partial p_i}\right] + \frac{\partial \alpha_2(\mathbf{p})}{\partial p_i} \frac{y}{\alpha_2(\mathbf{p})}. \tag{1.38}$$

Thus, although the demand functions may be complicated functions of prices, they are linear in income. In many microeconometric studies, we are dealing with cross-section data and are able to assume that every individual in the sample faces the same prices. If that is the case, then every term in (1.38) except for y itself is constant across individuals, and we have a very simple linear Engel curve to be estimated. Figure 1.10 illustrates this distinction between homothetic and quasi-homothetic preferences.

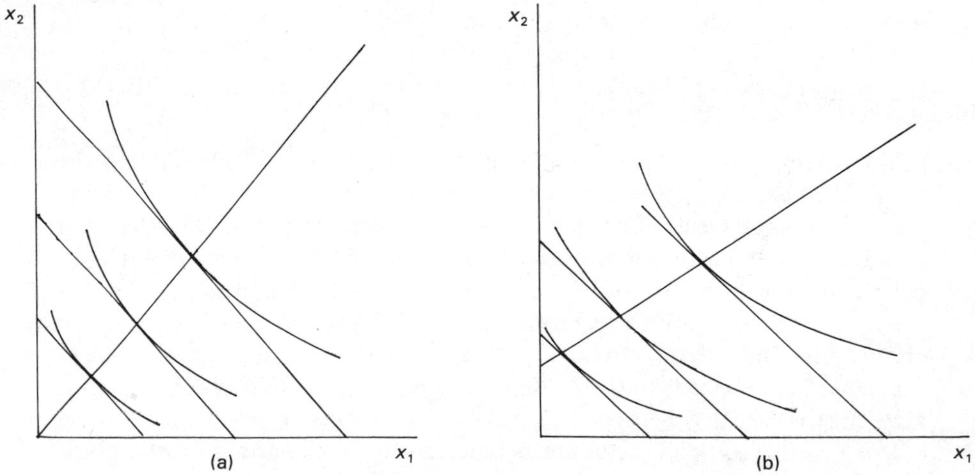

Figure 1.10 (a) Homothetic preferences; (b) quasi-homothetic preferences.

1.6 The distance function

In a number of microeconomic problems, and particularly in the discrete choice problems discussed in the next chapter, we require a measure of the similarity between two alternatives in the choice set Ψ. Since we are dealing with models of human behaviour, what is important is usually the consumer's perception of the similarity between alternatives rather than any technical relation between them. Consider, for example, the two vectors $\mathbf{x}^1$ and $\mathbf{x}^2$, illustrated in figure 1.11. These are both vectors in Ψ, and may contain quantities of both goods and characteristics among their elements.

The most natural way in which to compare $\mathbf{x}^1$ and $\mathbf{x}^2$ is to use a measure based on the difference between the utilities which they yield, $V(\mathbf{x}^1) - V(\mathbf{x}^2)$. The objection to this is that the utility function $V(\mathbf{x})$ is a purely ordinal concept, which means that only the sign of $V(\mathbf{x}^1) - V(\mathbf{x}^2)$, and not its numerical value, is of any significance. Debreu (1951) proposed (in the context of production, rather than consumption) a measure defined as the reciprocal of the proportion by which $\mathbf{x}^1$ must be expanded in order to move the consumer onto the indifference curve passing through the point $\mathbf{x}^2$. This measure will be a function of $\mathbf{x}^1$ and u^2, $D(\mathbf{x}^1, u^2)$ say, which is defined implicitly by the following equation:

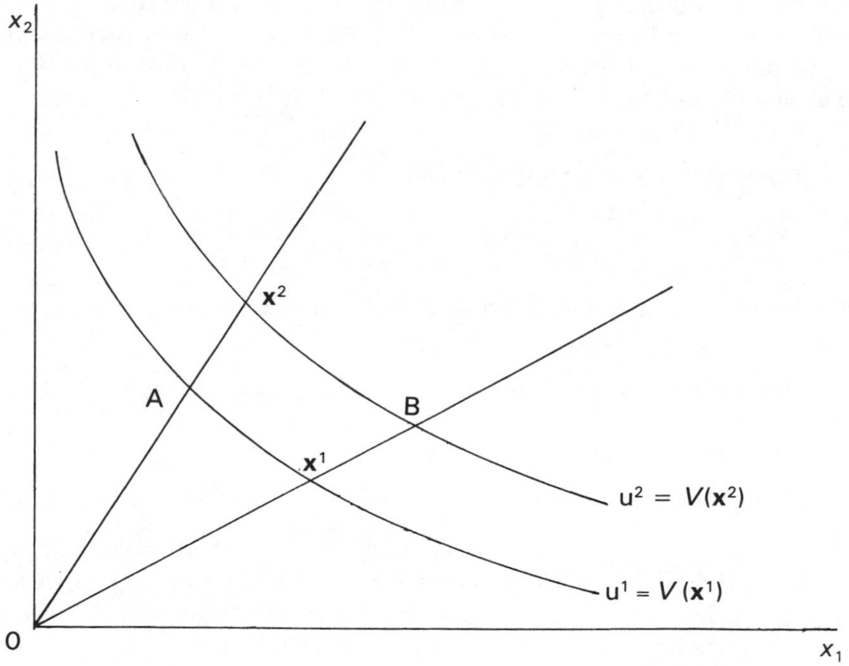

Figure 1.11 Measures of similarity between $\mathbf{x}^1$ and $\mathbf{x}^2$.

$$u^2 = V[\mathbf{x}^1/D(\mathbf{x}^1, u^2)]. \tag{1.39}$$

The value of $D(\mathbf{x}^1, u^2)$ is clearly invariant to monotonic transformations of $V(\mathbf{x})$, and it certainly captures the required idea of similarity of alternatives; however, there is an element of arbitrariness in its definition. We have chosen to compare these alternatives in terms of $\mathbf{x}^1$ and u^2; we could, with equal justification, have made the comparison in terms of $\mathbf{x}^2$ and u^1, leading to a measure $D(\mathbf{x}^2, u^1)$ defined implicitly by

$$u^1 = V[\mathbf{x}^2/D(\mathbf{x}^2, u^1)]. \tag{1.40}$$

In the example in figure 1.11, these two definitions are given by the ratios of Ox^1 to OB and Ox^2 to OA. There is no reason in general why these should be identical, so there is some ambiguity here; the problem is essentially identical with the one that arises in index number theory, where the reference standard of living to be used for the comparison is also arbitrary. However, there is one case in which this ambiguity is not present. When preferences are homothetic, $D(\mathbf{x}^1, u^2)$ is equal to u^1/u^2 and $D(\mathbf{x}^2, u^1)$ is equal to u^2/u^1 (assuming $V(\mathbf{x})$ to have been normalized to be homogeneous of degree one). In this case, $D(\mathbf{x}^2, u^1)$ is merely the reciprocal of $D(\mathbf{x}^1, u^2)$, so the two are essentially equivalent.

In recent years, the distance function has been the subject of considerable interest in the literature on demand analysis. Its importance extends well beyond its application as a measure of similarity, since the equation $D(\mathbf{x}, u) = 1$ can be used as an alternative characterization of preferences, with compensated demand functions derivable in inverse form through an analogue of Shephard's lemma. If we define the normalized price vector $\mathbf{p}^* = \mathbf{p}/y$, the cost function is

$$\begin{aligned} C(\mathbf{p}^*, u) &= \min_{\mathbf{x}} [\mathbf{p}^{*\prime}\mathbf{x} \mid u = V(\mathbf{x})] \\ &= \min_{\mathbf{x}} [\mathbf{p}^{*\prime}\mathbf{x} \mid D(\mathbf{x}, u) = 1]. \end{aligned} \tag{1.41}$$

The distance function is a perfect dual to the cost function, since (assuming convexity of preferences) it can be defined equivalently as

$$D(\mathbf{x}, u) = \min_{\mathbf{x}} [\mathbf{p}^{*\prime}\mathbf{x} \mid C(\mathbf{p}^*, u) = 1]. \tag{1.42}$$

The analogue of Shephard's lemma is

$$p_i^* = \partial D(\mathbf{x}, u)/\partial x_i. \tag{1.43}$$

These conditions give an inverse representation of the Hicksian demand functions. If $D(\mathbf{x}, u) = 1$ can be solved for u, its substitution in (1.43) yields the Marshallian demands in inverse form. Deaton (1979) gives a full analysis of this approach to the modelling of optimal behaviour.

There is a difficulty with the distance function when the utility function is

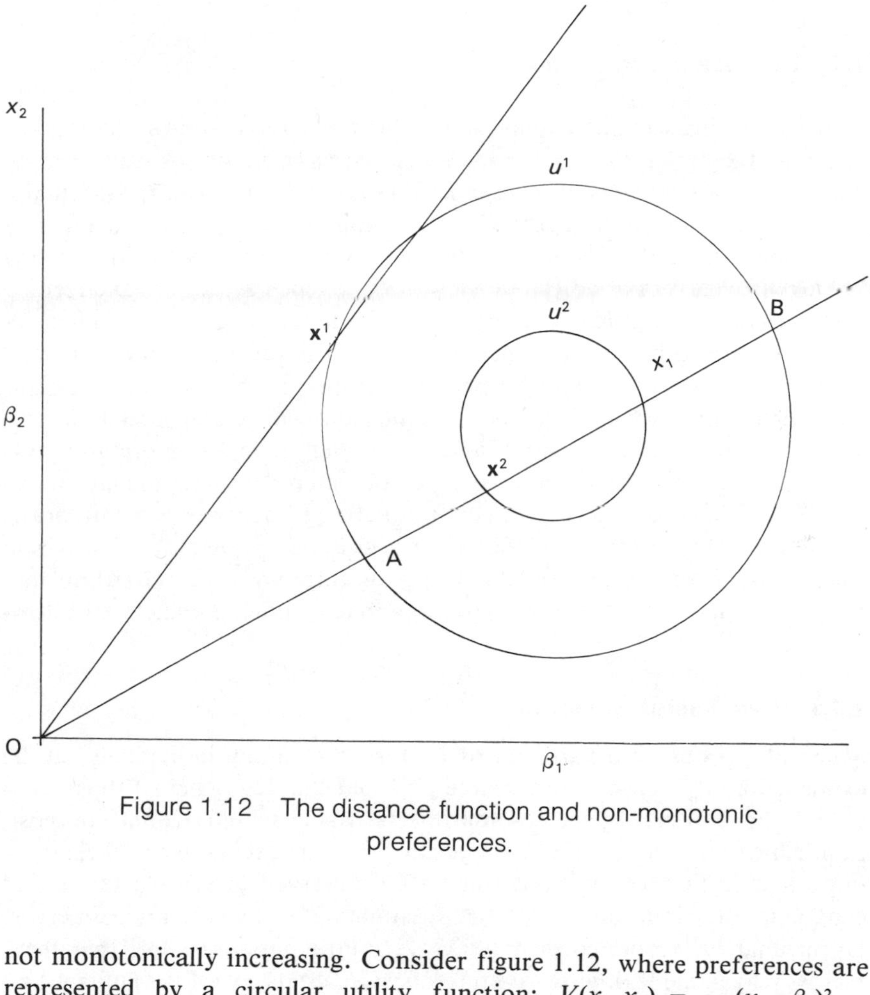

Figure 1.12 The distance function and non-monotonic preferences.

not monotonically increasing. Consider figure 1.12, where preferences are represented by a circular utility function: $V(x_1, x_2) = -(x_1 - \beta_1)^2 - (x_2 - \beta_2)^2$.

The problem here is that the distance function is either non-existent or over-determined almost everywhere: the equation $V(\mathbf{x}/D) = u$ has a unique solution only in very special cases. Consider the problem of constructing a measure of distance between points $\mathbf{x}^1$ and $\mathbf{x}^2$. Since the ray $O\mathbf{x}^1$ does not intersect the indifference curve u^2, the distance function $D(\mathbf{x}^1, u^2)$ does not exist. On the other hand, the measure $D(\mathbf{x}^2, u^1)$ can be defined either as $O\mathbf{x}^2/OA$ or $O\mathbf{x}^2/OB$. Such indeterminacies can always be resolved, for instance by defining distance as $\min(OA/O\mathbf{x}^2, O\mathbf{x}^2/OB)$. However, the distance function must be used with care when preferences are not guaranteed to be monotonic.

1.7 Variation in preferences

In the preceding sections we have made the implicit assumption that preferences are fixed: that different individuals share a common system of preferences which does not change over time. This is obviously absurd, particularly if we bear in mind that the agent whose decisions are being modelled is often a household rather than a single individual; a household with three young babies will clearly take a different view of goods such as nappies and feeding bottles than a household consisting of an old-age pensioner. Individual tastes are also likely to be heavily dependent on factors such as social status and education. However, everyday experience strongly suggests that even people who come from similar social backgrounds and who are in similar circumstances can have different tastes, and thus not all variation in preferences is likely to be explicable solely in terms of observed demographic and social factors. A final problem is that one cannot always infer the precise nature of decision-making directly from observed decisions: people make mistakes in their planning, or they depart from their plans through accident or whim, and it is usually desirable when specifying an applied model to make some allowance for this.

1.7.1 Deterministic preferences

Much of the observed variation of preferences among individuals can be explained by reference to observable personal characteristics of those individuals. Factors such as age, sex, marital status, household size and composition, educational achievement, social class, race and religion are likely to be important influences, and these are often observed in sample surveys of economic behaviour, albeit with the possibility of some measurement error. Unfortunately, economic theory says very little about the role that these factors play in the formation of preferences and thus gives little guidance on the use of these data in applied work.

What we seek is some flexible way of introducing demographic and social variables into the specification of preferences, while still preserving in our model some fundamental core which is common to all individuals and therefore capable of being estimated. We shall achieve this by extending the function $V(\mathbf{x})$ to include a vector of unobserved shift factors, or substitution parameters, β:

$$u = V(\mathbf{x}; \beta). \tag{1.44}$$

Individuals with different β vectors will have indifference maps displaying different substitution possibilities, and we can therefore explain preference variation by making some assumption about the determination of β and the way that it enters the utility function. For the time being, assume that β is related to the vector of observed personal attributes, $\mathbf{z}$, through a non-stochastic relation $\beta(\mathbf{z})$.

It should be noted that the assumption of a common utility function $V(.;.)$ does not carry with it any implication that utility is comparable across individuals: interpersonal comparisons are essentially political, not behavioural. Each individual's utility indicator could be subjected to a different monotonic transformation without altering the behavioural implications of the model in any way, despite the fact that the units in which utility is measured and compared would be completely disrupted. Therefore (1.44) does not necessarily provide a basis for welfare comparisons.

There are two main approaches to the incorporation of demographic variables. The most common is to adopt a convenient functional form for utility, in either its direct or indirect representation (for instance the direct or indirect translog utility function (Christensen, Jorgenson and Lau, 1975), the Klein–Rubin direct utility function (Stone, 1954) or the AIDS cost function (Deaton and Muellbauer, 1980b)), and to specify some or all of the parameters of this function to be (say) linear functions of $\mathbf{z}$. We shall see many examples of this in later chapters.

An alternative approach, often used in modelling family size and composition effects in demand analysis, is to specify a single universal utility function whose arguments are adjusted forms of the quantity variables $\mathbf{x}$. Assume that there exists a universal utility function $V^*(.)$ common to all individuals. This function has constant parameters, and its form is invariant to $\mathbf{z}$. However, its arguments are not the quantities $x_1, \ldots, x_q$ but rather transformations of these quantities, $x_1^*, \ldots, x_q^*$, where $x_i^* = x_i^*[x_i, \beta_i(\mathbf{z})]$.

A very common example of this is the use of per capita variables in family expenditure analysis; if $\mathbf{z}$ contains the single variable family size, $\beta_i = \mathbf{z}$ for all i and $x_i^*(x_i, \beta_i) = x_i/\beta_i$, then it is admissible to adjust for demographic variation by estimating demand functions defined in terms of expenditure per head and income per head. This is a special case of *demographic scaling*. Suppose that $x_i^* = x_i/\beta_i(\mathbf{z})$. Then the utility maximization problem can be reformulated:

$$\max_{\mathbf{x}^*} u = V^*(\mathbf{x}^*) \tag{1.45}$$

subject to

$$\sum_{i=1}^{q} x_i^* p_i^* = y \tag{1.46}$$

where $p_i^* = \beta_i(\mathbf{z})p_i$. In terms of the starred variables, this is a standard utility maximization problem, possessing as its solution the Marshallian demand functions $\tilde{x}_i^*(p_1^*/y, \ldots, p_q^*/y)$. The forms of the functions $\tilde{x}_i^*(.)$ are invariant to $\mathbf{z}$, but the demands expressed in terms of natural prices and quantities are

$$\tilde{x}_i(\mathbf{p}/y; \beta) = \beta_i(\mathbf{z})\, \tilde{x}_i^* [\beta_1(\mathbf{z})p_1/y, \ldots, \beta_q(\mathbf{z})p_q y]. \tag{1.47}$$

Optimal behaviour can also be represented in dual form. If $H^*(.)$ and $C^*(.)$ are the indirect utility and cost functions corresponding to a utility function $V^*(.)$, then the indirect utility and cost functions expressed in terms of natural variables are clearly

$$H(\mathbf{p}/y; \beta) = H^* [\beta_1(\mathbf{z})p_1/y, \ldots, \beta_q(\mathbf{z})p_q/y] \tag{1.48}$$

and

$$C(\mathbf{p}, u; \beta) = C^* [\beta_1(\mathbf{z})p_1, \ldots, \beta_q(\mathbf{z})p_q, u]. \tag{1.49}$$

If the commodity-specific scale factors β_i are identical, as in the per capita case, then the homogeneity of the cost function implies that individual cost functions are simply multiples of one another. To quote Gorman's (1976) celebrated schoolteacher, 'when you have a wife and child, a penny bun costs threepence'.

Other transformations are possible. If $x_i^* = x_i - \beta_i(\mathbf{z})$, then we have the case of *demographic translating*, leading to a budget constraint

$$\sum_{i=1}^{q} p_i x_i^* = y^* \tag{1.50}$$

where $y^* = y - \Sigma p_i \beta_i(\mathbf{z})$. Thus the demand functions, indirect utility function and cost function are

$$\tilde{x}_i(\mathbf{p}/y; \beta) = \beta_i(\mathbf{z}) + \tilde{x}_i^* (p_1/y^*, \ldots, p_q/y^*) \tag{1.51}$$

$$H(\mathbf{p}/y; \beta) = H^* (p_1/y^*, \ldots, p_q/y^*) \tag{1.52}$$

and

$$C(\mathbf{p}, u; \beta) = \Sigma p_i \beta_i(\mathbf{z}) + C^* (p_1, \ldots, p_q, u). \tag{1.53}$$

Combinations of these forms are possible, and also more complex transformations involving interactions between goods. Further discussion and an application to cross-section demand analysis can be found in Pollak and Wales (1981).

1.7.2 Random preferences

There are two distinct senses in which preferences could be regarded as random. Behaviour may be inherently unpredictable, in the sense that a consumer, repeatedly faced with the same choice problem under identical circumstances, might be observed to make a variety of different choices. In this case, preferences are random both to the outside observer and to the individual concerned, and the axioms of choice discussed in section 1.1 are no longer applicable. Conditions for the existence of a stochastic utility indicator (which is a random function $V(.)$ such that $\Pr(\mathbf{x}^1 > \mathbf{x}^2)$ and

$\Pr[V(\mathbf{x}^1) > V(\mathbf{x}^2)]$ are always equal) are given by Block and Marschak (1960), Marschak (1960) and McFadden and Richter (1971).

A second interpretation of randomness is as a device to represent factors which determine the nature of preferences but which are not known to the outside observer. Call these factors β, and represent preferences by a utility function $V(\mathbf{x}; \beta)$. The vector β summarizes the psychological makeup of this rational individual and thus, if β is held fixed, individual choices are strictly rational and deterministic. However, to the outside observer examining a group of individuals or a single individual over time, choices will appear to display random inconsistencies. This randomness is apparent rather than real.

The distinction between these two interpretations is interesting but of little practical importance. The important question is whether we can represent these random factors, however they arise, by a single value for β, drawn from the β population and held constant through all utility comparisons at a particular time (we do not exclude the possibility that β may evolve through time). In this case, a choice between $\mathbf{x}^1$ and $\mathbf{x}^2$ can be made by comparing $V(\mathbf{x}^1; \beta)$ and $V(\mathbf{x}^2; \beta)$. An alternative form of random variation can arise either because preference comparisons are inherently unpredictable or because there are some unobserved attributes of the opportunity set which are excluded from the vector $\mathbf{x}$ and treated instead as random. In this case, each element of the opportunity set is associated with a different β, and a choice between $\mathbf{x}^1$ and $\mathbf{x}^2$ requires a comparison of $V(\mathbf{x}^1; \beta^1)$ with $V(\mathbf{x}^2; \beta^2)$, where β^1 and β^2 are different drawings from the β population (this population may itself vary with $\mathbf{x}$). Randomness of the latter type is clearly much harder to handle in general. If the opportunity set is dense, as is usually the case, then conventional statistical methods are not available and the model is intractable except in very special cases. The one major applied field where this type of specification is widely used is the modelling of choice between discrete alternatives, for in this case there is only a limited number of drawings from the β population to be considered. Except in this one field, we shall avoid this formulation of random utility.

We shall normally write the nth individual's random utility indicator as

$$\mathrm{u}_n = V(\mathbf{x}; \beta_n) \tag{1.54}$$

where β_n is a random vector drawn from a population with conditional c.d.f.

$$\Pr(\beta_n \leqslant \beta \,|\, \mathbf{z}_n) = G_\beta(\beta \,|\, \mathbf{z}_n) \tag{1.55}$$

and $\mathbf{z}_n$ is a vector of observed personal attributes such as age, education, family size and composition. The non-random preferences discussed in section 1.7.1 are a special case of this, with β_n having a degenerate conditional distribution. Note that β_n might have a distribution that is at least partly discrete, representing distinctions between different types of preferences: those of vegetarians and non-vegetarians, for instance. Thus β_n might not possess a p.d.f. with respect to all its elements. An example of discrete preference shifts is discussed in chapter 4, section 4.3.2.

As a means of building random variation into a model of choice, specification (1.54) and (1.55) is very appealing, since it fits neatly into the economic theorist's world of optimizing behaviour whilst allowing for more variability than can be explained with measured variables. However, its insistence on strict rationality is sometimes a severe practical drawback, since it is not unusual for applied researchers to observe behaviour which is undoubtedly irrational in the context of a particular model. This is illustrated in figure 1.13, which shows the piecewise-linear frontier of a non-convex income–leisure opportunity set. Non-convexities of this form might arise from the payment of an overtime premium for weekly hours of work corresponding to the segment AB. Unless individuals have kinked indifference curves (for example, because income and leisure are perfect complements), it is clearly impossible for rational behaviour to lead to observed choices in the neighbourhood of point B. As we consider altering an individual's preferences by changing β in the direction β^1, β^2, β^3, the optimal consumption of leisure will increase continuously along segment AB until point x_1^* is reached, and then it will jump to x_1^{**} and continue increasing along segment BC. Thus no observation could ever be made between x_1^* and x_1^{**}.

Although few of the participants in a statistical survey would normally be

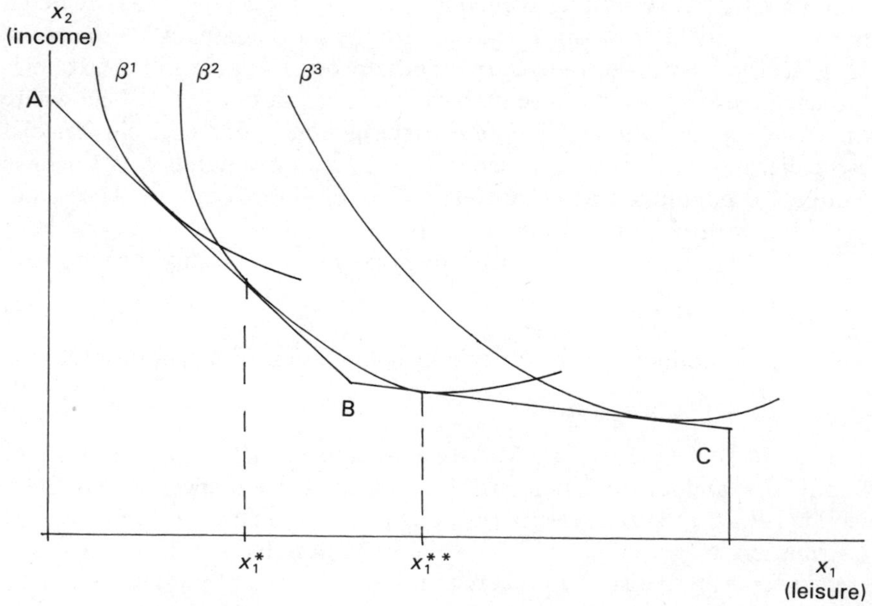

Figure 1.13 Regions of irrationality.

observed in regions of this kind, it is not unusual to find some individuals behaving in an apparently irrational way. One cannot definitely conclude from this that inherent randomness is a feature of observed behaviour, since there are many other things that could lead to this sort of problem: rationing, aggregation over members of a household and the failure to execute rational decisions perfectly, for instance. However, the important point is that apparently irrational individuals cannot be accommodated by a pure random parameter model, and 'nearly' irrational behaviour may cause severe distortion of the estimated utility function. For this reason, it is unusual to find applied models which assume randomness of preferences alone; mixed models involving also some random deviations from optimality are much more common.

1.7.3 Random inefficiency

It is usual in most branches of econometrics to maintain a complete separation between the deterministic economic part of the model and the random disturbances. This might be termed the random inefficiency specification: the individual solves a deterministic optimization problem to find the planned or desired demand $\tilde{\mathbf{x}}$ but is then observed to depart randomly from this optimal solution because of a host of trivial obstructions, whims, measurement errors etc. Thus the observed and planned values of $\mathbf{x}$ are related by

$$\mathbf{x}_n = \tilde{\mathbf{x}}_n + \epsilon_n \tag{1.56}$$

where ϵ_n is a vector of random disturbances with zero mean. This specification allows irrationality but asserts that behaviour is rational on average. Thus, two individuals n and n', with identical personal characteristics (and therefore substitution parameters β) and facing identical opportunity sets, would have the same optimal consumption vector $\tilde{\mathbf{x}}(\beta)$ but different observed consumption vectors $\mathbf{x}_n = \tilde{\mathbf{x}}(\beta) + \epsilon_n$ and $\mathbf{x}_{n'} = \tilde{\mathbf{x}}(\beta) + \epsilon_{n'}$.

Although it is quite reasonable to assert that people fail to execute their plans to perfection, this very simple stochastic specification is not beyond criticism. One objection is that the random disturbances do not grow naturally from the economic theory: for example, on economic grounds one would expect that the probability of making an execution error of a certain size would depend upon the cost (in terms of utility foregone) associated with that error. Put more simply, people are generally much more careful in carrying out important decisions than relatively unimportant ones, an argument that suggests that the distributional form for ϵ_n may display heteroscedasticity of a form related to the determinants of preferences, $\mathbf{z}_n$.

Consider the example of figure 1.14, illustrating the case of an individual under two alternative configurations of preferences, corresponding to β^1 and β^2. Under β^1, one would expect a distribution for observed consumption which has less dispersion than the distribution prevailing under β^2: large errors are less costly under β^2 and are thus more likely to be made. This is

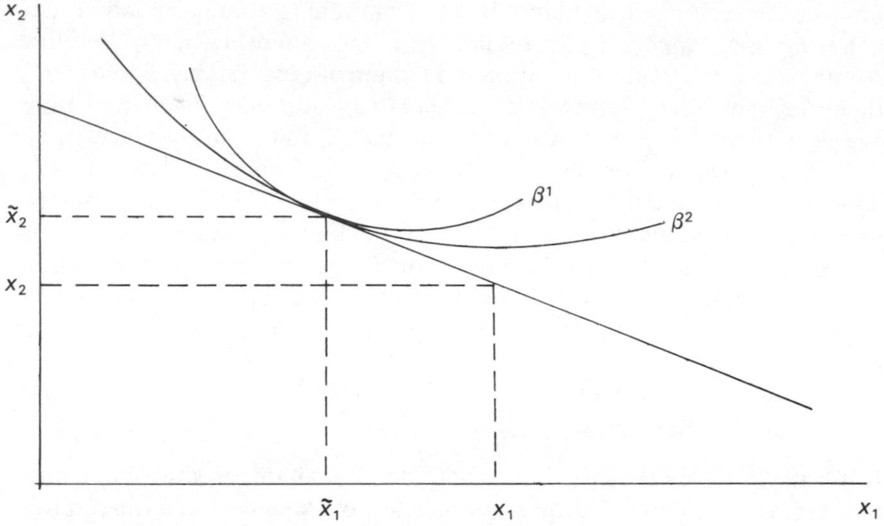

Figure 1.14 Variable costs of suboptimality.

because a higher indifference curve passes through the typical suboptimal point (x_1, x_2) under β^2.

A second objection concerns the very limited form that inefficiency is assumed to take. We are prepared to entertain the notion that consumers deviate from the optimal point $\tilde{\mathbf{x}}$, yet we still insist that their consumption takes place on the boundary, rather than the interior, of the opportunity set (in the terminology of production theory, we assume management inefficiency but not technical inefficiency). In practice there is no compelling reason why this should be the case: in any given decision period, the total available resources y may not be completely exhausted, and it is also quite possible for the resource constraint to be treated as an intended rather than actual limit on behaviour. In other words, provided there is some residual element, such as savings, in the individual's budget, it is quite possible to overspend in the short term. It is hard to accommodate this type of random error in applied models, since intended spending is unobservable and cannot be measured in the usual way as the sum of individual expenditures. The problem of the budget constraint is discussed further in chapter 4, section 4.2.

A third difficulty with the random inefficiency specification arises when we deal with non-standard opportunity sets of the type discussed in the section 1.6. In many instances, we are particularly interested in only a subset of the commodities involved in the microeconomic problem: for example, we might build a model of the leisure–income choice because we are interested in the supply of labour. In this case our model provides us with an expression

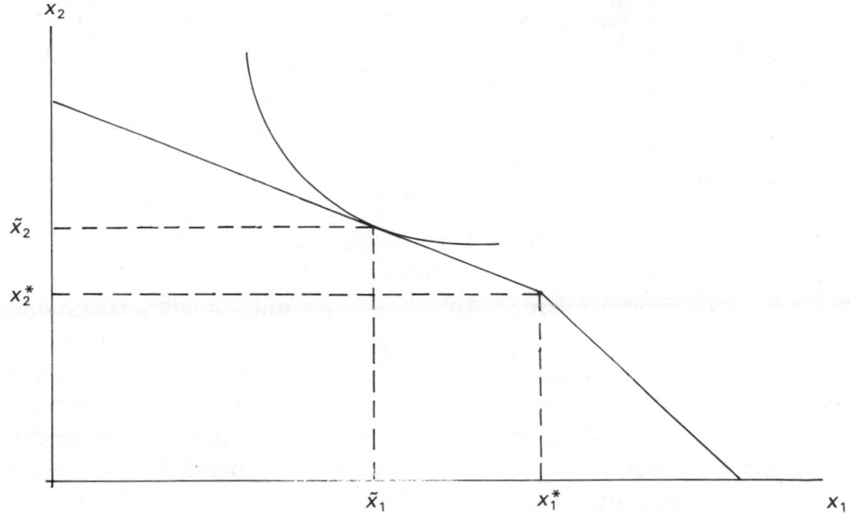

Figure 1.15 Random inefficiency with a kinked budget constraint.

for the optimal number of hours of leisure ($\tilde{x}_1$) for each individual, and actual hours of leisure are assumed to follow some convenient distribution (often the normal), with mean $\tilde{x}_1$. However, the implied distribution for the other decision variable, income (x_2), may be very odd indeed. Consider the example in figure 1.15.

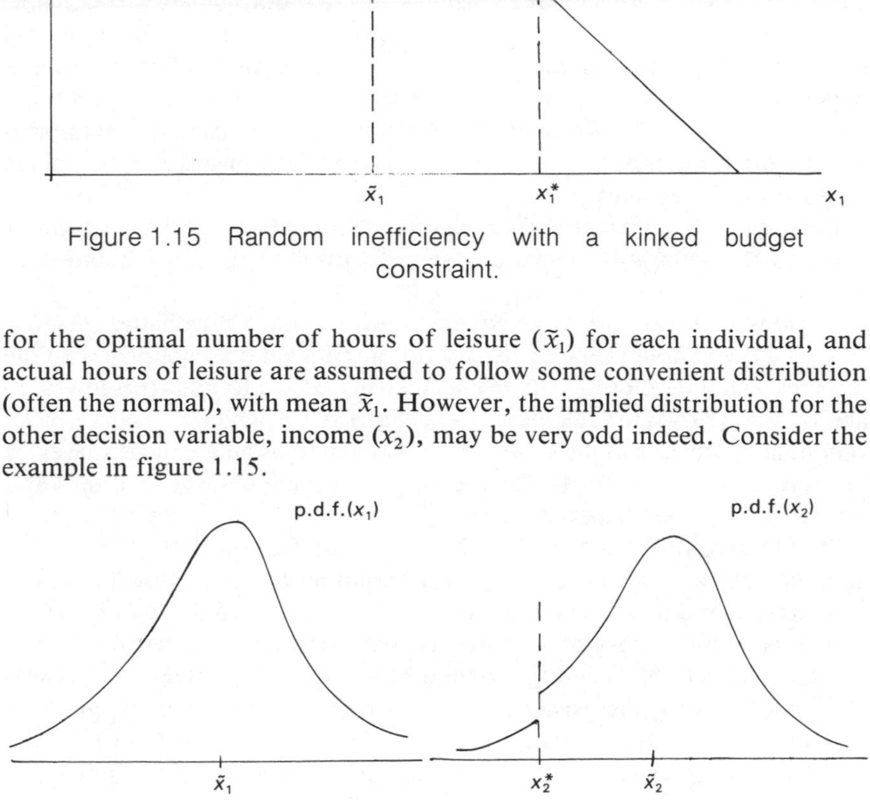

Figure 1.16 Assumed and induced distributions.

If the p.d.f. of x_1 is as illustrated in figure 1.16, then the kinked budget constraint (on which x_1 and x_2 must lie) induces a distribution for x_2 which is discontinuous at $x_2 = \tilde{x}_2$. This is an unnatural assumption (x_2 does not necessarily have mean $\tilde{x}_2$, for instance), which would presumably not have been chosen had x_2 been the focus of the analysis. Thus, the simple application of stochastic specification (1.56) can lead to an asymmetry in the estimated model which is hard to justify. This problem, and an alternative approach to stochastic specification, are discussed further in chapter 5, section 5.4.

Against these objections, this approach to model specification has the important virtues of simplicity and familiarity, and plays a very important role in applied work.

Further reading

The subject matter of section 1.1 is covered by most advanced micro-economics textbooks, although indivisibility and preferences defined over characteristics are topics which usually receive only cursory treatment. Deaton and Muellbauer (1980a) and Simmons (1974) are excellent general references. On the existence of utility functions, Debreu (1954) is the seminal paper, and his work is taken much further in the various contributions to Chipman *et al.* (1971). Kagel *et al.* (1975) describe an ingenious attempt to test the implications of the theory of rational choice by means of experiments with laboratory animals.

Deaton and Muellbauer (1980a, chapter 1) provide a useful discussion of many of the awkward opportunity sets discussed in section 1.2 and later chapters.

Sections 1.3–1.6 are covered by Deaton and Muellbauer (1980a, chapter 2); Simmons (1974) is also useful, although it does not deal with the distance function. Gorman (1976), Blackorby, Primont and Russell (1978) and Diewert (1974) are valuable references on the use of duality theory in conventional optimizing models. Deaton (1986) contains an excellent survey of alternative functional forms for the various representations of utility and their role in applied demand analysis.

Deaton and Muellbauer (1980, chapter 8) and Deaton (1986) discuss the methods that are commonly used to incorporate the effects of household composition and other demographic variables in demand analysis.

Inherent randomness of preferences has been analysed by Block and Marschak (1960), Marschak (1960) and McFadden and Richter (1971), who give conditions for the existence of a stochastic utility indicator. See also McFadden (1982) for a survey of stochastic choice theory. However, the applied literature contains very little discussion of the choice of a stochastic specification; analytical convenience usually has to be the overriding consideration.

2

Survey methods and cross-section econometrics

Let observation with extensive view
Survey mankind from China to Peru.

Samuel Johnson

Every day, thousands of people are asked thousands of questions about their behaviour, attitudes, habits, circumstances and opinions. Regular sample surveys are conducted by most governments to satisfy various national accounting needs: the construction of weights for the retail price index, the index of industrial production etc. and for a host of other policy-related purposes. Commercial market research surveys are conducted regularly to provide information on demand conditions for producers and to assess the effectiveness of advertising campaigns. Many research bodies and pressure groups carry out surveys to meet the needs of their research or supply evidence to support their case. A particularly interesting form of cross-section enquiry, carried out in several parts of the USA during the 1970s, is the social experiment, in which families' economic circumstances are not only observed but are also modified by subjecting them to some controlled change - an experimental form of negative income tax, for instance.

With the exception of these experimental enquiries, econometricians have played a surprisingly small part in this survey activity. It is still a comparative rarity for economists to commission a survey enquiry dedicated to the objectives of a specific piece of econometric research; it remains normal practice to make use of survey data which is collected for entirely different purposes, by methods over which the econometrician has no control. Although this is to be deplored, since it imposes severe constraints on the kind of research that is possible, we shall neglect the topic of optimal sample survey design and instead discuss the theory of sample surveys from the more realistic point of view of the econometrician who must use survey data gathered by a sampling technique which he or she is powerless to influence.

In section 2.1 we briefly survey the theory of common sampling methods.

Section 2.2 deals with some of the difficulties associated with the practical form of the enquiry. Section 2.3 discusses a specific example: the UK Family Expenditure Survey. Sections 2.4 and 2.5 are concerned with the econometric implications of exogenous and endogenous biased sampling methods, and section 2.6 deals with the problem of non-response, attrition and other forms of extraneous sample truncation.

2.1 Sampling techniques

We begin with some definitions. The *sampling unit* is the individual subject of our analysis; sampling units may be single persons, households, firms etc. Sometimes there may be some problems of definition here: if an aunt comes to visit in the week of the survey, is she counted as a member of the household? These definitional problems must be resolved by the survey designer, often arbitrarily.

The relevant attributes of these sampling units we represent by two (vector) variables: $\mathbf{x}$ is the subject of our economic model, for instance expenditure on food, hours of labour supplied etc.; ζ is a vector containing all attributes which are to be used as explanatory variables - income, prices, wage rates, family size and structure, age etc. Thus $\mathbf{x}$ is endogenous and ζ exogenous to our model.

2.1.1 The population

The *actual population* is simply the full set of sampling units in existence: the group from which the sample is chosen. For example, the population of individual persons in the UK comprises some 56 million sampling units. In virtually all practical cases, this actual population has a finite number of members, and therefore the distribution of the observable variables $\mathbf{x}$ and ζ is discrete - there are at most 56 million distinct possible values for any set of individual attributes observed at any one time. This is so even for quantities such as income that are potentially continuously variable. We denote the number of units in the actual population by N^a and the empirical c.d.f. of $\mathbf{x}$ and ζ by $G^a(.,.)$, where $G^a(\mathbf{X}, \mathbf{Z})$ is the probability of observing $\mathbf{x} \leqslant \mathbf{X}$ and $\zeta \leqslant \mathbf{Z}$ in a unit drawn at random from the actual population.

Note that, for it to be possible to sample members of this population, it is necessary that there exist some practical means of identifying sampling units. This list of sampling units is known as the *sample frame*. Ideally, one would like the sample frame to cover the whole of the population that the enquiry attempts to survey. However, this is rarely achievable in practice; sample frames are generally based on lists assembled for other purposes - the electoral register, the telephone directory etc. These are often highly unsatisfactory, omitting certain types of individual in a systematic way, and the possible consequences of a poor sampling frame should always be borne in mind.

Most statistical sampling theory (see, for instance, Cochran, 1963; Kish, 1965) is concerned with the problem of estimating characteristics of the actual population: quantities such as the average age, the quartiles of the income distribution, and so on. Our perspective is rather different, since we are interested in the construction of structural models. Such models are not designed to describe the actual population but rather to answer hypothetical questions: what would happen to the demand for bread if its price were to double? How would labour supply change in response to an increase in the tax rate? If such changes were actually to occur, there would be no reason why the stochastic factors affecting behaviour should remain fixed at the values they happen to take in the actual population. Thus the hypothetical worlds described by an econometric model have no particular relationship with the actual population that supplies the data from which it is estimated. To reflect this, we introduce the idea of a *super-population*, consisting of a continuum of 'potential' individuals. The actual sample is regarded as a set of N^a individuals drawn (by 'nature') at random from this super-population, which is characterized by a c.d.f. $G(\mathbf{X}, \mathbf{Z}) = \Pr(\mathbf{x} \leqslant \mathbf{X}, \boldsymbol{\zeta} \leqslant \mathbf{Z})$ or, equivalently, by a probability density/mass function $g(\mathbf{x}, \boldsymbol{\zeta})$, which is the function $G(.,.)$ partially differentiated with respect to all elements of $\mathbf{x}$ and $\boldsymbol{\zeta}$ that are (locally) continuously variable and differenced with respect to any elements (such as dummy variables) that are discrete.

2.1.2 Exogeneity and the statistical model

The econometric model that we seek to estimate from sample information attempts to 'explain' $\mathbf{x}$ in terms of $\boldsymbol{\zeta}$, and thus amounts to an assumed parametric form for the distribution of $\mathbf{x}$ conditional on $\boldsymbol{\zeta}$, in the super-population. Let the vector of unknown parameters that define the precise form of this distribution be $\boldsymbol{\theta}$, and write the model as $g(\mathbf{x} \mid \boldsymbol{\zeta}; \boldsymbol{\theta})$. For this to be an autonomous model (or, equivalently, for $\boldsymbol{\zeta}$ to be *weakly exogenous* or *ancillary* for $\boldsymbol{\theta}$), the marginal distribution of $\boldsymbol{\zeta}$ must be independent of $\boldsymbol{\theta}$, in which case it is uninformative for $\boldsymbol{\theta}$. By Bayes' rule

$$g(\mathbf{x}, \boldsymbol{\zeta}) = g(\mathbf{x} \mid \boldsymbol{\zeta}; \boldsymbol{\theta})\, g(\boldsymbol{\zeta}) \tag{2.1}$$

where we are using $g(.)$ as generic notation for any population density/mass function.

The exogeneity assumption (2.1) is often questionable. A particular problem concerns the use of prices as explanatory variables, since prices are determined simultaneously with quantities within the market. Few applied workers give any justification for the assumption of exogenous prices, but there is an implicit assumption that, in a large market with a uniform average price, the price variable is approximately exogenous.

To illustrate the issues involved, consider a very simple market model with an actual population of N^a consumers (drawn at random from the super-population). We follow conventional practice by specifying the demand curve for each consumer in structural form. For the simplest linear case

$$x_n = \gamma_0 + \gamma_1 p_n + \epsilon_n \tag{2.2}$$

where p_n (the sole element of ζ) is the price faced by individual n, and ϵ_n is a behavioural disturbance term, with an $N(0, \sigma_{\epsilon\epsilon})$ distribution (say). The typical cross-section demand analysis proceeds by translating (2.2) into the assumption that $x_n|p_n$ has an $N(\gamma_0+\gamma_1 p_n, \sigma_{\epsilon\epsilon})$ in the population. The parameters of interest are thus $\theta' = (\gamma_0\, \gamma_1\, \sigma_{\epsilon\epsilon})$.

Assume now that there is a single producer, operating under constant costs and having perfect knowledge of all aspects of the market. The retail system is such that individual prices p_n deviate randomly and uncontrollably from the mean price P fixed by the producer:

$$p_n = P + v_n \tag{2.3}$$

where v_n is normally distributed with zero mean and variance σ_{vv}. Assume that ϵ_n and v_n are independent. The producer's profit function is

$$\Pi(P) = \sum_{n=1}^{N^a} (P + v_n - c)\,[\gamma_0 + \gamma_1(P+v_n) + \epsilon_n] \tag{2.4}$$

where c is unit cost, which we assume to be known. The profit-maximizing price is $P = c - \bar{x}/\gamma_1 - \bar{v}$, where bars denote averages over all N^a consumers. Thus the actual price is

$$p_n = c - \bar{x}/\gamma_1 - \bar{v} + v_n. \tag{2.5}$$

Equations (2.2) and (2.5) have the reduced form

$$p_n = \frac{c\gamma_1 - \gamma_0}{2\gamma_1} - \frac{1}{2\gamma_1}\bar{\epsilon} - \frac{1}{2}\bar{v} + v_n \tag{2.6}$$

$$x_n = \frac{c\gamma_1 + \gamma_0}{2} - \frac{1}{2}\bar{\epsilon} - \frac{\gamma_1}{2}\bar{v} + \gamma_1 v_n + \epsilon_n \tag{2.7}$$

and these expressions imply that p_n and x_n have a bivariate normal distribution with means

$$\mu_p = (c\gamma_1 - \gamma_0)/2\gamma_1 \tag{2.8}$$

$$\mu_x = (c\gamma_1 + \gamma_0)/2 \tag{2.9}$$

and covariances

$$\sigma_{pp} = \sigma_{vv} + \frac{1}{4N^a}\left(\frac{\sigma_{\epsilon\epsilon}}{\gamma_1^2} - 3\,\sigma_{vv}\right) \tag{2.10}$$

$$\sigma_{xx} = \gamma_1^2\sigma_{vv} + \sigma_{\epsilon\epsilon} - \frac{3}{4N^a}(\gamma_1^2\sigma_{vv} + \sigma_{\epsilon\epsilon}) \tag{2.11}$$

$$\sigma_{xp} = \gamma_1 \sigma_{vv} - \frac{1}{4N^{\mathrm{a}}} \left(2\gamma_1 \sigma_{vv} - \frac{\sigma_{\epsilon\epsilon}}{\gamma_1} \right). \tag{2.12}$$

The marginal distribution of p_n is thus

$$p_n \sim N(\mu_p, \sigma_{pp}). \tag{2.13}$$

Since μ_p is a known function of $\boldsymbol{\theta}$, this distribution is informative for $\boldsymbol{\theta}$, and price is not exogenous in the sense of (2.1). We therefore lose information if we choose to work only with the conditional distribution of x_n. More seriously, the conditional distribution of x_n has the following form:

$$x_n | p_n \sim N[\mu_x + \sigma_{xp}(p_n - \mu_p)/\sigma_{pp}, \ \sigma_{xx} - (\sigma_{xp})^2/\sigma_{pp}]. \tag{2.14}$$

For finite N^{a}, this is not the $N(\gamma_0 + \gamma_1 p_n, \ \sigma\ \ )$ distribution that equation (2.2) suggests, and simple estimation of (2.2) by regression methods leads to biased estimates of γ_0 and γ_1. However, this problem disappears as N^{a} becomes large. If the limiting forms of σ_{xx}, σ_{pp} and σ_{xp} are substituted into (2.14), the result is the $N(\gamma_0 + \gamma_1 p_n, \ \sigma\ \ )$ distribution that we would assume if p_n were known to be exogenous.

The conclusion is therefore that, provided demand and supply side disturbances are independent and that the number of consumers is large,

i prices can be regarded as exogenous for the purpose of constructing the conditional distribution associated with the econometric model, but that

ii the marginal distribution of price may contain information on the demand parameters – so statistical methods based only on the conditional distribution may be inefficient.

Note that these conclusions are quite general and do not depend critically on normality or on the details of our model of supply.

In the remainder of the book we shall usually ignore the endogeneity of prices, since the cost is only a theoretical efficiency loss. However, in a few cases this endogeneity problem cannot be ignored. If, for instance, the consumer can choose between different qualities of the good, so that price is a choice variable, the price disturbance v_n is partly demand determined, and unlikely to be independent of ϵ_n. A second example concerns labour supply, where each individual commands a different specific wage, determined in part by his or her unobserved characteristics, which may also partly influence labour supply. For instance, an ambitious person is likely to supply more labour and be better paid than others, implying some correlation between the two random disturbances. In such cases, the price or wage must be regarded as endogenous, even if there are a large number of individuals in the market, and we are forced to estimate simultaneous models of demand and price. With these caveats in mind, we now return to the assumption that our explanatory variables $\boldsymbol{\zeta}$ are exogenous in the population (in the strong sense of (2.1) and consider the methods of sampling that underlie cross-section econometrics.

Sampling is a process by which we draw a subset of N individuals from the actual population so that their observed $\mathbf{x}$, ζ values can be used as the basis for inferences about the nature of the distribution $g(\mathbf{x} \mid \zeta; \theta)$, which is formally a feature of the super-population. There are several common methods of drawing a sample from a given sampling frame. In discussing these, we shall consider only the case where the size of sample to be drawn, N, is fixed. This is somewhat restrictive, since it excludes sequential sampling, in which successive observations are taken until some fixed criterion is reached, yielding a sample of random size. However, such sampling schemes are unusual in economic and social surveys. We shall adhere to the notation already established: distributions relating to the super-population have c.d.f. and p.d.f. written $G(.)$ and $g(.)$; the symbols $F(.)$ and $f(.)$ are used for distributions relating to the sample rather than the population.

2.1.3 Simple random sampling

Much of statistical theory is dominated by the concept of the random sample. A random sample of size N is a set of observations $(x_1, \zeta_1) \ldots (x_N, \zeta_N)$ chosen in such a way that their joint distribution, which has probability density/mass function $f(x_1, \zeta_1, \ldots, x_N, \zeta_N)$, displays two properties.

i The N pairs (x_n, ζ_n) are independently distributed:

$$f(x_1, \zeta_1, \ldots, x_N, \zeta_N) = \prod_{n=1}^{N} f_n(x_n, \zeta_n) \tag{2.15}$$

where $f_n(.,.)$ is the marginal density/mass function of (x_n, ζ_n).

ii Sampling is unbiased, in the sense that each observation has the same distribution as the super-population itself:

$$f(x_1, \zeta_1, \ldots, x_N, \zeta_N) = \prod_{n=1}^{N} g(x_n, \zeta_n)$$

$$= \prod_{n=1}^{N} g(x_n \mid \zeta_n; \theta)\, g(\zeta_n). \tag{2.16}$$

The term random sample is a very misleading one, since there are many possible methods of sampling which are random in character but do not possess these two properties; a better term would be unbiased independent sampling.

A random sample has tremendous analytical advantages. Because its distribution perfectly mirrors that of the population, statistical inference from a random sample is particularly simple and direct. However, despite this simplicity, and despite its prominent place in statistical theory, random samples are almost never encountered in practice. There are two main reasons for this.

Random samples are often a very inefficient way of collecting information which is representative of (as opposed to having the same theoretical distribution as) the population. For instance, if the survey designer is required to produce a sample with adequate representation of a number of subgroups in the population (e.g. workers in different industries, or consumers in different counties), it may be necessary to draw a very large and therefore expensive sample. Other sampling techniques can usually provide a much cheaper means of meeting the objectives of the body commissioning the survey.

A second reason is that the selection of a random sample requires the sample frame to cover the whole population and the method of choosing units from the frame to be by repeated random drawing. It is very unusual for a survey to be based on a perfect sampling frame. For instance, the electoral register omits the young and the transient, and therefore even if individuals were drawn at random from the electoral register the resulting sample would not be random in the present sense. In any case, many practical sampling schemes do not make repeated random drawings from the frame but instead use simpler methods such as interval sampling, which is discussed below.

2.1.4 Exhaustive sampling

Since the actual population is finite, it is in principle possible to adopt a policy of complete enumeration or exhaustive sampling, where the sample and actual population are identical. Many countries attempt to do this for the population of individual people by conducting a census every ten years, covering mainly demographic attributes. However, smaller-scale exhaustive samples are often conducted when the target population is small or when the required information is already gathered for some other administrative purpose. Unemployment statistics, for example, are usually compiled from an exhaustive sample (of the population of unemployed individuals), which is constructed for the purposes of paying unemployment benefits.

Exhaustive samples present no statistical problems, since they can be treated as simple random samples from the super-population. However, there are severe practical problems in most cases. Complete enumeration is usually very expensive, since it requires an enormous number of individual enquiries, and it therefore rather rare. Moreover, census data usually only become available after a long preparation delay, so that it is impossible to produce up-to-date econometric results. The latter problem is often avoided by the early publication of data for a small random sample of the full census, thus using census returns as a sampling frame for a smaller random sample. Perhaps the most serious problem with large exhaustive samples is that they simply generate too much data – the analysis of detailed statistical models using millions of observations is a practical impossibility, and one is forced either to use subsamples or to work with averaged data.

2.1.5 Interval sampling

Interval sampling is a particularly simple and widely used method of selecting a sample of units from a given sampling frame. Denote by $i \in \{1, \ldots, N^a\}$ the position of the typical sampling unit in the frame. In order to establish a relationship between the ordering of units in the frame and the distribution of individuals in the super-population, define also a continuous random variable $u \in (-\infty, \infty)$ which underlies this ordering. Thus we suppose that 'nature' selects N^a units from the super-population and arranges these within the frame in ascending u order. Write the probability density/mass function of $\mathbf{x}$, ζ and u in the super-population as

$$g(\mathbf{x}, \zeta, u) = g(\mathbf{x}, \zeta | u)\, g(u). \tag{2.17}$$

Interval sampling proceeds as follows: define k as the largest integer such that $k \leqslant N^a/N$; draw the first observation at random from the first k units in the sampling frame (suppose that this turns out to be the i_1th); then draw the remaining observations from positions $i_2 = i_1 + k$, $i_3 = i_1 + 2k$, . . ., $i_N = i_1 + (N-1)k$.

If viewed as a subsample of the actual population, this procedure clearly does not satisfy the requirements of random sampling. In particular, the observations are not independently distributed, *conditional on the sampling frame*, since (x_2, ζ_2), . . ., (x_N, ζ_N) are completely determined once the first observation is selected. However, this is necessarily so only if the frame is taken as given, whereas we are treating the units in the frame as a random sample from a super-population.

The distribution of the variables $\mathbf{x}$, ζ, u and i for the first sample observation has probability density/mass function

$$f(x_1, \zeta_1, u_1, i_1) = \frac{1}{k}\, g(x_1, \zeta_1 | u_1)\, g^{i_1}(u_1) \tag{2.18}$$

where $g^{i_1}(.)$ is the p.d.f. of the i_1-th smallest u value in a random sample of size N^a from the super-population. The joint distribution of the first two observations is similarly characterized:

$$f(x_1, \zeta_1, u_1, x_2, \zeta_2, u_2, i_1) = \frac{1}{k}\, g(x_1, \zeta_1 | u_1)\, g(x_2, \zeta_2 | u_2)\, g^{i_1 i_2}(u_1, u_2) \tag{2.19}$$

where $g^{i_1 i_2}(.,.)$ is the p.d.f. of the i_1th and i_2th smallest u values in a random sample of size N^a from the super-population. Continuing in this way for the full sample

$$f(x_1, \zeta_1, u_1, \ldots, x_N, \zeta_N, u_N, i_1) = \frac{1}{k}\left[\prod_{n=1}^{N} g(x_n, \zeta_n | u_n)\right] g^{i_1 \ldots i_N}(u_1, \ldots, u_N) \tag{2.20}$$

Then, summing over i_1 and integrating with respect to $u_1 \ldots u_N$,

$$f(x_1, \zeta_1, \ldots, x_N, \zeta_N) = \frac{1}{k} \sum_{i_1=1}^{k} \int_{-\infty}^{\infty} \int_{u_1}^{\infty} \cdots \int_{u_{N-1}}^{\infty} \prod_{n=1}^{N} g(x_n, \zeta_n | u_n) g^{i_1 \ldots i_N}(u_1, \ldots, u_N) \, du_N \ldots du_1 \tag{2.21}$$

In general, this joint distribution for the observables is very complicated and not the same as that yielded by a random sample.

However, provided that the mechanism for ordering the units within the sampling frame is independent of the mechanism generating $\mathbf{x}$ and ζ, the conditional distribution $g(\mathbf{x}, \zeta | u)$ does not depend on u and is identical with the marginal distribution $g(\mathbf{x}, \zeta) = g(\mathbf{x} | \zeta; \theta) g(\zeta)$. In that case, (2.21) reduces to the simple form (2.1) since $g^{i_1 \ldots i_N}(u_1, \ldots, u_N)$ integrates to unity. Therefore, if the organization of the sample frame is independent of $\mathbf{x}$ and ζ, interval sampling can be treated as random sampling for the purposes of drawing inferences about the super-population. Usually it is safe to make this independence assumption.

2.1.6 Stratified sampling

For stratified sampling, the population is divided into m sub-populations, or *strata*. Suppose that these strata are defined in terms of a variable (or variables) denoted $\mathbf{s}$, and that the joint density/mass function of $\mathbf{x}$, ζ and $\mathbf{s}$ in the super-population is $g(\mathbf{x}, \zeta, \mathbf{s})$, which can be decomposed as follows:

$$g(\mathbf{x}, \zeta, \mathbf{s}) = g(\mathbf{x} | \zeta, \mathbf{s}; \theta) g(\zeta, \mathbf{s}) \tag{2.22}$$

where $g(\mathbf{x} | \zeta, \mathbf{s}; \theta)$ is the essence of our (now extended) econometric model.

The typical stratum j is defined as that part of the population for which $\mathbf{s} \in S_j$, where $S_1, \ldots, S_m$ are non-overlapping regions in the domain of variation of $\mathbf{s}$. In practice, these strata represent particular groups of individuals that the survey designer wishes to see adequately represented in the sample. Often some of these groups are quite small and therefore unlikely to be well represented in a moderately sized random sample but are deemed to be of particular interest – single parent families, old people, the poor etc. Note that some of the criteria used for defining these strata may appear in the $\mathbf{x}$ or ζ vectors; for instance, the poor are a group defined in terms of income, which is a quantity that is also likely to be used as an endogenous or exogenous variable in an econometric study. In practice, the sub-populations are often defined by the use of multiple levels of stratification – for instance, the country may be divided into regions, each of which is subdivided into urban and rural areas.

Stratified sampling is merely the separate sampling of these strata, with the resulting subsamples finally merged to form the complete sample. We shall consider the case where the sample sizes, $N_1, \ldots, N_m$, drawn from the strata are fixed; other schemes are possible, and we shall encounter a different example in section 2.4 below. Assume that there is random sampling within strata. Then the distribution of an observation from stratum j is characterized by a density/mass function

$$f(\mathbf{x}, \zeta; j) = g(\mathbf{x}, \zeta \mid \mathbf{s} \in S_j). \tag{2.23}$$

However, this conditional function can be expressed as the ratio of the analogous joint and marginal functions:

$$g(\mathbf{x}, \zeta \mid \mathbf{s} \in S_j) = \int_{S_j} g(\mathbf{x}, \zeta \mid \mathbf{s}) \mathrm{d}G(\mathbf{s}) / P_j \tag{2.24}$$

where $G(\mathbf{s})$ is the c.d.f. of the marginal distribution of the stratification variable $\mathbf{s}$ and the integration is Lebesgue–Stieltjes integration, so that $\mathbf{s}$ may be discrete or continuous. The P_j are population proportions:

$$P_j = \int_{S_j} \mathrm{d}G(\mathbf{s}). \tag{2.25}$$

Therefore

$$f(\mathbf{x}, \zeta; j) = \frac{1}{P_j} \int_{S_j} g(\mathbf{x} \mid \zeta, \mathbf{s}; \theta)\, g(\zeta \mid \mathbf{s})\, \mathrm{d}G(\mathbf{s}). \tag{2.26}$$

Thus sample stratification generally leads to a distribution of the observable variables which is related to the econometric model $g(\mathbf{x} \mid \zeta, \mathbf{s}; \theta)$ in a rather complicated way.

However, in the important special case where our endogenous variable $\mathbf{x}$ is independent of the pattern of stratification, the conditional function $g(\mathbf{x} \mid \zeta, \mathbf{s}; \theta)$ does not depend on $\mathbf{s}$, and (2.13) simplifies to the much more tractable expression

$$f(\mathbf{x}, \zeta; j) = g(\mathbf{x} \mid \zeta; \theta)\, f(\zeta; j) \tag{2.27}$$

where the term

$$f(\zeta; j) = \frac{1}{P_j} \int_{S_j} g(\zeta \mid \mathbf{s}) \mathrm{d}G(\mathbf{s}) \tag{2.28}$$

is independent of $\boldsymbol{\theta}$. This is an example of exogenous sampling, discussed further in section 2.3.

Since the sample and population densities are not identical under stratified sampling, inference is sometimes less straightforward than for random sampling. For instance, consider the problem of estimating the super-population mean $E(\mathbf{x})$. The ordinary sample mean has expected value

$$\begin{aligned} E(\bar{\mathbf{x}}) &= \frac{1}{N} \sum_{n=1}^{N} E(\mathbf{x}_n) \\ &= \frac{1}{N} \sum_{j=1}^{m} \sum_{r=1}^{N_j} E(\mathbf{x} \mid \mathbf{s} \in S_j) \\ &= \sum_{j=1}^{m} \frac{N_j}{N} E(\mathbf{x} \mid \mathbf{s} \in S_j). \end{aligned} \tag{2.29}$$

However, since $E(\mathbf{x}) = \Sigma\, P_j E(\mathbf{x} \mid \mathbf{s} \in S_j)$, $\bar{\mathbf{x}}$ is generally biased unless the ratios N_j/N coincide with the population proportions P_j. This suggests the use of reweighted data, $\mathbf{x}_n^{\mathrm{w}} = P_j N \mathbf{x}_n / N_j$, where j is the stratum to which observation n belongs. The weighted mean $\bar{\mathbf{x}}^{\mathrm{w}} = N^{-1} \Sigma\, \mathbf{x}_n^{\mathrm{w}}$ is unbiased, and for this reason survey data are often made available in weighted form.

2.1.7 Multistage sampling

Ordinary stratification as described above involves the drawing of observations from all the strata. This can be thought of as exhaustive sampling of the population of strata, followed by non-exhaustive sampling within strata. In practice, this first stage is often not exhaustive, and instead samples are drawn only from a subset of the available strata (which are often called *primary sampling units* or PSUs in this context). For the simple two-stage case, a typical sampling process might be as follows.

i Draw a sample of $M \leqslant m$ strata from the set $\{S_1, \ldots, S_m\}$. Assume that this is done by making repeated independent drawings with probabilities $\Pi_1, \ldots, \Pi_m$ of selection for the strata, where the Π_j are chosen as part of the sample design.

ii From each stratum that is selected at the first stage, draw $k = N/M$ sampling units by random sampling.

This process yields observations on $\mathbf{x}$ and $\boldsymbol{\zeta}$ that are not generally independent (unless the stratification variable $\mathbf{s}$ is independent of both $\mathbf{x}$ and $\boldsymbol{\zeta}$). The marginal distribution of any single observation is

$$f(\mathbf{x}, \boldsymbol{\zeta}) = \sum_{j=1}^{m} \Pr(\text{stratum } j \text{ selected})\, g(\mathbf{x}, \boldsymbol{\zeta} \mid \mathbf{s} \in S_j)$$

$$= \sum_{j=1}^{m} \Pi_j \, g(\mathbf{x}, \zeta \mid \mathbf{s} \in S_j)$$

$$= \sum_{j=1}^{m} \frac{\Pi_j}{P_j} \int_{S_j} g(\mathbf{x} \mid \zeta, \mathbf{s}; \theta) \, g(\zeta \mid \mathbf{s}) \, \mathrm{d}G(\mathbf{s}). \tag{2.30}$$

However, the joint distribution of the full sample is more complicated. Define N_r as the index set of observations drawn from the rth stratum that is sampled (thus, if the observations are ordered by strata, N_r is the set $\{k(r-1)+1, \ldots, kr\}$). Then

$$f(\mathbf{x}_1, \zeta_1, \ldots, \mathbf{x}_N, \zeta_N) = \prod_{r=1}^{M} [\text{joint p.d.f. of observations in the set } N_r]$$

$$= \prod_{r=1}^{M} \left[\sum_{j=1}^{m} \frac{\Pi_j}{P_j} \prod_{n \in N_r} \int_{S_j} g(\mathbf{x}_n \mid \zeta_n, \mathbf{s}; \theta) \, g(\zeta_n \mid \mathbf{s}) \, \mathrm{d}G(\mathbf{s}) \right]. \tag{2.31}$$

Note that, in general, the inner summation and product operations cannot be interchanged, and so this joint distribution cannot be expressed in the product form $\Pi f_n(\mathbf{x}_n, \zeta_n)$. Therefore the observations are not independently distributed.

In the special case where the strata are defined independently of $\mathbf{x}$, the conditional distribution $g(\mathbf{x} \mid \zeta, \mathbf{s}; \theta)$ does not depend on $\mathbf{s}$, and (2.31) simplifies to

$$f(\mathbf{x}_1, \zeta_1, \ldots, \mathbf{x}_N, \zeta_N) = \left[\prod_{n=1}^{N} g(\mathbf{x}_n \mid \zeta_n; \theta) \right] f(\zeta_1, \ldots, \zeta_N) \tag{2.32}$$

where

$$f(\zeta_1, \ldots, \zeta_N) = \prod_{r=1}^{M} \left[\sum_{j=1}^{m} \frac{\Pi_j}{P_j} \prod_{n \in N_r} \int_{S_j} g(\zeta_n \mid \mathbf{s}) \, \mathrm{d}G(\mathbf{s}) \right]. \tag{2.33}$$

Thus, in the case of exogenously defined strata, the observations on the endogenous variables are independent conditional on $\zeta_1, \ldots, \zeta_N$, but the sample as a whole is not fully independent, unless ζ and $\mathbf{s}$ are independently distributed in the population. If, as is often the case in practice, the strata are sampled without replacement, then the marginal distribution of $\zeta_1, \ldots, \zeta_N$ becomes more complicated still, but the general form (2.32) still applies. As with ordinary stratification, problems arise in the estimation of population means, and to achieve unbiasedness observations must be reweighted by the factors P_j/Π_j.

Large-scale surveys generally make use of rather complex schemes involving both multiple levels of ordinary stratification and multistage sampling, sometimes with interval sampling used at the lowest level. The extension of our theory to such cases is straightforward in principle.

2.2 The survey enquiry

The way in which one asks a question often has a marked effect on the answer one receives. This is a fundamental truth in survey analysis, and the design of the survey questionnaire, the phrasing of questions, the duration of the period of observation etc. are at least as important to the user of survey data as the formal sampling technique used. Since these are essentially practical matters, there is only a limited amount that can be said that is of very wide validity: every field poses its own special problems for the survey designer.

One of the potential difficulties of the survey method is that the very act of observation may change the behaviour that is under study. Someone who is asked detailed questions about his or her current economic decisions may be forced into a re-evaluation of the way those decisions are made, and may become more cautious or moderate as a result. Alternatively, the attention of an external observer might cause departures from normal behaviour through conscious or unconscious attempts to impress the interviewer or to display behaviour that the subject feels will be regarded as normal or creditable. There is obviously little that can be done to investigate this suspicion: if the results of observation are suspect, then 'true' behaviour which is operative only in the absence of observation is unknowable, and there is no direct means of checking the validity of any given set of survey data. Thus most of the evidence on either side of this question is indirect and often anecdotal. However, one of the Family Budget Survey experiments carried out by the UK Office of Population Censuses and Surveys (see Kemsley, Redpath and Holmes, 1980) in 1976 did attempt to gain some information on this by asking households who had been interviewed for the Family Expenditure Survey (see section 2.6 below) whether they thought that keeping detailed expenditure records had affected their normal spending in any way. Of those questioned in this follow-up survey, 12.7 per cent believed that there had been some change, and this does not suggest that observation-induced bias is an especially serious problem.

Even if behaviour is itself unaffected by the survey, errors may still arise through various forms of misreporting. People may forget to record all the relevant events, or they may deliberately give inaccurate responses in order to conceal aspects of their behaviour that might seem shameful or that are felt to be too personal. This is particularly true of surveys covering sensitive areas such as drinking habits, sexual behaviour, participation in the black economy etc. Some individuals express the fear that complete information might be used against their interests in some way. For example, firms are usually very reluctant to provide accurate information about their commercial practices, and self-employed individuals frequently express suspicions that the results of income enquiries might be divulged to the Inland Revenue. People may also simply become impatient with the demands imposed on them by the enquiry and give superficial responses without troubling to ensure their accuracy.

Although there is no certain way of avoiding these reporting errors, the design of the enquiry does have an important bearing. Questions which are vague or complex are open to misunderstanding, or may allow the individual too much latitude to choose an interpretation, thus allowing a response that puts the subject in the most favourable light. As an example of this, consider table 2.1, which summarizes a subsample of data from the UK National Readership Survey (JICNARS 1971) for the fourth quarter of 1971. This annual survey asks a variety of questions about the readership of newspapers and magazines. The table gives the results of two questions about the readership of *The Times*. The first question is: 'How many issues of *The Times* do you look at or read in an average week these days?', a question which is vague, since the concept of an average week is not defined, and which is also hypothetical, since it is not concerned with any specific event or action. The second question is: 'On what day (before today) did you last read or look at an issue of *The Times*?'; the responses to this question are recoded as information on whether or not *The Times* had been looked at on the previous day of publication ('yesterday'). This is a much simpler, purely factual question.

The Times is generally perceived to be a 'highbrow' newspaper, and being a reader of *The Times* is widely felt to be a creditable attribute. As might be expected, the vague frequency question allows respondents much more freedom to cast themselves in the favourable role of a *Times* reader than does the simple question about readership on the previous day of publication.

The last row of the table gives the chance of observing readership on a randomly chosen day by a person with each given level of average readership. The actual proportions for each group of people with a common claimed readership frequency are consistently lower than the expected proportions, and overall roughly 31 per cent fewer copies of *The Times* were read 'yester-

Table 2.1 Claimed average frequency of readership of *The Times* against actual readership on the previous day of publication

Claimed number of copies seen per week	1	2	3	4	5	6
Number of respondents	89	56	32	6	26	69
Proportion of these who saw a copy yesterday (%)	7.9	12.5	31.3	16.7	65.4	84.1
Expected proportion (%)	16.7	33.3	50	66.7	83.3	100

day' than respondents claimed would be read on a typical day. Any econometrician seeking to model these frequency data would be led seriously astray by a reporting bias of this magnitude.

Survey enquiries are of two possible types: those that attempt to record activity as it occurs, usually by requiring that subjects keep continuous records of their behaviour for some period (the diary method); those that obtain information by retrospective interview, where the subject is asked to produce a record of past behaviour from memory (the recall method). These both have advantages and disadvantages and are best suited to different fields of enquiry. Some surveys use a combination of the two methods.

The diary method relies little on memory and can therefore be used to elicit information in much more detail. Its disadvantages are that it imposes a much greater burden on the respondent, and it is consequently hard to achieve a good response rate, particularly if the observation period is longer than one or two weeks. Moreover, because it is so intrusive, it risks causing some change in behaviour, which a retrospective enquiry cannot do.

The recall method usually produces much better co-operation, is cheaper to administer (and can therefore produce larger samples) but is highly suspect when the behaviour involved comprises numerous small-scale activities such as the purchase of household goods. In these circumstances, retrospective enquiry tends to produce underestimates of the level of activity, since minor events tend to be forgotten. The recall method is much better suited to surveys of infrequent events of a substantial magnitude, such as the purchase of major durables or the timing and duration of spells of unemployment. In these areas, the period of time covered by the retrospective interview can be much longer than would be feasible for a continuous diary-based enquiry.

The duration of the period over which the individual is observed is of major importance, and practice varies widely. For example, some countries conduct their household expenditure surveys with observation periods of one or two weeks, some a month, some (particularly in Eastern Europe) as long as a year. Economic theory is generally couched in terms of rates of flow: of demand, of labour supply, of production etc. However, this is an abstraction: in reality goods are purchased in discrete amounts at irregular intervals, for instance. If we view the theoretical rate of flow as a hypothetical average (holding external conditions constant) of this irregular sequence of actions, then there is some difficulty in interpreting the observed demand over, say, a two-week period as the true rate of demand. The two will differ by possibly large amounts which are entirely fortuitous – if someone happens to be interviewed in the week in which he or she buys a refrigerator, a naive interpretation of this as an observation of a rate of flow of one refrigerator a week is obviously wildly mistaken. As the length of the observation period is increased, the importance of these fortuitous errors diminishes, although a long observation period brings its own problems since external conditions (prices etc.) may change within the period. The length of the observation period is important because of its implications for survey methodology and response, and also for the specification of econometric models. In section 4.4 we shall examine models that take explicit account of the effects of a short observation period.

A major limitation of many of the surveys available for econometric analysis is the lack of repeated observation. Most surveys are simple cross-sections: observation is made only once for each individual, and the survey provides only a collection of snapshots of individual behaviour. For the purposes of modelling the dynamics of economic behaviour, a sequence of observations is desirable – a cine film rather than a snapshot. Such samples are known as panel data, and are still a comparative rarity (particularly outside the USA). For this reason, we shall concentrate almost exclusively on models intended for application to simple cross-section data. The analysis of panel data is discussed very fully by Hsiao (1986).

The chief problem associated with cross-section data is mis-specification: if individuals take time to adjust their behaviour to changed circumstances, then the lagged variables which should appear in the model to reflect this imperfect adjustment are unavailable without a sequence of repeated observations. An analogous static model must be estimated instead, and this may lead to an omitted variable bias. It is widely assumed that these dynamic specification errors can be safely consigned to the model's disturbance term, leaving a model whose coefficients are interpretable as long-run responses, but it is dangerous to take this for granted. Much depends on the horizon over which variables are measured and the speed with which adjustment takes place: if, in the estimation of a demand model, for instance, we are forced to use one week's observation on income, then the omission of lagged income is likely to have serious consequences; if it is measured as normal annual income, the problem is much less severe.

Perhaps the case where concern is greatest is when observation is linked directly to some change in the subject's circumstances. Many surveys make some payment to respondents as compensation for their effort; usually this payment is very small and cannot be expected to alter the resources available to the household significantly (although it may have some effect on response rates). However, in the case of the social experiments conducted in the USA, observation has been linked with the selective introduction of experimental programmes that do alter the economic circumstances of some participating households by substantial amounts. For instance, the Gary, New Jersey and Seattle–Denver experiments (see Hausman and Wise, 1982; Watts and Rees, 1974; and Spiegelman and Yaeger, 1980, for descriptions of these) involved groups of mainly low-income households participating in experimental income maintenance schemes that increased some families' incomes by large amounts; the Pheonix–Pittsburgh rent subsidy experiment (see Allen, Fitts and Glatt, 1981) gave substantial payments to some relatively poor families whose rents were above a critical level; various time-of-day electricity pricing experiments have changed the cost of electricity supply to some households (see Aigner, 1985).

There are two separate issues here. Since these programmes are of limited duration, households may not respond to them as fully as they might to the introduction of a similar permanent programme. Thus, quite apart from any dynamic adjustment problems, analysis of these experiments might give an unrepresentative picture of long-term behaviour, simply as a consequence of rational intertemporal choice: responses to transitory factors are less than responses to permanent factors. This problem has been investigated by Burtless and Greenberg (1982) in the context of a labour supply equation estimated from data on families subjected to a negative income tax programme in the Seattle–Denver experiment. Simple linear equations were estimated separately for families participating in schemes with three and five years' duration, and large differences were found in the coefficient estimates. Thus the transient nature of these schemes does seem to be a significant problem in the use of econometric methods to predict the consequences of any proposed permanent income support system.

The second difficulty that arises when the survey makes changes to individuals' circumstances is that it may take a long time before adjustment to the change is completed. For instance, to alter one's hours of work may necessitate finding a new job; to alter one's spending on rent will mean moving house. These responses are costly and time consuming, and will not be observed immediately. Depending on the timing of the observation, fitting an ordinary econometric model to a single cross-section generated by one of these experiments may yield very misleading results. In these circumstances, panel data allow the explicit modelling of the process of adjustment (possibly as a discrete change: moving house or changing job) and is therefore clearly preferable in principle, although it often raises almost as many econometric problems as it solves. The analysis of panel data is beyond the scope of this book.

2.3 An example: the UK Family Expenditure Survey

Many countries carry out regular surveys of household income and expenditure. In most cases, these surveys had their origins in the need to produce up-to-date weights for use in the construction of an aggregate retail price index, although now they are generally expected to meet many other needs, such as the measurement of welfare needs. The annual UK Family Expenditure Survey (FES) is fairly typical of these, and is used as the basis for a wide variety of econometric work.

2.3.1 The sample design

The basic sampling unit of the FES is the household. A household is defined as a group of one or more individuals (not necessarily related), who have the same address, whose meals are prepared together and who have exclusive use of at least one room. The sample design used in the FES is considerably more complicated than any of the simple techniques discussed in section 2.1 above; this is true of a vast majority of the sample surveys that are used in applied economic and social research.

There are four stages in the FES procedure; these are described in considerably greater detail in Kemsley, Redpath and Holmes (1980), on which this section is based. (Note that the design used since 1986 differs slightly from this.)

Stage 1 At the first stage, the whole of Great Britain (with the exclusion of some remote areas) is divided into 168 strata, which are the outcome of the application of three stratification factors: initially by region, then within region according to the degree of urbanization and the relative value of the private housing stock. Each of the strata is then divided into geographical areas belonging to different local administrative districts. One such area is drawn at random from each stratum, with each area's selection probability equal to its share of the stratum's total of registered electors.

Stage 2 Each area is composed of wards (the basic geographical unit of the electoral process), each ward being small enough to be covered by a single interviewer. Four of these wards are then drawn from each area (one for survey in each quarter of the year), using an adaptation of the interval sampling technique designed to give each ward a probability of selection proportional to the number of electors in that ward.

Stage 3 From each ward, sixteen addresses are selected by interval sampling from the electoral register. Thus (with some minor exceptions), an address has a probability of selection proportional to the number of electors resident there. If an address is ineligible because it is that of a hotel, public house, institution, vacant property etc., it is discarded and not replaced.

Stage 4 In 97 per cent of cases, an address contains only one household, and that household is selected for interview. For multi-household addresses, a further random sampling procedure is used to produce up to three households for interview.

2.3.2 The form of the enquiry

The FES is designed to gather information on general household characteristics, household income and also expenditures on all forms of goods and services over a two-week period. For each household, the enquiry proceeds as follows.

There is an initial interview at which all adult members (aged 16 and over) are present. This interview establishes whether or not all members are willing to participate; if any member refuses, then the entire household is classified as non-respondent and abandoned. However, if all adult household members are willing to co-operate, the interview continues and gathers a great deal of detailed information about household size and structure, housing costs, the income of all members of the household from all sources, and the household's regular expenditure commitments, such as rent, rates, gas and electricity bills etc. Finally, an expenditure diary is left with each household member, who is instructed to enter all expenditures on a daily basis.

Two intermediate interviews follow, to check the household's recording procedures and to collect the completed first week's diaries and leave diaries for the second week. These are collected in a final interview at the end of the 14-day period, and if (and only if) all diaries have been satisfactorily completed, arrangements are made for the payment of a £5 fee to each adult member of the household.

2.3.3 Response

It is always difficult to achieve an adequate rate of response in surveys of this kind. A detailed enquiry such as the FES involves a participating household in a considerable amount of effort and inconvenience, with very little direct benefit to the household. Experiments reported by Kemsley, Redpath and Holmes (1980) suggest that the way in which the survey is conducted has considerable bearing on response rates: a version conducted through the post, for example, met with a response rate that was less than a third of that of the interviewer-based survey. There is also evidence that the extension of the period of the enquiry from two to four or more weeks would reduce response by more than half. On the other hand, the payment of a small participation fee to each household member was found to have increased the response rate by about a third above the rate for an unpaid enquiry. Undoubtedly the main factor in the achievement of a good response rate is the personal encouragement given by the interviewers.

The FES attempts to reach a little over 10 000 eligible households every year. It is very successful in making these contacts: addresses are revisited for a month if necessary to establish the first interview, and only 1 or 2 per cent of households fail to be contacted at all. From the remaining households the survey usually meets with a response rate of approximately 70 per cent, which is low enough to cause some concern. It is desirable to know something about the types of households that are particularly likely to refuse to co-operate, since the under-representation of these households may bias the results of studies using data on respondents. It is possible to record some information for all non-respondents: the location of their dwelling and (from local authority records) its rateable value. Thus non-response is not a complete lack of information. Response tends to be relatively poor for households living in properties with high rateable values or situated in densely populated areas, and also varies seasonally, with a slight decline in co-operation in the fourth quarter of each year.

In census years, it is possible to go further than this: since participation in the census is compulsory, census information should be available for all households, including those who refused to co-operate with the FES. In 1971 and 1981, attempts were made to identify the census returns of all households that had been approached in the course of the 1971 and 1981 FES enquiries (see Kemsley, 1975, and Redpath, 1986); this proved possible in over 90 per cent of cases. For these, the responding and non-responding households were compared in terms of a number of general household characteristics recorded in the census. Significant differences were found for the age of the head of household (younger households being more likely to co-operate), for the number of children (the more children, the greater the likelihood of response), for employment status (much lower response for the self-employed) and for household size (better response for large households).

Unfortunately, census returns do not give information on income or expenditure, so it is not possible to find any direct evidence of a correlation between response and the variables which are most likely to be endogenous to an econometric study of individual behaviour. However, there are indications that wealthier and higher-spending households are less likely to respond: for example, multi-car households tend to have low response rates. Thus endogenous self-selection is definitely a potential difficulty. The econometric problems raised by this are examined in section 2.6 below.

2.3.4 Reliability of survey data

It is only possible to check the accuracy of survey data by indirect means, since any independent enquiry conducted for the purposes of checking is likely to be subject to the same inaccuracies as the FES itself. The major source of evidence about FES reliability is the comparison of grossed-up income and expenditure averages with the corresponding figures in the National Accounts. The latter figures are constructed from a wide variety of sources and are therefore a largely independent check. There are inevitable difficulties in putting FES and National Accounts data on a comparable basis, but attempts have been made. Table 2.2, containing comparisons for the year 1976, has been constructed from information given by Kemsley, Redpath and Holmes (1980) and Atkinson and Mickelwright (1983). The correspondence appears to be reasonably close except for the problem areas of expenditure on alcohol, tobacco, durables and catering, and income from self-employment, investment income and receipts of sickness benefit.

Table 2.2 Consumers' expenditure and income: comparison of UK Family Expenditure Survey and National Accounts (1976)

Variable	*(i) Grossed-up FES (£m)*	*(ii) National Accounts (£m)*	*(i)×100 / (ii) (%)*
Expenditures on			
(a) strictly comparable			
Food	13560	14085	96
Alcoholic drink	3238	5587	58
Tobacco	2381	3025	79
Housing	6591	6716	98
Fuel and light	3683	3528	104
Clothing and footwear	5200	5211	100
Total comparable	34653	38152	91
(b) less comparable			
Durables	3832	4842	79
Other goods	4805	4450	108
Transport	7782	8832	88
Catering	2820	2103	134
Services	4026	4365	92
Total less comparable	23265	24592	95
Total expenditure	57918	62744	92
Income from			
Employment	62305	66858	93
Self-employment	4651	10048	46
Occupational pensions	2350	2947	80
Investment	2594	5389	48
State pensions	5430	5509	99
Unemployment benefit	564	568	99
Sickness benefit	348	567	61
Child benefit	587	563	104
Supplementary benefit	1311	1525	86
Other benefits	923	1222	76
Total income	81063	95197	85

Source: Kemsley, Redpath and Holmes (1980) and Atkinson and Mickelwright (1983)

Much depends on the reasons for these apparent errors. If they are inaccuracies inherent in the survey method (for instance, if heavy drinkers feel guilty about their rates of consumption and either temporarily change their behaviour or lie about it) then little can be done – the data are simply wrong. On the other hand, if the discrepancies are due to differential response, for instance if heavy drinkers are reluctant to co-operate (or incapable!), then an attempt can be made to adjust for this endogenous sample selection.

Kemsley, Redpath and Holmes report an experiment which attempted to prevent the concealment or misrepresentation of expenditures by requiring households to keep much more detailed records, producing an income–expenditure account balanced to the last penny. This failed to reveal any hidden expenditures. There is some evidence, however, of survey-induced change in behaviour: the first few days' records for a household often show expenditures which are rather higher than is typical of the remainder of the 14 days. Expenditure tends to be 2 or 3 per cent higher in the first week of the survey than in the second. However, this effect is very small and in the wrong direction to explain FES understatement of national rates of expenditure, and it is necessary to look elsewhere for the explanation.

Since many consumer durables are purchased by instalment, and records of these committed expenditures are gathered at the initial interview rather than through a diary, the understatement of durables expenditure seems likely to be due mainly to memory bias. However, durable goods are relative luxuries, so the lower response rate of wealthier households is presumably also a factor. For alcohol and tobacco, differential response and limitations of the coverage of the survey seem to be mainly responsible. Consumption of alcohol is highly skewed in the cross-section, and many of the groups who are identified as heavy drinkers (publicans, hoteliers, seafarers etc.) are under-represented because they do not live in eligible households or because they are away from home for extended periods. The response rate is also lowest during December when consumption of alcohol is at its greatest. Since tobacco and alcohol consumption are highly correlated, the same response deficiencies would appear to account for the understatement of tobacco expenditures.

Atkinson and Mickelwright (1983) give a very detailed analysis of the FES income figures. They conclude that the understatement of income from self-employment is a roughly even mixture of three factors: differences in the time period to which the income figures refer; the relatively low response of the self-employed; and under-reporting. This under-reporting seems to be as much a consequence of a lack of knowledge of true income and difficulty in defining net profits as a deliberate attempt to conceal income. The measurement of individuals' investment incomes is also notoriously difficult, with most surveys encountering substantial understatement. There is little reliable evidence to suggest the reason for this, although both under-reporting and the relatively low response of the wealthy seem to be involved. The substantial understatement of income from state sickness benefit seems capable of being explained mainly in terms of differential response, since people who are ill are likely to be away from home or unwilling to co-operate at such a difficult time.

2.4 Estimation under exogenous sampling

The term exogenous sampling refers to the case where the mechanism used to collect the sample is independent of the behaviour that the economic model attempts to explain. In formal terms, this means that it is possible to write the probability density/mass function for the sample in the form

$$f(\mathbf{x}_1, \zeta_1, \ldots, \mathbf{x}_N, \zeta_N) = \left[\prod_{n=1}^{N} g(\mathbf{x}_n \mid \zeta_n; \theta)\right] f(\zeta_1, \ldots, \zeta_N) \tag{2.34}$$

where the marginal distribution of the ζ_n is independent of the parameter vector $\boldsymbol{\theta}$. If the sample is fully independent, then (2.34) can be written

$$f(\mathbf{x}_1, \zeta_1, \ldots, \mathbf{x}_N, \zeta_N) = \left[\prod_{n=1}^{N} g(\mathbf{x}_n \mid \zeta_n; \theta) f_n(\zeta_n)\right] \tag{2.35}$$

Random sampling (and, under our assumptions about the relationship of the actual population to a super-population, exhaustive sampling and interval sampling also) leads to the form (2.35) with

$$f_n(\zeta_n) = g(\zeta_n). \tag{2.36}$$

Under stratified random sampling, with the stratification variables $\mathbf{s}$ independent of $\mathbf{x}$, we also have (2.35) with

$$f_n(\zeta_n) = \int_{S_{j_n}} g(\zeta_n \mid \mathbf{s})\, \mathrm{d}G(\mathbf{s})/P_{j_n} \tag{2.37}$$

where j_n is the index of the stratum to which observation n belongs and P_j is the population frequency of stratum j. This is an instance of a sample of independent but not identically distributed (NID) observations, since the different strata generate different forms for $f_n(\zeta_n)$. For two-stage random sampling, with the strata exogenously defined, the observations are not fully independent, but the sample distribution is of the form (2.34) with $f(\zeta_1, \ldots, \zeta_N)$ given by expression (2.33) of section 2.1.

2.4.1 Maximum likelihood

There are three common estimation principles that we shall consider here: maximum likelihood, least-squares regression and instrumental variables. The maximum likelihood (ML) estimator is the most widely used in this field and is the technique we shall automatically consider whenever estimation is discussed in the remainder of this book. This merely reflects its dominance in applied work. The ML estimator $\hat{\theta}$ is the value of θ which maximizes the likelihood function $L(\theta)$ or, more conveniently, its logarithm:

$$\log L(\theta) = \sum_{n=1}^{N} \log f_n(\mathbf{x}_n, \zeta_n)$$

$$= \sum_{n=1}^{N} \log g(\mathbf{x}_n \mid \zeta_n; \theta) + \log f(\zeta_1, \ldots, \zeta_N). \tag{2.38}$$

Under our assumption that both ζ_n and the sampling process are exogenous, in the sense that the marginal density/mass function $f(\zeta_1, \ldots, \zeta_N)$ does not depend on θ, the ML estimator is also identical with the value of θ that maximizes the *conditional* log-likelihood function:

$$\log L^c(\theta) = \sum_{n=1}^{N} \log f(\mathbf{x}_n \mid \zeta_n)$$

$$= \sum_{n=1}^{N} \log g(\mathbf{x}_n \mid \zeta_n; \theta). \tag{2.39}$$

In later chapters, we make extensive use of ML estimators, and generally we shall assume that the sampling process is exogenous. Thus the log-likelihood functions we derive will usually be conditional on the exogenous variables, although for economy of notation we shall not make this conditioning explicit, as we have here.

The important consequence of the equivalence of (2.38) and (2.40) is that it is possible to compute the ML estimator without knowing the sampling distribution of the exogenous variables. This is an enormous practical advantage. Of course, the statistical properties of the ML estimator will depend on the nature of the sampling scheme: for example, a sampling process which collects observations from a very limited range of values for ζ will generate relatively imprecise estimates of θ. Moreover, the ease with which one can derive the asymptotic properties of the ML estimator certainly depends on the nature of the sampling process. Standard proofs (see, for instance, Le Cam, 1953) are based on the assumption that the sample observations are independently and identically distributed, and much less attention has been devoted to the general case. However, Bradley and Gart (1962) and Hoadley (1971) give regularity conditions under which standard asymptotic results remain valid.

Under these conditions, the ML estimator is consistent, asymptotically efficient and asymptotically normal. The usual asymptotic approximation to the covariance matrix of $\hat{\theta}$ is

$$\hat{\Sigma}_{\theta}^{1} = -\left[\sum_{n=1}^{N} \frac{\partial^2 \log g(\mathbf{x}_n \mid \zeta_n; \hat{\theta})}{\partial \hat{\theta}\, \partial \hat{\theta}'}\right]^{-1} \tag{2.40}$$

or the asymptotically equivalent expression

$$\hat{\Sigma}_{\theta}^{2} = \left[\sum_{n=1}^{N} \frac{\partial \log g(\mathbf{x}_n | \zeta_n; \hat{\theta})}{\partial \hat{\theta}} \frac{\partial \log g(\mathbf{x}_n | \zeta_n; \hat{\theta}}{\partial \hat{\theta}'} \right]^{-1}. \tag{2.41}$$

White (1982a) points out that the alternative formula

$$\hat{\Sigma}_{\theta}^{3} = \hat{\Sigma}_{\theta}^{1} (\hat{\Sigma}_{\theta}^{2})^{-1} \hat{\Sigma}_{\theta}^{1} \tag{2.42}$$

is a more robust estimate, in the sense that it remains valid even in cases where the model is mis-specified. We shall not normally trouble to give explicit forms for these expressions.

2.4.2 Least squares

Except in special cases, non-linear least-squares estimators are inefficient, since they are based only on the mean rather than the whole of the population distribution of **x** conditional on ζ. This mean is known as the regression function $\mu(\zeta; \theta)$,

$$\mu(\zeta; \theta) = E(\mathbf{x} | \zeta; \theta) \tag{2.43}$$

and is the basis for the structural form

$$\mathbf{x}_n = \mu(\zeta_n; \theta) + \epsilon_n \tag{2.44}$$

where $\epsilon_n = \mathbf{x}_n - \mu(\zeta_n; \theta)$ is a disturbance term with mean zero conditonal on ζ_n.

For some models, the density/mass function $g(\mathbf{x} | \zeta; \theta)$ is very awkward from the analytical or computational point of view, whereas the regression function is relatively tractable. In these cases, non-linear least-squares estimation has considerable practical advantages over the more efficient ML estimator. Consider the case where x is a scalar variable. The unweighted least-squares estimator $\tilde{\theta}$ is the value of θ that minimizes the following criterion:

$$s(\theta) = \sum_{n=1}^{N} [x_n - \mu(\zeta_n; \theta)]^2. \tag{2.45}$$

In the general non-linear case, $s(\theta)$ must usually be minimized by an iterative numerical algorithm. In the familiar linear case, where $\mu(\zeta_n; \theta) = \zeta_n'\theta$, the solution is the usual linear regression:

$$\tilde{\theta} = \left(\sum_{n=1}^{N} \zeta_n \zeta_n' \right)^{-1} \left(\sum_{n=1}^{N} \zeta_n x_n \right). \tag{2.46}$$

The asymptotic properties of $\tilde{\theta}$ have been studied by White (1980), who has shown that under weak conditions which also cover the NID case $\tilde{\theta}$ is strongly consistent and asymptotically normal, with covariance matrix approximated by

$$\tilde{\Sigma}_\theta = \tilde{\mathbf{A}}^{-1}\tilde{\mathbf{B}}\tilde{\mathbf{A}}^{-1} \tag{2.47}$$

where

$$\tilde{\mathbf{A}} = \sum_{n=1}^{N} \frac{\partial\mu(\zeta_n;\tilde{\theta})}{\partial\tilde{\theta}} \frac{\partial\mu(\zeta_n;\tilde{\theta})}{\partial\tilde{\theta}'} \tag{2.48}$$

and

$$\tilde{\mathbf{B}} = \sum_{n=1}^{N} [x_n - \mu(\zeta_n;\tilde{\theta})]^2 \frac{\partial\mu(\zeta_n;\tilde{\theta})}{\partial\tilde{\theta}} \frac{\partial\mu(\zeta_n;\tilde{\theta})}{\partial\tilde{\theta}'}. \tag{2.49}$$

Expression (2.47) has the advantage over the more usual formula $\tilde{\Sigma}_\theta = N^{-1}\mathbf{s}(\tilde{\theta})\tilde{\mathbf{A}}^{-1}$ that its validity does not depend on the assumption that the variance of $\mathbf{x}_n$ conditional on ζ_n is constant.

2.4.3 Instrumental variables

The least-squares estimator exploits the fact that the error $\epsilon_n = \mathbf{x}_n - \mu(\zeta_n;\theta)$ has zero mean, conditional on ζ_n. However, if the regression function $\mu(\zeta_n;\theta)$ is difficult to derive or to compute, least squares is not an appealing estimator. Occasionally, it is possible to find a simple function of observable variables, $\psi(\eta_n;\theta)$, such that

$$E\,\psi(\eta_n;\theta)\,|\,\zeta_n = \mu(\zeta_n;\theta) \tag{2.50}$$

where η_n is constructed from $\mathbf{x}_n$ and ζ_n in some way and $\psi(.)$ is a tractable function.

Condition (2.50) implies that $\mathbf{x}_n$ can be written in the structural form

$$\mathbf{x}_n = \psi(\eta_n;\theta) + v_n \tag{2.51}$$

where $v_n = \mathbf{x}_n - \psi(\eta_n;\theta)$ has zero mean conditional on ζ_n. The distinction between this expression and the regression model (2.44) is that there is no assumption here that the observed variables on the right-hand side are exogenous. In other words, v_n does not have zero mean conditional on η_n and there may be some correlation between the explanatory variables η_n and the error term v_n. We shall encounter several examples of such equations in the remainder of the book (see, for instance, equation (2.78) in the next section, which is the basis for Amemiya's (1973) two-step estimator).

The instrumental variable (IV) estimator proceeds by specifying a vector of exogenous instrumental variables ξ_n which are correlated with η_n but satisfy

$$Ev_n\,|\,\xi_n = 0. \tag{2.52}$$

The vector ξ_n can be identical with ζ_n or a subvector, or its elements may be transformations of ζ_n. Note that ξ_n must have at least as many elements as θ. The IV estimator is the vector $\breve{\theta}$ that minimizes the following criterion:

$$s(\theta) = \{\Sigma[\mathbf{x}_n - \psi(\eta_n;\theta)]\xi_n'\}(\Sigma\xi_n\xi_n')^{-1}\{\Sigma\xi_n[\mathbf{x}_n - \psi(\eta_n;\theta)]\}. \tag{2.53}$$

The objective function $s(\theta)$ can be thought of as a generalized vector norm $\|\Sigma(\mathbf{x}_n - \psi(\eta_n;\theta))\xi_n\|$, and so, in a sense, the IV estimator minimizes the covariance between the instruments and the residual. In the special case that $\psi(\eta_n\,\theta)$ is the linear function $\eta_n'\theta$, the IV estimator takes the form

$$\breve{\theta} = [\Sigma\eta_n\xi_n'(\Sigma\xi_n\xi_n')^{-1}\Sigma\xi_n\mathbf{x}_n]^{-1}\,\Sigma\eta_n\xi_n'(\Sigma\xi_n\xi_n)^{-1}\Sigma\xi_n\mathbf{x}_n \tag{2.54}$$

which specializes to the following form when η_n is of the same dimension as ξ_n:

$$\breve{\theta} = (\Sigma\xi_n\eta_n)^{-1}\Sigma\xi_n\mathbf{x}_n. \tag{2.55}$$

Under suitable regularity conditions, it can be shown (see White, 1982b) that $\breve{\theta}$ is consistent and asymptotically normal, with approximate covariance matrix

$$\Sigma_\theta = \mathbf{A}^{-1}\mathbf{B}\mathbf{A}^{-1} \tag{2.56}$$

where

$$\mathbf{A} = \Sigma\;\frac{\partial\psi(\eta_n;\hat{\theta})'}{\partial\hat{\theta}}\;\xi_n'(\Sigma\xi_n\xi_n')^{-1}\,\Sigma\xi_n\;\frac{\partial\psi(\eta_n;\hat{\theta})}{\partial\hat{\theta}'} \tag{2.57}$$

and

$$\mathbf{B} = \Sigma\;\frac{\partial\psi(\eta_n;\hat{\theta})'}{\partial\hat{\theta}}\;\xi_n'\{\Sigma[x_n - \psi(\eta_n;\hat{\theta})]^2\,\xi_n\xi_n'\}^{-1}\,\Sigma\xi_n\;\frac{\partial\psi(\eta_n;\hat{\theta})}{\partial\hat{\theta}'}. \tag{2.58}$$

Formula (2.56) remains valid when $v\,|\,\xi$ is heteroscedastic.

The best choice of instruments is usually not obvious. Under homoscedasticity the optimal choice is $\xi_n = \partial\mu(\zeta_n;\theta)/\partial\theta$, which is generally dependent on θ and thus unobservable. Moreover, if $\mu(\zeta_n;\theta)$ is intractable, it is often difficult to construct a very close approximation to this ideal.

2.5 Estimation under endogenous sampling

By the term endogenous sampling, we mean the case where sample selection proceeds according to a rule defined in terms of the endogenous variable or variables $\mathbf{x}$ (and possibly also ζ). Thus the variables determining an individual's likelihood of being included in the sample are both endogenous and observable. We leave until the next section the case where sample selection is based on variables that are unobservable. The formal distinction between these two cases is not very significant, but their implications for applied work are very different. Both cases can be characterized in the same general way. If s is the vector of variables on which sample selection is based and $g(\mathbf{x}, \zeta | \mathbf{s})$ is the conditional probability density/mass function in the population, for the nth sample observation we have

$$f_n(\mathbf{x}_n, \zeta_n) = \int g(\mathbf{x}_n, \zeta_n | \mathbf{s}) \, \mathrm{d}F_n(\mathbf{s}) \tag{2.59}$$

where $F_n(\mathbf{s})$ is the (possibly discrete) c.d.f. reflecting the sampling process by which observation n is drawn. Integration is over the full domain of variation of $\mathbf{s}$.

If $\mathbf{s}$ is observable, comprising a subset of the variables in $\mathbf{x}$ and ζ, the distribution of $\mathbf{x}$ and ζ conditional on $\mathbf{s}$ is degenerate with respect to those variables, and the integral reduces to

$$\begin{aligned} f_n(\mathbf{x}_n, \zeta_n) &= g(\mathbf{x}_n^-, \zeta_n^- | \mathbf{s}_n) \, f_n(\mathbf{s}_n) \\ &= [g(\mathbf{x}_n, \zeta_n)/g(\mathbf{s}_n)] \, f_n(\mathbf{s}_n) \\ &= g(\mathbf{x}_n | \zeta_n; \boldsymbol{\theta}) \, g(\zeta_n) \, f_n(\mathbf{s}_n)/g(\mathbf{s}_n) \end{aligned} \tag{2.60}$$

where $\mathbf{x}^-$ and ζ^- represent the elements of $\mathbf{x}$ and ζ that are not part of $\mathbf{s}$ and $f_n(\mathbf{s})$ is the density/mass function corresponding to $F_n(\mathbf{s})$. Under endogenous sampling, because $\mathbf{s}_n$ contains part of $\mathbf{x}_n$, the last two terms of (2.60) are generally dependent on $\boldsymbol{\theta}$. Rewriting their ratio as $\omega_n(\mathbf{s}_n; \boldsymbol{\theta}) = f_n(\mathbf{s}_n)/g(\mathbf{s}_n)$, ML estimation requires the maximization of

$$\log L(\boldsymbol{\theta}) = \sum_{n=1}^{N} [\log g(\mathbf{x}_n | \zeta_n; \boldsymbol{\theta}) + \log g(\zeta_n) + \log \omega_n(\mathbf{s}_n; \boldsymbol{\theta})]. \tag{2.61}$$

Although the second term in brackets is as usual independent of $\boldsymbol{\theta}$, the third is not, and therefore the simple procedure of maximizing the conventional objective function $\Sigma \log g(\mathbf{x}_n | \zeta_n; \boldsymbol{\theta})$ is not equivalent to ML estimation and generally yields inconsistent estimates. This is in sharp contrast with the case of exogenous sampling.

The true log-likelihood (2.61) is usually very awkward, and most applied work based on this type of sample uses instead a conditional log-likelihood function

$$\log L^c(\boldsymbol{\theta}) = \Sigma \log f_n(\mathbf{x}_n | \zeta_n; \boldsymbol{\theta}) \tag{2.62}$$

which is constructed from derived forms for the conditional sample density/mass functions $f_n(\mathbf{x}_n | \zeta_n; \boldsymbol{\theta})$. Econometricians often treat this objective function as if it were the true log-likelihood, assuming that the estimates possess the properties of consistency and asymptotic normality, with asymptotic standard errors computable from the information matrix. This is rather dangerous, since there do not appear to be any results of general validity on the asymptotic properties of conditional ML estimators. They certainly cannot be assumed to be asymptotically efficient, for instance.

Some specific examples will make all this rather more clear. The area where the theory has been most fully developed and applied is in discrete choice models; this will be discussed in the next chapter. For the present, we shall assume that x is a continuously variable scalar with unlimited range and concentrate on the normal regression model

$$x_n | \zeta_n \sim N(\gamma' \zeta_n, \sigma^2) \tag{2.63}$$

which implies the following p.d.f. and c.d.f.:

$$g(x_n | \zeta_n; \theta) = \sigma^{-1} \varphi \left(\frac{x_n - \gamma' \zeta_n}{\sigma} \right) \tag{2.64}$$

$$\Pr(x_n \leqslant X | \zeta_n) = G(X | \zeta_n; \theta) = \Phi \left(\frac{X - \gamma' \zeta_n}{\sigma} \right) \tag{2.65}$$

where $\varphi(.)$ and $\Phi(.)$ are the p.d.f. and c.d.f. of the $N(0, 1)$ distribution, and $\theta' = (\gamma' \sigma)$.

The techniques discussed here and in the next section can readily be extended to more complicated models and to distributions other than the normal. Since the appropriateness of these techniques is sensitive to distributional form, tests of the normality hypothesis are particularly important; Bera, Jarque and Lee (1984) and Lee (1984) discuss tests applicable to many of the cases we consider here.

We shall concentrate on two particular sampling schemes that have appeared in the applied literature: endogenous truncation and stratification.

2.5.1 Simple truncation

We shall consider two forms of truncation, both of which are widely encountered in applied work. These differ in the way in which observations are gathered. In both cases, we shall assume a convenient and very simple truncation rule; extension of this to more complicated truncation rules is straightforward. Suppose that sampling is to be done only from the part of the population for which $x > c$, where c is a known constant. For example, if x is hours of labour supplied, we might have a sample that excludes part-time and non-workers, where these are defined as people working fewer than c hours a week.

Fixed *N* For the first form of truncated sampling, a sample of fixed size N is drawn. In practice, this might be done either by making repeated drawings from a sampling frame covering the whole population but retaining only the first N for which $x > c$, or alternatively by using a frame that covers only the relevant sub-population. Whichever is the case, assume for simplicity that these drawings are purely random, so that sample and sub-population distributions are identical. The distribution of x and ζ in the sample is therefore the population distribution of x and ζ conditional on $x > c$:

$$
\begin{aligned}
f(x_n, \zeta_n) &= g(x_n, \zeta_n | x_n > c) \\
&= g(x_n, \zeta_n)/\Pr(x_n > c) \\
&= \sigma^{-1}\varphi\left(\frac{x_n - \gamma'\zeta_n}{\sigma}\right)\frac{g(\zeta_n)}{P(\gamma, \sigma)}
\end{aligned}
\tag{2.66}
$$

where

$$
\begin{aligned}
P(\gamma, \sigma) &= \int_{R_\zeta}\int_c^\infty g(x|\zeta;\theta)\,\mathrm{d}x\,\mathrm{d}G(\zeta) \\
&= 1 - \int_{R_\zeta}\Phi\left(\frac{c - \gamma'\zeta}{\sigma}\right)\mathrm{d}G(\zeta)
\end{aligned}
\tag{2.67}
$$

and R_ζ is the domain of variation of ζ. This is a special case of the general formulation (2.59) and (2.60) with $\mathrm{s}_n = x_n$ and the ratio $f_n(\mathrm{s}_n)/g(\mathrm{s}_n)$ being the constant

$$
\omega_n(\mathrm{s}_n;\theta) = 1/P(\gamma, \sigma). \tag{2.68}
$$

Thus the true log-likelihood is

$$
\begin{aligned}
\log L(\gamma, \sigma) = \sum_{n=1}^{N}\log g(\zeta_n) - \frac{N}{2}\log 2\pi - \frac{N}{2}\log\sigma^2 \\
- \frac{1}{2\sigma^2}\sum_{n=1}^{N}(x_n - \gamma'\zeta_n)^2 - N\log P(\gamma, \sigma).
\end{aligned}
\tag{2.69}
$$

This is very awkward and never used in practice. In order to evaluate $P(\gamma, \sigma)$ one must know the distributional form $G(\zeta)$ and also be able to perform the integration in (2.67), and this is too demanding for practical use. The difficulty cannot be circumvented by treating $P(\gamma, \sigma)$ as an unknown parameter to be estimated separately from γ and σ, since this would yield an ML estimator identical with inconsistent least-squares regression.

In practice, a conditional ML estimator is used. In the sample, the distribution of x_n conditional on ζ_n is

$$
\begin{aligned}
f(x_n|\zeta_n) &= g(x_n|\zeta_n, x_n > c) \\
&= g(x_n|\zeta_n)/\Pr(x_n > c|\zeta_n) \\
&= \frac{\sigma^{-1}\varphi[(c - \gamma'\zeta_n)/\sigma]}{1 - \Phi[(c - \gamma'\zeta_n)/\sigma]}.
\end{aligned}
\tag{2.70}
$$

Thus, conditional on ζ_n, x_n has an LTN($\gamma'\zeta_n$, σ^2) distribution, which is discussed in detail in appendix 2. This leads to the following conditional log-likelihood:

$$\log L^c(\gamma, \sigma) = -\frac{N}{2}\log 2\pi - \frac{N}{2}\log\sigma^2 - \frac{1}{2\sigma^2}\sum_{n=1}^{N}(x_n - \gamma'\zeta_n)^2$$

$$-\sum_{n=1}^{N}\log\left[1 - \Phi\left(\frac{c-\gamma'\zeta_n}{\sigma}\right)\right]. \tag{2.71}$$

The first-order conditions for a maximum are

$$\frac{\partial \log L}{\partial \gamma} = \frac{1}{\sigma^2}\sum_{n=1}[x_n - \gamma'\zeta_n - \sigma\lambda(c_n^*)]\,\zeta_n = 0 \tag{2.72}$$

$$\frac{\partial \log L}{\partial \sigma^2} = \frac{1}{2\sigma^4}\sum_{n=1}^{N}[(x_n - \gamma'\zeta_n)^2 - \sigma^2\lambda(c_n^*)c_n^*] - \frac{N}{2\sigma^2} = 0 \tag{2.73}$$

where $\lambda(.) = \varphi(.)/[1-\Phi(.)]$ is the inverse of Mills' ratio and c_n^* is the normalized truncation threshold $(c-\gamma'\zeta_n)/\sigma$.

These conditions can be manipulated to the more revealing forms

$$\hat{\gamma} = \left(\sum_{n=1}^{N}\zeta_n\zeta_n\right)^{-1}\left\{\sum_{n=1}^{N}\zeta_n[x_n - \hat{\sigma}\lambda(\hat{c}_n^*)]\right\} \tag{2.74}$$

$$\hat{\sigma}^2 = \sum_{n=1}^{N}(x_n - \hat{\gamma}'\zeta_n)^2 \Bigg/ \left[N + \sum_{n=1}^{N}\lambda(\hat{c}_n^*)\,\hat{c}_n^*\right] \tag{2.75}$$

where $\hat{c}_n^*$ is c_n^* evaluated at $\hat{\gamma}$ and $\hat{\sigma}$. Although (2.74) and (2.75) appear to be very simple modifications of the analogous regression formulae, they are non-linear in $\hat{\gamma}$ and $\hat{\sigma}$ and must be solved numerically by means of an iterative algorithm. Since the resulting estimator is not a true ML estimator, standard results on the asymptotic properties of ML estimators cannot be relied upon. However, the work of Amemiya (1973) can be used to show strong consistency and asymptotic normality, at least for the case where $\{\zeta_n\}$ is a non-stochastic sequence with convenient limiting properties. Amemiya also shows that the second derivative matrix of $\log L^c$ can be used for the calculation of asymptotic standard errors.

Alternative regression-based estimators have been proposed for this truncated model; these are based on the moments of $x_n \mid \zeta_n$, rather than the full distribution. From equations (A2.5) and (A2.7) of appendix 2, the conditional mean of x_n is

$$E(x_n \mid \zeta_n, x_n > c) = \gamma'\zeta_n + \sigma\lambda(c_n^*). \tag{2.76}$$

Thus, when the sample is gathered by means of a truncated sampling mechanism, the regression function of x_n is no longer the simple linear form $\gamma'\zeta_n$ but rather the non-linear form (2.76). Note, however, that the conditional mean of $x_n - \sigma\lambda(c_n^*)$ is equal to $\gamma'\zeta_n$, and so the ML estimator (2.72) can be interpreted as a regression of this corrected variable on ζ_n.

The conditional variance of x_n is

$$\mathrm{var}(x_n | \zeta_n, x_n > c) = \sigma^2[1 + c_n^* \lambda(c_n^*) - \lambda(c_n^*)^2]. \tag{2.77}$$

Therefore, although the full population regression has constant variance σ^2, this non-linear regression displays a complicated pattern of heteroscedasticity.

The expressions are specific to our assumption of a conditional normal distribution for x, and other distributional forms will give rise to different expressions; appendix 2 gives the truncated moments of some other common forms. However, whatever the true distribution, the linear regression model will always be mis-specified: truncation from below has the effect of increasing the mean of x by an amount that depends on the difference between $\gamma'\zeta_n$ and the threshold c. Thus there will be some covariation in the sample between the truncation effect which is omitted from the regression model and the explanatory variables ζ, and this will impart some omitted variable bias to the regression coefficients. The same will apply to the case of truncation from above. Unbiased estimation of γ by multiple regression is only possible if there happens to be exactly offsetting truncation both from above and below, and this is a case of no practical importance. Regression is an inappropriate technique in truncated samples, and can lead to seriously flawed empirical results.

For example, Hausman and Wise (1977) compare regression estimates with more appropriate ML estimates for a model of individual earnings fitted to a sample deriving from the New Jersey negative income tax experiment. This sample is quite severely truncated (from above, rather than below), with the truncation threshold equal to 150 per cent of the poverty level defined for each family (thus c is a function of ζ and varies from family to family). They find evidence of very serious biases, with the ML coefficients being two or three times as large as the corresponding regression coefficients.

One way of avoiding these biases is to treat (2.74) as the basis of a non-linear regression model, with $\hat{\gamma}$ and $\hat{\sigma}$ found by numerically minimizing the residual sum of squares:

$$S(\gamma, \sigma) = \sum_{n=1}^{N} [x_n - \gamma'\zeta_n - \sigma\lambda(c_n^*)]^2. \tag{2.78}$$

Since x_n is heteroscedastic, it is important that suitable expressions are used for computing asymptotic standard errors (for example, those of White, equations (2.69)–(2.71)). Although this least-squares estimator has seen some use (see Wales and Woodland, 1980), it has no obvious advantages over conditional ML estimation since it is inefficient but still requires an iterative computational algorithm.

In a slightly different context, Amemiya (1973) has proposed a simple estimator which, like non-linear least squares, is inefficient, but it has the advantage that iterative computations are not required. Combining equations (A2.5) and (A2.6) from appendix 2, we can show that

$$E(x_n(x_n - c) \mid \zeta_n, x_n > c) = \sigma^2 + \gamma' \zeta_n E(x_n \mid \zeta_n, x_n > c). \tag{2.79}$$

This suggests the regression model

$$x_n(x_n - c) = \sigma^2 + \gamma'(x_n \zeta_n) + v_n \tag{2.80}$$

where v_n is a random disturbance with $E(v_n \mid \zeta_n) = 0$. However, a regression of $x_n(x_n - c)$ on $x_n \zeta_n$ will not provide a consistent estimate of γ and σ, since x_n is correlated with v_n. Amemiya proposes a two-step procedure. First regress x_n on ζ_n and higher powers of the variables in ζ_n, and construct the fitted value $\hat{x}_n$. Then use the elements of the vector $\hat{x}_n \zeta_n$ as instrumental variables in estimating the regression of $x_n(x_n - c)$ on $x_n \zeta_n$. This procedure yields consistent estimates of γ and σ; Amemiya gives an expression for their asymptotic covariance matrix.

Random *N* It is quite common for samples to be truncated in such a way that the final sample size is random rather than fixed. This is sometimes done as part of a two-step estimation technique (see, for example, chapter 4, section 4.1) but is also sometimes a feature of the survey design (for instance, the New Jersey negative income tax experiment). In such cases, a sample of fixed size N^* is drawn from the whole population (assume again that this is a random sample), and the final sample is arrived at by deleting all observations which fail to satisfy the acceptance criterion $x > c$. This sample then contains a random number N of observations.

Consider the marginal distribution of N. Since a randomly drawn observation satisfies $x > c$ with probability $P(\gamma, \hat{\sigma})$, N has a binomial distribution with frequency function

$$\Pr(N) = \frac{N^*!}{N!\,(N^* - N)!} P(\gamma, \sigma)^N [1 - P(\gamma, \sigma)]^{N^* - N}. \tag{2.81}$$

Conditional on a specific positive value for N, the observations have a joint density/mass function

$$\begin{aligned} f(x_1, \zeta_1, \ldots, x_N, \zeta_N \mid N) &= \prod_{n=1}^{N} g(x_n, \zeta_n \mid x_n > c) \\ &= \prod_{n=1}^{N} \left[\sigma^{-1} \varphi \left(\frac{x_n - \gamma' \zeta_n}{\sigma} \right) \Big/ P(\gamma, \sigma) \right] \\ &= \sigma^{-N} P(\gamma, \sigma)^{-N} \prod_{n=1}^{N} \varphi \left(\frac{x_n - \gamma' \zeta_n}{\sigma} \right) g(\zeta_n). \end{aligned} \tag{2.82}$$

Thus the distribution of the full sample is

$$f(x_1, \zeta_1, \ldots, x_N, \zeta_N) = \frac{N^*! \, \sigma^{-N}[1-P(\gamma, \sigma)]^{N^*-N}}{N! \, (N^*-N)!} \times \prod_{n=1}^{N} \varphi\left(\frac{x_n - \gamma' \zeta_n}{\sigma}\right) g(\zeta_n) \tag{2.83}$$

where the product term is to be taken as unity if $N = 0$.

Ignoring inessential constants, the true log-likelihood is therefore

$$\log L(\gamma, \sigma) = -\frac{N}{2} \log \sigma^2 - \frac{1}{2\sigma^2} \sum_{n=1}^{N} (x_n - \gamma' \zeta_n)^2 + (N^* - N) \log [1 - P(\gamma, \sigma)]. \tag{2.84}$$

This is again intractable for most purposes, and in practice the conditional log-likelihood (2.71) is used, although now it must be regarded as conditional on both N and $\zeta_1, \ldots, \zeta_N$. The asymptotic properties of the conditional ML estimator have not been derived for this case; Amemiya's (1973) results do not apply directly, since they are asymptotic in N, whereas here N is random so the relevant theory must be asymptotic in N^*.

The previously discussed regression-based methods are also widely used, and there is no difficulty in showing that these have standard asymptotic properties in this case.

2.5.2 Endogenous stratification

Sample truncation can be thought of as an example of stratification of the population into two sub-populations, defined by $x > c$ and $x \leqslant c$, the latter having a sample of size zero drawn from it. Occasionally, more complicated forms of endogenous stratification are encountered. An example is the Gary income maintenance experiment, discussed by Hausman and Wise (1982), which used the following sampling technique. A pool of households was drawn at random from the relevant population and then divided into income classes, with limits defined as fixed multiples of a preselected poverty level. These endogenously defined income classes were sampled at different rates until a final sample of fixed size N was compiled. This is a somewhat simplified picture of the procedure that was followed in the Gary experiment, but it suffices to illustrate the ideas involved.

Define the m strata $S_1, \ldots, S_m$ as follows:

$$S_i = \{(x, \zeta) \mid c_{i-1} < x \leqslant c_i\} \qquad i = 1, \ldots, m \tag{2.85}$$

where $c_0 = -\infty$ and $c_m = \infty$. Note that, for the Gary experiment, $m = 5$ strata were used. In practice, the c_i depend on factors such as family size;

however, we shall simplify matters further by assuming them to be constant. We consider two different interpretations of the Gary sampling procedure.

Fixed stratum sample sizes Suppose that subsamples of fixed sizes $N_1, \ldots, N_m$ are drawn from the m strata. The result is an NID sample with the typical observation having the following density/mass function:

$$\begin{aligned} f_n(x_n, \zeta_n) &= g(x_n, \zeta_n \mid c_{i_n-1} < x_n \leqslant c_{i_n}) \\ &= g(x_n \mid \zeta_n; \theta)\, g(\zeta_n)/\Pr(c_{i_n-1} < x_n \leqslant c_{i_n}) \\ &= \sigma^{-1}\varphi[(x_n - \gamma'\zeta_n)/\sigma]/P(i_n; \theta) \end{aligned} \tag{2.86}$$

where

$$P(i;\theta) = \int_{R_\zeta} \left[\Phi\left(\frac{c_i - \gamma'\zeta}{\sigma}\right) - \Phi\left(\frac{c_{i-1} - \gamma'\zeta}{\sigma}\right)\right] \mathrm{d}G(\zeta) \tag{2.87}$$

This is a special case of our general formulation of endogenous sampling, equation (2.60), with

$$\omega_n(s_n; \theta) = 1/P(i_n; \gamma, \sigma) \tag{2.88}$$

and presents familiar problems: since the terms $P(i; \gamma, \sigma)$ require both knowledge of the form of $G(\zeta)$ and the evaluation of the integral (2.87), the true log-likelihood will be too awkward for applied work. Moreover, if, instead of being evaluated, they are treated as unknown parameters, ML estimation again reduces to the regression of x_n on ζ_n and yields inconsistent estimates of γ and σ (the $P(i; \gamma, \sigma)$ are also inconsistently estimated as N_i/N).

As usual, the conditional density $f_n(x_n/\zeta_n)$ leads to a much simpler conditional log-likelihood:

$$\begin{aligned} \log L(\gamma, \sigma) = &-\frac{N}{2}\log 2\pi - \frac{N}{2}\log\sigma^2 - \frac{1}{2\sigma^2}\sum_{n=1}^{N}(x_n - \gamma'\zeta_n)^2 \\ &- \sum_{n=1}^{N}\log\left[\Phi\left(\frac{c_{i_n} - \gamma'\zeta_n}{\sigma}\right) - \Phi\left(\frac{c_{i_n} - \gamma'\zeta_n}{\sigma}\right)\right]. \end{aligned} \tag{2.89}$$

A generalized version of Amemiya's estimator can also be constructed for this case.

Probabilistic stratum sampling In their applied work, Hausman and Wise (1982) favour a rather different interpretation of the Gary sampling procedure. They assume that the final sample is taken from the initial pool of households by repeated random drawings, with each draw being made from stratum i with probability Π_i, $i = 1, \ldots, m$. This leads to sample observations having a common density/mass function with discontinuities at the

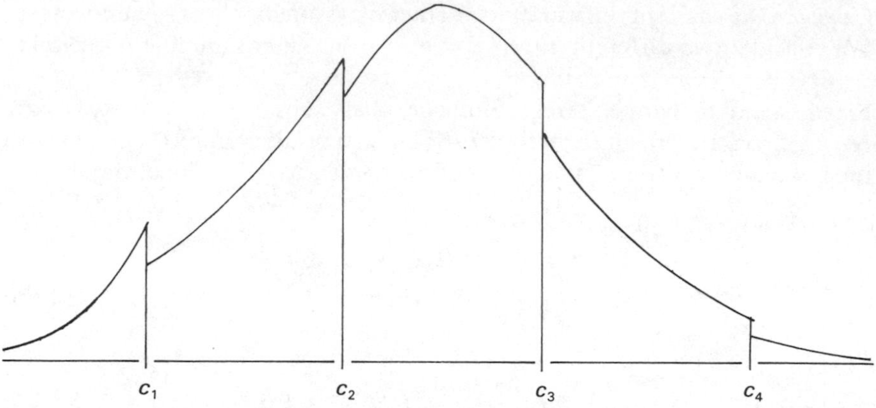

Figure 2.1 The distribution of x under probabilistic sampling of the strata.

boundaries of the strata, as in the example illustrated in figure 2.1. The ith segment of this density function has the following form:

$$\begin{aligned} f(x_n, \zeta_n) &= \Pi_i\, g(x_n, \zeta_n \mid c_{i-1} < x_n \leqslant c_i) \\ &= \Pi_i\, \sigma^{-1} \varphi \left(\frac{x_n - \gamma' \zeta_n}{\sigma} \right) \frac{g(\zeta_n)}{P(i; \gamma, \sigma)}. \end{aligned} \tag{2.90}$$

Again this is a special case of (2.60), with $\omega_n(s_n; \theta)$ being composed of the m segments $\Pi_i / P(i; \gamma, \sigma)$.

If the Π_i are constants (either known or unknown), then this leads to a log-likelihood function of the form

$$\begin{aligned} \log L(\gamma, \sigma) = & \sum_{i=1}^{m} N_i \log \Pi_i + \sum_{n=1}^{N} \log g(\zeta_n) - \frac{N}{2} \log 2\pi - \frac{N}{2} \log \sigma^2 \\ & - \frac{1}{2\sigma^2} \sum_{n=1}^{N} (x_n - \gamma' \zeta_n)^2 - \sum_{i=1}^{m} N_i \log P(i; \gamma, \sigma) \end{aligned} \tag{2.91}$$

where N_i is the random size of the sample drawn from stratum i.

However, suppose instead that the rates of oversampling, $\rho_i = \Pi_i / P(i; \gamma, \sigma)$, rather than the probabilities Π_i, are independent of γ and σ (this is the case that Hausman and Wise have in mind). Then this log-likelihood becomes

$$\begin{aligned} \log L(\gamma, \sigma) = & \sum_{i=1}^{m} N_i \log \rho_i + \sum_{n=1}^{N} \log g(\zeta_n) - \frac{N}{2} \log 2\pi - \frac{N}{2} \log \sigma^2 \\ & - \frac{1}{2\sigma^2} \sum_{n=1}^{N} (x_n - \gamma' \zeta_n)^2. \end{aligned} \tag{2.92}$$

Log-likelihoods (2.89) and (2.90) appear to be very different: evaluation of $P(i; \gamma, \sigma)$ is necessary for the former but not for the latter. However, this is misleading. The maximization of (2.92) with respect to γ leads to a simple regression of x_n on ζ_n, which is known to be inconsistent. To ensure consistency, it is necessary to maximize log L subject to the constraint

$$\sum_{i=1}^{m} \rho_i P(i; \gamma, \sigma) = 1. \tag{2.93}$$

Again, this is intractable.

The natural alternative to these unhelpful expressions is to use the conditional density function $f(x_n | \zeta_n) = f(x_n, \zeta_n)/f(\zeta_n)$. The marginal density of ζ_n is found by integrating and summing the forms (2.90):

$$f(\zeta_n) = g(\zeta_n) \sum_{i=1}^{m} \frac{\Pi_i(\Phi_{ni} - \Phi_{ni-1})}{P(i; \gamma, \sigma)} \tag{2.94}$$

where

$$\Phi_{ni} = \Phi\left(\frac{c_i - \gamma' \zeta_n}{\sigma}\right). \tag{2.95}$$

The conditional density function therefore has ith segment

$$f(x_n | \zeta_n) = \frac{\Pi_i \, \sigma^{-1} \varphi[(x_n - \gamma' \zeta_n)/\sigma]}{P(i; \gamma, \sigma) \sum_{j=1}^{m} \Pi_j(\Phi_{nj} - \Phi_{nj-1})/P(j; \gamma, \sigma)} \tag{2.96}$$

defined for $x_n \in (c_{i-1}, c_i)$, $i = 1, m$.

Although this conditional density also depends on the terms $P(i; \gamma, \sigma)$, conditional likelihood methods are feasible. The sampling rates $\rho_i = \Pi_i/P(i; \gamma, \sigma)$ can be treated as parameters and estimated independently of γ and σ by maximizing the unconstrained conditional log-likelihood

$$\log L^c(\rho_1, \ldots, \rho_m, \gamma, \sigma) = -\frac{N}{2} \log 2\pi - \frac{N}{2} \log \sigma^2 - \frac{1}{2\sigma^2} \sum_{n=1}^{N} (x_n - \gamma' \zeta_n)^2 + \sum_{i=1}^{m} N_i \log \rho_i - \sum_{n=1}^{N} \log \left[\sum_{j=1}^{m} \rho_j (\Phi_{nj} - \Phi_{nj-1}) \right]. \tag{2.97}$$

Note that, since (2.96) is homogenous of degree zero in the ρ_i, only the $m - 1$ ratios $\rho_2/\rho_1, \ldots, \rho_m/\rho_1$ (say) can be identified.

Although no formal derivation of the asymptotic properties of this conditional ML estimator is available, there appears to be little difficulty in extending Amemiya's (1973) results to this case, particularly if the ρ_i are known. Thus it is not necessary to impose restriction (2.93) to achieve consistency.

If the ρ_i are known or can be reliably estimated, an obvious weighted least-squares estimator is available. This weights each observation in inverse proportion to the square root of the degree of oversampling in its stratum, and requires only a regression of $x_n\sqrt{\rho_{i_n}}$ on $\zeta_n\sqrt{\rho_{i_n}}$:

$$\tilde{\gamma} = \left(\sum_{n=1}^{N} \frac{1}{\rho_{i_n}} \zeta_n \zeta_n'\right)^{-1} \left(\sum_{n=1}^{N} \frac{1}{\rho_{i_n}} \zeta_n x_n\right). \tag{2.98}$$

This estimator is easily shown to be consistent under weak conditions. However, Hausman and Wise present some calculations which suggest that it may be rather inefficient relative to conditional ML if the sampling scheme is very unbalanced.

2.6 Non-response and extraneous sample selection

With rare exceptions, participation in a sample survey is voluntary. Thus samples are in part self-selected, and any econometric analysis is conditional on individuals' decisions to co-operate with the survey. If this decision to co-operate is endogenous, in the sense that it is related to the behaviour under study, then this implicit conditioning will impart some bias to econometric results unless corrective action is taken.

2.6.1 Consequences of differential response

To illustrate the difficulties here, we shall continue to work with the simple normal regression model (2.63) and extend it by adding a related regression-like equation governing survey participation. Thus we have the following conditional bivariate normal model:

$$x_n, v_n | \zeta_n, \xi_n \sim N\left(\begin{bmatrix} \gamma'\zeta_n \\ \delta'\xi_n \end{bmatrix}, \begin{bmatrix} \sigma_x^2 & \sigma_{xv} \\ \sigma_{xv} & 1 \end{bmatrix}\right) \tag{2.99}$$

where v_n is an unobservable variable representing the individual's 'willingness to participate in the survey', ξ_n is a vector of exogenous variables explaining the participation decision and δ is the corresponding coefficient vector. The variance of v_n is normalized at unity: since v_n is unobserved, its scale is arbitrary.

Let us suppose (without any loss of generality, if $\delta'\xi_n$ includes an intercept term) that an individual decides to participate if 'willingness' is positive. Furthermore, assume for simplicity that the original sample of individuals (both respondents and non-respondents) is a random sample. Then the distribution of x and ζ in the sample is the population distribution of x and ζ conditional on the event $v > 0$. Now consider the regression estimator

$$\tilde{\gamma} = \left(\sum_n \zeta_n \zeta_n'\right)^{-1} (\Sigma\, \zeta_n x_n). \tag{2.100}$$

This has expected value

$$E(\tilde{\gamma}) = E\left[\left(\sum_n \zeta_n \zeta_n'\right)^{-1} \sum_n \zeta_n E(x_n \,|\, \zeta_n, \xi_n, v_n > 0)\right] \tag{2.101}$$

and bias

$$E(\tilde{\gamma} - \gamma) = E\left[\left(\sum_n \zeta_n \zeta_n'\right)^{-1} \sum_n \zeta_n E(x_n - \gamma' \zeta_n \,|\, \zeta_n, \xi_n, v_n > 0)\right]. \tag{2.102}$$

There are two principal circumstances under which this bias will be zero. If x and v are independent conditional on ζ and ξ, then

$$E(x_n - \gamma' \zeta_n \,|\, \zeta_n, \xi_n, v_n > 0) = E(x_n - \gamma' \zeta_n \,|\, \zeta_n, \xi_n) = 0.$$

Alternatively, consider the case where ζ_n and ξ_n are mutually independent, with distributions that do not vary with n. The regression model implies that $x_n - \gamma' \zeta_n$ is independent of ζ_n and therefore $E(x_n - \gamma' \zeta_n \,|\, \zeta_n, \xi_n, v_n > 0)$ is a function of ξ_n only, say $\mu(\xi_n)$. Therefore (2.101) can be factored as follows:

$$\begin{aligned} E(\tilde{\gamma} - \gamma) &= \sum_n E(A^{-1} \zeta_n)\, E[\mu(\xi_n)] \\ &= E\left(A^{-1} \sum_n \zeta_n\right) \mu \end{aligned} \tag{2.103}$$

where $A = \Sigma \zeta_n \zeta_n'$ and $\mu = E[\mu(\xi_n)]$. This is the regression of a constant, μ, on ζ; if, say, the first element of ζ is a unit variable so that γ_1 is the intercept term, then the bias vector is $E(\tilde{\gamma} - \gamma)' = (\mu\ 0 \ldots 0)$, and all slope coefficients are unbiased. This is because the conditional mean of x_n is greater than $\gamma' \zeta_n$ by a truncation factor that fluctuates randomly about the constant μ, independently of ζ_n.

It is often very difficult to justify making either of these two independence assumptions. Our discussion of the FES in section 2.3, for instance, suggested that response rates are likely to be related to many variables such as income, employment status, location, wealth and some types of expenditure. It is very unlikely that such variables are independent of the explanatory variables ζ_n, or, indeed, that the unobservable factors determining response are independent of the unobservable influences on x_n. Thus, least-squares regression and most other statistical techniques must be regarded as biased when applied to economic data originating from a sample survey in which response is voluntary. If response is low and non-uniform, then this bias may be substantial.

For the special case of normality, relation (2.99), the conditional expectation of $x_n - \gamma' \zeta_n$ is given by equation (A2.36) of appendix 2,

$$E(x_n - \gamma' \zeta_n | \xi_n, v_n > 0) = \sigma_{xv} \lambda^*(\delta' \xi_n) \tag{2.104}$$

and the least-squares bias is

$$E(\tilde{\gamma} - \gamma) = \sigma_{xv} E\left[\left(\sum_n \zeta_n \zeta_n'\right)^{-1} \sum_n \zeta_n \lambda^*(\delta' \xi_n)\right] \tag{2.105}$$

where $\lambda^*(z) = \lambda(-z) = \varphi(z)/\Phi(z)$ is the complement of the inverse Mills' ratio. Thus, in the case of a normal bivariate regression structure, the simple parameter restriction $\sigma_{xv} = 0$ is a sufficient condition for consistency of least squares in the presence of differential response.

Although we have considered the effects of differential response on a very simple regression model, the general considerations involved here are equally applicable to any statistical model and any estimation technique - the neglect of difficulties caused by non-response can have serious consequences.

2.6.2 Estimation without data on non-respondents

For obvious reasons it is extremely difficult to obtain worthwhile information about non-respondents. Most surveys yield no information at all, and those that do usually provide very limited and unreliable data on the characteristics of non-respondents. This is the fundamental problem faced by an applied worker attempting to correct for differential response.

Even if the sample is confined to respondents, correction for the effects of differential response still requires the specification of a model of response. We shall retain the normal regression model (2.99), assuming that x, ζ and ξ (but not v, of course) are observed. Since no information is available on the population of non-respondents (those for whom $v_n \leqslant 0$), the sample distribution has a joint probability density/mass function

$$\begin{aligned} f(x_n, \zeta_n, \xi_n) &= g(x_n, \zeta_n, \xi_n | v_n > 0) \\ &= \int_0^\infty g(x_n, v | \zeta_n, \xi_n) \mathrm{d}v \, g(\zeta_n, \xi_n)/\Pr(v_n > 0). \end{aligned} \tag{2.106}$$

The special case of (2.106) for our normal linear model can be found by decomposing the distribution of x and v (conditional on ζ and ξ) into marginal and conditional components (see appendix 3, section A3.5):

$$f(x_n, \zeta_n, \xi_n) = \left\{\sigma_x^{-1} \phi \left(\frac{x_n - \gamma' \zeta_n}{\sigma_n}\right) \Phi \left[\frac{\delta' \xi_n + \sigma_{xv}(x_n - \gamma' \zeta_n)/\sigma_x^2}{(1 - \sigma_{xv}^2/\sigma_x^2)^{1/2}}\right] \Big/ P(\delta)\right\} g(\zeta_n, \xi_n) \tag{2.107}$$

where

$$P(\delta) = \Pr(v_n > 0) = \int_{R_\xi} \Phi(\delta'\xi)\,\mathrm{d}G(\xi). \tag{2.108}$$

For the usual reasons, $P(\delta)$ is an intractable expression and an operational ML estimation technique must be based instead on the conditional density $f(x_n | \zeta_n, \xi_n)$, which is arrived at by replacing $P(\delta)$ in (2.107) by $\Pr(v_n > 0 | \xi_n) = \Phi(\delta'\xi_n)$ and deleting the term $g(\zeta_n, \xi_n)$ (see also equation (A2.34) of appendix 2). Thus the conditional log-likelihood is

$$\log L^c(\gamma, \delta, \sigma_x^2, \sigma_{xv}) = -\frac{N}{2}\log 2\pi - \frac{N}{2}\log \sigma_x^2 - \frac{1}{2\sigma_x^2}\sum_{n=1}^{N}(x_n - \gamma'\zeta_n)^2$$
$$+ \sum_{n=1}^{N}\log \Phi\left[\frac{\delta'\xi_n + \sigma_{xv}(x_n - \gamma'\zeta_n)/\sigma_x^2}{(1-\sigma_{xv}^2/\sigma_x^2)^{1/2}}\right]$$
$$- \sum_{n=1}^{N}\log \Phi(\delta'\xi_n). \tag{2.109}$$

Note that if a fixed number of individuals are approached initially, the number of respondents N is random, and therefore (2.108) must be interpreted as conditional on N also.

Non-likelihood methods are also available. From equation (A2.36) of appendix 2, the conditional expectation of x_n is

$$E(x_n | v_n > 0, \zeta_n, \xi_n) = \gamma'\zeta_n + \sigma_{xv}\lambda^*(\delta'\xi_n) \tag{2.110}$$

which suggests the non-linear least-squares estimator

$$\min_{\gamma,\,\delta,\,\sigma_{xn}} \sum_{n=1}^{N}[x_n - \gamma'\zeta_n - \sigma_{xv}\lambda^*(\delta'\xi_n)]^2. \tag{2.111}$$

Observe that this has a very simple interpretation as a correction of the least-squares bias (2.105). However, it has little to recommend it as an alternative to conditional ML since it is inefficient and yet still requires the use of an iterative computational algorithm.

Both the conditional ML and least-squares estimation techniques make very great demands on the sample. Information on x_n is assumed to be adequate for the simultaneous estimation of both the primary model itself and an additional model of survey response. Bearing in mind that ζ_n and ξ_n are likely to have variables in common, or at least to be highly correlated, it seems unlikely that one would be able to obtain good estimates of γ, δ, σ_x^2 and σ_{xv}. A simulation study by Muthén and Jöreskog (1981) tends to confirm this suspicion and suggests that $\hat{\delta}$ in particular is likely to be unreliable. Moreover, without direct observation of the response–non-response dichotomy and with no real behavioural theory as a guide to specification, it is very difficult to produce a convincing choice of variables for the vector ξ_n.

These considerations suggest that differential response bias is unlikely to be a curable ailment in most applied cross-section work. In the absence of reliable information on non-respondents, the best that can be done is probably to give some rough indication of the likely direction of any such bias. For instance, in the case of an analysis of the relationship between the demand for alcoholic drink and income using FES data, one could reasonably expect a downward bias in the estimated income coefficient, for the following reasons. The evidence described in section 2.3 suggests that the probability of non-response increases with alcohol consumption (implying $\sigma_{xv} < 0$) and with income (implying that $\delta'\xi_n$ decreases with income). Since $\lambda^*(.)$ is a decreasing function, the term $E(x_n - \gamma'\zeta_n | v_n > 0, \zeta_n, \xi_n) = \sigma_{xv}\lambda^*(\delta'\xi_n)$ will be negatively correlated with income. Since the least-squares bias can be seen as an omitted variable bias, with $\sigma_{xv}\lambda^*(\delta'\xi_n)$ as the omitted explanatory factor, the conventional analysis of mis-specification in linear regression indicates a downward bias in the income coefficient. For models more complicated than linear regression, the nature of non-response bias may, of course, be much more difficult to establish.

2.6.3 Estimation using data on non-respondents

Occasionally, it is possible to obtain useful information on the characteristics of non-respondents. If this is felt to be adequate for the specification of a model of survey participation, then estimation methods more efficient than those described above become available. Again, suppose that the simple model (2.99) is to be used. There are two observational regimes: for respondents x_n, ζ_n and ξ_n are all observed; for non-respondents only ξ_n is observable.

The sample distribution then consists of two parts. For respondents

$$f(x_n, \zeta_n, \xi_n) = \int_0^\infty g(x_n, v | \zeta_n, \xi_n)\mathrm{d}v \; g(\zeta_n, \xi_n)$$

$$= \sigma_x^{-1}\phi\left(\frac{x_n - \gamma'\zeta_n}{\sigma_x}\right)\Phi\left[\frac{\delta'\xi_n + \sigma_{xv}(x_n - \gamma'\zeta_n)/\sigma_x^2}{(1 - \sigma_{xv}^2/\sigma_x^2)^{1/2}}\right] g(\zeta_n, \xi_n) \tag{2.112}$$

and for non-respondents

$$f(v_n \leqslant 0, \xi_n) = \Pr(v_n \leqslant 0 | \xi_n)\, g(\xi_n)$$
$$= [1 - \Phi(\delta'\xi_n)]\, g(\xi_n). \tag{2.113}$$

Thus the log-likelihood function for a sample covering both respondents and non-respondents is

$$\log L(\gamma, \delta, \sigma_x, \sigma_{xv}) = K + \sum_{\mathrm{NR}} \log[1 - \Phi(\delta' \xi_n)] - \frac{N_r}{2} \log \sigma_x^2$$
$$- \frac{1}{2\sigma_x^2} \sum_{\mathrm{R}} (x_n - \gamma' \zeta_n)^2$$
$$+ \sum_{\mathrm{R}} \log \Phi \left[\frac{\delta' \xi_n + \sigma_{xv}(x_n - \gamma' \zeta_n)/\sigma_x^2}{(1 - \sigma_{xv}^2/\sigma_x^2)^{1/2}} \right] \tag{2.114}$$

where K is an inessential constant, R and NR represent the sets of observations on respondents and non-respondents, and N_r is the number of respondents. Note that there is no difficulty in evaluating and hence maximizing this log-likelihood, and that the resulting estimator is a true ML estimator. Thus standard asymptotic results apply.

Two-step regression-based techniques can also be used. These follow a suggestion made by Heckman (1976, 1979). The first step involves the estimation of a binary probit response model in isolation from the principal regression model. The probabilities of response and non-response are

$$\Pr(v_n > 0, \xi_n) = \Phi(\delta' \xi_n)\, g(\xi_n) \tag{2.115}$$

and

$$\Pr(v_n \leqslant 0, \xi_n) = [1 - \Phi(\delta' \xi_n)]\, g(\xi_n). \tag{2.116}$$

Thus a log-likelihood for the response–non-response dichotomy is

$$\log L(\delta) = \sum_{n=1}^{N} \log g(\xi_n) + \sum_{\mathrm{R}} \log \Phi(\delta' \xi_n) + \sum_{\mathrm{NR}} \log[1 - \Phi(\delta' \xi_n)]. \tag{2.117}$$

The maximizing value $\hat{\delta}$ is the widely used probit estimator, which is available in most statistical computing packages. The second stage of the Heckman procedure exploits expression (2.110). First an artificial variable $\hat{\lambda}_n^* = \lambda^*(\hat{\delta}' \xi_n)$ is constructed, and then a regression of x_n on ζ_n and $\hat{\lambda}_n^*$ yields coefficients which are the final estimates of γ and σ_{xv}. There is a complication, arising from the fact that $\hat{\lambda}_n^*$ depends on the estimate $\hat{\delta}$. This introduces an additional source of random variation into the final regression and invalidates the usual regression formula for the sampling variances of $\hat{\gamma}$ and $\hat{\sigma}_{xv}$. Heckman (1979) gives a formula for the correct asymptotic covariance matrix.

Heckman's estimator has been widely applied in cases where endogenous sample selection is due to deliberate truncation of the sample rather than differential survey response. For instance, a study of individual wage rates based on a sample including both labour force participants and non-participants would be essentially equivalent to our model (2.99) with v_n interpreted as hours of work (or, equivalently, as the difference between the actual wage and a reservation wage). Early examples of this type of model are those of Gronau (1974) and Heckman (1976). However, it is usually possible in this labour supply context to observe the extraneous truncation variable v_n (hours of work), and then more efficient techniques are available. These are described in chapter 4, section 4.5.

2.6.4 Multiple truncation factors

Cross-section samples are often subject to more than one type of extraneous truncation. Many surveys display both incomplete coverage and differential response. For example, a survey of earnings might exclude non-workers as part of the survey design, and also have a poor rate of response. In such cases, each observation is conditional on two events: that the individual is not excluded by the sample design (supplies a positive amount of labour), and that he or she is willing to co-operate with the survey. Thus, the equivalent of (2.97) in this case would consist of three equations, i.e. a primary earnings model and two sample participation equations:

$$x_n, v_{n1}, v_{n2} \mid \zeta_n, \xi_{n1}, \xi_{n2} \sim N\left(\begin{bmatrix} \gamma'\zeta_n \\ \delta_1'\xi_{n1} \\ \delta_2'\xi_{n2} \end{bmatrix}, \begin{bmatrix} \sigma_x^2 & \sigma_{x1} & \sigma_{x2} \\ & 1 & \sigma_{12} \\ & & 1 \end{bmatrix}\right) \tag{2.118}$$

Using the expressions derived in section A2.4 of appendix 2, it is straightforward to extend the ML estimation techniques derived above to this case, and we do not present the details here. The log-likelihood function is more difficult in this case, however, since bivariate normal probabilities are involved (see section A3.4 of appendix 3 for a review of computational methods).

For regression-based methods, we need the appropriate conditional expectation of x_n. This is found by adapting equation (A2.52) of appendix 2 to give

$$E(x_n \mid v_{n1} > 0, v_{n2} > 0, \zeta_n, \xi_{n1}, \xi_{n2}) = \gamma'\zeta_n + \sigma_{x1}\lambda_{n1}^+ + \sigma_{x2}\lambda_{x2}^+ \tag{2.119}$$

where

$$\lambda_{n1}^+ = \phi(\delta_1'\xi_{n1})\,\Phi\left[\frac{\delta_2'\xi_{n2} - \sigma_{12}\delta_1'\xi_{n1}}{1-\sigma_{12}^2}\right] \Bigg/ \Pr(v_{n1} > 0, v_{n2} > 0 \mid \xi_{n1}, \xi_{n2}) \tag{2.120}$$

$$\lambda_{n2}^+ = \phi(\delta_2'\xi_{n2})\,\Phi\left[\frac{\delta_1'\xi_{n1} - \sigma_{12}\delta_2'\xi_{n2}}{1-\sigma_{12}^2}\right] \Bigg/ \Pr(v_{n1} > 0, v_{n2} > 0 \mid \xi_{n1}, \xi_{n2}) \tag{2.121}$$

and $\Pr(v_{n1} > 0, v_{n2} > 0 \mid \xi_{n1}, \xi_{n2})$ is the integral of a bivariate $N(\delta_1'\xi_{n1}, \delta_2'\xi_{n2}, 1, 1, \sigma_{12})$ density over the positive quadrant. Thus the consistency of least squares regression now generally requires that both truncation processes are independent of $x_n(\sigma_{x1} = \sigma_{x2} = 0)$. A generalization of Heckman's two-step estimator is easily constructed. This involves bivariate probit analysis to give initial estimates of δ_1, δ_2 and σ_{12}, which are then used to form the artificial variables $\hat{\lambda}^+_{n1}$ and $\hat{\lambda}^+_{n2}$; these are included as explanatory variables in the second-stage regression. A study by Ham (1982) gives details of this estimator and its asymptotic distribution. He applies the technique to a model of labour supply that is estimated from a sample containing information subject to two types of constraint. The individual may choose not to work, and may be constrained by available employment opportunities to supply less than the desired number of hours of work. Ham finds a significant estimate of σ_{12} and thus rejects the much simpler model that results if v_{n1} and v_{n2} are independent. The final estimates of σ_{x1} and σ_{x2} are large and highly significant and a comparison with the regression estimator confirms that the truncation biases are indeed substantial.

2.6.5 Response in experimental surveys

Social experimentation programmes typically involve repeated observations. Households are first observed before being subjected to any experimental change (in the exogenous variables ζ) and then re-interviewed at some date after the experimental scheme has begun. Thus non-response can occur at two stages. A household might refuse to co-operate with the survey at all, or it might initially co-operate but then drop out of the programme before being re-interviewed. The latter phenomenon, the gradual decay of participation in a panel survey, is known as sample attrition.

A simple picture of this process is as follows: x_{n1} and v_{n1} are the dependent variable and the unobserved 'willingness to participate' variable at the time of the first interview; x_{n2} and v_{n2} are their analogues observed after the experimental treatment has begun. Assume that these four variables are generated by a conventional linear regression structure:

$$x_{n1}, v_{n1}, x_{n2}, v_{n2} \mid \zeta_{n1}, \xi_{n1}, \zeta_{n2}, \xi_{n2} \sim N(\mu_n, \Sigma) \tag{2.122}$$

where

$$\mu_n' = [\gamma_1'\zeta_{n1}\ \delta_1'\xi_{n1}\ \gamma_2'\zeta_{n2}\ \delta_2'\xi_{n2}] \tag{2.123}$$

and $\Sigma = \{\sigma_{ij}\}$, with σ_{22} and σ_{44} normalized to be unity. Note that (2.121) allows the possibility that the experimental change in ζ alters the whole relationship between x and ζ. The restriction $\gamma_1 = \gamma_2$ would be an important one to test.

The conditional distribution of x_{n1} and x_{n2} has components corresponding to three possible observational regimes: full participation; drop-out after the first interview; and refusal to participate at all. These three components are as follows.

i **Full participation** ($v_{n1} > 0, v_{n2} > 0$):

$$f(x_{n1}, x_{n2} \mid \zeta_{n1}, \xi_{n1}, \zeta_{n2}, \xi_{n2}) = \int_0^\infty \int_0^\infty \phi(x_{n1}, v_1, x_{n2}, v_2; \mu_n, \Sigma)\, \mathrm{d}v_2\, \mathrm{d}v_1 \tag{2.124}$$

where $\phi(\cdot\,; \mu, \Sigma)$ is general notation for the p.d.f. of the multivariate $N(\mu, \Sigma)$ distribution.

ii **Incomplete participation** ($v_{n1} > 0, v_{n2} \leqslant 0$):

$$f(x_{n1} \mid \zeta_{n1}, \xi_{n1}, \xi_{n2}) = \int_0^\infty \int_{-\infty}^0 \phi(x_{n1}, v_1, v_2; \mu_n^*, \Sigma^*)\, \mathrm{d}v_2\, \mathrm{d}v_1 \tag{2.125}$$

where

$$\mu_n^{*\prime} = [\gamma_1' \zeta_n\ \delta_1' \xi_{n1}\ \delta_2' \xi_{n2}] \tag{2.126}$$

and

$$\Sigma^* = \begin{bmatrix} \sigma_{11} & \sigma_{12} & \sigma_{14} \\ \sigma_{12} & 1 & \sigma_{24} \\ \sigma_{14} & \sigma_{24} & 1 \end{bmatrix} \tag{2.127}$$

iii **Non-participation** ($v_{n1} \leqslant 0$):

$$\begin{aligned} \Pr(\text{non-participation} \mid \xi_{n1}) &= \Pr(v_{n1} \leqslant 0 \mid \xi_{n1}) \\ &= 1 - \Phi(\delta_1' \xi_{n1}) \end{aligned} \tag{2.128}$$

If all required data were available (in particular, if ξ_{n1} were observed even for non-participants), then a full log-likelihood function could be defined and maximized numerically. This takes the form

$$\begin{aligned} \log L(\gamma_1, \delta_1, \gamma_2, \delta_2, \Sigma) &= K + \sum_{\mathrm{FP}} \log f(x_{n1}, x_{n2} \mid \zeta_{n1}, \xi_{n1}, \zeta_{n2}, \xi_{n2}) \\ &\quad + \sum_{\mathrm{IP}} \log f(x_{n1} \mid \zeta_{n1}, \xi_{n1}, \xi_{n2}) \\ &\quad + \sum_{\mathrm{NP}} \log \Pr(\mathrm{NP} \mid \xi_{n1}) \end{aligned} \tag{2.129}$$

where K is an inessential constant depending on the marginal distributions of the exogenous variables, and FP, IP and NP denote the three observational possibilities listed above. The maximization of the log-likelihood function is very demanding: a large number of parameters must be estimated simultaneously; the evaluation of log L requires the computation of large numbers of bivariate normal integrals (see appendix 3), and it is necessary to use information on individuals who refuse to co-operate even at the initial stage of the experiment.

For the last of these reasons, this sequential two-period model has not been estimated in practice. The nearest approach to it is the study by Hausman and Wise (1979) which concentrates on the problem of attrition and neglects the difficulties raised by initial non-response. The reason for this is that considerable information is available on people who drop out of the experiment after the first interview, whereas little is known about those who refuse any co-operation. The Hausman and Wise model can be seen as a special case of (2.122) and (2.123) with $\sigma_{12} = \sigma_{23} = \sigma_{24} = 0$. In this case, v_{n1} is independent of x_{n1}, v_{n2} and x_{n2}, and thus the joint density (2.124) which relates to full participants can be written

$$f(x_{n1}, x_{n2} \mid \zeta_{n1}, \xi_{n1}, \zeta_{n2}, \xi_{n2}) = \int_0^\infty \phi(x_{n1}, x_{n2}, v_2; \mu_n^+, \Sigma^+)\mathrm{d}v_2 \, \Phi(\delta_1' \xi_{n1}) \tag{2.130}$$

where

$$\mu_n^+ = [\gamma_1' \zeta_{n1} \; \gamma_2' \zeta_{n2} \; \delta_2' \xi_{n2}] \tag{2.131}$$

and

$$\Sigma^+ = \begin{bmatrix} \sigma_{11} & \sigma_{13} & \sigma_{14} \\ \sigma_{13} & \sigma_{33} & \sigma_{34} \\ \sigma_{14} & \sigma_{34} & 1 \end{bmatrix}. \tag{2.132}$$

Expression (2.125), which is the density of $\mathbf{x}_{n1}$ for those who drop out of the panel after the first interview, simplifies to the form

$$f(x_{n1} \mid \zeta_{n1}, \xi_{n1}, \xi_{n2}) = \left\{1 - \Phi\left[\frac{\delta_2' \xi_{n2} + \sigma_{14}(x_{n1} - \gamma_1' \zeta_{n1})/\sigma_{11}}{(1 - \sigma_{14}^2/\sigma_{11})^2}\right]\right\}$$
$$\times (\sigma_{11})^{-1/2} \, \phi\left[\frac{x_{n1} - \gamma_1' \zeta_{n1}}{\sqrt{\sigma_{11}}}\right] \Phi(\delta_1' \xi_{n1}). \tag{2.133}$$

In deriving (2.133), we have used the results of section A3.5 of appendix 3. Note that the integral term in (2.130) can also be expressed in terms of the univariate $\Phi(.)$ and $\phi(.)$ functions by decomposing the multivariate $\phi(.)$ into marginal and conditional components (see appendix 3 or Hausman and Wise, 1979). This yields a log-likelihood composed of two elements:

$$\log L(\gamma_1, \delta_1, \gamma_2, \delta_2, \Sigma) = \log L^{\mathrm{p}}(\delta_1) + \log L^{\mathrm{c}}(\gamma_1, \gamma_2, \delta_2, \Sigma^+) \tag{2.134}$$

where $\log L^{\mathrm{P}}(\delta_1)$ is the log-likelihood for a simple probit model of the initial participation decision, and

$$\log L^{\mathrm{c}}(\gamma_1, \gamma_2, \delta_2, \Sigma^+) = K + \sum_{\mathrm{FP}} \log f(x_{n1}, x_{n2} \mid \zeta_{n1}, \xi_{n1}, \zeta_{n2}, \xi_{n2}) + \sum_{\mathrm{IP}} \log f(x_{n1} \mid \zeta_{n1}, \xi_{n1}, \xi_{n2}). \tag{2.135}$$

Since $\log L^{\mathrm{P}}$ and $\log L^{\mathrm{c}}$ have no arguments in common, $\log L^{\mathrm{c}}(\gamma_1, \gamma_2, \delta_2, \Sigma^+)$ can be maximized independently of δ_1 and without knowledge of ξ_{n1}.

Hausman and Wise use this ML technique on an earnings model applied to a sample containing both individuals from a control group (subjected to no experimental treatment) and individuals experiencing an experimental change in their unearned income. They assume $\sigma_{11} = \sigma_{33}$ and $\gamma_1 = \gamma_2$, but allow for shifts in behaviour between control group and experimental group individuals and for individuals at interview one and interview two by including two appropriate dummy variables. Apart from the enforced exclusion of the temporal dummy variable, ξ_{n2} is identical with ζ_{n2}. They find that inclusion in the experimental group has a small but significant direct negative effect on earnings quite apart from its indirect effect through the change in unearned income; this could be interpreted as a consequence of delayed adjustment to the experimental change. Experimental treatment also has a strong negative effect on the probability of drop-out: as one would expect, people selected to receive additional payments are much less likely to leave the experiment than members of the control group. The parameter σ_{34} is small but statistically significant, and there is evidence that the estimation of γ using data on x_{n1} and x_{n2} without correction for attrition leads to appreciable biases.

Considerably more complex structures than this can arise from experimental surveys. People may withdraw from the experiment for a variety of reasons (ill-health, change of locality etc.), each governed by a different stochastic model. The allocation of people to experimental and control groups may be endogenous, either through an element of self-selection or because the programme administrator makes the allocation on the basis of endogenous characteristics. There may also be an element of truncated endogenous sampling, of the type discussed in the previous section. The generalization of our methods to these more complicated settings is straightforward in principle, although the practical problem of estimating the parameters of all the stochastic relations present in the data is likely to be formidable, particularly if no information is available on those who are excluded from the sample.

Further reading

Econometricians have only comparatively recently taken a major interest in the problems posed by cross-section data, and as a result very few econometrics texts have even the most rudimentary discussion of sampling methods. Most derivations of asymptotic results, for instance, are still based on the assumption that the exogenous variables are fixed in repeated samples. This assumption is generally valid only for controlled experiments, which are virtually non-existent in economics. Good general references on sampling techniques are Cochran (1963) and Kish (1965), but these are not primarily concerned with the problems of estimating structural models. The conference volume edited by Hausman and Wise (1985) contains useful summaries of the methodology of experimental surveys in several different fields, and also some discussion of their advantages and limitations as sources of statistical information.

Many of the most important problems associated with the use of cross-section data are practical rather than technical: the way one conducts an interview, the sort of questions that are asked etc. This is an area in which problems tend to be highly specific to the application, but Payne (1951) and Hyman (1954) are interesting general references.

A very good reference on the theory of ML, least-squares and IV estimation under exogenous sampling is Amemiya (1986, chapters 3, 4 and 8). Detailed analysis of a variety of sample selection problems can be found in Maddala (1983). Amemiya (1986) surveys many recent developments such as distribution-free estimation.

3

Choice among discrete alternatives

Whichever you please my little dears:
You pays your money and you takes your choice
You pays your money and what you sees is
A cow or a donkey just as you pleases.

Anonymous

Many of the most important choices that an individual is called upon to make are discrete, with only a limited number of separate possibilities available to be chosen. One must decide which profession to enter; whether or not to marry; the number of children to have; the area in which to live etc. Such decisions are of enormous importance for the welfare of the individual, yet have little in common with the textbook presentation of consumer choice theory, which assumes a continuum of alternatives and smooth substitution. We must therefore examine choice models in which the opportunity set consists of a finite (or at least countable) collection of isolated mutually exclusive alternatives. In doing this, we restrict attention to models arising from proper microeconomic choice problems, and we shall make full use of the assumption of economic rationality, represented by utility maximization. This means that there will be considerable differences between the presentation here and much of the statistical literature, which is usually concerned with general discrete response models lacking any explicit basis in choice theory. Less restrictive surveys can be found in Maddala (1983) and Amemiya (1981).

Our notation is as follows. Each alternative, indexed by j ($j = 1, \ldots, m$), is characterized completely by a vector $\mathbf{x}^j$, whose q elements may be quantities of goods, quantities of characteristics, dummy variables representing characteristics in qualitative form or, if we are dealing with indirect utility functions, prices divided by the individual's income. Some of the elements of $\mathbf{x}^j$ may be purely specific to alternative j, in which case they will not vary across individuals; other elements may vary (for instance, the cost of retirement will be less for a member of an occupational pension scheme than for a non-member). The examples given in the next section will clarify these distinctions.

Preferences will be represented by a utility function $u = V(\mathbf{x}; \beta)$ where β is a vector of unobservable preference shift variables. β will depend in some way on the observed personal characteristics $\mathbf{z}$ of the individual, and may also be random. Rational choice models are then founded on the assumption that observed decisions are based in some way on a comparison of the utilities $V(\mathbf{x}^1; \beta), \ldots, V(\mathbf{x}^m; \beta)$ yielded by each of the alternatives. The real content of the economic hypothesis is that the function $V(.;.)$ is common to all individuals and all alternatives, and displays all the generic properties of a utility function for every admissible β.

The econometric models we consider are all stochastic, and introduce random elements either into the utility function itself or into the comparison of the m utilities. This randomness makes it impossible to predict with certainty the alternative that any specific individual will choose; instead, the model generates expressions for the probabilities with which the individual will choose each alternative. Our notation for these choice probabilities is as follows.

Pr(alternative j is chosen | opportunity set $= \{\mathbf{x}^1, \ldots, \mathbf{x}^m | \mathbf{z}\}) = P(j | \zeta; \theta)$ where $\zeta' = (\mathbf{x}^{1\prime}, \ldots, \mathbf{x}^{m\prime}, \mathbf{z}')$ and θ is a vector containing all unknown parameters appearing in the statistical model. The econometric problem is to estimate θ; however, before discussing this estimation problem, we look at some examples involving discrete choice.

3.1 Applications of discrete choice models

As motivation for the theory to be presented in sections 3.2–3.7, we shall briefly consider some of the more important fields in which observed economic behaviour has been successfully modelled as choice between mutually exclusive discrete alternatives. The aim is not to provide a full survey of the applied literature, but rather to indicate the general nature of the models used in these fields and the difficulties which are typically encountered in applied work.

3.1.1 Choice between discrete quantities: indivisible goods

One important circumstance in which the consumer is faced with a choice among discrete alternatives is when one or more of the goods involved in the budget is indivisible and thus only capable of being purchased in multiples of some basic unit. This is the case with many goods but is only of practical importance when the units are large and costly, and this occurs mainly in the case of durable goods. Ignoring the problems of quality and intertemporal planning which durability raises, one might adopt the standard demand model in which the consumer is assumed to possess preferences represented by a utility function $u = V(x_1, \mathbf{x}_2; \beta)$; $x_1 \in I$ is the quantity of the indivisible good, where I is the set $\{0, 1, 2, \ldots\}$; $\mathbf{x}_2$ is the quantity vector for all other (divisible) goods; x_1 has price p_1 and the vector of prices for other goods is $\mathbf{p}_2$; income is y. Utility maximization can be expressed

$$\begin{aligned}\max_{x_1 \in I, \mathbf{x}_2} & [V(x_1, \mathbf{x}_2; \boldsymbol{\beta}) | p_1 x_1 + \mathbf{p}_2' \mathbf{x}_2 = y] \\ &= \max_{x_1 \in I} \{\max_{\mathbf{x}_2}[V(x_1, \mathbf{x}_2; \boldsymbol{\beta}) | \mathbf{p}_2' \mathbf{x}_2 = y - p_1 x_1]\} \\ &= \max_{x_1 \in I} \{H[x_1, \mathbf{p}_2/(y - p_1 x_1); \boldsymbol{\beta}]\} \end{aligned} \tag{3.1}$$

where H is the indirect utility yielded by the constrained maximization of $V(x_1, \mathbf{x}_2; \boldsymbol{\beta})$ with respect to $\mathbf{x}_2$ for any given x_1.

Frequently, detailed information on other goods, $\mathbf{x}_2$, is unavailable in cross-section surveys, and we must instead work with a utility function whose arguments are x_1 and a composite 'other consumption' good X_2 defined as $(y - p_1 x_1)/P_2$, where P_2 is a price aggregate. In this case, the consumer's discrete choice problem is

$$\max_{x_1 \in I} \{V[x_1, (y - p_1 x_1)/P_2; \boldsymbol{\beta}]\}. \tag{3.2}$$

Since prices p_1 and $\mathbf{p}_2$ or P_2 are often unavailable (and thus assumed constant across individuals), we have an objective function (3.1) or (3.2) that depends on the integer x_1 as the sole characteristic distinguishing the alternatives $j = 1, 2, \ldots$ corresponding to quantities $\mathbf{x}^j = 0, 1, \ldots$ units of good x_1. Thus a rational individual will make his or her decision by comparing the utilities $u^1 = V(0, y/P_2; \boldsymbol{\beta})$, $u^2 = V[1, (y - p_1)/P_2; \boldsymbol{\beta}]$ etc.

In practice, the two most important alternatives are usually $x_1 = 0$ and $x_1 = 1$, which correspond to consumption and non-consumption of the good. Frequently there is only a small number of individuals who consume more than one unit of the good, particularly in the case of durables, and it is common practice to keep the number of alternatives small by introducing an open-ended category, $x_1 > 2$ say, with the associated utility value defined in an ad hoc manner.

Applications of discrete choice models to indivisible durable goods are very numerous, although applied studies often do not adhere very closely to this theoretical structure. Noteable examples include those of Farrell (1954), Cramer (1962), Cragg and Uhler (1970) and Cragg (1971).

The economics of fertility involves a similar form of discreteness. Although children are not tradeable goods, one can think of their being obtained at implicit prices in terms of time and effort, and, in the majority of cases, 'demand' for children is the result of a conscious choice which has a definite economic dimension to it. There is a considerable body of economic theory (see, for instance, Becker, 1960, and Schultz, 1969) which uses the framework of utility maximization to analyse the determination of family size, and although much of this is rather unconvincing it has provided the basis for a large amount of applied literature (typical examples are Becker,

1960; Becker and Tomes, 1976; and Willis, 1973). Although the models to which this theory gives rise are discrete, common practice is to make incorrect use of conventional regression methods to explain numbers of children, and there are thus few good examples to be found in this literature.

A further difficulty with the economics of fertility is that the conventional static model of choice is hard to defend, even if discreteness is handled properly. A couple might make a Becker-type decision to have three children; however, they cannot go to a market and buy three children – it will usually be necessary to go through three pregnancies, a process that may take ten years or more. In that time, considerable unanticipated changes in economic circumstances, perceptions, tastes and even fecundity are likely to occur, necessitating revisions to the couple's original plus. Thus an explicit sequential model is more appropriate, and models of this general type are discussed in section 3.6 and chapter 6.

3.1.2 Discrete qualities of goods

Many goods are heterogeneous, in the sense that a range of different varieties or models of the goods is available. The most helpful way to approach this problem is to think of these differentiated products as bundles of characteristics. It is then the quantities of these characteristics that enter the utility function. A simple model might go as follows: $\mathbf{a}^j$ is the vector of characteristics yielded by a unit of the jth variety of good 1; v_1 is the quantity of good 1; $\mathbf{v}_2$ is the vector of quantities of all other goods (assumed undifferentiated). Variety j of good 1 costs p_1^j per unit, and the price vector for all other goods is $\mathbf{p}_2$. The individual's income is y. Assuming that quantities of characteristics are additive, the consumer's maximization problem will be the following:

$$\begin{aligned} \max_j \{ & \max_{v_1, \mathbf{v}_2} [V(v_1 \mathbf{a}^j, \mathbf{v}_2; \boldsymbol{\beta}) \mid p_1^j v_1 + \mathbf{p}_2' \mathbf{v}_2 = y]\} \\ &= \max_j [H(\mathbf{a}^j, p_1^j/y, \mathbf{p}_2/y; \boldsymbol{\beta})] \end{aligned} \tag{3.3}$$

where H is the indirect utility resulting from the constrained maximization of utility with respect to both v_1 and $\mathbf{v}_2$, for a given variety j. The criterion function that underlies the consumer's decision therefore involves a vector $\mathbf{x}^j = (\mathbf{a}^j, p^j/y)$, which includes both the physical characteristics of the jth variety and its normalized price. Because of its dependence on income, this last element of $\mathbf{x}^j$ varies across consumers in addition to alternatives.

The discrete choice literature includes a large range of applications which can be viewed as choice between differentiated products. The field that has seen most research activity is transport mode choice (see, for example, Quandt, 1968; McFadden, 1974; Domencich and McFadden, 1975; and Hausman and Wise, 1978). In transportation studies, the competing products are alternative modes of transport for a particular regular journey (usually the trip to work). The vector $\mathbf{a}^j$ represents the characteristics of the journey when made via the jth mode of transport, and its elements usually include in-vehicle and out-of-vehicle travel time as the two most important mode characteristics. These characteristics vary from one individual to another, since different people have different journeys to make. The object of many of these transportation studies is to construct choice models suitable for use in estimating the potential demand for proposed new modes of transport (a new underground railway, for instance) with any specified mode characteristics.

Applications to the demand for differentiated models of a durable good include those by Hausman (1979a) and Dubin and McFadden (1984), who consider energy-consuming electrical appliances, for which a major characteristic is operating cost. Choice of housing location has been treated as a discrete choice problem by Quigley (1976) and Lerman (1977). Others, notably Rosen (1979) and King (1980), also examine the demand for housing services, but treat the different forms of housing tenure (ownership, renting etc.), rather than locations, as discrete alternatives. Surprisingly, no separate tenure characteristics are allowed for, and $\mathbf{x}^j$ in this case contains only the normalized unit price of housing services in tenure j. Another major field of application is in educational and career decisions, where different combinations of course and educational establishment can be regarded as varieties of a single educational commodity. Kohn, Manski and Mundel (1976) and Venti and Wise (1983) give good examples. Occupational choice is a closely related problem and has been analysed in this way by Boskin (1974).

A difficulty that frequently arises in models of this type is that the alternative varieties may not be mutually exclusive – some individuals may, for instance, possess two different models of car simultaneously. When combinations of alternatives are possible, the applied researcher is faced with a major problem. To treat every possible combination as a separate alternative often involves working with an unmanageably large number of alternatives, and must be ruled out on computational grounds. On the other hand, to drop the observations corresponding to individuals who choose more than a single variety is to risk serious sample selection bias, since the sample is then chosen on an endogenous basis (see chapter 2). It is usual to adopt some ad hoc method of resolving such problems, and this is a potentially important defect in a number of studies.

A further striking feature of many of the models in this class is the possibility of exploiting information on the quantity purchased of the selected variety: in terms of the simplified theory underlying (3.3), we may often have a direct observation on v_1, in addition to the chosen j. In an analysis of the demand for energy-consuming durables, for instance, we may observe both the appliance which is purchased and its subsequent degree of utilization. In other fields, we may observe the individual's supply of labour in his or her chosen profession, or expenditure on housing in the chosen tenure etc. Thus many problems involve more than a simple discrete choice, and mixed discrete–continuous models are then available. These are examined in section 3.7.

3.1.3 Discrete choice as an approximation to continuous choice

Some problems of continuous choice are so complex that the analysis of a much simpler approximate problem seems more appealing. The most important examples are in labour supply, where the existence of a progressive tax system, income-related social security payments, retirement pensions, housing subsidies etc. cause the individual's budget constraint to take an extremely complicated piecewise-linear form. The associated estimation problems are particularly severe (see Chapter 5), and it is tempting to remove the possibility of continuous substitution from the problem and regard it as a choice between discrete regimes. This approach is taken by Zabalza, Pissarides and Barton (1980), who treat retirement, part-time work and full-time work as three discrete alternatives. Substitution within alternatives is disregarded, and each alternative is associated with representative hours which everyone choosing that alternative is assumed to work. Although this is viewed as an approximation, one could argue that many people are constrained in their choices – one might wish to work 30 hours a week, but find that only part-time work (20 hours) or full-time work (40 hours) is offered by employers. In such a case, the problem really is one of discrete choice, and its treatment as a continuous choice would be a definite mis-specification. Chapter 7 discusses these difficulties further.

Zabalza (1983) treats three segments of the kinked budget constraint as the available alternatives. These correspond to non-participation in the labour force, working below the tax threshold, and working as a tax-payer. His model assumes that continuous optimization does take place within these categories but avoids using observed hours of work in a full continuous analysis. Occasionally, methods of this kind are forced on the investigator by the nature of the survey data available. Individuals may be asked not for a specific figure for hours of work but rather which of a series of ranges their weekly hours fall into (e.g. 0–10 hours, 11–20 etc.). It is often felt that this practice results in more reliable responses. With this kind of data, each range must be treated as a separate alternative, and the utility corresponding to each would be the maximum attainable within that range.

3.1.4 Choice without markets

Many applications on the periphery of economics deal with problems which can usefully be regarded as rational choice between discrete alternatives. However, most of these have no market basis, and consequently none of the theory described above is applicable. The most interesting examples relate to the formation of public policy, for instance the analysis of voting in the US Congress by McKelvey and Zavoina (1975) and the study of incomes policy in the UK by Desai, Keil and Wadhwani (1984). Perhaps the best known of these studies is McFadden's (1975, 1976b) analysis of the California Division of Highways' choices of freeway routes. McFadden specifies a large number of characteristics that represent the costs, benefits and political and other implications of the competing routes. The study is also rather unusual in that the number of alternatives available varies from one planning problem to another, and thus across observations in the statistical work.

3.2 Estimation and testing

We shall discuss the estimation problem in general terms, postponing consideration of specific statistical models that might be used to generate particular forms for the choice probabilities, $P(j \mid \zeta; \theta)$. The ML estimation principle is dominant in this field, and we begin with the case of exogenous sampling. We maintain the distinction, introduced in the previous chapter, between a population probability (or density, in the case of continuous variables), denoted here by the generic symbol $P(.)$, and the corresponding sample probability, denoted by $\Pi(.)$. The arguments of these functions in each context specify precisely which probability is involved.

3.2.1 Maximum likelihood under exogenous sampling

For individual n, the probability of our observing the choice of the jth alternative, conditional on the exogenous variables ζ_n, is the choice probability implied by our economic model: $P(j \mid \zeta_n; \theta)$. Under exogenous sampling, the sample distribution of the exogenous variables is characterized by a probability density/mass function $\Pi_n(\zeta_n)$ that is independent of both j_n and the parameter vector θ. Thus the joint sample distribution of the observed choice j_n and ζ_n has density/mass function

$$\Pi(j_n, \zeta_n; \theta) = P(j_n \mid \zeta_n; \theta)\, \Pi_n(\zeta_n). \tag{3.4}$$

The log-likelihood function is merely the logarithm of the joint density/mass function of the full sample. If only one choice is observed for each individual, the sample consists of the N pairs $(j_1, \zeta_1), \ldots, (j_N, \zeta_N)$; assuming that the observations are independently drawn,

$$\begin{aligned} \log L(\theta) &= \prod_{n=1}^{N} \log \Pi(j_n, \zeta_n; \theta) \\ &= K + \sum_{n=1}^{N} \log P(j_n \mid \zeta_n; \theta) \end{aligned} \tag{3.5}$$

or, equivalently,

$$\log L(\theta) = K + \sum_{i=1}^{m} \sum_{n \in S_i} \log P(i \mid \zeta_n; \theta)$$

$$= K + \sum_{i=1}^{m} \sum_{n=1}^{N} d_{ni} \log P(i \mid \zeta_n; \theta) \tag{3.7}$$

where $S_i = \{n \mid j_n = i\}$, d_{ni} is a dummy variable equal to unity if $j_n = i$ and zero otherwise, and K is the inessential constant $\Sigma \log \Pi_n(\zeta_n)$.

The ML estimator $\hat{\theta}$ is the value of θ that maximizes $\log L$. Assuming that the choice probabilities are differentiable in θ and that the global maximum is at an interior point in the set of admissible θ-values, $\hat{\theta}$ satisfies the following system of first-order conditions:

$$\sum_{n=1}^{N} \sum_{i=1}^{m} d_{ni} \frac{\partial \log P(i \mid \zeta_n; \hat{\theta})}{\partial \hat{\theta}} = 0. \tag{3.8}$$

A slightly more revealing form of this condition can be derived by observing that $\Sigma\, P(i \mid \zeta_n; \hat{\theta}) = 1$, and hence $\partial\, \Sigma\, P(i \mid \zeta_n; \hat{\theta})/\partial \hat{\theta} = 0$. Thus

$$0 = \sum_{i=1}^{m} \frac{\partial P(i \mid \zeta_n; \hat{\theta})}{\partial \hat{\theta}} = \sum_{i=1}^{m} P(i \mid \zeta_n; \hat{\theta}) \frac{\partial \log P(i \mid \zeta_n; \hat{\theta})}{\partial \hat{\theta}}.$$

Subtracting this expression from the inner summation in (3.8) gives

$$\sum_{n=1}^{N} \sum_{i=1}^{m} [d_{ni} - P(i \mid \zeta_n; \hat{\theta})] \frac{\partial \log P(i \mid \zeta_n; \hat{\theta})}{\partial \hat{\theta}} = 0. \tag{3.9}$$

The condition (3.9) requires that $\hat{\theta}$ be chosen so that the residuals $d_{ni} - P(i \mid \zeta_n; \hat{\theta})$ are orthogonal to the $\hat{\theta}$-derivatives of the logarithmic choice probabilities. The ML estimator therefore has an IV interpretation, with these derivatives acting as the instruments. Equation (3.9) is generally non-linear in $\hat{\theta}$, in both the residual and derivative terms, and thus in practice it must be computed by means of an iterative algorithm.

Occasionally, it is possible to observe more than one choice per person. For example, suppose that a study of transport mode choice is based on a recall survey in which people are asked for the number of times that they have used each of m transport modes in their last r journeys to work. Assume that we observe only these totals and not the order in which the individual choices occur, and also that choices made on different days by any individual are independent. Then, provided that ζ_n remains unchanged over the recall period, the levels of usage of the competing transport modes have a conditional multinomial distribution:

$$\Pr(r_{n1}, \ldots, r_{nm} \mid \zeta_n) = \frac{r!}{r_{n1}! \ldots r_{nm}!} P(1 \mid \zeta_n; \theta)^{r_{n1}} \ldots P(m \mid \zeta_n; \theta)^{r_{nm}} \tag{3.10}$$

where r_{ni} is the number of times individual n uses mode i.

This model leads to a log-likelihood function

$$\log L(\theta) = K^* + \sum_{i=1}^{m} \sum_{n=1}^{N} r_{ni} \log P(i \mid \zeta_n; \theta) \tag{3.11}$$

where $K^* = K + N \log(r!) - \Sigma\Sigma \log(r_{ni}!)$. A comparison of this expression with (3.7) reveals that the effect of repeated observation is merely to change the weights associated with the log choice probabilities from the dummies d_{ni} to the occurrence counts r_{ni}.

3.2.2 McFadden's simulation estimator

Several of the most useful discrete choice models present formidable computational problems because the choice probabilities $P(j \mid \zeta; \theta)$ are very complicated and their evaluation requires a large amount of computer time. One solution to this problem is to compute unbiased estimates of the $P(j \mid \zeta; \theta)$ rather than attempt to evaluate the probabilities themselves. This is often easy to do by generating appropriate pseudo-random variables to represent unobservable factors and using these to simulate directly the process generating choices. The details of the simulation will depend on the particular model specification involved, but the method can be described in general terms.

Arrange all the unobservable random variables involved in the model in a vector ϵ suitably standardized so that its distribution involves no unknown parameters. For given vectors of exogenous variables ζ and parameters θ, this value ϵ completely determines the observed choice. Represent this choice by a vector of dummy variables, $d'(\epsilon, \zeta, \theta) = (d_1 \ldots d_m)$, where $d_i = 1$ if alternative i is chosen and $d_i = 0$ otherwise. Now suppose that we replicate (r times) the process generating the unobservable variables ϵ; this yields a sequence of r independent vectors $d(\epsilon^1, \zeta, \theta), \ldots, d(\epsilon^r, \zeta, \theta)$ that can be regarded as a random sample of choices drawn from a population conditioned on ζ and characterized by parameters θ. Since $E(d_j(\epsilon^i, \zeta, \theta) \mid \zeta) = P(j \mid \zeta; \theta)$, the following quantity is an unbiased estimator of $P(j \mid \zeta; \theta)$:

$$\hat{P}(j \mid \zeta; \theta) = \frac{1}{r} \sum_{i=1}^{r} d_j(\epsilon^i, \zeta, \theta). \tag{3.12}$$

The summation in (3.12) is the number of observed choices of alternative j in the r replications, and so these probability estimates are merely the relative frequencies of the simulated choices.

An obvious procedure, explored by Lerman and Manski (1981), is to use these to form a simulated log-likelihood function:

$$L^s(\theta) = \sum_{n=1}^{N} \log \hat{P}(j_n \mid \zeta; \theta_n) \tag{3.13}$$

where each $\hat{P}(j_n \mid \zeta_n; \theta)$ is based on a different set of simulated errors for each individual in the sample. However, maximization of this criterion does not result in a consistent estimator unless the number of replications r goes to infinity with the sample size. The reason is that, although $\hat{P}(j\,|\,\zeta;\theta)$ is an unbiased estimator of $P(j\,|\,\zeta;\theta)$, its unbiasedness is not preserved under the non-linear log transformation. Thus, if r remains fixed, as $N\to\infty$ the simulated log-likelihood and the true log-likelihood (both divided by N) do not approach the same limiting form. Moreover, the limiting form of $N^{-1}\log L^s(\theta)$ does not attain its maximum at the true parameter values. This inconsistency suggests that a very large number of replications is necessary to achieve good estimates, and thus the method is very expensive in terms of computer time.

McFadden (1988) observed that this problem does not arise for an objective function whose first-order conditions are linear in the simulated probabilities. As an example, consider the simplest possible IV estimator. This is based on an assumption that the residuals are asymptotically uncorrelated with a set of exogenous instrumental variables:

$$\operatorname*{plim}_{N\to\infty} N^{-1} \sum_{n=1}^{N} \sum_{j=1}^{m} \xi_{nj}\,[d_{nj} - P(j\,|\,\zeta_n;\theta)] = 0 \tag{3.14}$$

where ξ_{nj} is a $k \times 1$ vector of instrumental variables appropriate to alternative j for individual n, and k is the number of parameters in θ. Comparison with the ML first-order conditions, (3.9), suggests the use of approximations to the θ-derivatives of $\log P(j\,|\,\zeta_n;\theta)$ as an optimal set of instruments.

Now replace $P(j\,|\,\zeta_n;\theta)$ by its simulated estimate. The resulting terms inside the summation in (3.14) will all have zero expectation, and a law of large numbers thus establishes that the simulated analogue of (3.14) is valid. This suggests estimating θ by minimizing

$$S(\theta) = \left\| \sum_{n=1}^{N} \sum_{j=1}^{m} \xi_{nj}\,[d_{nj} - \hat{P}(j_n\,|\,\zeta_n;\theta)] \right\| \tag{3.15}$$

where $\|.\|$ denotes the Euclidean vector norm. The value of θ that minimizes $S(\theta)$ can be shown to be consistent for any positive value of r and to have good asymptotic efficiency even for quite small numbers of replications.

However, there are still difficulties associated with this estimator, and there is so far little experience of its use in practice. One problem is that, unless special simulation methods are used, the objective function (3.15) is not a continuous function of θ, and this means that most of the usual numerical optimization techniques are unsuitable for application to $S(\theta)$. For more detail on the construction of instruments, methods of simulation and derivation of the limiting distribution, the reader should consult McFadden (1988).

3.2.3 Estimation under endogenous sampling

Many of the samples used for the analysis of discrete choices are generated by endogenous (or choice-based) sampling schemes. As an example, consider the problem of drawing a sample relating to transport decisions. If individuals are selected on an exogenous basis, they must be interviewed at home, and this involves substantial travel costs for the interviewers. Moreoever, if people are interviewed during the normal working day, it is probable that commuters will not be found at home, so that interviews outside working hours become necessary. This will usually increase sampling costs, and may also affect the response rate. For these reasons, such surveys can be conducted much more cheaply if interviewing takes place at bus and train stations, car parks etc. Another advantage of this kind of sampling is that it is possible to ensure adequate representation of all choices by sampling to a quota for each alternative. If some alternatives are quite rarely chosen, ordinary exogenous sampling may require a very large (and therefore costly) sample size to achieve good coverage.

Sampling schemes of this type are endogenous, since the probability of an individual being included in the sample depends on the alternative that he or she has chosen. The significance of this endogeneity is that the reasoning that led to the simple log-likelihood function (3.7) or (3.11) no longer applies, and we are faced with more difficult estimation problems. Assume that the sampling scheme is such that the probability of an individual being interviewed depends only on the choice that he or she makes. If the sampling probabilities are $\Pi(1), \ldots, \Pi(m)$, then the probability density/mass function for an observation (j, ζ) is

$$\Pi(j, \zeta) = P(\zeta | j)\, \Pi(j). \tag{3.16}$$

This can be manipulated using the following identities, which hold in the population:

$$P(j, \zeta) = P(j | \zeta)\, P(\zeta) \tag{3.17}$$

$$P(j, \zeta) = P(\zeta | j)\, P(j) \tag{3.18}$$

where

$$P(\zeta) = \sum_{i=1}^{m} P(i, \zeta) \tag{3.19}$$

$$P(j) = \int P(j | \zeta)\, \mathrm{d}G(\zeta). \tag{3.20}$$

where $G(.)$ is the c.d.f. corresponding to $P(\zeta)$, and the integral in (3.20) is a Stieltjes–Lebesgue integral, representing integration with respect to continuous variables in ζ and summation with respect to discrete variables.

The conditional probability $P(j | \zeta)$ is of particular importance, since it contains the entire observational content of the econometric model of choice and is the medium through which the parameter vector θ enters the sample distribution $\Pi(j, \zeta)$. We must therefore manipulate expression (3.16) into a form involving $P(j \mid \zeta; \theta)$. Using (3.17)–(3.20) we have

$$\begin{aligned}\Pi(j, \zeta) &= P(j, \zeta)\, \Pi(j)/P(j) \\ &= P(j \mid \zeta)\, P(\zeta)\, \Pi(j)/\textstyle\int P(j \mid \zeta)\, \mathrm{d}G(\zeta).\end{aligned} \tag{3.21}$$

The log-likelihood function is therefore

$$\log L(\theta) = K^* + \sum_{n=1}^{N} \log P(j_n \mid \zeta_n; \theta) - \sum_{n=1}^{N} \log[\textstyle\int P(j \mid \zeta; \theta)\, \mathrm{d}G(\zeta)] \tag{3.22}$$

where $K^* = \Sigma \log P(\zeta_n) + \Sigma \log \Pi(j_n)$.

Unfortunately, in most practical cases it is not feasible to maximize log L owing to the complexity of the last term on the right-hand side. The function $G(\zeta)$ represents the joint distribution of all characteristics of the individuals, and the alternatives they face, in the population. Construction of the last term in (3.22) requires both knowledge of this joint distribution and the ability to perform the integration of $P(j \mid \zeta; \theta)$ with respect to this distribution. Neither is likely to be fulfilled in any real application. An alternative is to use semi-parametric methods to estimate the form of $\mathrm{d}G(\zeta)$ along with θ. Some progress has been made with this approach (see Amemiya, 1986, chapter 9, for a survey), but there is so far little practical experience of it.

Manski and Lerman (1977) showed that the last term of log $L(\theta)$ cannot be neglected without sacrificing consistency, and so unconstrained maximization of the conventional log-likelihood (3.5) is not an attractive alternative. Thus it is necessary to use estimators specific to this problem, and to depart from true ML. Suitable estimation techniques have been proposed by Manski and Lerman (1977), Cosslett (1981) and Manski and McFadden (1981), and these are of two types: those that require a priori knowledge of the population frequencies $P(j)$ and those that do not.

Consider first the former. If we know the proportions $P(j)$ of the population choosing each of the m alternatives, then it is possible to construct a reweighted pseudo-likelihood function that corrects for any bias present in the sampling scheme:

$$\log L^*(\theta) = \sum_{n=1}^{N} \gamma(j_n) \log P(j_n \mid \zeta_n; \theta) \tag{3.23}$$

where the weights $\gamma(j)$ are defined as $P(j)/\Pi(j)$. Note that it makes no real difference whether sampling is probabilistic, with the $\Pi(j)$ fixed as part of the sample design, or whether we sample to a quota N_j for each alternative. In the latter case, the $\Pi(j)$ are defined as the fixed sample frequencies N_j/N.

The estimator that maximizes log $L^*(\theta)$ is essentially the same as the weighted least-squares estimator used by Hausman and Wise (1982) in estimating linear regressions from endogenously stratified samples (see chapter 2, section 2.5). As in that case, the weighted estimator is consistent but asymptotically less efficient than the non-feasible true ML estimator.

Although (3.23) is widely used in applied work, it has one important limitation, since it is not suitable in cases where the aggregate distribution $P(j)$ is unknown. In that case the weights $\gamma(j)$ cannot be computed, and Cosslett (1981) has shown that to treat them as parameters and maximize (3.23) with respect to θ and $\gamma(1), \ldots, \gamma(m)$ leads to inconsistent estimators of both. In these circumstances, an alternative approach proves more fruitful. Consider a log-likelihood function defined not as the product of terms $\Pi(j_n, \zeta_n)$ but rather the conditional probabilities $\Pi(j_n | \zeta_n)$. Each of these probabilities can be re-expressed in the following form:

$$\begin{aligned}\Pi(j|\zeta) &= \Pi(j, \zeta)/\Pi(\zeta) \\ &= \Pi(j, \zeta)/\sum_i \Pi(i, \zeta).\end{aligned} \tag{3.24}$$

But, from (3.21), $\Pi(j, \zeta)$ is expressible as $P(j|\zeta)P(\zeta)\Pi(j)/P(j)$, and thus

$$\Pi(j|\zeta) = \frac{P(j|\zeta)\,\Pi(j)/P(j)}{\sum_{i=1}^{m} P(i|\zeta)\,\Pi(i)/P(i)}. \tag{3.25}$$

The ratios $\Pi(j)/P(j)$ in (3.25) are the reciprocals of the weights $\gamma(j)$, and so the conditional log-likelihood is

$$\log L^{c}(\theta) = \sum_{n=1}^{N} \log \left[\frac{P(j_n|\zeta_n; \theta)/\gamma(j_n)}{\sum_{i=1}^{m} P(i|\zeta_n; \theta)/\gamma(i)} \right]. \tag{3.26}$$

If the population choice proportions are known, then the $\gamma(j)$ weights can be constructed and log $L^c(\theta)$ can be maximized with respect to θ. This estimator is also consistent and asymptotically less efficient than true ML. It is tractable, however, since the summation in (3.26) is over alternatives which are relatively few in number. The estimators maximizing log L^* and log L^c cannot be ranked unambiguously in terms of efficiency, and so, when appropriate weights are available, log L^* is usually preferred on grounds of simplicity. When $P(1), \ldots, P(m)$ are unknown, however, log L^c can be maximized with respect to both θ and the $\gamma(j)$, subject to an arbitrary normalization such as

$$\Sigma\,\gamma(j) = 1 \tag{3.27}$$

and non-negativity constraints

$$\gamma(j) \geqslant 0 \qquad j = 1, \ldots, m. \tag{3.28}$$

Cosslett (1981) has shown the consistency of this estimator. Note that there may be identification problems when the $\gamma(j)$ are unknown; for instance, in the multinomial logit model with additive alternative-specific effects, these cannot be distinguished from the unknown weights.

3.2.4 Goodness of fit and diagnostic testing

Estimation is only part of the problem of statistical inference. For practical purposes, another question is equally important: how does one establish that the estimated model is well specified? This is important, since mis-specification will render estimators and standard errors inconsistent and test statistics misleading. A wide range of techniques is available for the detection of mis-specification in the traditional models of macroeconometrics, and also in some of the standard models commonly used in microeconomics. However, most of these are not applicable to models of discrete choice, and much useful work remains to be done in this field.

Although formal tests of model specification are desirable, most of the applied literature in econometrics uses simple heuristic measures of goodness of fit, intended to convey an overall impression of the success of the model in explaining the data. Alternative measures have been proposed by McFadden (1973), Efron (1978) and Lave (1970), among others. These measures can be regarded as informal specification tests, since a low value is usually regarded as a sign of inadequacy and a high value as desirable. It is worth considering the drawbacks of this practice before looking at more satisfactory formal techniques, and to begin by examining the analogy with the familiar linear regression model.

Regression results are usually accompanied by the coefficient of determination or R^2, which measures the goodness of fit of the equation. In a regression with Y_n the dependent variable, $\hat{Y}_n$ the predicted or fitted value and $e_n = Y_n - \hat{Y}_n$ the residual, R^2 can be interpreted in several different ways. It is the squared correlation between Y_n and $\hat{Y}_n$; it is the ratio of the explained sum of squares $\Sigma(\hat{Y}_n - \overline{Y})^2$ to the total sum of squares $\Sigma(Y_n - \overline{Y})^2$; it can be expressed as $1 - \Sigma e_n^2/\Sigma(Y_n - \overline{Y})^2$; and under normality it is equal to $1 - (L_1/L_0)^{2/N}$ where L_1 is the likelihood maximized without constraint and L_0 is the likelihood maximized subject to the constraint that all slope coefficients are zero. In this form, it is clearly related to the likelihood ratio statistic testing the latter constraint, and a simple transformation gives the usual F statistic.

This is the real limitation of R^2-like statistics: they derive whatever useful properties they have from this relation to a proper test statistic, yet the hypothesis involved is not one of particular practical interest. We are not usually worried about finding a 'significant' relationship – that is often not very hard to do – but rather with finding the 'correct' relationship – a much more challenging objective. If R^2 is separated from this hypothesis testing aspect, it becomes an arbitrary measure of fit, with no absolute standard against which it should be judged: a low R^2 does not necessarily mean that the model is mis-specified, since this can arise merely because the true model involves unusually large random elements (something that is commonly found in cross-section work). Similarly, a high R^2 does not necessarily imply that the model is well specified.

When we consider the case of discrete choice models, these problems of interpretation remain, but the situation is still worse since the convenient least-squares algebra is no longer operative and each of these different definitions of R^2 (equivalent in linear regression) leads to a different goodness-of-fit statistic, most of which cannot even be guaranteed to lie in the interval [0,1]. Moreover, it is not clear exactly what Y_n and $\hat{Y}_n$ are in this case. The model attempts to explain the choice made by individual n; this can be represented by the set of dummy variables $d_{n1}, \ldots, d_{nm}$, introduced above, and it seems reasonable to treat these as m observations on a dependent variable Y. There is more ambiguity over the definition of $\hat{Y}$. The model generates estimated probabilities $\hat{P}_{nj} = P(j \mid \zeta_n; \hat{\theta})$, $j = 1, \ldots, m$, and these could be regarded as m observations on $\hat{Y}$, with R^2 analogues defined accordingly.

Alternatively, one might attempt to predict the most likely choices rather than probabilities and define dummy variables $\hat{d}_{n1}, \ldots, \hat{d}_{nm}$, where $\hat{d}_{nj}$ is equal to unity if $\hat{P}_{nj}$ is the largest of the choice probabilities and zero otherwise; these dummies can be regarded as observations on a different definition of $\hat{Y}$. A common measure of goodness of fit is a simple count of the number of observations for which the vectors d_n and $\hat{\mathrm{d}}_n$, representing actual and predicted choices, are identical. However, any criterion based on $\hat{Y}$ defined in this way is especially misleading, since $P(j) = \operatorname{plim} N^{-1} \Sigma \, \mathrm{d}_{nj}$ and $\operatorname{plim} N^{-1} \Sigma \, \hat{d}_{nj}$ are not normally equal, even for a perfectly specified model. To illustrate this, consider an extreme case where alternative j is a possible, but unlikely, choice for every individual; as a consequence, $P(j)$ will be small but nonetheless positive. Since $\hat{\theta}$ is a consistent estimator, $P(j \mid \zeta_n; \hat{\theta})$ will tend to be small for all n, and hence $\hat{d}_{nj}$ will almost never indicate j as the most likely choice. As a result, $\operatorname{plim} N^{-1} \Sigma \, \hat{d}_{nj} = 0 < P(j)$.

Some more formal statistical tests for the detection of mis-specification are available. In the context of repeated choices, one can use a version of the conventional χ^2 goodness-of-fit test, yielding a statistic

$$\chi^2 = \sum_{n=1}^{N} \sum_{j=1}^{m} \frac{(r_{nj} - r\hat{P}_{nj})^2}{r\hat{P}_{nj}} \tag{3.29}$$

where r is the number of choices made by each individual. Under the null hypothesis of correct specification, this is asymptotically χ^2 with $N(m-1)-k$ degrees of freedom (where k is the number of estimated parameters) as $r \to \infty$. McFadden (1976a) finds this to be poorly behaved for small r, and particularly so for the usual case of $r = 1$.

Other forms of this test are possible. For instance, if we define residuals as $e_{nj} = d_{nj} - \hat{P}_{nj}$, we would expect $\bar{e}_j = N^{-1} \Sigma \, e_{nj}$, $j = 1, \ldots, m$, to be approximately zero in large samples if the model is well specified. It is not difficult to derive the limiting distribution of the scaled vector $\sqrt{N}(\bar{e}_1 \ldots \bar{e}_{m-1})$, and to construct an asymptotic test of the model's ability to explain the frequencies of observed choices ($\bar{e}_m$ is omitted because the $\bar{e}_i$ sum identically to zero). One can also extend this criterion to search for correlations between the residuals and any other variables. As an example, Pudney (1987) derives a test criterion based on the cross-products $N^{-1/2} \Sigma \hat{P}_{ni} e_{nj}$, $i = 1, \ldots, m, j = 1, \ldots, m-1$.

3.3 Random parameter models

The random parameter specification originates with the work of Quandt (1956, 1968). In its pure form, it has played a relatively minor role in the applied literature on discrete choice, although mixed specifications, involving additional sources of random variation, are now common. It is based on the assumption that preferences can be universally represented by a utility function of the form $u = V(\mathbf{x}; \beta)$, where β is a vector of substitution parameters or unobservable shift variables that vary randomly between individuals. Thus, a typical individual will derive from alternative j the following level of utility:

$$u_n^j = V(\mathbf{x}_n^j; \beta_n) \tag{3.30}$$

where $\mathbf{x}_n^j$ is the vector of characteristics of the jth alternative for this individual. In general, the vector β_n will be random with a joint c.d.f. $G_\beta(\beta \mid \mathbf{z}_n; \theta)$ whose form depends both on the observable personal characteristics of the individual, $\mathbf{z}_n$, and on the model's parameters θ. Note that we have considerable latitude in the way we represent the model; for instance, the utility function can always be written in such a way that θ appears only in $G_\beta(.)$ and not in $V(.)$ itself, or vice versa. For simplicity of notation, assume that $V(.)$ is independent of θ.

The econometric problem is to estimate θ by maximizing one of the objective functions derived in the previous section. For this, we require the choice probabilities $P(j \mid \zeta_n; \theta)$. If we assume that there is no inefficiency in decision-making, then alternative j will be observed to be chosen if and only if u_n^j is the greatest of the values $u_n^1, \ldots, u_n^m$ (under conventional distributional assumptions, ties occur with probability zero, so this possibility can be neglected). The ordering of these utility values will depend on the vector β_n, so the probability of selection for any particular alternative can be regarded as the probability that β_n falls in the region of β space that corresponds to the optimality of that alternative. Thus we can define B_n^j to be the following set:

$$B_n^j = \{\beta : V(\mathbf{x}_n^j; \beta) > V(\mathbf{x}_n^i; \beta), \text{all } i \neq j\}. \tag{3.31}$$

Whenever β_n falls in this region, individual n will choose the jth alternative, and the probability of this occurring is

$$P(j \mid \zeta_n; \theta) = \int_{B_n^j} \mathrm{d}G_\beta(\beta; \mathbf{z}_n, \theta). \tag{3.32}$$

This is as far as we can go without looking at specific examples, since the nature of the regions B_n^j and the c.d.f. $G_\beta(.)$ are completely problem specific. However, the main limitation of this approach is apparent from inspection of (3.32). If there are more than two or three substitution parameters in the vector $\boldsymbol{\beta}$, the integral in (3.32), which must usually be evaluated numerically, is likely to be computationally intractable. Moreover, even if the dimensions of the problem are moderate, the regions B_n^j are defined by the complicated set of inequalities (3.31), so the domain of integration may be very difficult to characterize conveniently. Although McFadden's (1988) simulation estimator offers some hope of a general solution to these problems, the random parameter approach has so far proved feasible only for particularly simple economic models. To illustrate these ideas, we shall consider an example based on the simple but highly non-linear constant elasticity of substitution (CES) form for the utility function.

The study of retirement by Zabalza, Pissarides and Barton (1980) is one of the most interesting applications of the random parameters specification. They approximate a very complex labour supply problem by a simple three-alternative discrete choice problem, with the alternatives being the options of retirement, part-time work and full-time work. In this model the three alternatives are distinguished by two characteristics, leisure (ℓ) and potential consumption or net income (y), so that the vector $\mathbf{x}_n^j$ has two elements, ℓ_n^j and y_n^j, being the hours of leisure and the size of income that individual n will receive under the jth of the three alternatives. The utility function is assumed to have the CES form

$$u_n^j = [\beta_{n1}(\ell_n^j)^{-\beta_2} + (1-\beta_{n1})(y_n^j)^{-\beta_2}]^{-1/\beta_2} \tag{3.33}$$

which is homothetic and therefore rather restrictive. The parameter β_2 controls the degree of substitution flexibility between ℓ and y, with the elasticity of substitution being the constant $1/(1+\beta_2)$. Variation in preferences is introduced through the distribution parameter β_{n1}, which is generated by a logistic relationship:

$$\beta_{n1} = [1 + \exp(\alpha' \mathbf{z}_n + \epsilon_n)]^{-1} \tag{3.34}$$

where ϵ_n is an $N(0, \sigma^2)$ random error and α is a vector of constant parameters. Thus, in this example, we have $\boldsymbol{\theta}' = (\beta_2\, \alpha'\, \sigma)$. The form (3.34) is used to ensure that β_{n1} falls in the unit interval, since this is required for convexity of preferences.

Zabalza et al. include in the $\mathbf{z}_n$ vector variables such as age, state of health and marital status, but also variables reflecting involuntary loss of job and the economic circumstances of the spouse, which should perhaps be regarded as aspects of the economic problem facing the individual rather than determinants of the preference ordering. The income variable y_n^j is only observed directly for the alternative j that the individual is actually observed to choose; for the other two alternatives, estimates based on predicted wage rates, state pension rules, etc. must be used. Hours of work are also observed only for the one state in which each individual is observed; to avoid this difficulty, leisure is defined arbitrarily as 65 hours per week minus a standard number of hours of work in each state. Standard hours are taken to vary between men and women but to be otherwise constant over n. These are common problems: we usually know much more about the attributes of the chosen alternatives than we do about those that were not chosen.

Let the three alternatives be ordered as follows: retirement ($\ell_n^1 = 65$ hours); part-time work ($\ell_n^2 = 49$ hours for women and 48 hours for men); and full-time work ($\ell_n^3 = 27$ hours for women and 23 hours for men). Zabalza et al. do not work with the (degenerate) joint distribution of the β_n vector, as we have done in (3.32), because it proves much simpler to conduct the analysis in terms of the standardized random error ϵ_n/σ. Straightforward manipulation of the inequality $u_n^1 > u_n^2$ establishes that alternative 1 is preferred to alternative 2 when $\epsilon_n/\sigma < \Psi_{n1}$, where

$$\Psi_{n1} = -\frac{1}{\sigma}\left\{\log\left[\frac{(y_n^2)^{-\beta_2} - (y_n^1)^{-\beta_2}}{(\ell_n^1)^{-\beta_2} - (\ell_n^2)^{-\beta_2}}\right] - \alpha'\mathbf{Z}_n\right\}. \tag{3.35}$$

The method used by Zabalza et al. for the construction of the ℓ_n^j and y_n^j ensures that the resulting opportunity set consists of three points on the boundary of a convex set in (ℓ, y) space. Together with the convexity of preferences, this implies that, whenever alternative 1 is preferred to alternative 2, it must also be preferred to alternative 3. Consequently, $\epsilon_n/\sigma < \Psi_{n1}$ is a necessary and sufficient condition for the observation of a choice of retirement. Similarly, the condition $\epsilon_n/\sigma > \Psi_{n2}$ is necessary and sufficient for a choice of alternative 3 (full-time work), where

$$\Psi_{n2} = -\frac{1}{\sigma}\left\{\log\left[\frac{(y_n^3)^{-\beta_2} - (y_n^2)^{-\beta_2}}{(\ell_n^2)^{-\beta_2} - (\ell_n^3)^{-\beta_2}}\right] - \alpha'\mathbf{z}_n\right\}. \tag{3.36}$$

Part-time work is chosen whenever the standardized error ϵ_n/σ falls in the interval (Ψ_{n1}, Ψ_{n2}). Thus the range of ϵ_n/σ is partitioned into three ordered subranges, with an alternative being selected whenever the choice determinant ϵ_n/σ falls in the associated subrange. The choice probabilities are then found by integrating the density function of ϵ_n/σ over these subranges. If we follow Zabalza et al. by assuming normality for ϵ_n,

$$P(1 \mid \zeta_n; \boldsymbol{\theta}) = \Phi(\Psi_{n1}) \tag{3.37}$$

$$P(2 \mid \zeta_n; \boldsymbol{\theta}) = \Phi(\Psi_{n2}) - \Phi(\Psi_{n1}) \tag{3.38}$$

$$P(3 \mid \zeta_n; \boldsymbol{\theta}) = 1 - \Phi(\Psi_{n3}). \tag{3.39}$$

Models involving choice probabilities with this structure are often referred to as *ordered models*. They were introduced by Aitchison and Silvey (1957), and were first used in the social sciences by McKelvey and Zavoina (1975) in a study of voting behaviour. The conventional ordered model is a discrete-response modification of regression analysis that specifies the break points Ψ_{ni} as linear forms: $\Psi_{ni} = \alpha^i - \alpha^{0\prime}\zeta_n$, where α^0 is a vector of underlying regression coefficients and the α^i are unknown thresholds. Ordered models have the important advantage that the dimension of the integrals involved is always one, no matter how many alternatives are present. In the present example, this simplicity is entirely due to the convenient forms chosen in (3.33) and (3.34), the small number of characteristics chosen to represent the alternatives, and the ingenuity of Zabalza et al. in transforming a difficult problem in β_{n1} to a simpler problem in ϵ_n/σ. Random parameter models cannot generally be expected to yield such neat choice probabilities.

A final difficulty with this type of model is the restrictiveness of its assumption that all observed behaviour is economically rational. As an example of the pitfalls, consider the Zabalza et al. model in the presence of a poverty trap. A poverty trap arises when a person taking part-time work rather than choosing retirement experiences a loss of social security benefit, which is not fully offset by the additional income from paid work. The result is the opportunity set of figure 3.1, where alternative 2 (part-time work) is dominated by alternative 1 (retirement) in the sense that it offers less income and less leisure. If leisure is always a 'good' (if $V(\ell, y)$ is increasing in ℓ for all y), then part-time working will never be an optimal state for a rational individual, and the random parameter model implies that no such choice will ever be observed.

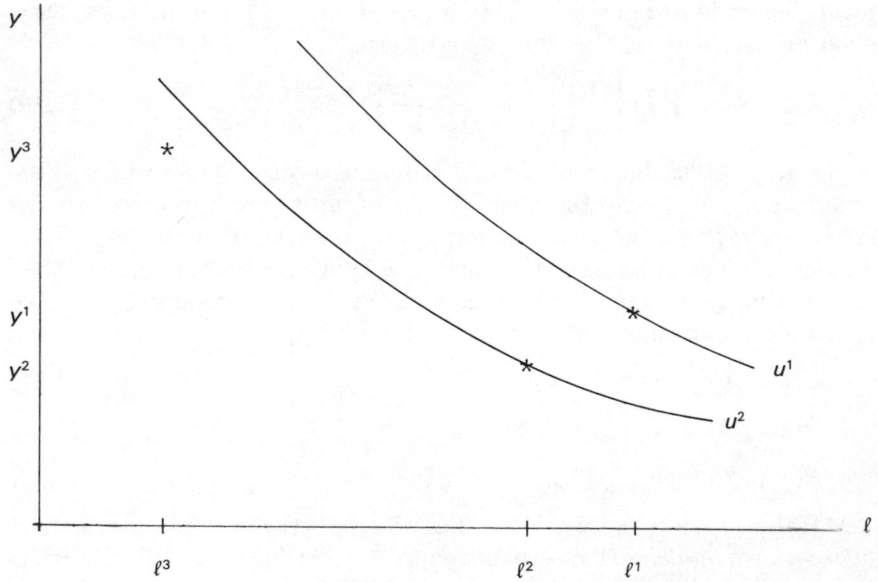

Figure 3.1 Discrete choice with dominated alternatives.

However, we could never rule out a priori the possibility that a particular set of survey data might contain such an observation. People may not correctly appreciate the full implications of the alternatives open to them; there may be other unobserved attributes of the alternatives that are unknown to the econometrician; people may simply make mistakes. Whatever the reason for such apparently 'impossible' observations, if they do occur, a pure random parameter model will be inapplicable. In less extreme cases, a single observation close to 'impossibility' may be responsible for severe distortion of the estimated model.

3.4 Alternative-specific random errors

The most commonly used models of discrete choice are based on the maximization of a random utility function but with random errors entering in a different manner from that of the previous section. These models express the utility associated with the jth alternative as the sum of a non-stochastic function of $\mathbf{x}_n^j$ and $\mathbf{z}_n$, and an unobserved random error specific to that alternative:

$$u_n^j = V^*(\mathbf{x}_n^j, \mathbf{z}_n; \alpha) + \epsilon_n^j \tag{3.40}$$

where α is a vector of parameters (a subvector of θ) and $E(\epsilon_n^j \mid \zeta_n)$ is zero (or some other constant independent of j).

It should be noted that the function $V^*(.)$ is not a utility function in the usual sense of the term. Although utility-maximizing behaviour is invariant to monotonic transformations of the sum $V^*(.) + \epsilon$, it is not invariant to non-linear transformations applied to $V^*(.)$ alone. This implies that the function $V^*(.)$ is a cardinal construct whose normalization is important: if we replace $V^*(.)$ by its logarithm, for instance, we have an essentially different model as a result.

There are several ways in which the formulation (3.40) could arise. Indeed, it is consistent with the random preference model of the previous section, provided that we interpret $V^*(\mathbf{x}_n^j, \mathbf{z}_n; \alpha)$ as $E[V(\mathbf{x}_n^j; \beta_n) \mid \zeta_n]$ and ϵ_n^j as $V(\mathbf{x}_n^j; \beta_n) - V^*(\mathbf{x}_n^j, \mathbf{z}_n; \alpha)$. A more common interpretation of the random error in (3.40) is that it represents unobservable (and hence, for our purposes, random) attributes of alternative j. For example, unobservable characteristics of transport modes might include such things as comfort and reliability; alternative labour supply states might yield social prestige or a sense of fulfilment. These are all attributes that are unmeasurable and that may vary in intensity from person to person. Write the vectors of observable and unobservable characteristics as $\mathbf{x}_n^j$ and v_n^j respectively, and represent preferences by a utility function

$$u_n^j = V(\mathbf{x}_n^j, v_n^j; \beta_n) \tag{3.41}$$

where $\boldsymbol{\beta}_n$ depends in some way on $\mathbf{z}_n$, and may be stochastic. Define a random vector $\boldsymbol{\nu}_n^{j\prime} = (v_n^{j\prime}\ \boldsymbol{\beta}_n^{\prime})$, and write its conditional c.d.f. as $G_\nu^j(\boldsymbol{\nu}^j \mid \zeta_n)$. Then the conditional expectation of u_n^j is

$$\begin{aligned} E(u_n^j \mid \zeta_n) &= \int V(\mathbf{x}_n^j, v_n^j; \boldsymbol{\beta})\, \mathrm{d}G_\nu^j(\boldsymbol{\nu}^j \mid \zeta_n) \\ &= V_j^*(\mathbf{x}_n^j, \mathbf{z}_n; \boldsymbol{\alpha}) \end{aligned} \tag{3.42}$$

say. Now define ϵ_n^j as $u_n^j - E(u_n^j \mid \zeta_n)$, and we have

$$u_n^j = V_j^*(\mathbf{x}_n^j, \mathbf{z}_n; \boldsymbol{\alpha}) + \epsilon_n^j. \tag{3.43}$$

This is of the form (3.40) except that there is, in general, a different $V^*(.)$ function for each alternative. Again, the $V_j^*(.)$ cannot be interpreted as utility functions, now for the additional reason that their nature depends on the opportunity set – classical utility theory is founded on the assumption that preferences are independent of the opportunities available. Only in very special cases will the $V_j^*(.)$ be identical for all j, for instance if all the $\boldsymbol{\nu}^1, \ldots, \boldsymbol{\nu}^m$ share a common distribution conditional on ζ_n. This is implausible in most cases (it is hard to believe that individual perceptions of the levels of comfort of cars and buses fluctuate randomly about a common mean, for instance), and one has to accept that the non-stochastic component of the utility function may not be invariant. In applied work, this problem is often tackled by including an alternative-specific additive constant in an otherwise invariant utility function:

$$V_j^*(\mathbf{x}_n^j, \mathbf{z}_n; \boldsymbol{\alpha}) = \alpha^j + V^*(\mathbf{x}_n^j, \mathbf{z}_n; \boldsymbol{\alpha}^0) \tag{3.44}$$

with α^1 normalized to zero (say) and $\alpha^2, \ldots, \alpha^m$ treated as unknown parameters; $\boldsymbol{\alpha}^0$ contains the remaining parameters of $V_j^*(.)$. In some applications, particularly when none of the attributes of the alternatives is observable, all the model's parameters are allowed to vary between alternatives. For example, the commonly used linear specification implies

$$V_j^*(\mathbf{x}_n^j, \mathbf{z}_n; \boldsymbol{\alpha}) = \boldsymbol{\alpha}^{j\prime} \mathbf{z}_n \tag{3.45}$$

where $\boldsymbol{\alpha}^1 = \mathbf{0}$ and the vectors $\boldsymbol{\alpha}^2, \ldots, \boldsymbol{\alpha}^m$ contain unknown parameters.

The chief disadvantages of (3.40) and (3.43) are that simple assumptions about the distribution of the ϵ^j, particularly independence, tend to have undesirable consequences in terms of the restrictiveness of the resulting model, and also that there is a tendency for more general assumptions to bring with them additional covariance parameters that are specific to each alternative, making the prediction of demand for new alternatives very problematic. This is, in any case, always so for models like (3.44) or (3.45), no matter how simple is the assumed distribution for the ϵ^j.

For any model based on (3.40) or (3.43), the implied selection probabilities have a common representation in terms of the joint distribution assumed for $\epsilon^1, \ldots, \epsilon^m$. Alternative j is chosen by individual n if $u_n^j > u_n^i$ for all $i \neq j$. This happens if and only if

$$\epsilon_n^i < \epsilon_n^j + V_j^*(\mathbf{x}_n^j, \mathbf{z}_n; \alpha) - V_i^*(\mathbf{x}_n^i, \mathbf{z}_n; \alpha)$$

or, defining $\psi_{ni}^j(\alpha)$ as the difference of the non-stochastic utilities,

$$\epsilon_n^i < \epsilon_n^j + \psi_{ni}^j(\alpha). \tag{3.46}$$

Since the inequalities (3.46) are defined only in terms of the utility differences $\psi_{ni}^j(\alpha)$ rather than the $V_j^*(\mathbf{x}_n^j, \mathbf{z}_n; \alpha)$ themselves, any additive component of $V_j^*(.)$ that is independent of j cannot be identified. Assuming that $\epsilon^1, \ldots, \epsilon^m$ have a continuous distribution, the conditional probability of the event defined by (3.46) is

$$P(j \mid \zeta_n; \theta) = \int_{-\infty}^{\infty} \left[\int_{-\infty}^{\epsilon^j + \psi_{n1}^j(\alpha)} \cdots \int_{-\infty}^{\epsilon^j + \psi_{nm}^j(\alpha)} g_\epsilon(\epsilon^1, \ldots, \epsilon^m) \prod_{i \neq j} \mathrm{d}\epsilon^i \right] \mathrm{d}\epsilon^j \tag{3.47}$$

where $g_\epsilon(.)$ is the joint p.d.f. of $\epsilon^1, \ldots, \epsilon^m$. Note that the density $g_\epsilon(.)$ may depend on ζ_n and some additional parameters.

Several alternative expressions are available for this probability. Define $G_\epsilon(.)$ to be the c.d.f. corresponding to $g_\epsilon(.)$, and differentiate with respect to its jth argument:

$$\Pr[\epsilon^j \in (E^j, E^j + \mathrm{d}E^j),\ \epsilon^i \leqslant E^i, \text{ all } i \neq j] = G_\epsilon^j(E^1, \ldots, E^m)\,\mathrm{d}E^j$$

where $G_\epsilon^j(.) = \partial G_\epsilon(.)/\partial E^j$. Setting E^i equal to $\epsilon^j + \psi_{ni}^j(\alpha)$ and integrating over the whole range of ϵ^j

$$P(j \mid \zeta_n; \theta) = \int_{-\infty}^{\infty} G_\epsilon^j[\epsilon^j + \psi_{n1}^j(\alpha), \ldots, \epsilon^j + \psi_{nm}^j(\alpha)]\,\mathrm{d}\epsilon^j. \tag{3.48}$$

This form is sometimes convenient as a starting point for the derivation of choice probabilities (see appendix 1, section A1.3, for an example).

In cases where the c.d.f. $G_\epsilon(.)$ is not available in a form convenient for computational purposes, it is sometimes possible to proceed by making a transformation from the joint p.d.f. of $\epsilon^1, \ldots, \epsilon^m$ to the p.d.f. of the $m-1$ differences $\eta^j, \ldots, \eta_m^j$, where

$$\eta_i^j = \epsilon^i - \epsilon^j \qquad i = 1, \ldots, m, i \neq j. \tag{3.49}$$

The advantage of this is that the dimensionality of the integral (3.47) can be reduced by one, since

$$\begin{aligned} P(j \mid \zeta_n; \theta) &= \Pr[\eta_i^j < \psi_{ni}^j(\alpha), \text{ all } i \neq j \mid \zeta_n] \\ &= G_\eta[\psi_{n1}^j(\alpha), \ldots, \psi_{nm}^j(\alpha)] \end{aligned} \tag{3.50}$$

$$= \int_{-\infty}^{\psi_{n1}^j(\alpha)} \cdots \int_{-\infty}^{\psi_{nm}^j(\alpha)} g_\eta(\eta_i^j, \ldots, \eta_m^j) \prod_{i \neq j} \mathrm{d}\eta_i^j \tag{3.51}$$

where $g_\eta(.)$ and $G_\eta(.)$ are the joint p.d.f. and c.d.f. of the η_i^j.

Despite this slight reduction in dimension, the computation of such expressions is a formidable task unless the number of alternatives is small (note that to evaluate the log-likelihood function even once, N of these quantities must be calculated). For this reason, most of the commonly used techniques are based on simple distributional assumptions for which $G_\epsilon(.)$ or $G_\eta(.)$ can be computed directly without any need for numerical integration. However, we begin by considering the most demanding of the standard models, for which this is not so.

3.4.1 The multinomial probit model

The probit model (which is often known as the multinomial probit model when the number of alternatives is greater than two) is based on the assumption that the $\epsilon_{n'} = (\epsilon_n^1, \ldots, \epsilon_n^m)$ have a multivariate normal distribution, conditional on ζ_n:

$$\epsilon_n \mid \zeta_n \sim N(0, \Sigma) \tag{3.52}$$

where $\Sigma = \{\sigma_{ij}\}$ is an $m \times m$ symmetric positive-definite matrix of constants. Since the utilities u_n^j can be multiplied by an arbitrary constant without altering the implications of the model, the scale of the vector ϵ_n is not defined. Therefore, some normalization restriction (such as $\sigma_{11} = 1$) is required for identification. We assume that such a restriction has been imposed.

The normality assumption implies that the error differences $\eta_i^j = \epsilon^i - \epsilon^j$ are also normally distributed. Define the $(m-1)$-dimensional vector $\boldsymbol{\eta}^{j'} = (\eta^j \ldots \eta_m^j)$; this has joint distribution

$$\boldsymbol{\eta}^j \sim N(0, \boldsymbol{\Omega}^j) \tag{3.53}$$

where $\boldsymbol{\Omega}^j$ is the matrix with typical (i, k)th element

$$\text{cov}(\epsilon^i - \epsilon^j, \epsilon^k - \epsilon^j) = \sigma_{ik} - \sigma_{\iota\sigma} - \sigma_{jk} + \sigma_{jj}. \tag{3.54}$$

Thus, for the probit model, expression (3.50) gives the choice probabilities as

$$P(j \mid \zeta_n; \boldsymbol{\theta}) = \Phi(\psi_n^j(\alpha); 0, \boldsymbol{\Omega}^j) \tag{3.55}$$

where $\psi_n^j(\alpha)$ is the $(m-1)$-dimensional vector containing the $\psi_{ni}^j(\alpha)$ and $\Phi(.; \mu, \Sigma)$ is the joint c.d.f. of the $N(\mu, \Sigma)$ distribution.

Note that there is an identification problem involving the elements of the covariance matrix Σ. An arbitrary choice probability $P(j \mid \zeta; \boldsymbol{\theta})$ is the probability of the vector inequality $\boldsymbol{\eta}^j < \psi^j(\alpha)$. But each $\boldsymbol{\eta}^j$ is expressible as a linear transformation of a single basis vector, $\boldsymbol{\eta}^1$ say, and therefore each choice probability can be constructed from knowledge of only $\boldsymbol{\Omega}^1$ (which has $m(m-1)/2 - 1$ free elements) rather than Σ (which has $m(m+1)/2 - 1$). Thus, the complete parameter vector $\boldsymbol{\theta}$ contains the utility parameters $\boldsymbol{\alpha}$ and the elements of Σ that remain free after normalization and identification restrictions are imposed.

The binary form of the probit model, where there are only two alternatives, has been particularly widely used as a general-purpose binary response model with no utility-based interpretation. When $m = 2$, the choice probability (3.55) becomes

$$P(2 \mid \zeta_n; \theta) = \Phi\left[\frac{V_2^*(\mathbf{x}_n^2, \mathbf{z}_n; \alpha) - V_1^*(\mathbf{x}_n^1, \mathbf{z}_n; \alpha)}{\sigma_{11} + \sigma_{22} - 2\sigma_{12}}\right] \tag{3.56}$$

with $P(1 \mid \zeta_n\, \theta) = 1 - P(2 \mid \zeta_n, \mathbf{z}_n)$. In normal use, a linear functional form is adopted, so that $V_2^*(\mathbf{x}_n^2, \mathbf{z}_n; \alpha) - V_1^*(\mathbf{x}_n^1, \mathbf{z}_n; \alpha) = \gamma'\zeta_n$, say. Since (3.56) is homogeneous of degree zero in γ and $\sigma_{11}+\sigma_{22}-2\sigma_{12}$, it is not possible to identify both, and it is usual to impose the normalization $\sigma_{11}+\sigma_{22}-2\sigma_{12} = 1$ and estimate γ only up to scale. In this linear case

$$P(1 \mid \zeta_n; \theta) = 1 - \Phi(\gamma'\zeta_n) \tag{3.57}$$

$$P(2 \mid \zeta_n; \theta) = \Phi(\gamma'\zeta_n). \tag{3.58}$$

In the general multinomial case, there are two substantial problems that have prevented the widespread use of the probit model. The first is purely practical: the evaluation of the multivariate normal c.d.f. in (3.55) requires an enormous amount of computer time when m is more than 3 or 4. The difficulty is discussed in appendix 3, section A3.4. Although McFadden's (1988) simulation estimator (see section 3.2 above) offers a solution to this problem, the computational burden remains formidable unless some restrictive structure is imposed on Σ. Some progress has been made with models in which Σ has a factor-analytic structure (see, for instance, Butler and Moffitt, 1982).

A second problem concerns the use of the model for forecasting purposes. If a new alternative were to be added to the opportunity set, the matrix Σ would have a new row and column added to it, and new parameters would enter the model. Predicting the response to an expansion of the opportunity set requires estimation of the values of these new parameters but, because the sample is collected before the new alternative is introduced, the data contain no information about them.

Hausman and Wise (1978) (see also Domencich and McFadden, 1975) use a mixed model that avoids the latter difficulty, although the random coefficient interpretation they give to their model is applicable only in cases where the functions $V_j^*(.)$ are linear in parameters. In this case, it is possible to define transformations $\xi_n^j = \xi(\mathbf{x}_n^j, \mathbf{z}_n)$ such that

$$V_j^*(\mathbf{x}_n^j, \mathbf{z}_n) = \alpha_n'\xi_n^j. \tag{3.59}$$

The Hausman–Wise specification rests on the assumption that $\epsilon_n^1, \ldots, \epsilon_n^m$ are a set of independent $N(0, 1)$ random errors; the restrictiveness of this assumption is overcome by treating α_n as a vector of random coefficients, with $\alpha_n \sim N(\alpha, \Sigma_\alpha)$. This structure implies that u_n^j can now be written

$$u_n^j = \alpha'\xi_n^j + \epsilon_n^{*j} \tag{3.60}$$

where

$$\epsilon_n^{*j} = \epsilon_n^j + (\alpha_n - \alpha)'\xi_n^j. \tag{3.61}$$

The covariance matrix of $\epsilon_n^{*1}, \ldots, \epsilon_n^{*m}$ is dependent on n and has the structure

$$\Sigma_n^* = \mathbf{I} + \Xi_n \Sigma_\alpha \Xi_n' \tag{3.62}$$

where Ξ_n is the matrix with jth row $\xi_n^{j\prime}$. This special structure for the error covariance matrix does not materially alter the computational problem.

Since Ξ_n is fully observed, and since the rows and columns of Σ_α contain parameters specific to characteristics rather than to alternatives, no extra parameters would be introduced if the opportunity set were to be expanded. What this model does is to tie the covariance structure of the ϵ_n^{*j} to the measured characteristics in ξ_n^j, since (3.62) implies

$$\text{cov}(\epsilon_n^{*i}, \epsilon_n^{*j}) = \xi_n^{i\prime} \Sigma_\alpha \xi_n^j. \tag{3.63}$$

Expression (3.63) can be regarded as a measure of the similarity between alternatives i and j, in terms of their observed attributes; to the extent that unobservable attributes are similar to observable ones, this is a reasonable structure to use. Hausman and Wise report some success with it in an application to a three-alternative model of transportation mode choice, although they restrict attention to the special case where Σ_α is diagonal.

Although the random coefficient model underlying (3.63) is intractable for non-linear $V_j^*(.)$, the covariance structure (3.63) can always be used. An alternative approach, more in the spirit of choice theory, would be to relate $\text{cov}(\epsilon_n^{*i}, \epsilon_n^{*j})$ to the distance function (see chapter 1, section 1.6) as a measure of similarity between alternatives i and j.

3.4.2 The multinomial logit model

In univariate problems requiring evaluation of the c.d.f., a traditional alternative to the awkward normal distribution is the logistic distribution, which provides a close approximation to the normal over much of its range (see appendix 1). The advantage of the logistic distribution is that both p.d.f. and c.d.f. are available as simple closed-form expressions. Thus, if we take the binary discrete choice problem (i.e. $m = 2$) and assume $\eta_n = \epsilon_n^1 - \epsilon_n^2$ to have the logistic distribution, its c.d.f. is

$$G_\eta(\psi) = [1 + \exp(-\psi)]^{-1} \tag{3.64}$$

and this yields a choice probability

$$\begin{aligned} P(2 \mid \zeta_n; \theta) &= \Pr[\eta_n < \psi_{n1}^2(\alpha) \mid \zeta_n] \\ &= \{1 + \exp[-\psi_{n1}^2(\alpha)]\}^{-1} \qquad (3.65) \\ &= \frac{\exp[V_2^*(\mathbf{x}_n^2, \mathbf{z}_n; \alpha)]}{\exp[V_1^*(\mathbf{x}_n^1, \mathbf{z}_n; \alpha)] + \exp[V_2^*(\mathbf{x}_n^2, \mathbf{z}_n; \alpha)]}. \qquad (3.66) \end{aligned}$$

An analogous expression gives the choice probability for alternative 1.

If a linear expression $\psi^2_{n1} = \alpha'\zeta_n$ is used, then (3.65) is the basis for the binary logit technique (sometimes known as logistic regression) that is used in many fields of statistics. In a series of papers, McFadden has laid the foundations for the extension of this model to the general m-alternative case (see particularly McFadden, 1973, 1976a). He showed that a necessary and sufficient condition for $\eta_n = \epsilon^1_n - \epsilon^2_n$ to have the logistic distribution is that ϵ^1_n and ϵ^2_n have independent and identical type I extreme value distributions, with p.d.f. and c.d.f.

$$g_\epsilon(\epsilon) = \exp[-\exp(-\epsilon) - \epsilon] \tag{3.67}$$

$$G_\epsilon(E) = \exp[-\exp(-E)]. \tag{3.68}$$

For the probit model, we can claim some justification for the normality assumption: the central limit theorem implies that, if a random error is composed of a large number of individually negligible components, then it is approximately normal. This is quite a convincing argument for normality of the errors of a well-specified model, in which only the most minor influences are not well represented by observable variables. On the other hand, the extreme value distribution is the limiting form of the distribution of the (rescaled) maximum of a set of random variables as their number increases (see appendix 1). It is hard to see any way in which this result can be used to justify the assumption of the extreme value distribution, and it is better to regard it as an arbitrary device for generating convenient logistic forms for the differences $\eta^j_{ni} = \epsilon^i_n - \epsilon^j_n$.

If $\epsilon^1_n, \ldots, \epsilon^m_n$ have identical independent extreme value distributions, the $m-1$ differences $\eta^j_{n1}, \ldots, \eta^j_{ni}$ have a joint distribution with c.d.f.

$$\begin{aligned} G_\eta(\psi^j_{n1}, \ldots, \psi^j_{nm}) &= \Pr(\eta^j_{ni} < \psi^j_{ni}, \text{ all } i \neq j) \\ &= \left[1 + \sum_{i \neq j} \exp(-\psi^j_{ni})\right]^{-1}. \end{aligned} \tag{3.69}$$

Expression (3.69) is derived in appendix 1. Since $\psi^j_{ni} = V^*_j(\mathbf{x}^j_n, \mathbf{z}_n; \alpha) - V^*_i(\mathbf{x}^i_n, \mathbf{z}_n; \alpha)$, the selection probability has the particularly simple form

$$P(j \mid \zeta_n; \hat{\theta}) = \frac{\exp[V^*_j(\mathbf{x}^j_n, \mathbf{z}_n; \alpha)]}{\exp[V^*_1(\mathbf{x}^1_n, \mathbf{z}_n; \alpha)] + \ldots + \exp[V^*_m(\mathbf{x}^m_n, \mathbf{z}_n; \alpha)]} \tag{3.70}$$

which is an obvious generalization of the binary model (3.66).

This multinomial logit model is the most widely applied technique of discrete choice analysis. It dominates research in transportation, in particular, following the work of McFadden and his associates (see Domencich and McFadden, 1975). The reason for the prevalence of the logit model is its simplicity: the evaluation of the choice probabilities and hence the likelihood function is very straightforward, even in problems involving a large number of alternatives. It has a further advantage in cases where it is possible to express the $V_j^*(.)$ as a linear function of $\mathbf{x}_n^j$ and $\mathbf{z}_n$ (or simple transforms of them), since the log-likelihood function (3.5) is then easily shown to be a globally concave function of $\boldsymbol{\theta}$. Thus, any stationary point that is located by the optimization algorithm is guaranteed to be the unique global maximum of the likelihood function.

However, the logit model has quite severe drawbacks when there are more than two alternatives. The stochastic specification is not very flexible: the joint distribution of $\epsilon_n^1, \ldots, \epsilon_n^m$ involves no unknown parameters and is consequently not capable of approximating a very wide range of stochastic structures. Most seriously, no correlation is permitted between different ϵ_n^i, and yet if these random errors do represent omitted unobserved characteristics we would expect alternatives that are similar in terms of these characteristics to have similar values of ϵ, leading to a definite pattern of correlation among $\epsilon_n^1, \ldots, \epsilon_n^m$.

It is this lack of correlation in the logit model that is largely responsible for its possessing a property known as 'independence from irrelevant alternatives' (IIA). The odds ratio between any two alternatives, say $P(i|\zeta)/P(j|\zeta)$, takes the form $\exp[V_i^*(\mathbf{x}^i, \mathbf{z}) - V_j^*(\mathbf{x}^j, \mathbf{z})]$, which is independent of the characteristics or even the existence of any alternative other than i and j. This implies that, if a new alternative were introduced, all the selection probabilities would be reduced in the same proportion. This is surely unreasonable as a general property of a choice model: one would expect $P(j|\zeta)$ to be affected by an amount dependent on the degree to which the individual regards the new alternative as a substitute for alternative j.

Moreover, the importance of the IIA property is not confined to applications involving the forecasting of demand for new alternatives: for example, it implies a very restrictive pattern of elasticities of $P(j|\zeta)$ with respect to the characteristics $\mathbf{x}^i$. Differentiation of $\log[P(j|\zeta)]$ with respect to $\log \mathbf{x}^i$ for any $i \neq j$ reveals, after some manipulation,

$$\frac{\partial \log P(j|\zeta)}{\partial \log \mathbf{x}^i} = -P(i|\zeta) \frac{\partial V_i^*(\mathbf{x}^i, \mathbf{z})}{\partial \log \mathbf{x}^i}. \tag{3.71}$$

This elasticity is dependent only on i, and not on j. All choice probabilities share a uniform set of cross-elasticities, and this imposes a severe restriction on the type of substitution responses that can be modelled successfully.

Since IIA is such a restrictive property, it is desirable to test its validity before using the logit model. A general test that does not require the specification of a particular alternative hypothesis has been proposed by Hausman and McFadden (1984). This is based on a further consequence of IIA: that if the opportunity set is contracted so that it contains (say) only a proper subset $S \subset \{1 \ldots m\}$ of the original m alternatives, the conditional probability $P(j|j \in S, \zeta)$ is also of logit form. Thus if we discard from the sample all individuals observed to choose alternatives not in the subset S, the relevant conditional choice probabilities for the remaining individuals will be

$$P(j \mid j \in S, \zeta_n; \theta) = \frac{\exp(V^*_{nj})}{\sum_{i \in S} \exp(V^*_{ni})} \tag{3.72}$$

where V^*_{nj} is shorthand for $V^*_j(\mathbf{x}^j_n, \mathbf{z}_n; \alpha)$. An implication of IIA, therefore, is that θ (which contains all the identifiable elements of α) can be estimated consistently from a sample truncated in this way. The Hausman–McFadden test is a comparison of the estimates $\hat{\theta}$ and $\tilde{\theta}$ obtained by maximizing the likelihoods derived respectively from (3.70) applied to the whole sample and (3.72) applied to the truncated sample. However, note that it may not be possible to identify all elements of α from (3.72); for instance, if there are alternative-specific parameters in $V^*_j(.)$, as in (3.44) and (3.45), these will not all be identifiable. In such cases, $\tilde{\theta}$ must be compared with the appropriate subvector of $\hat{\theta}$. The form of the test statistic is

$$\tau = (\tilde{\theta} - \hat{\theta})' \, [\tilde{\Sigma}_\theta - \hat{\Sigma}_\theta]^{-1} (\tilde{\theta} - \hat{\theta}) \tag{3.73}$$

where $\hat{\Sigma}_\theta$ and $\tilde{\Sigma}_\theta$ are the usual asymptotic approximations to the covariance matrices of $\tilde{\theta}$ and $\hat{\theta}$. Under the null hypothesis that the population displays the IIA property embodied in the logit model, this statistic has a limiting χ^2 distribution with degrees of freedom equal to the number of elements in θ. Under any form of mis-specification that gives rise to a non-zero probability limit for $\tilde{\theta} - \hat{\theta}$, τ will be of stochastic order N, leading to a rejection of the model with probability unity as $N \rightarrow \infty$. See Wills (1987) for further discussion of this and similar tests.

One of the drawbacks of this test is that the choice of the subset S is left open. Comparisons based on different definitions of S may lead to different conclusions, and, in this respect, the test is arbitrary. In cases where it is possible to partition alternatives into natural groups, the test is useful in detecting departures from IIA between these groups. However, as a general test, it may not have very good power.

3.4.3 Generalized extreme value models

Consider a function $Y(v_1, \ldots, v_m)$, defined for non-negative v_i, with the following properties. It is non-negative and linearly homogeneous; its limit as any $v_i \rightarrow \infty$ is $+\infty$; if it is partially differentiated with respect to any k distinct arguments, the derivative is non-negative for k odd and non-positive for k even. Any random variables $\epsilon^1, \ldots, \epsilon^m$ whose joint c.d.f. is expressible in the form

$$G_\epsilon(E^1, \ldots, E^m) = \exp\{-Y[\exp(-E^1), \ldots, \exp(-E^m)]\} \tag{3.74}$$

is said to have a generalized extreme value (GEV) distribution, so called because its univariate marginal distributions all have a type I extreme value form (see appendix 1). This very valuable class of distributions was introduced by McFadden (1978), who showed that the corresponding choice probabilities are

$$P(j \mid \zeta_n; \theta) = \frac{\partial \log Y[\exp(V^*_{n1}), \ldots, \exp(V^*_{nm})]}{\partial V^*_{nj}} \tag{3.75}$$

$$= \frac{\exp(V^*_{nj})\, Y_j[\exp(V^*_{n1}), \ldots, \exp(V^*_{nm})]}{Y[\exp(V^*_{n1}), \ldots, \exp(V^*_{nm})]} \tag{3.76}$$

where $Y_j(.)$ is the partial derivative of $Y(.)$ with respect to its jth argument. The restrictive multinomial logit model is a member of the GEV class, corresponding to $Y(v_1, \ldots, v_m) = (\Sigma v_i^\rho)^{1/\rho}$, where $\rho \geqslant 1$. However, other members of this family can be constructed to permit a wide variety of correlation patterns, whilst preserving the computational simplicity of the multinomial logit model.

Expression (3.73) implies elasticities of the form

$$\frac{\partial \log P(j \mid \zeta)}{\partial \log \mathbf{x}^i} = \left[\frac{Y_{ji}}{Y_j} \exp(V^*_{ni}) - P(i \mid \zeta) \right] \frac{\partial V^*_i(\mathbf{x}^i, \mathbf{z})}{\partial \log \mathbf{x}^i} \tag{3.77}$$

where Y_j and Y_{ji} are the first and second partial derivatives of $Y(.)$, evaluated at $\exp(V^*_{n1}) \ldots \exp(V^*_{nm})$. These elasticities are independent of j only if the cross-derivatives Y_{ji} are proportional to Y_j.

Most applied GEV models are of the hierarchical type, discussed in section 3.6, but there is no difficulty in constructing general-purpose discrete choice models by specifying $Y(.)$ to be a flexible functional form. Many of the functions commonly used to represent production and cost functions in applied microeconomics can be used with appropriate modification. As an arbitrary example, consider the function

$$Y(v_1, \ldots, v_m) = \sum_{i=1}^{m} \sum_{j=1}^{m} A_n^{ij}(v_i^\rho + v_j^\rho)^{1/\rho} \tag{3.78}$$

where $\rho \geqslant 1$ is a parameter that controls the general scale of correlation and A_n^{ij} is a quantity reflecting the similarity between alternatives i and j for individual n.

The implied choice probabilities are

$$P(j \mid \zeta_n; \theta) = \frac{\exp(\rho V^*_{nj}) \sum_{i=1}^{m} (A_n^{ij} + A_n^{ji})[\exp(\rho V^*_{ni}) + \exp(\rho V^*_{nj})]^{(1-\rho)/\rho}}{\sum_{i=1}^{m} \sum_{k=1}^{m} A_n^{ik}[\exp(\rho V^*_{ni}) + \exp(\rho V^*_{nk})]^{1/\rho}}. \tag{3.79}$$

As with the probit model, one might avoid the need for alternative-specific parameters by specifying each A_n^{ij} to be a function of ζ_n^i and ζ_n^j or, in the invariant case, by relating it to $D(\mathbf{x}_n^i, V^*_{nj}; \mathbf{z}_n)$, where $D(\mathbf{x}, u; \mathbf{z})$ is the distance function corresponding to $V^*(\mathbf{x}, \mathbf{z})$. In the latter case, since $D(\mathbf{x}_n^i, V^*_{nj}; \mathbf{z}_n) = 1$ indicates perfect similarity (in that alternatives i and j lie on the same pseudo-indifference surface), one might specify A_n^{ij} as the smaller of $D(\mathbf{x}_n^i, V_{nj}^*; \mathbf{z}_n)$ and $1/D(\mathbf{x}_n^i, V_{nj}^*; \mathbf{z}_n)$. However, models derived in this way have yet to be used in applied work.

3.5 Tversky's elimination model

Utility-based models view choice as a process involving a search amongst the competing alternatives for one which dominates all others. However, another view sees choice as a process involving the elimination of alternatives, with the process terminating when only a single alternative remains. If the criterion for elimination of an alternative is suitably chosen, these two approaches are clearly equivalent, and the distinction is without real significance. Nevertheless, psychologists have shown considerable interest in this approach, adopting particularly simple elimination criteria that are not equivalent to utility maximization. The best known of these models is due to Tversky (see Tversky, 1972a, 1972b; and Tversky and Sattath, 1979), and requires the existence of a complete set of purely qualitative characteristics that define and distinguish the alternatives. Choice behaviour is hypothesized to be the result of rational choice under random lexicographic preferences, for which no utility function representation exists.

The simplest way of explaining the model is by means of an example. Suppose our typical individual must choose between three models of car. Only four characteristics are regarded as important, all of them qualitative rather than quantitative: whether or not the car has (1) an automatic transmission, (2) power steering, (3) a turbo-charged engine and (4) a diesel engine. In our example, the three cars will have the following characteristics:

car 1 possesses characteristics 1 and 2
car 2 possesses characteristics 1 and 3
car 3 possesses characteristics 2 and 4

The individual is assumed to eliminate alternatives by first randomly selecting a characteristic and eliminating all alternatives not possessing it. Next, a second characteristic is selected, and all alternatives not possessing that are eliminated, and so on, with this sequence pursued until only a single alternative remains. To make clear the basis of this model in preference theory, we use the symbol $\gg$ to represent the lexicographic preference relation over qualitative characteristics. Thus, the statement $i \gg S$ means that, when asked to rank a group of alternative cars, the individual always ranks those possessing characteristic i (where $i \notin S$) above those possessing only characteristics from a set S.

Thus the probability that the individual chooses any particular car in our example is the probability that he or she has lexicographic preferences that eliminate all the others:

$$P(1\,|\,\zeta) = \Pr(1 \gg \{2,3,4\}, 2 \gg 3\,|\,\zeta) + \Pr(2 \gg \{1,3,4\}, 1 \gg 4\,|\,\zeta) \quad (3.80)$$

$$P(2\,|\,\zeta) = \Pr(1 \gg \{2,3,4\}, 3 \gg 2\,|\,\zeta) + \Pr(3 \gg \{1,2,4\}\,|\,\zeta) \quad (3.81)$$

$$P(3\,|\,\zeta) = \Pr(2 \gg \{1,3,4\}, 4 \gg 1\,|\,\zeta) + \Pr(4 \gg \{1,2,3\}\,|\,\zeta). \quad (3.82)$$

Another way of writing (3.80)–(3.82) is

$$P(1\,|\,\zeta) = P_{1.1234}P_{2.23} + P_{2.1234}P_{1.14} \quad (3.83)$$

$$P(2\,|\,\zeta) = P_{1.1234}P_{3.23} + P_{3.1234} \quad (3.84)$$

$$P(3\,|\,\zeta) = P_{2.1234}P_{4.14} + P_{4.1234} \quad (3.85)$$

where $P_{1.1234}$ denotes the probability that characteristic 1 is the dominant member of the set containing characteristics 1, . . ., 4 etc. Tversky models these probabilities using unknown parameters $V_1, \ldots, V_4$, interpreted as the 'utilities of the characteristics': $P_{1.1234} = V_1/(V_1+V_2+V_3+V_4)$, $P_{2.234} = V_2/(V_2+V_3+V_4)$ etc. Much more flexible expressions could be used in place of these.

In this form, the elimination model has severe drawbacks, which have prevented its use in economics. Firstly, its view of the choice process seems very restrictive, since it rules out any possibility of a trade off between characteristics. Secondly, the model can only cope with characteristics that are qualitative, and this is a great limitation in many economic problems. For instance, price is continuously variable, yet to play a role as a characteristic in Tversky's model it must be converted into qualitative form, perhaps by observing whether or not the good falls into a particular price range. This is arbitrary and fails to use all potentially relevant information. Thirdly, we must be able to specify and observe the relevant characteristics, and their configuration must be sufficient to guarantee an unambiguous conclusion to the elimination process. If, for instance, there were two cars in our example with automatic transmission and power steering as their only two characteristics, then the model would not be able to indicate a unique choice from that pair, and their choice probabilities would be left undefined. The last problem can easily be resolved by closing the model with an arbitrary rule or introducing an additional characteristic. Nevertheless, the theory of choice underlying Tversky's model has not found favour with economists, and remains largely untried.

3.6 Hierarchical and sequential discrete choice

In orthodox demand analysis, great use is made of the concept of separability. Separability refers to a particular structure of preferences that imparts to optimal behaviour a hierarchical form: the consumer first makes a global decision on the resources to be devoted to each of a set of natural groups of goods, and then determines expenditure on individual goods by considering only prices of other goods in the group together with total group expenditure. Related phenomena often arise in intertemporal models: the decision-maker can postpone decisions concerning future acts, while determining current policy on the basis of current prices and a single indicator of lifetime resources.

It is not hard to find casual evidence that people often do behave in this decentralized way, but the enthusiasm that econometricians have shown for the idea probably owes more to the considerable savings in computational effort that can be achieved by exploiting separability. For the same reason, hierarchical structures are appealing to econometricians working with discrete choice. For instance, if a probit model of choice between four alternatives is intractable because it requires the evaluation of a three-dimensional normal c.d.f., there is considerable advantage in re-specifying it as a binary choice between two pairs of alternatives followed by a binary choice within each pair. This would require only the evaluation of the univariate normal c.d.f.

We now consider such models, treating static hierarchical models and intertemporal or sequential models separately.

3.6.1 Static hierarchical models

To introduce the ideas involved here, we use an example based on the work of Cragg and Uhler (1970), who attempt to model car buying behaviour, treating it as a discrete choicc problem with four alternatives. Each individual who initially owns at least one car can do one of four things: (1) leave the stock of cars unchanged; (2) reduce the stock by selling a car; (3) change the quality of the stock by replacing a car; (4) expand the stock by purchasing an additional car. Cragg and Uhler estimate a conventional multinomial logit midel, but also a hierarchical model (which they reject, since it yields a much smaller likelihood value). The latter model views the choice process as following the decision tree depicted in figure 3.2.

This decision tree is based on the assumption that people first decide whether or not to buy a new car, and then whether that new car is to be a replacement for an existing car or an expansion of the stock. It should be observed that there is nothing natural about this hierarchy: one could, with equal justification, adopt the reverse view and think of a first-stage decision on whether or not to sell a car followed by a subsidiary decision on whether or not to buy a car. This arbitrariness is frequently a weakness of hierarchical specifications in practice.

In this example, the hierarchical model begins with a simple binary choice between branch A and branch B; adopting an explicit utility basis for this comparison, we must define u^A and u^B as random utility indicators such that branch A is pursucd if $u^A > u^B$ and branch B otherwise. The second stage

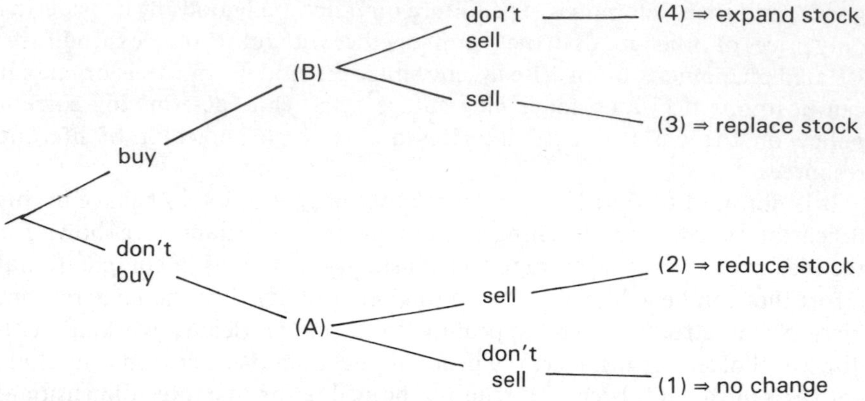

Figure 3.2 Decision tree for Cragg and Uhler's hierarchical model.

also involves a binary choice based on a comparison of utilities u^1 and u^2 (for branch A) or u^3 and u^4 (for branch B). This leads to selection probabilities of the form:

$$P(1\,|\,\zeta) = \Pr(u^A > u^B\,|\,\zeta)\Pr(u^1 > u^2\,|\,u^A > u^B, \zeta) \tag{3.86}$$

$$P(2\,|\,\zeta) = \Pr(u^A > u^B\,|\,\zeta)\Pr(u^2 > u^1\,|\,u^A > u^B, \zeta) \tag{3.87}$$

$$P(3\,|\,\zeta) = \Pr(u^B > u^A\,|\,\zeta)\Pr(u^3 > u^4\,|\,u^B > u^A, \zeta) \tag{3.88}$$

$$P(4\,|\,\zeta) = \Pr(u^B > u^A\,|\,\zeta)\Pr(u^4 > u^3\,|\,u^B > u^A, \zeta) \tag{3.89}$$

As it stands, this system is vacuous: we have only to define u^A and u^B as $\max(u^1, u^2)$ and $\max(u^3, u^4)$ to get back to the standard multiple choice problem with all its potential difficulties. However, if we require that u^A be definable independently of whether $u^1 > u^2$ or $u^2 > u^1$ and similarly for u^B, then this hierarchical decomposition has some additional content. Cragg and Uhler implicitly define u^A and u^B to be different linear functions of $\mathbf{x}_n$ with additive errors, and assume them independent of $u^1, \ldots, u^4$. This independence assumption means that the last term on the right-hand sides of each of (3.86)–(3.89) reduces to a probability conditioned only on ζ, and not on the events $u^A > u^B$ or $u^B > u^A$.

However, an important question remains unanswered. Under what conditions will a rational individual make decisions in this decentralized way? For u^A and u^B to be definable, a comparison of their values must give a correct indication of the branch in which the optimal alternative lies, independently of the outcomes of utility comparisons within branches. This requires

$$u^A > u^B \text{ iff } \min(u^1, u^2) > \max(u^3, u^4) \tag{3.90}$$

$$u^B > u^A \text{ iff } \min(u^3, u^4) > \max(u^1, u^2) \tag{3.91}$$

where iff means if and only if. For u^A and u^B to exist, it must be impossible for any configuration of $u^1, \ldots, u^4$ not satisfying one or other of the inequalities in (3.90) and (3.91) to arise. Inequality (3.90) implies that both u^1 and u^2 should be greater than both u^3 and u^4, while (3.91) implies the reverse. These conditions rule out the possibility of mixed orderings, such as $u^1 > u^3 > u^2 > u^4$. Thus, the stochastic structure must be such that they occur with probability zero, and the joint distribution of the u^i must display this particular kind of degeneracy. In formal terms

$$\Pr[\min(u^1, u^2) < \max(u^3, u^4), \min(u^3, u^4) < \max(u^1, u^2) \mid \zeta] = 0. \tag{3.92}$$

This is not a natural condition to impose. The random elements in the model are usually taken to represent unobseved variation in preferences and in the attributes of the alternatives, and so condition (3.92) places severe restrictions on the population distribution of both preferences and opportunity sets. In general, hierarchical behaviour is not rational.

However, one must distinguish between hierarchical behaviour and a hierarchical structure for the mathematical forms of the choice probabilities. Even if behaviour is not decentralized in the sense used above, it is still possible to devise choice models whose forms are based on natural groupings of alternatives. Such models were introduced by McFadden (1978) in an attempt to avoid the restrictive IIA property of the multinomial logit model. These are based on a GEV distribution whose c.d.f. displays strong separability between groups of alternatives whilst permitting correlations between utilities yielded by alternatives from a common group. Consider again the example of Cragg and Uhler, expressing each of the u^j and $V^*_{nj} + \epsilon^j_n$. If we assume strong separability between alternatives (1, 2) and (3, 4), the c.d.f. of $\epsilon^1, \ldots, \epsilon^4$ is

$$\begin{aligned} G_\epsilon(E^1, \ldots, E^4) &= \exp\{-Y^A[\exp(-E^1), \exp(-E^2)] - \\ &\qquad Y^B[\exp(-E^3), \exp(-E^4)]\} \end{aligned} \tag{3.93}$$

where $Y^A(.)$ and $Y^B(.)$ are functions satisfying the conditions given in section 3.4.3. This distribution leads to choice probabilities

$$P(1 \mid \zeta) = \frac{\exp(V^*_{n1})\, Y^{A1}[\exp(V^*_{n1}), \exp(V^*_{n2})]}{Y^A[\exp(V^*_{n1}), \exp(V^*_{n2})] + Y^B[\exp(V^*_{n3}), \exp(V^*_{n4})]} \tag{3.94}$$

where $Y^{A1}(.)$ is the partial derivative of $Y^A(.)$ with respect to its first argument. Similar expressions hold for $P(2 \mid \zeta)$, $P(3 \mid \zeta)$ and $P(4 \mid \zeta)$. The hierarchical structure of these probabilities can be seen by rewriting (3.94) as

$$P(1\,|\,\zeta_n) = \left\{\frac{Y^{A}[\exp(V_{n1}^*), \exp(V_{n2}^*)]}{Y^{A}[\exp(V_{n1}^*), \exp(V_{n2}^*)] + Y^{B}[\exp(V_{n3}^*), \exp(V_{n4}^*)]}\right\} \times \left\{\frac{\exp(V_{n1}^*)\, Y^{A1}[\exp(V_{n1}^*), \exp(V_{n2}^*)]}{Y^{A}[\exp(V_{n1}^*), \exp(V_{n2}^*)]}\right\}. \quad (3.95)$$

The first component on the right-hand side of (3.95) is the probability that the optimal choice is from branch A; the second component is the probability that alternative 1 is chosen, conditional on the event that the optimal choice is in branch A. The first of these has the binary logit form, corresponding to $\Pr(u_n^A > u_n^B\,|\,\zeta_n)$, where $u_n^A = \log\{Y^A[\exp(V_{n1}^*), \exp(V_{n2}^*)]\} + \epsilon_n^A$ and $u_n^B = \log\{Y^B[\exp(V_{n3}^*), \exp(V_{n4}^*)]\} + \epsilon_n^B$, with ϵ_n^A and ϵ_n^B defined as independent extreme value variates. Although u^A and u^B do exist in this case, there is no real decentralized decision-making here (in the strict sense used above), since condition (3.92) is violated by this model.

This is a model that can be expressed in the hierarchical form (3.95), despite the fact that the behaviour it describes is not strictly decentralized. Its main virtue is that it allows the relaxation of the IIA property of the multinomial logit model within selected groups of alternatives, without introducing too many additional parameters. It also permits relatively simple two-stage estimation, which avoids the need for simultaneous estimation of all the model's parameters. This is particularly useful when the total number of alternatives is large. A further advantage is that it is a simple matter to generalize the model to multilevel tree structures, allowing quite complex forms of interaction between alternatives.

However, against these must be set the disadvantage of the rigid nature of the hierarchy: in the case of transportation, for example, train and bus might be close substitutes, and therefore members of a natural group, for one individual, whilst another, who lives far from a railway station might view car and bus as a more natural pairing. As a consequence, there may not exist a single separable structure appropriate to all individuals in a particular sample.

The most common specification for the branch functions ($Y^A(.)$ and $Y^B(.)$ in our example) is the CES form

$$Y(v^1, \ldots, v^4) = \gamma^A[(v^1)^{\rho^A} + (v^2)^{\rho^A}]^{1/\rho A} + \gamma^B[(v^3)^{\rho^B} + (v^4)^{\rho^B}]^{1/\rho^B} \quad (3.96)$$

where $\gamma^A, \gamma^B > 0$ and $\rho^A, \rho^B \geqslant 1$. Consider the most common case, where utility can be expressed in the linear form $V_{nj}^* = \alpha'\xi_n^j$, where ξ_n^j is some elementary transformation of $\mathbf{x}_n^j$ and $\mathbf{z}_n$. Equation (3.96) leads to selection probabilities of the form

$$\begin{aligned} P(j\,|\,\zeta_n;\theta) &= P(A\,|\,\zeta_n;\theta)\, P(j\,|\,A, \zeta_n;\theta) \qquad \text{for } j = 1, 2 \\ &= P(B\,|\,\zeta_n;\theta)\, P(j\,|\,B, \zeta_n;\theta) \qquad \text{for } j = 3, 4 \end{aligned}$$

where, for instance,

$$P(1 \mid \mathrm{A}, \zeta_n; \theta) = \frac{\exp(\rho^{\mathrm{A}}\alpha'\xi_n^1)}{\exp(\rho^{\mathrm{A}}\alpha'\xi_n^1) + \exp(\rho^{\mathrm{A}}\alpha'\xi_n^2)} \tag{3.97}$$

and

$$P(\mathrm{A} \mid \zeta_n; \theta) = \frac{\exp(V_n^{\mathrm{A}})}{\exp(V_n^{\mathrm{A}}) + \exp(V_n^{\mathrm{B}})} \tag{3.98}$$

where

$$V_n^{\mathrm{A}} = \log \gamma^{\mathrm{A}} + \frac{1}{\rho^{\mathrm{A}}} \log[\exp(\rho^{\mathrm{A}}\alpha'\xi_n^1) + \exp(\rho^{\mathrm{A}}\alpha'\xi_n^2)] \tag{3.99}$$

Analogous expressions hold for V_n^{B} etc This structure suggests the following two-stage estimator.

Stage 1 Truncate the sample by omitting all observations for which $j_n = 3$ or $j_n = 4$; for this subsample, expression (3.97) and its analogue for alternative 2 are the appropriate conditional choice probabilities. Hence, estimate a simple binary logit model of the choice between alternatives 1 and 2; this yields a consistent estimate of $\rho^{\mathrm{A}}\alpha$. Do the same for the subsample of individuals choosing alternatives 3 and 4, to construct an estimate of $\rho^{\mathrm{B}}\alpha$.

Stage 2 Construct variables $\hat{I}_n^{\mathrm{A}} = \log[\exp(\hat{a}^{\mathrm{A}'}\xi_n^1) + \exp(\hat{a}^{\mathrm{A}'}\xi_n^2)]$ and $\hat{I}_n^{\mathrm{B}} = \log[\exp(\hat{a}^{\mathrm{B}'}\xi_n^3) + \exp(\hat{a}^{\mathrm{B}'}\xi_n^4)]$ (referred to by McFadden as inclusive values), where $\hat{a}^{\mathrm{A}}$ and $\hat{a}^{\mathrm{B}}$ are the stage 1 estimates. Use these values as in (3.99) to define linear utilities $\hat{V}_n^{\mathrm{A}}$ and $\hat{V}_n^{\mathrm{B}}$ which are then used as the basis for a single binary logit model of the choice between the two alternatives of branch A and branch B. This model is estimated from the full sample, and yields estimates of $\log \gamma^{\mathrm{A}}$, $\log \gamma^{\mathrm{B}}$, $1/\rho^{\mathrm{A}}$ and $1/\rho^{\mathrm{B}}$. From these, all the underlying parameters can be recovered.

For further details of this model and its multilevel extensions, see McFadden (1978, 1981, 1984). Amemiya (1978) and McFadden (1984) discuss the two-stage estimator and give its limiting distribution, and Hausman and McFadden (1984) put forward a test of the multinomial logit model against the alternative of a particular hierarchical GEV structure.

3.6.2 Sequential models

When a discrete choice problem involves the passage of time, hierarchical models arise naturally because the implementation of any decision requires a sequence of actions which are necessarily separated in time. Thus the consistency of the sequential choice process with static utility maximization is unimportant, since behaviour is of necessity sequential. In section 3.1 we discussed this in the context of the economics of human fertility; here, we shall consider another important example: the retirement decision. Retirement behaviour is of considerable importance: small changes in the average age of retirement can have significant effects on the level of unemployment and the cost of the state's social security system. As a consequence, economists have recently devoted a considerable amount of effort to the analysis of the timing of retirement, using individual data.

One approach to the problem is exemplified by the work of Fields and Mitchell (1984), who treat the timing decision as one involving a single static choice between discrete alternatives defined as the possible ages at which the individual might retire. These alternatives are characterized by two measures: expected future leisure and income. Both are discounted back to age 60, with expectations based on actuarial data on survival probabilities. The income variable is constructed from detailed knowledge of the pension provision for each individual, and takes account of the fact that the size of the pension depends on the chosen retirement age, as does leisure. They represent preferences by a very simple utility function:

$$u_n^j = V_{nj}^* + \epsilon_n^j \tag{3.100}$$

where

$$V_{nj}^* = \alpha_1 \log y_n(j) + \alpha_2 \log \ell_n(j) \tag{3.101}$$

j represents age of retirement ($j \geqslant 60$), and $y_n(j)$ and $\ell_n(j)$ are the discounted expected values of the income and leisure streams that the individual will receive if he or she retires at age j.

In this problem, the alternatives have a natural ordering, since they are successive ages. Thus it is reasonable to assume that any correlations between the errors $\epsilon_n^1, \ldots, \epsilon_n^m$ will be strongest for alternatives that are close together in this ordering. To capture this idea, they use a member of the class of *ordered GEV models* proposed by Small (1987). These are based on a GEV distribution with generating function

$$Y(v_1, \ldots, v_m) = \sum_{j=1}^{m+1} [v_{j-1}^\rho + v_j^\rho]^{1/\rho} \tag{3.102}$$

where $\rho \geqslant 1$ and $v_0 = v_m = 0$. In this case, m is the maximum number of separate retirement ages that we consider (the maximum possible retirement age minus 59). This leads to choice probabilities of the form

$$\begin{aligned} P_{60}(j \mid \zeta_n; \theta) = {} & \exp(\rho V_{nj}^*)\,[\exp(\rho V_{nj-1}^*) + \exp(\rho V_{nj}^*)]^{(1-\mathrm{p})/\rho} \\ & \times [\exp(\rho V_{nj}^*) + \exp(\rho V_{nj+1}^*)]^{(1-\mathrm{p})/\rho} \Big/ \sum_{i=60}^{m+60} \\ & \times [\exp(\rho V_{ni}^*) + \exp(\rho V_{ni-1}^*)]^{1/\rho} \end{aligned} \tag{3.103}$$

with the convention that $\exp(\rho V_{ni}^*) = 0$ for $i=0$ or $i=m+60$. In this expression, ζ_n represents the variables ($y_n(60)$, $\ell_n(60)$, $y_n(61)$, $\ell_n(61)$, . . .) and

$\boldsymbol{\theta} = (\alpha_1\ \alpha_2)$; we have also attached a subscript to the choice probability to indicate the age at which the retirement decision is being taken. The strong interaction between retirement at age j and at neighbouring alternatives, ages $j-1$ or $j+1$, is clear from (3.103). Fields and Mitchell use a limiting ($\rho \to \infty$) form of this model, and do not estimate ρ.

The Fields–Mitchell study provides valuable evidence on retirement behaviour, but this static view of the problem fails to reflect the necessarily sequential nature of the decision. Consider, for example, the problem facing a 60-year-old man currently in the labour force. He might indeed make a Fields–Mitchell type decision to retire at age 64, say, but much could happen between the present and his intended retirement date to upset his plans: he could become ill; he could lose his job; his circumstances or preferences could change in some other unforeseen way. To take the simplest possible example, retain the Fields–Mitchell utility function and the ordered GEV error structure but suppose that, at the start of his sixty-first year, his pension fund managers change the rules by which pension payments are determined in such a way as to favour earlier retirement. Thus $y_n(j)$ is now changed to $y_n^*(j)$ for $j = 61, 62, \ldots$, where $y_n^*(j)$ is greater than $y_n(j)$ for early retirement ages; this produces a new $\boldsymbol{\zeta}$ vector, say $\boldsymbol{\zeta}_n^*$. The change in the nature of his opportunity set will induce a revision of his plan (indeed, even in the absence of any change, there is no reason why he should feel bound by last year's decision). The outcome is a new set of choice probabilities. It is important to realize that these are conditional on the event that he is still in the labour force at the start of his sixty-first year: that he did not choose retirement at age 60. Write the revised choice probabilities in the form

$$\begin{aligned}&\Pr(\text{chooses retirement at age } j \mid \text{not yet retired at age } 61)\\&= P_{61}(j \mid \boldsymbol{\zeta}_n^*; \boldsymbol{\theta}).\end{aligned} \tag{3.104}$$

These could again be generated by the ordered GEV model based on (3.102) (presumably now with m reduced by one).

Both $P_{60}(j \mid \boldsymbol{\zeta}_n; \boldsymbol{\theta})$ and $P_{61}(j \mid \boldsymbol{\zeta}_n^*; \boldsymbol{\theta})$ are the probabilities of *planned* events. The probabilities associated with observed events are rather different, and must be built up sequentially. Our typical individual will be observed to retire at 60 if, when he makes his plan at age 60, it appears optimal for him to retire immediately. This decision is made before the change in pension rules, and the probability therefore depends only on $\boldsymbol{\zeta}_n$:

$$P(60 \mid \boldsymbol{\zeta}_n; \boldsymbol{\theta}) = P_{60}(60 \mid \boldsymbol{\zeta}_n; \boldsymbol{\theta}). \tag{3.105}$$

He will be observed to retire at age 61 if two things happen: he is still in the labour force at the start of his sixty-first year, and it then appears optimal for him to retire immediately. The resulting probability will involve both $\boldsymbol{\zeta}_n$ (which underlies his decision not to retire at age 60) and $\boldsymbol{\zeta}_n^*$ (which underlies his current decision):

$$\begin{aligned} P(61 \mid \zeta_n, \zeta_n^*; \theta) &= \Pr(\text{no retirement at } 60 \mid \zeta_n) \times \\ &\quad \Pr(\text{retire at } 61 \mid \text{no retirement at } 60, \zeta_n^*) \\ &= [1 - P_{60}(60 \mid \zeta_n; \theta)]\, P_{61}(61 \mid \zeta_n^*; \theta). \end{aligned} \tag{3.106}$$

Under the assumption that he continues this annual replanning (even if there is no further change in ζ), the next year's retirement probability is the product of the probabilities of three events: no retirement at 60; no retirement at 61; immediate retirement at 62. Thus

$$P(62 \mid \zeta_n, \zeta_n^*; \theta) = [1 - P_{60}(60 \mid \zeta_n; \theta)]\,[1 - P_{61}(61 \mid \zeta_n^*; \theta)]\, P_{62}(62 \mid \zeta_n^*; \theta). \tag{3.107}$$

Unless people make arrangements to enforce their current plans for the future, any intertemporal decision of this type wil involve replanning from year to year, and will result in event probabilities with a structure similar to (3.107). In the general case, where the vector ζ may change from year to year as new information becomes available or circumstances change, we have

$$P(j \mid Z_n; \theta) = \left(\prod_{i=60}^{j-1} \{1 - P_i[i \mid \zeta_n(i); \theta]\} \right) P_j[j \mid \zeta_n(j); \theta] \tag{3.108}$$

where $\zeta_n(i)$ represents the external variables relevant to the decision at age i, and $Z_n = (\zeta_n(60), \zeta_n(61), \ldots)$. Only in the special case where circumstances never change (when $\zeta_n(60) = \zeta_n(61) = \ldots$) is it possible to represent these probabilities by a simple static multinomial choice model.

This example is highly simplified in several respects. In modelling intertemporal choice under uncertainty, it is more satisfactory (although much more difficult) to use formal stochastic dynamic programming techniques to derive optimal decisions, rather than resorting to a simple model like (3.101). Moreover, our interpretation of $P_j(j+s \mid \zeta_n(j); \theta)$ as a probability conditional on the event that retirement has not occured prior to age j is inconsistent with the random utility formulation (3.100)–(3.102) unless the vectors of random errors that are involved in any two years' planning exercises are independent. If successive years' errors are correlated (as we would expect, since they represent slowly changing unobserved factors associated with the different retirement age), then the conditional probabilities in (3.108) will not have the simple GEV forms that we have assumed.

Another objection to this type of model is that its divison of time into discrete years is very arbitrary, and there is much to be said for conducting the analysis in continuous time. The system (3.108) is essentially a discrete-time hazard function model; such models are discussed further in a continuous time setting in chapter 6.

3.7 Composite discrete–continuous choices

Our brief review of applications of discrete choice models in section 3.1 suggests that the discreteness of alternatives is often found to be embedded in a much more general choice problem. Quite often, it is necessary to regard the separate alternatives as complex entities which include opportunities to make further choices. In such cases, the utilities which are compared within the process of choice are indirect utilities, representing the outcomes of these further decisions. The nature of the resulting model varies considerably from problem to problem, but a single example, based loosely on King's (1980) study of the demand for housing in the UK, will serve to illustrate the main ideas.

A microeconomic model of housing demand must do two things: explain the type of housing tenure chosen by the household, and explain its expenditure on housing given its choice of tenure. The discrete alternatives in this example are three tenure types: owner occupation, renting from a local authority and renting in the private sector. The household makes a conventional continuous choice between the quantity of housing services it consumes and its real expenditure on other consumption goods; however, the budget constraint it faces depends on the type of housing tenure it chooses, since the price of housing services differs between tenure types owing to imperfections in the housing market, tax relief, subsidies etc. To represent the resulting opportunity set on a conventional diagram, it is necessary to introduce a third characteristic that serves to distinguish the three types. Suppose that a factor in the choice is the household's subjective feelings of security, and that this can somehow be represented by a variable x_3, while the variables x_1 and x_2 represent the quantities of housing services and of other consumption respectively. The household's income is y and it faces a fixed price p_2 for non-housing consumption, but prices p_1^1, p_1^2 and p_1^3 for housing in tenures 1 (owner occupation), 2 (public sector rental) and 3 (private sector rental) respectively. For a typical household, the opportunity set would consist of the three triangles illustrated in figure 3.3, where x_3^1, x_3^2 and x_3^3 are the levels of security associated with tenures 1, 2 and 3.

The statistical analysis of this problem is based on observations of two endogenous variables for each household: the discrete variable j that indicates its selected tenure, and the continuous variable x_1 that represents its purchases of housing services. Thus a stochastic microeconomic model of the housing demand decision must generate a joint distribution for these two variables that can be characterized by a conditional probability density/mass function $P(j, x_1 \mid \zeta; \theta)$ that is continuous in x_1 but discrete in j, where ζ represents all relevant exogenous variables. This type of mixed distribution is very common in microeconometrics, and its interpretation is straightforward: the

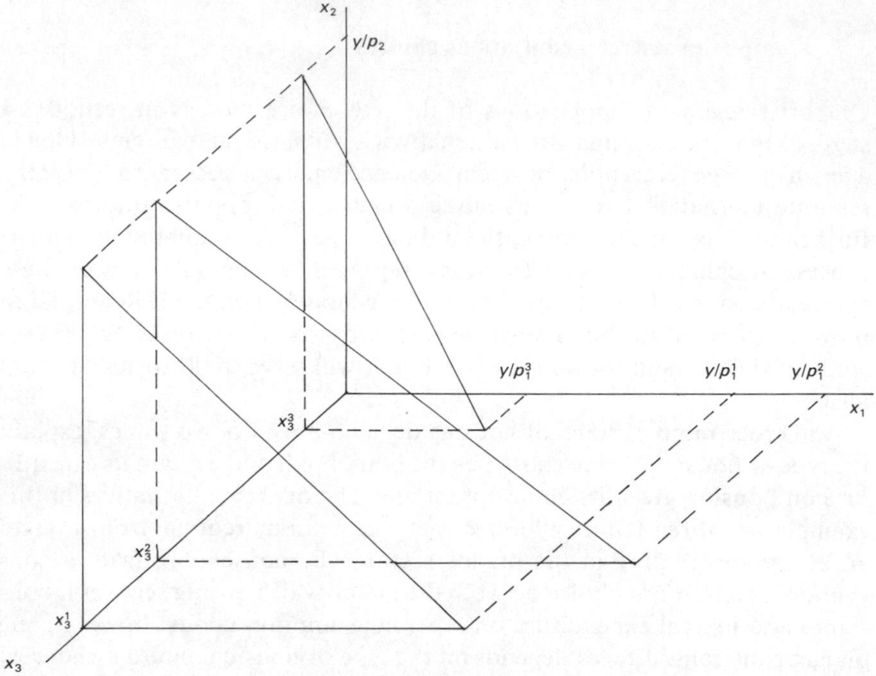

Figure 3.3 The opportunity set for the joint choice of tenure and quantity of housing.

conditional probability that a household simultaneously chooses tenure type j and purchases a quantity of housing of that type in the infinitesimal range $(x_1, x_1+\mathrm{d}x_1)$ is $P(j, x_1 \mid \zeta; \boldsymbol{\theta})\mathrm{d}x_1$. It is convenient to discuss the two aspects of the household's decision separately, and the law of conditional probability can be used to express this function in the corresponding form

$$P(j, x_1 \mid \zeta; \boldsymbol{\theta}) = P(j \mid \zeta; \boldsymbol{\theta})\, g(x_1 \mid j, \zeta; \boldsymbol{\theta}) \tag{3.109}$$

where $P(j \mid \zeta; \boldsymbol{\theta})$ is the usual discrete choice probability and $g(x_1 \mid j, \zeta; \boldsymbol{\theta})$ is the p.d.f. of x_1 conditional on ζ and the chosen tenure.

Under exogenous sampling, the log-likelihood function for a sample of N households will have the general form

$$\log L(\boldsymbol{\theta}) = K + \sum_{i=1}^{3} \sum_{n \in S_i} \log P(i, x_1 \mid \zeta_n; \boldsymbol{\theta}) \tag{3.110}$$

$$= K + \sum_{i=1}^{3} \sum_{n \in S_i} \log P(i \mid \zeta_n; \boldsymbol{\theta}) + \sum_{i=1} \sum_{n \in S_i} \log g(x_{n1} \mid i, \zeta_n; \boldsymbol{\theta}) \tag{3.111}$$

where $S_j = \{n | j_n = j\}$.

The first two components of (3.111) constitute the log-likelihood function for a standard discrete choice problem, and, if there were no information on x_1 in the sample, it is this which would yield our estimator. The third component of (3.111) arises from the availability of information on x_1, and, since the same preferences underlie both aspects of the demand decision, its presence leads to gains in the efficiency with which the preference parameters can be estimated.

We now turn to the economic theory that generates the terms $P(j | \zeta_n; \theta)$ and $g(x_{n1} | j, \zeta_n; \theta)$. In formal terms, the household's problem is the following:

$$\max_{j, x_1, x_2} [V(x_1, x_2, x_3^j; \beta) \mid p_1^j x_1 + p_2 x_2 \leqslant y, j \in \{1,2,3\}] \tag{3.112}$$

which can be split into two stages:

$$\max_j \{\max_{x_1, x_2} [V(x_1, x_2, x_3^j; \beta) \mid p_1^j x_1 + p_2 x_2 \leqslant y] | j \in \{1,2,3\}\}$$

$$= \max_j \left[H\left(\frac{p_1^j}{y}, \frac{p_2}{y}; x_3^j, \beta\right) \middle| j \in \{1,2,3\} \right] \tag{3.113}$$

where the function $H(.; x_3, \beta)$ is the conditional indirect utility function, indicating the highest indifference curve attainable at any price–income configuration, when x_3 is held constant, for a household with preference parameter β. The value of x_1 that solves this inner optimization problem is given by Roy's identity:

$$\tilde{x}_1 = \frac{\partial H / \partial p_1^j}{\partial H / \partial y}. \tag{3.114}$$

Thus, when a suitable stochastic specification is adopted, the expression (3.113), which involves a comparison of indirect utilities, will be the theoretical basis of the term $P(j | \zeta; \theta)$, while expression (3.114) will generate the p.d.f. $g(x_1 | j, \zeta; \theta)$. Together, these are used to construct the log-likelihood (3.111).

Following King, assume first that price is the only observable attribute of the three tenures relevant to the choice; this leaves the unobservable x_3^j to be represented by an alternative-specific additive random error ϵ_n^j. Assume (somewhat unrealistically) that the form of the deterministic component of utility is invariant to both j and $\mathbf{z}$, and that it takes the translog form

$$-\log H(\mathbf{p}/y) = \alpha_1 q_1 + \alpha_2 q_2 + \alpha_3 q_1^2 + \alpha_4 q_2^2 + \alpha_5 q_1 q_2 \tag{3.115}$$

where $q_i = \log(p_i/y)$ for $i = 1,2$, and $\alpha_1, \ldots, \alpha_5$ are constant parameters. For convenience, preferences are further assumed to be homothetic. For this to be the case, three restrictions must be satisfied: $\alpha_1 + \alpha_2 = 1$, $2\alpha_3 + \alpha_5 = 0$ and $2\alpha_4 + \alpha_5 = 0$. After imposing these on (3.115), we have the following expression for the random log utility yielded to household n by the jth tenure:

$$u_n^j = \alpha_1 \log(p_{n1}^j/p_{n2}) + \alpha_3[\log(p_{n1}^j/p_{n2})]^2 + \log(y_n/p_{n2}) + \epsilon_n^j$$
$$= \zeta_{n0} + \alpha'\zeta_n^j + \epsilon_n^j \tag{3.116}$$

where $\zeta_{n0} = \log(y_n/p_{n2})$, $\zeta_n^{j'} = (\log(p_{n1}^j/p_{n2}), [\log(p_{n1}^j/p_{n2})]^2)$ and $\alpha' = (\alpha_1, \alpha_3)$. The ϵ_n^j are assumed to have independent normal distributions, with var($\epsilon_n^1 = 1$, var$(\epsilon_n^2) = \sigma_2^2$ and var$(\epsilon_n^3) = \sigma_3^2$, leading to a restricted multinomial probit form for the discrete choice probabilities $P(j\,|\,\zeta_n; \theta)$.

Under homotheticity, $\partial \log H/\partial \log y = 1$ (see section 1.5), and this allows Roy's identity (3.113) to be rewritten in terms of logarithmic derivatives:

$$\tilde{x}_1^j = -\left(\frac{\partial \log H}{\partial \log p_1^j}\right)\frac{y}{p_1^j} \tag{3.117}$$

where $\tilde{x}_1^j$ denotes the optimal consumption of housing services in tenure j. If $H(.)$ is given by (3.115), this leads to the following housing demand function for household n:

$$x_{n1}^j = \alpha_1(y_n/p_{n1}^j) + 2\alpha_3(y_n/p_{n1}^j)\log(p_{n1}^j/p_{n2}) + \nu_n$$
$$= \alpha'\xi_n^j + \nu_n \tag{3.118}$$

where $\alpha' = (\alpha_1, \alpha_3)$ and $\xi_n^{j'} = (y_n/p_{n1}^j, 2(y_n/p_{n1}^j)\log(p_{n1}^j/p_{n2}))$. Note that this is a hypothetical demand function, since it generates demand for a fixed tenure type j, not necessarily identical with the actual tenure choice.

The disturbance term ν_n has been added to represent random inefficiencies in the execution of the optimal decision. If we assume that ν_n has an $N(0, \sigma_\nu^2)$ distribution conditional on ζ_n and is independent of ϵ_n^1, ϵ_n^2 and ϵ_n^3, then the conditional density $g(x_{n1}\,|\,j, \zeta_n; \theta)$ has a normal form and depends on j only through its mean:

$$g(x_{n1}\,|\,j, \zeta_n; \theta) = \sigma_\nu^{-1}\varphi[(x_{n1} - \alpha'\xi_n^j)/\sigma_\nu]. \tag{3.119}$$

Substituting this into the log-likelihood function (3.111) gives

$$\log L = K^* + \sum_{i=1}^{3}\sum_{n\in S_i}\log P(i\,|\,\zeta_n; \theta) - N\log\sigma_\nu$$
$$-\frac{1}{2}\sum_{i=1}^{m}\sum_{n\in S_i}\left[\frac{(x_{n1} - \alpha'\xi_n^j)^2}{\sigma_\nu^2}\right] \tag{3.120}$$

where K^* is the new constant $K - (N\log 2\pi)/2$. This log-likelihood must be maximized numerically with respect to the parameter vector $\theta' = (\alpha_1, \alpha_3, \sigma_\nu)$.

Thus, provided we are prepared to assume that the random error associated with the continuous decision is independent of the random errors involved in the discrete decision, the log-likelihood function takes a particularly simple form: it is the sum of the log-likelihoods that would be relevant to the two problems taken separately. Unfortunately, it is rather hard to defend this independence assumption. A person who is (randomly) disposed towards an expensive form of housing tenure might be expected to be similarly disposed towards higher spending on housing within that tenure, for instance. Such considerations suggest that it is unwise to rule out the possibility of some correlation between ν and the ϵ^j. King's study does attempt to provide a link between the two parts of the stochastic specification by adopting the random coefficient approach of Hausman and Wise (1978). He assumes that $\boldsymbol{\alpha}$ varies between households, and that this variable coefficient vector $\boldsymbol{\alpha}_n$ has a bivariate normal distribution with mean vector $\boldsymbol{\alpha}$ (which is common to all individuals) and diagonal covariance matrix Σ_α. Thus, for household n,

$$u_n^j = \zeta_{n0} + \boldsymbol{\alpha}'\zeta_n^j + \epsilon_n^{*j} \tag{3.121}$$

and

$$x_{n1}^j = \boldsymbol{\alpha}'\boldsymbol{\xi}_n^j + \nu_n^{*j} \tag{3.122}$$

where $\epsilon_n^{*j} = \epsilon_n^j + (\boldsymbol{\alpha}_n - \boldsymbol{\alpha})'\zeta_n^j$ and $\nu_n^{*j} = \nu_n + (\boldsymbol{\alpha}_n - \boldsymbol{\alpha})'\boldsymbol{\xi}_n^j$. These new composite error terms have $\boldsymbol{\alpha}_n - \boldsymbol{\alpha}$ in common, and therefore ν_n^{*j} is correlated with each of the ϵ_n^{*j}, even if ν_n and ϵ_n^j are independent (in fact $\text{cov}(\nu_n^{*j}, \epsilon_n^{*j}) = \boldsymbol{\xi}_n^{j\prime}\Sigma_\alpha\zeta_n^j$). This implies that housing demand x_{n1} is not independent of the choice of tenure and the conditional density $g(x_{n1}|j_n, \zeta_n)$ is not identical with the density of $x_{n1}|\zeta_n$. Thus a log-likelihood similar to (3.120) (which King used) is incorrect in this case.

The derivation of the correct log-likelihood function is straightforward, although it is rather more awkward from the computational point of view. It is easiest in this case to use the basic form (3.110), where the joint probability density/mass function $P(j, x_1 | \zeta_n; \boldsymbol{\theta})$ is derived from the structure (3.121) and (3.122). As an example, consider the form of $P(j=1, x_1 | \zeta_n; \boldsymbol{\theta})$. Similar expressions will arise for $j=2$ or $j=3$.

Tenure 1 is chosen if and only if $\nu_{n2}^1 = u_n^1 - u_n^2$ and $\nu_{n3}^1 = u_n^1 - u_n^3$ are both positive. Therefore the distribution $P(j=1, x_1 | \zeta_n; \boldsymbol{\theta})$ can be derived from the trivariate normal distribution of x_{n1}^1, ν_{n2}^1 and ν_{n3}^1. From (3.121)–(3.122) and the definitions of ν_n^{*1} and the ϵ_n^{*j}, this has mean vector

$$\boldsymbol{\mu}_n = \begin{pmatrix} \boldsymbol{\alpha}'\boldsymbol{\xi}_n^1 \\ \boldsymbol{\alpha}'(\zeta_n^1 - \zeta_n^2) \\ \boldsymbol{\alpha}'(\zeta_n^1 - \zeta_n^3) \end{pmatrix} \tag{3.123}$$

and covariance matrix

$$\Sigma_n = \begin{pmatrix} \sigma_\nu^2 + \boldsymbol{\xi}_n^{1\prime}\Sigma_\alpha\boldsymbol{\xi}_n^1 & \text{-----} & \text{-----} \\ \boldsymbol{\delta}_n^{2\prime}\Sigma_\alpha\boldsymbol{\xi}_n^1 & 1 + \sigma_2^2 + \boldsymbol{\delta}_n^{2\prime}\Sigma_\alpha\boldsymbol{\delta}_n^2 & \text{-----} \\ \boldsymbol{\delta}_n^{3\prime}\Sigma_\alpha\boldsymbol{\xi}_n^1 & 1 + \boldsymbol{\delta}_n^{3\prime}\Sigma_\alpha\boldsymbol{\delta}_n^2 & 1 + \sigma_3^2 + \boldsymbol{\delta}_n^{3\prime}\Sigma_\alpha\boldsymbol{\delta}_n^3 \end{pmatrix} \tag{3.124}$$

where $\boldsymbol{\delta}_n^i = \zeta_n^1 - \zeta_n^j$ for $i=2, 3$.

If we denote the joint p.d.f. of this distribution by $\varphi(x_1, \nu_2, \nu_3; \boldsymbol{\mu}_n, \Sigma_n)$, the discrete–continuous probability density/mass function $P(j=1, x_{n1} | \zeta_n; \theta)$ is obtained by integrating over the region corresponding to the selection of alternative 1 (i.e. $v_2 > 0$, $v_3 > 0$):

$$P(j=1, x_{n1} | \zeta_n; \theta) = \int_0^\infty \int_0^\infty \varphi(x_1, v_2, v_3; \mu_n, \Sigma_n)\, dv_3\, dv_2. \tag{3.125}$$

Thus, each of the N terms in the log-likelihood function requires two-dimensional integration of a trivariate normal density with a rather complicated covariance structure. Although this is quite a substantial computational problem, it is feasible with modern computing resources (see appendix 3 section A3.5). Duncan (1980) discusses this type of likelihood function in the context of a discrete–continuous production model. As a less demanding alternative, one can develop models based on extreme value or GEV distributions (see Dubin and McFadden, 1984, and Hanemann, 1984, for examples for this approach).

It should be borne in mind when applying this type of model that its economic foundation implies a very stringent restriction: that the parameters underlying the discrete decision are identical with those underlying the continuous decision. A test of this restriction is desirable, since it amounts to a test of the correctness of specification of the economic model. Following King, one could allow α to take different values in the two components of the model, by generalizing (3.123) to

$$\mu_n = \begin{pmatrix} \alpha' \xi_n^1 \\ \alpha^{*\prime}(\zeta_n^1 - \zeta_n^2) \\ \alpha^{*\prime}(\zeta_n^1 - \zeta_n^3) \end{pmatrix}. \tag{3.126}$$

This expression leads to a more general form for the density $\varphi(x_1, v_2, v_3; \mu_n, \Sigma_n)$, yielding a generalized log-likelihood function that must now be maximized with respect to the expanded parameter set $\{\alpha, \alpha^*, \Sigma_\alpha, \sigma_2, \sigma_3\}$. The hypothesis $\alpha^* = \alpha$ is then tested by means of a likelihood ratio test.

King's study in fact departs from the model described here. King reduces the dimension of the integrals involved by observing that the relative cost of tenure 3 (private sector rental) is very high, making it extremely unlikely that any individual will choose tenure 3. This restricts the demand side of the model to a choice between tenures 1 and 2 (so that only univariate probabilities are required), and the model is extended to allow rationing which might force households into a suboptimal tenure. We postpone consideration of these supply-side intrusions until chapter 7.

Further reading

The most prolific contributor to the econometric literature on discrete choice analysis is Daniel McFadden. His survey articles (1973, 1976a, 1984) provide a very good account of the development of the field and its relationship with similar work in psychology. Other useful references are Amemiya (1981; 1986, chapter 9) and Maddala (1983, chapters 2 and 3). Amemiya (1986, chapter 9) contains a very thorough discussion of the problems of statistical inference, particularly in the case of choice-based sampling. Chow (1983) provides a good introduction to the logit, probit and GEV techniques for the case of linear utilities.

An interesting extension of the basic model of discrete choice is to the case where observations are available on each individual's complete rank ordering of the alternatives, not merely the identity of the optimal choice. Beggs, Cardell and Hausman (1981) discuss the problem of modelling discrete choice behaviour using this type of data, and base their analysis on the multinomial logit model. So far, there are few economic surveys that provide data of this kind.

4

Zero expenditures and corner solutions

We are nothing; less than nothing; and dreams.
We are only what might have been.

Charles Lamb

Aggregate econometric analysis usually treats behavioural responses as the outcome of a smooth process: for instance, if a small reduction is made in the price of a good, we anticipate a corresponding marginal increase in aggregate demand. However, this apparently smooth variability is largely the result of the aggregation process since, beneath the surface of the aggregate, individuals may make non-marginal changes, switching from one behavioural regime to another. In reality, there are two distinct types of response involved. At the intensive margin, consumers of the good are prompted to consume marginally more; this sort of response is amenable to analysis with familiar regression-like methods. However, there is also an extensive margin, where people who were not previously consumers of the good are now induced to purchase it in positive quantities; this type of response is a discrete switch, rather than a smooth adjustment, and cannot be analysed satisfactorily with such simple techniques. Appropriate statistical methods must be based on composite distributions, containing a discrete probability mass at zero, representing non-consumption, and a continuous density function, describing positive consumption. Another important application is in labour supply analysis, where the two regimes are employment (positive hours of work) and non-participation in the labour force (zero hours of work).

These different behavioural regimes, and the transitions between them, are often of considerable interest in themselves. For instance, the recent growth in the rate of female labour force participation is a social development of profound significance; individual's decisions on whether or not to smoke and drink are important because of their consequences for health. These are not mere technical difficulties caused by the non-negativity of our dependent variable, and it is important to derive both types of response from an adequate economic model.

In this chapter, we are concerned with the ways in which zero observations can arise, and we shall examine the models and associated estimation techniques to which these phenomena give rise. The statistical theory involved here rests heavily on the notions of truncation and censoring of probability distributions, which are examined in detail in appendix 2. Section 4.1 deals with the Tobit, or censored regression, model, which is the most widely used method of dealing with samples containing observations limited in this way. Section 4.2 deals with extensions of this technique to the case of a system of behavioural equations, considering particularly the question of their consistency with the budget constraint. Section 4.3 examines models which are more in the spirit of standard economic theory, treating zero expenditures as the consequence of a corner solution to the conventional utility maximization problem. Section 4.4 deals with the difficulties raised by the fact that observed zero expenditures may reflect the short duration of the consumers' expenditure survey rather than true non-consumption. Finally, section 4.5 examines the econometric methods available in cases where price or wage information is unavailable for non-purchasing individuals.

4.1 Single-equation censored regression (Tobit) models

The most common technique for estimating a structural model that is subject to a non-negativity constraint is based on the censored regression model. This was first introduced to the econometric literature by Tobin (1958), and has become widely known as the Tobit ('Tobin's probit') model. It is essentially nothing more than an *ad hoc* modification of the regression model, allowing it to be used in cases where there are observations 'piled up' at a limiting value (usually zero), and has no convincing foundation in behavioural theory. For concreteness, we shall discuss it in the context of a cross-section demand function for a single commodity, although it can, of course, be used in many other fields (see Amemiya, 1986, chapter 10, for a survey).

The typical derivation of a model of demand proceeds as follows. The maximization of a non-stochastic utility function subject to the usual budget constraint leads to a demand function of the form

$$\tilde{x} = \tilde{x}[\mathbf{p}/y; \boldsymbol{\beta}(\mathbf{z})] \tag{4.1}$$

where we have omitted the subscript identifying the good concerned, and where $\mathbf{p}$ is the vector of prices of all goods, y is total expenditure and $\boldsymbol{\beta}(\mathbf{z})$ is a vector of unobserved preference parameters which are non-stochastic functions of a vector of observed personal characteristics $\mathbf{z}$. We shall initially follow common practice and assume that the function $\tilde{x}(.)$ is expressible as a linear function of observable variables constructed from **p**, y and **z**. If these variables are arranged in a vector ζ, then the demand function can be expressed

$$\tilde{x} = \gamma'\zeta \tag{4.2}$$

where γ is the vector of demand parameters. Note that our discussion of this model would apply equally to a demand function expressed in budget share or expenditure form, and that the common practice of assuming that prices do not vary between individuals in the cross-section also allows some models that are non-linear in prices to be treated as linear - all quasi-homothetic models, for instance.

If we use a conventional regression model, the observed demands are generated as

$$x_n = \gamma'\zeta_n + \epsilon_n \tag{4.3}$$

where ϵ_n is a random disturbance with mean zero and variance σ^2. Assuming normality, (4.3) could be expressed more succinctly as

$$x_n \,|\, \zeta_n \sim N(\gamma'\zeta_n, \sigma^2). \tag{4.4}$$

This normal distribution is untenable for two reasons. Since it has an unlimited range, it implies a non-zero probability that x_n takes an absurd negative value. One could retain the regression format and solve this non-negativity problem by assuming (say) a log-normal, rather than normal, conditional distribution for x_n, but this fails to solve a second problem: that any purely continuous density function implies that an observed value for x_n of exactly zero will occur with a probability that is essentially zero. This flatly contradicts most samples, since there is usually a substantial group of non-consumers of any particular good, certainly at low levels of aggregation over commodities.

Thus, the typical sample looks something like the configuration illustrated in figure 4.1, and we must specify a conditional distribution for x_n which could generate such a sample. The conventional regression model is not appropriate, since the deviations from the true demand relation are obviously not identically distributed with zero means conditional on ζ_n. Instead, we require a distribution that has both a continuous part to generate the positive observations and a discrete part to generate the zero observations. A convenient way of constructing such a distribution is to posit a fictional *censoring process*, which converts a purely continuous regression model into a mixed discrete–continuous model of the required kind. Define a latent variable x_n^*, which is conditionally normally distributed,

$$x_n^* \,|\, \zeta_n \sim N(\gamma'\zeta_n, \sigma^2) \tag{4.5}$$

and assume that the observed demand x_n is generated as follows:

$$x_n = \max(x_n^*, 0). \tag{4.6}$$

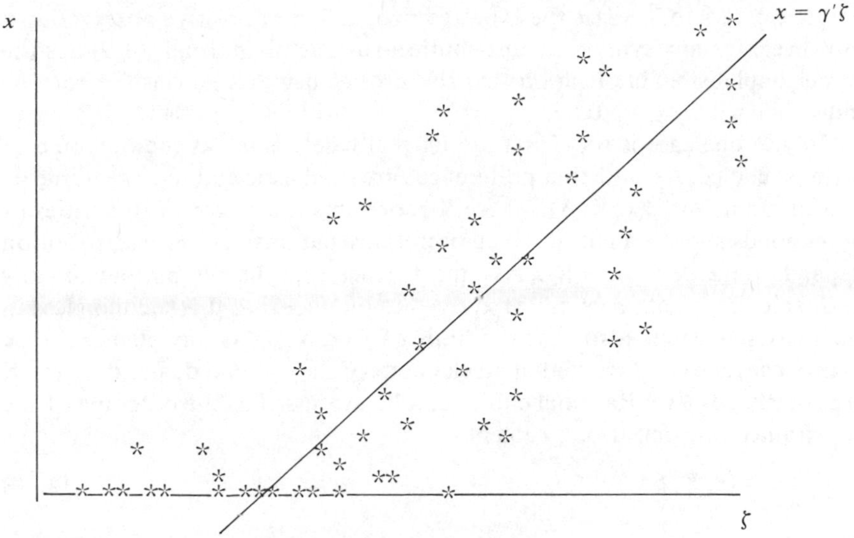

Figure 4.1 A censored sample.

Thus, whenever x_n^* is negative, it is replaced by zero; otherwise it is observed directly. This mechanism implies a conditional lower censored normal distribution for x_n, or, more concisely, $x_n | \zeta_n \sim \text{LCN}(\gamma'\zeta_n, \sigma^2, 0)$. This and other censored distributions are examined in appendix 2.

The interpretation of the coefficients of a Tobit model differs somewhat from that of an ordinary regression model, where the coefficient vector is expressible as $\partial E(x|\zeta)/\partial\zeta$ and thus indicates the expected response of x to a small change in ζ. The distribution (4.5) and (4.6) has mean vector (see appendix 2, equation (A2.31))

$$E(x_n | \zeta_n) = \gamma'\zeta_n \Phi(\gamma'\zeta_n/\sigma) + \sigma\varphi(\gamma'\zeta_n/\sigma). \tag{4.7}$$

Upon differentiation with respect to ζ_n,

$$\partial E(x_n | \zeta_n)/\partial\zeta_n = \gamma\, \Phi(\gamma'\zeta_n/\sigma) \tag{4.8}$$

which is the coefficient vector γ multiplied by the conditional probability that x_n is positive. This merely reflects the fact that marginal variations in ζ_n have no effect on individuals for whom x_n^* remains negative.

There is an obvious objection to our interpretation of the censored regression model. The observed demand x_n, is subject to an inviolable non-negativity restriction, and yet the term $\tilde{x}_n = \gamma'\zeta_n$, which is the economic model's prediction of x_n, may be negative for some observations. This is obviously unreasonable, and perhaps suggests the *ad hoc* modification

$$x_n | \zeta_n \sim \text{LCN}[\max(\gamma'\zeta_n, 0), \sigma^2, 0] \tag{4.9}$$

whose effect is to increase the expected proportion of positive observations. However, for any symmetric distribution such as the normal, (4.9) has the rather implausible implication that the probability of a zero is 0.5 for any individual with $\gamma'\zeta_n \leqslant 0$.

Only in one case is the Tobit model really defensible as the outcome of rational choice. Assume that preferences are stochastic and representable by a utility function $V(x, \mathbf{X}; \beta)$, where $\mathbf{X}$ represents the vector of quantities of other goods and β is an unobserved preference parameter whose distribution depends on $\mathbf{z}$ in some way. Assume further that $V(.)$ is mathematically definable for negative values of x, despite the fact that it is meaningless in such cases. Assume also that the limit of $V(x, \mathbf{X}; \beta)$ as any element of $\mathbf{X}$ approaches zero is $-\infty$, so that all elements of the optimal demand vector $\tilde{\mathbf{X}}$ are strictly positive. Rational choice can be expressed as the outcome of the constrained maximization problem

$$\max_{x, \mathbf{X}} V(x, \mathbf{X}; \beta) \tag{4.10}$$

subject to

$$px + \mathbf{P}'\mathbf{X} = y \tag{4.11}$$

where p and $\mathbf{P}$ are the prices corresponding to x and $\mathbf{X}$ and

$$x \geqslant 0. \tag{4.12}$$

In this special case, the solution to the non-negativity constrained problem (4.10)–(4.12) can be expressed in terms of the analogous unconstrained problem. Define $\check{\mathbf{x}}(p, \mathbf{P}, y; \beta)$ as the solution to (4.10) and (4.11) without the non-negativity constraint (4.12). Then the true demand $\tilde{x}$ can be written

$$\tilde{x}(p, \mathbf{P}, y; \beta) = \max[\check{\mathbf{x}}(p, \mathbf{P}, y; \beta), 0]. \tag{4.13}$$

Now suppose that the preference model is such that the expectation of $\check{\mathbf{x}}$, conditional on p, $\mathbf{P}$, y and $\mathbf{z}$, is of the linear form $\gamma'\zeta$, where ζ is some observable transformation of those variables. Define ϵ as $\check{\mathbf{x}} - \gamma'\zeta$, and assume β to have a distribution such that $\epsilon | \zeta \sim N(0, \sigma^2)$. Under these conditions, the non-negative constrained demand (4.11) is of the Tobit form (4.5) and (4.6). The further assumption that there are no errors in the implementation of this optimal demand, $x_n \equiv \tilde{x}_n$, then implies that observed demand is also of Tobit form.

As a justification of the Tobit model, this is rather far-fetched. If there is more than a single good that may be at a corner, or if demand is non-linear, or if there are other sources of randomness in observed behaviour, the data will be generated by a more complicated distribution than that implied by the Tobit model. It is usually best to regard censored regression as nothing more than a simple and convenient approximation; because of its practical advantages, we shall continue to make extensive use of it, both here and in later chapters.

4.1.1 Least-squares regression in censored samples

Before examining estimators which are appropriate to the censored regression model (4.5) and (4.6), it is useful to consider the consequences of inappropriate use of ordinary regression techniques in the context of a censored model. There are two regressions that one might reasonably compute: one with zero observations excluded, the other using the whole sample.

If the zeros are excluded, then the regression is computed from a truncated sample, with the sample inclusion rule being $x_n > 0$. This is a special case of the truncated sampling that was discussed in chapter 2, section 2.5.1. There it was shown that the conventional regression estimator is always biased.

On the other hand, if the zeros are retained in the sample, the vector of regression coefficients is

$$\hat{\gamma} = \left[\sum_{n=1}^{N} \zeta_n \zeta_n' \right]^{-1} \left[\sum_{n=1}^{N} \zeta_n x_n \right] \tag{4.14}$$

and this has bias

$$E(\hat{\gamma} - \gamma) = E \left\{ \left(\sum_n \zeta_n \zeta_n' \right)^{-1} \left[\sum_n \zeta_n E(x_n - \gamma' \zeta_n \mid \zeta_n) \right] \right\}. \tag{4.15}$$

Manipulation of equation (A2.31) of appendix 2 gives the conditional mean of the censored random variable $x_n - \gamma'\zeta_n$ as

$$E(x_n - \gamma'\zeta_n \mid \zeta_n) = \sigma[1 - \Phi(b_n)]\,[\lambda(b_n) - b_n] \tag{4.16}$$

where $b_n = \gamma'\zeta_n/\sigma$ and $\lambda(.)$ is the inverse of Mills' ratio. Note that (4.16) is a negative decreasing function of b_n. It it thus correlated with ζ_n, and the bias in $\hat{\gamma}$ is non-zero even in large samples. The reason is clear from the two-variable example of figure 4.1: zero observations tend to occur more frequently to the left of the true regression line than to the right, and if the true slope coefficient is positive these zeros pull the fitted regression line towards the horizontal, imparting a downward bias to the slope coefficient. In the multi-regressor case, it is not possible to give a definite sign to the bias on each coefficient.

4.1.2 Maximum likelihood estimation

The Tobit model leads to a conditional LCN($\gamma'\zeta_n$, σ^2, 0) distribution for x_n, which (see appendix 2, section A2.2) has a mixed discrete-continuous distribution of the form

$$\begin{aligned} \Pr(x_n = 0 \mid \zeta_n) &= \Pr(x_n^* \leqslant 0 \mid \zeta_n) \\ &= \Phi[(0 - \gamma'\zeta_n)/\sigma] \\ &= 1 - \Phi(b_n) \end{aligned} \tag{4.17}$$

$$g(x_n|\zeta_n) = \sigma^{-1}\varphi[(x_n-\gamma'\zeta_n)/\sigma]$$
$$= (2\pi)^{-½}\,\sigma^{-1}\exp[-(x_n-\gamma'\zeta_n)^2/2\sigma^2]. \qquad (4.18)$$

Under exogenous sampling, this leads to a log-likelihood

$$\log L(\gamma,\sigma) = K - N^+\log\sigma - \frac{1}{2\sigma^2}\sum_+ (x_n-\gamma'\zeta_n)^2 + \sum_0 \log[1-\Phi(b_n)] \qquad (4.19)$$

where K is an inessential constant, N^+ is the number of positive observations on x, and the suffixes + and 0 denote summation over the observations for which x is respectively positive and zero. The gradient expressions for log L are

$$\frac{\partial \log L}{\partial\gamma} = \frac{1}{\sigma^2}\sum_0 (x_n-\gamma'\zeta_n)\zeta_n - \frac{1}{\sigma}\sum_+ \lambda(b_n)\zeta_n \qquad (4.20)$$

and

$$\frac{\partial \log L}{\partial\sigma^2} = \frac{1}{2\sigma^4}\sum_+ (x_n-\gamma'\zeta_n)^2 - \frac{N^+}{2\sigma^2} + \frac{1}{2\sigma^3}\sum_0 \lambda(b_n)b_n. \qquad (4.21)$$

Equating $\partial \log L/\partial\gamma$ to zero, the ML estimator $\hat{\gamma}$ can be characterized as follows:

$$\hat{\gamma} = \left[\sum_+ \zeta_n\zeta_n'\right]^{-1}\left[\sum_+ \zeta_n x_n - \hat{\sigma}\sum_0 \lambda(\hat{b}_n)\zeta_n\right] \qquad (4.22)$$

where $\hat{b}_n$ is the value $\hat{\gamma}'\zeta_n/\hat{\sigma}$. Equating $\partial \log L/\partial\sigma^2 + \frac{1}{2}\gamma'(\partial \log L/\partial\gamma)/\sigma^2$ to zero yields

$$\hat{\sigma}^2 = \frac{1}{N^+}\sum_0 [(x_n-\hat{\gamma}'\zeta_n)^2 + (x_n-\hat{\gamma}'\zeta_n)\gamma'\zeta_n]$$
$$= \frac{1}{N^+}\sum_0 (x_n-\hat{\gamma}'\zeta_n)_n. \qquad (4.23)$$

These expressions are non-linear in $\hat{\gamma}$ and $\hat{\sigma}$ and cannot be solved analytically; many iterative algorithms are available, however.

Equation (4.22) expresses the ML estimator of γ as a simple modification of least squares applied to the subsample of observations for which $x_n > 0$. Another way of looking at (4.22) is that it is the regression on ζ_n of a variable x_n^+ equal to x_n when $x_n > 0$ and to an estimate of $E(x_n|x_n \leqslant 0, \zeta_n) = \gamma'\zeta_n - \sigma\lambda(b_n)$ when $x_n = 0$. The normal equations which must be solved to obtain this regression are

$$\sum_{n=1}^{N} \zeta_n\zeta_n'\,\hat{\gamma} = \sum_{n=1}^{N} \zeta_n x_n^+ \qquad (4.24)$$

or

$$\left[\sum_{0} \zeta_n \zeta_n' + \sum_{+} \zeta_n \zeta_n' \right] \hat{\gamma} = \sum_{+} \zeta_n x_n + \sum_{0} \zeta_n \zeta_n' \hat{\gamma} - \hat{\sigma} \sum_{0} \zeta_n \lambda(\hat{b}_n) \quad (4.25)$$

which is clearly equivalent to (4.22). This interpretation of the ML first-order condition is exploited for computational purposes by the widely used EM algorithm of Dempster, Laird and Rubin (1977).

It is easily shown (see Olsen, 1978) that log L is globally concave in the transformed parameters $\delta = \gamma/\sigma$ and $\omega = \sigma^{-1}$, and thus log L can have at most one maximum with respect to β and σ^2. Together with the truncated regression model and the binary probit and logit models, this is one of the few examples of an interatively calculated estimator for which there is no possibility of multiple local optima. The asymptotic properties of $\hat{\gamma}$ and $\hat{\sigma}^2$ have been examined by Amemiya (1973).

An alternative to the Tobit ML estimator is to truncate the sample by discarding all zero observations and then to use the conditional ML estimator appropriate to the truncated regression model (this is discussed in chapter 2, section 2.5.1, the relevant conditional log-likelihood being (2.71)). It is obviously inefficient to throw away the information contained in the zero observations, and the truncated estimator seems also to be less robust against heteroscedasticity and non-normality (see the results of Arabmazar and Schmidt, 1981, 1982, and the discussion of table A2.1 in appendix 2). However, it is not always possible to use the full-sample Tobit technique: limited observations are frequently discarded, as part of the sample design, before the data are made available to the econometrician. Very often, the vector ζ_n is only partly observable when $x_n = 0$: for instance, in a model of labour supply, a major explanatory variable is the individual's market wage rate, which is unobserved for people who are not employed. To cope with the latter problem in a correct manner greatly increases the econometric burden, and in such cases it is often sensible to resort to sample truncation instead. The problems raised by partial observability of ζ_n are discussed further in section 4.5.

4.1.3 Two-step estimation

The log-likelihood function for the Tobit model is usually very well behaved and easy to maximize numerically. Thus there is little need for alternatives to the ML estimator. However, other estimators have been proposed and are sometimes used in applied work; both have been discussed in a slightly different context in chapter 2.

The Heckman (1976) estimator uses the binary probit technique applied to the zero demand/positive demand dichotomy to generate an initial estimate of the vector $\delta = \sigma^{-1}\gamma$. This is then used to form a new explanatory variable $\hat{\lambda}_n^* = \lambda^*(\hat{\delta}'\zeta_n)$, where $\lambda^*(.)$ is the complement of Mills' ratio $\varphi(.)/\Phi(.)$. At the second stage, x_n is regressed on ζ_n and $\hat{\lambda}_n^*$, using only the observations for which $x_n > 0$. The inclusion of the additional variable compensates for the increased conditional mean of x_n in the truncated sample and thus yields consistent estimates of γ and σ^2.

Amemiya (1973) also proposes a two-step estimator which is based on the truncated sample. The first step involves a regression of x_n on ζ_n and higher powers of the variables in ζ_n to form the fitted value $\hat{x}_n$, and then the use of $\hat{x}_n \zeta_n$ as a vector of instrumental variables in a regression of x_n^2 on $x_n \zeta_n$.

Since these are inefficient estimators, and since the Tobit likelihood function is generally well behaved, there seems little advantage to be gained in using these techniques. Their real value lies in the more elaborate extensions of this model. Maddala (1983, chapter 8) is a good reference.

4.1.4 Extensions of the Tobit model

We have so far considered only a very simple form of the censored regression model. Many extensions are possible. The more important of these include multiple and variable censoring thresholds, non-linearity of the regression function, non-normality of the underlying distributional form and heteroscedasticity of the conditional distribution of x_n^*.

Multiple and variable censoring thresholds In some practical examples, the observed dependent variable x_n may be subject to more than a single bound. For example, in a study of a rationed market, x_n must be non-negative and must not exceed the rationed quantity. In some cases, these limits will vary from individual to individual, and they may not be observable. As an example of this more general setting, consider the following two-limit model:

$$x_n^* \mid \zeta_n \sim N(\gamma' \zeta_n, \sigma^2) \tag{4.26}$$

$$x_n = c_{n1} \qquad \text{if } x_n^* \leqslant c_{n1} \tag{4.27}$$

$$x_n = x_n^* \qquad \text{if } c_{n1} < x_n^* < c_{n2} \tag{4.28}$$

$$x_n = c_{n2} \qquad \text{if } x_n^* \geqslant c_{n2}. \tag{4.29}$$

This generates a conditional distribution for x_n that has two discrete components: $\Pr(x_n = c_{n1} \mid \zeta_n, c_{n1}, c_{n2}) = \Phi(c_{n1}^*)$ and $\Pr(x_n = c_{n2} \mid \zeta_n, c_{n1}, c_{n2}) = 1 - \Phi(c_{n2}^*)$, where $c_{ni}^* (i = 1, 2)$ is the standardized limit $(c_{ni} - \gamma' \zeta_n)/\sigma$. Thus the log-likelihood conditional on ζ, c_1 and c_2 is

$$\log L(\gamma, \sigma^2) = K + \sum_{x_n = c_{n1}} \log \Phi(c_{n1}^*) + \sum_{x_n = c_{n2}} \log[1 - \Phi(c_{n2}^*)]$$
$$- N^* \log \sigma - \frac{1}{2\sigma^2} \sum_{x_n \in I_n} (x_n - \gamma' \zeta_n)^2 \tag{4.30}$$

where K is an inessential constant, I_n is the open interval (c_{n1}, c_{n2}) and N^* is the number of observations for which $x_n \in I_n$. Similar modifications of the truncated ML estimator and the Heckman and Amemiya two-step estimators are also straightforward.

Censoring limits are not always observable. For instance, an individual buying a house may be limited in his or her decision by the size of mortgage that potential lenders are prepared to advance. In such circumstances, it would not usually be possible to make direct observations of these lending limits, at least for people who are not at their limit. This suggests a stochastic model for the c_{ni} (in the case of the two-limit model, the stochastic specification would have to be such that the upper and lower limits cannot cross over). There would be two possible cases to consider. We may have information on whether or not each observation is at its limit, in which case the censoring threshold is recorded as the value of x_n for some observations. However, it may be unknown whether or not any given household is at its limit, and in such cases it can be extremely difficult to achieve good estimates of both the primary model and the model of the ration. Discussion of these problems is postponed until chapter 7.

Another common application of the model with random censoring threshold is in the study of labour supply. In this case, x_n is interpreted as the individual's wage, and the single random lower limit c_n as the reservation wage (the lowest wage at which the person is prepared to work at all). Examples of this approach can be found in the work of Gronau (1974) and Nelson (1977). This application has the special feature that when the limit is binding, and x_n and c_n are equal, their common value is unobserved. This contrasts with the more usual case where x_n is observed as c_n whenever the limit is binding. Both forms of censoring are distinguished from sample truncation by the fact that ζ_n and ξ_n are observed in all circumstances. We shall postpone discussion of this type of model to section 4.5, where a more general model is used. This exploits the fact that, when the wage exceeds the reservation wage, the individual enters the labour force, and labour supply then also becomes observable.

Non-linearity We have so far made the assumption that the regression function underlying the Tobit model is a linear form. In fact the character of the various Tobit estimators is not greatly altered if this expression is replaced by a smooth, well-behaved non-linear function $\tilde{x}(\zeta_n; \gamma)$. The effect of this non-linearity is to replace the term $\gamma'\zeta_n$ by $\tilde{x}(\zeta_n; \gamma)$ in the likelihood function (4.19), and the term ζ_n (representing the derivative of $\gamma'\zeta_n$ with respect to γ) by $\partial\tilde{x}(\zeta_n; \gamma)/\partial\gamma$ in the corresponding gradient expression (4.20). The chief complication is that the log-likelihood can no longer be assumed to have a unique maximum, and computation may therefore be a little more difficult. There is no longer any advantage to be gained from the Heckman and Amemiya two-step estimators, since they become considerably more complicated, with iterative non-linear estimation necessary in the second stage of both.

Heteroscedasticity Heteroscedasticity is always likely to be a serious problem in cross-section econometrics, and the problem is particularly serious for the Tobit and related models since the ML estimator is generally inconsistent if the conditional variance of x_n^* is not a constant. Arabmazar and Schmidt (1981) give some examples of these asymptotic biases. There is no difficulty in generalizing the censored regression ML estimator to cope with heteroscedasticity if a parametric model of the conditional variance can be specified. Suppose that $\text{var}(x_n^* \mid \zeta_n)$ is known to have the form $v_n = v(\zeta_n; \sigma)$, where σ is a vector of parameters and $v(.)$ is a known positive function. For instance, v_n might be specified as the square of the regression function $\gamma'\zeta_n$. Under normality, the generalized log-likelihood is

$$\log L(\gamma, \sigma) = K + \sum_0 \log\left(1 - \Phi\left\{\frac{\gamma'\zeta_n}{[v(\zeta_n; \sigma)]^{1/2}}\right\}\right) - \frac{1}{2}\sum_+ \log v(\zeta_n; \sigma)$$
$$- \frac{1}{2}\sum_+ \frac{(x_n - \gamma'\zeta_n)^2}{v(\zeta_n; \sigma)}. \qquad (4.31)$$

Once again, the main impact of this generalization is to increase the computational burden somewhat: $\log L$ is a little more complicated now and can no longer be assumed to possess a single maximum.

Semi-parametric methods which do not require the specification of a particular functional form for the conditional variance are a major topic of current theoretical research, although so far these methods have played little part in applied work.

Non-normality Most applications of the censored regression model are based on the assumption of normality, which we have maintained above. However, there is no compelling reason for this, and the consequences of departures from normality can be severe. If the underlying distributional form is mis-specified, then the estimator than maximizes the incorrect normal log-likelihood is generally inconsistent; Arabmazar and Schmidt (1982) give some examples of the consequences.

These considerations have led some researchers to estimate models based on censored distributions other than the normal, particularly distributions exhibiting skewness. Most observable economic variables are highly skewed in the cross-section, and there seems no obvious reason why the unobserved effects represented by the disturbance term ϵ_n should not also be highly skewed.

There is no difficulty in defining the ML estimator of the Tobit model for an arbitrary non-normal distribution of known parametric form. The conditional normality assumption (4.5) can be replaced by an assumed specific form for the conditional p.d.f. of x_n:

$$g(x_n \mid \zeta_n) = \sigma_1^{-1}\psi\left[\frac{x_n - \gamma'\zeta_n}{\sigma_1}; \sigma_2\right] \tag{4.32}$$

where σ_1 is a scale parameter, σ_2 is a vector containing any additional parameters necessary to define $g(x_n \mid \zeta_n)$, and $\psi(.)$ is a known standardized p.d.f. If the c.d.f. corresponding to $\psi(.)$ is denoted $\Psi(.)$, then the log-likelihood function is

$$\begin{aligned}\log L(\gamma, \sigma_1, \sigma_2) = & \sum_0 \log \Psi\left[\frac{-\gamma'\zeta_n}{\sigma_1}; \sigma_2\right] - N^+ \log \sigma_1 \\ & + \sum_+ \log \Psi\left[\frac{x_n - \gamma'\zeta_n}{\sigma_1}; \sigma_2\right].\end{aligned} \tag{4.33}$$

Applied examples of this parametric approach are the study by Amemiya and Boskin (1974) of the duration of welfare dependency, based on a two-parameter log-normal distribution, and the use by Atkinson, Gomulka and Stern (1984b) of the gamma distribution in their analysis of the demand for alcoholic drink. Both of these forms imply a distribution for x_n with a limited range which depends on the estimated parameters. This raises difficulties for asymptotic sampling theory, and, in Amemiya and Boskin's case, some computational problems also.

Perhaps a more promising approach is to use semi-parametric methods that do not require the specification of a parametric form for $\psi(.)$. This is the subject of much current research, and many alternative techniques have been proposed. A natural extension of the conventional ML technique is the semi-parametric ML estimator (SPMLE), which treats the log-likelihood (4.33) as a functional, to be maximized with respect to both $\boldsymbol{\theta} = (\gamma, \sigma_1)$ and the functional form $\Psi(.)$. For given $\boldsymbol{\theta}$, the solution to this problem in the calculus of variations is the product-limit estimator of Kaplan and Meier (1958), $\hat{\Psi}(.; \boldsymbol{\theta})$, which is a step function with jumps at points corresponding to the standardized residuals $(x_n - \gamma'\zeta_n)/\sigma_1$ for the uncensored observations. Buckley and James (1979) propose a version of the EM algorithm based on $\hat{\Psi}(.; \boldsymbol{\theta})$. However, the basic form of the EM algorithm relies on the assumption that $\Psi(.)$ belongs to the exponential family, and as a result the Buckley–James procedure has not been shown to have any desirable asymptotic properties in the general semi-parametric setting.

The great problem with the SPMLE is that the concentrated log-likelihood obtained by substituting $\hat{\Psi}(.; \boldsymbol{\theta})$ into $\log L$ yields an objective function that is not continuous in $\boldsymbol{\theta}$. This causes both computational and theoretical problems, and some form of smoothing is required. Duncan (1986) approximates $\psi(.)$ with a continuous linear spline function and assumes that the number of linear segments is allowed to increase with the sample size. Fernandez (1986) proposes Fourier smoothing of $\hat{\Psi}(.; \boldsymbol{\theta})$. Both these techniques can be shown to be consistent although no asymptotic approximation to their sampling distributions is available.

Perhaps the only semi-parametric estimators which are yet suitable for widespread applied use are the least absolute deviations (LAD) and symmetrically censored least-squares (SCLS) estimators of Powell (1984, 1986). The LAD estimator is based on the conditional median function of x_n:

$$m(\gamma; \zeta_n) = \max(\gamma'\zeta_n, 0) \tag{4.34}$$

which is particularly convenient since it coincides with the median function of the underlying x_n^* whenever $x_n > 0$. Powell (1984) uses the following estimation criterion:

$$\min_{\gamma} \sum_{n=1}^{N} |x_n - \max(\gamma'\zeta_n, 0)| \tag{4.35}$$

He proves that this LAD estimator is $\sqrt{N}$ consistent and derives the asymptotic approximation to its sampling distribution. Although the covariance matrix of this distribution depends on the specific form of $\Psi(.)$, Powell is able to construct a consistent non-parametric estimator which can be used to generate asymptotic standard errors. The LAD estimator is therefore entirely operational; moreover, it is extremely robust – the median function (4.34) remains correctly specified in heteroscedastic models (and also in the modified Tobit structure (4.9)). Its principal drawback is the difficulty of the computational problem (4.35), and there is some evidence that it has rather poor small-sample efficiency. Simulations presented by Fernandez (1986) and others suggest that alternative approaches, particularly the SPMLE, may have much smaller sampling variances.

Powell's (1986) SCLS estimator is less robust, since it requires the additional assumption that the conditional distribution of x_n^* is symmetric. Under symmetry, the censoring from below can be compensated by suitable censoring from above. This involves the definition of a new variable $x_n^+ = \min(x_n, 2\gamma'\zeta_n)$, which has a distribution symmetric about $\gamma'\zeta_n$ provided that $\gamma'\zeta_n > 0$. This suggests that we use an estimator that solves the following modification of the least-squares normal equations:

$$\sum_{n \in N(\gamma)} [x_n^+ - \gamma'\zeta_n]\zeta_n = 0 \tag{4.36}$$

where $N(\gamma) = \{n | \gamma'\zeta_n > 0\}$. Since the solution to (4.36) may not be unique, Powell defines the estimator as the solution to a corresponding minimization problem:

$$\min_{\gamma} \sum_{n=1}^{N} [x_n - \max(\tfrac{1}{2}x_n, \gamma'\zeta_n)]^2 + \sum_{n \in N^*(\gamma)} [(\tfrac{1}{2}x_n)^2 - \max(\gamma'\zeta_n, 0)^2] \tag{4.37}$$

where $N^*(\gamma) = \{n | x_n > 2\gamma'\zeta_n\}$. This estimator is something of a compromise: it is not efficient in general, but it is robust to heteroscedasticity. It is also robust to non-normality, but only within the class of symmetric distributions: it does not retain its consistency in the presence of skewness, for instance. Its main advantage is that (4.37) is a relatively simple computational problem and that its limiting distribution is known.

4.1.5 Tobit specification tests

In all applied work, it is extremely important to test the main assumptions underlying the estimation technique in use, and this is especially so for techniques such as Tobit analysis, where even the basic property of consistency is sensitive to heteroscedasticity and non-normality. Fortunately, there is now a wide range of Tobit specification tests available to the applied researcher.

General specification tests The most accessible general-purpose Tobit specification test is that of Nelson (1981), which amounts to a formal comparison of the sample moment $\tilde{\mathbf{m}} = N^{-1}\Sigma\zeta_n x_n$ with an estimate of the corresponding population moment implied by the Tobit model: $\hat{\mathbf{m}} = \hat{\sigma}N^{-1}\Sigma\zeta_n[\hat{b}_n\Phi(\hat{b}_n) + \varphi(\hat{b}_n)]$. This leads to a statistic of the form

$$Z = (\hat{\mathbf{m}} - \tilde{\mathbf{m}})'[\tilde{\mathbf{V}} - \hat{\mathbf{V}}]^{-1}(\hat{\mathbf{m}} - \tilde{\mathbf{m}}) \tag{4.38}$$

where $\tilde{\mathbf{V}}$ and $\hat{\mathbf{V}}$ are the asymptotic approximations to the sampling covariance matrices of $\tilde{\mathbf{m}}$ and $\hat{\mathbf{m}}$. Expressions for these are given by Nelson (1981). Under the null hypothesis of correct specification, the statistic Z is asymptotically χ^2, with degrees of freedom equal to the number of parameters in γ; in the presence of mis-specification (particularly omitted variables, heteroscedasticity and non-normality), Z is $O_p(N)$ and will yield a significant result if the sample is sufficiently large.

There are other approaches to specification testing. Lee and Maddala (1985) constructed a Lagrange multiplier (LM) test against a generalized version of Cragg's (1971) double-hurdle model (see section 4.3.2 below); see also Blundell and Meghir (1987). Newey (1987) proposes a test based on a direct comparison of the ML Tobit estimator and the more robust SCLS estimator of Powell (1986); this test can be viewed as a combined test for heteroscedasticity and (certain forms of) non-normality.

Testing for non-normality Although general specification tests should detect any departure from normality in a sufficiently large sample, better power can be expected from a test specifically designed for the purpose. Bera, Jarque and Lee (1984) propose a test of the normality assumption against the alternative hypothesis that the true distributional form belongs to the Pearson family (see Johnson and Kotz, 1970, chapter 12). Imposing a zero mean, this is the class of distributions with p.d.f. $g(\epsilon)$ satisfying the following differential equation:

$$\frac{\mathrm{d}\log g(\epsilon)}{\mathrm{d}\epsilon} = \frac{\alpha_1 - \epsilon}{\alpha_0 - \alpha_1\epsilon + \alpha_2\epsilon^2} \tag{4.39}$$

which has the general solution

$$g(\epsilon) = K(\alpha_0, \alpha_1, \alpha_2)\exp[q(\epsilon; \alpha_0, \alpha_1, \alpha_2)] \tag{4.40}$$

where $q(\epsilon)$ is the indefinite integral of the right-hand side of (4.39) and K is the factor required to make $g(\epsilon)$ integrate to unity. This family has as special cases the beta ($\alpha_2 = -\alpha_1$) and gamma ($\alpha_2 = 0$) distributions, among others, and thus provides a wide class of alternative forms. Note, however, that this is not a convenient form to use for the estimation of a generalized Tobit model: since the function $q(\epsilon)$ cannot be expressed in closed form, the evaluation of $g(\epsilon)$ and its associated c.d.f. as components of the general non-normal log-likelihood function (4.33) would be very difficult. However, Bera, Jarque and Lee use the LM testing principle which does not require the estimation of the model under the alternative hypothesis.

The construction of the test statistic is somewhat complicated, and we shall not present it here; the reader is referred to Bera, Jarque and Lee (1984) for the details. However, the statistic does have a simple interpretation as a criterion based on the third and fourth conditional moments of ϵ_n. Under normality, the following restrictions hold:

$$E(\epsilon_n^{*3} \mid \zeta_n) = \sigma^3(b_n^2 + 2)\varphi(b_n) \tag{4.41}$$

$$E(\epsilon_n^{*4} \mid \zeta_n) = \sigma^4[3\Phi(b_n) - 3b_n\varphi(b_n) - b_n^3\varphi(b_n)] \tag{4.42}$$

where $\epsilon_n^* = x_n - \gamma'\zeta_n$ if $x_n > 0$ and $\epsilon_n^* = 0$ otherwise. The test statistic is interpretable as a direct comparison of estimates of the right-hand sides of these relations with the sample analogues of the left-hand sides computed from the Tobit residuals. Under normality, the statistic is asymptotically χ^2 with two degrees of freedom.

Testing for heteroscedasticity Jarque (1981) and Lee and Maddala (1985) have derived the LM test statistic for heteroscedasticity in the case where the conditional variance of ϵ_n is believed to depend on an observed vector of exogenous variables ξ_n. The form of the relationship is immaterial. Again, the details of the test are too complicated to be presented here, but it has a simple interpretation as a quadratic form in the vector $\Sigma\xi_n v_n$, where v_n is equal to the standardized squared residual $(x_n - \hat{\gamma}'\zeta_n)^2/\hat{\sigma}^2 - 1$ for positive observations and to the quantity $\hat{b}_n\lambda(\hat{b}_n)$, which is an estimate of $E(\epsilon^2/\sigma^2 \mid x_n = 0) - 1$, for censored observations.

Testing exogeneity There is often reason to suspect that one or more of the variables appearing in the vector ζ_n is endogenous. A common example arises in the analysis of labour supply of married women. Most investigators develop their econometric models under the assumption that the earnings of the woman's husband are exogenous to her labour supply decision, but it is quite conceivable that husbands' and wives' labour supply behaviour is the outcome of a single joint decision, implying the endogeneity of husbands' earnings. Smith and Blundell (1986) have constructed a particularly simple test of the exogeneity assumption, based on the following model:

$$x_n^* = \gamma'\zeta_n + \epsilon_n \tag{4.43}$$

$$x_n = \max(x_n^*, 0) \tag{4.44}$$

$$\zeta_{n1} = \delta'\xi_n + \nu_n \tag{4.45}$$

where the first element of the vector ζ_n is the husband's income ζ_{n1} and where ξ_n is a vector of exogenous variables believed to determine ζ_{n1}. This is not a particularly convincing model in its own right: it does not respect the non-negativity of ζ_{n1} for instance; nevertheless, it is probably adequate for the limited purposes of specification testing.

Under normality, the random disturbance ϵ_n can always be written as

$$\epsilon_n = \psi\nu_n + \upsilon_n \tag{4.46}$$

where ψ is a constant and υ_n is a normal variate independent of ν_n. Thus (4.43) can be re-expressed as

$$x_n^* = \gamma'\zeta_n + \psi\nu_n + \upsilon_n. \tag{4.47}$$

Equations (4.44) and (4.47) represent a new Tobit model, conditioned on ν_n. The exogeneity hypothesis states that the two sources of randomness, ϵ_n and ν_n, are mutually independent; a necessary and sufficient condition for this is the restriction $\psi = 0$.

Smith and Blundell show that the following simple procedure provides an asymptotically optimal test of H_0: $\psi = 0$:

i regress ζ_{n1} on ξ_n and form the residual $\hat{\nu}_n = \zeta_{n1} - \hat{\delta}'\xi_n$;

ii substitute the residual $\hat{\nu}_n$ for ν_n in the conditional Tobit model (4.47) and estimate it using the conventional Tobit ML estimator. Conduct a t test of the restriction $\psi = 0$.

4.2 Systems of censored regression equations

Applied work frequently requires the simultaneous analysis of a number of variables, some or all of which may be subject to non-negativity constraints. For example, one might wish to model the allocation of consumers' expenditure among a group of goods or, in an analysis of labour supply, one might attempt to model the simultaneous determination of the husband's and wife's labour supply.

The obvious extension of the single-equation Tobit model to the case of q equations is the following structure:

$$\mathbf{x}_n^* \mid \zeta_n \sim N(\tilde{\mathbf{x}}_n, \Sigma) \tag{4.48}$$

$$x_{ni} = \max(x^*_{ni}, 0) \qquad i=1, \ldots, q \tag{4.49}$$

$$\tilde{\mathbf{x}}_n = \tilde{\mathbf{x}}(\zeta_n; \gamma) \tag{4.50}$$

where $\mathbf{x}^*_n$ is the unobserved $q \times 1$ vector $(x^*_{n1} \ldots x^*_{nq})'$ and $\tilde{\mathbf{x}}_n$ is a vector of non-stochastic functions (linear or non-linear) of a $k \times 1$ vector of explanatory variables ζ_n and a fixed parameter vector γ. Σ is a $q \times q$ covariance matrix, and the observed endogenous variables are $\mathbf{x}_n = (x_{n1} \ldots x_{nq})'$. The variables x_{ni} might be expenditures on individual goods by family n (possibly expressed in the form of quantities purchased or budget shares) or, say, hours of labour supplied by different members of family n. Many other applications are possible.

4.2.1 Estimation without a budget constraint

To begin with, we shall discuss the estimation of system (4.48)–(4.50) treated as an arbitrary group of correlated censored regression equations, without considering the problems raised by the existence of a budget constraint.

Denote the conditional joint p.d.f. and c.d.f. of the latent vector $\mathbf{x}^*_n$ by $g_*(.\,|\,\zeta_n;\gamma, \Sigma)$ and $G_*(.\,|\,\zeta_n; \gamma, \Sigma)$. In general, an observed $\mathbf{x}_n$ vector will contain r positive demands (r may be equal to q) and $q-r$ zero demands. Re-order the goods so that the non-zero demands occur first. Then the mixed discrete-continuous distribution of $\mathbf{x}_n|\,\zeta_n$ is found by integrating $g_*(.)$ over the region $\mathbf{x}^*_i < 0, i=r+1, \ldots, q$. This leads to the following function, which is a continuous p.d.f. with respect to the positive $\mathbf{x}_i$ and a discrete probability mass function with respect to the zero $\mathbf{x}_i$:

$$f(x_{n1} \ldots x_{nq}\,|\,\zeta_n; \gamma, \Sigma)$$

$$= \int_{-\infty}^{0} \cdots \int_{-\infty}^{0} g_*(x_{n1} \ldots x_{nr}, \mathbf{x}^*_{r+1} \ldots \mathbf{x}^*_q\,|\,\zeta_n; \gamma, \Sigma) \prod_{j=r+1}^{q} \mathrm{d}\mathbf{x}^*_j \tag{4.51}$$

$$= G_*^{1 \cdots r}(x_{n1} \ldots x_{nq}\,|\,\zeta_n; \gamma, \Sigma) \tag{4.52}$$

where the superscripts denote partial differentiation with respect to the first r arguments of $G_*(.)$. The log-likelihood function for this model is the sum of the logarithm of an expression of the form (4.51) or (4.52) for each individual in the sample.

If we make the normality assumption (4.48), then $G_*(.) = \Phi(.; \tilde{\mathbf{x}}_n, \Sigma)$ and $g_*(.) = \varphi(.; \tilde{\mathbf{x}}_n, \Sigma)$, and computation of $f(x_{n1} \ldots x_{nq}\,|\,\zeta_n; \gamma, \Sigma)$ requires the evaluation of a partially integrated multivariate normal p.d.f., since the c.d.f. $\Phi(.; \tilde{\mathbf{x}}_n, \Sigma)$ is not available in closed form (see appendix 3, section A3.5). Consequently, if the sample were to include individuals who are non-purchasers of a significant number of goods, this joint ML approach to estimation would be computationally expensive at best, and probably infeasible. These computational problems could certainly be avoided by estimating the system one equation at a time, applying the Tobit technique to each equation in turn; however, such an estimator is inefficient since it fails to take account of the intercorrelations between the equations. Moreover, the cross-equation symmetry restrictions which are implied by any underlying choice theory cannot be imposed if single equation methods are used.

An alternative would be to use some multivariate distribution other than the normal, and the GEV class of distributions (see appendix 1) seems particularly useful in this context. There are two ways one might proceed: either assume that $\mathbf{x}_n^*$ itself has a GEV distribution or, alternatively, assume that each x_{ni}^* is the difference of two GEV variates, and thus has a pseudo-logistic distribution. So far, this approach has seen little use in applied work.

4.2.2 Estimation in the presence of a budget constraint

When behavioural models are derived from the theory of optimal choice, their constituent equations will satisfy a budget constraint of the form

$$\sum p_{ni} x_{ni} = y_n \tag{4.53}$$

where p_{ni} is the price of good i and y_n is the constraint on total spending.

In the conventional theory of demand, the requirement that expenditures on individual goods should sum to total expenditure implies cross-equation restrictions both on the demand functions and on the error covariance matrix (see Deaton and Muellbauer, 1980a, chapter 1). These adding-up restrictions cause little difficulty, since they merely imply that any one of the demand equations can be deduced from the others and can therefore be ignored. In the case of multi-equation censored models, however, the presence of a budget constraint is more problematic. The difficulty is that no parametric restrictions on the underlying distribution (4.48) are sufficient to guarantee that (4.53) is satisfied. Even if the latent demands $\mathbf{x}_n^*$ satisfy the budget constraint, the Tobit formulation is inconsistent with the presence of a budget identity in the data. There are three obvious solutions to this problem.

One possibility is to treat one of the expenditure categories as a residual with no specific demand equation of its own. Thus, the full model would be specified as a system of $q-1$ Tobit equations together with an identity defining the residual expenditure category as the difference between y_n and spending on the first $q-1$ categories. The implications of such a model will not be invariant to the choice of the residual good, but if there is a natural choice for this residual, then this is an appealing model, both plausible and simple. The main drawback is that predicted expenditure on the residual good may be negative for some individuals, although this should happen with negligible probability if the residual category is always relatively large.

Two alternative approaches are to follow Wales and Woodland (1983) in modifying the Tobit model to enforce adding-up, or to argue that the resource constraint used in the individual's planning is an *ex ante* rather than *ex post* concept which is respected by planned expenditures but not necessarily by observed expenditures. These two approaches are motivated by different interpretations of the random error on each equation. If a random error represents unmeasured factors which are unknown to the econometrician but known (and therefore taken account of in the planning of expenditures) to the individual, then observed behaviour corresponds to perfect execution of an apparently random plan, which, since it is rational, must respect the budget constraint. On the other hand, if random errors represent, at least in part, accidents, whims or mistakes, then observed expenditures embody some random departures from optimal plans. If individual expenditures do depart from their planned values, there is no obvious reason why their sum should not depart from planned total expenditure, provided that there is some residual component of the overall household budget, such as savings, which is able to absorb these random errors.

The Wales–Woodland generalized Tobit system In order to impose adding-up, Wales and Woodland (1983) modify system (4.48)–(4.50) by introducing an intermediate step which involves a second set of latent expenditures. Their specification is most conveniently phrased in terms of budget shares, rather than quantities. If the ith share is $s_{ni} = p_{ni}x_{ni}/y_n$, the budget constraint is $\Sigma\, s_{ni} = 1$, and this is imposed in the following manner:

$$\mathbf{s}_n^* \sim N(\tilde{\mathbf{s}}_n, \Sigma) \tag{4.54}$$

$$s_{ni}^{**} = \max(s_{ni}^*, 0) \qquad i = 1, \ldots, q \tag{4.55}$$

$$s_{ni} = \frac{s_{ni}^{**}}{\sum_{j=1}^{q} s_{nj}^{**}} \qquad i = 1, \ldots, q \tag{4.56}$$

where $\tilde{\mathbf{s}}_n$ is the vector with ith element $p_{ni}\tilde{x}_{ni}/y_n$.

In this model, (4.54) plays the role of the demand system, with the latent shares satisfying adding-up restrictions implying that $\Sigma\, s_{ni}^* = 1$ and $\mathbf{e}'\Sigma\mathbf{e} = 0$, where $\mathbf{e}' = (1 \ldots 1)$. Equations (4.55) then impose non-negativity on the resulting demands,.and equations (4.56) constitute an arbitrary device for re-imposing adding-up on the censored demands.

This model gives rise to formidable computational problems. Consider a typical outcome for the expenditure vector $\mathbf{s}_n$; suppose that r of these expenditures are positive, and re-order the goods so that these occur first. Since the budget constraint holds with probability one, the budget shares have a degenerate joint distribution, so any one of them may be dropped as redundant; make this the last of the zeros, s_{nq}. The expression given by Wales and Woodland for the probability density/mass of $(s_{n1}, \ldots, s_{nr}, 0, \ldots, 0)$ is

$$f(s_{n1} \ldots s_{nq} | \zeta_n; \gamma, \Sigma)$$

$$= \int_{s_{n1}}^{\infty} \int_{\alpha_{nr+1}}^{0} \ldots \int_{\alpha_{nq-1}}^{0} g_* \left(s_1^*, \frac{s_1^* s_{n2}}{s_{n1}}, \ldots, \frac{s_1^* s_{nr}}{s_{n1}}, s_{r+1}^*, \ldots, s_{q-1}^* | \zeta_n; \gamma, \Sigma \right)$$

$$J(\mathrm{s}_n)\, \mathrm{d}s_{q-1}^* \ldots \mathrm{d}s_{r+1}^*\, \mathrm{d}s_1^* \tag{4.57}$$

where $g_*(.)$ is now the p.d.f. of $s_{n1}^* \ldots s_{nq-1}^* | \zeta_n$, $J(\mathrm{s}_n)$ is the constant $[1 + (s_{n2}/s_{n1})^2 + \ldots + (s_{nr}/s_{n1})^2]^{1/2}$ and the $\alpha_{nr+1}, \ldots, \alpha_{nq-1}$ are given by

$$\alpha_{nr+1} = 1 - \sum_{i=1}^{r} s_1^* \frac{s_{ni}}{s_{n1}} \tag{4.58}$$

$$\alpha_{nj} = \alpha_{nr+1} - \sum_{i=r+1}^{j-1} s_i^* \qquad j = r+2, \ldots, q-1.$$

Thus the inner limits of integration depend on the outer variable of integration, s_1^*. For applications in which individuals are non-purchasers of more than two or three goods, the evaluation of the expressions (4.57), which are the components of the likelihood function, will be very costly. However, using the multivariate normal form for $g_*(.)$, Wales and Woodland do manage to estimate a three-good version of the linear expenditure system.

***Ex ante* budget constraints** If we interpret the budget constraint as an *ex ante* concept relevant to the formation of the consumer's expenditure plans, rather than an *ex post* concept reflected in the data as an identity, then the adding-up problem is removed. However, if individual expenditures no longer necessarily sum to the value of planned total expenditure y_n^*, then the latter variable cannot be measured as the sum of individual expenditures and is therefore unobservable. Much depends on whether or not the optimal demands are linear in y_n^*. If so, preferences are quasi-homothetic, and it is possible to write

$$\tilde{\mathbf{x}}_n = \boldsymbol{\alpha}_{n0} + \boldsymbol{\alpha}_{n1} y_n^* \tag{4.59}$$

where $\boldsymbol{\alpha}_{n0} = \boldsymbol{\alpha}_0(\zeta_n; \gamma)$ and $\boldsymbol{\alpha}_{n1} = \boldsymbol{\alpha}_1(\zeta_n; \gamma)$ are vectors of functions independent of y_n^* but homogeneous of degree 0 and -1 respectively in prices. Without further information, nothing can be done with this model – we require an additional relationship determining y_n^*. In the case of a complete demand system, this relationship will be a cross-section consumption function; if we are dealing with a branch of the budget, it will be a group expenditure function, presumably derived from the maximization of a separable utility function (see Deaton and Muellbauer, 1980a, chapter 5). Again, for simplicity, assume linearity and normality, and write this additional relation in the form

$$y_n^* \sim N(\delta'\xi_n, \sigma_y^2) \tag{4.60}$$

where ξ_n is a vector of explanatory variables and δ is the corresponding coefficient vector. Relations (4.48), (4.59) and (4.60) imply

$$\mathbf{x}_n^* | \alpha_{n0}, \alpha_{n1}, \xi_n \sim N(\mu_n, \Omega_n) \tag{4.61}$$

where

$$\mu_n = \alpha_{n0} + \alpha_{n1}\delta'\xi_n \tag{4.62}$$

$$\Omega_n = \Sigma + \sigma_y^2 \alpha_{n1}\alpha_{n1}' + \alpha_{n1}\sigma_{xy}' + \sigma_{xy}\alpha_{n1s}' \tag{4.63}$$

and σ_{xy} is the $q \times 1$ vector of covariances between the random components of $\mathbf{x}_n^*$ and y_n^*. Equations (4.48) and (4.49) and (4.61)–(4.63) together constitute the observable model, which is a non-linear Tobit system, conforming to the assumptions made in section 4.2.1 above. Consequently the same estimation methods can be applied. Note, however, that the estimation problem is much more demanding, since μ_n and Ω_n are considerably more complicated than $\tilde{\mathbf{x}}_n$ and Σ, and since one is attempting to estimate simultaneously the parameters of both a demand system and a consumption function.

It should also be observed that this approach, treating the budget constraint as *ex ante* and planned total expenditure as a latent variable, still requires that, somewhere in the consumer's budget, there is a residual element which absorbs random disturbances. This element permits the relevant observable accounting identity to be satisfied while the planning constraint is randomly violated. However, there is a sense in which the behaviour represented by this model is irrational: the budget identity is not respected on average, since the structure based on (4.61)–(4.63) does not satisfy $E(\Sigma p_{ni}x_{ni} | y_n^*) = y_n^*$. This is a consequence of the *ad hoc* nature of the Tobit specification.

This treatment of the budget constraint is not easy to use if the optimal demands (4.50) are non-linear in y_n^*, since it is only possible to derive an analogue of (4.61) by integrating the joint distribution of $\tilde{\mathbf{x}}_n, y_n^*$ with respect to y_n^*. This rarely leads to a convenient closed-form expression for the resulting non-normal marginal distribution for $\tilde{\mathbf{x}}_n$.

4.3 Corner solutions

The models of the previous two sections arise from a very superficial view of the problem of zero expenditures. They merely take a non-stochastic demand model and generate a corresponding statistical structure by introducing additive random disturbances distributed in such a way that observed expenditures are necessarily non-negative. Thus non-negativity is imposed, almost as an afterthought, as a feature of the stochastic specification. This approach is not very satisfactory, since it provides no convincing explanation of the process generating zeros.

At least three mechanisms are possible. A person may make no purchase of a particular good simply because the observation period is too short - most people consume the services of furniture, for instance, yet few purchases are observed in the one- or two-week period of the typical family expenditure enquiry. Models based on this interpretation are discussed in the next section. Alternatively, observed zeros may be purely involuntary - labour supply may be zero because an individual cannot find a job, for instance. Problems of this kind are discussed in chapter 7. A third interpretation, which we now examine, is that the observed zero is not an observational artifice and that it is the outcome of a completely free choice. In other words, at current prices and current income, the individual will never consume the good, and is therefore at a corner solution to his or her utility maximization problem.

It should be emphasized that this interpretation is probably mistaken for most goods for most individuals in demand analysis. Very few people never consume any particular good (except at the most detailed level of disaggregation), and it is usually more plausible to treat zeros as a consequence of the short duration of most expenditure surveys. However, some people are vegetarians or non-smokers, for instance, and true corner solutions can never be ruled out completely.

Most applied models are derived without explicit consideration of non-negativity conditions. If one simply takes such a model and uses a Tobit-type stochastic specification to impose non-negativity, the result is unsatisfactory, since it allows the absurd possibility that a rational person might plan to consume negative amounts of a good but be forced by purely random factors to do otherwise. In section 4.1.4 we considered an *ad hoc* solution in the case of a single equation by modelling planned expenditure as $\max(\gamma'\zeta_n, 0)$ rather than $\gamma'\zeta_n$ itself, and, of course, this simple solution could be extended to the case of a system of equations. However, optimal demands are not generally of this simple piecewise-linear form, and it is certainly never optimal to impose non-negativity by conducting an unconstrained planning exercise and replacing negative demands with zeros. Indeed, there is not necessarily even a one-to-one correspondence between negative unconstrained demands and zero constrained demands. Only in the trivial case where only one particular good can be at a corner is it certain that a good with a negative unconstrained demand will not be consumed when non-negativity constraints are imposed explicitly. We must therefore derive applied models which have non-negativity constraints built into their structure, and we do this separately for two cases: non-random and random preferences.

4.3.1 Non-random preferences

If an individual has preferences represented by a utility function $V(\mathbf{x}; \beta_n)$, where β_n is a vector of unobserved preference parameters, then the problem of non-negative choice is

$$\max_{\mathbf{x}} \; V(\mathbf{x}; \beta_n) \tag{4.64}$$

subject to

$$x_i \geqslant 0 \qquad i=1,\ldots,q \tag{4.65}$$

$$\sum_{i=1}^{q} p_{ni}x_i = y_n. \tag{4.66}$$

The solution is a system of optimal demands:

$$\tilde{x}_{ni} = \tilde{x}_i(\mathbf{p}_n, y_n; \beta_n) \qquad i=1,\ldots,q \tag{4.67}$$

which are not smooth functions of $\mathbf{p}_n$ and y_n: they are kinked at all points at which any good is on the margin of being consumed. However, apart from this special feature (which introduces isolated discontinuities into the gradient of the corresponding likelihood function), there is in principle no difficulty in using the methods of the previous section, with the vector of unconstrained demand functions $\tilde{\mathbf{x}}_n$ in (4.48) replaced by this vector of constrained optimal demand functions. Under this approach, individual heterogeneity would be introduced by specifying β_n as a vector of non-stochastic functions of observed personal characteristics $\mathbf{z}_n$.

However, there is a major practical difficulty here. The mathematical programming problem (4.64)–(4.66) must be solved for each individual at every evaluation of the likelihood function, and this may be a formidable task, since the standard computational algorithms (see, for instance, Luenberger, 1972 are iterative. This problem would not arise if we could assume that $x_{ni} = 0$ always implies $\tilde{x}_{ni} = 0$, since $\tilde{\mathbf{x}}_n$ could then be found very simply by maximizing utility with respect to the consumed goods only. However, the existence of random differences between $\tilde{\mathbf{x}}_n$ and the observed vector $\mathbf{x}_n$ means that the observed and optimal patterns of non-consumption may differ, and thus it is necessary to solve the full problem (4.64)–(4.66) in order to compute $\tilde{\mathbf{x}}_n$. The combined complexities of the non-linear programming problem and the multivariate Tobit likelihood function have prevented the use of this type of model in applied work.

An alternative approach is to assume that there are no deviations from optimal behaviour but that preferences contain random elements – factors that are known to, and taken account of by, the individual but which are not observable. Under this interpretation, β_n is a random vector. There are several ways in which these random preference models can be specified.

4.3.2 Discrete random preference regimes: the double-hurdle model

Most empirical corner solution models treat non-consumption (or non-participation in the labour force) as a strictly economic decision – goods are not consumed when they are too expensive; people do not work unless they are adequately paid. However, non-consumption is often the result of a social, psychological or ethical distinction, and is unconnected with the levels of prices and income. Most vegetarians do not abstain from eating meat because it is too expensive; many non-smokers would not smoke even if tobacco were a free good; teetotallers often have some ethical basis for their non-consumption. This suggests that, in many cases, zero expenditures may be best modelled by means of a discrete shift variable altering the nature of individual preferences. Consider the case of a single good x_{n1} (tobacco, say) whose demand is subject to this type of distinction, with $\mathbf{x}_{n2}$ representing the vector of quantities of all other goods. Their prices are p_{n1} and $\mathbf{p}_{n2}$, and total expenditure is y_n. We model the distinction between those who would never smoke under any circumstances and those for whom smoking or non-smoking is an economic decision by means of a discrete preference parameter β_{n1}. We assume this to be generated by a probit structure:

$$\Pr(\beta_{n1}=1\,|\,\mathbf{z}_n) = \Phi(\alpha'\mathbf{z}_n) \tag{4.68}$$

$$\Pr(\beta_{n2}=0\,|\,\mathbf{z}_n) = 1 - \Phi(\alpha'\mathbf{z}_n) \tag{4.69}$$

where $\mathbf{z}_n$ is a vector of observed personal characteristics which are relevant to the distinction and $\boldsymbol{\alpha}$ is the corresponding parameter vector.

Consider the following preference relation:

$$u = \beta_{n1} V(x_1, \mathbf{x}_2; \boldsymbol{\beta}_{n2}) + (1-\beta_{n1}) V^*(\mathbf{x}_2; \boldsymbol{\beta}_{n2}) \tag{4.70}$$

where $\boldsymbol{\beta}_{n2}$ contains all other preference parameters besides β_{n1} and $V(.; \boldsymbol{\beta}_2)$ and $V^*(.; \boldsymbol{\beta}_2)$ are the utility functions representing the preferences of (potential) smokers and non-smokers respectively. For non-smokers ($\beta_{n1}=0$), x_1 does not affect preferences and, since $p_{n1}>0$, the rational decision is $\tilde{x}_{n1} = 0$. For actual and potential smokers ($\beta_{n1}=1$), $\tilde{x}_{n1}$ is the solution to the problem

$$\max_{x_1, x_2} V(x_1, \mathbf{x}_2; \boldsymbol{\beta}_{n2}) \tag{4.71}$$

subject to

$$p_{n1}x_{n1} + \mathbf{p}_{n2}'\mathbf{x}_{n2} = y_n \tag{4.72}$$

and the non-negativity conditions $x_{n1} \geqslant 0$, $\mathbf{x}_{n2} \geqslant 0$. For simplicity, assume that the solution for x_{n1} can be adequately approximated by a Tobit model:

$$x_{n1}\,|\,\beta_{n1}=1, \zeta_n \sim \text{LCN}(\gamma'\zeta_n, \sigma^2, 0). \tag{4.73}$$

The resulting statistical structure is thus a mixture of a censored and degenerate distribution,

with probability $\Phi(\alpha'\mathbf{z}_n)$

$$x_{n1}\,|\,\zeta_n \sim \text{LCN}(\gamma'\zeta_n, \sigma^2, 0)$$

with probability $1 - \Phi(\alpha'\mathbf{z}_n)$

$$x_{n1} = 0$$

implying the following conditional distribution for x_{n1}:

$$\Pr(x_{n1}=0\,|\,\zeta_n, \mathbf{z}_n) = 1 - \Phi(\alpha'\mathbf{z}_n) + \Phi(\alpha'\mathbf{z}_n)[1 - \Phi(b_n)]$$
$$= 1 - \Phi(b_n)\Phi(\alpha'\mathbf{z}_n) \tag{4.74}$$

$$g(x_{n1}\,|\,\zeta_n, \mathbf{z}_n) = [1 - \Phi(\alpha'\mathbf{z}_n)]\,\sigma^{-1}\varphi[(x_{n1}-\gamma'\zeta_n)/\sigma] \qquad x_{n1}>0 \tag{4.75}$$

where $b_n=\gamma'\zeta_n/\sigma$. The regression function associated with this structure is

$$E(x_{n1}\,|\,\zeta_n, \mathbf{z}_n) = \sigma[1 - \Phi(\alpha'\mathbf{z}_n)]\,[\Phi(b_n)b_n + \varphi(b_n)]. \tag{4.76}$$

This model incorporates two mechanisms for generating zeros, one intended to represent a fundamental non-economic decision, the other representing an ordinary corner solution. This gives it additional flexibility, which is often valuable in applied work (see Atkinson, Gomulka and Stern, 1984a, for an example of its use in a study of the demand for tobacco).

This, and other related structures, was first proposed by Cragg (1971), who called it the double-hurdle model. However, Cragg did not motivate it with any formal basis in choice theory, and therefore could give no guidance on the variables that should be included in each of the two forms $\alpha'\mathbf{z}_n$ and $\gamma'\zeta_n$. This is a serious problem: for instance, Atkinson, Gomulka and Stern (1984a) experience considerable difficulty in allocating variables to the two hurdles, and eventually select a model with income included in both. Under our interpretation, only personal characteristics should appear in $\alpha'\mathbf{z}_n$, not prices or income.

We have derived this model assuming that only one good is the subject of discrete preference shifts, that the demand functions for potential and actual consumers are well approximated by a censored linear model, and that the Tobit and probit components are independent. None of these is essential to the argument - we could specify separate discrete shifts for each of a set of goods, generated by a system of probit-type relations, and use more sophisticated demand functions than the Tobit type. Moreover, we could allow some correlation between the random factors underlying the two hurdles. However, these extensions do complicate matters considerably.

4.3.3 Random preferences: Kuhn–Tucker models

When zeros are the result of an economic decision, rather than a discrete preference shift, econometric analysis is much more difficult. The problem can be approached either by direct means, using the standard Kuhn–Tucker conditions, or by indirect means, using virtual prices. The Kuhn–Tucker conditions, which are both necessary and sufficient, provided that preferences are strictly convex (see Kuhn and Tucker, 1951; and Arrow and Enthoven, 1961) are

$$\frac{\partial V(\tilde{\mathbf{x}}; \beta_n)}{\partial \tilde{\mathbf{x}}_i} = \lambda p_{ni} \qquad \text{if } \tilde{\mathbf{x}}_i > 0 \tag{4.77}$$

$$\frac{\partial V(\tilde{\mathbf{x}};\beta_n)}{\partial \tilde{\mathbf{x}}_i} \leqslant \lambda p_{ni} \qquad \text{if } \tilde{\mathbf{x}}_i = 0 \tag{4.78}$$

for $i=1, \ldots, q$. Wales and Woodland (1983) propose a stochastic specification for which the random disturbances enter the left-hand side of (4.77) in a simple additive fashion. This corresponds to a utility function that is expressible as a monotonic transformation of

$$u_n = \bar{V}(\mathbf{x};\mathbf{z}_n) + \mathbf{x}'\boldsymbol{\epsilon}_n \tag{4.79}$$

where $\boldsymbol{\epsilon}_n$ is a $q \times 1$ vector of zero mean random disturbances. Then conditions (4.77) and (4.78) are

$$\bar{V}_{ni} + \epsilon_{ni} = \lambda_n p_{ni} \qquad \text{if } \tilde{x}_{ni} > 0 \tag{4.80}$$

$$\bar{V}_{ni} + \epsilon_{ni} \leqslant \lambda_n p_{ni} \qquad \text{if } \tilde{x}_{ni} = 0 \tag{4.81}$$

where $\bar{V}_{ni} = \partial \bar{V}(\tilde{\mathbf{x}};\mathbf{z}_n)/\partial \tilde{\mathbf{x}}_i$. Assume, without loss of generality, that individual n is a consumer of the first good. Then, at the optimum,

$$\lambda_n = (\bar{V}_{n1} + \epsilon_{n1})/p_{n1} \tag{4.82}$$

which implies

$$\eta_{ni} = \psi_i(\tilde{\mathbf{x}};\mathbf{z}_n,\mathbf{p}_n) \qquad \text{if } \tilde{x}_{ni} > 0 \tag{4.83}$$

$$\eta_{ni} \leqslant \psi_i(\tilde{\mathbf{x}};\mathbf{z}_n,\mathbf{p}_n) \qquad \text{if } \tilde{x}_{ni} = 0 \tag{4.84}$$

for $i=2, \ldots, q$, where η_{ni} and $\psi_i(\tilde{\mathbf{x}};\mathbf{z}_n,\mathbf{p}_n)$ are

$$\eta_{ni} = p_{n1}\epsilon_{ni} - p_{ni}\epsilon_{n1} \tag{4.85}$$

$$\psi_i(\tilde{\mathbf{x}};\mathbf{z}_n,\mathbf{p}_n) = p_{ni}\bar{V}_{n1} - p_{n1}\bar{V}_{ni}. \tag{4.86}$$

Since the budget constraint always holds at the optimum, $\tilde{x}_{n1}$ can be expressed as an exact function of $\tilde{x}_{n2}, \ldots, \tilde{x}_{nq}$:

$$\tilde{x}_{n1} = (y_n - p_{n2}\tilde{x}_{n2} - \ldots - p_{nq}\tilde{x}_{nq})/p_{n1} \tag{4.87}$$

and thus each of $\psi_{n2}, \ldots, \psi_{nq}$ can be regarded as a function of $\tilde{x}_{n2} \ldots \tilde{x}_{nq}$. Consider the case of an individual who consumes only r of the q goods $(1 \leqslant r \leqslant q)$, and let the goods be re-ordered so that these occur first. Make the assumption that $\epsilon_{n1}, \ldots, \epsilon_{nq}$ have a multivariate normal distribution with mean vector zero and covariance matrix $\Sigma_n = \{\sigma_{ij}\}$. Then $\eta_{n2}, \ldots, \eta_{nq}$ also have a multivariate normal distribution with mean vector zero and covariance matrix $\boldsymbol{\Omega}_n = \{p_{n1}^2\sigma_{ij} - p_{ni}p_{n1}\sigma_{ii} - p_{nj}p_{n1}\sigma_{1j} + p_{ni}p_{nj}\sigma_{11}\}$. Write the p.d.f. of this distribution $\varphi(\eta_2, \ldots, \eta_q; 0, \boldsymbol{\Omega}_n)$. Then the observed demands $x_{n2} \ldots x_{nq}$ have a joint distribution which is of mixed discrete–continuous form, characterized by a probability density/mass function

$$g(x_{n2}, \ldots, x_{nq} | \zeta_n)$$

$$= \int_{-\infty}^{\psi_{r+1n}} \cdots \int_{-\infty}^{\psi_{qn}} \varphi(\psi_{2n}, \ldots, \psi_{rn}, \eta_{r+1}, \ldots, \eta_q; 0, \Omega_n) |J_n| \, d\eta_q \ldots d\eta_{r+1} \tag{4.88}$$

where $\psi_{in} = \psi_i(\mathbf{x}_n; \mathbf{z}_n)$ and J_n is the Jacobian term

$$\det \begin{bmatrix} \dfrac{\partial\psi_2(x_{n2}, \ldots, x_{nr}, 0, \ldots, 0; \mathbf{z}_n)}{\partial x_{n2}} & \cdots & \dfrac{\partial\psi_2(x_{n2}, \ldots, x_{nr}, 0, \ldots, 0; \mathbf{z}_n)}{\partial x_{nr}} \\ \vdots & & \vdots \\ \dfrac{\partial\psi_r(x_{n2}, \ldots, x_{nr}, 0, \ldots, 0; \mathbf{z}_n)}{\partial x_{n2}} & \cdots & \dfrac{\partial\psi_r(x_{n2}, \ldots, x_{nr}, 0, \ldots, 0; \mathbf{z}_n)}{\partial x_{nr}} \end{bmatrix} \tag{4.89}$$

Note that if $r = q$ and all goods are consumed, then (4.88) reduces to the simple expression

$$f(x_{n2}, \ldots, x_{nq} | \zeta_n) = \varphi(\psi_{2n}, \ldots, \psi_{qn}; 0, \Omega_n) \, |J_n| . \tag{4.90}$$

Given a particular parametric form for the utility function $\bar{V}(\mathbf{x}; \mathbf{z}_n)$, estimation proceeds by numerically maximizing the log-likelihood function, which is the sum of the logarithm of a term of the form (4.88) for each individual. Wales and Woodland (1983) give more detailed expressions for the case of the quadratic utility function and manage to compute estimates for a $q=3$ model of the demand for beef, lamb and other meats. However, with currently available computing resources, the estimation of this type of model is probably impractical for larger-scale cases, where families may be observed as non-purchasers of more than two or three goods. This is because the complexity of expression (4.88) necessitates the repeated use of expensive multidimensional numerical integration methods within the iterative optimization algorithm used to locate the maximum of the log-likelihood function. One also wonders whether the 34 per cent of families who are non-purchasers in Wales and Woodland's data set would really never consume the meat categories concerned, as this model assumes.

4.3.4 Random preferences: virtual prices

One drawback of the Kuhn–Tucker approach to model specification is that it provides no opportunity for the specification of preferences through the indirect utility function (see chapter 1, section 1.4), which has considerable advantages in terms of analytical convenience. An alternative approach to the problem is available if we exploit the analytical techniques which are used in the theory of rationing – after all, a non-negativity constraint is merely rationing from below at zero rather than rationing from above at some positive quantity. For many purposes it is convenient to use a characterization of the non-negativity constrained optimum which is phrased in terms of prices rather than quantities. These conditions make use of the notion of *virtual prices*, introduced by Rothbarth (1941) (see also Neary and Roberts, 1980; and Deaton, 1981).

Virtual prices are merely shadow, or reservation, prices. They are widely used in economic analysis; for instance, in labour supply theory the reservation wage is the virtual price of leisure for a person not in the labour force. Virtual prices are those prices at which the non-negativity constrained demands solve the analogous unconstrained utility maximization problem; in other words, they are prices at which the consumer would be on the margin of consuming non-purchased goods. This is illustrated, for the case of two goods, in figure 4.2. The indifference curves cut the x_1 axis, allowing the possibility of a corner solution at zero for good x_2. Denote the price of good 1 by p_1 and total spending by y; then, if the price of good 2 is p_2^*, there is a point of tangency at $x_2 = 0$, and the individual is on the margin of consuming good 2. If the price were to fall to p_2^a, the point of tangency would move to point A in the interior of the choice set, and the individual would become a consumer of good 2. If the price were to increase to p_2^b, there would be no tangency within the choice set, and the optimum decision is to consume none of good 2. The tangency illustrated at point B is merely a useful technical device: strictly speaking, indifference curves are not definable outside the choice set.

The price p_2^* is the virtual price of good 2. It depends on the nature of preferences and on y and p_1, and characterizes the constrained optimum: given y

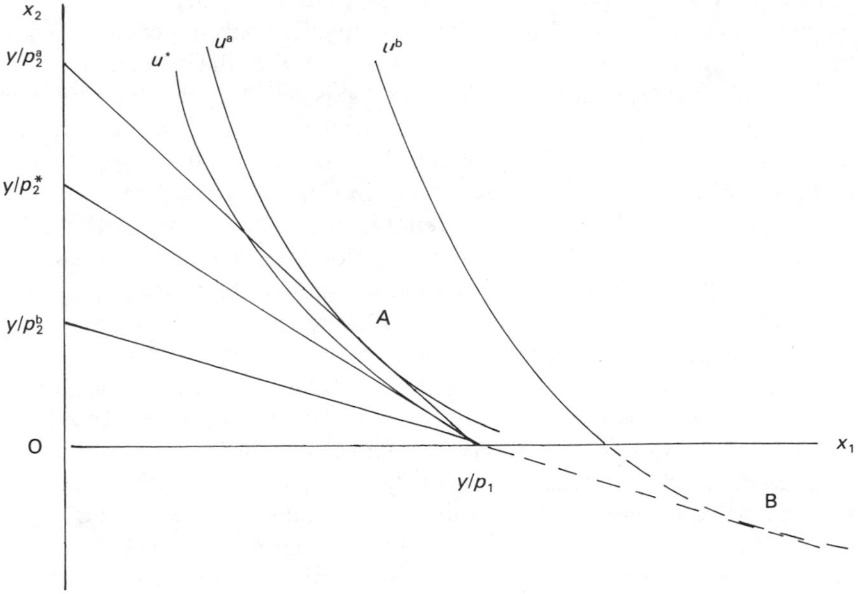

Figure 4.2 The virtual price.

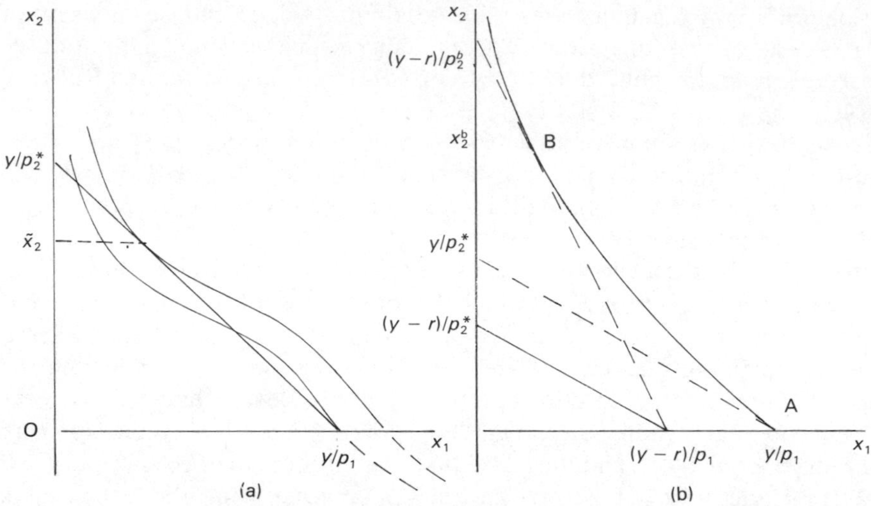

Figure 4.3 Counter-examples: (a) non-convex preferences; (b) fixed costs.

and p_1, $\tilde{x}_2$ is zero whenever $p_2 \geqslant p_2^*$ and is positive otherwise. However, this is true only under certain assumptions, and figure 4.3 illustrates two important cases where this characterization breaks down.

In figure 4.3(a), preferences are non-convex and drawn in such a way that it is never optimal to consume none of good 2, despite the fact that there is a point of tangency for price p_2^* at $x_2 = 0$. The virtual price of x_2 can be defined in either of two ways, which are generally equivalent only under convexity. A 'local' definition relates the virtual price to the slope of the indifference curve at its point of intersection with the $x_2 = 0$ axis, yielding the quantity illustrated as p_2^*. A proper 'global' definition is as the value of p_2 at which $\tilde{x}_2 = 0$ is the optimal choice; in our example this yields no finite value for p_2^*. It is the global definition that gives a true characterization of optimal behaviour, and the simpler local definition is only reliable if preferences are certain to be convex. If they are not, then dominant interior solutions may exist, and one must check that a tangency does represent a global optimum. In principle, there is no difficulty here if we believe that preferences are convex, but there are obvious potential technical problems if we approximate the preference map with a utility function that is not constrained to be globally quasi-concave. Note also that *local* convexity is not adequate to remove this problem: in our example, preferences are locally convex when x_2 is zero.

A second pathological case is illustrated in figure 4.3(b), where there are fixed costs associated with the consumption of good 2; an example is a good like electricity, for which one must pay a flat connection charge before being able to consume at all. This implies a discontinuous budget constraint consisting of an isolated point A and the unbroken linear segment defined only for $x_2 > 0$. At point A, the illustrated value p_2^* satisfies both local and global definitions of the virtual price. However, as p_2 falls from this value, $\tilde{x}_2$ does not increase but remains at zero until the price reaches the level p_2^b, when the optimal consumption level jumps to x_2^b. The discontinuity in the demand function for x_2 implies that the virtual price is not unique, since any value in the range (p_2^*, p_2^b) satisfies the global definition. Note that this difficulty can occur even for continuous linear budget constraints, since there may be 'psychological' fixed costs (or benefits). The most important case is perhaps labour supply, where a person may, for example, derive some self-esteem from the mere fact of having a job. For the remainder of this section we assume there are no such discontinuities, either in the budget constraint or in preferences; discussion of these problems is postponed until the next chapter.

Consider a consumer with preferences represented by a quasi-concave utility function $u = V(\mathbf{x}_1, \mathbf{x}_2; \beta)$, where $(\mathbf{x}_1' \ \mathbf{x}_2')$ is a partition of $\mathbf{x}'$ into subvectors of dimensions r and $q-r$, with corresponding price subvectors $\mathbf{p}_1$ and $\mathbf{p}_2$. Total spending is constrained to be y. Suppose that this individual is at a corner solution with $\tilde{\mathbf{x}}_2 = 0$, and that the solution to the unconstrained choice problem $\max[V(\mathbf{x}_1, \mathbf{x}_2; \beta) \mid \mathbf{p}_1'\mathbf{x}_1 + \mathbf{p}_2'\mathbf{x}_2 = y]$ is given by the demand functions

$$\check{\mathbf{x}}_1 = \check{\mathbf{x}}_1(\mathbf{p}_1, \mathbf{p}_2, y; \beta) \tag{4.91}$$

$$\check{\mathbf{x}}_2 = \check{\mathbf{x}}_2(\mathbf{p}_1, \mathbf{p}_2, y; \beta). \tag{4.92}$$

The virtual prices which support the constrained demands $(\tilde{\mathbf{x}}_1, 0)$ are given by the (unique) solution $\mathbf{p}_1^*$ and $\mathbf{p}_2^*$ to the equations

$$\tilde{\mathbf{x}}_1 = \check{\mathbf{x}}_1(\mathbf{p}_1^*, \mathbf{p}_2^*, y; \beta) \tag{4.93}$$

$$0 = \check{\mathbf{x}}_2(\mathbf{p}_1^*, \mathbf{p}_2^*, y; \beta). \tag{4.94}$$

Since (4.93) and (4.94) satisfy the marginal conditions for an interior optimum, we must have

$$\lambda \mathbf{p}_1^* = \left.\frac{\partial V(\mathbf{x}; \beta)}{\partial \mathbf{x}_1}\right|_{\mathbf{x}_1 = \tilde{\mathbf{x}}_1, \mathbf{x}_2 = 0} \tag{4.95}$$

$$\lambda \mathbf{p}_2^* = \left.\frac{\partial V(\mathbf{x}; \beta)}{\partial \mathbf{x}_2}\right|_{\mathbf{x}_1 = \tilde{\mathbf{x}}_1, \mathbf{x}_2 = 0} \tag{4.96}$$

But (4.95) is merely the Kuhn–Tucker condition (4.77) with $\mathbf{p}_1 = \mathbf{p}_1^*$. Hence, for consumed goods, virtual prices and actual prices are equal. Moreover, a comparison of (4.96) with (4.78) reveals that the Kuhn–Tucker inequality for non-consumed goods is equivalent to

$$\mathbf{p}_2 \geqslant \mathbf{p}_2^* \tag{4.97}$$

where the vector inequality means that all elements of $\mathbf{p}_2 - \mathbf{p}_2^*$ are non-negative. Relation (4.97) merely says that goods are not consumed when they are too expensive.

A thorough treatment of the theory of virtual prices can be found in Neary and Roberts (1980). Assuming that utility is strictly quasi-concave, increasing and continuous, they show that the analysis of any rationing problem of this type can be conducted in terms of virtual prices. A further advantage of the Kuhn–Tucker inequality expressed in the price form (4.97) is that the vector of virtual prices is derived from the system of unconstrained demand functions, and this may be constructed in any way we find convenient - from an indirect utility function using Roy's identity, for instance. Thus the process of constructing a corner solution model may be very much easier using the virtual price conditions than using the Kuhn–Tucker conditions in direct form.

In outline, the derivation of the distribution of observed demands proceeds as follows. Consider system (4.93) and (4.94); setting $\mathbf{p}_1^* = \mathbf{p}_1$ and solving (4.93) for $\mathbf{p}_2^*$

$$\mathbf{p}_2^* = \mathbf{p}_2^*(\mathbf{p}_1, y; \boldsymbol{\beta}) \tag{4.98}$$

$$\begin{aligned}\tilde{\mathbf{x}}_1 &= \check{\mathbf{x}}_1(\mathbf{p}_1, \mathbf{p}_2^*, y; \boldsymbol{\beta}) \\ &= \tilde{\mathbf{x}}_1(\mathbf{p}_1, y; \boldsymbol{\beta}).\end{aligned} \tag{4.99}$$

Thus the vector $(\tilde{\mathbf{x}}_1', \mathbf{p}_2^{*\prime})$ is merely a function of the underlying random variables $\boldsymbol{\beta}$. Again, one element of $\tilde{\mathbf{x}}_1$ is redundant, since the budget constraint must be satisfied exactly. Hence the first element, say, of $\tilde{\mathbf{x}}_1$ can be recovered from the condition $\mathbf{p}_1{}'\tilde{\mathbf{x}}_1 = y$, and $(\tilde{\mathbf{x}}_1', \mathbf{p}_2{}^{*\prime})$ is to be regarded as a $(q-1)$-dimensional vector. If we can derive the joint distribution of $(\tilde{\mathbf{x}}_1', \mathbf{p}_2^{*\prime})$ from that of $\boldsymbol{\beta}$, then the probability density/mass function of the observed quantity vector $\mathbf{x}_n' = (x_{n2} \ldots x_{nr}\, 0 \ldots 0)$ is

$$f(\mathbf{x}_n \mid \zeta_n) = \int_{-\infty}^{p_{nr+1}} \cdots \int_{-\infty}^{p_{nq}} g(x_{n2} \ldots x_{nr}, \mathbf{p}_{r+1}^* \ldots \mathbf{p}_q^* \mid \zeta_n) \mathrm{d}p_q^* \ldots \mathrm{d}p_{r+1}^* \tag{4.100}$$

where $g(.; \zeta_n)$ is the p.d.f. of the derived distribution of $\tilde{\mathbf{x}}_1$ and $\mathbf{p}_2^*$.

An example will make this clear. Lee and Pitt (1984) give a very general treatment of the case of a transcendental logarithmic indirect utility function, and also present an applied production model estimated from Indonesian survey data. Instead, we shall sketch the derivation of a simpler family labour supply model, based on a similar indirect utility function, written as follows:

$$\begin{aligned}-\log H(p, w_1, w_2; \beta_n) = {} & \beta_{n0} \log\left(\frac{p}{y}\right) + \beta_{n1} \log\left(\frac{w_1}{y}\right) + \beta_{n2} \log\left(\frac{w_2}{y}\right) \\ & + \tfrac{1}{2}\beta_{00}\left[\log\left(\frac{p}{y}\right)\right]^2 + \beta_{01} \log\left(\frac{p}{y}\right) \\ & \log\left(\frac{w_1}{y}\right) + \beta_{02} \log\left(\frac{p}{y}\right) \log\left(\frac{w_2}{y}\right) \\ & + \tfrac{1}{2}\beta_{11}\left[\log\left(\frac{w_1}{y}\right)\right]^2 + \beta_{12} \log\left(\frac{w_1}{y}\right) \\ & \log\left(\frac{w_2}{y}\right) + \tfrac{1}{2}\beta_{22}\left[\log\left(\frac{w_2}{y}\right)\right]^2.\end{aligned} \tag{4.101}$$

This function represents the value of a utility index $u = V(c, -h_1, -h_2)$ maximized subject to the budget constraint $pc - w_1h_1 - w_2h_2 = y$. The variables c and p are respectively the quantity and price of a single composite consumption good, h_1 and h_2 are the hours of labour supplied by the husband and wife, w_1 and w_2 are their wage rates and y is their joint unearned income. We assume that only the linear coefficients in the quadratic (4.101) vary across individuals, with

$$\begin{bmatrix}\beta_{n0}\\ \beta_{n1}\\ \beta_{n2}\end{bmatrix} \sim N\left(\begin{bmatrix}\bar{\beta}_0(\mathbf{z}_n)\\ \bar{\beta}_1(\mathbf{z}_n)\\ \bar{\beta}_2(\mathbf{z}_n)\end{bmatrix}, \begin{bmatrix}\sigma_{00} & \sigma_{01} & \sigma_{02}\\ \sigma_{01} & \sigma_{11} & \sigma_{12}\\ \sigma_{02} & \sigma_{12} & \sigma_{22}\end{bmatrix}\right) \tag{4.102}$$

where the $\bar{\beta}_i(\mathbf{z}_n)$ are suitable functions of a vector $\mathbf{z}_n$ of observable family characteristics. Since the scale of the indirect utility function is arbitrary, some normalizing restriction is necessary, and we impose the constraint $\beta_{n0} + \beta_{n1} + \beta_{n2} = 1$, which implies $\bar{\beta}_0(\mathbf{z}_n) + \bar{\beta}_1(\mathbf{z}_n) + \bar{\beta}_2(\mathbf{z}_n) = 1$ and $\sigma_{i0} + \sigma_{i1} + \sigma_{i2} = 0$ for $i = 0, 1, 2$.

By Roy's identity (see chapter 1, equation (1.20)) the three behaviour equations are the following:

$$\frac{p\,\tilde{c}}{y} = \frac{\beta_{n0} + \beta_{00}\log(p/y) + \beta_{01}\log(w_1/y) + \beta_{02}\log(w_2/y)}{D} \tag{4.103}$$

$$\frac{-w_1\tilde{h}_1}{y} = \frac{\beta_{n1} + \beta_{01}\log(p/y) + \beta_{11}\log(w_1/y) + \beta_{12}\log(w_2/y)}{D} \tag{4.104}$$

$$\frac{-w_2\tilde{h}_2}{y} = \frac{\beta_{n2} + \beta_{02}\log(p/y) + \beta_{12}\log(w_1/y) + \beta_{22}\log(w_2/y)}{D} \tag{4.105}$$

where

$$D = 1 + (\beta_{00}+\beta_{01}+\beta_{02})\log(p/y) + (\beta_{01}+\beta_{11}+\beta_{12})\log(w_1/y) + (\beta_{02}+\beta_{12}+\beta_{22})\log(w_2/y). \tag{4.106}$$

Since $c_n = 0$ is a practical impossibility, there are only four cases that might be encountered in an actual sample. In all cases, equation (4.103) can be ignored as redundant since the dependent variables sum to unity as an identity.

Both husband and wife work In this case, the variables $-w_{n1}h_{n1}/y_n$ and $-w_{n2}h_{n2}/y_n$ have a conditional bivariate normal distribution, with mean vector $\boldsymbol{\mu}_n' = (\mu_{n1}\ \mu_{n2})$, where μ_{n1} and μ_{n2} are the expected right-hand sides of (4.104) and (4.105) respectively, for family n. The covariance matrix is

$$\boldsymbol{\Omega}_n = \frac{1}{D_n^2}\begin{bmatrix}\sigma_{11} & \sigma_{12}\\ \sigma_{12} & \sigma_{22}\end{bmatrix} \tag{4.107}$$

and we can therefore write the p.d.f. of this distribution (conditional on $\zeta_n = (p_n/y_n, w_{n1}/y_n, w_{n2}/y_n)$)

$$f\left[\frac{-w_{n1}h_{n1}}{y_n}, \frac{-w_{n2}h_{n2}}{y_n}\,\middle|\,\zeta_n\right] = \varphi\left[\frac{-w_{n1}h_{n1}}{y_n}, \frac{-w_{n2}h_{n2}}{y_n}; \boldsymbol{\mu}_n, \boldsymbol{\Omega}_n\right] \tag{4.108}$$

where $\varphi(.;\boldsymbol{\mu};\boldsymbol{\Omega})$ is the p.d.f. of the multivariate $N(\boldsymbol{\mu},\boldsymbol{\Omega})$ distribution.

Neither husband nor wife works In this case, the right-hand sides of (4.104) and (4.105) must be equated to zero and solved for the virtual wages w_{n1}^* and w_{n2}^*. We thus have

$$\beta_{n1} + \beta_{01}\log(p_n/y_n) + \beta_{11}\log(w_{n1}^*/y_n) + \beta_{12}\log(w_{n2}^*/y_n) = 0 \quad (4.109)$$

$$\beta_{n2} + \beta_{02}\log(p_n/y_n) + \beta_{12}\log(w_{n1}^*/y_n) + \beta_{22}\log(w_{n2}^*/y_n) = 0 \quad (4.110)$$

These have a solution

$$\begin{bmatrix}\log(w_{n1}^*/y_n)\\ \log(w_{n2}^*/y_n)\end{bmatrix} = -\begin{bmatrix}\beta_{11} & \beta_{12}\\ \beta_{12} & \beta_{22}\end{bmatrix}^{-1}\begin{bmatrix}\beta_{n1} + \beta_{01}\log(p_n/y_n)\\ \beta_{n2} + \beta_{02}\log(p_n/y_n)\end{bmatrix} \quad (4.111)$$

which is linear in β_{n1} and β_{n2} and therefore also normally distributed, with mean vector

$$\boldsymbol{\mu}_n^* = -\begin{bmatrix}\beta_{11} & \beta_{12}\\ \beta_{12} & \beta_{22}\end{bmatrix}^{-1}\begin{bmatrix}\bar{\beta}_1(\mathbf{z}_n) + \beta_{01}\log(p_n/y_n)\\ \bar{\beta}_2(\mathbf{z}_n) + \beta_{02}\log(p_n/y_n)\end{bmatrix} \quad (4.112)$$

and covariance matrix

$$\boldsymbol{\Omega}_n^* = \begin{bmatrix}\beta_{11} & \beta_{12}\\ \beta_{12} & \beta_{22}\end{bmatrix}^{-1}\begin{bmatrix}\sigma_{11} & \sigma_{12}\\ \sigma_{12} & \sigma_{22}\end{bmatrix}\begin{bmatrix}\beta_{11} & \beta_{12}\\ \beta_{12} & \beta_{22}\end{bmatrix}^{-1}. \quad (4.113)$$

Since utility is decreasing in h_1 and h_2, the virtual wage inequality (4.97) is reversed. Thus the discrete probability of neither husband nor wife joining the labour force, conditional on ζ_n, is the probability of the events $w_{n1} < w_{n1}^*$ and $w_{n2} < w_{n2}^*$:

$$\begin{aligned} f(h_{n1}=0, h_{n2}=0\,|\,\zeta_n) &= \Pr[\log(w_{n1}^*/y_n) > \log(w_{n1}/y_n),\\ &\qquad \log(w_{n2}^*/y_n) > \log(w_{n2}/y_n)]\\ &= \int_{\log(w_{n1}/y_n)}^{\infty}\int_{\log(w_{n2}/y_n)}^{\infty} \varphi(\eta_1, \eta_2; \boldsymbol{\mu}_n^*, \boldsymbol{\Omega}_n^*)\, \mathrm{d}\eta_2\, \mathrm{d}\eta_1. \end{aligned} \quad (4.114)$$

Only the husband works For this case, $h_{n1} > 0$ and $h_{n2} = 0$, and we must derive the appropriate mixed discrete–continuous distribution. The virtual wages in this case are $w_{n1}^* = w_{n1}$ and w_{n2}^* given by the solution to

$$\beta_{n2} + \beta_{02}\log(p_n/y_n) + \beta_{12}\log(w_{n1}/y_n) + \beta_{22}\log(w_{n2}^*/y_n) = 0 \quad (4.115)$$

which is

$$\log\left(\frac{w_{n2}^*}{y_n}\right) = \frac{-[\beta_{n2} + \beta_{02}\log(p_n/y_n) + \beta_{12}\log(w_{n1}/y_n)]}{\beta_{22}}. \quad (4.116)$$

Substituting $\log(w_{n2}^*/y_n)$ for $\log(w_{n2}/y_n)$ in (4.104),

$$\frac{-w_{n1}h_{n1}}{y_n} = \frac{\beta_{n1}\beta_{22}-\beta_{12}\beta_{n2} + b_1\log(p_n/y_n) + b_2\log(w_{n1}/y_n)}{\beta_{22}D_n} \tag{4.117}$$

where $b_1 = \beta_{22}\beta_{01}-\beta_{12}\beta_{02}$ and $b_2 = \beta_{11}\beta_{22}-\beta_{12}^2$. Since (4.116) and (4.117) are linear in β_{n1} and β_{n2}, $-w_{n1}h_{n1}/y_n$ and $\log(w_{n2}^*/y_n)$ have a bivariate normal distribution with mean vector

$$\mu_n^+ = -\begin{bmatrix} \bar{\beta}_1(\mathbf{z}_n)\beta_{22}-\beta_{12}\bar{\beta}_2(\mathbf{z}_n) + b_1\log(p_n/y_n) + b_2\log(p_n/y_n)]/\beta_{22}D_n \\ -[\bar{\beta}_2(\mathbf{z}_n) + \beta_{02}\log(p_n/y_n) + \beta_{12}\log(w_{n1}/y_n)]/\beta_{22} \end{bmatrix} \tag{4.118}$$

and covariance matrix

$$\Omega_n^+ = \begin{bmatrix} (\sigma_{11}\beta_{22}^2-2\sigma_{12}\beta_{22}\beta_{12}+\sigma_{22}\beta_{12}^2)/\beta_{22}^2D_n & (\sigma_{22}\beta_{12}-\sigma_{12}\beta_{22})/\beta_{22}^2 \\ (\sigma_{22}\beta_{12}-\sigma_{12}\beta_{22})/\beta_{22}^2 & \sigma_{22}/\beta_{22}^2 \end{bmatrix}. \tag{4.119}$$

Thus the required density/mass function is

$$f\left[\frac{-w_{n1}h_{n1}}{y_n}, h_{n2}=0\,|\,\zeta_n\right] = \int_{\log(w_{n2}/y_n)}^{\infty} \varphi\left[\frac{-w_{n1}h_{n1}}{y_n}, \eta; \mu_n^+, \Omega_n^+\right] d\eta. \tag{4.120}$$

Only the wife works This case is identical with the previous one, with subscripts 1 and 2 interchanged.

These expressions are relatively straightforward, involving only the integration of bivariate normal densities (see appendix 3 for methods of evaluating these integrals). The reason for this simplicity is that the indirect translog utility function is a particularly convenient one, yielding virtual wages which are easily computable as the solution to a system of linear equations. Moreover these solutions are themselves conveniently linear in the stochastic preference parameters β_{n1} and β_{n2}.

Things are not always this easy: in the labour supply example, the income variable y_n may be zero for some households, rendering the translog specification unusable unless it is modified (e.g. by replacing y_n by $y_n + Y$, where Y is fixed a priori or estimated). For most other common utility functions virtual prices cannot be derived in closed form, and even for those utility functions where this is possible there is no natural stochastic specification yielding simple distributional forms for the virtual price vector associated with each possible regime. Note also that this indirect translog utility function is not a globally convex representation of preferences; as a result, the derived expressions for $f(h_{n1}, h_{n2}\,|\,\zeta_n)$ may not constitute a proper distribution.

Given a sample of observations on N families, with wage rates fully observed, the conditional log-likelihood function for this model would be

$$\log L = \sum_{\substack{h_{n1}>0\\h_{n2}>0}} \log f\left(\frac{-w_{n1}h_{n1}}{y_n}, \frac{-w_{n2}h_{n2}}{y_n} \mid \zeta_n\right)$$
$$+ \sum_{\substack{h_{n1}>0\\h_{n2}=0}} \log f\left(\frac{-w_{n1}h_{n1}}{y_n}, h_{n2}=0 \mid \zeta_n\right)$$
$$+ \sum_{\substack{h_{n1}=0\\h_{n2}>0}} \log f\left(h_{n1}=0, \frac{-w_{n2}h_{n2}}{y_n} \mid \zeta_n\right)$$
$$+ \sum_{\substack{h_{n1}=0\\h_{n2}=0}} \log f(h_{n1}=0, h_{n2}=0 \mid \zeta_n). \tag{4.121}$$

However, it is extremely unlikely that this log-likelihood could ever be computable in practice, since the potential wage of each non-worker is required for the limits of integration in the expressions (4.114) and (4.120) and the analogous expression for the $h_{n1}=0$, $h_{n2}>0$ case. These potential wages are generally not available – if someone does not work it is usually not possible to observe the wage that he or she would have earned. (The situation may be different in the case of demand, since it is more plausible and often unavoidable to make the assumption that there is no inter-individual price variation.) There are two possible ways of solving this problem: one is to extend the model to include wage equations which essentially predict these missing wage observations. This technique is discussed in section 4.5. Alternatively, one might estimate the model from a truncated sample, discarding all observations on families with one or more non-working spouse. The probability of this conditioning event is the integral of p.d.f. (4.108) over negative values for $-w_1h_1/y$ and $-w_2h_2/y$:

$$\Pr(h_{n1}>0, h_{n2}>0 \mid \zeta_n) = \int_{-\infty}^{0}\int_{-\infty}^{0} \varphi(\eta_1, \eta_2; \mu_n, \Omega_n)\, d\eta_2\, d\eta_1. \tag{4.122}$$

Thus the conditional log-likelihood function for a truncated sample is

$$\log L = \sum_{\substack{h_{n1}>0\\h_{n2}>0}} \left[\log f\left(\frac{-w_{n1}h_{n1}}{y_n}, \frac{-w_{n2}h_{n2}}{y_n} \mid \zeta_n\right) - \log \Pr(h_{n1}>0, h_{n2}>0 \mid \zeta_n)\right] \tag{4.123}$$

and this would be maximized numerically with respect to β_{00}, β_{01}, β_{02}, β_{11}, β_{12}, β_{22}, σ_{11}, σ_{12}, σ_{22} and whatever parameters appear in the specified functions $\bar{\beta}_1(\mathbf{z}_n)$ and $\bar{\beta}_2(\mathbf{z}_n)$.

So far there has been little applied used of this type of model, and therefore little experience of the computational difficulties. Studies by Pitt and Lee

(1983) and Lee and Pitt (1984), applying this approach to consumers' demand and to the choice of energy source of manufacturers, appear to be the only examples. Of these, the latter application seems the more persuasive, since it is plausible that producers' decisions on energy usage represent equilibrium plans as this model assumes. In contrast, consumers' expenditure patterns observed over a short survey period are likely to be affected by substantial purely fortuitous elements, making it much harder to justify the treatment of zeros as corner solutions.

A natural development of the methods discussed in this and the previous section would be the specification of models with mixed stochastic specifications, allowing random preferences, giving rise to optimal plans that may be corner solutions, and also random errors in the execution of those plans. Unfortunately, such mixed models, although more realistic than either of the two extreme specifications, tend to be very complicated, even for problems involving few goods. If q is at all large, they are completely intractable.

The reason for this is that execution errors may lead to positive observed expenditures on goods that are not planned to be consumed, and conversely zero observed expenditures on goods that are. Therefore the actual configuration of zero and non-zero demands is not necessarily the same as the configuration in the optimal plan. There are 2^{q-1} such configurations (a very large number, unless q is small), and thus for any observed demand regime there are 2^{q-1} planned regimes that might have generated the observation, rather than just one as in the cases above. Therefore, the p.d.f. of the observed positive demands will have 2^{q-1} components, each taking the form of a multiple integral. Generally, such distributions are hopelessly unfeasible as a basis for applied work. We shall, however, consider mixed models in the simple labour supply examples (where $q = 2$) of the next chapter.

4.4 Consumption and purchases: the *P*-Tobit model

A major problem in cross-section demand analysis stems from the fact that most household expenditure surveys are based on a very short observation period – perhaps only one or two weeks. The demand model that the econometrician seeks to estimate is concerned with true rates of *consumption* of commodities, since it is presumably the consumption of goods that yields 'utility', and therefore consumption that is the individual's real objective. However, cross-section surveys are usually only able to observe *purchases* of commodities, and, since it is assumed that the act of purchasing does not itself yield 'utility', observed purchase data are only directly relevant if consumption and purchases are always equal. In short-duration surveys, consumption and purchases can differ markedly for many goods, and there is a serious problem in fitting a model of consumption directly to data on purchases. For instance, a good which is purchased regularly once every four weeks will have a 75 per cent probability of no purchase being observed in a one-week enquiry, and a 25 per cent probability of purchase being observed in a quantity four times as large as the underlying average weekly rate of consumption. Thus a zero observation may not correspond to a corner solution to the consumer's utility maximization problem, and a non-zero observation may not be an accurate measurement of the rate of consumption.

The seriousness of this problem will depend on the good and the consumer involved. The corner solution model is probably a good one for labour supply, since the labour force participation decision is usually a long-term one; it may also be a good description of *some* individuals' behaviour at a very detailed level - many people never eat smoked salmon or wear a hat. It is also a reasonable model to use for goods which are non-storable and consumed frequently and regularly - tobacco, for example. It is generally a very poor model, however, for durable or storable goods and broad aggregates of goods - a person may not buy any clothes during a particular week, but nevertheless presumably does not go naked. Personal characteristics may play an important role - families owning a car and a freezer will be in a position to make large and infrequent food purchases. Such characteristics vary systematically between households, so it is not reasonable to expect these effects to be adequately represented by the stochastic error term.

The shortcomings of survey data on purchases have been known to practitioners in this field since the very earliest days of Engel curve analysis. However, this concern has only recently been translated into a formal econometric technique, by Deaton and Irish (1984), who propose a very simple modification of the Tobit model. Their *P*-Tobit structure has two components: a true demand model, defined in terms of unobservable consumption (which may be zero), and a purchasing model which provides a link between consumption and purchases and allows for the possibility of purely fortuitous non-purchasing of a good which is consumed in the longer run. In their specification, both these components are very simple, and many generalizations are possible.

Define a variable $\tilde{x}_n$ to be the unobservable true rate of consumption of the good by household n. This depends on all the factors affecting household preferences, as well as prices and income; its interpretation is the following. Suppose that all these influences could be held fixed indefinitely, and the resulting sequence of household expenditures observed over a long period; the average rate of expenditure on the good in this hypothetical long run is the true rate of consumption $\tilde{x}_n$ which is determined by the household's demand function. The precise way in which this planned consumption rate is translated into actual purchases will vary across households, depending on such things as shopping habits, the ownership of cars and freezers etc. Represent all relevant observable factors by a vector of exogenous variables ξ_n. Then purchasing behaviour can be represented by the probability (conditional on $\tilde{x}_n$ and ξ_n) that we will observe at least one purchase of the good in a randomly chosen period of the same length as the survey period; call this probability $P_n = P(\tilde{x}_n, \xi_n)$. By definition, consumption and expenditure are equal on average, and so

$$E(x_n \mid \tilde{x}_n, \xi_n) \equiv \tilde{x}_n \tag{4.124}$$

But the left-hand side of (4.124) can be written

$$E(x_n \mid \tilde{x}_n, \xi_n) = E(x_n \mid x_n > 0, \tilde{x}_n, \xi_n)\, P(\tilde{x}_n, \xi_n) \tag{4.125}$$

and thus

$$E(x_n \mid x_n > 0, \tilde{x}_n \xi_n) = \frac{\tilde{x}_n}{P(\tilde{x}_n, \xi_n)} \tag{4.126}$$

Therefore, conditionally on $\tilde{x}_n$ and ξ_n, the *P*-Tobit model implies the following distribution for x_n:

with probability $1 - P_n$

$$x_n = 0 \tag{4.127}$$

with probability P_n

x_n is a random drawing from a distribution with mean $\tilde{x}_n/P_n$, described by a p.d.f. $g(x_n \mid \tilde{x}_n/P_n, \xi_n)$ (4.128)

As it stands, the model is incomplete: it is nothing more than a statistical device for relating the observable x_n to the unobservable $\tilde{x}_n$. To complete the model, we require specific forms for $P(\tilde{x}_n, \xi_n)$ and $g(x_n \mid \tilde{x}_n/P_n, \xi_n)$, and some assumption about $\tilde{x}_n$. In principle, anything is possible here; $\tilde{x}_n$ could be specified as one of the demand functions from a stochastic Kuhn–Tucker model, for instance. However, a simpler model seems more reasonable, and we could follow Deaton and Irish in assuming that $\tilde{x}_n$ is determined by a conventional Tobit model:

$$\tilde{x}_n \mid \zeta_n \sim \text{LCN}(\gamma'\zeta_n, \sigma^2, 0). \tag{4.129}$$

The zeros generated by this Tobit model are to be interpreted as permanent non-consumption – in other words, the Tobit model approximates a proper corner solution model. On the other hand, the zeros generated by (4.127) are to be interpreted as purely fortuitous – cases where the good is consumed but no purchase happens to be observed.

Alternative approximations may perform better than (4.129) in some cases. Some goods are necessarily consumed by everyone – clothing, for instance – and it is more plausible to use a model for $\tilde{x}_n$ that does not permit non-consumption. A log-normal model may be suitable (see Blundell and Meghir, 1987, and Pudney, 1988b) for instance

$$\log \tilde{x}_n \mid \zeta_n \sim N(\gamma'\zeta_n, \sigma^2). \tag{4.130}$$

Some work using the structure (4.127) and (4.128) has assumed a simple linear regression model for $\tilde{x}_n | \zeta_n$ (see Kay, Keen and Morris, 1984; Keen, 1986; Blundell and Meghir, 1987). This may be adequate as an approximation, but fails to respect the non-negativity of $\tilde{x}_n$.

4.4.1 A simple least-squares estimator

Except in very special cases, the structure (4.127) and (4.128) implies a very complicated distribution for x_n. Moreover, in order to estimate such a structure by ML, we are forced to specify a model of purchasing behaviour (through the probability P_n). Economists are often not interested in the way people organize their shopping, and the necessity of producing such a model is a drawback of the P-Tobit structure. However, there is a general estimation principle (see Pudney, 1985, 1988b; and Keen, 1986) that is applicable to any model of this form, irrespective of the nature of P_n. This estimator, which is not asymptotically efficient, proceeds by fitting an expression for the expected value of x_n by non-linear least-squares. If we operate on identity (4.124) with the expectations operator conditioned only on the exogenous variables ζ_n and ξ_n, the result is

$$E(x_n | \zeta_n, \xi_n) = E(\tilde{x}_n | \zeta_n, \xi_n). \tag{4.131}$$

This expectation depends only on the underlying demand relation, and is independent of P_n; it is therefore unaffected by the assumptions we make about the purchase probability. Relation (4.131) can be rewritten in the form of a non-linear regression equation:

$$x_n = \mu(\zeta_n; \theta) + v_n \tag{4.132}$$

where $\mu(\zeta_n; \theta)$ is the mean function of $\tilde{x}_n$ implied by our demand model, $v_n = x_n - \mu(\zeta_n; \theta)$ is a random disturbance term, and θ is the vector of model parameters.

If we assume a Tobit demand function, the mean function of $\tilde{x}_n$ is

$$\mu(\zeta_n; \theta) = \sigma[b_n \Phi(b_n) + \varphi(b_n)] \tag{4.133}$$

(from equation (A2.31) of appendix 2, after some manipulation), where b_n is again $\gamma' \zeta_n / \sigma$. For the alternative log-normal model (4.130), the mean function of $\tilde{x}_n$ is

$$\mu(\zeta_n; \theta) = \exp(\gamma' \zeta_n + \tfrac{1}{2}\sigma^2). \tag{4.134}$$

The least-squares estimator of γ and σ solves the following minimization problem:

$$\min_{\theta} \sum_{n=1}^{N} v_n^2 \tag{4.135}$$

where the v_n are defined implicitly by (4.132). Since $\mu(\zeta_n; \theta)$ is non-linear in γ

and σ, this minimization problem cannot be solved analytically; thus a suitable iterative algorithm must be used to locate the minimum.

In addition to the non-linearity of (4.133) and (4.134), there are further practical difficulties. The random error v_n is generally heteroscedastic, and the precise form of the heteroscedasticity depends on the nature of P_n. Thus, a more efficient estimator, such as non-linear generalized least squares, would require the specification of a model of the purchase probability, which we wish to avoid. In the interests of simplicity, it seems best to ignore this heteroscedasticity at the estimation stage but to take proper account of it when estimating the covariance matrix of the least-squares estimator. This can be achieved by using the expressions proposed by White (1980) (see chapter 2, section 2.4.2). A second problem is that the parameters γ and σ of the demand model are sometimes impossible or difficult to identify from the mean function $\mu(\zeta_n; \theta)$ alone. For instance, in the case of the log-normal model (4.134) σ^2 cannot be distinguished from the constant term appearing in the linear form $\gamma' \zeta_n$. In less extreme cases, such as (4.133), we often encounter convergence difficulties in the application of an iterative optimization algorithm to the problem (4.135), and the least-squares estimator sometimes has very poor precision.

Despite these difficulties, this approach to estimation seems very promising – it provides estimates of the underlying demand relation without any need for the specification of a full model of purchasing frequency. However, in cases where the least-squares estimator is unsuccessful, it is necessary to construct a formal model of purchasing behaviour and derive the full distribution of observed expenditure. We now turn to these fully specified models.

4.4.2 The constant-*P* model

The standard Tobit model is a special case of the *P*-Tobit structure (4.127)–(4.129). It assumes that $\tilde{x}_n \equiv x_n$ (implying a degenerate form for the distribution of $g(x_n | \tilde{x}_n, \xi_n)$) and takes the purchase probability to be the unit step function

$$P(\tilde{x}_n, \xi_n) = 0 \qquad \text{for } \tilde{x}_n = 0 \tag{4.136}$$

$$P(\tilde{x}_n, \xi_n) = 1 \qquad \text{for } \tilde{x}_n > 0 \tag{4.137}$$

Deaton and Irish (1984), in proposing the *P*-Tobit model, make the simplest possible generalization of the Tobit model, retaining the assumption of exact equality between x_n and $\tilde{x}_n/P_n$ but replacing (4.137) with

$$P(\tilde{x}_n, \xi_n) = P \qquad \text{for } \tilde{x}_n > 0. \tag{4.138}$$

The constant value P is regarded as a fixed characteristic of the good concerned, and is treated as a parameter to be estimated. The resulting distribution of x_n conditional on ζ_n has two components:

$$\begin{aligned}\Pr(x_n=0\,|\,\zeta_n) &= 1 - \Pr(x_n>0\,|\,\zeta_n)\\ &= 1 - P\Pr(\tilde{x}_n>0\,|\,\zeta_n)\\ &= 1 - P\,\Phi(b_n)\end{aligned} \tag{4.139}$$

$$\begin{aligned}f(x_n\,|\,\zeta_n) &= P\,\sigma^{-1}\,\varphi\left(\frac{Px_n-\gamma'\zeta_n}{\sigma}\right)\left|\frac{\partial\tilde{x}_n}{\partial x_n}\right|\\ &= P^2\,\sigma^{-1}\,\varphi\left(\frac{Px_n-\gamma'\zeta_n}{\sigma}\right).\end{aligned} \tag{4.140}$$

This yields a log-likelihood function of the form

$$\begin{aligned}\log L(\gamma,\sigma^2,P) &= K + \sum_0 \log[1-P\Phi(b_n)] - N^+\log\sigma + 2N^+\log P\\ &\quad - \frac{1}{2\sigma^2}\sum_+ (Px_n-\gamma'\zeta_n)^2\end{aligned} \tag{4.141}$$

where K is the usual inessential constant and N^+ is the number of positive observations. As Deaton and Irish point out, this is equivalent to the log-likelihood function for a misreporting model, in which x_n is generated by a Tobit mechanism but there is a probability P that any positive purchase will be misreported as a zero.

Unfortunately, Deaton and Irish's results are not encouraging: although they are able to reject the Tobit model against the P-Tobit model, the parameter P is generally estimated to be significantly greater than unity – a result which is meaningless under either interpretation of their model. A possible explanation of these poor results might be the restrictiveness of the assumptions that P_n is constant for all $\tilde{x}_n>0$ and that the relation $x_n=\tilde{x}_n/P_n$ is exact. We sketch some possible generalizations of their model in the next section.

There is no obvious two-step estimator available for the Deaton–Irish model. This is because there are two separate mechanisms at work generating zeros, and it is not possible to disentangle these in any simple way – both mechanisms must be estimated simultaneously. In contrast, if it is known a priori that there is no non-consumption, then all observed zeros must be fortuitous, and it is possible to estimate P consistently in a first stage as the sample proportion $\hat{P}=N^+/N$. If we adopt (say) the log-normal model (4.134) for $\tilde{x}_n$, the variable $\log(Px_n)$ has an $N(\gamma'\zeta_n,\sigma^2)$ distribution conditional on ζ_n and $x_n > 0$, and thus one can regress $\log(\hat{P}x_n)$ on ζ_n, using only the positive observations, to achieve consistent estimates of γ and σ^2. For ML estimation of this 'P-log-normal' model, we must maximize the conditional log-likelihood function

$$\begin{aligned}\log L(\gamma,\sigma^2,P) &= K^* + (N-N^+)\log(1-P) - N^+\log\sigma + N^+\log P\\ &\quad - \frac{1}{2\sigma^2}\sum_+ (\log x_n + \log P - \gamma'\zeta_n)^2\end{aligned} \tag{4.142}$$

where $K^* = -(N^+/2)\log 2\pi - \Sigma_+ \log x_n$.

4.4.3 Generalized *P*-Tobit models

Exogenously variable purchase frequency It is a simple matter to generalize the *P*-Tobit or *P*–log-normal model by replacing the constant *P* with a parameterized function of exogenous variables (see Blundell and Meghir, 1987). For instance, if the purchasing–non-purchasing distinction is modelled via a probit relationship, we would have

$$P_n = \Phi(\delta'\xi_n) \tag{4.143}$$

where δ is a vector of coefficients requiring estimation along with γ and σ. This expands the parameter space, but otherwise does not materially alter either of the two likelihood functions (4.141) or (4.142). The two-step estimator for the *P*-log-normal model is also easily modified: we first run a simple probit analysis of the purchase–non-purchase dichotomy to estimate δ and then form $\hat{P}_n = \Phi(\hat{\delta}'\xi_n)$ and regress $\log(\hat{P}_n x_n)$ on ζ_n, using only data on purchasers. Note that this procedure is still consistent (except for the intercept term in $\gamma'\zeta_n$) even if x_n deviates randomly from $\tilde{x}_n/P_n$.

Endogenous frequency and random purchase quantities Although these limited generalizations of Deaton and Irish's work are valuable, they retain the assumption that P_n is independent of $\tilde{x}_n$; this seems unreasonable, since it implies that a family which almost never consumes a good will have the same probability of being observed to purchase it during the survey period as a similar family which consumes heavily. Thus, the former household is assumed to make many tiny purchases while the latter makes roughly the same number of large purchases. Everyday experience tends to contradict this, and one would expect P_n to be a smoothly increasing function of $\tilde{x}_n$, *ceteris paribus*, rather than a step function. It may also depend on other extraneous variables ξ_n. We shall assume the following general relation:

$$P_n = P(\tilde{x}_n, \xi_n) \tag{4.144}$$

where $P(.)$ is a (presumably increasing) function satisfying $P(0, \xi_n) = 0$ for all ξ_n.

A second restrictive feature of the Deaton–Irish form of the model is the non-stochastic nature of the relation $x_n = \tilde{x}_n/P_n$, which implies that, given the prevailing rate of consumption and frequency of purchase, goods are always bought in the same quantity. This also seems unreasonable, and a more realistic model could be constructed by equating x_n to $\tilde{x}_n/P_n$ only on average. Thus, when x_n is non-zero, it should have some appropriate distribution with mean $\tilde{x}_n/P_n$ and p.d.f. $g(x_n \mid \tilde{x}_n, \xi_n)$. In general terms, the distribution of x_n resulting from this structure is the following:

$$\Pr(x_n = 0 \mid \zeta_n, \xi_n) = 1 - \int_0^\infty P(\tilde{x}, \xi_n)\, \tilde{g}(\tilde{x} \mid \zeta_n)\, d\tilde{x} \tag{4.145}$$

$$f(x_n \mid \zeta_n, \xi_n) = \int_0^\infty g(x_n \mid \tilde{x}, \xi_n)\, P(\tilde{x}, \xi_n)\, \tilde{g}(\tilde{x} \mid \zeta_n)\, \mathrm{d}\tilde{x} \tag{4.146}$$

where $\tilde{g}(.)$ is the p.d.f. of the strictly positive part of the distribution of $\tilde{x}_n \mid \zeta_n$. For the Tobit model (4.129), $\tilde{g}(\tilde{x} \mid \zeta_n)$ is $\sigma^{-1}\varphi[\tilde{x}-\gamma'\zeta_n)/\sigma]$, and for the log-normal model (4.130) it is $(\sigma\tilde{x}_n)^{-1}\varphi[(\log \tilde{\mathbf{x}} - \gamma'\zeta_n)/\sigma]$. The conditional log-likelihood function resulting from this distribution is

$$\log L(\theta) = \sum_{+} \log f(x_n \mid \zeta_n, \xi_n) + \sum_{0} \log \Pr(x_n = 0 \mid \zeta_n, \xi_n) \tag{4.147}$$

where θ contains γ, σ and any parameters involved in $P(\tilde{x}_n, \xi_n)$ and $g(x_n \mid \tilde{x}_n, \xi_n)$.

This log-likelihood is complicated, since numerical integration is generally necessary for the evaluation of (4.145) and (4.146). However, it is feasible: in Pudney (1988) a model is successfully estimated, based on a log-normal regression for $\tilde{x}_n$ and the following conditional probit purchasing model:

$$P(\tilde{x}_n, \xi_n) = \Phi(\delta_1'\xi_n + \delta_2 \log \tilde{x}_n). \tag{4.148}$$

The density $g(x_n \mid \tilde{x}_n, \xi_n)$ is specified to be the log-normal form

$$g(x_n \mid \tilde{x}_n, \xi_n) = (\sigma^* x_n)^{-1}\, \varphi\left[\frac{\log x_n - \log(\tilde{x}_n/P_n) - \sigma^{*2}/2}{\sigma^*}\right] \tag{4.149}$$

where σ^{*2} is the variance of $\log x_n$ about its mean. This is the p.d.f. of a log-normal distribution with mean $\tilde{x}_n/P_n$. Note that, for this specification, (4.145) can be written in the simple form $\Phi[\delta_1'\xi_n + \delta_2\gamma'\zeta_n)/(1+\delta_2^2\sigma^2)^{1/2}]$. Gaussian quadrature (see appendix 3) is used for the evaluation of the expressions (4.146).

The budget constraint One of the most serious problems associated with short-duration budget surveys is the obvious endogeneity of total expenditure. Orthodox demand analysis assumes the size of the budget to be exogenously determined. In the long run this may be a reasonable assumption, but it is a dangerous one to make when spending is observed for only one or two weeks. This is largely due to the durability and indivisibility of many goods: for example, if a member of the household happens to buy an expensive coat during the survey week (say), this may account for a very large proportion of the normal weekly budget. Such purchases are typically financed by borrowing, or from accumulated savings, and one would not expect the household to reduce its standard of living for a week to make room for the item within a fixed weekly budget. This implies that total expenditure varies randomly with the pattern of purchases that happens to be observed, and there is likely to be a spuriously high correlation between the observed size of the budget and the dependent variable, particularly in very short surveys or for durable goods with high unit value. Provided that identity (4.124) holds for every good, measured total expenditure will be equal to planned spending on average, but it will deviate randomly from it, causing a particularly difficult non-linear measurement error problem.

All this is well known (see Liviatan, 1961), and the traditional remedy is to use income as an instrument for the total expenditure variable. However, in *P*-Tobit models IV techniques are not easily applicable since the model structure is of complicated non-linear form. Keen (1986) does use an IV estimator, but he is forced to justify it under the assumption that $\tilde{x}_n$ is generated by a regression structure linear in total expenditure. This is rather hard to defend, since it does not guarantee the non-negativity of $\tilde{x}_n$, and since the linearity assumption for Engel curves is rather restrictive.

4.5 Partially observed explanatory variables

In cross-section demand analysis, one can rarely rule out the possibility of variation in prices between individuals in the sample. Prices may vary between regions and between different retail outlets, and they may vary seasonally, so that families interviewed at different times of the year face different prices. There is a further problem here, since a large part of the variability in observed prices may be due to the choice by consumers of different qualities of goods, implying that prices cannot be regarded as exogenous to the consumer. Prais and Houthakker (1955, chapter 8) discuss the consequences of quality variation and give estimates which suggest that its impact is very substantial for many goods. True constant-quality prices would presumably vary much less than observed prices, so there is perhaps a case for using only the average price for the region and season as the relevant explanatory variable, rather than the partially observed recorded prices. This would avoid the present problem completely, since regional and seasonal average prices are usually fully observable.

A more frequently encountered example of inter-individual price variation is the wage rate, which reflects quality differences in the labour supplied by different individuals and which usually displays a very large range of variation across the cross-section. In the case of labour supply, it is more reasonable to regard these quality-specific wages as exogenous, since they are largely determined by factors such as education, ability and experience.

The difficulty raised by this variability is that the price of a good is unique to the individual, and is therefore unobservable if that individual chooses to make no purchase of it during the observation period. Similarly, if a person chooses not to participate in the labour force, we are unable to record the wage at which he or she would have been employed. Since prices and wage rates are important explanatory variables, the econometric models we have discussed in previous sections are not operational in a full sample which includes zero observations.

There are two courses open to the applied worker. The zero observations can be discarded and the model estimated from the resulting truncated sample. It is then important to use the correct statistical procedures which take proper account of this truncation. These are described in the preceding sections and in chapter 2. Alternatively, rather than truncating the sample, we can attempt to expand the model by specifying equations whose function is to predict the values of the missing explanatory variables. In the demand and labour supply cases, these will take the form of statistical models explaining individual prices or wage rates in terms of observable variables.

The choice between these two approaches is not clear-cut. Methods based on the truncated sample are inefficient, since they waste information, and they also tend to be rather less robust to departures from normality than full-sample methods; however, they do not require the specification (possibly mis-specification) of additional relationships, and they are also computationally simpler. Thus sample truncation may be a perfectly sensible policy in many cases. Nevertheless, in this section we concentrate on full-sample methods requiring extension of the model, and, for concreteness, we examine the special case of a very simple labour supply model. Wales and Woodland (1980) give a more complete survey of the available estimation techniques for models of this simple type. Generalization to the more complicated models discussed in previous sections is straightforward, at least in principle.

Consider the following linear labour supply equation:

$$h_n^* = \gamma_1 w_n + \gamma_2 y_n + \gamma_3' \mathbf{z}_n + \epsilon_n \tag{4.150}$$

where h_n^* is latent hours of work, w_n is the wage, y_n is unearned income, $\mathbf{z}_n$ is a vector of observed personal characteristics and ϵ_n is a random disturbance term.

This equation may be either an *ad hoc* Tobit model or it could arise from an explicit foundation in choice theory. On assuming that all households face the same consumption good price level, which can then be normalized at unity, Hausman (1980) has shown that (4.150) is consistent with rational choice if preferences are representable by a stochastic indirect utility function:

$$H(w, y; \mathbf{z}_n) = \exp(\gamma_2 y)\left[y + \frac{\gamma_1}{\gamma_2} w - \frac{\gamma_1}{\gamma_2^2} + \frac{\gamma_3' \mathbf{z}_n + \epsilon_n}{\gamma_2}\right] \tag{4.151}$$

with $\gamma_1 \geqslant 0$ and $\gamma_2 \leqslant 0$. Since this is a simple two-good choice problem, a corner solution for hours of work is equivalent to the operation of the usual Tobit censoring mechanism:

$$h_n = \max(h_n^*, 0). \tag{4.152}$$

The variable w_n is unobservable for those who do not participate in the labour force, and therefore a model of the wage is required. In specifying this wage equation, the applied worker can draw on a large theoretical and applied literature on the determinants of individual earnings (see Mincer, 1974; and Griliches, 1977). In view of the linearity of equation (4.150), the most convenient specification for w_n would be a linear regression model. However, this is unsatisfactory since w_n must always be positive, and a more appealing model is the widely used semi-log specification:

$$\log w_n = \delta' \xi_n + \nu_n \tag{4.153}$$

where ξ_n is a vector of explanatory variables such as educational attainment, length of work experience, job characteristics etc., δ is the corresponding coefficient vector and ν_n is a random disturbance.

A very simple two-stage estimator is widely used; the study by Layard, Barton and Zabalza (1980) is a typical example. The two stages are the following.

i Compute $\hat{\delta}$ by regressing log w_n on ξ_n, using only observations on individuals who are in the labour force; construct $\hat{w}_n = \exp(\hat{\delta}'\xi_n)$ for all observations.

ii Estimate the labour supply model by the Tobit technique, with $\hat{w}_n$ used as the wage variable.

This procedure has two major drawbacks: unless ϵ_n and ν_n are independent, $\hat{\delta}$ is an inconsistent estimator, since least-squares regression is an inappropriate technique for use in a sample truncated with respect to a related variable (h_n^* in this case). Secondly, the use of $\hat{w}_n$ rather than w_n introduces an additional source of random variation, which invalidates the conventional theory of the Tobit estimator. The usual formulae for asymptotic standard errors and test statistics are incorrect, and in our example the Tobit estimator is generally inconsistent, even if a consistent $\hat{\delta}$ is used at the first stage.

Proper ML estimation is clearly preferable, although rather more complicated. Assume that ϵ_n and ν_n have a bivariate normal distribution with zero means and covariance matrix

$$\Sigma = \begin{bmatrix} \sigma_{\epsilon\epsilon} & \sigma_{\epsilon\nu} \\ \sigma_{\epsilon\nu} & \sigma_{\nu\nu} \end{bmatrix}. \tag{4.154}$$

Write the p.d.f. of this distribution $\varphi(\epsilon, \nu; 0, \Sigma)$. The Jacobian of the transformation from (ϵ, ν) to $(h^*, \log w)$ is

$$J(h^*, w) = \det \begin{bmatrix} 1 & \gamma_1 w \\ 0 & 1 \end{bmatrix} = 1 \tag{4.155}$$

and thus the joint distribution of h^* and log w has p.d.f.

$$f(h^*, \log w \mid y_n, \mathbf{z}_n, \xi_n) = \varphi(h^* - \gamma_1 w - \gamma_2 y_n - \gamma_3' \mathbf{z}_n, \log w - \delta'\xi_n; 0, \Sigma). \tag{4.156}$$

The probability that h_n is zero (and thus w_n unobserved) is

$$\Pr(h_n=0|y_n, \mathbf{z}_n, \xi_n) = \int_{-\infty}^{\infty}\int_{-\infty}^{0} \varphi[h^* - \gamma_1 \exp(W) - \gamma_2 y_n - \gamma_3'\mathbf{z}_n, W - \delta'\xi_n; 0, \Sigma)\, \mathrm{d}h^*\, \mathrm{d}W. \tag{4.157}$$

The log-likelihood for the full sample is therefore

$$\log L(\gamma_1, \gamma_2, \gamma_3, \delta, \Sigma) = K - \frac{N^+}{2}\log(\sigma_{\epsilon\epsilon}\sigma_{\nu\nu} - \sigma_{\epsilon\nu}^2) - \frac{1}{2}\sum_{h_n>0} \mathbf{d}_n'\Sigma^{-1}\mathbf{d}_n$$

$$+ \sum_{h_n=0} \log\left\{\int_{-\infty}^{\infty}\int_{-\infty}^{0} \varphi[h^* - \gamma_1 \exp(W) - \gamma_2 y_n - \gamma_3'\mathbf{z}_n, W - \delta'\xi_n; 0, \Sigma]\, \mathrm{d}h^*\, \mathrm{d}W\right\} \tag{4.158}$$

where N^+ is the number of positive observations and $\mathbf{d}_n' = [(h_n - \gamma_1 w_n - \gamma_2 y_n - \gamma_3'\mathbf{z}_n), (\log w_n - \delta'\xi_n)]$. Even for this simple model, the computational problems raised by the double integral in (4.158) are quite severe, although the decomposition of $\varphi(.; 0, \Sigma)$ into a conditional and marginal component can reduce this to a univariate integral (see appendix 3).

The difficulty here arises from the fact that we have specified this example as a non-linear system: (4.150) is linear in the wage, whereas (4.153) is linear in the logarithm of the wage. Looking at it another way, the complicated probability (4.115) is the probability that the actual wage does not exceed the reservation wage w_n^r, which is

$$w_n^r = -(\gamma_2 y_n + \gamma_3'\mathbf{z}_n + \epsilon_n)/\gamma_1. \tag{4.159}$$

The problem then is that $\log w_n - \log w_n^r$ is non-linear in the fundamental random variables ϵ_n and ν_n.

One can often avoid these problems by using an expedient stochastic specification or a more convenient functional form for labour supply. For instance, if the latent labour supply function were re-specified as

$$h_n^* = \gamma_1 \exp(-\epsilon_n)\, w_n + \gamma_2 y_n + \gamma_3'\mathbf{z}_n \tag{4.160}$$

then the log reservation wage would be

$$\log w_n^r = \log[-(\gamma_2 y_n + \gamma_3'\mathbf{z}_n)/\gamma_1] + \epsilon_n \tag{4.161}$$

provided that $(\gamma_2 y_n + \gamma_3'\mathbf{z}_n)/\gamma_1 < 0$. Thus, the non-participation probability would be

$$\begin{aligned}\Pr(h_n=0|y_n, \mathbf{z}_n, \xi_n) &= \Pr(\nu_n - \epsilon_n < \log[-(\gamma_2 y_n + \gamma_3'\mathbf{z}_n)/\gamma_1] - \delta'\xi_n \\ &= \Phi\left\{\frac{\log[-(\gamma_2 y_n + \gamma_3'\mathbf{z}_n)/\gamma_1 - \delta'\xi_n}{(\sigma_{\epsilon\epsilon} + \sigma_{\nu\nu} - 2\sigma_{\epsilon\nu})^{1/2}}\right\} \quad \text{if } (\gamma_2 y_n + \gamma_3'\mathbf{z}_n)/\gamma_1 < 0 \\ &= 0 \quad \text{if } (\gamma_2 y_n + \gamma_3'\mathbf{z}_n)/\gamma_1 \geqslant 0\end{aligned} \tag{4.162}$$

and there is no need for numerical integration at all. However, stochastic specifications chosen like this purely on grounds of convenience are rarely convincing.

In most of the applied literature, the problem is avoided in a different way, by using the same transformation of w_n in the hours equation as in the wage equation. For example, Heckman (1974), after some unsuccessful experimentation with Box–Cox transformations, uses the log wage in both equations (Stern, 1986, discusses the form of individual preferences from which such a supply function arises). If the wage enters (4.150) in a log-linear rather than linear fashion, the log reservation wage is

$$\log w_n^{\mathrm{r}} = -(\gamma_2 y_n + \gamma_3' \mathbf{z}_n + \epsilon_n)/\gamma_1 \tag{4.163}$$

yielding a non-participation probability

$$\begin{aligned} \Pr(h_n = 0 \mid y_n, \mathbf{z}_n, \xi_n) &= \Pr(\nu_n + \epsilon_n/\gamma_1 < -[\delta'\xi_n + (\gamma_2 y_n + \gamma_3'\mathbf{z}_n)/\gamma_1]) \\ &= 1 - \Phi\left[\frac{\delta'\xi_n + (\gamma_2 y_n + \gamma_3'\mathbf{z}_n)/\gamma_1}{(\sigma_{\nu\nu} + \sigma_{\epsilon\epsilon}/\gamma_1^2 + 2\sigma_{\epsilon\nu}/\gamma_1)^{1/2}}\right]. \end{aligned} \tag{4.164}$$

Again, integration is not required.

The point to be made here is that, by choosing model specifications with an eye to computational convenience, it is often possible to avoid the apparent complexity of expressions like (4.157). However, one would prefer to choose a specification for its ability to approximate a wide range of behaviour rather than its computational convenience, and, as Stern (1986) points out, the nature of applied results may be very sensitive to such specification changes.

Further reading

Amemiya (1986, chapter 10) contains a very extensive review of the Tobit model and various extensions of it, concentrating on the statistical structure of these models rather than their relationship to choice theory. Maddala (1983, chapters 6–8) is also a valuable reference. Three special issues of the *Journal of Econometrics* (*Annals 1984–1*, *1986–1* and *1987–1*) contain many of the recent developments in the statistical theory of the Tobit model and related structures. Research activity is particularly intense in the area of distribution-free estimation, although little of this work has yet seen application to applied problems. Robinson (1986a, 1986b) surveys the alternative approaches to non-parametric estimation that appear in this theoretical literature.

Simultaneous systems of censored, truncated and discrete variables have been widely discussed in the econometric literature, and the subject matter of sections 4.2 and 4.3 can be regarded as a special case of this class of models. Maddala (1983, chapter 7) provides a good survey. Without further restriction, these general structures are difficult to specify, since they must be forced to satisfy coherency conditions for logical consistency (see Amemiya, 1974; Heckman, 1978; and Schmidt, 1981). The theory of choice imposes a very specific structure on an econometric model, and this structure naturally leads to a coherent model; see Ransom (1987) for an example of the link between the convexity of preferences and these coherency conditions.

5

Non-linear budget frontiers

Be thy intents wicked or charitable,
thou com'st in such a questionable shape

Hamlet

The real world can be appallingly complicated. The standard economic model of the consumer's allocation problem envisages fixed prices, leading to an opportunity set with a simple linear frontier. Yet a moment's thought suggests that, in practice, this is the exception rather than the rule. One is charged a smaller unit price for the contents of a large box of cornflakes than for a small box. Electricity usage is charged on a multipart tariff. Progressive income taxation and social security contribution schedules make the net wage vary with hours worked. The rules governing social security benefits complicate the budget constraint for the labour supply decision still further. The rate of return on savings is better for large savers than for small savers.

These are typical examples of non-linearity in the frontiers of actual opportunity sets. Generally, these non-linearities take the form of kinks and breaks in a piecewise-linear frontier. In many cases, these frontiers turn out to be exceedingly complicated, making the task of the econometrician (and also the individual decision-maker, of course) very difficult indeed.

In section 5.1 we examine a few of the ways in which these opportunity sets can arise in practice. To avoid undue complication, we then restrict attention to the simplest one-dimensional labour supply example. Section 5.2 discusses this in the context of a very simple stochastic specification, with preferences assumed to be non-stochastic. Section 5.3. generalizes this to allow for stochastic variation in one of the preference parameters. Section 5.4 outlines the difficulties associated with these conventional stochastic specifications, and discusses alternative approaches.

5.1 Some examples

There are an immense number of practical examples of non-linear constraints on economic behaviour. In this section, we introduce a few of the more common cases.

5.1.1 Non-linear pricing schemes

An example of non-linear pricing, involving discounts for bulk buying, has already been discussed in chapter 1, section 1.2.4. More complicated cases are also common. For instance, many suppliers, especially those operating in the presence of high fixed costs, use multipart pricing schemes. Examples are gas, electricity and telephone utilities. These pricing schemes have at least two components. One is a fixed amount (usually in the form of a rental for the physical connection to the supply) entitling the consumer to purchase the good but independent of the amount purchased. Additional to this is a normal pricing schedule, usually with a constant unit price. Some pricing schemes also offer alternative rental–price combinations, intended for different classes of consumer, or allow the price per unit to depend in some way on total consumption.

A hypothetical example is illustrated in figured 5.1. In this case, the good x_1 can be bought under either of two schedules characterized by rentals r^a and r^b and prices p_1^a and p_1^b. Schedule b has a high rental but low unit price and is aimed at larger consumers. The resulting budget frontier consists of three parts: an isolated point corresponding to non-payment of either rental (and thus non-consumption of x_1) at co-ordinates $(0, y/p_2)$; a linear segment characterized by prices p_1^a and p_2 and (virtual) income $y - r^a$; a linear segment characterized by prices p_1^b and p_2 and virtual income $y - r^b$.

This form of multipart pricing always leads to a non-convex opportunity set because of the isolated point $(0, y/p_2)$ produced by the rental charge. In our example, the choice of schedules leads to a further non-convexity. When the opportunity set is non-convex, a tangency between the budget constraint and an indifference curve no longer necessarily implies an optimal choice. In our example, there is a tangency at (x_1^*, x_2^*), but optimal behaviour corresponds to the point $(0, y/p_2)$.

Another example of non-linear pricing is the season ticket. Many transportation authorities and suppliers of other services offer a choice between simple constant unit pricing and a flat-rate price for a season ticket which allows unlimited access to the service. Consider the example of figure 5.2, where x_1 is the number of bus journeys per year, priced either at p_1 per journey or at a flat rate s for unlimited travel.

Again, the opportunity set is non-convex. In this case, it is optimal to buy a season ticket and make x_1^* journeys per year, despite the tangency at x_1^{**}

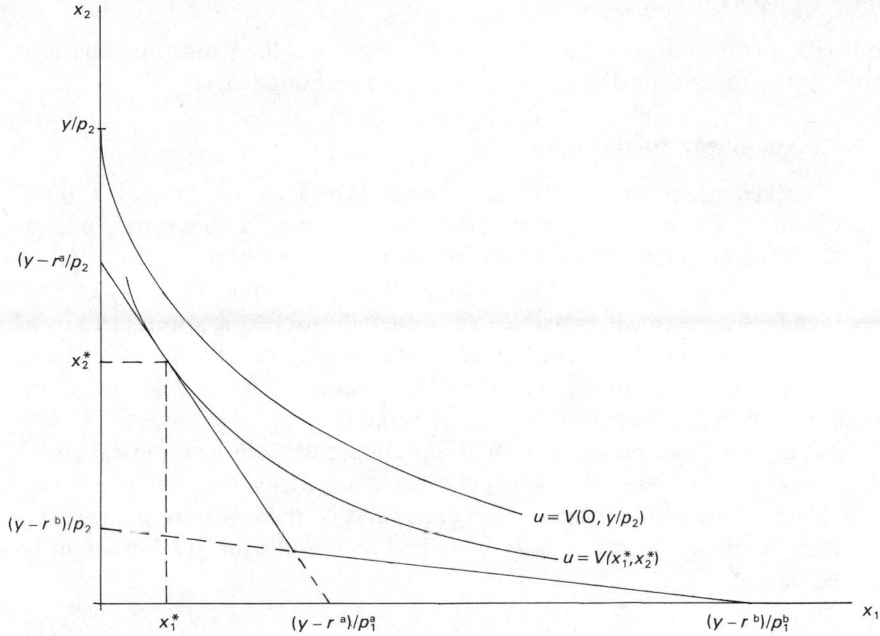

Figure 5.1 A multipart pricing scheme.

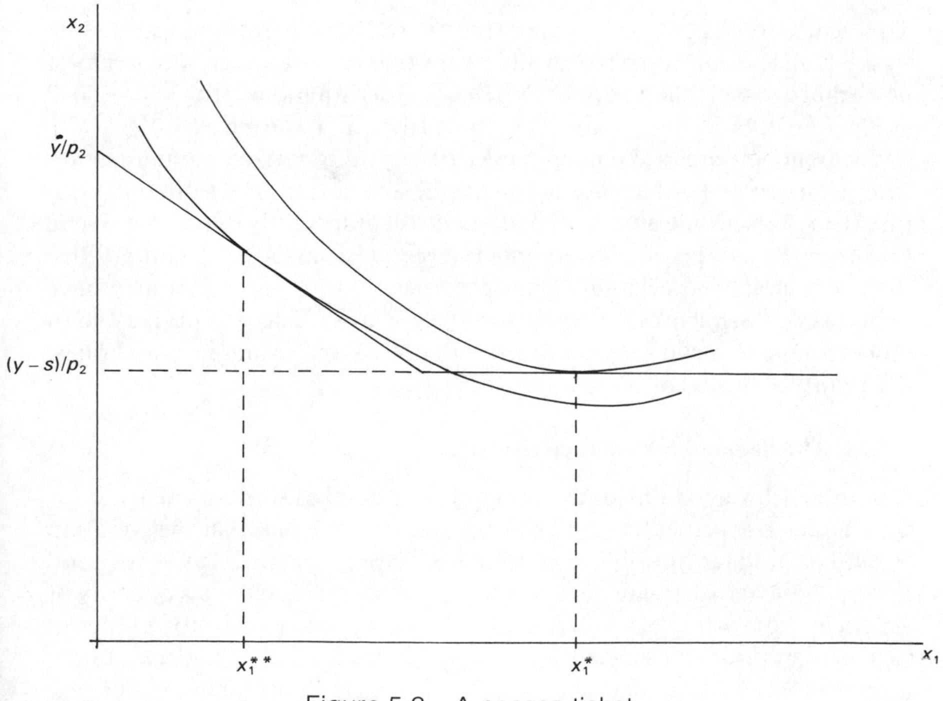

Figure 5.2 A season ticket.

journeys on the non-season ticket segment. Note that there must be satiation with respect to x_1 if the demand for travel is to be bounded.

5.1.2 Non-linear interest rates

If one walked into a bank in the UK in late 1986 and asked to borrow £1000, one would have to pay an interest rate of approximately 15 per cent. To lend £1000 to the same bank through the medium of a deposit account would yield a rate of return of 5 per cent. On the other hand, if a larger sum, say £5000, were available, it would be possible to open a high-interest account, yielding a return of 8 per cent. This dependence of the interest rate on the size of the debt contradicts the assumption of perfect capital markets that underlies most intertemporal models of consumer behaviour.

Consider the example of an individual allocating consumption expenditures between two years. These expenditures are denoted x_1 and x_2. If the fixed levels of income in the two years are y_1 and y_2, there is no initial wealth, and the interest rate schedule is as described above, the budget constraint is the following:

$$1.15x_1 + x_2 = 1.15y_1 + y_2 \qquad \text{for } y_1 < x_1 \tag{5.1}$$

$$1.05x_1 + x_2 = 1.05y_1 + y_2 \qquad \text{for } 0 < y_1 - x_1 < 5000 \tag{5.2}$$

$$1.08x_1 + x_2 = 1.08y_1 + y_2 \qquad \text{for } y_1 - x_1 \geqslant 5000. \tag{5.3}$$

This leads to a non-convex opportunity set of the form illustrated in figure 5.3. The non-convexity again means that tangency conditions cannot be assumed to yield the true optimum, and corner solutions, at $x_1 = y_1 - 5000$ as illustrated, or at $x_1 = y_1$, are likely to be frequent occurrences.

The common practice among banks of imposing a fixed administration charge on accounts which are not in credit would lead to a second discontinuity in the schedule at $x_1 = y_1$, making it still more costly to borrow. These breaks in the frontier imply very much larger costs associated with positive than with negative deviations from a corner solution, and thus may have important consequences for stochastic specification, since people may go to more trouble to avoid expensive errors than to avoid inconsequential ones. We return to this issue in section 5.4.

5.1.3 The demand for characteristics

It is often helpful to think of the demand for a good as a derived demand for the characteristics that the good embodies or for a service that the good can be used to produce (possibly in conjunction with other goods). We buy food for the characteristics of taste and nutrition; a television set and a quantity of electricity together yield entertainment; a car and a quantity of petrol together produce transportation services. In each case, it is these fundamental services, rather than the good itself, that are the real objects of pre-

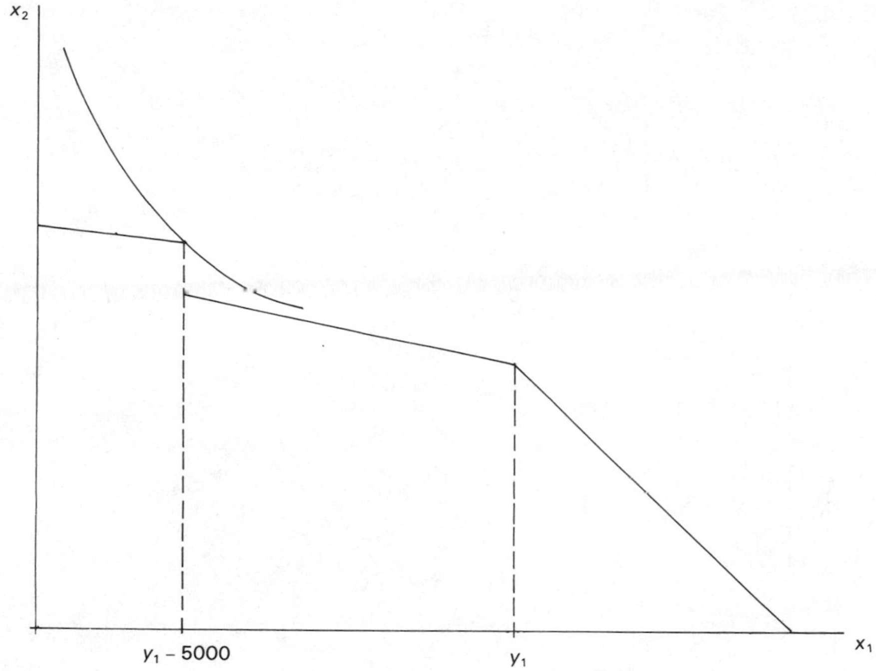

Figure 5.3 The intertemporal budget constraint under variable interest rates.

ferences. If the analysis is conducted in terms of characteristics rather than goods, the opportunity set has a non-linear frontier, whose form depends on the technological relationship between the purchased goods and the services or characteristics they yield.

Consider the following example (essentially the model of Gorman, 1956, and Lancaster, 1971), based on a linear goods–characteristics technology. There are four perfectly divisible goods, purchased in quantities $\xi_1, \ldots, \xi_4$ at prices $p_1, \ldots, p_4$, and these goods yield two distinct characteristics x_1 and x_2. Preferences are represented in characteristics space by a utility function $V(x_1, x_2)$. The linear technology is as follows:

$$x_1 = \alpha_{11}\xi_1 + \ldots + \alpha_{41}\xi_4 \tag{5.4}$$

$$x_2 = \alpha_{12}\xi_1 + \ldots + \alpha_{42}\xi_4. \tag{5.5}$$

We assume also that there is no free disposal of characteristics: (5.4) and (5.5) are strict equalities, not inequalities. The opportunity set in (x_1, x_2) space is as illustrated in figure 5.4.

The four marked points are the combinations of characteristics yielded by the four extreme cases in which only a single good is purchased. The linearity and divisibility assumptions imply an opportunity set that is the convex hull

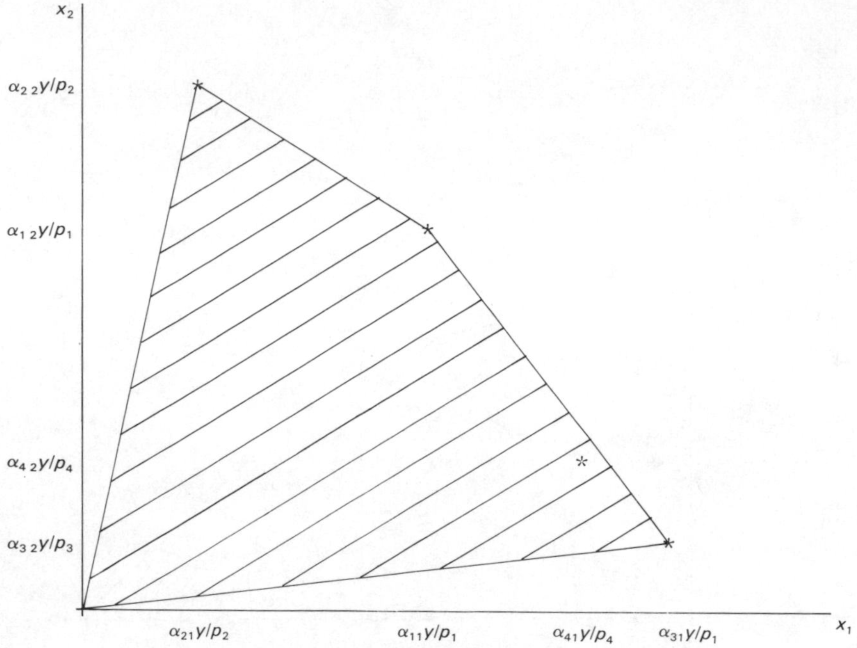

Figure 5.4 The opportunity set for a linear goods–characteristics technology.

of these four points and the origin. The set does not reach the axes since there is no free disposal assumption: if we buy only good 2, for instance, it is not possible to throw away its complement of characteristic 1 to reach the point $(x_1=0, x_2=\alpha_{22}y/p_2)$.

As drawn in figure 5.4, good 4 will never be consumed by a strictly rational individual: a suitable combination of goods 1 and 3 allows a higher indifference curve to be reached. Moreover, since every point on the frontier can be achieved by consuming either a single good (at a vertex) or a pair of goods (on a facet), it is never rational to buy more than two goods. We could, of course, handle this model in ξ space, rather than x space, and maximize a utility function $V(\Sigma\alpha_{i1}\xi_i, \Sigma\alpha_{i2}\xi_i)$ subject to $\Sigma p_i\xi_i = y$. However, this merely exchanges the difficulty of a piecewise-linear budget constraint for the difficulty of the corner solutions implied by preferences of this form.

The implications of strict rationality in this type of model are often unacceptable – we tend to observe consumption of a very wide range of goods, including goods that appear to be inefficient as sources of the obvious measurable characteristics. To avoid the prediction of widespread non-consumption, one must adopt a stochastic specification that allows consumption at points in the interior of the opportunity set, or allow different individuals to have different perceptions of the goods (by specifying the α_{ij} as random), or else allow the goods to have some direct utility of their own (through a desire for variety in consumption, perhaps). The last device simplifies the analysis enormously, and has been exploited by Gorman (1956) and Pudney (1981).

A rather different approach must be taken for many problems involving durable goods. There is typically a variety of models of any durable goods from which to choose, and the selected model is used in conjunction with a divisible good such as gas, electricity or petrol to provide a service such as room heating or transportation. The structure of this problem is identical with the multipart pricing scheme illustrated in figure 5.1 above. The annualized purchase and maintenance costs of the durable are equivalent to the rental charge, and the efficiencies with which the alternative models use energy, together with the price of energy, determine the effective unit price of the derived service. There may be a tradeoff between the cost of the durable and its efficiency in use, yielding non-convexities of the type illustrated in figure 5.1.

The only major difference between the durables purchase–utilization problem and the multipart pricing problem is that durable goods tend to have other specific (and often unmeasurable) characteristics, such as appearance, size, social prestige etc. This suggests that the utilities associated with the different budget segments may have unobserved random components, and thus lead to a mixed discrete–continuous choice problem of the type discussed in chapter 3, section 3.7. Empirical studies of this type have been conducted by Dubin and McFadden (1984) and Hausman (1979a).

5.1.4 The UK tax–social security system

In chapter 1, section 1.2.3, we examined some very simple convex opportunity sets in the context of labour supply and income taxation. In practice, the problem is much more difficult, because taxation and social security systems are usually extremely complicated. To illustrate the immense complexity of the opportunity sets confronting many individuals, we shall consider, as an example, the treatment of a hypothetical low-income household by the UK tax–social security system as it existed in 1986. This illustrative household consists of a single parent and three children aged under ten years, two of whom are of school age. The parent is able to earn income at the low wage rate of £3 per hour, increasing to £4.50 for overtime hours (which begin at 40 hours per week), and also receives on behalf of the children a maintenance payment of £20 per week from an ex-spouse. The (fixed) rent on the family home is £30 per week, the cost of midday school meals for the two children attending school is £5 per week, and the hourly cost of nursery facilities for the child of pre-school age is £1.

The relevant taxation and social security systems are governed by the following rules. These are given in the forms prevailing in mid-1986, and are taken largely from Kay and King (1986), Cohen and Lakhani (1986) and Smith and Rowland (1986).

Income tax The basic rate of income tax is 29 per cent, applying to taxable income up to the limit of £311.50 per week, after which the marginal rate increases to 40 per cent, with further progression in higher income brackets. Taxable income in this case is based on the earned income of the parent only, and does not include social security benefits or the children's maintenance receipts. Subtracted from this is a tax allowance of £66.44 per week, comprising the single person's and single parent's allowances of £42.40 and £24.04 respectively.

National Insurance Contributions A person earning less than £35.50 per week pays no national insurance contribution. Over this threshold, contributions are made at a rate of 5 per cent of total earnings up to a second threshold at £55 per week. If this is exceeded, contributions are made at the rate of 7 per cent of total earnings up to the final threshold of £90 per week, where the rate raises to 9 per cent. The fact that these higher contribution rates apply to the whole of earnings rather than to earnings in excess of the threshold leads to discontinuities in the hours–earnings frontier.

Child benefit All households receive a payment of £7 per week for every child under the age of 16 years.

One-parent benefit A single parent receives £4.55 per week for each child under 16 years of age.

Supplementary benefit The supplementary benefit system is extremely complicated. Supplementary benefit is payable only to people working less than 30 hours per week. The weekly payment is calculated as the difference between a measure of needs and a measure of resources. Ignoring any special requirements and assuming that the basic rather than the long-term rate applies, in our example needs will be assessed as £29.50 per week for the parent and £10.10 per week for each of the children, plus the total housing cost (which is paid in full under a linked scheme known as certificated housing benefit). Resources include receipts of maintenance, child benefit, one-parent benefit, family income supplement (see below) and an amount related to earnings. The last item consists of net earnings less the cost of child care for hours spent at work, less a personal allowance of £4 per week and less a single-parent allowance of half the earnings between £4 and £20 per week.

Free school meals School meals are free for children whose parents are in receipt of supplementary benefit. In our example, this amounts to a payment in kind of £5 per week.

Family income supplement Family income supplement (FIS) can be claimed by anyone who has at least one dependent child and who is in full-time work (defined as a minimum of 24 hours per week for a single parent). FIS is calculated as 50 per cent of the difference between a measure of normal gross income and a prescribed income level. The income measure comprises gross weekly earnings and maintenance receipts. The prescribed income level is £97.50 for a one-child family plus an extra £11.50 for each additional child, making a total of £120.50 for our example. There is an upper limit on weekly FIS payments, however, computed as £25 for a one-child family plus £2.50 for each additional child, yielding a maximum possible payment of £30 per week in our example.

Housing benefit People receiving supplementary benefit usually receive full relief for their housing costs. However, there is an additional housing benefit system applying to people who are on low incomes but do not receive supplementary benefit. The amount of housing benefit again depends on a comparison of needs and resources. Needs are defined as £47.70 per week for the parent plus £14.50 for each child: £91.20 in our example. Resources are defined as receipts of child benefit, one-parent benefit, FIS and maintenance plus any gross weekly earnings above an allowance of £17.30 per week. The housing benefit payment is calculated as 60 per cent of rent (including rates) and either *plus* 33 per cent of the difference between needs and resources if needs exceed resources, or *less* 42 per cent of the difference between resources and needs, if resources exceed needs.

In fact, this is a highly simplified picture of the UK system: there are in addition many special irregular benefits and also exclusions, and the rules for multi-earner households and for people suffering involuntary unemployment, sickness or disability are more complicated still. The civil servants who administer the system also have considerable discretionary powers over the application of some of these rules. A more detailed description can be found in Kay and King (1986), Cohen and Lakhani (1986) and Smith and Rowland (1986).

If we assume that our hypothetical parent is free to choose his or her hours of work, the budget constraint for this choice problem is the work–income frontier of figure 5.5. Its complexity is astonishing.

The opportunity set for this hypothetical individual is hopelessly non-convex. Moreover, its frontier has no less than five discontinuities. The first of these is caused by the loss of entitlement to supplementary benefit, and thus of free school meals, at roughly 9 hours of work per week. The next two discontinuities, at 12 and 18 hours, are caused by the initial impact of national insurance contributions and then their increase to 7 per cent. At 24 hours per week, the family qualifies for FIS payments, and this causes a very large discontinuity. Finally, at 30 hours, the last increase in national

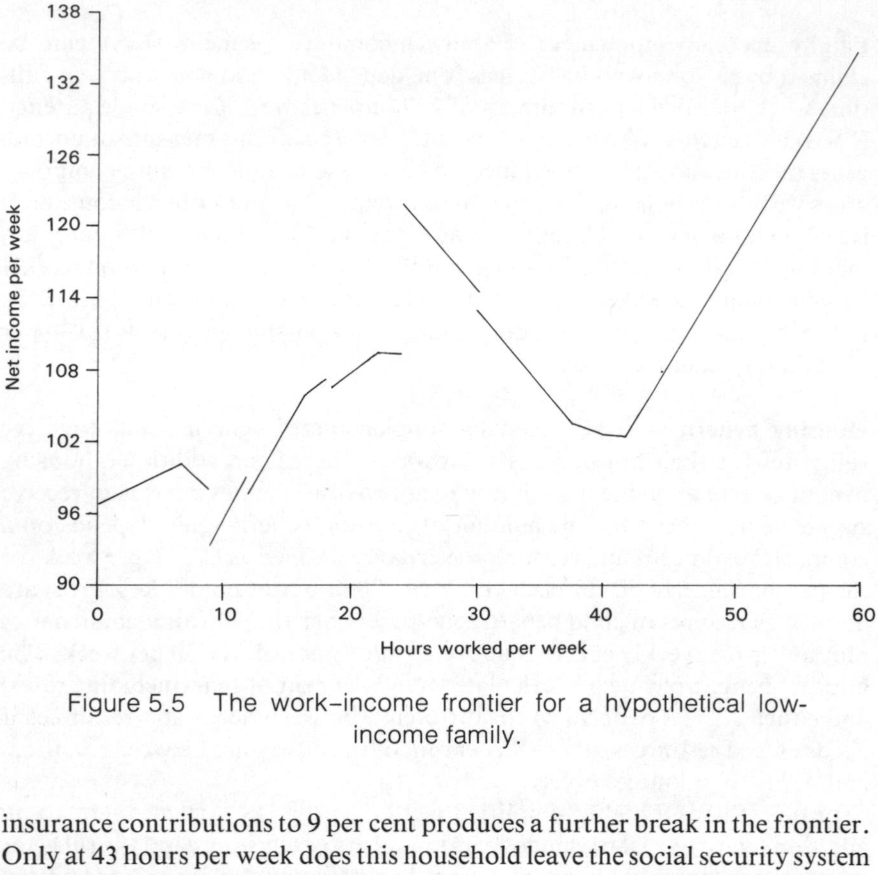

Figure 5.5 The work–income frontier for a hypothetical low-income family.

insurance contributions to 9 per cent produces a further break in the frontier. Only at 43 hours per week does this household leave the social security system completely. Thus, our hypothetical family suffers particularly badly from the poverty trap: for most low levels of labour supply, any effort to improve the standard of living by working marginally longer hours is self-defeating, since it leaves the household worse off.

There are several important points to make about these labour supply problems, particularly where low-income households are involved. The complexity of the budget frontier makes it very difficult to characterize optimal behaviour, and thus construct and estimate a behavioural model. Complexity of this order also makes it much harder to believe in the hypothesis of utility maximization: it may simply be beyond the analytical power of many individuals to decide on the best policy. (The author's initial attempt to construct this budget frontier without the aid of a computer was a sobering experience.) Moreover, people often have only a hazy appreciation of the social security system: the perceived budget constraint may differ substantially from the actual constraint. This conjecture is supported by evidence of considerable shortfalls in the take-up of many social security benefits (see, for instance, Townsend, 1979; and Duncan, 1984). If the individual is aware of the uncertainty surrounding his or her treatment by the social security system, then the maximization of expected rather than actual utility is appropriate; Hausman (1985) discusses one such case.

A further characteristic of many of these labour supply problems is the wide variation across individuals in the forms of opportunity sets. Variation in personal circumstances and in the potential wage can completely alter the nature of the budget constraint. This is illustrated in figure 5.6, which shows the work–income frontier for a household identical with that of figure 5.5 but with the wage rate doubled to £6 per hour. The kinks and discontinuities become much less pronounced and the complexities of the social security system are left behind at 21 hours rather than 43 hours as before.

A final point that we ignore in the remainder of this chapter, but return to in chapter 7, is that labour supply decisions (unlike most demand decisions) are often subject to rationing. In figure 5.5, it is highly likely that the individual will decide to work 24 hours per week. In practice, it may not be possible to find an employer willing to take on employees at 24 hours per week (at least, not at the full potential wage of £3). Thus, observed and optimal decisions may differ widely. The models we discuss in this chapter assume that these deviations are purely random with zero means, but this

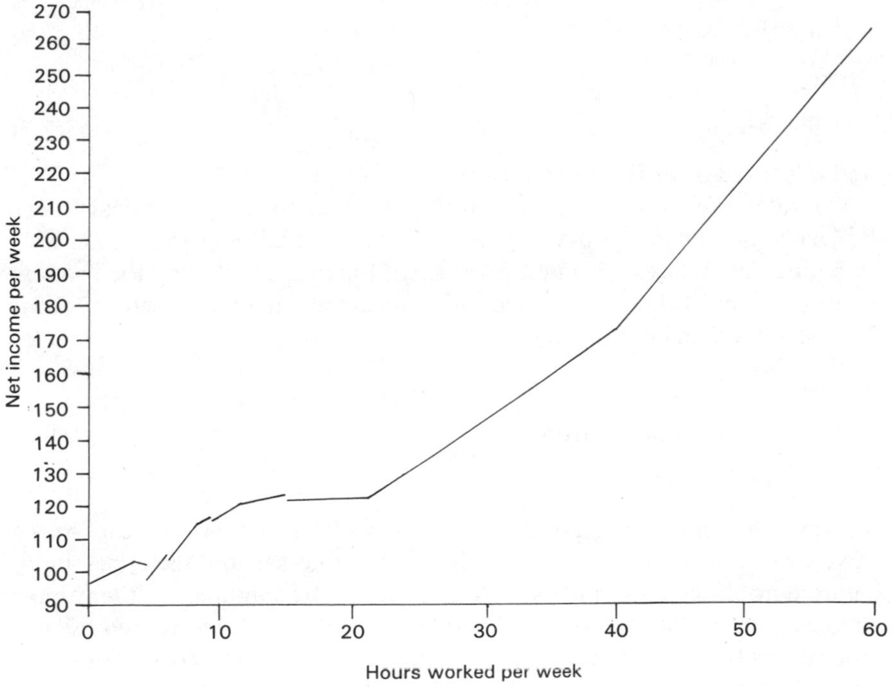

Figure 5.6 The effect of doubling the wage.

may be a dangerous assumption: casual empiricism suggests that demand-side constraints on hours worked are very important and operate in a systematic rather than random fashion. We defer consideration of this problem until chapter 7.

5.2 Models with deterministic preferences

We begin by assuming that preferences are non-stochastic, and thus that any variation in tastes is due exclusively to observable personal attributes $\mathbf{z}_n$. Our model is extremely simple, involving only a choice between two goods (consumption and hours of leisure, say) made by a single individual. It thus abstracts from many of the complexities of real examples, where there may be more than one potential supplier of labour in the household and many goods with non-linear pricing schemes.

5.2.1 The behavioural model

Let the quantities of the two goods concerned be x_1 and x_2. Good 1 (leisure, say) is subject to a piecewise-linear pricing schedule. Good 2 (composite consumption, say) is sold at a constant price p_2. Preferences, which we assume to be strictly convex, are represented by the following direct utility function:

$$u = V(x_1, x_2; \beta) \tag{5.6}$$

where

$$\beta = \beta(\mathbf{z}; \alpha) \tag{5.7}$$

and α is a vector of fixed parameters.

Consider the maximization of utility subject to a hypothetical linear budget constraint $p_1x_1 + p_2x_2 = y$. Note that, in the labour supply case, with x_1 defined as leisure, y is interpreted as full income, including the shadow value of the individual's total time endowment (see chapter 1, section 1.2.3). This yields a demand function

$$x_1 = \breve{x}_1(p_1, p_2, y; \beta) \tag{5.8}$$

and an indirect utility function

$$u = H(p_1, p_2, y; \beta). \tag{5.9}$$

Now consider the actual budget frontier, which is piecewise linear. As we have seen in the examples discussed in the previous section, the opportunity set need not be convex, and its frontier need not be continuous: it may have breaks, and there may also be isolated feasible points. A general representation of this frontier is in the form of the union of a number (r, say) of open-ended linear segments, each defined by an equation

$$p_1^i x_1 + p_2 x_2 = y^i \tag{5.10}$$

on the interval

$$a^i < x_1 < b^i \qquad i = 1, \ldots, r \tag{5.11}$$

together with a number (s, say) of discrete points:

$$\begin{aligned} x_1 &= \bar{x}_1^i \\ x_2 &= \bar{x}_2^i \end{aligned} \qquad i = 1, \ldots, s \tag{5.12}$$

In most practical examples, the linear segments are closed at one or both ends, and thus the majority of the points defined by (5.12) will close one end of one or more of the intervals (5.11).

As an illustration of this, consider figure 5.7, which represents both a convex opportunity set with a continuous frontier and a more complicated non-convex case with a discontinuous frontier.

The problem illustrated in figure 5.7(a) might apply to labour supply, with x_1 being hours of leisure, x_2 the quantity of consumption goods, and the budget set arising from a progressive tax system with three tax rates applied to an individual with unearned income equal to $p_2\bar{x}_2^4$. There are $r = 3$ linear segments, each characterized by different (p_1, y) pairs, and $s = 4$ points $\bar{x}^i = (\bar{x}_1^i, \bar{x}_2^i)$, which are merely the end points of these segments. Thus, we have $a^1 = \bar{x}_1^1 = 0$, $b^1 = a^2 = \bar{x}_1^2$, $b^2 = a^3 = \bar{x}_1^3$ and $b_3 = \bar{x}_1^4$.

Figure 5.7(b) might arise from the treatment of a similar individual under a two-part income support system that applies only to people in employment: hence the downward jump of the frontier at $x_1 = \bar{x}_1^4$, since this point corresponds to non-participation. Note that a similar *upward* jump might occur if there were fixed costs associated with participation in the labour force: see Hausman (1980) and Cogan (1981) for examples. Figure 5.7(b) also shows a frontier comprising three linear segments and four isolated points. However, although we still have $a^1 = \bar{x}_1^1 = 0$, $b^1 = a^2 = \bar{x}_1^2$ and $b^2 = a^3 = \bar{x}_1^3$, there are now discontinuities at $\bar{x}^2$ and $\bar{x}^4$, so that segments 1 and 3 cannot be defined on closed intervals. Moreover, $\bar{x}^4$ is not the end point of any segment.

5.2.2 The use of simple regression methods

Because of the complexity of most systems of direct taxation, it is common practice to analyse labour supply behaviour by ignoring all segments of the budget constraint except the one that the individual is observed to be on. Consider the example of figure 5.7(a), and denote the marginal tax rates associated with the three budget segments τ^1, τ^2 and τ^3. Individual n is on the i_nth segment. The marginal price of leisure there is $p_{n1} = w_n(1 - t_n)$, where w_n is the individual's wage rate and $t_n = \tau^{i_n}$ is the tax rate on the i_nth budget segment. If we extend this segment forward to zero hours of labour (in other words to $x_1 = \bar{x}_1^4$), its ordinate there is the virtual (full) income for segment i_n,

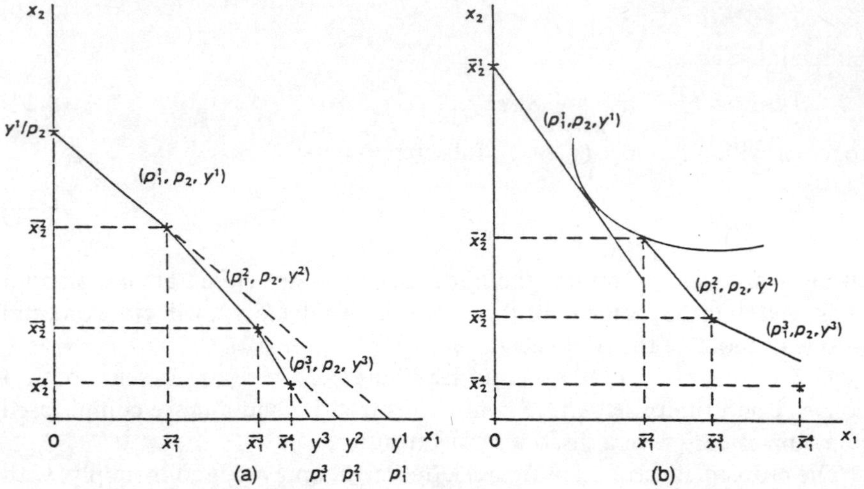

Figure 5.7 Convex and non-convex opportunity sets.

y_n^* say. We could then take the generic demand function for leisure and evaluate it at prices p_{n1}, p_{n2} and income y_n^*; ignoring the problem of censoring at $\bar{x}^4$, this implies an approximate regression model:

$$x_{n1} = \check{x}_1(p_{n1}, p_{n2}, y_n^*; \beta_n) \tag{5.13}$$

where v_n is the regression residual. Many other approximations are possible: for instance, one might use the person's average, rather than marginal, tax rate as the variable t_n and actual, rather than virtual, full income for y_n.

For simplicity, assume that the generic demand function is expressible in linear-in-parameters form:

$$x_{n1} = \gamma' \zeta_n + v_n \tag{5.14}$$

where ζ_n is a vector of observable variables defined as transformations of p_{n1}, p_{n2}, y_n^* and $\mathbf{z}_n$; γ is a vector of coefficients derived in some way from the underlying α.

The simple regression estimator is

$$\hat{\gamma} = \left[\sum_{n=1}^{N} \zeta_n \zeta_n'\right]^{-1} \left[\sum_{n=1}^{N} \zeta_n x_{n1}\right]. \tag{5.15}$$

Now assume that the true model is of regression form

$$x_{n1} = \tilde{x}_{n1} + \epsilon_n \tag{5.16}$$

where $\tilde{x}_n$ is the solution to the true utility maximization problem. The model (5.16) implies an estimation error of the form

$$\hat{\gamma} - \gamma = \left(\frac{1}{N}\sum_n \zeta_n\zeta_n'\right)^{-1}\left[\frac{1}{N}\sum_n \zeta_n\epsilon_n + \frac{1}{N}\sum_n \zeta_n(\tilde{x}_{n1} - \zeta_n'\gamma)\right]. \tag{5.17}$$

There are two sources of bias here. The first is a simultaneity problem: the person's work decision is affected by the rate of tax that he or she faces, but that rate of tax is also affected by the chosen level of labour supply, and the simple regression approach fails to distinguish between these two causal links. ζ_n is endogenous because it depends on the tax rate t_n, which depends on the individual's gross income, which is in turn a function of labour supply. This is manifested in a non-zero correlation between ϵ_n and one or more of the elements in ζ_n, implying a non-zero probability limit for the term $N^{-1}\Sigma\zeta_n\epsilon_n$ in (5.17).

A second source of bias lies in the mis-specification of the regression function $\tilde{x}_{n1}$. The simple regression approach is based on the assumption that if a person is observed on one segment of the budget frontier then the optimal demand for leisure, $\tilde{x}_{n1}$, must also be located at an interior point of that segment. It is this assumption that allows us to use the generic demand function $\check{x}_1(.)$ to characterize the optimum, and to identify unambiguously the relevant marginal tax rate. However, this assumption is incorrect, at least for some individuals: the presence of the random disturbance ϵ_n implies that the observed and optimal demands for leisure need not lie on the same segment. Moreover, it is possible that the optimal demand is at a vertex; at such a point, the optimum does not satisfy the marginal conditions which underlie $\check{x}_1(.)$, and so demand cannot be characterized by $\check{x}_1(.)$ evaluated at any observable tax rate. Thus, $\tilde{x}_{n1}$ differs systematically from $\zeta_n'\gamma$, and the term $N^{-1}\Sigma\zeta_n(\tilde{x}_{n1} - \zeta_n'\gamma)$ in (5.17) also converges to a non-zero probability limit.

If we believe that observed labour market behaviour is the outcome of free rational choice subject to the constraints imposed by the tax–benefit system, there is a very strong case for making an attempt to use econometric techniques that take proper account of the complexity of the opportunity set. We now turn our attention to this.

5.2.3 The maximum likelihood estimator

The conventional model with deterministic preferences proceeds as follows. Let $\tilde{x}_{n1}(\alpha)$ be the solution for x_1 to the following maximization problem facing individual n:

$$\max_{x_1, x_2} V(x_1, x_2; \boldsymbol{\beta}_n) \tag{5.18}$$

subject to

$$x_2 = \frac{y_n^i - p_{n1}^i x_1}{p_{n2}} \qquad \text{for } x_1 \in (a_n^i, b_n^i),\ i = 1, \ldots, r \tag{5.19}$$

and

$$x_2 = \bar{x}_2^i \qquad \text{for } x_1 = \bar{x}_1^i, i=1, \ldots, s. \tag{5.20}$$

Note that in the non-convex case there is no certainty that $\tilde{x}_{n1}$ will be unique: in the example of figure 5.7(b), for instance, the indifference curve as drawn yields two utility maximizing solutions for x_1. In real applications, such ambiguities will almost never arise: however, if necessary, some arbitrary rule must be specified for choosing between the alternative optima.

If departures from this optimum are purely random, and if there is no censoring at the extreme points $x_{n1} = 0$ and $x_{n1} = \bar{x}_{n1}^4$, then our stochastic model is the following:

$$x_{n1} = \tilde{x}_{n1}(\alpha) + \epsilon_n \tag{5.21}$$

where $E(\epsilon_n | \tilde{x}_{n1}) = 0$. This is a non-linear regression model, but it is considerably more complicated than the approximate model (5.13). Under the assumption of homoscedasticity and normality, the non-linear least-squares and ML estimators are identical:

$$\min_{\alpha} \sum_{n=1}^{N} [x_{n1} - \tilde{x}_{n1}(\alpha)]^2. \tag{5.22}$$

However, there is likely to be censoring at one or both ends of the range of admissible values for x_{n1}: people may not buy the good in question, or may not participate in the labour force. Suppose censoring is only encountered at the point $x_{n1} = \bar{x}^4{}_{n1}$ (which corresponds to non-participation in the labour force, if x is leisure). Redefine the vector ζ_n to contain all relevant exogenous variables $(p_{n1}^1 \ldots p_{n1}^r, p_{n2}, y_n^1 \ldots y_n^r, \bar{x}_1^1 \ldots \bar{x}_1^s, \bar{x}_2^1 \ldots \bar{x}_2^s, \mathbf{z}_n)$. Conditional on ζ_n, the observed x_{n1} has a UCN$(\tilde{x}_{n1}(\alpha), \sigma^2, \bar{x}_{n1}^4)$ distribution (see appendix 2), yielding a log-likelihood function

$$\log L(\alpha, \sigma) = K - N^+ \log \sigma - \frac{1}{2\sigma^2} \sum_{x_{n1} < \bar{x}^4{}_{n1}} [x_{n1} - \tilde{x}_{n1}(\alpha)]^2$$

$$+ \sum_{x_{n1} = \bar{x}_{n1}^4} \log \left\{ 1 - \Phi\left[\frac{\bar{x}_{n1}^4 - \tilde{x}_{n1}(\alpha)}{\sigma} \right] \right\} \tag{5.23}$$

where N^+ is the number of uncensored observations and K is the usual inessential constant.

In the case of labour supply, the gross wage which underlies the net wages $p_{n1}^1 \ldots p_{n1}^r$ is observed for individuals working zero hours, and this log-likelihood cannot be computed. This is the partial observability problem discussed in chapter 4, section 4.5. If the model is extended to include an equation explaining the gross wage, maximum likelihood becomes very complicated; for this reason, many applied researchers use simple least-squares predictions of the gross wage for non-workers. A better alternative may be to delete non-participants from the sample and use the conditional log-likelihood function based on the appropriate truncated normal distribution. This is merely a non-linear version of the truncated regression model discussed in chapter 2, section 2.5.

Even if $\tilde{x}_{n1}(\alpha)$ can be computed easily, the problem of optimizing the log-likelihood (5.23) or the residual sum of squares (5.22) may not be straightforward, since $\tilde{x}_{n1}(\alpha)$ (and hence the objective function) is not a smooth function of α; this is because there are kinks in $\tilde{x}_{n1}(\alpha)$ at every point at which some individual is on the margin of switching from one side of a budget kink point to the other. Moreover, there are typically ranges of α values for which the typical individual's optimum is 'stuck' at a vertex of the opportunity set, and thus $\tilde{x}_{n1}(\alpha)$ is flat over these ranges. The implication is that the least-squares or ML objective function is likely to have a large number of (very small) flat sections, and the estimator may not be unique, as a result. Indeed, if the budget frontier has discontinuities, $\tilde{x}_{n1}(\alpha)$ is not even a continuous function of α, and this means that there may not exist any values of α that minimize the residual sum of squares (5.22) or maximize the log-likelihood function (5.23).

Under normal conditions, provided that there is sufficient variability in preferences and opportunity sets, these problems disappear in large samples, since the influence of any one observation (and its concomitant flats and discontinuities) becomes negligible. However, there may be computational problems in practice. In their applied work, Burtless and Hausman (1978) and Blomquist (1983) encounter no difficulties in the use of gradient-based optimization algorithms to compute these estimators, but both authors work with a simple continuous problem. Computational problems may be much more severe in a more general setting.

We now turn to the details of computing the optimal point $\tilde{x}_{n1}(\alpha)$. Since there are few available models for which the generic demands (5.8) and direct and indirect utility functions (5.6) and (5.9) are known in closed form, it is particularly important to establish which of these three are required for the analysis.

The convex case If the opportunity set is convex, then computation of $\tilde{x}_{n1}(\alpha)$ presents few difficulties and requires only knowledge of the generic demand function $\breve{x}_1(.)$ defined by (5.8).

Consider the example of figure 5.7(a). An optimum on the first segment would lead to a value of $\breve{x}_1(p_1^1, p_2, y^1; \beta)$; if this lies in the admissible range (a^1, b^1), then $\tilde{x}_1$ corresponds to a classical tangency at this point. If $\breve{x}_1(p_1^1, p_2, y^1; \beta) \leqslant 0$, however, convexity implies that the global optimum must be a corner solution at the point $(0, y^1/p_2)$. If $\breve{x}_1(p_1^1, p_2, y^1; \beta) \geqslant \bar{x}_1^2$, then the optimum must lie at or beyond the point b_1, and further examination is necessary. For this, we move to the second segment, where a tangency occurs at the point $\breve{x}_1(p_1^2, p_2, y^2; \beta)$. If this lies at or to the left of $\bar{x}_1^2$, then a corner solution occurs at the point $(\bar{x}_1^2, \bar{x}_2^2)$; however, if $\check{x}_1(p_1^2, p_2, y^2; \beta) \in (\bar{x}_1^2, \bar{x}_1^3)$, then the optimum is a tangency at this point. If $\check{x}_1(p_1^2, p_2, y^2; \beta) \geqslant \bar{x}_1^3$, then the third segment must be used to determine where the optimum lies.

Thus, for the three-segment problem of figure 5.7(a), the solution $\tilde{x}_{n1}(\alpha)$ is as follows:

$$
\begin{aligned}
\tilde{x}_{n1}(\alpha) &= 0 && \text{if } \check{x}_{n1}^1 \leqslant 0 \\
&\quad \check{x}_{n1}^1 && \text{if } 0 < \check{x}_{n1}^1 < \bar{x}_{n1}^2 \\
&\quad \bar{x}_{n1}^2 && \text{if } \check{x}_{n1}^1 \geqslant \bar{x}_{n1}^2 \text{ and } \check{x}_{n1}^2 \leqslant \bar{x}_{n1}^2 \\
&\quad \check{x}_{n1}^2 && \text{if } \bar{x}_{n1}^2 < \check{x}_{n1}^2 < \bar{x}_{n1}^3 \\
&\quad \bar{x}_{n1}^3 && \text{if } \check{x}_{n1}^2 \geqslant \bar{x}_{n1}^3 \text{ and } \check{x}_{n1}^3 \leqslant \bar{x}_{n1}^3 \\
&\quad \check{x}_{n1}^3 && \text{if } \bar{x}_{n1}^3 < \check{x}_{n1}^3 < \bar{x}_{n1}^4 \\
&\quad \bar{x}_{n1}^4 && \text{if } \check{x}_{n1}^3 \geqslant \bar{x}_{n1}^4
\end{aligned} \tag{5.24}
$$

where

$$\check{x}_{n1}^i = \check{x}_1[p_{n1}^i, p_{n2}, y_n^i; \beta(\mathbf{z}_n; \alpha)]. \tag{5.25}$$

A simple computational scheme thus requires only the sequential examination of values of demand for successive segments of the budget frontier. This can be done at relatively small computational cost and requires only knowledge of the generic demand function (5.8) and not the direct or indirect utility function. Thus, the model could be used with an arbitrary flexible specification of demand possessing no convenient representation in terms of preferences, provided that the demand model is consistent with a strictly quasi-concave utility function. A further convenient aspect of this simple specification is that the sequential algorithm can be easily generalized to problems in more than two dimensions; see Hausman (1979b) and Hausman and Ruud (1984) for further discussion.

The general case Unfortunately, as we saw in the examples of section 5.1, the opportunity sets encountered in applied problems are often not convex. In such cases, the simple sequential search for an optimum described above cannot be guaranteed to generate the global utility maximum. The case illustrated in figure 5.7(b) is an example of this: sequential search will lead to a tangency on segment 1 being chosen as the optimum, despite the fact that the point $(\bar{x}_1^2, \bar{x}_2^2)$ lies on the same indifference curve. If preferences were such that the indifference curves had slightly less curvature than that illustrated, the latter point would dominate the erroneously chosen point of tangency.

Thus, a proper computational scheme must be based on a global examination of the budget frontier, with every possible type of local optimum being explicitly considered. Unfortunately, this requires the availability of a closed-form expression for the indirect utility function, so the class of models that can be conveniently handled is restricted to those for which such an expression is known.

Consider the example of figure 5.7(b). In principle, corner solutions at the points $(\bar{x}_1^1, \bar{x}_2^1)$ and $(\bar{x}_1^2, \bar{x}_2^2)$ are possibilities; solutions at $(\bar{x}_1^3, \bar{x}_2^3)$ and $(\bar{x}_1^4, \bar{x}_2^4)$ can be ruled out *a priori* because of the local non-convexities there. Interior solutions at points $x_1 = \check{x}_1(p_1^1, p_2, y^1; \beta)$, $\check{x}_1(p_1^2, p_2, y; \beta)$ and $\check{x}_1(p_1^3, p_2, y^3; \beta)$ are also possible, provided these lie within their admissible ranges of $(0, \bar{x}_1^2)$, $(\bar{x}_1^2, \bar{x}_1^3)$ and $(\bar{x}_1^3, \bar{x}_1^4)$ respectively. The indifference curves passing through these five (or fewer) points have associated with them utility values $V(\bar{x}_1^1, \bar{x}_2^1; \beta)$, $V(\bar{x}_1^2, \bar{x}_2^2; \beta)$, $H(p_1^1, p_2, y^1; \beta)$, $H(p_1^2, p_2, y^2; \beta)$ and $H(p_1^3, p_2, y^3; \beta)$ respectively. The global optimum $\tilde{x}_1$ corresponds to the greatest of these. In the case of a tie, some additional systematic rule must be adopted to resolve the ambiguity.

The algorithm implicitly defined by this description can be conveniently formalized as a two-stage procedure: first the opportunity set is split up into convex subsets (in our example, these subsets would correspond to the ranges $[0, \bar{x}_1^2)$, $[\bar{x}_1^2, \bar{x}_1^3]$ and $[\bar{x}_1^3, \bar{x}_1^4)$ for x_1), the utility maximum is located for each subset (using the sequential algorithm described above), and then the global maximum is chosen from these.

As it stands, this characterization of the optimum requires, in addition to the demand function $\check{x}_1(.)$, the availability of both direct and indirect utility functions. However, only the latter is usually necessary. Consider the evaluation of $V(\bar{x}_1^i, \bar{x}_2^i; \beta)$. If the demand function $\check{x}_1(.)$ is of simple form, it is usually feasible to solve the following equations for the virtual prices (see chapter 4, section 4.3.4) $\bar{p}_1^i$ and $\bar{p}_2^i$ that support the point $(\bar{x}_1^i, \bar{x}_2^i)$ (possibly using an iterative numerical algorithm):

$$\bar{x}_1^i = \check{x}_1(\bar{p}_1^i, \bar{p}_2^i, y; \beta) \tag{5.26}$$

$$\bar{p}_1^i \bar{x}_1^i + \bar{p}_2^i \bar{x}_2^i = y \tag{5.27}$$

where y can be set at an arbitrary value. These virtual prices can then be substituted into the indirect utility function to give

$$V(\bar{x}_1^i, \bar{x}_2^i; \beta) = H(\bar{p}_1^i, \bar{p}_2^i, y; \beta). \tag{5.28}$$

Thus, at the cost of a certain amount of extra effort, it is usually possible to solve the computational problems associated with this model even when the direct utility function is not available.

5.3 Models with random preferences

A restrictive feature of the model of the previous section is its assumption that all variation in preferences is attributable entirely to a vector of observed attributes $\mathbf{z}_n$. If, in addition to $\mathbf{z}_n$, there are some unobserved influences on preferences, then β_n must be assumed to be random rather than a non-stochastic function of $\mathbf{z}_n$. Thus we assume a utility function $u = V(x_1, x_2; \beta)$ as before but now regard β as a vector of unobserved random quantities with a joint distribution, conditional on $\mathbf{z}$, characterized by a c.d.f. $G_\beta(.\,|\,\mathbf{z};\boldsymbol{\alpha})$, where $\boldsymbol{\alpha}$ is a vector of fixed parameters.

5.3.1 The behavioural model

For a given $\boldsymbol{\beta}$, the individual's problem is identical with that discussed in the previous section. Write the value of x_1 that maximizes utility over the opportunity set as $\tilde{x}_{n1}(\boldsymbol{\beta})$. Now assume that deviations from this optimal choice have a conditional normal distribution, censored from above at $\bar{x}^4_{n1}$. The distribution of x_{n1} conditional on the vector ζ_n, containing all prices, income and $\mathbf{z}_n$, and on $\boldsymbol{\beta}_n$ is UCN$(\tilde{x}_{n1}(\boldsymbol{\beta}_n), \sigma^2, \bar{x}^4_{n1})$. Thus

$$\Pr(x_{n1}=\bar{x}^4_{n1}\,|\,\zeta_n,\boldsymbol{\beta}_n) = 1 - \Phi\left[\frac{\bar{x}^4_{n1}-\tilde{x}_{n1}(\boldsymbol{\beta}_n)}{\sigma}\right] \tag{5.29}$$

$$f(x_{n1}\,|\,\zeta_n,\boldsymbol{\beta}_n) = \sigma^{-1}\,\varphi\left[\frac{x_{n1}-\tilde{x}_{n1}(\boldsymbol{\beta}_n)}{\sigma}\right]. \tag{5.30}$$

Since $\boldsymbol{\beta}_n$ is unobserved, we must derive the unconditional distribution by integrating these expressions with respect to the marginal distribution of $\boldsymbol{\beta}_n$:

$$\Pr(x_{n1}=\bar{x}^4_{n1}\,|\,\zeta_n) = \int_B \left[1 - \Phi\left[\frac{\bar{x}^4_{n1}-\tilde{x}_{n1}(\boldsymbol{\beta})}{\sigma}\right]\right]\mathrm{d}G_\beta(\boldsymbol{\beta}\,|\,\mathbf{z}_n;\boldsymbol{\alpha}) \tag{5.31}$$

$$f(x_{n1}\,|\,\zeta_n) = \int_B \sigma^{-1}\,\varphi\left[\frac{x_{n1}-\tilde{x}_{n1}(\boldsymbol{\beta})}{\sigma}\right]\mathrm{d}G_\beta(\boldsymbol{\beta}\,|\,\mathbf{z}_n;\boldsymbol{\alpha}) \tag{5.32}$$

where B is the domain of variation of $\boldsymbol{\beta}$.

The corresponding log-likelihood function has the usual form for a censored distribution:

$$\log L(\boldsymbol{\alpha},\sigma) = \sum_{x_{n1}=\bar{x}^4_{n1}} \log \Pr(x_{n1}=0\,|\,\zeta_n) + \sum_{x_{n1}<\bar{x}^4_{n1}} \log f(x_{n1}\,|\,\zeta_n). \tag{5.33}$$

The difficulty with the representation (5.31) and (5.32) is that the function $\tilde{x}_{n1}(\boldsymbol{\beta})$ is neither simple nor smooth: indeed, in many cases it is not even continuous. To simplify the problem, it is necessary to split up the integrals in (5.31) and (5.32) into components that correspond to the different regimes that are possible. There are up to $r+s$ of these, since every linear segment and every corner may yield a potential optimal regime. Each one of these regimes is generated (given the form of the frontier) by a different set of outcomes for $\boldsymbol{\beta}$. Thus B may be regarded as the union of $r+s$ subsets $B_{n1}, \ldots, B_{nr}$ and $\bar{B}_{n1}, \ldots, \bar{B}_{ns}$, yielding respectively the r different interior optima and the s different corner solutions (note that suboptimal points such as $(\bar{x}^3_{n1}, \bar{x}^3_{n2})$ in the example of figure 5.7(b) yield correspondingly empty subsets). After partitioning B in this way, (5.34) and (5.35) become

$$\Pr(x_{n1}=\bar{x}^4_{n1}\,|\,\zeta_n) = \sum_{i=1}^{r}\int_{B_{ni}}\left[1-\Phi\left[\frac{\bar{x}^4_{n1}-\check{x}^i_{n1}(\beta)}{\sigma}\right]\right]\mathrm{d}G_\beta(\beta\,|\,\mathbf{z}_n;\alpha)$$

$$+\sum_{i=1}^{s}\left[1-\Phi\left(\frac{\bar{x}^4_{n1}-\bar{x}^i_{n1}}{\sigma}\right)\right]\int_{\bar{B}_{ni}}\mathrm{d}G_\beta(\beta\,|\,\mathbf{z}_n;\alpha) \quad (5.34)$$

$$f(x_{n1}\,|\,\zeta_n) = \sum_{i=1}^{r}\int_{B_{ni}}\sigma^{-1}\varphi\left[\frac{x_{n1}-\check{x}_{n1}(\beta)}{\sigma}\right]\mathrm{d}G_\beta(\beta\,|\,\mathbf{z}_n;\alpha)$$

$$+\sum_{i=1}^{s}\sigma^{-1}\varphi\left(\frac{x_{n1}-\bar{x}^i_{n1}}{\sigma}\right)\int_{\bar{B}_{ni}}\mathrm{d}G_\beta(\beta\,|\,\mathbf{z}_n;\alpha) \quad (5.35)$$

where $\check{x}^i_{n1}(\beta)$ is the generic demand function $\check{x}_1(p^i_{n1}, p_{n2}, y^i_n; \beta)$ and $\bar{x}^i_{n1}$ is the location of the ith isolated point in the budget frontier.

There are two specific difficulties with (5.34) and (5.35). One is that the regions of integration B_{ni} and $\bar{B}_{ni}$ are defined only implicitly, by the following complicated system of inequalities. For B_{ni},

$$H(p^i_{n1}, p_{n2}, y^i_n; \beta) > H(p^j_{n1}, p_{n2}, y^j_n; \beta) \quad \text{for all } j=1,\ldots,r \text{ such that } j\neq i \text{ and } a^j_n < \check{x}^j_{n1}(\beta) < b^j_n$$

and

$$H(p^i_{n1}, p_{n2}, y^i_n; \beta) > V(\bar{x}^j_{n1}, \bar{x}^j_{n2}; \beta) \quad \text{for all } j=1,\ldots,s. \quad (5.36)$$

For $\bar{B}_{ni}$,

$$V(\bar{x}^i_{n1}, \bar{x}^i_{n2}; \beta) > V(\bar{x}^j_{n1}, \bar{x}^j_{n2}; \beta) \quad \text{for all } j=1,\ldots,s \text{ such that } j\neq i$$

and

$$V(\bar{x}^i_{n1}, \bar{x}^i_{n2}; \beta) > H(p^j_{n1}, p_{n2}; \beta) \quad \text{for all } j=1,\ldots,r \text{ such that } a^j_n < \check{x}^j_{n2}(\beta) < b^j_n \quad (5.37)$$

The second difficulty associated with (5.34) and (5.35) is that $\check{x}^i_{n1}$ may be a complicated function of β, so that the integrands in the first element of (5.34) and (5.35) are awkward unless we specify a utility function consistent with some simple form for the generic demand.

This is as far as we can go, working in general terms, but we are still left with potentially difficult integrals to evaluate. Further progress requires a specific example, and we shall work with the linear model used in applied work by Hausman (1980) and Blomquist (1983). This has generic demand function

$$\check{x}_1 = \beta_0 + \beta_1\frac{y}{p_2} + \beta_2\frac{p_1}{p_2} \quad (5.38)$$

which corresponds to direct and indirect utility functions

$$V(x_1, x_2; \beta) = \left[\frac{x_1}{\beta_1} + \frac{\beta_2}{\beta_1^2}\right] \exp\left[\frac{\beta_1^2 x_2 - \beta_1 x_1 + \beta_0 \beta_1}{\beta_2 + \beta_1 x_1}\right] \tag{5.39}$$

$$H(p_1, p_2, y; \beta) = \left[\frac{y}{p_2} + \frac{\beta_2 p_1}{\beta_1 p_2} + \frac{\beta_2}{\beta_1^2} + \frac{\beta_0}{\beta_1}\right] \exp\left[-\frac{\beta_1 p_1}{p_2}\right]. \tag{5.40}$$

See Hausman (1980), Deaton and Muellbauer (1981) and Stern (1986) for further discussion of the properties of this model. Convexity of preferences requires that the second derivative of the cost function with respect to p_1 be negative, and this is easily seen to imply the condition $\beta_1 \check{x}_1 + \beta_2 \leqslant 0$. This is a rather restrictive model, particularly in labour supply problems, since it rules out a *priori* the possibility of a backward-bending labour supply curve. Nevertheless, linearity traditionally plays a very important role in econometrics, and the model is extremely convenient for analytical purposes. For these reasons, it has been widely used in applied work. Stern (1986) discusses many alternative specifications, in the context of labour supply.

We now turn to the problem of evaluating expressions (5.36) and (5.37), which are required for the computation of the likelihood function. Consider first the problem of defining the regions B_{ni} and $\bar{B}_{ni}$. If all three elements of $\boldsymbol{\beta}' = (\beta_0, \beta_1, \beta_2)$ are random, then the joint probability of these events is very complicated, and certainly not feasible from a computational point of view. Thus it is sensible to restrict the specification by allowing only one source of randomness in the utility function. This can be done in many ways: we could, for instance, take $\boldsymbol{\beta}$ as the product of a fixed vector and a scalar random variable, or we could assume that only one particular element of $\boldsymbol{\beta}$ is stochastic.

In the labour supply context, Hausman (1980) and Blomquist (1983) have argued for the income coefficient β_1 to be treated as a random variable with constant mean α_1, with β_0 specified as a non-stochastic function $\alpha_0'\mathbf{z}$ and β_2 as a fixed parameter α_2. They employ distributional forms restricted to ensure convexity of preferences. We shall do the same, but since our model is in terms of leisure rather than hours of work it is parameterized rather differently, and the required restriction on the range of β_1 is therefore also different. Since we need $\beta_1 \check{x}_1 + \beta_2 \leqslant 0$ for convexity, and since x_1 cannot exceed $\bar{x}_1^4$, the range of β_1 should satisfy $\beta_1 \leqslant -\beta_2/\bar{x}_1^4$. Assume, then, that β_1 has a $\text{UTN}(\alpha_1, \sigma_\alpha^2, -\alpha_2/\bar{x}_1^4)$ distribution, and that it is independent of the deviation $x_1 - \tilde{x}_1(\boldsymbol{\beta})$. Thus, the p.d.f. of β_1 is

$$g_\beta(\beta_1) = \sigma_\alpha^{-1} \varphi\left[\frac{\beta_1 - \alpha_1}{\sigma_\beta}\right]\left[1 - \Phi\left(\frac{\alpha_2/\bar{x}_1^4 + \alpha_1}{\sigma_\beta}\right)\right]^{-1} \tag{5.41}$$

This completes the specification of the behavioural model. The problem of evaluating the likelihood elements (5.34) and (5.35) is considerably simplified if the opportunity set is convex, and we begin with that case.

5.3.2 The convex case

Consider once again the example of figure 5.7(a). Suppose that, initially, individual n has a value of β_1 which is such that there is an interior optimum on the first segment of the budget frontier. Now consider the effect of increasing β_1. Along the first segment, p^1_{n1}, p_{n2} and y^1_n remain fixed; since y^1_n/p_{n2} is positive, the increase in β_1 causes $\check{x}^1_{n1}(\beta)$ to increase, and so the optimum moves to the right. However, once this tangency moves beyond the kink point at $\bar{x}^2_{n1}$, we have a transition to a corner solution. The value of β_1 at which this occurs equates $\check{x}^1_{n1}(\beta)$ and $\bar{x}^2_{n1}$; call this value $\bar{\beta}^1_{n1}(\alpha)$:

$$\bar{\beta}_{n1}(\alpha) = \frac{\bar{x}^2_{n1} - \alpha_2 p^1_{n1}/p_{n2} - \alpha_0' \mathbf{z}_n}{y^1_n/p_{n2}}. \tag{5.42}$$

As β_1 continues to increase, the optimum remains at the corner solution until β_1 becomes sufficiently large that we switch to a tangency on the second budget segment. This occurs when $\check{x}^2_{n1}(\beta) = \bar{x}^2_{n1}$, which corresponds to the following value of β_1:

$$\bar{\beta}^2_{n1}(\alpha) = \frac{\bar{x}^2_{n1} - \alpha_2 p^2_{n1}/p_{n2} - \alpha_0' \mathbf{z}_n}{y^2_n/p_{n2}}. \tag{5.43}$$

As β_1 increases further, the tangency on the second budget segment moves rightward, until we have a switch to a corner solution at $\bar{x}^3_{n1}$, followed by a tangency on segment 3 and then finally a corner solution at $\bar{x}^4_{n1}$. Define also the following values:

$$\bar{\beta}^3_{n1}(\alpha) = \frac{\bar{x}^3_{n1} - \alpha_2 p^2_{n1}/p_{n2} - \alpha_0' \mathbf{z}_n}{y^2_n/p_{n2}} \tag{5.44}$$

$$\bar{\beta}^4_{n1}(\alpha) = \frac{\bar{x}^3_{n1} - \alpha_2 p^3_{n1}/p_{n2} - \alpha_0' \mathbf{z}_n}{y^3_n/p_{n2}} \tag{5.45}$$

$$\bar{\beta}^5_{n1}(\alpha) = \frac{\bar{x}^4_{n1} - \alpha_2 p^3_{n1}/p_{n2} - \alpha_0' \mathbf{z}_n}{y^3_n/p_{n2}} \tag{5.46}$$

and note that convexity of the opportunity set implies $\bar{\beta}^1_{n1}(\alpha) < \bar{\beta}^2_{n1}(\alpha) < \ldots < \bar{\beta}^5_{n1}(\alpha)$.

Thus the sets of β_1 values corresponding to the different types of optimum are simple intervals, $B_{ni} = (c^i_n(\alpha), d^i_n(\alpha))$ and $\bar{B}_{ni} = (\bar{c}^i_n(\alpha), \bar{d}^i_n(\alpha))$, defined as follows:

tangency on segment 1

$$B_{n1} = (-\infty, \bar{\beta}^1_{n1}(\alpha))$$

corner solution at $\bar{x}^2_{n1}$

$$\bar{B}_{n2} = (\bar{\beta}^1_{n1}(\alpha), \bar{\beta}^2_{n1}(\alpha))$$

tangency on segment 2

$$\bar{B}_{n2} = (\bar{\beta}^2_{n1}(\alpha), \bar{\beta}^3_{n1}(\alpha))$$

corner solution at $\bar{x}^3_{n1}$

$$\bar{B}_{n3} = (\bar{\beta}^3_{n1}(\alpha), \bar{\beta}^4_{n1}(\alpha))$$

tangency on segment 3

$$\bar{B}_{n3} = (\bar{\beta}^4_{n1}(\alpha), \bar{\beta}^5_{n1}(\alpha))$$

corner solution at $\bar{x}^4_{n1}$

$$\bar{B}_{n4} = (\bar{\beta}^5_{n1}(\alpha), -\alpha_2/\bar{x}^4{}_{n1}).$$

Note that we are assuming here that the probabilities of a corner solution at $x_1 = 0$ (no leisure) and of β_1 lying exactly on one of the boundaries are essentially zero.

In this convex case, then, (5.34) and (5.35) reduce to the simpler forms

$$\Pr(x_{n1}=0\,|\,\zeta_n) = \sigma_\beta^{-1}\sum_{i=1}^{3} \frac{\displaystyle\int_{c_n^i(\alpha)}^{d_n^i(\alpha)} \left[1 - \Phi\left(\frac{\alpha_0'\mathbf{z}_n + \beta_1 y_n^i/p_{n2} + \alpha_2 p_{n1}^i/p_{n2}}{\sigma}\right)\right]\varphi\left(\frac{\beta_1-\alpha_1}{\sigma_\beta}\right)\mathrm{d}\beta_1}{1 - \Phi\left(\dfrac{\alpha_2/\bar{x}^4_{n1}+\alpha_1}{\sigma_\beta}\right)}$$
$$+\ \sigma_\beta^{-1}\sum_{i=2}^{4} \frac{\left[1-\Phi\left(\dfrac{\bar{x}^i_{n1}}{\sigma}\right)\right]\left\{\Phi\left[\dfrac{\bar{d}^i_n(\alpha)-\alpha_1}{\sigma_\beta}\right] - \Phi\left[\dfrac{\bar{c}^i_n(\alpha)-\alpha_1}{\sigma_\beta}\right]\right\}}{\left[1-\Phi\left(\dfrac{\alpha_2/\bar{x}^4_{n1}+\alpha_1}{\sigma_\beta}\right)\right]} \quad (5.47)$$

$$f(x_{n1}\,|\,\zeta_n) = \sigma^{-1}\sigma_\beta^{-1}\sum_{i=1}^{3} \frac{\displaystyle\int_{c_n^i(\alpha)}^{d_n^i(\alpha)} \varphi\left(\frac{x_{n1} - \alpha_0'\mathbf{z}_n - \beta_1 y_n^i/p_{n2} - \alpha_2 p_{n1}^i/p_{n2}}{\sigma}\right)\varphi\left(\frac{\beta_1-\alpha_1}{\sigma_\beta}\right)\mathrm{d}\beta_1}{1 - \Phi\left(\dfrac{\alpha_2/\bar{x}^4_{n1}+\alpha_1}{\sigma_\beta}\right)}$$
$$+\ \sigma^{-1}\sigma_\beta^{-1}\sum_{i=2}^{4} \frac{\varphi\left(\dfrac{x_{n1}-\bar{x}^i_{n1}}{\sigma}\right)\left\{\Phi\left[\dfrac{\bar{d}^i_n(\alpha)-\alpha_1}{\sigma_\beta}\right] - \Phi\left[\dfrac{\bar{c}^i_n(\alpha)-\alpha_1}{\sigma_\beta}\right]\right\}}{\left[1-\Phi\left(\dfrac{\alpha_2/\bar{x}^4_{n1}+\alpha_1}{\sigma_\beta}\right)\right]} \quad (5.48)$$

It is possible to simplify this still further by expressing the integral in (5.47) as a volume under a bivariate normal density, and by expressing the product of normal densities in (5.48) as a multiple of a single normal density, and thus its integral in terms of $\Phi(.)$. Blomquist (1983) gives details of this.

Thus, despite the apparent complexity of (5.47) and (5.48) and the log-likelihood based upon them, the computational problems raised by this model are not severe. However, it should be borne in mind that this tractability is based on several special features: the simple nature of the generic demand function and its parameterization, the single source of preference randomness, the convenient properties of the distributional assumptions, and, most importantly, the convexity of the opportunity set.

5.3.3 The general case

In the general non-convex case, the analysis is much less straightforward because it is necessary to make explicit global comparisons based on the inequalities (5.36) and (5.37). Even when the space of random β is one dimensional, this is rather difficult to translate into a simple computational scheme.

What is required is an algorithm that can be used to determine the ranges of values for β_1 that correspond to the different types of optimum. In the general case, these ranges need not be simple intervals: it is possible, for some utility functions and some budget sets, for an increase in β_1 to cause a transition to a new optimal regime, and a further increase to bring a return to the original regime. In special cases involving simple budget frontiers, it is often possible to determine the sequence of optimal regimes as β_1 increases, and to determine the boundaries of the B_{ni} and $\overline{B}_{ni}$ by solving (numerically) the equation counterparts of the inequalities (5.36) and (5.37) for the critical values of β_1. Examples of this include studies by Burtless and Hausman (1978) and Hausman and Wise (1980).

However, in cases where the budget frontier is very complicated, particularly when its character varies markedly between individuals, this semi-analytical approach is not feasible. Perhaps the simplest general computational method would be to use some form of grid search. This would proceed by examining equally spaced points in the interval $(\beta_{\min}, -\alpha_2/\bar{x}^4_{n1})$ to determine the optimal regime at each; $\beta_{\min}$ would be chosen so that $\Pr(\beta_1 < \beta_{\min})$ is negligible. Then, whenever there is a regime change between one search point and the next, a further search is used to locate, within that small interval, the point at which the transitional occurs. The expressions (5.47) and (5.48) for the distribution of x_{n1} in the convex case can then be generalized to this non-convex case by replacing the intervals $(c^i_n(\alpha), d^i_n(\alpha))$ and $(\bar{c}^i_n(\alpha), \bar{d}^i_n(\alpha))$ with the equivalent ranges (not necessarily simple intervals) indicated by this search algorithm.

Provided that the initial search grid is sufficiently fine, this type of algorithm should be adequate. Its main drawback, of course, is the high computational cost of performing this search for every individual in the sample at each evaluation of the likelihood function. The treatment of the general non-convex problem, using random-parameter models, seems to be at the limits of computational feasibility, and there is no applied example of the analysis of a problem as complicated as our example of the UK social security system, discussed in section 5.1.4.

5.4 More on stochastic specification

The stochastic specifications discussed in the previous two sections are both open to objection. As an illustration, we shall consider a model of housing demand based loosely upon a study by Hausman and Wise (1980).

The individual is faced with a choice problem in two dimensions: x_1 is the quantity of housing services and x_2 is the quantity of a composite good representing all other forms of consumption. The corresponding prices are p_1 and p_2, and the individual has preferences representable by a utility function

$$u = V(x_1, x_2; \beta) \tag{5.49}$$

where β is the usual vector of preference parameters.

The non-linear budget frontier arises in this case from an experimental rent subsidy to low-income households. If a qualifying household spends more than a critical amount x_1^* on housing, it receives a rent subsidy of an amount $\rho p_1 x_1$. Thus the budget constraint is as illustrated in figure 5.8. This differs slightly from the Hausman and Wise problem in that the two budget segments have different slopes. For $x_1 < x_1^*$, the price ratio is p_1/p_2, but this reduces to $(1-\rho)p_1/p_2$ for $x_1 \geqslant x_1{}^*$.

A pure random-preference specification has the implication that certain ranges of x_1 will never be observed and for this reason is unlikely to be successful in practice. In our example, rational choice could never lead to an observation of x_1 in the interval (x_1^{**}, x_1^*) and, except in special cases involving perfect complementarity between x_1 and x_2, the range of impossibility will be substantially larger than this. Hausman and Wise solve this problem by allowing, in addition to random variation in preferences, random departures from optimal decisions, with the observed x_1 having a conditional normal distribution centred on the optimal rental $\tilde{x}_1$. As we pointed out in chapter 1, section 1.7, there are two objections to this specification: that it fails to take into account the relative costs of different deviations from $\tilde{x}_1$, and that it introduces an asymmetry in the treatment of the two variables x_1 and x_2. We begin with the problem of asymmetry.

5.4.1 Symmetric specifications: the Wales–Woodland model

Wales and Woodland (1979) analyse a labour supply problem and propose a symmetric specification based on the use of variables analogous to budget shares. We shall discuss their stochastic specification in the housing demand

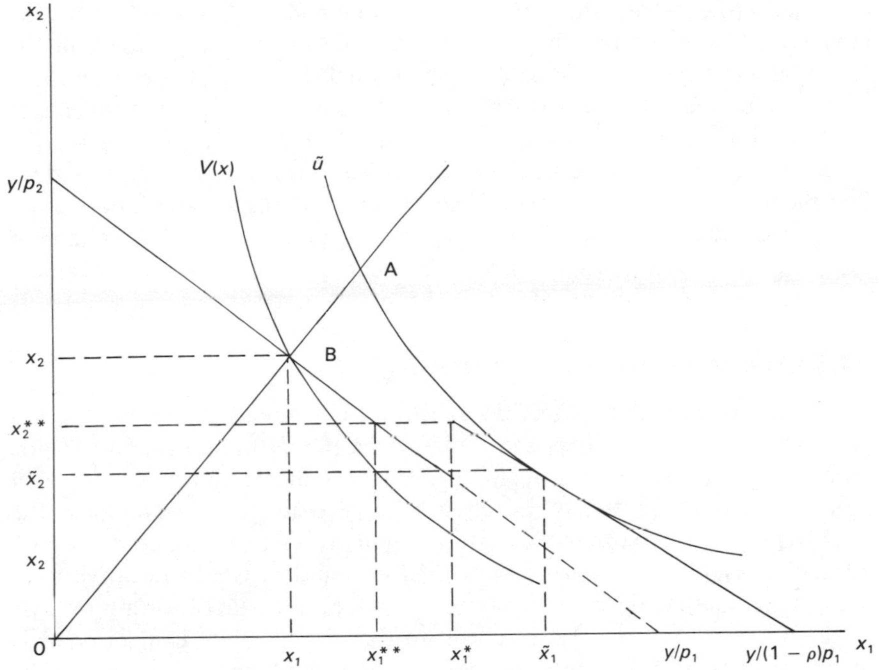

Figure 5.8 The budget constraint for a rent subsidy scheme.

context described above. Demand models expressed in budget share form are often successful in applied work, since the conventional assumption of homoscedasticity is much more reasonable for budget shares than for expenditures or quantities. The problem with a share formulation is that there is no natural definition of a budget share when the opportunity set has a non-linear frontier, since the prices used to construct the shares are not exogenous but depend on the chosen budget segment.

Wales and Woodland resolve this ambiguity by defining notional expenditures, valued at the exogenous gross price (p_1) rather than the endogenous net price (a function of x_1 taking values p_1 or $(1-\rho)p_1$). In the more common labour supply application, the gross price is the pre-tax wage. The notional expenditures are then normalized to share form, yielding $s_{n1} = p_{n1}x_{n1}/(p_{n1}x_{n1} + p_{n2}x_{n2})$ and $s_{n2} = p_{n2}x_{n2}/(p_{n1}x_{n1} + p_{n2}x_{n2})$. These are treated as the dependent variables and are assumed to be generated by the following non-linear structure:

$$s_{ni} = p_{ni}\tilde{x}_{ni}/(p_{n1}\tilde{x}_{n1} + p_{n2}\tilde{x}_{n2}) + \epsilon_{ni} \qquad i = 1, 2 \tag{5.50}$$

where the ϵ_{ni} are jointly normally distributed, conditional on $\tilde{x}_{n1}$ and $\tilde{x}_{n2}$. The optimal demands $\tilde{x}_{ni}$ can be generated by any deterministic model of preferences. Note that the total expenditure terms $p_{n1}x_{n1} + p_{n2}x_{n2}$ and $p_{n1}\tilde{x}_{n1}$ +

$p_{n2}\tilde{x}_{n2}$ used to construct the actual and optimal budget shares in (5.50) need not be equal, since it is possible for actual and optimal behaviour to lie on different budget segments. The actual and optimal shares must both sum identically to unity, and therefore the model (5.50) satisfies the budget constraint provided that ϵ_{n1} and ϵ_{n2} sum to zero. This implies that $\text{var}(\epsilon_{n1}) = \text{var}(\epsilon_{n2}) = -\text{cov}(\epsilon_{n1}, \epsilon_{n2})$, and thus the stochastic specification is symmetric in x_1 and x_2. For the purposes of estimation, one of the two behaviour equations is redundant and can be ignored. Since $\tilde{x}_{n1}$ and $\tilde{x}_{n2}$ are not smooth functions of the model parameters, there may be difficulties relating to the existence, uniqueness or computation of the estimator.

5.4.2 Testing the stochastic specification

The usual stochastic specification assumes that individuals make optimal plans and then deviate from those plans in a purely random manner. For example, if someone is maximizing utility at the discontinuity at $x_1 = x_1^*$ in figure 5.8, this implies that we are equally likely to observe an outcome to the left of x_1^* as we are to observe one to the right, at least under a conventional normality assumption. This is despite the fact that the cost of a negative error is much greater than the cost of a similar positive error, since it entails the loss of the housing subsidy. The assumption that the likelihood of an error is independent of its associated cost is contentious, and may have serious consequences: if it is incorrect, the statistical fitting procedure will generate values of the preference parameters that reduce the frequency of predicted optima near the point x_1^*. This may result in a misleading picture of consumer behaviour and of the effects of the subsidy; it may also be a possible explanation for the implausibly high degree of stochastic variation that is sometimes found in estimated preferences. It is desirable to make some attempt to test this feature of the specification, although there has so far been no formal attempt to do this in applied work.

There are many ways in which one could construct such a test. An appealing approach is to partition the range of x_{n1} into intervals that correspond to the different segments of the budget constraint and to examine the actual and predicted frequencies with which observations fall in those intervals. Consider the example of figure 5.8. There is a natural partition of the x_1 axis into three intervals: $(0, x_1^{**})$, (x_1^{**}, x_1^*) and $(x_1^*, y/(1-\rho)p_1)$. If our criticism of the conventional specification is correct, we would expect to see fewer observations in the 'irrational' interval (x_1^{**}, x_1^*) than is predicted by the model, and conversely under-prediction in one or both of the other two intervals. A similar natural partition is usually obvious for any choice problem involving a non-linear budget frontier, with the boundaries of the intervals being kink points, break points and possible interior points marking the limits of irrational areas.

Note that these intervals must be defined independently of θ, but that they will vary between individuals facing different opportunity sets. Some of the intervals may be null for some individuals, and if there is censoring of x_1, one or more of the intervals may consist of a single point. In addition, one of the intervals is redundant, since its frequency can be deduced from those of the others.

Return to the example of figure 5.8; we refer to any two of the three intervals as R_{n1} and R_{n2} and define corresponding dummy variables d_{n1} and d_{n2} such that $d_{ni} = 1$ if $x_{n1} \in R_{ni}$ and $d_{ni} = 0$ if $x_{n1} \notin R_{ni}$. The sample frequencies are the means of these dummies, $N^{-1}\Sigma d_{ni}$. The analogous predicted frequencies are the sample means of the following estimated conditional probabilities:

$$\hat{\Pi}_{ni} = \Pr(x_{n1} \in R_{ni} \mid \zeta_n; \hat{\theta}) \tag{5.51}$$

where ζ_n is the vector of exogenous variables and $\hat{\theta}$ is the estimated parameter vector. The discrepancy between these two frequencies is

$$\delta_i = \frac{1}{N} \sum_{n=1}^{N} [d_{ni} - \hat{\Pi}_{ni}]. \tag{5.52}$$

In large samples, if the model is well specified, the vector $\sqrt{N}\delta' = \sqrt{N}(\delta_1 \ \delta_2)$ has an approximate $N(0, \Sigma_\delta)$ distribution whose covariance matrix can be consistently estimated by

$$\hat{\Sigma}_\delta = \mathbf{A} - \mathbf{B}\hat{\Sigma}_\theta\mathbf{B}' \tag{5.53}$$

where $\hat{\Sigma}_\theta$ is a consistent estimate of the covariance matrix of the limiting distribution of $\sqrt{N}(\hat{\theta} - \theta)$ and $\mathbf{A}$ and $\mathbf{B}$ are matrices with typical elements

$$a_{ij} = \delta_{ij} N^{-1}\Sigma\, \hat{\Pi}_{ni} - N^{-1}\Sigma\, \hat{\Pi}_{ni}\hat{\Pi}_{nj} \tag{5.54}$$

$$b_{ij} = N^{-1}\Sigma\, \partial\hat{\Pi}_{ni}/\partial\hat{\theta}_j \tag{5.55}$$

where δ_{ij} is the Kronecker delta. The resulting test statistic is

$$\tau = N\delta'(\hat{\Sigma}_\delta)^{-1}\delta \tag{5.56}$$

and this is asymptotically χ^2 with two degrees of freedom if the model is well specified. If the model is mis-specified in such a way that these frequencies are mis-predicted, the statistic τ is $O_p(N)$ rather than $O_p(1)$, and the test has unit asymptotic power. It is straightforward to extend this to more general cases with more than three intervals and with censoring. The statistic has an interpretation as an application of the Hausman (1978) approach to specification testing, since the means of $\hat{\Pi}_{ni}$ and d_{ni} can be regarded as alternative estimators of the corresponding population frequency, and expression (5.53) is the difference of their asymptotic covariance matrices.

The probabilities $\hat{\Pi}_{ni}$ must be derived by integrating the conditional distribution of x_{n1} over the intervals R_{n1} and R_{n2}. For the case of non-stochastic preferences this is a simple matter, and $\hat{\Pi}_{ni}$ can be expressed as the difference of $\Phi(.)$ evaluated at the standardized limits of R_{ni}. For models based on random preferences, one must integrate a more complicated density function, of the general form (5.48), with respect to x_{n1} over R_{ni}. See Pudney (1988a) for more detail on this test and the derivation and calculation of the probabilities $\hat{\Pi}_{ni}$ and their θ derivatives.

5.4.3 Specifications based on the distance function

There is a case for the use of a stochastic specification that takes some account of the relative costs of various deviations from optimal behaviour, particularly when discontinuous constraints are involved. However, a difficulty with this idea is that there is no natural measure of cost: the incurred cost is in terms of utility foregone, and this is not, even in principle, a measurable quantity. Traditional measures of welfare loss, such as the compensating variation, are based on the cost function, which presents enormous analytical difficulties in the case of a non-convex budget frontier. Thus, a measure constructed directly in (x_1, x_2) space is required, but this should be independent of any specific normalization of the utility function.

Debreu (1951) studied an identical problem posed in terms of production theory and proposed the distance function (see chapter 1, section 1.6) as a suitable measure. In figure 5.8, the ratio OB:OA provides a simple indicator of the degree of optimization efficiency of the point (x_1, x_2) relative to $(\tilde{x}_1, \tilde{x}_2)$, and this ratio is Debreu's coefficient of resource utilization or the distance function $D(x_1, x_2, \tilde{u})$. Our aim is to construct a stochastic specification in which observed outcomes are distributed along the budget frontier in relation to this distance measure.

The budget constraint for our example is

$$p_1x_1 + p_2x_2 = y \qquad \text{for } x_1 < x_1^* \tag{5.57}$$

$$(1-\rho)p_1x_1 + p_2x_2 = y \qquad \text{for } x_1 \geqslant x_1^*. \tag{5.58}$$

For points along the budget frontier, the distance function is therefore

$$D^*(x_1, u) = \begin{cases} D[x_1, (y-p_1x_1)/p_2, u] & \text{for } x_1 < x_1^* \\ D\{x_1, [y-(1-\rho)p_1x_1]/p_2, u\} & \text{for } x_1 \geqslant x_1^*. \end{cases} \tag{5.59}$$

A simple stochastic specification can be constructed by assuming a conditional p.d.f. for x that is proportional to $D^*(x_1, \tilde{u})$ (or to some parameterized transformation of it) and therefore reflects the notion that the likelihood of an error is inversely related to its associated cost.

Thus, for individual n,

$$f(x_{n1} | \tilde{x}_{n1}) = K_n^{-1} h[D^*(x_{n1}, \tilde{u}_n); \sigma] \tag{5.60}$$

where $h(.; \sigma)$ is the chosen transformation, σ is a vector of parameters governing the form of the distribution, and K_n is the normalizing constant required to make $f(x_{n1} | \tilde{x}_{n1})$ integrate to unity along the budget frontier:

$$K_n = \int_0^{y_n/(1-\rho)} h\{D[x_1, x_2(x_1), \tilde{u}_n]; \sigma\} \, dx_1 \tag{5.61}$$

where $x_2(x_1) = (y_n - p_{n1}x_1)/p_{n2}$ for $x_1 < x_1^*$ and $[y_n - (1-\rho)p_{n1}x_1]/p_{n2}$ otherwise. Note that this assumes that there is no discrete probability of either of the two extreme events $x_{n1} = 0$ or $x_{n2} = 0$.

The model of preferences used by Hausman and Wise is homothetic, with utility defined as a monotonic transformation of the linearly homogeneous Cobb–Douglas function

$$u_n = x_1^{\beta_n} x_2^{1-\beta_n} \tag{5.62}$$

where β_n is a specified function of the observed personal characteristics:

$$\beta_n = \beta(\mathbf{z}_n; \alpha). \tag{5.63}$$

(Hausman and Wise assume β_n to be a linear stochastic function; we shall instead use the deterministic form (5.63).) For convenience, we parameterize the error distribution by taking the transformation $h(.; \sigma)$ to be the simple form $h(D; \sigma) = D^{1/\sigma}$, where σ is a positive parameter governing the dispersion of the implied conditional density of x_{n1}. Homotheticity of preferences implies that the distance function is a simple ratio of utilities expressed in homogeneous form: $D(x_1, x_2, u) = V(x_1, x_2)/u$. Thus the distribution of observed housing expenditure is

$$f(x_{n1} \mid \tilde{u}_n) = K_n^{-1} \tilde{u}_n^{-1/\sigma} x_{n1}^{\beta_n/\sigma} x_2(x_{n1})^{(1-\beta_n)/\sigma} \tag{5.64}$$

where the normalizing constant is

$$\begin{aligned} K_n &= \tilde{u}_n^{-1/\sigma} \left\{ \int_0^{x_1^*} x_1^{\beta_n/\sigma} \left(\frac{y_n - p_{n1}x_1}{p_{n2}} \right)^{(1-\beta_n)/\sigma} dx_1 \right. \\ &\quad \left. + \int_{x_1^*}^{y_n/(1-\rho)} x_1^{\beta_n/\sigma} \left[\frac{y_n - (1-\rho)p_{n1}x_1}{p_{n2}} \right]^{(1-\beta_n)/\sigma} dx_1 \right\} \\ &= \tilde{u}_n^{-1/\sigma} \{ d_{n1} B_{c_{n1}}(a_n, b_n) + d_{n2}[B(a_n, b_n) - B_{c_{n2}}(a_n, b_n)] \}. \end{aligned} \tag{5.65}$$

In this expression, $B(a, b) = \Gamma(a)\Gamma(b)/\Gamma(a+b)$ is the complete beta function, $B_c(a, b) = \int_0^c x^{a-1}(1-x)^{b-1} \, dx$ is the incomplete beta function and

$$a_n = 1 + \beta_n/\sigma \tag{5.66}$$

$$b_n = 1 + (1-\beta_n)/\sigma \tag{5.67}$$

$$c_{n1} = p_{n1}x_1^*/y_n \tag{5.68}$$

$$c_{n2} = (1-\rho)p_{n1}x_1^*/y_n \tag{5.69}$$

$$d_{n1} = [y_n/p_{n1}]^{(\sigma+\beta_n)/\sigma}\,[y_n/p_{n2}]^{(1-\beta_n)/\sigma} \tag{5.70}$$

$$d_{n2} = [y_n/(1-\rho)p_{n1}]^{(\sigma+\beta_n)/\sigma}\,[y_n/p_{n2}]^{(1-\beta_n)/\sigma}. \tag{5.71}$$

As a consequence of the homotheticity assumption, the term $\tilde{u}_n^{-1/\sigma}$ is common to both the numerator and denominator of (5.64) and thus the computation of the density function does not require explicit evaluation of $\tilde{u}_n$. In this example, the log-likelihood function is

$$\log L(\alpha;\sigma) = \sum_{n=1}^{N} \beta(\mathbf{z}_n;\alpha)\log x_{n1} + \sum_{n=1}^{N} [1-\beta(\mathbf{z}_n;\alpha)]\log x_{n2}$$

$$- \sum_{n=1}^{N} \log\{d_{n1}B_{c_{n1}}(a_n, b_n) + d_{n2}[B(a_n, b_n) - B_{c_{n2}}(a_n, b_n)]\}. \tag{5.72}$$

The calculation of this log-likelihood is fairly straightforward since fast computational algorithms for the complete and incomplete beta functions are widely available. From the analytical point of view, it is rather simpler than the log-likelihood that arises from Hausman and Wise's model, since it is not necessary to derive the regions in β space corresponding to the three different types of optimum.

The present example is restrictive in two respects. Preferences are assumed to be homothetic, and this avoids the necessity for computation of the optimal utility level $\tilde{u}_n$. A second special feature of the housing demand problem is that there is no censoring: everyone spends some amount on housing, so there is no parallel to the participation decision in a labour supply setting. We now consider some possible extensions.

Non-homothetic preferences In general, the stochastic specification (5.60) and (5.61) requires the calculation of $\tilde{u}_n$. We have already looked at the problem of locating the optimum in this type of model in section 5.2 above. For practical purposes, this can only be done if we have available the indirect utility function in closed form. Thus, to implement the present approach to stochastic specification, we need a model of preferences for which both the distance function and the indirect utility function are known. This presents problems: for example, there is no explicit expression available for the distance function corresponding to Hausman's (1980) linear model.

However, although many existing models are intractable from this point of view, it is not difficult to construct new models starting from the distance function itself. For example, Hausman's model of preferences is based on a cost function of the form

$$C(p_1, p_2, u) = -\psi(u)p_2\exp(\alpha_1 p_1/p_2) + \alpha_2 p_1 + \alpha_3 p_2 \tag{5.73}$$

where $\psi(.)$ is an arbitrary decreasing function and $\alpha_1, \ldots, \alpha_3$ are positive parameters (see Deaton and Muellbauer, 1981). The distance function is merely the dual to the cost function, so a dual Hausman model would be based on the following distance function:

$$D(x_1, x_2, u) = -\psi^*(u)x_2 \exp(\alpha_1 x_1/x_2) + \alpha_2 x_1 + \alpha_3 x_2 \tag{5.74}$$

where $\psi^*(.)$ is an arbitrary increasing function. This leads to a direct utility function

$$u = \psi^{*-1}\left[\frac{\alpha_2 x_1 + \alpha_3 x_2 - 1}{x_2 \exp(\alpha_1 x_1/x_2)}\right]. \tag{5.75}$$

The demand functions can be found most easily by equating the first partial derivative of $D(x_1, x_2, u)$ to p_1/y (see chapter 1, equation (1.43)) and using the budget constraint to eliminate x_2. This yields

$$\tilde{x}_1 = \frac{\alpha_1 p_2 - p_1 + (\alpha_2 - \alpha_1\alpha_3)y}{[\alpha_1\alpha_2 p_2 + (\alpha_2 - \alpha_1\alpha_3)p_1]y - p_1^2}\, y \tag{5.76}$$

and, upon substitution in the budget constraint,

$$\tilde{x}_2 = \frac{\alpha_1\alpha_2 y - \alpha_1 p_1}{[\alpha_1\alpha_2 p_2 + (\alpha_2 - \alpha_1\alpha_3)p_1]y - p_1^2}\, y \tag{5.77}$$

If these expressions are substituted into the direct utility function (5.75) the indirect utility function is found immediately. Thus, for preferences representable in the form (5.74), the distance function and direct and indirect utility functions are all available in closed form, and a distance-based stochastic specification is feasible. It is not difficult to construct other models for which this is the case.

In general, the evaluation of the likelihood function will usually be rather more difficult than is the case for the Cobb–Douglas model, since the calculation of K_n requires numerical integration. The difficulty of this numerical integration problem depends on the form of the distance function. However, it should be noted that the optimal utility level $\tilde{u}$ is a continuous function of α, even if $\tilde{x}_1$ and $\tilde{x}_2$ are not. Thus, this approach avoids the discontinuity problems encountered in estimating non-stochastic preference models on discontinuous budget sets.

Censoring In some applications, the sample contains observations 'piled up' at either or both extremes of the budget frontier. This is particularly so in problems involving labour supply, where non-participation in the labour force is frequently observed. The stochastic specification described above must be modified if it is to accommodate this type of censored sample.

An obvious way of generating the required discrete probabilities is to relate them to the degree of suboptimality of the extreme points. For instance, in the context of labour supply, with x_1 interpreted as leisure, non-participation in the labour force corresponds to the extreme event $x_1 = T$, where T is the total time endowment. The degree of optimizing efficiency at this corner is $D^*(T, \tilde{u}_n)$, and if we again use $h(d; \sigma) = d^{1/\sigma}$ a natural specification is the following:

$$\Pr(x_{n1} = T \mid \tilde{u}_n) = K_n^{-1} \rho D^*(T, \tilde{u}_n)^{1/\sigma} \tag{5.78}$$

$$f(x_{n1} \mid \tilde{u}_n) = K_n^{-1} D^*(x_{n1}, \tilde{u}_n)^{1/\sigma} \tag{5.79}$$

where

$$K_n = \rho D^*(T, \tilde{u}_n)^{1/\sigma} + \int_0^T D^*(x_1, \tilde{u}_n)^{1/\sigma} \, dx_1. \tag{5.80}$$

The additional parameter ρ governs the overall relative frequency with which non-participation occurs, and makes this approach somewhat more flexible than conventional censoring.

It should be observed, however, that the close relation between this specification and the structure of preferences does require that the model of preferences be carefully chosen. For instance, in the Hausman–Wise housing model, the assumption of Cobb–Douglas preferences implies that the distance measure is zero at the extreme points $x_1 = 0$ and $x_2 = 0$. Thus a distribution based on the distance function could never generate extreme observations, and a different utility function would be needed for application to a censored sample.

Further reading

Hausman (1985) gives the most complete available survey of the econometric literature. Deaton and Muellbauer (1980a, chapters 1, 10, 11 and 12) give useful background discussion of the examples described in section 5.1. Early work in this field was based on simple *ad hoc* procedures: for instance, to ignore the non-linearity of the budget frontier and estimate a labour supply function based on the pre-tax rather than post-tax wage rate. Some researchers used the post-tax wage and attempted to cope with its endogeneity by using IV estimation techniques (see Hausman and Wise, 1976; Rosen, 1976). However, these techniques fail to take account of the fact that the labour supply equation is inoperative for individuals whose optimal behaviour is at a corner, and hence are generally inconsistent. The earliest references on the ML estimation of models with piecewise-linear budget constraints are Burtless and Hausman (1978) and Wales and Woodland (1979). Since then, there has been a large number of published studies, including those of Brown (1981); Blomquist (1983), Hausman (1980), Hausman and Ruud (1984) (who consider a three-dimensional labour supply problem), Zabalza (1983), Yatchew (1985) on labour supply; Hausman and Wise (1980) and Venti and Wise (1984) on the effect of housing subsidies; and Hausman, Kinnucan and McFadden (1979) on electricity demand. Lee and Pitt (1984) use the theory of virtual prices to derive the likelihood function for a random-parameter model of choice in the presence of a convex opportunity set with a piecewise-linear frontier.

6

Sequential choice in continuous time: duration analysis

This suspense is terrible. I hope it will last.

Oscar Wilde

The passage of time is an essential part of many of the decision problems facing people in practice: the choice of retirement age is a continuous sequence of choices between retirement now and continuation in the labour force; the length of an individual's spell of unemployment depends on a sequence of events comprising the arrival (or non-arrival) of employment opportunities and the individual's acceptance or rejection of them; a strike continues until the first return-to-work decision in a sequence of choices between termination and continuation of the action. The econometric analysis of these and similar problems involves the modelling of the duration of some state or condition: of labour force participation, of unemployment and of withdrawal of labour in our three examples. In practice, these decision sequences are in discrete time, with the day or week or year as the fundamental decision period. Nevertheless, for simplicity and because these decision periods are often sufficiently short that discreteness is unimportant, we shall assume throughout that all events occur in continuous time.

Although the modelling of durations is a common problem in biometrics, actuarial science, operations research and other fields of statistics, the methods developed there have been in widespread use in econometrics for only a short time, with most applied work being done in the study of unemployment duration. However, potential applications (and technical problems) abound, and consequently this is a field in which developments are occurring very rapidly.

Our discussion of duration models is organized as follows: section 6.1 defines the important concept of the hazard function and examines its relation to the underlying distribution of duration; section 6.2 deals with the way in which the hazard function arises from simple microeconomic theories of individual behaviour, concentrating particularly on applications to unemployment duration and the retirement decision, and section 6.3 deals with some extensions of the simple duration model. Sections 6.4 and 6.5 discuss parametric and semi-parametric approaches to the estimation of these models from samples of various types.

6.1 The hazard function

The random variable whose behaviour we are studying is a duration, denoted δ. It is important to bear in mind that δ is a *length* of time and not a *point* in time. Instead we use the symbol t to represent points in time, measured from the beginning of the state whose duration is under study. Thus the same value of t may correspond to different calendar dates for different individuals. For our discussion of the basic theory, we shall maintain the assumption that the date of commencement of the spell, and the fact that the spell occurs at all, are exogenous. In effect, this means that we work with distributions that are to be interpreted as conditional on these events, and it is important that econometric models are constructed with this in mind if we are to avoid serious sample selection problems.

All the models we consider lead to a distribution for δ which can be characterized by a p.d.f. and c.d.f. of the form

$$\text{p.d.f.}(\delta) = g(\delta \mid \zeta; \theta) \tag{6.1}$$

$$\Pr(\delta \leqslant \Delta) = G(\Delta \mid \zeta; \theta) \tag{6.2}$$

where θ is a vector of parameters requiring estimation and ζ is a vector containing the values taken by a set of explanatory variables, which we assume for the moment to be time invariant. For given ζ, the function $G(\Delta \mid \zeta; \theta)$ represents the proportion of observed durations which are expected to be less than Δ; its complement, $1 - G(\Delta \mid \zeta; \theta)$, represents the expected proportion of durations greater than Δ, and is known as the *survivor function*, from its extensive use in the analysis of mortality.

However, most economic models are constructed in a way which does not lead directly to (6.1) or (6.2). Models of economic choice are usually phrased as statements about the behaviour of individuals at a particular time, taking the past as given, and are therefore conditional in nature. Such models lead naturally to the *hazard function* $h(t, \zeta; \theta)$, which is a measure of the local rate at which individuals leave the state whose duration is under study. The quantity $h(t, \zeta; \theta)\mathrm{d}t$ is the probability of departure from the state in the infinitesimal time interval $(t, t + \mathrm{d}t)$, conditional on the event that departure has not already occurred. The terminology derives again from the study of mortality, where the hazard rate represents the current risk of death given that the subject has survived until the present. Note that the hazard function is not a conditional density function for δ in the usual sense, because it does not integrate to unity over $(0, \infty)$.

If δ denotes the duration of the completed spell, the hazard function is related to $g(.)$ and $G(.)$ in the following way:

$$h(t, \zeta; \theta)\mathrm{d}t = \frac{\Pr(\delta \in (t, t+\mathrm{d}t) \mid \zeta)}{\Pr(\delta \geqslant t \mid \zeta)} = \frac{g(t \mid \zeta; \theta)\mathrm{d}t}{1 - G(t \mid \zeta; \theta)}.$$

Thus

$$h(t, \zeta; \theta) = \frac{g(t \mid \zeta; \theta)}{1 - G(t \mid \zeta; \theta)}. \tag{6.3}$$

Equation (6.3) is a relationship that tells us how to construct the hazard function from knowledge of the underlying $g(.)$ and $G(.)$. However, it is usually necessary to work in the opposite direction and to start from the hazard function, since this is the form our economic model naturally takes, and one must then derive $g(.)$ and $G(.)$ from the assumed form for $h(.)$. Thus (6.3) (which is a differential equation in G) must be solved for $g(.)$ and $G(.)$ in terms of $h(.)$.

Consider the derivative of the log of the survivor function:

$$\frac{\mathrm{d}\log[1 - G(t \mid \zeta; \theta)]}{\mathrm{d}t} = \frac{-g(t \mid \zeta; \theta)}{1 - G(t \mid \zeta; \theta)}$$
$$= -h(t, \zeta; \theta).$$

Now integrate over the range $(0, \Delta)$:

$$\int_0^\Delta \mathrm{d}\log[1 - G(t \mid \zeta; \theta)] = -\int_0^\Delta h(t, \zeta; \theta)\mathrm{d}t.$$

Since $G(0 \mid \zeta; \theta) = 0$,

$$\log[1 - G(\Delta \mid \zeta; \theta)] = -\int_0^\Delta h(t, \zeta; \theta)\mathrm{d}t$$

which leads to the solution

$$G(\Delta \mid \zeta; \theta) = 1 - \exp\left[-\int_0^\Delta h(t, \zeta; \theta)\mathrm{d}t\right] \tag{6.4}$$

and, using (6.3),

$$g(\delta \mid \zeta; \theta) = h(\delta, \zeta; \theta)\,[1 - G(\delta \mid \zeta; \theta)]. \tag{6.5}$$

The definite integral in (6.4) is an important variable known as the *integrated* or *cumulated hazard*:

$$I(\Delta, \zeta; \theta) = \int_0^{\Delta} h(t, \zeta; \theta)\mathrm{d}t. \tag{6.6}$$

The Jacobian term for a transformation from δ to $I(\delta, \zeta; \theta)$ is $(\partial I/\partial \delta)^{-1} = 1/h(\delta, \zeta; \theta)$, and thus the conditional distribution of the integrated hazard has density function

$$\begin{aligned} \text{p.d.f.}(I \mid \zeta; \theta) &= g(\delta \mid \zeta; \theta)/h(\delta, \zeta; \theta) \\ &= 1 - G(\delta \mid \zeta; \theta) \\ &= \exp(-I). \end{aligned} \tag{6.7}$$

This is the density function of the standard exponential distribution, with unit mean and variance. Since this distribution is independent of the structure of the model and of ζ, it is a particularly convenient way of checking the validity of a specified model: the integral of the estimated hazard function should have an approximate exponential distribution in the sample. An alternative criterion arises from a transformation to $v = -\log I(\delta, \zeta; \theta)$, which has inverse $I = \exp(-v)$ and Jacobian $|\partial I/\partial v| = I$. Thus

$$\begin{aligned} \text{p.d.f.}(v \mid \zeta; \theta) &= I \exp(-I) \\ &= \exp[-v - \exp(-v)] \end{aligned} \tag{6.8}$$

This is the p.d.f. of the type I extreme value distribution.

For $g(.)$ and $G(.)$ to represent a proper distribution, it is necessary that $G(\infty \mid \zeta; \theta) = 1$. Inspection of (6.4) reveals that for this to be so the following condition must be satisfied:

$$\lim_{\Delta \to \infty} \int_0^{\Delta} h(t, \zeta; \theta)\mathrm{d}t = +\infty. \tag{6.9}$$

Condition (6.9) imposes a considerable restriction on the class of functions which are admissible for use as hazard functions. If it is not satisfied, then $G(\infty \mid \zeta; \theta) < 1$ and there is a discrete probability of $1 - G(\infty \mid \zeta; \theta)$ that the spell will never be completed (such a distribution is termed *defective*). Defective distributions do not possess finite moments. This possibility may be acceptable for some applications, such as employment duration, where there may be a positive probability that a worker will never want to change his or her job; an interesting example of this is the model of Jovanovich (1979). We shall refer to (6.9) as the *admissibility condition*, despite the fact that some operational models may violate it.

The nature of the relationship between h and t is known as its *duration dependence*; if $\partial h/\partial t > 0$, there is positive duration dependence and the conditional probability of a departure from the state increases with the length of the spell; if $\partial h/\partial t < 0$, there is negative duration dependence, and departure from the state becomes less likely as the current duration increases. In most applications, and particularly in the analysis of the duration of individuals' spells of unemployment, the detection of the existence and form of any duration dependence is a major research objective.

Most applications of the hazard function involve special forms that offer some simplification. One is the *accelerated failure time* model, in which the effect of the explanatory variables ζ is to define an individual-specific scaling of duration $\tau = h_1(\zeta; \gamma)t$, which is the argument of an invariant hazard function

$$h(t, \zeta; \theta) = h_2(\tau; \alpha). \tag{6.10}$$

More widely used is the *proportional hazards* specification:

$$h(t, \zeta; \theta) = h_1(\zeta; \gamma)h_2(t; \alpha) \tag{6.11}$$

where $\theta = (\gamma, \alpha)$. This specification implies that the explanatory variables influence the scale of the hazard rate, but not the form of its dependence on time. The function $h_2(t; \alpha)$ is known as the *baseline hazard* function. Since $h_1(\zeta; \gamma)$ must be non-negative, a natural form to choose is $h_1 = \exp(\gamma'\zeta)$. This implies that minus the log of the integrated baseline hazard (η, say) is generated by a linear regression equation:

$$-\log\left[\int_0^\delta h_2(t; \alpha)\mathrm{d}t\right] = \log h_1(\zeta; \gamma) - \log I(\delta, \zeta; \theta)$$

or

$$\eta = \gamma'\zeta + \upsilon \tag{6.12}$$

where $\upsilon = -\log I$ has a type I extreme value distribution (see equation (6.8) above).

Table 6.1 gives some widely used forms for the function $h_2(t; \alpha)$, together with the associated admissibility conditions, type of duration dependence and the c.d.f. and mean of the implied unconditional duration distribution. Cox and Oakes (1984) give more details of these and other functional forms. These standard specifications are used mainly for analytical convenience, since they lead to simple closed-form expressions for $g(.)$ and $G(.)$. For other functional forms, it may be necessary to compute the integrated hazard by numerical quadrature, which involves considerable computational costs.

Expressions (6.3)–(6.5) are fundamental relationships which we use repeatedly in the remainder of the chapter: they allow us to make the transition from an economic model to the implied duration distribution which underlies the statistical analysis of that model. However, for practical purposes, this rather simple structure is often inadequate as it stands, and we consider some extensions in section 6.3.

Table 6.1 Common specifications for proportional hazard functions (h_1 represents $h_1(\zeta; \gamma)$)

$h_2(t; \boldsymbol{\alpha})$	Admissibility condition	Duration dependence	$G(\Delta \mid x; \boldsymbol{\theta})$	$E(\delta \mid x; \boldsymbol{\theta})$
1	—	None	Exponential: $1 - \exp(-h_1\Delta)$	$1/h_1$
$\alpha t^{\alpha-1}$	$\alpha > 0$	$\alpha > 1$: positive $\alpha < 1$: negative	Weibull: $1 - \exp(-h_1\Delta^{\alpha})$	$\frac{1}{h_1^{1/\alpha}}\Gamma\left[\frac{\alpha+1}{\alpha}\right]$
$\exp(\alpha t)$	$\alpha \geqslant 0$	$\alpha > 0$: positive	Gompertz: $1 - \exp\left\{\frac{-h_1(\exp(\alpha\Delta) - 1]}{\alpha}\right\}$	No closed form
$(t+1)^{-1}$	—	Negative	Pareto: $1 - (\Delta + 1)^{-h_1}$	$(h_1 - 1)^{-1}$ for $h_1 > 1$

6.2 Applications of duration models

Applied duration analysis in econometrics has been confined largely to the field of labour economics, and especially to problems involving labour supply. We shall, somewhat arbitrarily, consider as representatives of this literature the analysis of the retirement decision and of job search by the unemployed. A much more general analysis involving multiple states such as full participation, retirement, semi-retirement and unemployment could be attempted using the methods described in section 6.3.4 below.

6.2.1 The retirement decision

In chapter 3, section 3.6.2, we examined a hypothetical model of retirement as an illustration of the sequential discrete choice model. The following probability was derived for a person of fixed initial age (0, say) to retire at age δ (where δ is a whole number):

$$P(\delta \mid \mathbf{Z}) = \left(\prod_{t=0}^{\delta-1} \{1 - P_t[t \mid \zeta(t)]\} \right) P_\delta[\delta \mid \zeta(\delta)] \tag{6.13}$$

where $P(\delta \mid \mathbf{Z})$ is the probability that the individual is observed to retire at age δ, conditional on $\mathbf{Z} = \{\zeta(0), \zeta(1), \ldots\}$ and $P_t[t \mid \zeta(t)]$ is the probability that, when the individual reaches age t, it appears optimal to retire immediately, given the current environment described by a vector of exogenous variables $\zeta(t)$. The theory underlying the terms $P_t[t \mid \zeta(t)]$ involved a comparison of the utility derived from immediate retirement with the greatest of the utilities yielded by retirement in each of the subsequent years. Since retirement is only a possibility in year t if the individual is not already retired (we are assuming no 'comebacks' from retirement), the probability $P_t[t \mid \zeta(t)]$ is clearly conditional on the latter event and is therefore the discrete-time analogue of the hazard function. The probability $P(\delta \mid \mathbf{Z})$ is conditioned only on the exogenous variables and is therefore the analogue of the duration p.d.f.

To establish the parallel between (6.13) and the continuous density (6.5), allow the unit of discrete time (the 'year') to become very small. Then each of the component probabilities $P_t[t \mid \zeta(t)]$ becomes small, and the linear approximation $\exp\{-P_t[t \mid \zeta(t)]\} \cong 1 - P_t[t \mid \zeta(t)]$ approaches an equality. Thus, for *nearly* continuous time,

$$P(\delta \mid \mathbf{Z}) \cong \left[\exp\left\{ - \sum_{t=0}^{\delta-1} P_t[t \mid \zeta(t)] \right\} \right] P_\delta[\delta \mid \zeta(\delta)]. \tag{6.14}$$

Now allow the unit time interval to approach zero, replacing the sum by an integral, and use the symbols $g(\delta \mid \mathbf{Z})$ and $h[t \mid \zeta(t)]$ rather than $P(\delta \mid \mathbf{Z})$ and $P_t[t \mid \zeta(t)]$. Then (6.14) approaches the equality

$$g(\delta \mid \mathbf{Z}) = \exp\left\{ - \int_0^\delta h[t \mid \zeta(t)] \, \mathrm{d}t \right\} h(\delta). \tag{6.15}$$

This is identical with expression (6.5) relating the duration density to the hazard function, except that we are considering a generalized case where ζ is time dependent so that the duration distribution is a functional of the whole time path of ζ. We return to this case in section 6.3.1.

The economic model which generates these selection probabilities is often much harder to translate into continuous time. Define $u(a, t)$ to be the continuously discounted utility stream which a person currently of age a expects to derive from following a policy of retiring at age t ($t \geqslant a$). The continuous time analogue of a Thurstone–McFadden discrete choice model decomposes $u(a, t)$ into a non-stochastic component $V(a, t)$ and a continuous-time two-dimensional random function $\epsilon(a, t)$, where the t dimension represents unobservable factors, known to the individual, that are associated with hypothetical retirement ages. The a dimension represents the unobservable and unanticipated evolution of preferences and prospects as the individual ages. Thus

$$u(a, t) = V(a, t) + \epsilon(a, t) \qquad a \geqslant 0, t \geqslant a. \tag{6.16}$$

The age δ of retirement is the first age at which

$$u(\delta, \delta) \geqslant \sup_{t>\delta} u(\delta, t) \tag{6.17}$$

Two-dimensional stochastic processes of this type are unfamiliar, and it is difficult to specify a process for $\epsilon(a, t)$ that yields a tractable distribution for the waiting time defined by (6.17). The situation is easier if we assume that the decision problem does not evolve with age, in which case $\epsilon(a, t)$ can be replaced by a one-dimensional process $\epsilon(t)$. For simple processes such as Brownian motion, it is sometimes possible to derive the duration distribution and hazard function, but this does not exploit the ability of hazard-based models to incorporate the effects of ageing and other changes in circumstances.

Models incorporating random preference parameters rather than alternative-specific random disturbances are more promising (see chapter 3, section 3.4.1, for the discrete choice analogue). As an example, consider the following very simple model. The individual, while in the labour force, earns an income y and has leisure ℓ; after retirement at age t, these change to $y^r(t)$ and ℓ^r. Post-retirement income $y^r(t)$ is increasing in t, reflecting the loss of benefits through early retirement, and for simplicity, we assume it to be continuously differentiable in t. At age a, this person expects to derive a lifetime utility of $V(a, t)$ if he or she retires at age t, where

$$\begin{aligned} V(a, t) &= \int_a^t \exp[-\rho(\tau - a)]\,[v_1(y) + \beta\, v_2(\ell)]\,d\tau \\ &\quad + \int_t^\infty \exp[-\rho(\tau - a)]\,\{v_1[y^r(t)] + \beta\, v_2(\ell^r)\}\,d\tau \\ &= \frac{v_1(y) + \beta\, v_2(\ell)}{\rho} - \frac{\exp[-\rho(t-a)]}{\rho} \times \\ &\quad \{v_1(y) - v_1[y^r(t)] + \beta[v_2(\ell) - v_2(\ell^r)]\} \end{aligned} \tag{6.18}$$

$v_1(.)$ and $v_2(.)$ are instantaneous utilities associated with income and leisure, ρ is the discount rate and β is a random preference parameter. $V(a, t)$ is a smooth function of t, and has first derivative

$$\frac{\partial V(a, t)}{\partial t} = \exp[-\rho(t-a)]\, K(t) \tag{6.19}$$

where

$$K(t) = \frac{v_1'[y^r(t)]y^{r\prime}(t)}{\rho} + v_1(y) - v_1[y^r(t)] + \beta[v_2(\ell) - v_2(\ell^r)] \tag{6.20}$$

where $v_1'(.)$ and $y^{r\prime}(.)$ are the derivatives of v_1 and y^r.

If $\partial V(a, t)/\partial t$ is positive at $t = a$, it cannot be optimal for this individual to retire immediately. Thus a necessary condition for immediate retirement is $\partial V(a, t)/\partial t \leqslant 0$ at $t = a$. Assume this to be satisfied; for this to be the case, $K(a)$ must be non-positive. On the assumption that the second derivatives of v_1 and y^r are also non-positive, $K(t)$ is a non-increasing function of t and thus $K(t) \leqslant 0$ for all $t > a$. Therefore $\partial V(a, t)/\partial t$ is non-positive for all $t > a$, and

$V(a, t)$ must attain its maximum on $[a, \infty]$ at $t = a$. Under our assumptions, a necessary and sufficient condition for retirement at age a is $K(a) \leqslant 0$ and, provided that the optimal policy has been pursued in the past and there have been no revisions or discontinuities in the decision problem, the equality must hold. Thus, if δ is the optimal retirement age, it must satisfy

$$K(\delta) = 0. \tag{6.21}$$

This occurs if the preference parameter β satisfies

$$\beta = \Psi(\delta; \zeta) \tag{6.22}$$

where

$$\Psi(\delta; \zeta) = \frac{v_1(y) - v_1[y^r(\delta)] + v_1'[y^r(\delta)]y^{r\prime}(\delta)}{v_2(\ell^r) - v_2(\ell)} \tag{6.23}$$

and ζ represents all exogenous information.

Condition (6.22) and (6.23) states that, if the income difference between retirement and non-retirement is large, or if the pension entitlement is increasing rapidly with age, then a large leisure coefficient β is required to make immediate retirement an attractive option. Assume that, conditional on a set of personal characteristics $\mathbf{z}$, the coefficient β has a continuous c.d.f. and p.d.f. $G_\beta(.|\mathbf{z})$ and $g_\beta(.|\mathbf{z})$. Then the optimal duration is $\delta = \Psi^{-1}(\beta; \zeta)$, which has p.d.f.

$$g(\delta|\zeta) = g_\beta(\Psi(\delta; \zeta)|\mathbf{z})\, |\partial\Psi(\delta; \zeta)/\partial\delta|. \tag{6.24}$$

If we assume that retirement at $t = 0$ is impossible (in other words $G_\beta[\Psi(0; \zeta)|\mathbf{z}] = 1$), the corresponding c.d.f. is

$$\begin{aligned} G(\delta|\zeta) &= \int_0^\delta g_\beta[\Psi(t; \zeta)|\mathbf{z}] \left| \frac{\partial\Psi(t; \zeta)}{\partial t} \right| \mathrm{d}t \\ &= -\int_{\Psi(0; \zeta)}^{\Psi(\delta; \zeta)} g_\beta(\Psi|\mathbf{z})\, \mathrm{d}\Psi \\ &= 1 - G_\beta[\Psi(\delta; \zeta)|\mathbf{z}]. \end{aligned} \tag{6.25}$$

The hazard function is $g(\delta|\zeta)/[1 - G(\delta|\zeta)]$, and this takes the form

$$h(t; \zeta) = \frac{g_\beta[\Psi(t; \zeta)|\mathbf{z}]}{G_\beta[\Psi(t; \zeta)|\mathbf{z}]} \left| \frac{\partial\Psi(t; \zeta)}{\partial t} \right| . \tag{6.26}$$

Expression (6.26) has two components: the density of β conditional on the event that $\Psi(t; \zeta)$ has not passed the threshold β prior to time t; and the rate at which $\Psi(t; \zeta)$ is changing.

The hazard function is particularly useful when this type of model is generalized to allow some evolution of the individual's decision problem over time. For example, suppose that preferences are subject to random (and unforeseeable) discrete shifts, through the preference parameter β, and that the probability of a fresh drawing from the β population in any infinitesimal time interval $[t, t+\mathrm{d}t]$ is $\lambda\ \mathrm{d}t$, where λ is an unknown parameter. This gives rise to a hazard function

$$h(t; \zeta) = \frac{g_\beta[\Psi(t; \zeta)\,|\,\mathbf{z}]}{G_\beta[\Psi(t; \zeta)\,|\,\mathbf{z}]}\left|\frac{\partial \Psi(t; \zeta)}{\partial t}\right| + \lambda\{1 - G_\beta[\Psi(t; \zeta)\,|\,\mathbf{z}]\}. \qquad (6.27)$$

The additional term $\lambda\{1 - G_\beta[\Psi(t; \zeta)\,|\,\mathbf{z}]\}$ is the probability that a change in preferences occurs, multiplied by the probability that the new value of β exceeds the critical value $\Psi(t; \zeta)$. In cases like this, it is much simpler to derive the duration distribution through the hazard function than by direct means.

The same is also true if there is some change in the pension rules. Suppose that the individual's pension entitlement is altered at time a^* to conform with a new, more generous, pension rule $y^{r*}(t)$. Define a new exogenous vector ζ^*, and the corresponding ratio $\Psi(t; \zeta^*)$. Immediate retirement after the change is optimal if $\beta \geqslant \Psi(a^*, \zeta^*)$. The resulting hazard function is given by expression (6.26) for $t < a^*$, by the same expression with ζ replaced by ζ^* for $t > a^*$, and by a discrete probability mass at $t = a^*$:

$$h^*(a^*; \zeta, \zeta^*) = \frac{G_\beta[\Psi(a^*; \zeta)\,|\,\mathbf{z}] - G_\beta[\Psi(a^*; \zeta^*)\,|\,\mathbf{z}]}{G_\beta[\Psi(a^*; \zeta)\,|\,\mathbf{z}]}. \qquad (6.28)$$

Expression (6.28) is the probability that β exceeds the new threshold $\Psi(a^*, \zeta^*)$ conditional on the event that it has not previously exceeded $\Psi(a^*, \zeta)$. Thus, the integrated hazard $I(\delta, \zeta)$, which is used to construct the duration distribution *via* expressions (6.4)–(6.6), is the sum of up to three components:

$$I(\delta, \zeta) = \int_0^{\delta^*} h(t; \zeta)\,\mathrm{d}t + d_1 h^*(a^*; \zeta, \zeta^*) + d_2 \int_{a^*}^{\delta} h(t; \zeta^*)\,\mathrm{d}t \qquad (6.29)$$

where $\delta^* = \min(\delta, a^*)$, $d_1 = 1$ if $\delta \geqslant a^*$ and 0 otherwise, and $d_2 = 1$ if $\delta > a^*$ and 0 otherwise. Discontinuities in the relation $y^r(t)$ result in similar breaks in the hazard function.

This simple model serves only to illustrate the way in which a duration distribution can be derived from a continuously evolving choice problem. It has many limitations, not least its assumption that retirement is purely voluntary – people are not forced to retire by their employers or by ill health. This may be an unreasonable assumption, and a hazard function of this sort is perhaps best viewed only as one component of a model that allows for alternative reasons for retirement. Such structures are known as *competing risks* models, and are discussed in section 6.3.3 below. Diamond and Hausman (1984) use this approach.

There are few studies of the retirement decision that are based on the hazard function and that exploit its ability to accommodate variations in the nature of the choice problem over time. An exception is the study by Diamond and Hausman (1984). There remains considerable scope for the development of the economic foundations of duration analysis in this area.

6.2.2 Job search

In economics, duration models have found their widest application in the study of the transition from unemployment to employment. The reason for focusing particularly on the duration of individual spells of unemployment is that this seems to be the main determinant of the aggregate unemployment rate. The aggregate rate of job loss is usually found to vary less than the average length of unemployment spells over the trade cycle.

Consider a typical individual, currently unemployed, and assume that it is not possible for this person to leave the labour force. Then, in order to leave the state of unemployment, he or she must get a job. Getting a job generally comprises three events:

i finding and applying for a job vacancy;
ii receiving an offer of that job;
iii deciding that the pay and conditions of that job are acceptable.

Thus, a realistic model of job search might look something like this.

i The population of job vacancies is characterized by a distribution function $G_1(\mathbf{c}\,|\,\boldsymbol{\xi})$ where $\mathbf{c}$ is a vector describing the characteristics of the job (its requirements for specialized training and experience, the nature of the work, and prospects for current and future pay). The vector $\boldsymbol{\xi}$ contains exogenous variables describing the current condition of the local labour market.

ii The intensity with which the individual samples this population of vacancies is described by a function $g_2(\mathbf{c}, \mathbf{z}, \boldsymbol{\xi})$, where $\mathbf{z}$ is a vector of exogenous personal characteristics of the individual. Thus, the effort a person devotes to job search will depend in some way on local conditions ($\boldsymbol{\xi}$) and the person's circumstances ($\mathbf{z}$). Different amounts of effort will also be devoted to different types of job ($\mathbf{c}$): unemployed labourers are not likely to be actively searching the managerial job market, for instance. The probability (or probability density, if $\mathbf{c}$ is continuous) that a vacancy in a job of type $\mathbf{c}$ will come to the attention of this person, and be applied for, in a short interval $(t, t+\mathrm{d}t)$ is therefore $g_1(\mathbf{c}\,|\,\boldsymbol{\xi})g_2(\mathbf{c}, \mathbf{z}, \boldsymbol{\xi})\mathrm{d}t$, where $g_1(.)$ is the probability density/mass function corresponding to $G_1(.)$.

iii An application for a job of type $\mathbf{c}$ has a probability of success of $g_3(\mathbf{c}, \mathbf{z}, \boldsymbol{\xi})$. The vectors $\mathbf{c}$ and $\mathbf{z}$ reflect the quality of the match between the individual and the job, while $\boldsymbol{\xi}$ reflects the degree of competition for the job – when times are hard, vacancies attract more applicants.

iv The wage the potential employer is prepared to offer the successful applicant is random, with c.d.f. $G_4(w|\mathbf{c}, \mathbf{z}, \xi)$ that depends on the attributes of the job and the applicant, and on local conditions.

v The offer of a job of type $(\mathbf{c}, w)$ under local labour market conditions ξ will be accepted by an individual with characteristics $\mathbf{z}$ if $w > w^r(\mathbf{c}, \mathbf{z}, \xi)$, where $\mathbf{z}$ is assumed to include such things as the person's entitlement to unemployment benefits. This occurs with conditional probability $1 - G_4(w^r(\mathbf{c}, \mathbf{z}, \xi)|\mathbf{c}, \mathbf{z}, \xi)$. Thus we are assuming that search behaviour displays the *reservation wage property*: for each possible type of job, the individual decides on a cut-off point, or reservation wage. If the offered wage is less than this, the offer is declined; otherwise it is accepted. Although it is possible to construct examples of circumstances in which optimal behaviour requires a more complicated acceptance criterion than this, most models of the search process do display the reservation wage property.

As it stands, this structure generates a hazard function of the form

$$h(t, \zeta) = \int_{R_c} g_2(\mathbf{c}, \mathbf{z}, \xi) g_3(\mathbf{c}, \mathbf{z}, \xi) \, [1 - G_4(w^r(\mathbf{c}, \mathbf{z}, \xi)|\mathbf{c}, \mathbf{z}, \xi)] \, dG_1(\mathbf{c}|\xi) \tag{6.30}$$

where R_c is the domain of variation of $\mathbf{c}$.

Although this theoretical framework is rather more general than any model used in the applied literature, in one important respect it is extremely restrictive. The right-hand side of expression (6.30) defining the hazard function is completely independent of t, the current length of the individual's unemployment spell. This is therefore a stationary structure, displaying no duration dependence, and implying an exponential distribution for δ. There are many ways in which non-stationarity might enter a model of this type.

- i The variables $\mathbf{z}$ and ξ, reflecting the characteristics of the individual and the labour market, may evolve through time.
- ii The effort with which a person searches for work (g_2) may depend on t: a long stay on the unemployment register might induce either desperation (positive dependence) or discouragement (negative dependence).
- iii The individual's chance of success (g_3) may depend negatively on t, through stigma: employers might treat a long history of unemployment as an indication of poor qualities on the part of the job applicant.
- iv The reservation wage w^r may decline as the duration of the spell increases. This could happen because a long spell has a direct disutility of its own, or because the individual anticipates the effects of stigma, or because some of the personal attributes in $\mathbf{z}$ (such as income from unemployment benefit or social security payments) may be negatively related to the length of time spent out of work.

The majority of empirical studies have found some evidence of duration dependence (usually negative), but there have so far been few attempts to locate the source of this dependence, largely because of the difficulty of identifying the individual components of a detailed model from an estimated hazard function.

In fact, most studies which do have an explicit theoretical basis use a much simpler model than that outlined above. Jobs are generally assumed to be homogeneous in all respects but the wage they offer: thus **c** drops out of the model, and the integral in (6.30) is removed. Job vacancies are assumed to be costlessly found and applied for (although see Narendranathan and Nickell, 1985, for an exception): thus g_2 may be taken as unity. The probability of success for a job application, g_3, is usually taken to be the same for all individuals (Narendranathan and Nickell, 1985, again give an exception). These modifications lead to a simpler form for the hazard rate:

$$h(t, \zeta) = \{1 - G_4[w^r(\mathbf{z}, \xi) \,|\, \mathbf{z}, \xi]\}\ g_3. \tag{6.31}$$

Most of the early work in this field (see, for instance, Kiefer and Neumann, 1979; Lancaster, 1979; and Nickell, 1979) had a model of this simple form as its implicit foundation.

A major problem is the intricacy of the theory underlying the hazard function, which, in our example, is built up from five elementary functions $G_1(.)$, $g_2(.)$, $g_3(.)$, $G_4(.)$ and $w^r(.)$, each representing a different aspect of the problem. Since these functional forms are unknown, and since many explanatory variables will appear in more than one component, it is a practical impossibility to identify them solely from the structure of an estimated hazard function. The only way to make progress is to exploit further sources of statistical information.

One possibility is to use data on the wage rates associated with accepted job offers to allow separate estimation of the wage distribution and the reservation wage. Assuming homogeneous jobs, accepted wages have a truncated distribution, with p.d.f.

$$f(w \,|\, \mathbf{z}, \xi) = \frac{g_4(w \,|\, \mathbf{z}, \xi)}{1 - G_4[w^r(\mathbf{z}, \xi) \,|\, \mathbf{z}, \xi]}. \tag{6.32}$$

Kiefer and Neumann (1981) use wage data to estimate parametric forms for G_4 and w^r, and Flinn and Heckman (1982b) use non-parametric methods to estimate w^r under the assumption of a constant reservation wage.

One can go further by obtaining direct survey information on the underlying behavioural elements: for example, there is no reason why one should not attempt to conduct a survey of the unemployed to determine their rates of job application and the resulting offers and refusals. More ambitious still, Lancaster and Chesher (1983) exploited the results of a survey which asked unemployed people to nominate a wage below which they would not work and the wage they would expect to receive on finding a job. This type of data makes it possible to determine the general characteristics of the implied hazard function without using formal estimation methods.

The major input of economic theory into a model of job search is through the reservation wage. Theories of the reservation wage can be very simple. For instance, a semi-log Tobit labour supply model (see chapter 4) would yield

$$h = \max[\gamma_1 \log(w) + \boldsymbol{\gamma}_2'\mathbf{z} + \boldsymbol{\gamma}_3'\boldsymbol{\xi} + \epsilon, 0] \tag{6.33}$$

where h is hours worked and ϵ is an $N(0, \sigma^2)$ random disturbance. Assuming $\gamma_1 > 0$, the condition $h > 0$ is equivalent to $w > w^r$, where the reservation wage w^r is

$$w^r = \exp[-(\boldsymbol{\gamma}_2'\mathbf{z} + \boldsymbol{\gamma}_3'\boldsymbol{\xi} + \epsilon)/\gamma_1]. \tag{6.34}$$

This provides a simple form for $w^r(.)$ and also introduces random heterogeneity in a natural way through the error term ϵ. However, it is an unsatisfactory model since it assumes that individual decisions are completely myopic. For instance, when deciding whether or not to accept a job, the individual should surely take into account such factors as the likely wait until the next job offer, yet the simple Tobit model excludes this.

The full theory of optimal job search is beyond the scope of this brief survey, and the reader is referred to the excellent exposition in Lippman and McCall (1976). In these models, the individual is assumed to know the distribution of wages associated with potential jobs and the probability that any application will be successful. He or she then uses this knowledge in choosing the reservation wage to maximize expected discounted lifetime utility. The basic ideas can be illustrated with the following simple model.

Jobs are homogeneous and, once obtained, last forever. The individual ignores leisure, and his or her choice criterion is to maximize expected lifetime income discounted at a rate ρ; call this criterion V. The model is stationary, so the probability that a successful job application is made in any interval $(t, t+\mathrm{d}t)$ is $g_2(\mathbf{z}, \boldsymbol{\xi})g_3(\mathbf{z}, \boldsymbol{\xi})\mathrm{d}t = \lambda\, \mathrm{d}t$, say, where λ may depend on $\mathbf{z}$ and $\boldsymbol{\xi}$ but not on t. Job offers are therefore generated by a Poisson process, and the time intervals between successive offers are distributed exponentially, with p.d.f. $\lambda \exp(-\lambda t)$ (see, for example, Karlin and Taylor, 1975). For simplicity, we assume rather than prove that this model has the reservation wage property.

Consider an instant ($t = 0$, say) at which a job opportunity arrives. Define $\tilde{V}$ to be the value of the choice criterion resulting from pursuit of the optimal policy. If the job is accepted ($w > w^r$), the individual has a perpetual constant income of w, with present value w/ρ. Denote by R the expected return from rejection of the current offer and the pursuit of an optimal policy thereafter. Then

$$\tilde{V} = \max_{w^r}\left[\int_{w^r}^{\infty} \frac{w}{\rho}\,\mathrm{d}G_4(w) + R\int_0^{w^r} \mathrm{d}G_4(w)\right] \tag{6.35}$$

Performing this maximization, the optimal choice for the reservation wage is $w^r = \rho R$ and thus, after some manipulation of (6.35),

$$\tilde{V} = \int_{w^r}^{\infty} \frac{w - w^r}{\rho} \, \mathrm{d}G_4(w) + \frac{w^r}{\rho}. \tag{6.36}$$

Now assume that, when unemployed, the individual is entitled to a regular benefit payment of size B, and that this amount is independent of the time spent in unemployment. Moreover, it is unaffected by any rejections of employment opportunities. Let τ be the random waiting time until the next opportunity arrives. Then

$$\begin{aligned} R &= E\left[\int_0^{\tau} \exp(-\rho t)\, B \, \mathrm{d}t + \exp(-\rho\tau)\, \tilde{V}\right] \\ &= \frac{B}{\rho} + \left(\tilde{V} - \frac{B}{\rho}\right) E \exp(-\rho\tau). \end{aligned} \tag{6.37}$$

Since τ has an exponential distribution, $E \exp(-\rho\tau)$ is $\lambda/(\rho+\lambda)$, and therefore (6.37) implies $R = (B+\lambda\tilde{V})/(\rho+\lambda)$. Since $w^r = \rho R$, this gives

$$\tilde{V} = \frac{(\rho+\lambda)w^r - \rho B}{\rho\lambda}. \tag{6.38}$$

Equating expressions (6.36) and (6.38)

$$w^r = B + \frac{\lambda}{\rho} \int_{w^r}^{\infty} (w - w^r) \, \mathrm{d}G_4(w). \tag{6.39}$$

Even for this very simple model, it is not possible to write an explicit solution to this equation for w^r, and a theoretically consistent econometric model thus requires repeated numerical solution of equation (6.39) for each individual to evaluate the reservation wage.

However, it is possible to derive some qualitative implications of the theory that assist in the evaluation of an estimated hazard function: the stationarity of the model implies a constant hazard rate, and therefore an exponential duration distribution; differentiation with respect to the benefit rate reveals that $\partial \log w^r/\partial \log B \in [0, 1]$ and $\partial \log h(t; \zeta)/\partial \log B \leqslant 0$. The chief policy issue is the magnitude of the latter effect of unemployment benefit on re-employment probabilities, and most investigators have detected a moderate but significant negative elasticity. However, many studies also find negative duration dependence, which casts some doubt on this static model. Atkinson et al. (1984) are critical of the use of this simple search model and find that the significance of the benefit effect is very sensitive to the way in which the theory is implemented empirically.

Although this approach does not suffer from the drawback of myopia, it is still based upon very strong assumptions about the information available to individuals and their capacity to use it efficiently. Moreover, if one introduces duration dependence into the theory, or attempts to extend the optimality principle by generating simultaneously optimal strategies for finding vacancies, applying for jobs and accepting offers, then no empirically tractable model seems to be available.

6.2.3 Other applications

Duration models have been used in a few other areas of economics. Early examples are Horvath's (1968) and Lancaster's (1972) use of the Weibull and inverse Gaussian hazard function respectively in modelling the duration of strikes. Further work on strikes has been carried out by Kennan (1985), who used a discrete-time beta-logistic hazard function incorporating a high-order polynomial in t. Estimates of this very flexible model indicate that the hazard rate for the duration of a strike is U-shaped, and that duration varies systematically with industrial production, moving in a counter-cyclical fashion. These results are confirmed by Harrison and Stewart (1987), using a different specification, and contrast strongly with empirical findings on the incidence, rather than duration, of strikes.

Most other applications are in the area of demography, where duration models have been used to estimate the importance of the economic factors influencing demographic phenomena. For example, Tuma, Hannan and Groenwald (1979) use the proportional hazards model to analyse the determinants of the duration of marriages. Olsen and Wolpin (1983) and Olsen and Farkas (1985) use a regression-based technique to investigate the impact of infant mortality and economic constraints on fertility.

Other applications are possible: the timing of promotions for individual workers and pay increases at the level of bargaining groups; the waiting time for the take-up of new technology by producers or of new products by consumers; the timing of interest rate and other discrete policy changes by governments and financial institutions. In these and other fields, techniques based on the hazard function are likely to be of value.

6.3 Some extensions

As these practical examples suggest, the simple theory presented in section 6.1 is often inadequate for applied analysis. We now consider some extensions.

6.3.1 Time-varying explanatory variables

In many applications it is unreasonable to make the assumption that ζ is time invariant. Indeed, one of the major advantages of the hazard function is that it provides a natural way of taking account of changing external conditions in a model of sequential choice. This is often important: in a study of retirement, for instance, the state of the individual's health is an important consideration, and this evolves through time; in a model of unemployent duration, the individual's entitlement to benefits may decline with duration (in the USA, for instance, benefits cease after 26 weeks of unemployment).

In such cases, we have a hazard function of the form $h[t, \zeta(t); \theta]$. The distribution of δ which corresponds to this hazard rate is now characterized by a p.d.f. and c.d.f. of the form $g(\delta | \mathbf{Z}; \theta)$ and $G(\Delta | \mathbf{Z}; \theta)$ respectively, where the symbol $\mathbf{Z}$ refers to the complete time path of the vector $\zeta(t)$ over the period $[0, \infty]$. Thus g and G are *functionals*, rather than functions, with respect to the explanatory variables, since they depend on the form of the time path $\zeta(t)$ rather than on the value of ζ at a particular point in time.

Using the same derivation as in section 6.1, we have in this case

$$h[t, \zeta(t); \theta] = \frac{g(t | \mathbf{Z}; \theta)}{1 - G(t | \mathbf{Z}; \theta)} \tag{6.40}$$

$$G(\Delta | \mathbf{Z}; \theta) = 1 - \exp\left\{ - \int_0^\Delta h[t, \zeta(t); \theta] \mathrm{d}t \right\} \tag{6.41}$$

$$g(\delta | \mathbf{Z}; \theta) = h[\delta, \zeta(\delta); \theta] \, [1 - G(\delta | \mathbf{Z}; \theta)]. \tag{6.42}$$

The important implication of these expressions is that the construction of $G(.)$ and $g(.)$ from a specified form for the instantaneous hazard rate now require observation of the explanatory variables continuously. This is possible for variables like age and for many dummy variables, but it is a practical impossibility for factors such as income, which are continuously variable. In practice, the best one can do for such variables is to collect observations on ζ at a limited number of points in time and assume some arbitrary, analytically convenient time path passing through the observed points (see the study of retirement by Diamond and Hausman, 1984, as an example of this approach).

6.3.2 Random heterogeneity

In the simple hazard function model, all inter-individual heterogeneity in the hazard rate is assumed to be due to the observable vector ζ. This assumption is usually felt to be an unduly strong one, and most applied workers attempt to relax it by assuming the presence of unobservable random factors in the hazard function. Let these random effects be represented by a single disturbance term ν, with p.d.f. $g_\nu(.)$, defined over a range R_ν. This distribution is referred to as a *mixing distribution*.

It we proceed with the analysis conditional on ν, (6.3)–(6.5) remain valid, although $h(.)$, $g(.)$ and $G(.)$ must now be written $h(t, \zeta \mid \nu; \theta)$, $g(\delta \mid \zeta, \nu; \theta)$ and $G(\Delta \mid \zeta, \nu; \theta)$ respectively. To generate the unconditional distribution of δ, the conditional p.d.f. and c.d.f. must be multiplied by $g_\nu(\nu)$ and integrated over the range R_ν:

$$G(\Delta \mid \zeta; \theta) = \int_{R_\nu} G(\Delta \mid \zeta, \nu; \theta) g_\nu(\nu)\, \mathrm{d}\nu$$

$$= 1 - \int_{R_\nu} \exp\left[- \int_0^\Delta h(t, \zeta \mid \nu; \theta) \mathrm{d}t \right] g_\nu(\nu)\, \mathrm{d}\nu \tag{6.43}$$

$$g(\delta \mid \zeta; \theta) = \int_{R_\nu} h(\delta, \zeta \mid \nu; \theta)\, [1 - G(\delta \mid \zeta, \nu; \theta)] g_\nu(\nu)\, \mathrm{d}\nu. \tag{6.44}$$

From these two unconditional quantities, one could then construct a corresponding unconditional hazard function $h(t, \zeta; \theta)$ as the ratio of $g(t \mid \zeta; \theta)$ to $1 - G(t \mid \zeta; \theta)$. In all subsequent discussion in this chapter, it is to be understood that the hazard functions in use may have been arrived at in this way, and the parameter vector $\boldsymbol{\theta}$ may therefore contain parameters of the $g_\nu(.)$ function. Alternatively, we can regard all our analysis as conditional on ν and add a final stage in which ν is integrated out to yield an unconditional distribution. It is usual practice to select a functional form for $g_\nu(.)$ that yields a convenient closed-form expression for the unconditional c.d.f. and p.d.f. For instance, a common specification involves a Weibull hazard function and a gamma distribution for ν (see Lancaster, 1979):

$$h(t, \zeta \mid \nu; \theta) = \exp(\gamma' \zeta + \log \nu)\, \alpha t^{\alpha - 1} \tag{6.45}$$

$$g_\nu(\nu) \sim \nu^{(1-\sigma^2)/\sigma^2} \exp(-\nu/\sigma^2) \tag{6.46}$$

leading to

$$G(\Delta \mid \zeta; \theta) = 1 - Y(\Delta, \zeta)^{-1/\sigma^2} \tag{6.47}$$

$$g(\delta \mid \zeta; \theta) = \alpha \delta^{\alpha - 1} \exp(\gamma' \zeta)\; Y(\delta, \zeta)^{-(1+\sigma^2)/\sigma^2} \tag{6.48}$$

$$h(t, \zeta; \theta) = \alpha t^{\alpha - 1} \exp(\gamma' \zeta)\; Y(t, \zeta)^{1+\sigma^2} \tag{6.49}$$

where $Y(t, \zeta) = 1 + \sigma^2 \exp(\gamma' \zeta)\, t^\alpha$. A commonly used combination for discrete data is the beta-logistic model of Heckman and Willis (1977).

Essentially, the role of this random heterogeneity is to generalize an overly simple model – if we begin with a restrictive specification for the hazard function, this can be made more flexible by introducing the additional function $g_\nu(.)$ into the problem. A simple alternative to doing this is merely to specify directly a very general functional form for $g(.)$, and indeed, if we were only interested in providing a close fit to the data, this would be a perfectly acceptable strategy. However, the hazard function usually arises from some economic theory, and the main object of applied work is therefore to draw inferences about its nature, particularly its duration dependence. Unfortunately, as Heckman and Singer (1982) point out, there exists in general more than one pair of functions $h(.)$, $g_\nu(.)$ yielding any particular distribution for the duration (although this is not the case if the hazard function is known a priori to be of proportional form; see Elbers and Ridder, 1982). In this sense, the functional forms of the hazard rate and the distribution of random heterogeneity are unidentifiable from data on durations alone, and the correctness of a priori choices of functional form therefore plays a very important role.

There is nothing especially surprising in this – parametric statistical techniques usually do depend critically on the correctness of assumed functional forms. However, the problem is an especially important one here for two reasons: for a given specification of the hazard, alternative arbitrary forms for $g_\nu(.)$ can yield quite different parameter estimates (see Heckman and Singer, 1982); secondly, a failure to accommodate random heterogeneity is likely to lead to spurious negative duration dependence (see the discussion in Lancaster and Nickell, 1980, and the formal analysis of asymptotic bias for the Weibull model given by Lancaster, 1985). The latter problem arises since, in a group of individuals with identical observable attributes and current spell lengths, those whose ν effects (representing unobservables such as ambition or initiative, perhaps) predispose them towards short durations will tend to be the first to depart from the state, leaving behind a group of individuals who are on average predisposed towards longer durations. This will be reflected in the data as apparent negative duration dependence, even though ν is not in fact directly related to duration.

Thus specification problems are particularly severe: to ignore random heterogeneity is to commit a serious error, yet there is no theoretical guidance available on the nature of such heterogeneity, and the parameter estimates may be sensitive to the arbitrary form assumed. Because of these problems, considerable attention is being paid to the estimation of models by non-parametric methods which do not require the specification of specific functional forms. These are surveyed in section 6.4.

6.3.3 Competing risks

Typically, the economic theory underlying the hazard function deals with a single process acting to terminate the spell: unemployment ends when the individual finds a job; retirement occurs when the individual's expectation is that the benefits will outweigh the costs. However, in most practical examples, it is unrealistic to assume that there is only one way in which a spell can end: unemployment may terminate because the individual decides to leave the labour force completely; retirement may occur as a result of ill health or redundancy. Models which accommodate multiple causes of termination have so far seen little application in econometrics, although in biometrics and operations research models of *competing risks* are widely used (see, for instance, Kalbfleish and Prentice, 1980; and Cox and Oakes, 1984).

We shall consider only the case of independent risks. Suppose there are m distinct processes which might lead to the termination of the spell, and that each of these is represented by a hazard function

$$h_i(t, \zeta_i; \theta_i) \qquad i = 1, \ldots, m \tag{6.50}$$

where ζ_i and θ_i are vectors of explanatory variables and parameters respectively. If process i were the only cause of termination, the completed duration δ_i would be distributed with the usual c.d.f. and p.d.f.:

$$G_i(\Delta_i | \zeta_i; \theta_i) = 1 - \exp\left[- \int_0^{\Delta_i} h_i(t, \zeta_i; \theta_i)\, dt \right] \tag{6.51}$$

$$g_i(\delta_i | \zeta_i; \theta_i) = h_i(\delta_i, \zeta_i; \theta_i)[1 - G_i(\delta_i | \zeta_i; \theta_i)] \tag{6.52}$$

However, the spell in fact ends when the *first* of the m processes causes termination. Thus, the actual duration is the smallest of the m hypothetical durations generated by (6.51) and (6.52):

$$\delta = \min(\delta_1, \ldots, \delta_m). \tag{6.53}$$

Consider first the c.d.f. of δ:

$$\begin{aligned} G(\Delta | \mathbf{Z}; \Theta) &= \Pr(\delta \leqslant \Delta | \mathbf{Z}; \Theta) \\ &= 1 - \Pr(\delta > \Delta | \mathbf{Z}; \Theta) \\ &= 1 - \prod_{i=1}^{m} \Pr(\delta_i > \Delta | \zeta_i; \theta_i) \\ &= 1 - \prod_{i=1}^{m} [1 - G_i(\Delta | \zeta_i; \theta_i)] \\ &= 1 - \prod_{i=1}^{m} \exp\left[- \int_0^{\Delta} h_i(t, \zeta_i; \theta_i)\, dt \right] \end{aligned} \tag{6.54}$$

where now $\mathbf{Z} = \{\zeta_1 \ldots \zeta_m\}$ and $\Theta = \{\theta_1 \ldots \theta_m\}$. Thus, after a little further manipulation,

$$G(\Delta | \mathbf{Z}; \Theta) = 1 - \exp\left[- \int_0^{\Delta} h(t, \mathbf{Z}; \Theta) dt \right] \tag{6.55}$$

where

$$h(t, \mathbf{Z}; \Theta) = \sum_{i=1}^{m} h_i(t, \zeta_i; \theta_i). \tag{6.56}$$

Differentiate $G(\Delta | \mathbf{Z}; \Theta)$ with respect to Δ:

$$\frac{\partial G(\Delta | \mathbf{Z}; \Theta)}{\partial \Delta} = -\left\{ \exp\left[-\int_0^{\Delta} h(t, \mathbf{Z}; \Theta)\mathrm{d}t \right] \right\} \left[-\frac{\partial}{\partial \Delta} \int_0^{\Delta} h(t, \mathbf{Z}; \Theta)\mathrm{d}t \right]$$

$$= \left\{ \exp\left[-\int_0^{\Delta} h(t, \mathbf{Z}; \Theta)\mathrm{d}t \right] \right\} h(\Delta, \mathbf{Z}; \Theta).$$

Thus, using (6.55), the p.d.f. of the completed duration is

$$g(\delta | \mathbf{Z}; \Theta) = [1 - G(\delta | \mathbf{Z}; \Theta)] h(\delta, \mathbf{Z}; \Theta) \tag{6.57}$$

which yields

$$h(t; \mathbf{Z}; \Theta) = \frac{g(t | \mathbf{Z}; \Theta)}{1 - G(t | \mathbf{Z}; \Theta)}. \tag{6.58}$$

Expressions (6.58), (6.55) and (6.57) are identical in form with (6.3)–(6.5): for the competing risks model, all that is required is to sum the hazard rates of the separate risks and then apply standard theory.

In some cases, it may be possible to observe both the duration δ and the identity, j say, of the process responsible for the ending of the spell. For example, in a study of retirement behaviour, we may know when each person retired and also whether retirement was due to choice, redundancy or ill health. The joint distribution of δ and j can be characterized by the following function, which is a c.d.f. with respect to δ and a discrete frequency function with respect to j:

$$G(j, \Delta | \mathbf{Z}; \Theta) = \Pr(j, \delta \leqslant \Delta | \mathbf{Z}; \Theta)$$

$$= \int_0^{\Delta} g_j(\delta_j | \zeta_j; \theta_j) \Pr(\delta_i > \delta_j, i = 1, \ldots, m, i \neq j | \delta_j, \mathbf{Z}; \Theta) \, \mathrm{d}\delta_j$$

$$= \int_0^{\Delta} g_j(\delta_j | \zeta_j; \theta_j) \prod_{i \neq j} [1 - G_i(\delta_j | \zeta_i; \theta_i)] \, \mathrm{d}\delta_j.$$

Using (6.54) and the definition of $h_j(.)$

$$G(j, \Delta | \mathbf{Z}; \Theta) = \int_0^{\Delta} h_j(t, \zeta_j; \theta_j) \, [1 - G(t | \mathbf{Z}; \Theta) \, \mathrm{d}t. \tag{6.59}$$

Differentiation of this function yields the corresponding frequency–density function:

$$g(j, \delta \,|\, \mathbf{Z}; \Theta) = h_j(\delta, \zeta_j; \theta_j)\,[1 - G(\delta \,|\, \mathbf{Z}; \Theta)]. \tag{6.60}$$

Observe also that the ratio of (6.60) to (6.57) yields the frequency function of j conditional on duration:

$$g(j \,|\, \delta, \mathbf{Z}; \Theta) = \frac{h_j(\delta, \zeta_j; \theta_j)}{h(\delta, \mathbf{Z}; \Theta)}. \tag{6.61}$$

The unconditional probabilities $g(j \,|\, \mathbf{Z}; \Theta)$ are typically quite complicated, requiring integration of $g(j, \delta \,|\, \mathbf{Z}; \Theta)$ with respect to δ over $(0, \infty)$.

In many cases, we are not interested in modelling all the potential causes of termination. If that is so, it is tempting to discard from the analysis all observations on people whose spells terminated for economically uninteresting reasons: for instance, those who retire for reasons of ill health. If this were done, the conditional distribution relevant to the remaining individuals would be $g(\delta \,|\, j, \mathbf{Z}; \Theta)$, where j is the identifier of the process of interest (free choice, say). This has the form:

$$\begin{aligned} g(\delta \,|\, j, \mathbf{Z}; \Theta) &= g(j, \delta \,|\, \mathbf{Z}; \Theta)/g(j \,|\, \mathbf{Z}; \Theta) \\ &= g(j, \delta \,|\, \mathbf{Z}; \Theta) \bigg/ \int_0^\infty g(j, t \,|\, \mathbf{Z}; \Theta)\mathrm{d}t. \end{aligned} \tag{6.62}$$

The implication of (6.62) is that it is unwise to make this sort of sample truncation – the result is a conditional distribution of complicated form, which still depends on all the underlying $h_i(.)$. Thus, we cannot escape the need to model all causes of termination, even if the underlying risks are independent. This is because an *observed* termination caused by an uninteresting process (ill health) is not independent of the interesting process (free choice), since the forced retirement that we observe at time δ is only possible if there has been no freely chosen retirement prior to δ.

6.3.4 Multiple spells and multiple states

We have so far considered the case of a single transition between two states: a move from unemployment into employment, or from employment into retirement, for instance. However, in practice, one often finds a multiplicity of states or spells. For instance, a combination of our unemployment and retirement examples would involve three states: employment and unemployment and withdrawal from the labour force. Multiple spells might arise if it were possible to observe people who return to the labour force after retirement or who are unemployed more than once in an observation period.

Assume that there are S possible states. A complete specification of the pattern of transitions between them requires a hazard function representing the rate of exit from every state r, say, to every other state s: thus $h_{rs}(t, \zeta_{rs}; \theta_{rs})$ governs the rate of exit from state r into state s for all $r, s = 1, \ldots, S, r \neq s$. An S-state problem therefore requires the specification of $S(S-1)$ hazard functions, each with a possibly distinct set of parameters θ_{rs} and explanatory variables ζ_{rs}. If these hazard functions are all independent of current (and past) durations, this multistate process is known as a *Markov process*; if the hazard functions are independent of past durations but exhibit some current duration dependence, then the model is said to be a *semi-Markov process*.

Because of the resulting complexity and dimensionality of multistate models, there is so far little experience of their use in econometrics, apart from the work of Flinn and Heckman (1982a, 1982b) and Burdett, Kiefer and Sharma (1985). Consider the distribution of a sequence of pairs (δ_p, j_p), $p = 1, \ldots, P$, where δ_p is the duration of the pth observed spell and j_p is the index of the state into which a transition is made at the end of the pth spell (thus the pth spell is actually spent in state j_{p-1}).

We assume away difficulties with the initial state by conditioning on j_0. The distribution of the remaining $2P$ random variables can be characterized by a function $g(\delta_1, j_1, \ldots, \delta_P, j_P | \mathbf{Z}, j_0; \Theta)$, which is a p.d.f. with respect to $\delta_1, \ldots, \delta_P$ and a discrete frequency function with respect to $j_1, \ldots, j_P$, where now $\mathbf{Z} = \{\zeta_{rs}\}$ and $\Theta = \{\theta_{rs}\}$. Repeated use of the law of conditional probabilities yields

$$g(\delta_1, j_1, \ldots, \delta_P, j_P | \mathbf{Z}, j_0; \Theta) = g(\delta_1, j_1 | \mathbf{Z}, j_0; \Theta) g(\delta_2, j_2 | \mathbf{Z}, j_0, \delta_1, j_1; \Theta) \times \ldots \times g(\delta_P, j_P | \mathbf{Z}, j_0, \delta_1, j_1, \ldots, \delta_{P-1}, j_{P-1}; \Theta). \quad (6.63)$$

Consider the pth component on the right-hand side of (6.63), and for simplicity assume that it is independent of $\delta_1, \ldots, \delta_{p-1}$ and $j_0, \ldots, j_{p-2}$ so that it can be written $g(\delta_p, j_p | \mathbf{Z}, j_{p-1}; \Theta)$. It has the form of a joint frequency–density function of the duration and exit destination from a spell in state j_{p-1}, with the $S-1$ possible destination states acting as competing risks. If these are assumed to be independent, they can be characterized by separate hazard functions:

$$h_{j_{p-1}s}(t, \zeta_{j_{p-1}s}; \theta_{j_{p-1}s}) \qquad s = 1, \ldots, S, s \neq j_{p-1}.$$

Since the exit from state j_{p-1} is governed by a competing risks structure, each right-hand side component of (6.63) is given by expressions analogous to (6.55), (6.56) and (6.60) above:

$$g(\delta_p, j_p | \mathbf{Z}, j_{p-1}; \Theta) = h_{j_{p-1}j_p}(\delta_p, \zeta_{j_{p-1}j_p}; \theta_{j_{p-1}j_p}) \, [1 - G(\delta_p | \mathbf{Z}, j_{p-1}; \Theta)] \quad (6.64)$$

where

$$G(\Delta_p | \mathbf{Z}, j_{p-1}; \Theta) = 1 - \exp\left[- \int_0^{\Delta_p} h_{j_{p-1}}(t, \mathbf{Z}; \Theta) \, dt \right] \quad (6.65)$$

and

$$h_{j_{p-1}}(t, \mathbf{Z}; \Theta) = \sum_{\substack{i=1 \\ i \neq j_{p-1}}}^{S} h_{j_{p-1}i}(t, \zeta_{j_{p-1}i}; \theta_{j_{p-1}i}). \tag{6.66}$$

There are two important generalizations of this structure. If we allow the hazard function to depend on the number of previous spells in each state, or if the parameter vector Θ changes in some other way from spell to spell, then this is a case of *occurrence dependence* (see Heckman and Borjas, 1980; and Flinn and Heckman, 1982a). If the hazard functions governing the exit from state j_{p-1} depend on past durations $\delta_1, \ldots, \delta_{p-1}$ (and possibly also on past states $j_0, \ldots, j_{p-2}$), then we have *lagged duration dependence*; such dependence may be important – for instance, individuals with a history of unemployment may be more likely to become unemployed in the future. Both of these generalizations remove the model from the class of semi-Markov processes.

6.4 Parametric estimation

We begin our discussion of the estimation of duration models by assuming that the hazard rate is known to belong to a specific parametric family of functions whose members are uniquely defined by a vector of unknown parameters $\boldsymbol{\theta}$. In practice, some members of $\boldsymbol{\theta}$ will derive from the component relationships of the underlying economic model and some will come from the assumed distribution of the random heterogeneity term ν. It must be borne in mind that the assumption that we are able to associate particular values of $\boldsymbol{\theta}$ uniquely with particular mathematical forms for these various components of the hazard is a strong one, and is generally hard to defend. Methods which attempt to avoid this identification problem are considered in section 6.4.

Many different observational schemes are encountered in the literature on duration analysis. For simplicity, we shall concentrate on the simplest case, where only a single duration is observed for each individual. The generalization to problems involving multiple spells and multiple states is straightforward in most cases, and is left to the reader.

6.4.1 Maximum likelihood with exogenous initial state

In our discussion of the theory of the hazard function in section 6.1, we made the assumption that the initial state was non-stochastic: for instance, in an analysis of the duration of a spell of unemployment or of a strike, the fact that the individual has become unemployed, or that the strike has occurred at all, would be assumed exogenous. These two examples should be sufficient to convince the reader that this may be an assumption that it is unwise to make, but for simplicity we begin by following common practice and ignore the possible endogeneity of the initial state. Sometimes this is in any case a reasonable thing to do: few people start their adult life by going into retirement, for instance.

The log-likelihood function has the following additive form:

$$\log L(\theta) = \ell_1(\theta) + \ldots + \ell_N(\theta). \tag{6.67}$$

There are several types of observation that might be encountered in practice, each giving rise to a different form for $\ell_n(\theta)$. We discuss these with reference to the retirement example, where the assumption of an exogenous initial state is usually a reasonable one. The sample is assumed to be generated by an exogenous sampling scheme: a random sample of the over-65s, for instance, with a retrospective survey questionnaire revealing details of the respondent's retirement age and other characteristics.

A completed duration observed unconditionally If the *n*th person happens to have retired before he or she is interviewed, and if the survey provides a precise observation of the retirement age δ_n, then the relevant likelihood component is based on the density at δ_n:

$$\ell_n(\theta) = \log g(\delta_n \mid \zeta_n; \theta). \tag{6.68}$$

An incomplete duration observed unconditionally If the person is interviewed before retirement, all we know about retirement age is that it must exceed that person's age Δ_n at the time of the interview. Thus the observation is censored from above at the exogenous threshold Δ_n, and the *n*th likelihood component is therefore

$$\begin{aligned}\ell_n(\theta) &= \log \Pr(\delta > \Delta_n \mid \zeta_n; \theta)\\ &= \log[1 - G(\Delta_n \mid \zeta_n; \theta)].\end{aligned} \tag{6.69}$$

An observation of the current state but not its duration Surveys are rarely conducted specifically to produce data for econometric use. This means that, in practice, one is often forced to use relatively uninformative data. For example, when the individual is interviewed at age Δ_n, the survey might reveal whether he or she is retired, but not the age at which retirement occurred. In such a case, if the *n*th individual is not yet retired, (6.69) gives the required likelihood component, and if he or she is retired it is

$$\begin{aligned}\ell_n(\theta) &= \log \Pr(\delta < \Delta_n \mid \zeta_n; \theta)\\ &= \log G(\Delta_n \mid \zeta_n; \theta).\end{aligned} \tag{6.70}$$

Discrete observation periods It is quite common for the process under study to operate continuously (or nearly so) but for observations to be recorded in discrete time: for instance, the retirement decision can be made on a daily basis, whereas many surveys will record the age of retirement only in whole years. The most common approach to the use of such data is to develop the model in discrete time, when it takes the same general form as the sequential discrete choice model discussed in chapter 3, section 3.6. An alternative procedure is to keep the theoretical model in continuous time but to take proper account of the discreteness of the observations when constructing the likelihood function. Assume that δ_n is measured in years and that we observe for individual n the age, in whole years, at which retirement took place; call this a_n. The corresponding log-likelihood component is based on the probability that δ_n falls in the interval $(a_n, a_n + 1)$:

$$\ell_n(\theta) = \log[G(a_n + 1 \mid \zeta_n; \theta) - G(a_n \mid \zeta_n; \theta)]. \tag{6.71}$$

6.4.2 Maximum likelihood under endogenous sampling

Sampling is often endogenous. A survey of retirement behaviour might be designed to make initial contact with a sample of unretired workers and then observe their subsequent decisions. Studies of unemployment duration are often based on samples drawn from the stock of people who are unemployed at a particular time. This type of sampling means that the initial state is not exogenous. In these two examples, people who tend to retire late or suffer long spells of unemployment are more likely to be caught by the sampling procedure than those who retire early or experience little unemployment.

We shall consider unemployment duration as our example. Assume that at a fixed time 0 a random sample is drawn from the stock of unemployed people. Thus we are sampling from the population of unemployment spells that contain time 0. The situation is as illustrated in figure 6.1. It is important to understand that, under this sampling scheme, the point $t = 0$ is exogenously fixed as part of the sample design. The length δ of the spell and its partition into pre-interview (δ_1) and post-interview (δ_2) components are random, as are the dates t_1 and t_2 at which the sampled spell starts and finishes. The nature of the likelihood function depends on which of δ, δ_1 and δ_2 are observable, and whether we are prepared to make assumptions about the way unemployment spells are generated.

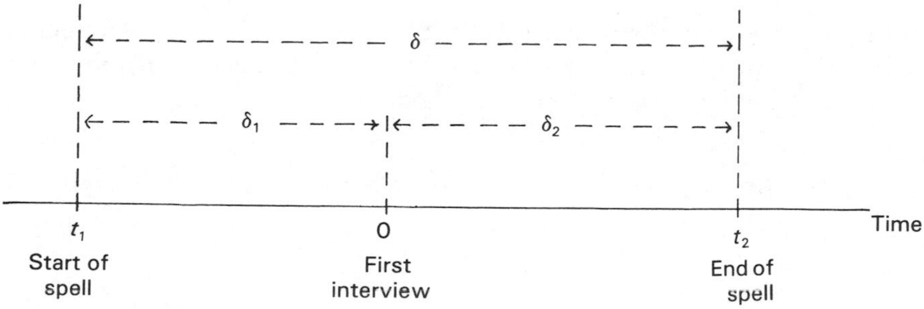

Figure 6.1 The structure of re-interview data.

We begin with the distribution of a sample duration δ conditional on ζ, and make an additional assumption that the process generating spells of unemployment and their durations is time invariant. An individual of type ζ has duration p.d.f. $g(\delta \mid \zeta)$, but, since sampling only takes place amongst the unemployed, this person is only at risk of being sampled for a period of length δ. Thus the p.d.f. of durations which are captured by the sampling process comprises two components: the length of the period during which the person might be sampled, multiplied by the likelihood of that duration being generated for that person. Thus, for a *sampled* duration,

$$f(\delta \mid \zeta; \boldsymbol{\theta}) = \delta\, g(\delta \mid \zeta; \boldsymbol{\theta}) / E(\delta \mid \zeta; \boldsymbol{\theta}) \tag{6.72}$$

where the term $E(\delta \mid \zeta; \boldsymbol{\theta})$ enters as the factor required to make $f(.)$ integrate to unity. Expression (6.72) is the density of a completed duration conditional on both ζ and the event that the spell contains the time 0 at which sampling occurs.

Now consider the post-interview component of duration. For a given complete duration δ, under random sampling all values of δ_2 are equally likely, up to the limit δ. Thus the p.d.f. of δ_2 conditional on δ and ζ is a constant, and, since this must integrate to unity over $(0, \delta)$, we have the specific form

$$f(\delta_2 \mid \delta) = 1/\delta. \tag{6.73}$$

Thus, conditional on ζ, the joint sample density of δ_2 and δ is

$$\begin{aligned} f(\delta_2, \delta \mid \zeta; \boldsymbol{\theta}) &= f(\delta \mid \zeta; \boldsymbol{\theta}) f(\delta_2 \mid \delta) \\ &= g(\delta \mid \zeta; \boldsymbol{\theta}) / E(\delta \mid \zeta; \boldsymbol{\theta}). \end{aligned} \tag{6.74}$$

Now integrate with respect to δ over (δ_2, ∞) to give the marginal density of δ_2:

$$f(\delta_2 \mid \zeta; \boldsymbol{\theta}) = [1 - G(\delta_2 \mid \zeta; \boldsymbol{\theta})] / E(\delta \mid \zeta; \boldsymbol{\theta}). \tag{6.75}$$

An identical line of reasoning establishes the same distribution for δ_1:

$$f(\delta_1 \mid \zeta; \boldsymbol{\theta}) = [1 - G(\delta_1 \mid \zeta; \boldsymbol{\theta})] / E(\delta \mid \zeta; \boldsymbol{\theta}). \tag{6.76}$$

The form of the log-likelihood function depends on the nature of the available observations.

Only total spell lengths are observed If the survey information is presented only in the form of total spell lengths (without being broken down into δ_1 and δ_2), the distribution (6.72) is applicable, and the nth likelihood component is either

$$\ell_n(\boldsymbol{\theta}) = \log \delta_n + \log g(\delta_n \mid \zeta_n; \boldsymbol{\theta}) - \log E(\delta \mid \zeta_n; \boldsymbol{\theta}) \tag{6.77}$$

or

$$\ell_n(\boldsymbol{\theta}) = \log \left[\int_0^{\Delta_n} t g(t \mid \zeta_n; \boldsymbol{\theta}) \mathrm{d}t \right] - \log E(\delta \mid \zeta_n; \boldsymbol{\theta}) \tag{6.78}$$

depending on whether observation n is observed as a completed duration or is censored at Δ_n.

Only incomplete spells are observed If there is no re-interview and our data come from a single survey conducted amongst the unemployed, then we observe only an uncompleted duration δ_{n1} for each person. Nickell (1979) used data of this kind. In this case, distribution (6.76) is applicable and the typical log-likelihood component is

$$\ell_n(\theta) = \log[1 - G(\delta_{n1} \mid \zeta_n; \theta)] - \log E(\delta \mid \zeta_n; \theta). \tag{6.79}$$

Pre-interview durations observed If the survey does not provide information on the length of time that the person had been unemployed before the first interview, then δ_{n1} is unobservable, and distribution (6.75) is the basis for the log-likelihood function. Thus, for completed spells,

$$\ell_n(\theta) = \log[1 - G(\delta_{n2} \mid \zeta_n; \theta)] - \log E(\delta \mid \zeta_n; \theta) \tag{6.80}$$

and for incomplete spells

$$\ell_n(\theta) = \log\left\{ \int_0^{\Delta_n} [1 - G(t \mid \zeta_n; \theta)]\mathrm{d}t \right\} - \log E(\delta \mid \zeta_n; \theta). \tag{6.81}$$

Full observation If both pre- and post-interview durations are observed, the distribution (6.74) is relevant and leads to a log-likelihood component of the form

$$\ell_n(\theta) = \log g(\delta_n \mid \zeta_n; \theta) - \log E(\delta \mid \zeta_n; \theta) \tag{6.82}$$

for a completed duration and

$$\ell_n(\theta) = \log[1 - G(\Delta_n \mid \zeta_n; \theta)] - \log E(\delta \mid \zeta_n; \theta) \tag{6.83}$$

for an observation censored at Δ_n.

These likelihood functions are not particularly appealing, since they are based on the questionable assumption that the rate of entry into unemployment is constant. They also require the evaluation of the expectation $E(\delta \mid \zeta_n; \theta)$ and other integrals, which may not be available in closed form.

Truncation from below One way of avoiding explicit consideration of entry rates is to follow Lancaster (1979) in working with the distribution of spell lengths conditional on the pre-interview duration δ_{n1}, which must be observable for this approach to be possible. Using (6.74) and (6.76).

$$f(\delta \mid \delta_1, \zeta; \theta) = g(\delta \mid \zeta; \theta)/[1 - G(\delta_1 \mid \zeta; \theta)]. \tag{6.84}$$

This leads to a log-likelihood function with completed and censored components

$$\ell_n(\theta) = \log g(\delta_n \mid \zeta_n; \theta) - \log[1 - G(\delta_{n1} \mid \zeta_n; \theta)] \tag{6.85}$$

and

$$\ell_n(\theta) = \log[1 - G(\Delta_n \mid \zeta_n; \theta)] - \log[1 - G(\delta_{n1} \mid \zeta_n; \theta)]. \tag{6.86}$$

Expressions (6.85) and (6.86) are much simpler than (6.77)–(6.83) and are more robust in an economic sense, since they do not require explicit assumptions about entry into the state of unemployment. The cost of this robustness is a loss of asymptotic efficiency.

6.4.3 Least-squares estimation

An obvious alternative to ML estimation is to fit an appropriate regression function to the sample of observed durations or log durations. We shall consider only the case of the proportional hazards model with random heterogeneity:

$$h(t, \zeta_n \mid \nu; \theta) = \exp(\gamma'\zeta_n + \log \nu) h_2(t; \alpha). \tag{6.87}$$

This leads naturally to a regression structure

$$\eta = -\log\left[\int_0^\delta h_2(t; \alpha)\mathrm{d}t\right] = \gamma'\zeta + \log \nu + \upsilon \tag{6.88}$$

where υ has a type I extreme value distribution (see section 6.1, equation (6.12)).

Conditional on ν, this is a fixed effects regression structure, with a different $\log \nu$ for each individual. However, unconditionally, the composite error term $\epsilon = \log \nu + \upsilon$ is a constant mean random disturbance term whose known mean can be absorbed into the intercept term in $\gamma'\zeta$. Provided that ν is homoscedastic, ϵ is also. Thus, if η were observable and all observed durations complete, a simple regression of η on ζ would provide consistent estimates of ζ and var(ν), and would be semi-parametric in the sense that no assumption about the distributional form of ν is required.

Consider the example of the Weibull model, where

$$h_2(t; \alpha) = \alpha t^{\alpha - 1} \tag{6.89}$$

and thus

$$\eta = -\alpha \log \delta. \tag{6.90}$$

Normalize ν so that $E \log \nu = 0$, and divide (6.88) by $-\alpha$. Using the fact that the type I extreme value distribution has mean $\psi(1) = \Gamma'(1)/\Gamma(1)$, we then have the following regression model:

$$\log \delta_n = b_0 + \mathbf{b}_1'\zeta_n + \epsilon_n \tag{6.91}$$

where $b_0 = -\psi(1)/\alpha$, $\mathbf{b}_1 = -\gamma/\alpha$ and ϵ_n is a homoscedastic random deviation with zero mean conditional on ζ_n. The least-squares regression estimator applied to (6.91) has the great virtue of simplicity: no integration or even iterative optimization is required.

However, this approach does have severe drawbacks. If an intercept term is included in the $\gamma'\zeta_n$ expression, then it is not possible to identify α and γ separately. Since ϵ_n has a non-normal distribution, least squares will be inefficient, even in favourable circumstances. Worse than this, there is no simple way of handling censored or truncated samples, since the appropriate conditional expectation of log δ is a complicated function of ζ_n and ν; thus the method will only give consistent estimates of b_0 and $\mathbf{b}_1$ if the length of the survey period is so great that the probability of encountering an incomplete spell is essentially zero. It is also difficult to modify regression techniques to deal with the case of time-varying explanatory variables (however, see Olsen and Wolpin, 1983, for an attempt at this).

The least-squares method can be applied in less simple models than the Weibull; in such cases, the dependent variable in (6.88) is a non-linear function of α and δ_n, and the minimum of the residual sum-of-squares function must be located numerically. In multi-spell models with lagged durations included in the ζ vector, the individual effects log ν_n are correlated with ζ_n, and IV techniques are then appropriate.

6.4.4 Specification testing

There are many sources of uncertainty in the specification of duration models in economics: the choice of functional forms, of explanatory variables, of distributional assumptions for unobservable heterogeneity. It is important to attempt some sort of diagnostic checking once a model has been fitted, and several methods are available. A useful concept here is the generalized residual, which was introduced by Cox and Snell (1968). Consider, for example, the integrated hazard

$$I(\delta, \zeta; \theta) = \int_0^\delta h(t, \zeta; \theta)\mathrm{d}t. \tag{6.92}$$

This is a monotonically increasing function of δ and is invertible. Write this inverse

$$\delta = \delta(I, \zeta; \theta). \tag{6.93}$$

Thus the duration δ is generated by a non-linear regression structure, involving observed exogenous variables ζ, unknown parameters θ, and an unobserved random variable I. We know from section 6.1 that I has a distribution that is completely independent of the structure of the underlying economic model and of ζ and θ. It can therefore be regarded as a *generalized error*, analogous to a standardized regression disturbance. Since its construction requires knowledge of θ, it is unobserved (as are regression disturbances), but it can be estimated by substituting $\hat{\theta}$ for θ in (6.95). Thus the *generalized residuals* are

$$\hat{I}_n = \int_0^{\delta_n} h(t, \zeta; \hat{\theta})\, dt. \qquad (6.94)$$

Note that these generalized residuals are not uniquely defined – any elementary transformation of $\hat{I}_n$ has a known distribution and thus satisfies the definition. We have seen that $-\log I(\delta, \zeta; \theta)$ has a type I extreme value distribution, and so $-\log \hat{I}_n$ would also serve as a generalized residual, for instance.

If the model is well specified, $I(\delta_n, \zeta_n; \theta)$ has a unit exponential distribution, and, in large samples, we expect $\hat{I}_n$ to have the same distribution, to a good approximation. Thus, if the $\hat{I}_n$ have an empirical distribution that departs substantially from the exponential form, there is reason to suspect that the assumed hazard function is incorrectly specified. A simple plot of the empirical distribution of $\hat{I}_n$ and tabulations of $\hat{I}_n$ against the ζ_n are often very useful in detecting specification problems. However, note that if there is censoring of the durations, $I(\delta_n, \zeta_n; \theta)$ also has a censored distribution, but with censoring thresholds that vary in quite a complicated way. The interpretation of residual plots is made more difficult by the presence of both estimation error and censoring.

More formal specification tests can be constructed, and these can often be expressed in terms of the generalized residuals. As an example consider the test for random heterogeneity developed by Kiefer (1984) and Lancaster (1985). This can be derived from the following mixed model, incorporating a random heterogeneity term ν:

$$h(\delta, \zeta \mid \nu; \theta) = \nu\, h^*(\delta, \zeta; \theta) \qquad (6.95)$$

where ν has a positive distribution with p.d.f. $g_\nu(.)$, a unit mean and variance σ^2. The integrated hazard conditional on ν is $\nu\, I^*(\delta, \zeta; \theta)$, where $I^*(.)$ is the integral of $h^*(.)$, and thus $G(\delta \mid \nu, \zeta; \theta) = 1 - \exp[\nu I^*(\delta, \zeta; \theta)]$. Therefore

$$G(\delta \mid \zeta; \theta) = 1 - \int_{R_\nu} \exp[-\nu\, I^*(\delta, \zeta, \nu; \theta)] g_\nu(\nu)\, d\nu$$
$$= 1 - E \exp[-\nu I^*(\delta, \zeta; \theta)]. \qquad (6.96)$$

Now expand the exponential term about $\nu = 1$ up to second order and collect terms:

$$G(\delta \mid \zeta; \theta) \approx 1 - [1 + (\sigma I^*)^2/2] \exp(-I^*) \qquad (6.97)$$

Upon differentiation

$$g(\delta \mid \zeta; \theta) \approx h^*(\delta, \zeta; \theta)\,[1 + \sigma^2(I^{*2}/2 - I^*)]\,\exp(-I^*) \tag{6.98}$$

where $I^* = I^*(\delta, \zeta; \theta)$.

These approximations can be used as an alternative to the null hypothesis of non-heterogeneity. A test for random heterogeneity is thus a test of H_0: $\sigma^2 = 0$. Lancaster (1985) shows that, for an uncensored sample, an LM (or score) test of this hypothesis is based on the quantity

$$\frac{2}{N} \left.\frac{\partial \log L(\theta)}{\partial \sigma^2}\right|_{\sigma^2=0} = N^{-1} \sum_{n=1}^{N} (\hat{I}_n^{*2} - 2\hat{I}_n^*) \tag{6.99}$$

where $\hat{I}_n^* = I^*(\delta_n, \zeta_n; \hat{\theta})$. If the log hazard is linear with an intercept, the sample mean of $\hat{I}_n^*$ is identically unity, and so (6.99) can be written

$$\frac{2}{N} \left.\frac{\partial \log L(\theta)}{\partial \sigma^2}\right|_{\sigma^2=0} = s^2 - 1 \tag{6.100}$$

where $s^2 = N^{-1} \Sigma\, (\hat{I}_n^* - 1)^2$ is the generalized residual variance. Thus a test for heterogeneity can be regarded as a test for the unit variance implied by the exponential distribution of the true integrated hazard.

An asymptotic approximation to the sampling variance of (6.100) is derived as $v = 4[1 - 1/\psi'(1)]/N$, where $\psi'(.)$ is the second derivative of $\log \Gamma(.)$. Thus, under H_0: $\sigma^2 = 0$, the following statistic has an approximate $N(0, 1)$ distribution:

$$\begin{aligned} T &= \frac{\sqrt{N}\,(s^2 - 1)}{2[1 - 1/\psi'(1)]^{1/2}} \\ &= 0.7985\,\sqrt{N}\,(s^2 - 1). \end{aligned} \tag{6.101}$$

Kiefer (1984) derives the same test, with a different variance approximation, for the special case of an exponential model. The extension to the case of censored samples is straightforward, with (6.99) redefined as

$$\frac{2}{N} \left.\frac{\partial \log L(\theta)}{\partial \sigma^2}\right|_{\sigma^2=0} = N^{-1} \sum^{N} [\hat{I}_n^{*2} - 2\, d_n \hat{I}_n^*] \tag{6.102}$$

where d_n is a dummy variable taking the value 1 for uncensored observations and 0 for censored observations, and each $\hat{I}_n^*$ is evaluated at the observed δ_n or Δ_n as appropriate. Variance approximations can easily be derived, but take a more complicated form in this case.

Tests for distributional form are usually made by estimating a flexible hazard function and then testing restrictions on it. For instance, a test of the exponential hypothesis can be made by testing H_0: $\alpha = 1$ in the Weibull model, and this is very common practice. Kiefer (1985) proposes a more comprehensive test, based on an alternative hypothesis

$$g(\delta \mid \zeta) = h_1 \exp(-h_1\delta) \, [1 + \psi_1 L_1(h_1\delta) + \ldots + \psi_r L_r(h_1\delta)] \tag{6.103}$$

where $h_1 = h_1(\zeta; \gamma)$ and $L_i(t)$ is the ith Laguerre polynomial (see appendix 3). These polynomials form an orthogonal set over $(0, \infty)$ with respect to the function $\exp(-t)$, and the coefficients ψ_i reflect the degree to which the ith moment of δ about zero deviates from the value $i!/h_1^i$ implied by the exponential distribution. Kiefer derives the LM test of the hypothesis that the ψ_i are zero. The resulting statistic is rather complicated, and the reader is referred to his paper for details.

6.5 Semi-parametric methods

In common with most statistical techniques in microeconometrics, the correctness of distributional assumptions is extremely important in duration analysis: mis-specification of distributional forms results not only in estimation inefficiency but also in inconsistency. What makes the problem worse in this field than in the case of the Tobit model, say, is that the distributions involved cannot be recovered uniquely from observed data, even in principle, without strong and untestable assumptions. Thus it is only possible to go part of the way towards freeing the analysis from reliance on specific distributional forms.

The central identification problem here is that the heterogeneous distribution of duration $g(\delta \mid \nu, \zeta; \theta)$ and the mixing distribution $g_\nu(\nu)$ are not uniquely recoverable from knowledge of the observable distribution $g(\delta \mid \zeta; \theta)$. There are therefore two approaches that we might take. One is to assume (or derive from economic theory) a specific form for $g(\delta \mid \nu, \zeta; \theta)$ and attempt to estimate θ without making any assumptions about the form of $g_\nu(\nu)$. The other possibility is to assume a specific form for $g_\nu(\nu)$ (usually the degenerate form corresponding to the assumption that there is no ν term in the model) and to attempt to infer the general nature of $g(\delta \mid \nu, \zeta; \theta)$.

It should be noted, however, that for applications in which there is a strong structural economic model underlying $g(\delta \mid \nu, \zeta; \theta)$, and where there is available additional information relevant to the components of this structure, it is often possible to draw further inferences by non-parametric means. For example, Flinn and Heckman (1982b) discuss the possibilities for the estimation of job search models which are opened up by the availability of data on accepted wage offers. We do not go into these extensions here.

6.5.1 An unknown mixing distribution

Consider first the case of a known duration distribution $g(\delta \mid \nu, \zeta; \theta)$ and a mixing distribution characterized by a c.d.f. $G_\nu(.)$ whose form is unknown. Heckman and Singer (1982, 1984) have studied this problem, and they propose a semi-parametric ML estimator which solves the following maximization problem:

$$\max_{\theta,\, G_\nu(.)} \sum_{n=1}^{N} \log\left[\int_{R_\nu} g(\delta \mid \nu, \zeta_n; \theta)\mathrm{d}G_\nu(\nu)\right]. \qquad (6.104)$$

They show that the resulting estimated form for $G_\nu(.)$ must be that of a step function, with $\iota \leqslant N$ discrete points. Thus (6.104) is equivalent to the rather less unusual problem

$$\max_{\theta,\, \iota,\, P_1, \ldots, P_\iota,\, \nu_1, \ldots, \nu_\iota} \sum_{n=1}^{N} \log\left[\sum_{i=1}^{\iota} P_i\, g(\delta \mid \nu_i, \zeta_n; \theta)\right] \qquad (6.105)$$

subject to

$$\sum_{i=1}^{\iota} P_i = 1 \qquad (6.106)$$

$$P_i \geqslant 0 \qquad i = 1, \ldots, \iota. \qquad (6.107)$$

Thus, it is valid to treat the mixing distribution as an unrestricted discrete frequency distribution, provided that a sufficiently large number of discrete points is allowed. In a limited simulation exercise, Heckman and Singer (1982) produce evidence that the required number of discrete points may be very small: for $N = 1000$, values for ι of 4 or 5 were found to be sufficient, and attempts to estimate more points merely led to duplication of these. It is interesting to note that Nickell's (1979) treatment of random heterogeneity amounts to a special case of this approach, with ι fixed at a value of 2.

Heckman and Singer (1984) prove that, provided ι is allowed to increase appropriately with N, this estimator provides strongly consistent estimates of both $\boldsymbol{\theta}$ and $G_\nu(.)$ under standard assumptions. However, there are no results available on its limiting distribution. It is incorrect to construct asymptotic standard errors from the information matrix, since conventional theory does not cover cases such as this, where the dimension of the parameter space varies with N. The little simulation evidence that is available suggests that non-parametric estimation of $\boldsymbol{\theta}$ is rather successful but that estimated mixing distributions may be very inaccurate, even in large samples.

Heckman and Singer also propose a computational algorithm, based on the EM algorithm of Dempster, Laird and Rubin (1977), for the solution of problem (6.105) with ι fixed. This appears to work well, although there is evidence of the existence of a large number of local optima, so that a good deal of experimentation with alternative starting points is called for. The absence of any practical guidance on the choice of a value for ι also necessitates a certain amount of experimentation. Thus the method seems to be very demanding from the computational point of view.

6.5.2 An unknown baseline hazard

A second type of analysis, which can be regarded as semi-parametric in the sense that it removes part of the necessity for specifying functional forms, seeks to determine the nature of duration dependence displayed by the hazard function without imposing a particular parametric form. For this to be possible, some definite assumptions must be made about the way in which the vector ζ enters the hazard function, and also about the form of the distribution of ν. Virtually all work of this type has been based on the proportional hazard specification, with no unobserved heterogeneity. This is the case we shall consider, with the duration distribution being based on the following hazard function:

$$h(t, \zeta; \theta) = h_1(\zeta; \gamma)\, h_2(t) \tag{6.108}$$

where $h_1(\zeta; \gamma)$ is completely known, up to a finite vector of parameters γ, but $h_2(.)$ is an arbitrary function whose form we seek to estimate. This is the approach of Cox (1972).

The technique proceeds in two stages. The first is to estimate the parameters of the scale function $h_1(\zeta; \gamma)$ independently of $h_2(t)$. Define η to be minus the log of the integrated baseline hazard:

$$\eta = -\log\left[\int_0^\delta h_2(t)\mathrm{d}t\right]. \tag{6.109}$$

Since η is a monotonic transformation of δ, we can conduct the analysis in terms of η: a high value of η indicates early termination of the spell. But it was shown in section 6.1 (see equation (6.12)) that η is generated by a regression mechanism of the form

$$\eta = \log h_1(\zeta; \gamma) + v \tag{6.110}$$

where $v \mid \zeta$ has a type I extreme value distribution. Consider an arbitrary set S of individuals indexed by $k \in S$. The individual with the shortest duration in this group is the one with the largest value of η, and the identity of this individual is therefore generated by a statistical mechanism formally identical to a discrete choice model. We can think of the η_k as random 'utilities', decomposed into stochastic and non-stochastic components v_k and $\log h_1(\zeta_k; \gamma)$, with the shortest duration being selected by 'nature' to maximize utility. Since individuals are assumed to be independent, and since the v_k have type I extreme value distributions, the resulting 'choice' probabilities are of the multinomial logit form (see chapter 3, section 3.4.2). Thus, the probability that the nth duration is the shortest in the set S is

$$\Pr[\delta_n \leqslant \delta_k, k \in S \mid S, \mathbf{Z}(S)] = \frac{h_1(\zeta_n; \gamma)}{\sum_{k \in S} h_1(\zeta_k; \gamma)} \tag{6.111}$$

where $\mathbf{Z}(S)$ represents all ζ_k, for $k \in S$.

This suggests a multinomial logit analysis based on a sequence of sets of individuals ranked by their observed durations. Assume that there are no ties and define the ranking $n(r)$ to be an integer function such that

$$\delta_{n(1)} < \delta_{n(2)} < \ldots < \delta_{n(N)}. \tag{6.112}$$

Thus $n(r)$ represents the identity (i.e. its position in the original sample) of the rth ranked duration. Now define the set

$$S(t) = \{n \mid \delta_n \geqslant t\}. \tag{6.113}$$

$S(t)$ is the set of individuals in the sample who have not completed their spells before time t; it is therefore the set of individuals who are at risk of generating an observation after this time. For this reason, $S(t)$ is known as the *risk set* at t. Note that the sequences $\{n(r)\}$ and $\{S(\delta_n)\}$ are logically equivalent and are both random. Consider the joint probability of the observed sequence $n(1) \ldots n(N)$ (implicitly conditioned on the exogenous variables). Repeated application of the law of conditional probability yields

$$\begin{aligned}
\Pr[n(1) \ldots n(N)] &= \Pr[n(N) \mid n(1) \ldots n(N-1)] \\
&\quad \Pr[n(1) \ldots n(N-1)] \\
&= \Pr[n(N) \mid n(1) \ldots n(N-1)] \\
&\quad \Pr[n(N-1) \mid n(1) \ldots n(N-2)] \\
&\quad \Pr[n(1) \ldots n(N-2)] \\
&\quad \ldots \\
&= \left\{ \prod_{r=2}^{N} \Pr[n(r) \mid n(1) \ldots n(r-1)] \right\} \Pr[n(1)].
\end{aligned} \tag{6.114}$$

But the risk set $S(\delta_{n(r)})$ can be deduced uniquely from knowledge of $n(1) \ldots n(r-1)$. Moreover, it is easy to show that $n(r)$ is statistically independent of the ordering of $n(1) \ldots n(r-1)$. Thus, although the single risk set $S(\delta_{n(r)})$ contains less information than the sequence $n(1) \ldots n(r-1)$, it is still possible to write (6.114) in the form

$$\Pr[n(1) \ldots n(N) = \left\{ \prod_{r=1}^{N} \Pr[n(r) \mid S(\delta_{n(r)}] \right\}. \tag{6.115}$$

This suggests a partial log-likelihood function based only on the ordering of the observations by duration:

$$\begin{aligned}
L^{\mathrm{P}}(\gamma) &= \sum_{n \ni 1}^{N} \log \Pr[n(n) \mid S(\delta_n)] \\
&= \sum_{n=1}^{N} \log \left[\frac{h_1(\zeta_n; \gamma)}{\sum_{k \in S(\delta_n)} h_1(\zeta_k; \gamma)} \right].
\end{aligned} \tag{6.116}$$

Cox (1975) and Tsiatis (1981) show that the value of γ that maximizes $L^p(\gamma)$ is a consistent estimator of γ, with a limiting normal distribution whose covariance matrix can be estimated in the usual way from the second derivatives of $L^p(\gamma)$. It is an inefficient estimator, since it uses only information on the identity of the individual terminating at each δ_n and not on the magnitude of the δ_n. It also has two further drawbacks. There is no simple extension of the method to handle unobserved heterogeneity, since the form of the probability (6.111) then becomes much more complicated. The method is also not strictly applicable in cases other than the standard one, involving an exogenous initial state, with durations either observed exactly or censored from above. Some *ad hoc* adjustments are available in cases of tied discrete observations (see Cox and Oakes, 1984, section 7.6).

The second stage of the Cox procedure is to estimate the baseline hazard function non-parametrically. Several alternative methods can be used, including the following. The number of individuals in the risk set $S(t)$ who are expected to terminate (not through censoring) in the short interval $(t, t+\mathrm{d}t)$ is approximately

$$\sum_{n\in S(t)} h_1(\zeta_n;\gamma)\, h_2(t)\, \mathrm{d}t.$$

Thus, the quantity

$$\frac{\text{number of spells terminating in } (t, t+\mathrm{d}t)}{\sum_{n\in S(t)} h_1(\zeta_n;\gamma)} \tag{6.117}$$

can be regarded loosely as an estimator of $h_2(t)\mathrm{d}t$. Now integrate with respect to t over $(0, t)$ and substitute the first stage estimate $\hat{\gamma}$, to arrive at the following estimator of the integrated baseline hazard:

$$\hat{I}_2(t) = \sum_{n:\delta_n<t} \frac{1}{\sum_{k\in S(\delta_n)} h_1(\zeta_n;\hat{\gamma})} \tag{6.118}$$

where we have assumed that durations are continuously observable, and therefore distinct, implying that the numerator of (6.117) is always 0 or 1. The corresponding estimate of the duration c.d.f. conditional on ζ_n is

$$\hat{G}(\delta\,|\,\zeta_n) = 1 - \exp[-h_1(\zeta_n;\hat{\gamma})\, \hat{I}_2(\delta)]. \tag{6.119}$$

This estimate is not continuous, and some form of smoothing must be used if an estimated p.d.f. or hazard function is required.

Further reading

For thorough background references on duration analysis, the reader must go to the statistical literature in other fields. Kalbfleisch and Prentice (1980) and Cox and Oakes (1984) give good accounts of the basic statistical theory. Some knowledge of discrete-state continuous-time stochastic processes is valuable, and Karlin and Taylor (1975) and Cox and Isham (1980) are good references here. Amemiya (1986, chapter 11) discusses duration analysis in econometrics, and stresses its relationship with Markov chain models.

Much applied econometric work based on the hazard function is *ad hoc*, with economic theory used only to suggest explanatory variables and the signs of their coefficients. Few formal models of sequential decision-making have been developed and estimated through the hazard function, despite its advantages. For instance, in the study of retirement decisions, there are two standard approaches. One is to treat behaviour as the result of a single optimal plan, constructed under perfect certainty, which is never revised or departed from; this is exemplified by the work of Gustman and Steinmeier (1986). The other is to assume that individuals are uncertain about future prospects but know the random process that generates the future and are able to cope with this uncertainty in an optimal way. The study by MaCurdy (1981) is a good example. A drawback of the latter type of model is that it is very difficult to derive the implied relationship between retirement behaviour and the opportunity set, and this limits its use for policy analysis. The prototype model sketched in section 6.2 is more limited in its view of retirement as an irreversible transition from a fixed level of labour supply to zero hours, and in its assumption that all change in the choice problem is unforeseen. Nevertheless, this approach has some promise.

7

Barriers to choice

Lane: There were no cucumbers in the market
this morning, sir. I went down twice.
Algernon: No cucumbers!
Lane: No sir. Not even for ready money.

Oscar Wilde

People cannot always do what they want. One might walk into a shop to buy a loaf of bread, and find it out of stock. One might apply for a loan to buy a new car and have the application rejected completely, or have agreement given only for an amount smaller than that requested. One might attempt to fulfil one's childhood ambitions by becoming an engine-driver but only receive an offer of work as a guard, or perhaps be refused a job at all. Many (perhaps most) jobs allow the individual little or no choice over hours of work. Someone seeking to rent a house from a local authority is likely to be consigned to a years-long waiting list.

All these barriers to the exercise of free choice are examples of rationing: cases where some mechanism other than the adjustment of a price is used to allocate the supply of a good to all the competing individual demands. At the micro level, over the short observation periods typical of cross-section surveys, price adjustment usually plays a minor role. Rationing is the inconvenient obverse side to the convenient fact that prices are predetermined at the individual level, in the sense that they are effectively invariant to any particular individual's actions.

There are many reasons for price stickiness and the non-clearing of micro-markets: restrictive labour agreements, asymmetric inventory and sell-out costs, informational and reaction lags in the setting of administered prices, transactions costs etc. Some of these barriers may be insubstantial and unsystematic in operation, and consequently capable of being absorbed into stochastic disturbance terms without inducing any significant specification errors. However, in many important cases this is clearly not so, and an analysis that neglects the role of these barriers may prove to be seriously misleading. Indeed, in some areas of applied economics, particularly labour supply, it is hard to escape the conclusion that the great majority of econometric studies are seriously flawed in this respect.

Consider the labour supply example of figure 7.1. Ignore all determinants of labour supply (ℓ) except the wage (w). Desired labour supply is given by the supply function $\tilde{\ell}(w)$. Suppose that preferences are such that many people want to supply a moderate number of hours per week but that, for technical or administrative reasons, there is a shortage of jobs with normal hours in the range (ℓ_1, ℓ_2). As a result, many people are forced off the labour supply schedule into full-time work ($\ell = 40$, say) or out of the labour force ($\ell = 0$). This will generate the illustrated clusters of observations above and below the supply curve, whose effect is to cause the fitted supply function $\hat{\ell}(w)$ to have too steep a slope. The neglect of hours constraints may therefore lead us to overestimate the wage sensitivity of labour supply.

This example is not conclusive. Different forms of rationing may have different implications, and the consequences of ignoring the problem are often obscure. However, figure 7.1 does suggest that it is extremely dangerous to regard rationing as an unimportant phenomenon that can be consigned to the error term. In the remaining sections of this chapter, we

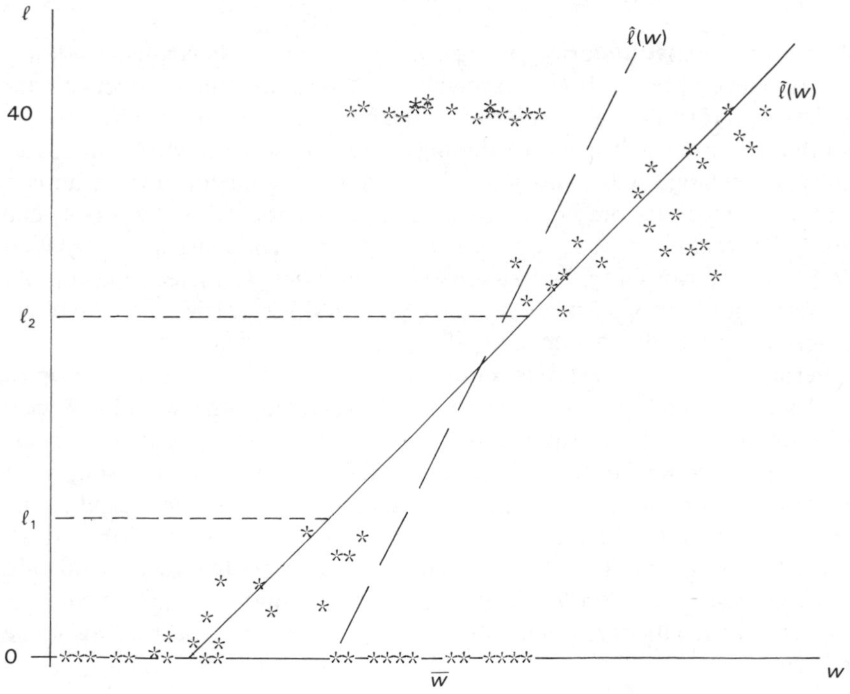

Figure 7.1 Possible consequences of the neglect of quantity constraints.

examine some of the econometric models that can be used to account for direct constraints on behaviour. Section 7.1 examines the case of point rationing, where a choice variable is fixed at a given value, and no choice is possible. Section 7.2 deals with the case where there is a barrier that imposes a limit on the magnitude of the choice variable but allows free choice within that limit. Finally, section 7.3 considers cases in which rationing takes the form of a limited collection of discrete possibilities offered by the market.

In all these applications, the nature of the econometric problem depends on several important distinctions. Is it known whether or not each individual is constrained? Is the size of the ration observed or unobserved? Is the ration constant or variable across individuals? Is the rationing mechanism exogenous or endogenous? The first of these is particularly important: it is extremely difficult to identify the parameters of both the underlying demand function and the rationing mechanism unless we can directly observe the incidence of quantity constraints. It is still very rare for surveys to include questions designed to reveal constrained behaviour, but this kind of information (if it can be trusted) is very valuable to the econometrician.

7.1 Point rationing

If someone is involuntarily unemployed, then his or her consumption of leisure is set extraneously at a fixed value, equal to the total number of hours in the week. If someone is unable to adjust his or her demand for housing in a continuous manner because of the high fixed costs of moving house, then short-run behaviour is constrained by having the consumption of housing services fixed at its pre-determined value. If a good is out of stock, consumers' purchases of that good are fixed at zero. These are all examples of simple point rationing, a phenomenon that has attracted considerable interest from economic theorists in recent years (see particularly Barro and Grossman, 1976; and Malinvaud, 1977).

Perhaps the most pervasive example of this type of rationing arises in the field of labour supply, since many jobs are associated with a working week of a fixed length that is determined by technological or institutional factors and is outside the control of the individual worker. In terms of labour supply, the models we examine in this section are assuming that the individual cannot control the length of his or her working week by choosing a job with the desired hours of work as its fixed requirement; models based on this idea are discussed in section 7.3.2 below. Here, we maintain the assumption that any constraint the individual encounters is entirely beyond his or her influence.

7.1.1 The effect of point rationing on demand for unrationed goods

Suppose that we have a vector of rationed goods, whose quantities are denoted by $\mathbf{x}_1$ and which are rationed at a fixed vector $\mathbf{R}$. The quantities of other non-rationed goods are arranged in a vector $\mathbf{x}_2$, and there is a linear budget constraint with price vectors $\mathbf{p}_1$ and $\mathbf{p}_2$ and total expenditure y. We ignore any complications caused by the non-negativity of $\mathbf{x}_1$ and $\mathbf{x}_2$, and assume that demand is generated by an interior solution to the utility maximization problem. In the absence of any quantity constraint on $\mathbf{x}_1$, the consumer's problem is the following:

$$\max_{\mathbf{x}_1, \mathbf{x}_2} V(\mathbf{x}_1, \mathbf{x}_2; \boldsymbol{\beta}) \tag{7.1}$$

subject to

$$\mathbf{p}_1^{\prime}\mathbf{x}_1 + \mathbf{p}_2^{\prime}\mathbf{x}_2 = y \tag{7.2}$$

where $\boldsymbol{\beta}$ is the usual vector of preference parameters. This has a solution of the general form

$$\mathbf{x}_1 = \tilde{\mathbf{x}}_1(\mathbf{p}_1, \mathbf{p}_2, y; \boldsymbol{\beta}) \tag{7.3}$$

$$\mathbf{x}_2 = \tilde{\mathbf{x}}_2(\mathbf{p}_1, \mathbf{p}_2, y; \boldsymbol{\beta}). \tag{7.4}$$

Now impose the quantity constraints. The consumer's problem becomes

$$\max_{\mathbf{x}_2} V(\mathbf{R}, \mathbf{x}_2; \boldsymbol{\beta}) \tag{7.5}$$

subject to

$$\mathbf{p}_2^{\prime}\mathbf{x}_2 = y - \mathbf{p}_1\mathbf{R} \tag{7.6}$$

which has solution

$$\mathbf{x}_2 = \check{x}_2(\mathbf{p}_2, y - \mathbf{p}_1^{\prime}\mathbf{R}, \mathbf{R}; \boldsymbol{\beta}) \tag{7.7}$$

Variations in the rationed quantity $\mathbf{R}$ have two separate effects: an income effect, since they change the resource variable $y - \mathbf{p}_1^{\prime}\mathbf{R}$, and a substitution effect, since $\mathbf{R}$ appears in the utility function (7.5).

We are often interested in studying the effect that rationing of one good has on the demands for other goods: if a husband becomes unemployed, does the wife work more or less? What are the consequences for the household's consumption pattern? In such problems, it is the nature of the restricted demand (7.7) that is at issue. Much will depend on whether we specify preferences to be directly separable in $\mathbf{x}_1$ and $\mathbf{x}_2$. Under separability, $V(\mathbf{x}_1, \mathbf{x}_2; \boldsymbol{\beta})$ can be written

$$V(\mathbf{x}_1, \mathbf{x}_2; \boldsymbol{\beta}) = V^*(\mathbf{x}_1, v(\mathbf{x}_2; \boldsymbol{\beta}); \boldsymbol{\beta}) \tag{7.8}$$

where $V^*(.)$ and $v(.)$ have all the generic properties of a utility function. In this case, the maximization of $V(\mathbf{R}, \mathbf{x}_2; \beta)$ is equivalent to the maximization of $v(\mathbf{x}_2; \beta)$, and there is no substitution effect at all. Thus, under separability, all that is required for the imposition of rationing is a re-definition of the income variable.

However, in general, there is no compelling reason why separability should be imposed: for instance, if $\mathbf{x}_1$ is leisure, there are many consumption activities requiring the input of time, and this would lead to specific interactions between $\mathbf{x}_1$ and certain elements of $\mathbf{x}_2$, contradicting any separability assumption.

Thus it is usually a rather complicated matter to specify a theoretical model that generates tractable rationed and unrationed demands. The key to this lies in the vector of virtual prices that support the rationed quantity. These are prices $\mathbf{p}_1^*$ at which it is optimal to consume at the level $\mathbf{x}_1 = \mathbf{R}$, even in the absence of a direct constraint. Thus $\mathbf{p}_1^*$ is the solution to the following equality:

$$\mathbf{R} = \tilde{\mathbf{x}}_1(\mathbf{p}_1^*, \mathbf{p}_2, y; \beta). \tag{7.9}$$

Write these virtual prices as follows:

$$\mathbf{p}_1^* = \mathbf{p}_1^*(\mathbf{p}_2, y, \mathbf{R}; \beta) \tag{7.10}$$

and substitute in (7.4) to give the rationed demands for $\mathbf{x}_2$:

$$\check{\mathbf{x}}_2(\mathbf{p}_2, y - \mathbf{p}_1'\mathbf{R}, \mathbf{R}; \beta) = \tilde{\mathbf{x}}_2(\mathbf{p}_1^*(\mathbf{p}_2, y, \mathbf{R}; \beta), \mathbf{p}_2, y, \beta). \tag{7.11}$$

Thus, everything hinges on the virtual prices (7.10). If these can be derived analytically by solving equation (7.9), then we can easily find the rationed demands $\check{\mathbf{x}}_2$. Unfortunately, this has proved impossible for most common models of consumer preferences. Deaton (1981) and Deaton and Muellbauer (1981) give some examples for which both $(\tilde{\mathbf{x}}_1, \tilde{\mathbf{x}}_2)$ and $\check{\mathbf{x}}_2$ are available in closed form, but these are all models with rather restrictive properties, and there is as yet no flexible specification available for application in problems where the sample contains a mixture of rationed and unrationed individuals, or where estimates based on unrationed behaviour are to be used to predict the consequences of rationing (or *vice versa*).

For this reason, there has so far been no applied analysis of general multi-good demand behaviour under quantity constraints. Deaton (1981) and Blundell and Walker (1982), however, do estimate rationed demand models under the strong assumption that every individual in the sample experiences rationing. Deaton treats housing as a constrained quantity in the context of a complete system of aggregate demand equations and Blundell and Walker treat the husband's hours of work as a rationed good in a model of the joint determination of husbands' and wives' labour supply and household consumption. Both studies attempt an informal comparison with results from models based on similar functional forms for the unrationed demand problem, although in the former case, the comparison is not very convincing, since the rationed and unrationed models implicitly assume different forms for $V(\mathbf{x}_1, \mathbf{x}_2)$.

There are also other difficulties associated with quantity constraints: rationing may not be exogenous, and its operation may not be fully observed. To investigate these problems, we have to be more modest in our objectives and adopt a much simpler model. We now restrict attention to a single demand function (of simple Tobit form) and dispense with any explicit foundation in utility theory.

7.1.2 Demand for the constrained good: fully observed rationing

We now focus attention on the demand for the rationed good itself. To simplify matters as far as possible, we shall suppose that the unconstrained demand $\tilde{x}_{n1}$ is generated by a Tobit structure involving a vector of explanatory variables ζ_n containing all relevant prices, observed personal attributes and income (or suitable transformations of these). Thus, in the absence of rationing, our estimation problem would be to fit the following censored regression model:

$$\tilde{x}_{n1} \mid \zeta_n \sim \mathrm{LCN}(\gamma'\zeta_n, \sigma^2, 0). \tag{7.12}$$

In this section we confine attention to cases where the rationing mechanism is fully observed: we know which individuals are rationed, and we observe the rationed quantities also.

The case where every individual is point rationed is trivial: no individual is on his or her demand curve, and so its parameters are not estimatable. For the non-trivial case in which the sample contains a mixture of constrained and unconstrained individuals, there are three possibilities.

Exogenous rationing Define a dummy variable d_n acting as an indicator of the *sample separation*: the division of individuals into rationed and unrationed subsamples. d_n takes the value 1 if individual n is rationed and 0 otherwise, and, where rationing exists, R_n is the rationed quantity. The observational scheme is thus

$$\begin{aligned} x_{n1} &= \tilde{x}_{n1} \qquad \text{if } d_n = 0 \\ x_{n1} &= R_n \qquad \text{if } d_n = 1. \end{aligned} \tag{7.13}$$

Rationing is said to be fully exogenous if (d_n, R_n) is independent of $\tilde{x}_{n1}$ (conditional on ζ_n), in other words, if the barriers to free choice are independent of those choices.

Since in this case it is only the unrationed observations that yield information on γ and σ^2, and since we know precisely which observations these are, efficient estimation is straightforward. The exogeneity of the rationing mechanism implies that the quantity-constrained observations can be deleted from the sample without inducing any truncation bias. The standard Tobit estimator is then applied to the remaining unconstrained observations.

Partially exogenous rationing In many applied examples, the process that determines which individuals encounter some quantity constraint is endogenous, but the constrained quantity R_n is exogenous. Usually this occurs when R_n is a constant value common to all individuals. For instance, if x_{n1} is labour supply and the rationing in question represents involuntary unemployment, we have a case where R_n is identically zero. The situation is not different if R_n does vary but remains exogenous. For example, some jobs may be associated with exogenously fixed lengths of the working day, with these hours requirements varying from job to job.

It is usually hard to rule out the possibility that there are unobserved (and hence random) characteristics of the individual that determine both the choices that a person makes and also the obstacles that he or she encounters. For instance, an individual with little personal ambition might tend to supply relatively little labour and also to have difficulty convincing potential employers of his or her worth. In this example, there would be some negative stochastic dependence between x_{n1} and d_n as a result, and d_n would be an endogenous variable.

However, there is another consideration that militates against the assumption that d_n is exogenous. Suppose we are considering an application to labour supply. If d_n is defined independently of $\tilde{x}_{n1}$, the mechanism (7.13) implies a particularly Draconian form of rationing. Even if the individual wishes to supply no labour ($\tilde{x}_{n1} = 0$), he or she is forced to supply a positive number of hours R_n if d_n takes the value 1. In practice, people always have the option to drop out of the labour force, and so the structure (7.13) can only hold if the indicator d_n is defined appropriately in terms of $\tilde{x}_{n1}$. The following model is the simplest that meets this objection. Define latent variables $\tilde{x}^*_{n1}$ and d^*_n such that

$$\tilde{x}^*_{n1}, d^*_n \mid \zeta_n, \xi_n \sim N(\mu_n, \Sigma) \tag{7.14}$$

where

$$\mu'_n = (\gamma'\zeta_n \quad \delta'\xi_n) \tag{7.15}$$

$$\Sigma = \begin{bmatrix} \sigma & \sigma\rho_{xd} \\ \sigma\rho_{xd} & 1 \end{bmatrix} \tag{7.16}$$

and where ξ_n is a vector of exogenous variables used to explain the incidence of rationing. In the case of labour supply, for example, ξ_n might include variables such as the local rate of unemployment in the individual's place of residence and the individual's educational attainment and length of work experience.

Now assume that rationing is recorded by the survey enquiry only if desired labour supply $\tilde{x}_{n1}$ is positive (implying that its latent analogue $\tilde{x}^*_{n1}$ is positive) and d^*_n crosses a (zero) threshold to induce the constraint $x_{n1} = R_n$. Thus the full mechanism is

$$\tilde{x}_{n1} = \max[\tilde{x}^*_{n1}, 0] \tag{7.17}$$

and

$$\begin{aligned} d_n &= 1 \qquad \text{if } \tilde{x}_{n1} > 0 \text{ and } d^*_n > 0 \\ &= 0 \qquad \text{if } \tilde{x}_{n1} = 0 \text{ or} \\ & \qquad\quad \text{if } \tilde{x}_{n1} > 0 \text{ and } d^*_n \leqslant 0. \end{aligned} \tag{7.18}$$

The structure comprising equations (7.13)–(7.18) displays dual censoring of x_{n1}, both with respect to its own underlying latent variable $\tilde{x}^*_{n1}$ and with respect to the extraneous variable d^*_n. In this respect, it is similar to Cragg's (1971) double-hurdle model and Amemiya's (1984, 1986, chapter 10) type 2 Tobit model.

Although (7.18) is a more reasonable observational mechanism than the assumption of exogeneity for d_n, it is still open to objection. Suppose that our typical individual wishes to work 10 hours per week ($\tilde{x}_{n1} = 10$) but can only find a 40-hour full-time job ($d_n = 1$, $R_n = 40$). In reality, it is quite likely that the individual will decline the job offer and decide instead to drop out of the labour force, on the grounds that $x_{n1} = 0$ is closer to $\tilde{x}_{n1}$ than is $x_{n1} = 40$. However, the model (7.18) assumes that this can never happen. Since jobs with requirements for very low hours are comparatively rare, the restrictiveness of this assumption may be a serious problem. A better approach would be to model an explicit utility comparison between the alternatives of zero hours and R_n hours whenever rationing arises. Such models, which view rationing as a process generating a limited number of discrete job opportunities, raise substantial technical difficulties, but have considerable advantages. We return to this issue in sections 7.2.3 and 7.3.2.

With rationing endogenous, it is no longer appropriate to drop the quantity-constrained observations and apply the Tobit estimator to the remainder, since the resulting subsample is then truncated with respect to an endogenous variable (see chapter 2, section 2.6). To correct this bias or to use the efficient ML estimator, it is necessary to derive the distribution of the observed variables d_n and x_{n1}. There are three observational regimes: observations can be censored, rationed or completely unconstrained. Thus the conditional distribution for the observables x_{n1} and d_n has the following three components:

$$\begin{aligned} \Pr(x_{n1} = 0, d_n = 0 \mid \zeta_n, \xi_n, R_n) &= \Pr(\tilde{x}^*_{n1} \leqslant 0 \mid \zeta_n) \\ &= 1 - \Phi(\gamma' \zeta_n / \sigma) \end{aligned} \tag{7.19}$$

$$\begin{aligned} \Pr(x_{n1} = R_n, d_n = 1 \mid \zeta_n, \xi_n, R_n) &= \Pr(\tilde{x}^*_{n1} > 0, d^*_n \leqslant 0 \mid \zeta_n, \xi_n) \\ &= \int_0^{\infty} \int_{-\infty}^{0} \varphi(\tilde{x}^*_1, d^*; \mu_n, \Sigma)\, \mathrm{d}d^*\, \mathrm{d}\tilde{x}^*_1 \end{aligned} \tag{7.20}$$

$$f(x_{n1}, d_n = 0 \mid \zeta_n, \xi_n, R_n) = \int_{-\infty}^{0} \varphi(x_{n1}, d^*; \mu_n, \Sigma)\, \mathrm{d}d^*$$

$$= \sigma^{-1}\phi\left[\frac{x_{n1} - \gamma'\zeta_n}{\sigma}\right]$$

$$\left\{1 - \Phi\left[\frac{\delta'\xi_n + \rho_{xd}(x_{n1} - \gamma'\zeta_n)/\sigma}{(1-\rho_{xd}^2)^{1/2}}\right]\right\} \qquad (7.21)$$

where $\varphi(.; \mu_n, \Sigma)$ denotes the p.d.f. of the bivarite $N(\mu_n, \Sigma)$ distribution. The continuous component of the distribution of x_{n1} and d_n, (7.21), is expressed as the product of two terms: the marginal density of x_{n1}, and the probability of the event $d_n = 0$ conditional on x_{n1} (see appendix 3, section A3.5). Note that R_n is not involved in the right-hand sides of any of (7.16)–(7.18) and thus need not be observed at all provided that d_n is available.

The log-likelihood function takes the following general form:

$$\log L(\gamma, \sigma, \delta, \rho_{xd}) = \sum_{d_n=1} \log \Pr(x_{n1} = R_n, d_n = 1 \mid \zeta_n, \xi_n, R_n)$$

$$+ \sum_{\substack{d_n=0 \\ x_{n1}=0}} \log \Pr(x_{n1} = 0, d_n = 0 \mid \zeta_n, \xi_n, R_n)$$

$$+ \sum_{\substack{d_n=0 \\ x_{n1}>0}} \log f(x_{n1} \mid \zeta_n, \xi_n, R_n) \qquad (7.22)$$

Note that the endogeneity of d_n gives rise to quite a substantial computational burden since it is necessary, in evaluating the second component of this log-likelihood, to compute expression (7.20), which is a volume under a bivariate normal density function; section A3.4 of appendix 3 examines this type of computational problem.

Applications based on the distribution (7.19)–(7.21) and log-likelihood (7.22) are rare in the applied literature, since most attempts to use double-hurdle structures have been made in the context of samples for which the classification variable d_n is unobserved (see, for example, Blundell, Ham and Meghir, 1987). However, the study by Ham (1982) does exploit information of this form but uses a slightly different model, estimated by means of Heckman-type truncated regression estimators (see chapter 2, section 2.6.4).

Rationing with d_n and R_n endogenous In some cases, the constrained quantity varies between individuals, and if we suspect the endogeneity of the rationing process it seems wise to treat both d_n and R_n as endogenous. For example, if x_{n1} represents hours of labour supply, we might suspect the possibility that some individuals are not free to choose their hours of work. If our sample survey asks each individual whether or not this is the case, then d_n is observed. However, we assume R_n to be observed only when the quantity constraint is binding.

We now have to choose between two approaches to estimation. If we truncate the sample by deleting all observations on constrained individuals, no knowledge of R_n is required. Thus we might use one of the estimation techniques appropriate to a sample truncated with respect to the extraneous variable d_n^* and avoid the necessity for modelling R_n. Section 2.6 of chapter 2 discusses this type of estimation problem.

If we are more ambitious and attempt to model R_n, we run the risk of misspecifying the additional relationship but stand to achieve some gain in terms of asymptotic efficiency. In practice, sample truncation may be preferable, since the new equation may be hard to specify convincingly. For instance, in our labour supply example, we would have to explain the distribution of weekly hours of work that various firms impose on their various employees.

Since we are assuming x_{n1} to be censored from below at zero, we must also ensure that R_n cannot be negative. There are many ways in which this could be done. We could, for example, specify a censored regression structure for this variable too:

$$R_n \sim \mathrm{LCN}(\delta'\xi_{n2}, \sigma_r^2, 0) \tag{7.23}$$

where ξ_{n2} is a second vector of exogenous explanatory variables, not necessarily identical with the vector (which we now call ξ_{n1}) explaining d_n. We thus assume that the three underlying latent variables in the problem arise from the following trivariate normal regression structure:

$$\tilde{x}_{n1}^*, d_n^*, R_n^* \mid \zeta_n, \xi_{n1}, \xi_{n2} \sim \mathrm{N}(\mu_n, \Sigma) \tag{7.24}$$

where μ_n and Σ are now redefined as

$$\mu_n' = [\gamma'\zeta_n \quad \delta_1'\xi_{n1} \quad \delta_2'\xi_{n2}] \tag{7.25}$$

$$\Sigma = \begin{bmatrix} \sigma^2 & \sigma_{xd} & \sigma_{xr} \\ \sigma_{xd} & 1 & \sigma_{rd} \\ \sigma_{xr} & \sigma_{rd} & \sigma_r^2 \end{bmatrix}. \tag{7.26}$$

Although the Tobit model (7.23) is a simple way of specifying the rationed quantity, it may not accord very well with observation; in the case of labour supply, for instance, one usually observes a distinctly trimodal distribution of working hours, with peaks at zero for the unemployed, at around 15–20 hours for part-time jobs and around 40 hours for most full-time jobs (see Zabalza, Pissarides and Barton, 1980). Of course, it is possible that this might be a supply-side phenomenon but, as Dickens and Lundberg (1985) have pointed out, conventional labour supply models alone do not fit this distribution very well. If, instead, we regard this as a feature of the demand for labour, then we require the Tobit model (7.23) to be able to generate such a distribution, and yet there is nothing in the stochastic specification or the explanatory variables of such a model that is likely to achieve this. The discrete models examined in section 7.3 are perhaps more plausible in this respect.

However, returning to model (7.23), the two observed variables are again x_{n1} and d_n, but there are now four observational regimes, and so their conditional distribution has four components. If the individual is constrained at zero (is involuntarily unemployed, for example), this occurs because $d_n = 1$ and $R_n = 0$ (implying $d_n^* > 0$ and $R_n^* < 0$). Assume that individuals only declare themselves to be rationed if $\tilde{x}_{n1} > 0$. Thus

$$\Pr(x_{n1}=0, d_n=1 \mid \zeta_n, \xi_{n1}, \xi_{n2}) = \Pr(\tilde{x}_{n1}^* > 0, d_n^* > 0, R_n^* < 0 \mid \zeta_n, \xi_{n1}, \xi_{n2}) \tag{7.27}$$

$$= \int_0^{\infty}\int_0^{\infty}\int_{-\infty}^{0} \varphi(\tilde{x}_1, d^*, R^*; \mu_n, \Sigma)\, \mathrm{d}R^*\, \mathrm{d}d^*\, \mathrm{d}\tilde{x}_1 \tag{7.28}$$

On the other hand, if the individual is constrained at a positive number of hours of labour supply, we must have $d_n = 1$ (implying $d_n^* > 0$) and R_n equal to the positive value observed for x_{n1}; we also know that $\tilde{x}_{n1}$ must be positive for rationing to be recorded. Thus

$$f(x_{n1}, d_n=1 \mid \zeta_n, \xi_{n1},\xi_{n2}) = \int_0^{\infty}\int_0^{\infty} \varphi(\tilde{x}_1, d^*, x_{n1}; \mu_n, \Sigma)\, \mathrm{d}d^*\, \mathrm{d}\tilde{x}_1 \tag{7.29}$$

If the individual supplies no hours of labour, but does this voluntarily, we have $\tilde{x}_{n1} = 0$ (implying $\tilde{x}_{n1}^* \leqslant 0$); in this case we have no information about d_n^* or R_n^*. Thus

$$\Pr(x_{n1}=0, d_n=0 \mid \zeta_n, \xi_{n1}, \xi_{n2}) = \int_{-\infty}^{0}\int_{-\infty}^{\infty}\int_{-\infty}^{\infty} \varphi(\tilde{x}_1, d^*, R^*; \mu_n, \Sigma)\, \mathrm{d}R^*\, \mathrm{d}d^*\, \mathrm{d}\tilde{x}_1 \tag{7.30}$$

$$= 1 - \Phi\left[\frac{\gamma' \zeta_n}{\sigma}\right] \tag{7.31}$$

Finally, the individual is in work and able to choose the length of his or her working week if $d_n = 0$ (implying $d_n^* < 0$) and $\tilde{x}_{n1}$ is observed as x_{n1}. Nothing is known about R_n^*, and hence

$$f(x_{n1}, d_n=0 \mid \zeta_n, \xi_{n1}, \xi_{n2}) = \int_{-\infty}^{0}\int_{-\infty}^{\infty} \varphi(x_{n1}, d^*, R^*; \mu_n, \Sigma)\, \mathrm{d}R^*\, \mathrm{d}d^* \tag{7.32}$$

$$= \sigma^{-1} \varphi \left[\frac{x_{n1} - \gamma' \zeta_n}{\sigma}\right] \left\{1 - \Phi\left[\frac{\delta_1' \xi_{n1} + \rho_{xd}(x_{n1} - \gamma' \zeta_n)/\sigma}{(1 - \rho_{xd}^2)^{1/2}}\right]\right\}. \tag{7.33}$$

In expressions (7.27)–(7.33), $\varphi(.; \mu, \Sigma)$ denotes the p.d.f. of the multivariate $N(\mu, \Sigma)$ distribution, and ρ_{rd} and ρ_{xd} are the correlation coefficients σ_{rd}/σ_r and σ_{xd}/σ. The final expression (7.33) is arrived at by decomposing the relevant bivariate marginal density into univariate conditional and marginal components (see appendix 3, section A3.5).

The log-likelihood function arising from this type of model has the following general form:

$$\begin{aligned} \log L(\gamma, \delta_1, \delta_2, \Sigma) &= \sum_{\substack{d_n = 1 \\ x_{n1} = 0}} \log \Pr(x_{n1} = 0, d_n = 1 \mid \zeta_n, \xi_{n1}, \xi_{n2}) \\ &+ \sum_{\substack{d_n = 0 \\ x_{n1} = 0}} \log \Pr(x_{n1} = 0, d_n = 0 \mid \zeta_n, \xi_{n1}, \xi_{n2}) \\ &+ \sum_{\substack{d_n = 1 \\ x_{n1} > 0}} \log f(x_{n1}, d_n = 1 \mid \zeta_n, \xi_{n1}, \xi_{n2}) \\ &+ \sum_{\substack{d_n = 0 \\ x_{n1} > 0}} \log f(x_{n1}, d_n = 0 \mid \zeta_n, \xi_{n1}, \xi_{n2}). \end{aligned} \tag{7.34}$$

In the form (7.27)–(7.33), this model is rather unusual and quite difficult to handle, since every rationed zero observation will give rise to the trivariate normal probability (7.28). As a result, computational difficulties are severe, and this is one reason why this type of model has seen little use in applied work. The structure becomes rather more tractable if we assume that when $d_n^* > 0$ and $R_n^* < 0$, the observation is always recorded as a case of rationing, even if desired labour supply $\tilde{x}_{n1}$ is zero. In that case, equation (7.27) is replaced by the less natural equality

$$\Pr(x_{n1} = 0, d_n = 1 \mid \zeta_n, \xi_{n1}, \xi_{n2}) = \Pr(d_n^* > 0, R_n^* < 0 \mid \zeta_n, \xi_{n1}, \xi_{n2}), \tag{7.35}$$

which gives a more convenient bivariate probability. Expressions (7.29)–(7.31) also require modification in this case. Note, however, that σ_{xr} no longer appears in the log-likelihood function for this variant, and is not identifiable, even in principle.

Statistical structures of this latter type are now common in econometrics: apart from the censoring at zero that we have imposed on $\tilde{x}_{n1}$ and R_n, our illustrative model is identical with one commonly known as the endogenous switching model (see Maddala and Nelson, 1975; and Maddala, 1983, chapters 8, 9 and 10), since we can view it as the operation of an endogenous switching rule (7.13) allocating observations randomly to the two regression models for $\tilde{x}_{n1}$ and R_n. Amemiya (1984, 1986, chapter 10) refers to this structure as a type 5 Tobit model. Applications include Lee's (1978) study of trade union membership and many studies of markets in disequilibrium (see Maddala, 1983, chapter 10, for a survey). The latter application may be seen as a problem in rationing, but there does not appear to have been any use of this type of model in the analysis of quantity constraints using individual data. A particularly important potential field of application is in labour supply, where the availability of direct evidence on hours constraints would be extremely valuable.

7.1.3 Demand for the constrained good: unobserved rationing

We now turn to the case where it is unknown whether or not any particular individual in the sample is constrained: in other words, the sample separation, indicated by d_n, is not observed. We can still only draw inferences about γ and σ^2 from unconstrained behaviour, but now it is not possible to select the unconstrained observations with certainty. Thus, truncated sample methods are no longer available, and we are forced to model d_n; consequently, there is little to be gained by maintaining the distinction between endogenous and exogenous rationing, and we shall assume it to be endogenous.

Thus our model is again

$$\tilde{x}^*_{n1}, d^*_n, R_n \mid \zeta_n, \xi_{n1}, \xi_{n2} \sim N(\mu_n, \Sigma) \tag{7.36}$$

where μ_n and Σ are given by (7.25) and (7.26).

We observe only x_{n1}, which is generated from (7.36) by the usual mechanism:

$$\tilde{x}_{n1} = \max(\tilde{x}^*_{n1}, 0) \tag{7.37}$$

and

$$\begin{aligned} x_{n1} &= \tilde{x}_{n1} \qquad \text{if } \tilde{x}_{n1} = 0 \text{ or } d^*_n \leqslant 0 \text{ and } \tilde{x}_{n1} > 0 \\ x_{n1} &= R_n \qquad \text{if } d^*_n > 0 \text{ and } \tilde{x}_{n1} > 0. \end{aligned} \tag{7.38}$$

The conditional distribution of x_{n1} has a discrete and a continuous component, each of which is the sum of two terms arising from the two observational regimes in (7.38). These are merely the two relevant parts of the distribution (7.27)–(7.33) which we derived for the case of full observation. Thus the log-likelihood for samples in which the separation of rationed and unrationed observations is impossible has the form

$$\log L(\gamma, \delta_1, \delta_2, \Sigma) = \sum_{x_{n1}=0} \log[\Pr(x_{n1}=0, d_n=0 \mid \zeta_n, \xi_{n1}, \xi_{n2}) + \Pr(x_{n1}=0, d_n=1 \mid \zeta_n, \xi_{n1}, \xi_{n2})] + \sum_{x_{n1}>0} \log[f(x_{n1}, d_n=0 \mid \zeta_n, \xi_{n1}, \xi_{n2}) + f(x_{n1}, d_n=1 \mid \zeta_n, \xi_{n1}, \xi_{n2})] \quad (7.39)$$

where the components of this expression come from (7.26)–(7.29).

Most applications of the endogenous switching model have been to problems in which the sample separation d_n is observed. However, it is the exception rather than the rule to have such information available when modelling individual choices. Few survey enquiries include direct questions on such things as hours constraints, loan refusals and unsatisfied demand generally. The great practical problem facing any econometrician attempting to estimate the importance of rationing is that estimation on the basis of log-likelihood (7.39) is much more difficult than estimation on the basis of log-likelihood (7.35).

Most experience has been with the disequilibrium market model, in which x_{n1} is interpreted as market demand, R_n^* as the quantity supplied and d_n^* as the excess demand $\tilde{x}_{n1}^* - R_n^*$, with no censoring imposed on $\tilde{x}_{n1}^*$ and R_n^*. In this special case, x_{n1}, d_n^* and R_n^* have a singular joint distribution and $\delta_1' \xi_{n1}$ is equal to $\gamma' \zeta_n - \delta_2' \xi_{n2}$. Thus it is a simpler structure, with fewer parameters. Nevertheless, the log-likelihood function is badly behaved, being unbounded with respect to σ and σ_r in some regions of the parameter space (see Goldfeld and Quandt, 1975). Despite this unboundedness, Amemiya and Sen (1977) and Kiefer (1978) have shown (in the context of rather simpler models) that there is a local maximum of the log-likelihood function that yields a consistent and asymptotically efficient estimator. Nevertheless, Goldfeld and Quandt (1975) and Kiefer (1979) have demonstrated that the non-observability of d_n imposes a very high cost in terms of estimation precision.

Blundell, Ham and Meghir (1987) manage to compute plausible estimates of a labour supply function under the assumption that rationing only produces complete unemployment (this is the case where $R_n = 0$ with probability one: in other words, $\sigma_r = \sigma_{xr} = \sigma_{rd} = 0$ and $\delta_2 = 0$). Arellano and Meghir (1987) go further, presenting estimates of a more general labour supply model, identical with the one discussed here except for the simplifying assumption that R_n, $\tilde{x}_{n1}^*$ and d_n^* are independent (hence $\sigma_{xr} = \sigma_{rd} = \sigma_{xd} = 0$). Perhaps rather surprisingly, they report no difficulty in computing reasonably precise estimates. Both studies find estimated labour supply responses to be very sensitive to these attempts to incorporate hours constraints.

7.2 Bounds on behaviour

Quantity constraints are not always found in the strict form of point rationing. Frequently there is some constraint imposed on behaviour in the weaker form of a bound. Thus, rationing only comes into effect when there is a potential conflict between behaviour and this bound. There are many examples, usually arising from some kind of institutional rigidity. In the UK, most mortgage lenders set limits on the size of a mortgage as arbitrary multiples of the gross income of the individual and the value of the property. Many employers insist on a minimum length for the working week but allow individual employees some freedom to choose the number of overtime hours they work, thus setting a lower bound on labour supply. Rationing during wartime or during national shortages usually takes the form of an upper bound, set in relation to a few characteristics of the household.

We shall restrict attention to very simple Tobit-type demand models and not discuss the problem of specifying and estimating a general system of demand equations in the presence of this type of rationing; such models have not appeared in the applied literature, largely because of their extreme complexity. The difficulties involved are very similar to those associated with non-negativity restrictions, which were discussed in chapter 4, section 4.3.2.

7.2.1 Demand for the constrained good: fully observed rationing

To avoid the complexities of a proper treatment of the consumer's utility maximization problem in the presence of inequality restrictions, we focus attention on a single rationed good and assume that rationing takes the form of a simple upper bound:

$$x_{n1} \leqslant R_n. \tag{7.40}$$

We retain our previous assumption that the Tobit model is an adequate representation of its unconstrained demand function:

$$\tilde{x}_{n1} \mid \zeta_n \sim \mathrm{LCN}(\gamma' \zeta_n, \sigma^2, 0). \tag{7.41}$$

Now define d_n to be a dummy variable distinguishing between the two possibilities of constrained and unconstrained behaviour:

$$\begin{aligned} d_n &= 1 \qquad \text{if } x_{n1} = R_n \\ d_n &= 0 \qquad \text{if } x_{n1} < R_n. \end{aligned} \tag{7.42}$$

We assume in this section that rationing is observed, in the sense that d_n and x_{n1} are always observed. This is necessarily the case if the value of R_n is known both for constrained and unconstrained individuals, since d_n can be deduced from a comparison of x_{n1} and R_n. On the other hand, if we do not observe the constraints that would have been applied to individuals who do not reach their bounds, then we must assume the existence of some survey question providing direct information on d_n. Such questions are comparatively rare in practice.

Exogenous rationing With rationing in the form of a bound, d_n is always an endogenous variable, since it is defined in terms of an event $x_{n1} = R_n$ that involves the endogenous variable x_{n1}. This distinguishes it from the point rationing model discussed in section 7.1, where there was a quite separate mechanism generating d_n, which could be either endogenous or exogenous. In the present case, we use the term exogenous rationing to refer to any situation where R_n is a directly observed non-negative exogenous variable.

The effect of rationing in this case is very simple: it merely transforms the simple one-limit Tobit model (7.41) into a two-limit Tobit model, with an upper limit R_n that may be variable. The implied conditional distribution for x_{n1} is mixed discrete–continuous with the following three components:

$$\Pr(x_{n1}=0 \mid \zeta_n, R_n) = 1 - \Phi(\gamma'\zeta_n/\sigma) \tag{7.43}$$

$$f(x_{n1} \mid \zeta_n, R_n) = \sigma^{-1}\varphi\left[\frac{x_{n1}-\gamma'\zeta_n}{\sigma}\right] \quad 0<x_{n1}<R_n \tag{7.44}$$

$$\Pr(x_{n1}=R_n \mid \zeta_n, R_n) = 1 - \Phi\left[\frac{R_n-\gamma'\zeta_n}{\sigma}\right]. \tag{7.45}$$

This is a well-known variant of the Tobit model, and has been discussed by Rosett and Nelson (1975) and applied in a number of cases: for instance to the demand for health insurance, where there is both a maximum and minimum coverage.

This doubly censored regression model shares most of the convenient properties of the standard Tobit model. Its log-likelihood function is

$$\begin{aligned} \log L(\gamma, \sigma) &= K + \sum_{x_{n1}=0} \log\left[1 - \Phi\left(\frac{\gamma'\zeta_n}{\sigma}\right)\right] - N^{+}\log\sigma \\ &\quad - \frac{1}{2\sigma^2}\sum_{x_{n1}\in(0,R_n)} (x_{n1}-\gamma'\zeta_n)^2 \\ &\quad + \sum_{x_{n1}=R_n} \log\left[1 - \Phi\left[\frac{R_n-\gamma'\zeta_n}{\sigma}\right]\right] \end{aligned} \tag{7.46}$$

where N^{+} is the number of observations for which $x_{n1} \in (0, R_n)$ and K is an inessential constant. This log-likelihood is globally concave in terms of the reparameterization $\theta = (\gamma/\sigma, 1/\sigma)$ and its maximization presents no special computational problems.

Endogenous rationing Whenever the maximum permitted level of x_1 is variable across individuals, there is a possibility that its variation is related in some way to variation in desired consumption $\tilde{x}_1$. For example, the fact that someone asks for a large mortgage might signal to a potential lender that the individual is rash, and consequently a more risky prospect than the typical borrower. As a result, R_n may have some correlation with $\tilde{x}_{n1}$.

A natural approach to this problem is to specify a bivariate normal distribution for the two underlying latent variables $\tilde{x}^*_{n1}$ and R^*_n:

$$\tilde{x}^*_{n1}, R^*_n \mid \zeta_n, \xi_n \sim N(\mu_n, \Sigma) \tag{7.47}$$

where μ_n and Σ are now

$$\mu'_n = (\gamma'\zeta_n \quad \delta'\xi_n) \tag{7.48}$$

$$\Sigma = \begin{bmatrix} \sigma^2 & \sigma_{xr} \\ \sigma_{xr} & \sigma_r^2 \end{bmatrix} \tag{7.49}$$

and where ξ_n contains the exogenous variables that determine the size of the ration: in the mortgage example, for instance, ξ_n would include the individual's age, income, marital status etc.

The observational scheme is as follows:

$$\begin{aligned} x_{n1} &= \min(\tilde{x}_{n1}, R_n) \\ &= \min[\max(\tilde{x}^*_{n1}, 0), \max(R^*_n, 0)]. \end{aligned} \tag{7.50}$$

Thus x_{n1} is censored from below at zero to impose non-negativity, and is also censored from above at the stochastic threshold $R_n = \max(R^*_n, 0)$, which has a conditional $\mathrm{LCN}(\delta'\xi_n, \sigma_r^2, 0)$ distribution. This structure reflects the fact that there are two ways in which we can observe a zero value for x_{n1}: the individual may not seek a mortgage ($\tilde{x}_{n1} = 0$) or may apply for one and be refused ($\tilde{x}_{n1} > 0$ and $R_n = 0$).

If both x_{n1} and the rationing indicator d_n, are observed, we have a four-part conditional distribution for each sample observation. Whenever $\tilde{x}^*_{n1}$ is non-positive (implying $\tilde{x}_{n1} = 0$), no mortgage application is made, and so d_n will never indicate that rationing has been encountered. Thus

$$\begin{aligned} \Pr(x_{n1}=0, d_n=0 \mid \zeta_n, \xi_n) &= \Pr(\tilde{x}^*_{n1} \leqslant 0 \mid \xi_n) \\ &= 1 - \Phi(\gamma'\zeta_n/\sigma) \end{aligned} \tag{7.51}$$

If a mortgage application is made ($\tilde{x}^*_{n1} > 0$), the individual will fail to receive any mortgage offer if R_n is zero, which is the event $R^*_n \leqslant 0$. Thus

$$\begin{aligned} \Pr(x_{n1}=0, d_n=1 \mid \zeta_n, \xi_n) &= \Pr(\tilde{x}^*_{n1}>0, R^*_n \leqslant 0 \mid \zeta_n, \xi_n) \\ &= \int_0^\infty \int_{-\infty}^0 \varphi(\tilde{x}^*_1, R^*; \mu_n, \Sigma)\, \mathrm{d}R^*\, \mathrm{d}\tilde{x}^*_1. \end{aligned} \tag{7.52}$$

If both $\tilde{x}^*_{n1}$ and R^*_n are positive (and hence equal to $\tilde{x}_{n1}$ and R_n), a mortgage application is made and a positive limit is set on its size. If this limit is larger than the amount requested ($R_n^* \geqslant \tilde{x}_{n1}^*$), then d_n will indicate an absence of rationing. Thus, all we know about R_n^* is that it exceeds x_{n1}, and hence

$$f(x_{n1}, d_n = 0 \mid \zeta_n, \xi_n) = \int_{x_{n1}}^{\infty} \varphi(x_{n1}, R^*; \mu_n, \Sigma)\, \mathrm{d}R^*$$
$$= \sigma^{-1} \varphi\left[\frac{x_{n1} - \gamma'\zeta_n}{\sigma}\right]$$
$$\left\{1 - \Phi\left[\frac{x_{n1} - \delta'\xi_n - \rho_{xr}(x_{n1} - \gamma'\zeta_n)/\sigma}{(1 - \rho_{xr}^2)^{½}}\right]\right\}. \tag{7.53}$$

If, on the other hand, a mortgage application is made and is frustrated by the lending limit, then we observe x_{n1} as $R_n(=R_n^*)$, and all we know about the size of the mortgage request $\tilde{x}_{n1}(=\tilde{x}_{n1}^*)$ is that it exceeds x_{n1}. Hence

$$f(x_{n1}, d_n = 1 \mid \zeta_n, \xi_n) = \int_{x_{n1}}^{\infty} \varphi(\tilde{x}_1, x_{n1}; \mu_n, \Sigma)\, \mathrm{d}\tilde{x}_1$$
$$= \sigma_r^{-1} \varphi\left[\frac{x_{n1} - \zeta'\xi_n}{\sigma_r}\right]$$
$$\left\{1 - \Phi\left[\frac{x_{n1} - \gamma'\zeta_n - \rho_{xr}(x_{n1} - \delta'\xi_n)/\sigma}{(1 - \rho_{xr}^2)^{½}}\right]\right\}. \tag{7.54}$$

In these expressions $\varphi(.; \mu, \Sigma)$ is the p.d.f. of the bivariate $N(\mu, \Sigma)$ distribution and $\rho_{xr} = \sigma_{xr}/\sigma\sigma_r$. In (7.53) and (7.54) we have again used the decomposition of the bivarite normal density into univariate marginal and conditional components.

Assuming that we can observe the division of the sample into constrained and unconstrained individuals, the appropriate log-likelihood is

$$\log L(\gamma, \delta, \Sigma) = \sum_{\substack{d_n = 0 \\ x_{n1} = 0}} \log \Pr(x_{n1} = 0, d_n = 0 \mid \zeta_n, \xi_n)$$
$$+ \sum_{\substack{d_n = 1 \\ x_{n1} = 0}} \log \Pr(x_{n1} = 0, d_n = 1 \mid \zeta_n, \xi_n)$$
$$+ \sum_{\substack{d_n = 0 \\ x_{n1} > 0}} \log f(x_{n1}, d_n = 0 \mid \zeta_n, \xi_n)$$
$$+ \sum_{\substack{d_n = 1 \\ x_{n1} > 0}} \log f(x_{n1}, d_n = 1 \mid \zeta_n, \xi_n). \tag{7.55}$$

Note that we are assuming here that R_n is unobserved when the quantity constraint is not binding. This is the most usual case, since it is extremely unlikely that a mortgage lender, for instance, will be prepared to supply us with information on the maximum loan that would be offered to any particular individual. We are also assuming that we cannot directly observe the size of the mortgage request $\tilde{x}_{n1}$ when it differs from the mortgage actually granted. This is a stronger assumption, since it is perfectly feasible to include a question on this in the survey that provides our data. If $\tilde{x}_{n1}$ were directly observed, then expression (7.54) would be replaced by the bivariate normal density evaluated at $(\tilde{x}_{n1}, x_{n1})$. The additional sample information would improve the asymptotic efficiency of the ML estimates.

7.2.2 Demand for the constrained good: unobserved rationing

Suppose now that rationing is unobserved. For any individual, it is unknown whether or not the quantity constraint is binding, and all we observe is x_{n1}. We shall retain our previous assumption that demand $\tilde{x}_{n1}$ and the quantity constraint R_n are generated by a pair of correlated censored regressions, with the actual quantity x_{n1} being observed as the smaller of these two.

In the previous section, we derived for this model the joint distribution (7.51)–(7.54) of x_{n1} and a dummy variable d_n representing the division of the sample into constrained and unconstrained observations. When rationing is unobserved, d_n is not part of the available sample, and so we require the marginal distribution for x_{n1} implied by (7.51)–(7.54). This only requires the summation of components over the two events $d_n = 0$ and $d_n = 1$, yielding the following:

$$\Pr(x_{n1}=0 \mid \zeta_n, \xi_n) = 1 - \Phi(\gamma'\zeta_n/\sigma) + \int_0^{\infty}\int_{-\infty}^{0} \varphi(\tilde{x}_n^*, R^*; \mu_n, \Sigma)\, dR^*\, d\tilde{x}_1^* \tag{7.56}$$

$$\begin{aligned} f(x_{n1} \mid \zeta_n, \xi_n) = {} & \sigma^{-1}\varphi\left[\frac{x_{n1} - \gamma'\zeta_n}{\sigma}\right] \\ & \left\{1 - \Phi\left[\frac{x_{n1} - \delta'\xi_n - \rho_{xr}(x_{n1} - \gamma'\zeta_n)/\sigma}{(1-\rho_{xr}^2)^{1/2}}\right]\right\} \\ & + \sigma_r^{-1}\varphi\left[\frac{x_{n1} - \delta'\xi_n}{\sigma_r}\right] \\ & \left\{1 - \Phi\left[\frac{x_{n1} - \gamma'\zeta_n - \rho_{xr}(x_{n1} - \delta'\xi_n)/\sigma}{(1-\rho_{xr}^2)^{1/2}}\right]\right\}. \end{aligned} \tag{7.57}$$

The log-likelihood function is then

$$\log L(\gamma, \delta, \Sigma) = \sum_{x_{n1}=0} \log \Pr(x_{n1}=0 \mid \zeta_n, \xi_n) + \sum_{x_{n1}>0} \log f(x_{n1} \mid \zeta_n, \xi_n). \tag{7.58}$$

This model is essentially identical (apart from the censoring at zero) to the simple disequilibrium market model first discussed by Fair and Jaffee (1972) (see Maddala, 1983, chapter 10, for an exposition), since the Tobit model for R_n can be regarded as an individual-specific labour demand function. The log-likelihood (7.58) is unbounded with respect to σ and σ_r in some regions of the parameter space, and so the computational problems are likely to be more severe in the present case of unobserved rationing than for the fully observed case of the previous section. Perhaps for this reason, the model has so far seen little application at the individual level, although applied studies at the market level based on time-series data are numerous; see Sealey (1979), Rosen and Quandt (1978) and Portes and Winter (1980).

7.2.3 Rationing as a lower bound

One of the few attempts to estimate a cross-section model involving rationing in the form of a bound is the study of labour supply by Moffitt (1982). Moffitt represents hours restrictions by a stochastic *lower* bound, representing the idea of a mimimum length for the working week and free choice of overtime hours. The bound is unobservable and is assumed to be generated by an independent uncensored normal regression structure; labour supply is also uncensored, and in this respect Moffitt's model is more restrictive than the one outlined above.

However, Moffitt introduces an important innovation designed to overcome one of the limitations of this model when applied to a problem involving a lower bound. We have made the assumption that, whenever the stochastic limit is binding, the individual is automatically committed to operating at that limit. This is perfectly reasonable when rationing imposes an upper limit on x_1, but is clearly unreasonable for the case of a lower limit. Suppose, for example, that desired hours of work $\tilde{x}_{n1}$ were very small but the hours limit R_n were large; in such a case, one would expect the individual to drop out of the labour market completely ($x_{n1} = 0$) rather than working an unacceptably long week ($x_{n1} = R_n$), as the model of the previous two sections assumes. Thus the model fails to cope adequately with the fact that individuals always have the option of choosing not to work.

What is required here is a mechanism to produce a zero observation if desired hours are too far below the job offer produced by the demand side of the labour market. The ideal way of specifying such a mechanism is to base it on an explicit utility comparison: the individual compares the utility attainable at the zero hours option with the utility attainable at the limit imposed by the labour market, and is then observed in the better of the two states. Unfortunately, such a model presents considerable technical difficulties (as we shall see in section 7.3.2 when discussing the model of Dickens and Lundberg, 1985, which is an elaboration of this idea). Instead, Moffitt uses an *ad hoc* mechanism of very simple form: if desired hours is within a constant distance D of the market constraint, then the individual chooses to accept the constraint; on the other hand, if desired hours are outside this neighbourhood, the individual chooses to supply no labour.

We shall generalize Moffitt's model somewhat by retaining the structure (7.47)–(7.49) discussed in the preceding two sections. However, we replace the observational mechanism (7.50) by the following:

$$\text{if } \tilde{x}^*_{n1} \leqslant 0 \quad \text{then } x_{n1} = 0 \tag{7.59}$$

$$\text{if } 0 < \tilde{x}^*_{n1} < R^*_n - D \quad \text{then } x_{n1} = 0 \tag{7.60}$$

$$\text{if } \tilde{x}^*_{n1} > 0 \text{ and } \tilde{x}^*_{n1} > R^*_n \quad \text{then } x_{n1} = \tilde{x}^*_{n1} \tag{7.61}$$

$$\text{if } \tilde{x}^*_{n1} > 0 \text{ and } R^*_n - D \leqslant \tilde{x}^*_{n1} \leqslant R^*_n \quad \text{then } x_{n1} = R^*_n \tag{7.62}$$

The form of the model, then, is this: a latent desired hours variable $\tilde{x}^*_{n1}$ and a latent hours constraint R^*_n are generated from a bivariate regression structure. The rationing–censoring mechanism (7.59)–(7.62) then partitions $(\tilde{x}^*_{n1}, R^*_n)$ space into the regions shown in figure 7.2, each corresponding to a different type of outcome.

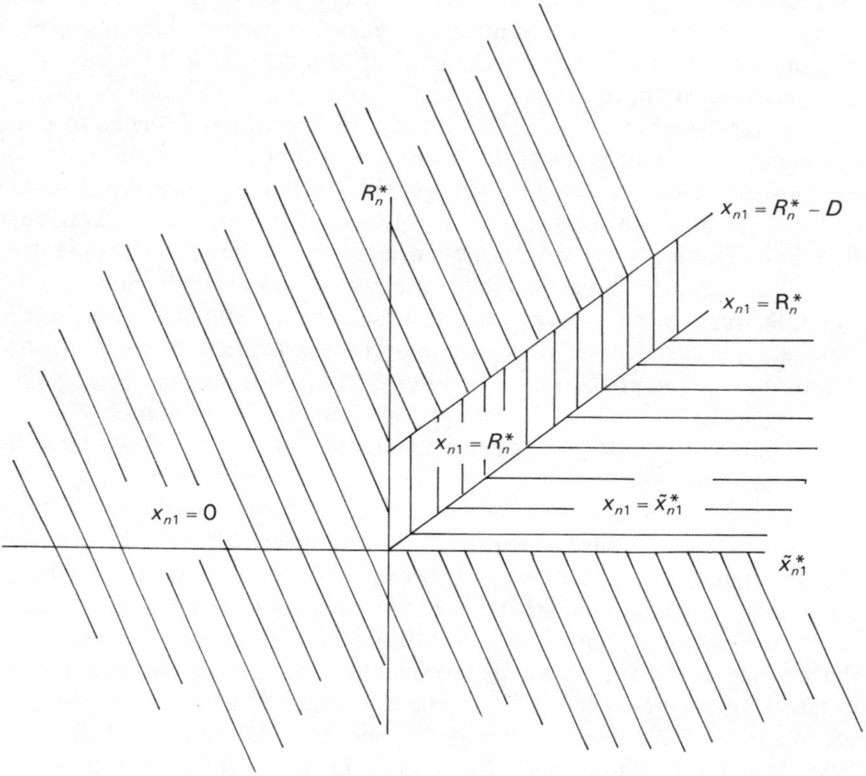

Figure 7.2 The censoring and rationing mechanisms in a Moffitt-type model.

We assume that only x_{n1} is observed, and that we have no direct information on the operation of hours constraints. The mechanism (7.59)–(7.62) implies a mixed discrete–continuous distribution for x_{n1}. A zero observation can occur either because the individual is in regime (7.59) and does not want to work or because he or she is in regime (7.60) and wants to work substantially fewer hours than the labour market offers. Therefore

$$\Pr(x_{n1}=0 \mid \zeta_n, \xi_n) = \Pr(\tilde{x}^*_{n1} \leqslant 0 \mid \zeta_n) + \Pr(\tilde{x}^*_{n1} > 0, \tilde{x}^*_{n1} + D - R^*_n < 0 \mid \zeta_n, \xi_n)$$

$$= 1 - \Phi\left(\frac{\gamma' \zeta_n}{\sigma}\right) + \int_0^{\infty} \int_{-\infty}^{0} \varphi(\tilde{x}^*_1, \eta; \mu^*_n, \Sigma^*)\, \mathrm{d}\eta\, \mathrm{d}\tilde{x}^*_1 \qquad (7.63)$$

where $\varphi(.; \mu^*_n, \Sigma^*)$ is the p.d.f. of the bivariate $N(\mu^*_n, \Sigma^*)$ distribution and μ^*_n and Σ^* are the conditional mean vector and covariance matrix of $\tilde{x}^*_{n1}$ and $\eta_n = \tilde{x}^*_{n1} + D - R^*_n$:

$$\mu^{*\prime}_n = (\gamma' \zeta_n \quad D + \gamma' \zeta_n - \delta' \xi_n) \qquad (7.64)$$

$$\Sigma^* = \begin{bmatrix} \sigma^2 & \sigma^2 - \sigma_{xr} \\ \sigma^2 - \sigma_{xr} & \sigma^2 + \sigma_r^2 - 2\sigma_{xr} \end{bmatrix}. \qquad (7.65)$$

The continuous component of the conditional distribution of x_{n1} is the sum of two parts. The first arises from regime (7.61), where x_{n1} is equal to desired hours $\tilde{x}^*_{n1}$ and all we know about the lower bound R^*_n is that it is less than x_{n1}. The second part corresponds to regime (7.62), where x_{n1} is constrained by the bound and we know only that desired hours exceeds this level. Thus

$$f(x_{n1} \mid \zeta_n, \xi_n) = \int_{-\infty}^{x_{n1}} \varphi(x_{n1}, R^*; \mu_n, \Sigma)\, \mathrm{d}R^* + \int_0^{D} \varphi(\eta, x_{n1}; \mu^*_n, \Sigma^*)\, \mathrm{d}\eta. \qquad (7.66)$$

The log-likelihood function to be maximized with respect to γ, δ, σ, σ_r, σ_{xr} and the threshold parameter D is of the familiar form (7.58), with the likelihood elements given by these two expressions.

Working with a special case of the model presented here, Moffitt finds that hours restrictions are extremely important, with average desired labour supply being 21 hours per week, compared with an average minimum working week of 39 hours; however, D is estimated at 37 hours, implying that almost everyone opts for the offered minimum rather than for nonparticipation. These findings are in sharp contrast with those of Dickens and Lundberg (1985), discussed in section 7.3.2, who use a less restrictive model of hours constraints and find that most individuals are restricted to work considerably *less* than their desired number of hours. This casts some doubt on Moffitt's model, but there has so far been no systematic attempt to determine whether or not actual hours restrictions can be adequately approximated by a simple lower bound of this form. Moreover, it is unlikely that this could be done convincingly without direct observation of the rationing process.

7.3 Discrete opportunities

The possibility of rationing is not confined to the continuous choice problems examined above. People are often faced with a choice among discrete alternatives, only to find the chosen option barred by some extraneous process. A similar type of problem arises when continuous choice is possible in principle but the individual's decision is frustrated by a rationing mechanism that excludes all but a limited number of discrete possibilities. Models of these types are the subject of this section.

7.3.1 Barriers to discrete choice

Because it is so implausible to assume that workers are able to vary the length of their working week freely, some econometricians have treated labour supply behaviour as choice among three discrete alternatives: non-participation, part-time working and full-time working (see Zabalza, Pissarides and Barton, 1980, for example). Although this approach meets some of the criticisms levelled against continuous labour supply models, it still makes the unreasonable assumption that everyone has these three options open to them. In practice, one might look for a part-time job and be unable to find one, or one might be unable to find a job of any description. In other words, one or more of the alternatives in the opportunity set may turn out to be unavailable.

Another case that has appeared in the applied literature is that of tenure choice in housing, where government rent controls and institutional restrictions on the mortgage market have led to considerable unsatisfied demand for both private rented and owner-occupied housing. Most work on the determinants of tenure choice at the individual level ignores the severe problems raised by this rationing. However, an exception is the study by King (1980), described in chapter 3, section 3.7. We shall base our discussion (rather loosely) on King's model.

There are three alternatives available. These are owner occupation, public rental and private rental, referred to as alternatives A^1, A^2 and A^3 respectively. Since rationing has the effect of preventing entry to the preferred alternative and forcing the adoption of the second or third best alternative, we need to specify not just the probabilities of the three possible optimal choices, as we did in chapter 3, but the probabilities associated with every possible ordering of the alternatives. Using $\succcurlyeq$ to represent the 'preferred to' relation, our notation for these six choice probabilities is the following:

$$P_n(ijk) = \Pr(A^i \succcurlyeq A^j \succcurlyeq A^k \mid \zeta_n; \theta) \tag{7.67}$$

where ijk represents any permutation of 1, 2 and 3, and ζ_n is the vector containing all measured variables relevant to the choice. In this example, ζ_n will represent household characteristics and resources and the relative prices and other attributes of the three housing types. The vector $\boldsymbol{\theta}$ contains all the unknown parameters involved in the specification of household preferences and the distribution of any random elements involved in the choice problem.

Any parametric model could be used to generate these probabilities. As an example, consider the trinomial probit specification, where alternative A^j is associated with a utility level

$$u_n^j = V(\mathbf{x}_n^j, \mathbf{z}_n; \alpha) + \epsilon_n^j \tag{7.68}$$

where $V_n^j = V(\mathbf{x}_n^j, \mathbf{z}_n; \alpha)$ is the non-stochastic component of the household's utility function. The elements of $\mathbf{x}_n^j$ are the measured attributes of alternatives j, $\mathbf{z}_n$ is the vector of characteristics of household n and α is a vector of fixed preference parameters. The random terms ϵ_n^1, ϵ_n^2 and ϵ_n^3 have a trivariate $N(0, \Sigma)$ distribution conditional on $\zeta_n = (\mathbf{z}_n, \mathbf{x}_n^1, \mathbf{x}_n^2, \mathbf{x}_n^3)$, where Σ is subject to suitable normalizing restrictions. The full parameter vector $\boldsymbol{\theta}$ contains α and the free elements of Σ. The choice probabilities implied by this structure are of the general form

$$\begin{aligned} P_n(ijk) &= \Pr(u_n^i > u_n^j > u_n^k \mid \zeta_n; \boldsymbol{\theta}) \\ &= \Pr(u_n^j - u_n^i < 0, u_n^k - u_n^j < 0 \mid \zeta_n; \boldsymbol{\theta}) \\ &= \int_{-\infty}^{0} \int_{-\infty}^{0} \varphi(\eta_1, \eta_2; \mu_n^{ijk}, \Sigma^{ijk})\, \mathrm{d}\eta_2\, \mathrm{d}\eta_1 \end{aligned} \tag{7.69}$$

where $\varphi(.; \mu_n^{ijk}, \Sigma^{ijk})$ is the p.d.f. of the bivariate $N(\mu_n^{ijk}, \Sigma^{ijk})$ distribution, and μ_n^{ijk} and Σ^{ijk} are the mean vector and covariance matrix of the utility differences $\eta_1 = u_n^j - u_n^i$ and $\eta_2 = u_n^k - u_n^j$:

$$\mu_n^{ijk\prime} = (V_n^j - V_n^i \quad V_n^k - V_n^j) \tag{7.70}$$

$$\Sigma^{ijk} = \begin{bmatrix} \sigma_{ii} + \sigma_{jj} - 2\sigma_{ij} & \sigma_{ij} + \sigma_{jk} - \sigma_{ik} - \sigma_{jj} \\ \sigma_{ij} + \sigma_{jk} - \sigma_{ik} - \sigma_{jj} & \sigma_{jj} + \sigma_{kk} - 2\sigma_{jk} \end{bmatrix}. \tag{7.71}$$

King (1980) departs from this structure by assuming that A^3 is never preferred to A^1 or A^2, and thus that $P_n(312)$, $P_n(321)$, $P_n(132)$ and $P_n(231)$ are identically zero. A simple probit model is used to generate the remaining probabilities $P_n(123)$ and $P_n(213)$.

For simplicity, we shall assume through that rationing is exogenous in the sense that the random elements involved in the individual's decision-making are independent of those involved in the rationing mechanism. This makes it possible to construct the probabilities of observed outcomes by combining the choice probabilities (7.67) with corresponding rationing probabilities in a very simple way.

Our notation for each of these rationing probabilities is as follows:

$$\Pi_n(ij\ldots) = \Pr(A^i, A^j, \ldots \text{ are open to individual } n \mid \xi_n; \delta) \tag{7.72}$$

where ξ_n is a vector of observed exogenous variables that are involved in the rationing process and δ is a vector of unknown parameters. We shall follow King in assuming that the private rental market is able to absorb unsatisfied demand where necessary, so that entry into tenure 3 is always possible. This means that the list $\{i, j, \ldots\}$ is never empty and always includes alternative 3. Thus four probabilities must be specified: $\Pi_n(123)$, $\Pi_n(13)$, $\Pi_n(23)$ and $\Pi_n(3)$.

King (1980) adopts a very simple model. He defines two constants Q_1 and Q_2, interpreted as the fixed probabilities that an applicant will be successful in seeking admission to tenures 1 and 2 respectively. If we make the further strong assumption that these two events are statistically independent, the required probabilities are

$$\Pi_n(123) = Q_1 Q_2 \tag{7.73}$$

$$\Pi_n(13) = Q_1(1 - Q_2) \tag{7.74}$$

$$\Pi_n(23) = (1 - Q_1)Q_2 \tag{7.75}$$

$$\Pi_n(3) = (1 - Q_1)(1 - Q_2). \tag{7.76}$$

The assumption that every individual faces the same probability of admission is clearly invalid: mortgages are much more easily obtained by the wealthy and the young, and public housing priorities are much higher for those in obvious need. The independence assumption is also rather hard to defend.

It is not difficult to generalize King's model by specifying a pair of correlated probit-type equations governing entry into tenures 1 and 2:

$$v_{n1} = \delta_1'\xi_n + \nu_{n1} \tag{7.77}$$

$$v_{n2} = \delta_2'\xi_n + \nu_{n2} \tag{7.78}$$

where ν_{n1} and ν_{n2} have a bivariate normal distribution with zero means, unit variances and correlation coefficient ρ. Entry into tenure 1 is possible if v_{n1} is positive, and entry into tenure 2 is possible if v_{n2} is positive. Thus

$$\Pi_n(123) = \Pr(v_{n1}>0, v_{n2}>0 \mid \xi_n; \delta_1, \delta_2, \rho) \tag{7.79}$$

$$\Pi_n(13) = \Pr(v_{n1}>0, v_{n2}\leqslant 0 \mid \xi_n; \delta_1, \delta_2, \rho) \tag{7.80}$$

$$\Pi_n(23) = \Pr(v_{n1}\leqslant 0, v_{n2}>0 \mid \xi_n; \delta_1, \delta_2, \rho) \tag{7.81}$$

$$\Pi_n(3) = \Pr(v_{n1}\leqslant 0, v_{n2}\leqslant 0 \mid \xi_n, \delta_1, \delta_2, \rho). \tag{7.82}$$

These probabilities are computed by integrating the bivariate normal density of v_{n1}, v_{n2} over the relevant region. For example

$$\Pi_n(3) = \int_{-\infty}^{0} \int_{-\infty}^{0} \varphi(v_1, v_2; \boldsymbol{\mu}_n, \boldsymbol{\Sigma})\, \mathrm{d}v_2\, \mathrm{d}v_1 \tag{7.83}$$

where $\boldsymbol{\mu}_n$ and $\boldsymbol{\Sigma}$ are now defined as

$$\mu_n' = (\delta_1'\xi_n \quad \delta_2'\xi_n) \tag{7.84}$$

$$\Sigma = \begin{bmatrix} 1 & \rho \\ \rho & 1 \end{bmatrix} \tag{7.85}$$

The computation of these bivariate probit probabilities can be done without any special difficulty (see appendix A3, section A3.4).

Other approaches are possible. For example, Ilmakunnas and Pudney (1987), in the context of a discrete choice labour supply model, obtained a better fit with a simple multiple logit model, yielding probabilities of the form

$$\Pi_n(123) = \frac{\exp(\delta_1'\xi_n)}{1 + \exp(\delta_1'\xi_n) + \exp(\delta_2'\xi_n) + \exp(\delta_3'\xi_n)} \tag{7.86}$$

with similar expressions for $\Pi_n(13)$, $\Pi_n(23)$ and $\Pi_n(3)$, where δ_1, δ_2 and δ_3 are parameter vectors specifically associated with the combinations 123, 13 and 23 respectively.

The nature of the log-likelihood function resulting from a rationed discrete choice model depends on the information that is available in the sample. If we only observe the actual outcome and have no information on the constraints that each individual has faced, then we have the following form:

$$\log L(\theta, \delta) = \sum_{n \in S_1} \log P_{n1} + \sum_{n \in S_2} \log P_{n2} + \sum_{n \in S_3} \log P_{n3} \tag{7.87}$$

where P_{ni} is the probability of observing individual n in tenure type i and S_i is the index set of such observations. Our assumed structure implies that the P_{ni} have the following forms:

$$P_{n1} = [P_n(123) + P_n(132)]\,[\Pi_n(123) + \Pi_n(13)] + P_n(213)\,\Pi_n(13) \tag{7.88}$$

$$P_{n2} = [P_n(213) + P_n(231)]\,[\Pi_n(123) + \Pi_n(23)] + P_n(123)\,\Pi_n(23) \tag{7.89}$$

$$P_{n3} = 1 - P_{n1} - P_{n2}. \tag{7.90}$$

However, it is often difficult to achieve good estimates of both the choice and the rationing mechanisms from data on actual outcomes alone, and the econometric problems associated with this type of model are considerably eased if it is possible to use information on desired choices as well as actual outcomes. Consider a hypothetical extension of King's model. Suppose that people in the private rental sector are asked two supplementary questions: 'Have you applied for and been refused a mortgage ?' and 'Are you on the waiting list for council accommodation ?' In this case there are six, rather than three, states that an individual can be observed to be in. These states have associated probabilities

$$\begin{aligned} P_{n1} &= \Pr(\text{owner-occupier} \mid \zeta_n, \xi_n) \\ &= [P_n(123) + P_n(132)]\,[\Pi_n(123) + \Pi_n(13)] + P_n(213)\,\Pi_n(13) \end{aligned} \tag{7.91}$$

$$P_{n2} = \Pr(\text{public sector rental} \mid \zeta_n, \xi_n)$$

$$= [P_n(213) + P_n(231)]\,[\Pi_n(123) + \Pi_n(23)] + P_n(123)\,\Pi_n(23) \qquad (7.92)$$

$$P_{n3} = \Pr(\text{private rental, refused mortgage} \mid \zeta_n, \xi_n)$$
$$= [P_n(132)\,[\Pi_n(23) + \Pi_n(3)] \qquad (7.93)$$

$$P_{n4} = \Pr(\text{private rental, refused public housing} \mid \zeta_n, \xi_n)$$
$$= [\mathrm{P}_n(231)\,[\Pi_n(13) + \Pi_n(3)] \qquad (7.94)$$

$$P_{n5} = \Pr(\text{private rental, refused mortage and public housing} \mid \zeta_n, \xi_n)$$
$$= [P_n(123) + P_n(213)]\,\Pi_n(3) \qquad (7.95)$$

$$P_{n6} = \Pr(\text{private rental, no refusals} \mid \zeta_n, \xi_n)$$
$$= P_n(312) + P_n(321). \qquad (7.96)$$

The log-likelihood function formed from these probabilities is

$$\log L(\boldsymbol{\theta}, \boldsymbol{\delta}) = \sum_{j=1}^{6} \sum_{n \in S_j} \log P_{nj} \qquad (7.97)$$

where the six observational regimes are as listed above and S_j is the index set of individuals observed to be in the *j*th regime.

Information relating to preferred rather than actual occurrences is comparatively rare, so methods of this type are not widely used. However, Ilmakunnas and Pudney (1987) use rather complicated data on perceived constraints on hours of work in a discrete choice model of labour supply.

7.3.2 Discrete random opportunities

Consider the problem of modelling labour supply. Most people sell their labour through the medium of a job. A job is an arrangement, more or less formal, covering hours, conditions and type of work, and associating this complex with some rate of pay (or perhaps a scale of rates). Many jobs give one or both parties to this agreement some discretion in choosing the precise outcome of the arrangement: within limits, the employer may be free to determine the tasks that are to be performed and the employee may be free to choose overtime hours. However, this scope for variation in hours of work within a job is usually very limited in comparison with the variation in hours of work between different jobs. Thus the main avenue open to an individual in controlling his or her labour supply lies in the choice of a job. However, although desired hours is a continuously variable quantity, a job is a discrete entity. Thus, it is natural to attempt to model labour supply behaviour as the result of free choice from a limited number of available job opportunities.

This approach leads to discrete choice models that are considerably more complicated than those discussed in chapter 3, for we have to construct a simultaneous model of two processes: choice amongst discrete opportunities and the random generation of those opportunities. We shall discuss this approach in the context of a variant of the model used by Dickens and Lundberg (1985); this is so far the only example of this type of model in the applied literature.

Individual n has a number m_n of job opportunities from which to choose. This number of alternatives varies between individuals: some can find no job at all; others have considerable scope for choice. The variable m_n, conditional on a vector $\boldsymbol{\xi}_n$ of relevant exogenous variables (age, work experience, educational attainment etc.), has a discrete probability function $g_m(.\,|\,\xi_n)$ defined on the integers $(0, 1, \ldots, M)$.

The hours of work associated with any set of m job opportunities are denoted $R_1, \ldots, R_m$ and are assumed to be m independent drawings from a population with a discrete probability function $g_r(.\,|\,\xi_n)$, defined on the integers $(1, 2, \ldots, \bar{R})$. Since non-participation is always a possibility, if individual n draws m job offers, he or she will face an opportunity set $\Omega = \{0, R_1, \ldots, R_m\}$.

Assume that the individual has preferences that can be represented by a utility function $V(x_1, x_2; \beta_n)$, where x_1 is labour supply, $x_2 = w_n x_1 + y_n$ is total income, w_n is the wage, y_n is unearned income and β_n is an unobserved preference parameter which we assume, for simplicity, to be scalar and to possess a continuous distribution with p.d.f. $g_\beta(.\,|\,\mathbf{z}_n)$. The vector $\mathbf{z}_n$ contains all observed exogenous variables affecting preferences. Furthermore, we assume that w_n is exogenous and common to all job opportunities facing individual n. This may be a dangerous assumption, since there is considerable evidence of apparently random variation in the wage rates associated with otherwise similar jobs, and also of a tradeoff between the length of the working week and the hourly wage. However, a joint analysis of wages and hours in the presence of rationing raises further difficulties which we do not consider here.

Define $Q_n(x_1, \beta)$ as the probability that a random draw from the offered hours distribution yields an inferior outcome to x_1 for a person with preference parameter β, where $\zeta_n = (w_n, y_n, \mathbf{z}_n)$. Thus

$$\begin{aligned} Q_n(x_1, \beta) &= \Pr(x_1 \succcurlyeq R\,|\,\beta, \zeta_n, \xi_n) \\ &= \sum_{S_n(x_1,\, \beta)} g_r(R\,|\,\xi_n) \end{aligned} \tag{7.98}$$

where $S_n(x_1, \beta)$ is the inferior set $\{R: x_1 \succcurlyeq R\}$, and where $x_1 \succcurlyeq R$ represents the inequality $V(R, w_n R + y_n; \beta) \leqslant V(x_1, w_n x_1 + y_n; \beta)$.

For this model, observed hours x_{n1} has a discrete distribution defined on $\{0, \ldots, \bar{R}\}$. We begin by examining this distribution conditional on ζ_n, ξ_n and β_n. The probability at zero hours is the sum of two parts: a probability that no employment opportunities are found, and a probability that opportunities are available but none is preferred to the option of non-participation. Thus

$$\Pr(x_{n1}=0\,|\,\zeta_n,\xi_n,\beta_n) = \Pr(m_n=0\,|\,\xi_n) + \sum_{m=1}^{M} g_m(m\,|\,\xi_n)\Pr(0>R_1,\ldots,0>R_m\,|\,\zeta_n,\xi_n,\beta_n)$$

$$= g_m(0\,|\,\xi_n) + \sum_{m=1}^{M} g_m(m\,|\,\xi_n)\,[Q_n(0,\beta_n)]^m \qquad (7.99)$$

where $0 > R_j$ represents the inequality $V(0, y_n; \beta_n) > V(R_j, w_nR_j+y_n; \beta_n)$.

Consider now the probability of observing a particular positive value for x_{n1}. Conditional on ζ_n, ξ_n and β_n, this has the form

$$\Pr(x_{n1}\,|\,\zeta_n,\xi_n,\beta_n) = \sum_{m=1}^{M} g_m(m\,|\,\xi_n)\,\{Q_n(x_{n1},\beta_n)^m - [Q_n(x_{n1},\beta_n)-g_r(x_{n1}\,|\,\xi_n)]^m\}. \qquad (7.100)$$

The term Q^m in (7.100) is the conditional probability of the event $\{x_{n1} \geqslant R_1, \ldots, x_{n1} \geqslant R_m\}$, where $R_1, \ldots, R_m$ are independent random drawings from the offered hours distribution, while $(Q - g_r)^m$ is the conditional probability of the event $\{x_{n1} > R_1, \ldots, x_{n1} > R_m\}$ (we assume that β_n is such that $x_{n1} \sim R_j$ can only occur if R_j and x_{n1} are equal). Thus their difference represents the probability that at least one of the m drawings is equal to x_{n1} and that the remainder are suboptimal.

Since β_n is not observable, (7.99) and (7.100) cannot be used as the basis for econometric work. If we remove the conditioning on β_n, these expressions take the more complicated forms

$$\Pr(x_{n1}=0\,|\,\zeta_n,\xi_n) = g_m(0\,|\,\xi_n) + \sum_{m=1}^{M} g_m(m\,|\,\xi_n)\int_{-\infty}^{\infty} Q_n(0,\beta_n)^m\, g_\beta(\beta\,|\,\mathbf{z}_n)\,\mathrm{d}\beta \qquad (7.101)$$

$$\Pr(x_{n1}\,|\,\zeta_n;\xi_n) = \sum_{m=1}^{M} g_m(m\,|\,\xi_n)\int_{-\infty}^{\infty} P_n(x_{n1},\beta,m)\, g_\beta(\beta\,|\,\mathbf{z}_n)\,\mathrm{d}\beta \qquad (7.102)$$

where $P = Q^m - (Q-g_r)^m$.

The two functions Q and P in (7.101) and (7.102) are step functions in the preference parameter β, with jumps at points in β space where any of the elements of the inferior set $S_n(x_1, \beta)$ is on the margin of indifference with x_1. The point at which an offer of R hours passes out of the inferior set is denoted $\beta_n(x_1, R)$ and solves the equation

$$V[x_1, w_nx_1+y_n; \beta_n(x_1,R)] = V[R, w_nR+y_n; \beta_n(x_1,R)]. \qquad (7.103)$$

We assume that preferences are specified in such a way that these jump points can be readily computed, and that they are unique and monotonically increasing in R. These last two assumptions are not critical but do simplify the analysis considerably. If we assume that $\beta_n | \mathbf{z}_n \sim N(\alpha_1' \mathbf{z}_n, \sigma^2)$, expressions (7.101) and (7.102) take the forms

$$\Pr(x_{n1} = 0 | \zeta_n, \xi_n) = g_m(0 | \xi_n) + \sum_{m=1}^{M} g_m(m | \xi_n) \Big\{ \Phi_n(0, 1) + \sum_{R=2}^{\bar{R}} Q_n[0, \beta_n(0, R)]^m [\Phi_n(0, R) - \Phi_n(0, R-1)] + Q_n[0, \beta_n(0, \bar{R})] [1 - \Phi_n(0, \bar{R})] \Big\} \tag{7.104}$$

$$f(x_{n1} | \zeta_n, \xi_n) = \sum_{m-1}^{M} g_m(m | \xi_n) \sum_{R=1}^{\bar{R}} \{P_n[x_{n1}, \beta_n(x_{n1}, R), m] \times [\Phi_n(x_{n1}, R) - \Phi_n(x_{n1}, R-1)] + P_n[x_{n1}, \beta_n(x_{n1}, \bar{R}), m] [1 - \Phi_n(x_{n1}, \bar{R})]\} \tag{7.105}$$

where $\Phi_n(x_{n1}, R) = \Phi\{[\beta_n(x_{n1}, R) - \alpha_1' \mathbf{z}_n]/\sigma\}$. Note that the value $\beta_n(x_{n1}, x_{n1})$ that occurs in the inner summation in (7.105) is left undefined by the equality (7.103). However, the inferior set $S_n(x_1, \beta)$ is invariant over the interval $(\beta_n(x_1, x_1 - 1), \beta_n(x_1, x_1 + 1))$, and so $\beta_n(x_{n1}, x_{n1})$ can be set to an arbitrary value such as $\beta_n(x_{n1}, x_{n1} + 1)$ for this term.

The log-likelihood function for this model is

$$\log L = \sum_{n=1}^{N} \log \Pr(x_{n1} | \zeta_n, \xi_n) \tag{7.106}$$

and this must be maximized numerically with respect to all parameters appearing in the functions $V(.)$, $g_r(.)$, $g_m(.)$ and $g_\beta(.)$.

Dickens and Lundberg (1985) represent preferences by the following utility function:

$$V(x_1, x_2; \beta) = -\exp(\beta_n) x_1^{\alpha_2} + x_2^{\alpha_3}. \tag{7.107}$$

The number m_n of job opportunities is assumed to have a binomial (10, p) distribution, and the distribution $g_r(.)$ of offered hours is specified as an unrestricted step function, uniform within each of nine ranges of weekly hours. This specification implies, perhaps unreasonably, that all individuals face exactly the same population of job opportunities, irrespective of their personal characteristics. The full parameter vector thus contains α_1, α_2, α_3, p and eight of the nine probabilities making up the function $g_r(.)$ (the ninth is fixed by the condition that they sum to unity).

Using this specification, Dickens and Lundberg manage to produce plausible ML estimates from a sample of low-wage males. These estimates imply that the mean number of job offers is approximately 3 and that, on average, individuals work roughly 10 hours per week less than the 47 hours desired. Their most important conclusion is that estimated preferences are dramatically changed when hours constraints are taken account of in this way. In particular, they find that desired hours of work are much less wage sensitive than is usually the case for unconstrained models.

This is an important area for further research, although it is unclear how far one can go in generalizing Dickens and Lundberg's model (for example by allowing $g_m(.)$ and $g_r(.)$ to vary with ξ_n) in the absence of information on the incidence of constraints.

Further reading

To a large extent, quantity constraints have been ignored by applied workers in most areas of choice modelling. This is principally because of the difficulty of identifying both desired behaviour and rationing mechanisms in the absence of any observation of such constraints. The few available applications of the models discussed in this chapter include those by King (1980), Moffitt (1982), Ham (1982), Dickens and Lundberg (1985), Blundell, Ham and Meghir (1987), Arellano and Meghir (1987) and Ilmakunnas and Pudney (1987), and are mostly in the field of labour supply. The most important reference on the theory of rationing is Neary and Roberts (1980), and their analysis in terms of virtual prices is exploited by Lee and Pitt (1984), who established general econometric techniques (see also section 4.3.2 above).

Appendices

And such a deal of skimble-skamble stuff.

Henry IV part 1

Appendix 1

Logistic, extreme value and generalized extreme value distributions

The normal distribution is the most widely assumed distributional form in the majority of branches of econometrics. There are good reasons for this. The central limit theorem can be used to justify the normality assumption whenever it is reasonable to view random errors as comprising a large number of individually insignificant components. Moreover, normality is very convenient: it is preserved under linear transformations, the multivariate form of the distribution permits unrestricted correlation structures, and all marginal and conditional distributions derived from the multivariate normal are themselves normal. However, offsetting these advantages is one great disadvantage: there is no explicit closed-form expression for the c.d.f. of the normal distribution, and its computation must therefore be performed indirectly, usually by means of numerical integration or one of the other approximations discussed in appendix 3. In multivariate problems, with more than two or three random variates involved, these methods require amounts of computer time that are sufficiently large to make iterative estimators in particular prohibitively expensive.

An alternative approach is to dispense with the normality assumption and use instead some other distributional form which should ideally be unrestrictive, have a p.d.f. and c.d.f. which are easily computable, and be sufficiently flexible to allow a close approximation to the normal form if this is felt desirable.

A1.1 The univariate logistic distribution

A traditional alternative to the univariate normal is the logistic distribution, which provides a very close approximation except in the extreme tails. The standard logistic distribution has mean 0 and variance $\pi^2/3$, and a p.d.f. and c.d.f. of the form

$$f(\eta) = \frac{\exp(\eta)}{[1 + \exp(\eta)]^2} \tag{A1.1}$$

$$F_\eta(\psi) = \Pr(\eta \leqslant \psi) = [1 + \exp(-\psi)]^{-1} \tag{A1.2}$$

The general form, adjusted to have mean μ and variance σ^2, is thus

$$f(\eta) = \frac{\pi}{\sigma\sqrt{3}} \exp\left[\frac{(\eta - \mu)\pi}{\sigma\sqrt{3}}\right]\left\{1 + \exp\left[\frac{(\eta - \mu)\pi}{\sigma\sqrt{3}}\right]\right\}^{-2} \tag{A1.3}$$

$$F_\eta(\psi) = \left\{1 + \exp\left[\frac{-(\psi - \mu)\pi}{\sigma\sqrt{3}}\right]\right\}^{-1} \tag{A1.4}$$

Note that no integration is required for the evaluation of the c.d.f.

A1.2 The type I extreme value distribution

The logistic distribution can be used directly in place of the normal in any univariate problem. However, in some cases, notably binary discrete choice problems of the kind discussed in chapter 3, the random variable involved is in fact the difference of two more fundamental random errors: the random components of the two utilities under comparison. With the normality assumption, this is perfectly straightforward: the difference of two normal variates is itself normal (moreover, the difference can *only* be normal if the underlying variates are jointly normal). However, this is not generally the case with other distributions: the difference of two logistic variates is not logistic. The question then arises: if the difference of two random variables is to have a logistic distribution, what form must their underlying joint distribution take? It can be shown that the required joint distribution is that of two independent variates, each having a type I extreme value distribution. This distribution is skewed, with a long right-hand tail and a mode at zero. In its standard form, it has mean 0.57722 and variance $\pi^2/6$, and is characterized by a p.d.f. and c.d.f. of the form

$$f(\epsilon) = \exp[-\epsilon - \exp(-\epsilon)] \tag{A1.5}$$

$$F_\epsilon(E) = \Pr(\epsilon \leqslant E) = \exp[-\exp(-E)]. \tag{A1.6}$$

Again, appropriate adjustments can be made to produce a type I extreme value distribution with unrestricted mean and variance.

This distributional form is known as an extreme value distribution, because if $x_1, \ldots, x_n$ are identically and independently distributed and $m_n = \max\{x_1 \ldots x_n\}$, then, for a wide class of x distributions, $m_n - \log(n)$ converges in distribution to a type I extreme value random variable. The central limit theorem is often quite plausibly used to justify the assumption of normality, but it is rather hard to see how this limiting result can be used to justify the assumption of extreme value errors. It is probably more realistic to view the extreme value distributional form as nothing more than a convenient device for generating logistic (i.e. approximately normal) errors in cases where differences are involved. The reader should consult Johnson and Kotz (1970), chapter 21, for more detail on this and other types of extreme value distributions.

A1.3 Multivariate logistic distributions

In the univariate case, the logistic c.d.f. is a fairly good approximation to the normal c.d.f., so there is generally little to be lost by assuming logistic errors rather than normal errors, even if the latter is the true distributional form. However, it is precisely in the univariate case that the need for an alternative to the normal is least pressing. The univariate normal c.d.f. can be evaluated very rapidly on modern computers (see appendix 3), and the logistic distribution therefore offers little practical advantage.

Unfortunately, in the multivariate context, where there is a definite need for a computationally simple alternative to the normal c.d.f., we find that the various multivariate logistic distributional forms are inadequate. Gumbel (1961) considers two different joint distributions which each yield marginal distributions of the form (A1.2) and can therefore be thought of as multivariate logistic distributions. In the m-dimensional case, these have c.d.f.s of the form

$$F_\eta(\psi_1, \ldots, \psi_m) = \left[1 + \sum_{i=1}^{m} \exp(-\psi_i)\right]^{-1} \tag{A1.7}$$

$$F_\eta(\psi_1, \ldots, \psi_m) = \left\{1 + \alpha \exp\left(-\sum_i \psi_i\right) \prod_i [1+\exp(-\psi_i)]^{-1}\right\} \prod_i [1+\exp(-\psi_i)]^{-1} \tag{A1.8}$$

Neither of these forms is capable of providing a good approximation to the multivariate normal, even after adjustment for means and variances: neither form yields a symmetric joint density function, and neither permits an unrestricted correlation structure. (A1.7) embodies a fixed correlation of $\frac{1}{2}$ between any pair of variates, while the correlation in (A1.8) varies with the parameter α but cannot be greater in magnitude than 0.30396. It appears not to be known whether it is possible to construct a less restrictive joint distribution possessing logistic marginals.

Despite the shortcomings of the logistic distribution in a multivariate context, the form (A1.7) is very widely used, principally because of its great simplicity. In particular, the multinomial logit model of discrete choice, discussed in chapter 3, is based on variate differences assumed to possess a joint c.d.f. of this form. Again, there is a link with the extreme value distribution: if the $m+1$ random variables $\epsilon_0, \ldots, \epsilon_m$ have independent type I extreme value distributions, then the m differences $\eta_1 = \epsilon_1 - \epsilon_0, \ldots, \eta_m = \epsilon_m - \epsilon_0$ have a joint distribution characterized by the c.d.f. (A1.7). This can be shown as follows:

$$
\begin{aligned}
\Pr(\eta_i \leqslant \psi_i, i=1, \ldots, m) &= \Pr(\epsilon_0 \leqslant \infty, \epsilon_i \leqslant \epsilon_0 + \psi_i, i=1, \ldots, m) \\
&= \int_{-\infty}^{\infty} f(\epsilon_0) F(\epsilon_0+\psi_1) \ldots F(\epsilon_0+\psi_m)\, \mathrm{d}\epsilon_0 \\
&= \int_{-\infty}^{\infty} I(\epsilon_0)\, \mathrm{d}\epsilon_0
\end{aligned}
$$

say, where $f(.)$ and $F(.)$ denote the type I extreme value p.d.f. and c.d.f. But the integrand $I(\epsilon_0)$ can be re-expressed as follows:

$$
\begin{aligned}
I(\epsilon_0) &= \exp[-\epsilon_0 - \exp(-\epsilon_0)] \prod_{i=1}^{m} \exp[-\exp(-\epsilon_0 - \psi_i)] \\
&= \exp(-\epsilon_0) \exp[-\exp(-\epsilon_0)] \prod_{i=1}^{m} \{\exp[-\exp(-\epsilon_0)]\}^{\exp(-\psi_i)} \\
&= \exp(-\epsilon_0) \{\exp[-\exp(-\epsilon_0)]\}^{\rho}
\end{aligned}
$$

where

$$\rho = 1 + \sum_{i=1}^{m} \exp(-\psi_i).$$

Thus

$$
\begin{aligned}
I(\epsilon_0) &= \exp(-\epsilon_0) \exp[-\rho \exp(-\epsilon_0)] \\
&= \exp(-\epsilon_0) \exp[-\exp(\rho^*) \exp(-\epsilon_0)]
\end{aligned}
$$

where $\rho^* = \log \rho$. Now define $\epsilon_0^* = \epsilon_0 - \rho^*$, so that $I(\epsilon_0)$ becomes

$$
\begin{aligned}
I(\epsilon_0) &= \exp(-\epsilon_0) \exp[-\exp(-\epsilon_0^*)] \\
&= \exp(-\rho^*) \exp(-\epsilon_0^*) \exp[-\exp(-\epsilon_0^*)] \\
&= \exp(-\rho^*) \exp[-\epsilon_0^* - \exp(-\epsilon_0^*)].
\end{aligned}
$$

But the exponential term in square brackets in this expression is simply the p.d.f. of the type I extreme value distribution (A1.5) and therefore integrates to unity. Thus

$$\int_{-\infty}^{\infty} I(\epsilon_0)\, d\epsilon_0 = \exp(-\rho^*) \int_{-\infty}^{\infty} \exp[-\epsilon_0^* - \exp(-\epsilon_0^*)]\, d\epsilon_0^* = \exp(-\rho^*).$$

But

$$\exp(-\rho^*) = \exp(-\log \rho) = \rho^{-1} = \left[1 + \sum_{i=1}^{m} \exp(-\psi_i)\right]^{-1}$$

which is the multivariate logistic distribution given in (A1.7).

A1.4 Generalized extreme value distributions

The restrictiveness of the multivariate logistic distribution (A1.7) is largely due to the restrictiveness of the assumption that the underlying extreme value variates $\epsilon_0, \ldots, \epsilon_m$ are independent and identically distributed. Less restrictive distributional forms can be generated if we work with a more flexible, non-independent class of distribution for $\epsilon_0, \ldots, \epsilon_m$. McFadden (1978) achieved this when he introduced the important notion of a generalized extreme value distribution. This is not a specific distribution but rather a means of generating suitable distributions. Suppose that $Y(.)$ is a function possessing the following properties:

i $Y(v_0, \ldots, v_m)$ is a non-negative function of non-negative arguments;
ii $Y(v_0, \ldots, v_m)$ is linearly homogeneous in its $m+1$ arguments;
iii $\lim_{v_i \to \infty} Y(v_0, \ldots, v_m) = +\infty$ for all $i = 0, \ldots, m$;
iv The partial derivative $\partial^k Y / \partial v_{i_1} \partial v_{i_2} \ldots \partial v_{i_k}$ is non-negative for k odd and non-positive for k even, provided that $i_1, \ldots, i_k$ are distinct.

The random variables $\epsilon_0, \ldots, \epsilon_m$ are said to have a generalized extreme value (GEV) distribution if their c.d.f. is expressible in the form

$$F_\epsilon(E_0, \ldots, E_m) = \exp\{-Y[\exp(-E_0), \ldots, \exp(-E_m)]\} \qquad \text{(A1.9)}$$

and the joint p.d.f. is found in the usual way by partially differentiating with respect to each of the ϵ_i. The form of this p.d.f. is too awkward to be worth presenting here.

The distribution defined by (A1.9) is known as the GEV distribution because its marginal distributions are all of displaced univariate extreme value form. The marginal c.d.f. of (say) ϵ_0 is defined as $F_\epsilon(E_0, \infty, \ldots, \infty)$, which in the present case is $\exp\{-Y[\exp(-E_0), 0, \ldots, 0]\}$. But $Y(.)$ is homogeneous of degree one, so $Y[\exp(-E_0), 0, \ldots, 0]$ is equal to $Y(1, 0, \ldots, 0)\exp(-E_0)$. Thus the marginal c.d.f. of ϵ_0 is $\exp\{-\exp[-(E_0 - \log h_0)]\}$, where $h_0 = Y(1, 0, \ldots, 0)$. This is a displaced form of (A1.6), and therefore $\epsilon_0 - \log h_0$ has a standard type I extreme value distribution.

An important special case of the GEV class of distributions corresponds to linearity of the function $Y(.)$. If $Y(v_0, \ldots, v_m) = h_0 v_0 + \ldots + h_m v_m$, then the expression (A1.9) factors into individual terms of the form $\exp\{-\exp[-(E_i - \log h_i)]\}$, and thus $\epsilon_0, \ldots, \epsilon_m$ are $m+1$ independent extreme value random variables; thus a more general non-independent distribution requires non-linearity of $Y(.)$

Most applications of the GEV distribution in econometrics have been in the field of discrete choice modelling. For those applications (see chapter 3) we require the distribution of the differences $\epsilon_1 - \epsilon_0, \ldots, \epsilon_m - \epsilon_0$ (say). Under the GEV assumption, these differences have what may be loosely described as a generalized logistic distribution. To derive this distribution, we must find the following probability:

$$\Pr(\epsilon_1 - \epsilon_0 \leqslant \psi_1, \ldots, \epsilon_m - \epsilon_0 \leqslant \psi_m) = \int_{-\infty}^{\infty} F_0(\epsilon_0, \psi_1 + \epsilon_0, \ldots, \psi_m + \epsilon_0)\, d\epsilon_0 \qquad (A1.10)$$

where $F_0(.)$ is the derivative of the c.d.f. of $\epsilon_0, \ldots, \epsilon_m$ with respect to ϵ_0:

$$\begin{aligned} F_0(\epsilon_0, \psi_1 + \epsilon_0, \ldots, \psi_m + \epsilon_0) = {} & \exp(-Y\{\exp(-\epsilon_0), \exp[-(\psi_1 + \epsilon_0)], \ldots, \\ & \exp[-(\psi_m + \epsilon_0)]\}) \\ & \times\ Y_0\{\exp(-\epsilon_0), \exp[-(\psi_1 + \epsilon_0)], \ldots, \\ & \exp[-(\psi_m + \epsilon_0)]\}\ \exp(-\epsilon_0) \end{aligned} \qquad (A1.11)$$

where $Y_0(.)$ is the partial derivative of $Y(.)$ with respect to its zeroth argument. Since $Y(.)$ is homogeneous of degree one and $Y_0(.)$ of degree zero, (A1.11) can be expressed in the simpler form

$$\begin{aligned} F_0(\epsilon_0, \psi_1 + \epsilon_0, \ldots, \psi_m + \epsilon_0) &= \exp[-\exp(-\epsilon_0) Y^*]\ Y_0^*\ \exp(-\epsilon_0) \\ &= \exp\{-\exp[-(\epsilon_0 - \log Y^*)]\} \\ &\quad \exp[-(\epsilon_0 - \log Y^*)]\ Y_0^*/Y^* \\ &= \exp[-\epsilon_0^* - \exp(-\epsilon_0^*)]\ Y_0^*/Y^* \end{aligned}$$

where Y^* and Y_0^* are the non-random quantities $Y[1, \exp(-\psi_1), \ldots, \exp(-\psi_m)]$ and $Y_0[1, \exp(-\psi_1), \ldots, \exp(-\psi_m)]$ respectively, and ϵ_0^* is the new random variate $\epsilon_0 - \log Y^*$. Since the Jacobian of the transformation from ϵ_0 to ϵ_0^* is unity, the probability (A1.10) is

$$\begin{aligned} \Pr(\epsilon_1 - \epsilon_0 \leqslant \psi_1, \ldots, \epsilon_m - \epsilon_0 \leqslant \psi_m) &= \int_{-\infty}^{\infty} \exp[-\epsilon_0^* - \exp(-\epsilon_0^*)] \frac{Y_0^*}{Y^*}\, d\epsilon_0^* \\ &= Y_0^*/Y^* \end{aligned}$$

since $\exp[-\epsilon_0^* - \exp(-\epsilon_0^*)]$ is the p.d.f. of the extreme value distribution and thus integrates to unity. Thus the c.d.f. of the m differences $\eta_i = \epsilon_i - \epsilon_0$ is

$$F_\eta(\psi_1, \ldots, \psi_m) = \frac{Y_0[1, \exp(-\psi_1), \ldots, \exp(-\psi_m)]}{Y[1, \exp(-\psi_1), \ldots, \exp(-\psi_m)]}. \qquad (A1.12)$$

To see the form of the corresponding marginal distributions, allow $\psi_2, \ldots, \psi_m$ to go to infinity:

$$F_{\eta_1}(\psi_1) = \frac{Y_0[1, \exp(-\psi_1), 0, \ldots, 0]}{Y[1, \exp(-\psi_1), 0, \ldots, 0]}. \tag{A1.13}$$

But by Euler's theorem the denominator can be expressed as the sum $Y_0[1, \exp(-\psi_1), 0, \ldots, 0] + Y_1[1, \exp(-\psi_1), 0, \ldots, 0]\exp(-\psi_1)$ and, dividing through by $Y_0(.)$, we have

$$F_{\eta_1}(\psi_1) = \{1 + \exp[-(\psi_1 - \gamma)]\}^{-1} \tag{A1.14}$$

where $\gamma = \log\{Y_1[1, \exp(-\psi_1), 0, \ldots, 0]/Y_0[1, \exp(-\psi_1), 0, \ldots, 0]\}$. Although (A1.14) looks vaguely similar to a displaced univariate logistic distribution (compare (A1.2)), it is not a true logistic distribution since the quantity γ is in general a function of ψ_1; it is only in special cases (including linearity of $Y(.)$) that the GEV distribution leads to a true multivariate logistic form for the differences.

Although this type of pseudo-logistic distribution will not generally give a close approximation to the multivariate normal (for example, it is not generally symmetric, since $F_\eta(-\psi_1, \ldots, -\psi_m) \neq 1 - F_\eta(\psi_1, \ldots, \psi_m)$), suitable choices for the function $Y(.)$ can at least give a reasonably flexible and unrestrictive form, which may be useful in cases where the multivariate normal c.d.f. is computationally intractable. For instance, in the systems of Tobit equations considered in chapter 4, the likelihood function is expressed in terms of multivariate functions which are distribution functions with respect to a subset of the variables of the problem but density functions with respect to the remaining variables. In the case of the normal, the evaluation of such a function requires numerical integration of the joint p.d.f., whereas for pseudo-logistic distribution, with c.d.f. available in closed form, all that is required is differentiation of (A1.12). Consider the following concrete example: $\eta_1, \ldots, \eta_k$ are observed as continuous variables, while for $\eta_{k+1}, \ldots, \eta_m$ we know only that each η_i is less than some value ψ_i. The corresponding likelihood component will be the expression

$$\frac{\partial^k F_\eta(\eta_1, \ldots, \eta_k, \psi_{k+1}, \ldots, \psi_m)}{\partial\eta_1 \ldots \partial\eta_k}. \tag{A1.15}$$

Define the function $G(.)$ to be $\log Y(.)$, and observe that $F_\eta(.)$ is the derivative of $G(.)$ with respect to its zeroth argument. Then differentiate a further k times to arrive at the combined distribution–density function:

$$\begin{aligned} f_\eta(\eta_1, \ldots, \eta_k, \psi_{k+1}, \ldots, \psi_m) = {} & G_{0\ldots k}[1, \exp(-\eta_1), \ldots, \exp(-\eta_k), \\ & \exp(-\psi_{k+1}), \ldots, \exp(-\psi_m)] \\ & \exp\left(-\sum_{i=1}^{k} \eta_i\right)(-1)^k \end{aligned} \tag{A1.16}$$

where the subscripts on $G(.)$ denote partial differentiation with respect to each of its arguments $0, \ldots, k$. The use of this pseudo-logistic distribution, or the GEV distribution directly, thus permits some econometric analysis to be made with models which would be completely non-feasible under the normality assumption. Whether the data will support this kind of distributional assumption is another matter.

Appendix 2

Truncated and censored distributions

Truncation and censoring arise in models involving endogenous variables which must satisfy some inequality constraint. For example, expenditure on a good cannot normally be negative, and this requires the use of models based on probability distributions with suitably restricted range. A simple way of imposing (say) a non-negativity constraint would be to employ a conventional non-negative distribution such as the log-normal, but distributions of this kind suffer from the drawback that, in imposing non-negativity, one is also imposing the assumption that small positive observations occur with small probability, and zero observations are essentially impossible. Truncated and censored distributions avoid this restrictiveness, and are widely used in microeconometrics.

To keep the analysis as simple as possible, we shall consider only censoring and truncation from below, so that the random variables concerned are not permitted to be less than some threshold. Moreover, all random variables considered here are scalars rather than vectors. The extension to other types of truncation and censoring and to multvariate problems is mostly straightforward, and is made where necessary in the text. There are several cases to be considered.

A2.1 Simple truncation

Suppose that ϵ is a random variable with c.d.f. $\Pr(\epsilon \leqslant E) = F(E)$ and p.d.f. $f(\epsilon)$. This distribution is subject to a process of (lower) truncation at the point c if realizations of ϵ which are less than c are simply discarded. This amounts to conditioning the distribution on the event $\epsilon \geqslant c$ or, in simple terms, taking the part of the density to the right of the point c and scaling it up so that the area under its curve is unity. Since $\Pr(\epsilon \geqslant c) = 1 - F(c)$, the truncated density is

$$f(\epsilon; c) = f(\epsilon \mid \epsilon \geqslant c) = f(\epsilon)/[1 - F(c)] \qquad c \leqslant \epsilon \leqslant \infty \qquad \text{(A2.1)}$$

This is illustrated in figure A2.1; note that the shaded areas, representing transferred probability mass, must be equal.

The mean of a distribution truncated in this way is

$$E(\epsilon \mid \epsilon \geqslant c) = \int_c^\infty \frac{\epsilon f(\epsilon)\,\mathrm{d}\epsilon}{1 - F(c)}. \qquad \text{(A2.2)}$$

From this definition, it is clear that $E(\epsilon \mid \epsilon \geqslant c)$ must always be at least as great as both c and the mean $E(\epsilon)$. The second moment about zero is defined analogously, with the integrand in (A2.2) replaced by $\epsilon^2 f(\epsilon)$. We shall not consider moments higher than the second.

We now examine a few of the most useful specific truncated distributions, concentrating particularly on the case of the normal, which is the most widely used special case.

A2.1.1 The truncated normal distribution

Consider the case where $\epsilon \sim N(\mu, \sigma^2)$, truncated from below at the point c. A simple shorthand for this lower truncated normal distribution is LTN(μ, σ^2, c). In discussing this case, we shall make use of the standard notation $\phi(.)$ and $\Phi(.)$ to denote the p.d.f. and c.d.f. of the $N(0,1)$ distribution, where $\phi(x) = (2\pi)^{-1/2} \exp(-x^2/2)$ and $\Phi(E) = \int_{-\infty}^{E} \phi(x)\,\mathrm{d}x$. Thus

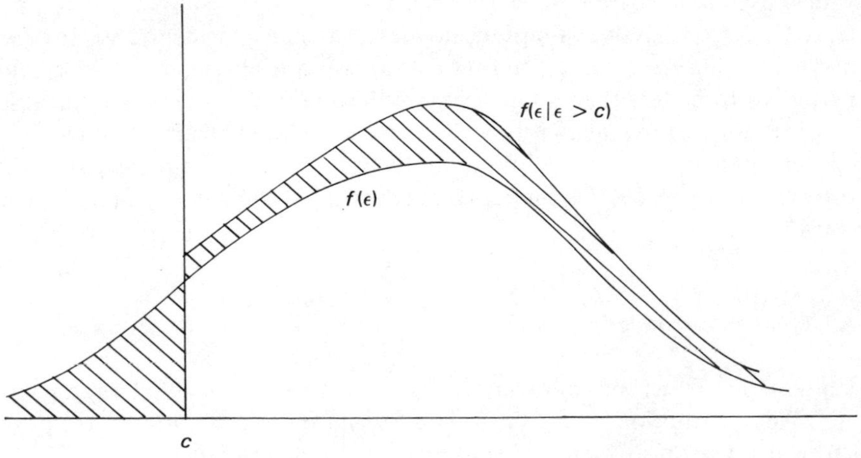

Figure A2.1 Lower truncation of a density function.

the p.d.f. and c.d.f. of the general $N(\mu,\ \sigma^2)$ distribution are expressed as $f(\epsilon) = \sigma^{-1}\phi[(\epsilon-\mu)/\sigma]$ and $F(E) = \Phi[(E-\mu)/\sigma]$. From (A2.1), an LTN$(\mu, \sigma^2, c)$ distribution has density function

$$f(\epsilon \mid \epsilon \geqslant c) = \frac{\phi[(\epsilon-\mu)/\sigma]}{\sigma\{1 - \Phi[(c-\mu)/\sigma]\}} \qquad c \leqslant \epsilon \leqslant \infty. \tag{A2.3}$$

This can be written as $\phi(\epsilon^*)/\sigma[1 - \Phi(c^*)]$, where ϵ^* and c^* are the standardized quantities $(\epsilon-\mu)/\sigma$ and $(c-\mu)/\sigma$. The moments of the LTN(μ, σ^2, c) distribution can be found directly from this expression. The mean is derived using definition (A2.2) as follows:

$$E(\epsilon \mid \epsilon \geqslant c) = \int_c^\infty \frac{\epsilon\, \phi(\epsilon^*)\, d\epsilon}{\sigma[1-\Phi(c^*)]}$$

$$= \int_{c^*}^\infty \frac{(\sigma\epsilon^* + \mu)\, \Phi(\epsilon^*)\, d\epsilon^*}{1-\Phi(c^*)}$$

$$= \mu + \sigma \int_{c^*}^\infty \frac{\epsilon^*\, \phi(\epsilon^*)\, d\epsilon^*}{1-\Phi(c^*)}. \tag{A2.4}$$

But it is easily seen from the definition of $\phi(.)$ that $d\phi(\epsilon^*) = -\epsilon^*\phi(\epsilon^*)d\epsilon^*$, and thus $\int\epsilon^*\phi(\epsilon^*)d\epsilon^* = -\int d\phi(\epsilon^*) = -\phi(\epsilon^*)$, and (A2.4) can therefore be expressed

$$E(\epsilon \mid \epsilon \geqslant c) = \mu + \sigma\{0 - [-\phi(c^*)]\}/[1-\Phi(c^*)]$$

$$= \mu + \sigma\lambda(c^*) \tag{A2.5}$$

where $\lambda(c^*) = \phi(c^*)/[1-\Phi(c^*)]$ is the quantity known as the inverse of Mills' ratio (Mills, 1926), or, in some contexts, the hazard rate.

Employing a similar argument, and making use of the fact that $d\phi'(\epsilon^*) = \epsilon^{*2}\phi(\epsilon^*)d\epsilon^* - \phi(\epsilon^*)d\epsilon^*$, and hence $\int\epsilon^{*2}\phi(\epsilon^*)d\epsilon^* = \Phi(\epsilon^*) - \epsilon^*\phi(\epsilon^*)$, the second truncated moment can be derived as

$$E(\epsilon^2 \mid \epsilon \geqslant c) = \sigma^2[1 + c^*\lambda(c^*) + 2(\mu/\sigma)\lambda(c^*) + (\mu/\sigma)^2] \tag{A2.6}$$

and, upon subtracting the squared truncated mean,

$$\mathrm{var}(\epsilon \mid \epsilon \geqslant c) = \sigma^2[1 + c^*\lambda(c^*) - \lambda(c^*)^2]. \tag{A2.7}$$

Table A2.1 gives values for the p.d.f., the c.d.f. and $E(\epsilon \mid \epsilon \geqslant c)$ at various points c, for the case where $\epsilon \sim N(0, 1)$.

For the case of upper truncation, the UTN(μ, σ^2, c) distribution has p.d.f.

$$f(\epsilon \mid \epsilon \leqslant c) = \frac{\phi[(\epsilon-\mu)/\sigma]}{\sigma\Phi[(c-\mu)/\sigma]} \qquad -\infty \leqslant \epsilon \leqslant c \tag{A2.8}$$

Table A2.1 Cumulative distribution functions, probability density functions and truncated and censored mean functions for six representative standardized symmetric distributions

c =	−3.0	−2.4	−1.8	−1.2	−0.6	0.0	0.6	1.2	1.8	2.4	3.0
$F(c)$											
Normal	0.0013	0.0082	0.0359	0.1151	0.2743	0.5000	0.7257	0.8849	0.9641	0.9918	0.9987
Logistic	0.0043	0.0127	0.0368	0.1019	0.2519	0.5000	0.7481	0.8981	0.9632	0.9873	0.9957
Laplace	0.0072	0.0168	0.0392	0.0916	0.2140	0.5000	0.7860	0.9084	0.9608	0.9832	0.9928
$t(5)$	0.0059	0.0135	0.0339	0.0910	0.2368	0.5000	0.7632	0.9090	0.9661	0.9865	0.9941
$t(10)$	0.0037	0.0115	0.0359	0.1047	0.2588	0.5000	0.7412	0.8953	0.9641	0.9885	0.9963
$t(20)$	0.0024	0.0100	0.0362	0.1102	0.2671	0.5000	0.7329	0.8898	0.9638	0.9900	0.9976
$f(c)$											
Normal	0.0044	0.0224	0.0790	0.1942	0.3332	0.3989	0.3332	0.1942	0.0790	0.0224	0.0044
Logistic	0.0078	0.0227	0.0643	0.1660	0.3418	0.4534	0.3418	0.1660	0.0643	0.0227	0.0078
Laplace	0.0102	0.0237	0.0555	0.1296	0.3027	0.7071	0.3027	0.1296	0.0555	0.0237	0.0102
$t(5)$	0.0173	0.0381	0.0848	0.1777	0.3081	0.3796	0.3081	0.1777	0.0848	0.0381	0.0173
$t(10)$	0.0114	0.0319	0.0831	0.1857	0.3203	0.3891	0.3203	0.1857	0.0831	0.0319	0.0114
$t(20)$	0.0080	0.0276	0.0814	0.1899	0.3267	0.3940	0.3267	0.1899	0.0814	0.0276	0.0080
$E(\epsilon \mid \epsilon \geqslant c)$											
Normal	0.004	0.023	0.082	0.219	0.459	0.798	1.215	1.688	2.197	2.732	3.283
Logistic	0.015	0.038	0.090	0.202	0.416	0.764	1.235	1.781	2.362	2.955	3.553
Laplace	0.027	0.053	0.102	0.192	0.356	0.707	1.307	1.907	2.507	3.107	3.707
$t(5)$	0.023	0.044	0.088	0.185	0.384	0.735	1.237	1.844	2.509	3.205	3.919
$t(10)$	0.013	0.034	0.087	0.205	0.428	0.773	1.226	1.754	2.329	2.934	3.559
$t(20)$	0.008	0.028	0.085	0.213	0.445	0.787	1.220	1.718	2.258	2.826	3.411
$E[\max(\epsilon, c)]$											
Normal	0.000	0.003	0.014	0.056	0.169	0.399	0.769	1.256	1.814	2.403	3.000
Logistic	0.002	0.007	0.021	0.059	0.160	0.382	0.760	1.259	1.821	2.407	3.002
Laplace	0.005	0.012	0.028	0.065	0.151	0.354	0.751	1.265	1.828	2.412	3.005
$t(5)$	0.022	0.034	0.052	0.084	0.162	0.368	0.762	1.284	1.852	2.434	3.022
$t(10)$	0.004	0.010	0.024	0.063	0.164	0.387	0.764	1.263	1.824	2.410	3.004
$t(20)$	0.001	0.005	0.018	0.058	0.166	0.393	0.766	1.258	1.818	2.405	3.001

and this has mean

$$E(\epsilon \mid \epsilon \leqslant c) = \mu - \sigma\lambda^*(c^*) \tag{A2.9}$$

where $\lambda^*(c^*) = \phi(c^*)/\Phi(c^*)$ is the complement of Mills' ratio.

The two Mills' ratios $\lambda(.)$ and $\lambda^*(.)$ have the following properties:

$$\lambda(c) = \lambda^*(-c) > 0 \tag{A2.10}$$

$$\frac{\mathrm{d}\lambda(c)}{\mathrm{d}c} = \lambda(c)[\lambda(c) - c] > 0 \tag{A2.11}$$

$$\frac{\mathrm{d}\lambda^*(c)}{\mathrm{d}c} = -\lambda^*(c)[\lambda^*(c)+c] < 0. \tag{A2.12}$$

A2.1.2 Other truncated distributions

Table A2.1 compares the LTN(0, 1, c) distribution with a number of other truncated distributions.

The truncated logistic distribution The standard form of the logistic distribution with c.d.f. $L(E) = [1 + \exp(-E)]^{-1}$ has untruncated mean and variance of 0 and $\pi^2/3$ respectively. Its truncated mean takes the form (see, for instance, Arabmazar and Schmidt, 1982)

$$E(\epsilon^* \mid \epsilon^* \geqslant c^*) = c - \frac{\log L(c^*)}{1-L(c^*)}. \tag{A2.13}$$

To derive the general form, construct a new variable $\epsilon = \mu + \sigma\sqrt{3}\epsilon^*/\pi$, which has mean μ and variance σ^2. Then $E(\epsilon \mid \epsilon \geqslant c) = E(\mu+\sigma\sqrt{3}\epsilon^*/\pi \mid \mu+\sigma\ 3\epsilon^*/\pi \geqslant c) = \mu + \sigma\sqrt{3}E(\epsilon^* \mid \epsilon^* \geqslant c^*)/\pi$, where c^* is now the specific value $(c-\mu)\pi/\sigma\sqrt{3}$. Using (A2.13) for the conditional expectation in this expression, we find, after some manipulation,

$$E(\epsilon \mid \epsilon \geqslant c) = c - \frac{\sigma\sqrt{3}}{\pi}\,\frac{\log L(c^*)}{1-L(c^*)}. \tag{A2.14}$$

The second moment of the truncated logistic distribution is available only in a rather awkward form involving infinite series (see Arabmazar and Schmidt, 1982, for details).

The p.d.f., c.d.f. and truncated expectation of the standardized (i.e. $\mu=0$ and $\sigma^2=1$) form of the logistic distribution are given in table A2.1 for various values of c. It should be noted that, although the logistic c.d.f. provides a reasonably close approximation to that of the normal distribution (with a maximum discrepancy of approximately 0.023), the difference between their truncated expectations is considerably greater, with the discrepancy as great as 0.27 at the positive end of the tabulated range.

The truncated Laplace distribution The Laplace or double exponential distribution has been used by Arabmazar and Schmidt (1982) and Goldberger (1983) as an alternative to the normal distribution for the purpose of examining the sensitivity of conventional econometric techniques to departures from normality. In its natural untruncated form, which has mean zero and a variance of 2, and p.d.f. and c.d.f. are

$$f(\epsilon^*) = \tfrac{1}{2}\exp(-|\epsilon^*|) \tag{A2.15}$$

$$F(E^*) = \begin{cases} \tfrac{1}{2}\exp(E^*) & E^* \leqslant 0 \\ 1 - \tfrac{1}{2}\exp(-E^*) & E^* > 0. \end{cases} \tag{A2.16}$$

In this form, the distribution has truncated mean

$$E(\epsilon^* \mid \epsilon^* > c^*) = \begin{cases} c^* + 1 & c^* \geqslant 0 \\ (c^* - 1)/[1 - 2\exp(-c^*)] & c^* < 0. \end{cases} \tag{A2.17}$$

When transformed to generate a variate $\epsilon = \mu + \sigma\epsilon^*/\sqrt{2}$, which has mean μ and variance σ^2, (A2.15)–(A2.17) become

$$f(\epsilon) = (2\sigma^2)^{-1/2}\exp[-|\sqrt{2}(\epsilon-\mu)/\sigma|] \tag{A2.18}$$

$$F(E) = \begin{cases} \tfrac{1}{2}\exp[\sqrt{2}(E-\mu)/\sigma] & E \leqslant \mu \\ 1 - \tfrac{1}{2}\exp[-\sqrt{2}(E-\mu)/\sigma] & E > \mu \end{cases} \tag{A2.19}$$

$$E(\epsilon \mid \epsilon \geqslant c) = \begin{cases} c + \sigma\sqrt{2} & c \geqslant \mu \\ \dfrac{c - \sigma/\sqrt{2} - 2\mu\exp(-c^*)}{1 - 2\exp(-c^*)} & c < \mu \end{cases} \tag{A2.20}$$

where $c^* = \sqrt{2}(c-\mu)/\sigma$. From table A2.1, it is evident that the Laplace distribution differs considerably from the normal and logistic distributions. One unusual feature is that its p.d.f. is not differentiable at the mean, μ. See Johnson and Kotz (1970), chapter 23, for further details of the Laplace distribution.

The truncated *t* distribution Student's t distribution is well known from classical hypothesis-testing theory. Like the normal distribution, it is symmetric and bell shaped. Its precise form depends on the degrees-of-freedom parameter q, and the distribution approaches the limiting $N(0, 1)$ form as $q \rightarrow \infty$. Thus the t distribution provides a natural alternative to the normal, with the parameter q controlling the degree of non-normality. In its natural form, the t distribution has mean zero and variance $q/(q-2)$, and has the following density function:

$$t(\epsilon^*) = \frac{1}{\sqrt{q}\,B(\tfrac{1}{2}, q/2)}\left(1 + \frac{\epsilon^{*2}}{q}\right)^{-(q+1)/2} \tag{A2.21}$$

where $B(.\,,\,.)$ is the beta function. The t distribution suffers from the same practical drawback as the normal distribution in that its c.d.f. is not available in closed form. We shall denote the c.d.f. corresponding to the natural form (A2.21) $T(E^*) = \int_{-\infty}^{E^*} t(\epsilon^*)d\epsilon^*$. Adjusting the distribution to have mean μ and variance σ^2, the p.d.f. becomes

$$f(\epsilon) = \frac{1}{\sigma(q-2)^{1/2}B(\frac{1}{2}, q/2)}\left[1 + \frac{(\epsilon-\mu)^2 q}{\sigma^2(q-2)}\right]^{-(q+1)/2}. \tag{A2.22}$$

The truncated mean of this generalized t distribution takes the following form:

$$E(\epsilon \mid \epsilon \geqslant c) = \mu + \frac{q^{1/2}}{(q-2)^{1/2}}\left[\frac{(c-\mu)^2 + \sigma^2(q-2)}{\sigma(q-1)}\right]\left[\frac{t(c^*)}{1 - T(c^*)}\right]. \tag{A2.23}$$

The absence of a convenient expression for the c.d.f. $T(.)$ has prevented the use of the t distribution as a serious alternative to the normal in applied work; however, Arabmazar and Schmidt (1982) and Goldberger (1983) have used it to examine the robustness of econometric techniques to non-normality. Table A2.1 presents values of $f(c)$, $F(c)$ and $E(\epsilon \mid \epsilon \geqslant c)$ for $q = 5$, 10 and 20. It should be noted again that the c.d.f. gives a fairly close approximation to the normal c.d.f. after adjustment for their different variances; however, the truncated expectations differ quite considerably. Thus one must conclude from table A2.1 that methods based on truncated distributions will tend to be very sensitive to even quite small departures from normality.

Asymmetric truncated distributions The normal, logistic, Laplace and t distributions are all of the form conventionally assumed for random disturbances in econometric models: symmetric and bell shaped. Other distributional forms have occasionally been tried in an attempt to allow for possible skewness in the underlying distribution. Examples are given by Amemiya and Boskin (1974), who use the truncated log-normal distribution, and Atkinson, Gomulka and Stern (1984a), who use the truncated gamma distribution. Other obvious possibilities are the exponential and Pareto forms. A feature of these distributions is that their ranges are limited, and this may occasionally cause difficulties in the specification and estimation of the resulting econometric models. A skewed distribution with unlimited range is the type I extreme value form (see appendix 1), which could be used in truncated form. However, its degree of skewness is fixed and does not permit estimation. For details of these and other truncated distributions, see the various chapters of Johnson and Kotz (1970).

A2.2 Censored distributions

Since truncated distributions imply that the probability of an observation at the truncation point c is essentially zero, their principal use is in the analysis of models involving limited dependent variables, with observations at the limit point excluded from the sample in use. However, in many applications, observations of random variables at their limit points are available, and this leads naturally to models based on censored, rather than truncated, distributions. In the case of (lower) censoring, realizations of the underlying random variable which are less than c are not discarded, but rather are observed instead as equal to c. Thus the lower tail of the density function is not redistributed over the remainder of the distribution but accumulated as discrete probability mass at the point c. A censored distribution is therefore mixed discrete–continuous. Censoring has the effect of defining a new random variable ϵ^c such that

$$\begin{aligned} \epsilon^c &= c \qquad \text{if } \epsilon < c \\ \epsilon^c &= \epsilon \qquad \text{if } \epsilon > c \end{aligned} \tag{A2.24}$$

or, more concisely,

$$\epsilon^c = \max(\epsilon, c). \tag{A2.25}$$

Thus the censored distribution has the following mixed discrete–continuous form:

$$\begin{aligned} \Pr(\epsilon^c = c) &= F(c) \\ f(\epsilon^c) &= f(\epsilon) \qquad c < \epsilon \leqslant \infty \end{aligned} \tag{A2.26}$$

where $f(.)$ and $F(.)$ are the p.d.f. and c.d.f. of the underlying variate ϵ.

The moments of a censored distribution are related in a very simple way to those of the corresponding truncated distribution. In particular, the mean and second moment about zero are

$$\begin{aligned} E(\epsilon^c) &= \Pr(\epsilon^c = c)\, c + \int_c^\infty \epsilon f(\epsilon)\, \mathrm{d}\epsilon \\ &= F(c)\, c + [1 - F(c)]\, E(\epsilon \mid \epsilon \geqslant c) \end{aligned} \tag{A2.27}$$

$$E[(\epsilon^c)^2] = F(c)\, c^2 + [1 - F(c)]\, E(\epsilon^2 \mid \epsilon \geqslant c). \tag{A2.28}$$

Thus the general rth order censored moment about zero is a convex combination of c^r and the corresponding truncated moment, with the weights being the probabilities of the events $\epsilon^c = c$ and $\epsilon^c > c$ respectively. From these expressions, it is clear that censoring increases moments by less than truncation, and consequently we have the inequality

$$\max[c^r, E(\epsilon^r)] \leqslant E[(\epsilon^c)^r] \leqslant E(\epsilon^r \mid \epsilon \leqslant c) \tag{A2.29}$$

for moments of any order r.

Because it is so straightforward to determine the characteristics of censored distributions from knowledge of the analogous truncated distributions, we shall not examine any specific censored distributions except for the lower censored normal (LCN(μ, σ^2, c)). Table A2.1 gives the censored means of standardized normal, logistic, Laplace and t distributions. The important point that emerges from the table, and which is an obvious consequence of the inequality (A2.29), is that the censored mean is rather less affected by departures from normality than is the truncated mean. This suggests that techniques based on censored, rather than truncated, distributions are likely to be more robust in this sense.

If ϵ^c has an LCN(μ, σ^2, c) distribution, obervations are generated as follows:

$$\begin{aligned} \epsilon^c &= c \text{ with probability } \Phi\left[\frac{c-\mu}{\sigma}\right] \\ f(\epsilon^c) &= \frac{1}{\sigma}\sigma\left[\frac{\epsilon^c-\mu}{\sigma}\right] \qquad c < \epsilon^c \leqslant \infty. \end{aligned} \tag{A2.30}$$

This distribution has mean

$$\begin{aligned} E(\epsilon^c) &= \Phi(c^*)c + [1-\Phi(c^*)][\mu + \sigma\lambda(c^*)] \\ &= \mu + \sigma[\Phi(c^*)c^* + \phi(c^*)]. \end{aligned} \tag{A2.31}$$

The second moment can be derived from expressions (A2.28) and (A2.6).

A2.3 Truncation with respect to an extraneous variable

We have so far considered only cases of truncation defined in terms of an inequality applying directly to the variable ϵ itself. However, in many practical problems, truncation involves some extraneous variable. For instance, in a study of labour supply, it is usual to employ samples from which the unemployed are excluded. If unemployment occurs, for example, because the productivity of the invididual is less than some critical market threshold, then the sample of observations on labour supply is truncated with respect to an extraneous variable, productivity. Further examples are given in chapter 2.

In such cases, the distribution involved is conditional, with density function $f(\epsilon_1 \mid \epsilon_2 \geqslant c_2)$. It should be noted that our analysis will apply equally to the case where the principal variate ϵ_1 is a vector rather than a simple scalar; however, we assume that the truncating variate ϵ_2 is scalar. The case of multiple truncation rules is considered in the next section. The truncated density of ϵ_1 is derived from the following truncated joint density:

$$f(\epsilon_1, \epsilon_2 | \epsilon_2 \geqslant c_2) = f(\epsilon_1, \epsilon_2)/\Pr(\epsilon_2 \geqslant c_2) \qquad \begin{matrix} -\infty \leqslant \epsilon_1 \leqslant \infty \\ c \leqslant \epsilon_2 \leqslant \infty \end{matrix} \tag{A2.32}$$

where the denominator is given by

$$\Pr(\epsilon_2 \geqslant c_2) = \int_{c_2}^{\infty} \int_{-\infty}^{\infty} f(\epsilon_1, \epsilon_2)\, d\epsilon_1\, d\epsilon_2. \tag{A2.33}$$

Integrating (A2.32) with respect to ϵ_2, the marginal distribution of ϵ_1 truncated with respect to ϵ_2 is

$$f(\epsilon_1 | \epsilon_2 \leqslant c_2) = \int_{c_2}^{\infty} \frac{f(\epsilon_1, \epsilon_2)\, d\epsilon_2}{\Pr(\epsilon_2 \geqslant c_2)}. \tag{A2.34}$$

Alternatively, this can be expressed in terms of ordinary conditional densities:

$$\begin{aligned} f(\epsilon_1 | \epsilon_2 \geqslant c) &= \int_{c_2}^{\infty} \frac{f(\epsilon_2 | \epsilon_1) f(\epsilon_1)\, d\epsilon_2}{\Pr(\epsilon_2 \geqslant c_2)} \\ &= f(\epsilon_1) \frac{\Pr(\epsilon_2 \geqslant c_2 | \epsilon_1)}{\Pr(\epsilon_2 \geqslant c_2)} \end{aligned} \tag{A2.35}$$

where $f(\epsilon_1)$ is the marginal density of ϵ_1.

From (A2.34), the truncated expectation of ϵ_1 is

$$\begin{aligned} E(\epsilon_1 | \epsilon_2 \geqslant c_2) &= \int_{-\infty}^{\infty} \epsilon_1 \int_{c_2}^{\infty} \frac{f(\epsilon_1, \epsilon_2)\, d\epsilon_2\, d\epsilon_1}{\Pr(\epsilon_2 \geqslant c_2)} \\ &= \int_{c_2}^{\infty} \left[\int_{-\infty}^{\infty} \epsilon_1 f(\epsilon_1 | \epsilon_2)\, d\epsilon_1 \right] \frac{f(\epsilon_2)\, d\epsilon_2}{\Pr(\epsilon_2 \geqslant c_2)} \\ &= \int_{c_2}^{\infty} \frac{E(\epsilon_1 | \epsilon_2) f(\epsilon_2)\, d\epsilon_2}{\Pr(\epsilon_2 \geqslant c_2)} \end{aligned} \tag{A2.36}$$

where $f(\epsilon_2)$ is the marginal density of ϵ_2. Expression (A2.36) can be thought of as $E_2[E_1(\epsilon_1 | \epsilon_2) | \epsilon_2 \geqslant c_2]$, where the subscript on the $E(.)$ operator indicates the variate involved in the operation.

The only specific example we consider is that of the bivariate normal distribution. Suppose that ϵ_1 and ϵ_2 are jointly normal, with means μ_1 and μ_2, variances σ_1^2 and σ_2^2, and covariance σ_{12}. We shall use two properties of the normal distribution: its marginal and conditional distributions are of univariate normal form, and the conditional expectation is a linear function of the conditioning variable. Thus, in the present case,

$$E(\epsilon_1 | \epsilon_2) = \mu_1 + \frac{\sigma_{12}}{\sigma_2^2}(\epsilon_2 - \mu_2) = \left[\mu_1 - \frac{\sigma_{12}}{\sigma_2^2}\mu_2\right] + \frac{\sigma_{12}}{\sigma_2^2}\epsilon_2 \tag{A2.37}$$

$$\text{var}(\epsilon_1 | \epsilon_2) = \sigma_1^2 - \sigma_{12}^2/\sigma_2^2. \tag{A2.38}$$

For the normal distribution, therefore, the truncated marginal density (A2.35) can be expressed as follows:

$$f(\epsilon_1 | \epsilon_2 \geqslant c_2) = \frac{1}{\sigma_1}\phi\left(\frac{\epsilon_1 - \mu_1}{\sigma_1}\right)\left\{1 - \Phi\left[\frac{c_2 - \mu_2 - \sigma_{12}(\epsilon_1 - \mu_1)/\sigma_1^2}{(\sigma_2^2 - \sigma_{12}^2/\sigma_1^2)^{1/2}}\right]\right\}$$
$$\left[1 - \Phi\left(\frac{c_2 - \mu_2}{\sigma_2}\right)\right]^{-1} \tag{A2.39}$$

The truncated expectation of ϵ_1 is found from (A2.36) and (A2.37):

$$\begin{aligned} E(\epsilon_1 | \epsilon_2 \geqslant c_2) &= E(\mu_1 - \sigma_{12}\mu_2/\sigma_2^2 + \sigma_{12}\epsilon_2/\sigma_2^2 | \epsilon_2 \geqslant c_2) \\ &= \mu_1 - \frac{\sigma_{12}}{\sigma_2^2}\mu_2 + \frac{\sigma_{12}}{\sigma_2^2}E(\epsilon_2 | \epsilon_2 \geqslant c_2). \end{aligned} \tag{A2.40}$$

Expression (A2.40) allows us now to make use of results from section A2.1 on univariate truncation:

$$\begin{aligned} E(\epsilon_1 | \epsilon_2 \geqslant c_2) &= \mu_1 - \frac{\sigma_{12}}{\sigma_2^2}\mu_2 + \frac{\sigma_{12}}{\sigma_2^2}\left[\mu_2 + \sigma_2\lambda\left(\frac{c_2 - \mu_2}{\sigma_2}\right)\right] \\ &= \mu_1 + \sigma_1\rho\lambda\left[\frac{c_2 - \mu_2}{\sigma_2}\right] \end{aligned} \tag{A2.41}$$

where ρ is the correlation coefficient $\sigma_{12}/\sigma_1\sigma_2$.

A2.4 Multiple truncation

In applied work, it is not unusual to encounter problems involving more than a single truncation rule. For instance, either unemployment or ill health may be sufficient grounds for the rejection of a potential participant in a survey of labour supply behaviour. For generality, we shall consider a p-dimensional joint distribution which is truncated with respect to the last $p-1$ variates. The first untruncated variate may be either a scalar or a vector. Suppose this distribution has p.d.f. $f(\epsilon_1, \ldots, \epsilon_p)$, and define the compound event Ξ to be

$$\Xi = \{\epsilon_2 \geqslant c_2, \ldots, \epsilon_p \geqslant c_p\}. \tag{A2.42}$$

Since violation of any one of the $p-1$ component conditions is sufficient to prevent an observation's being made, the truncated distribution we seek is

$$f(\epsilon_1, \ldots, \epsilon_p \mid \Xi) = f(\epsilon_1, \ldots, \epsilon_p)/\Pr(\Xi) \tag{A2.43}$$

where

$$\Pr(\Xi) = \int_{-\infty}^{\infty}\int_{c_2}^{\infty} \cdots \int_{c_p}^{\infty} f(\epsilon_1, \ldots, \epsilon_p)\, d\epsilon_p \ldots d\epsilon_1. \tag{A2.44}$$

If we are interested in the marginal truncated distribution of ϵ_1 alone,

$$f(\epsilon_1 \mid \Xi) = \int_{c_2}^{\infty} \cdots \int_{c_p}^{\infty} \frac{f(\epsilon_1, \ldots, \epsilon_p)\, d\epsilon_p \ldots d\epsilon_2}{\Pr(\Xi)} \tag{A2.45}$$

which, as in the previous section, can be expressed as

$$f(\epsilon_1 \mid \Xi) = f(\epsilon_1) \frac{\Pr(\Xi \mid \epsilon_1)}{\Pr(\Xi)}. \tag{A2.46}$$

A similar argument to that underlying (A2.36) can then be used to derive the truncated mean:

$$E(\epsilon_1 \mid \Xi) = E[E(\epsilon_1 \mid \epsilon_2 \ldots \epsilon_p) \mid \Xi]. \tag{A2.47}$$

This is as far as we can go in the general case; however, under normality, rather more useful expressions can be obtained. Suppose that $\epsilon' = (\epsilon_1 \ldots \epsilon_p)$ has a multivariate normal distribution with mean vector μ and covariance matrix Σ. Partition ϵ; μ and Σ as follows:

$$\epsilon = \begin{bmatrix} \epsilon_1 \\ \epsilon^+ \end{bmatrix} \qquad \mu = \begin{bmatrix} \mu_1 \\ \mu^+ \end{bmatrix} \qquad \Sigma = \begin{bmatrix} \sigma_{11} & \sigma^{+\prime} \\ \sigma^+ & \Sigma^+ \end{bmatrix} \tag{A2.48}$$

where ϵ^+, μ^+ and σ^+ are $(p-1) \times 1$ vectors and Σ^+ is a $(p-1) \times (p-1)$ matrix. Under normality, we have the following results (see Anderson, 1958, chapter 2):

$$\epsilon_1 \mid \epsilon_2 \ldots \epsilon_p \sim N\{\mu_1 + \sigma^{+\prime}(\Sigma^+)^{-1}(\epsilon^+ - \mu^+)], [\sigma_{11} - \sigma^{+\prime}(\Sigma^+)^{-1}\sigma^+]\} \tag{A2.49}$$

$$\epsilon_2 \ldots \epsilon_p \mid \epsilon_1 \sim N\{[\mu^+ + \sigma^+(\epsilon_1 - \mu_1)/\sigma_{11}], [\Sigma^+ - \sigma^+\sigma^{+\prime}\sigma_{11}^{-1}]\}. \tag{A2.50}$$

Thus (A2.46) takes the form

$$f(\epsilon_1 \mid \Xi) = \frac{1}{(\sigma_{11})^{1/2}} \phi \left[\frac{\epsilon_1 - \mu_1}{(\sigma_{11})^{1/2}}\right] \frac{\Pr(\Xi \mid \epsilon_1)}{\Pr(\Xi)} \tag{A2.51}$$

where $\Pr(\Xi \mid \epsilon_1)$ is arrived at by integrating the normal density function of (A2.50) over the region $\{(c_2, \infty), \ldots, (c_p, \infty)\}$, and $\Pr(\Xi)$ by integrating an $N(\mu^+, \Sigma^+)$ density over the same region.

Using (A2.49), the truncated expectation (A2.47) simplifies to

$$E(\epsilon_1 | \Xi) = \mu_1 - \sigma^{+\prime}(\Sigma^+)^{-1}\mu^+ + \sigma^{+\prime}(\Sigma^+)^{-1}E(\epsilon^+ | \Xi) \tag{A2.52}$$

which is a clear generalization of (A2.40). The expected value on the right-hand side of (A2.52) is

$$E(\epsilon^+ | \Xi) = \int_{c_2}^{\infty} \cdots \int_{c_p}^{\infty} \frac{\epsilon^+ f(\epsilon_2, \ldots, \epsilon_p)\, d\epsilon_p \ldots d\epsilon_2}{\Pr(\Xi)} \tag{A2.53}$$

where $f(\epsilon_2, \ldots, \epsilon_p)$ is the p.d.f. of an $N(\mu^+, \Sigma^+)$ distribution. Differentiating such a p.d.f., we have

$$\frac{\partial f}{\partial \epsilon^+} = f(\epsilon_2, \ldots, \epsilon_p)\,[-(\Sigma^+)^{-1}(\epsilon^+ - \mu^+)].$$

Thus

$$\int_{c_2}^{\infty} \cdots \int_{c_p}^{\infty} \epsilon^+ f(\epsilon_2, \ldots, \epsilon_p)\, d\epsilon_p \ldots d\epsilon_2 = \mu^+ \Pr(\Xi) - \Sigma^+ \begin{bmatrix} \partial \Pr(\Xi)/\partial c_2 \\ \vdots \\ \partial \Pr(\Xi)/\partial c_p \end{bmatrix}. \tag{A2.54}$$

Expressions (A2.52)–(A2.54) yield

$$E(\epsilon_1 | \Xi) = \mu_1 - \sum_{i=2}^{p} \sigma_{1i} \frac{\partial \Pr(\Xi)}{\partial c_i} \Big/ \Pr(\Xi) \tag{A2.55}$$

or

$$E(\epsilon_1 | \Xi) = \mu_1 + \sum_{i=2}^{p} \sigma_{1i} \left[\frac{\int_{c_2}^{\infty} \cdots \int_{c_p}^{\infty} f(\epsilon_2, \ldots, \epsilon_{i-1}, c_i, \epsilon_{i+1}, \ldots, \epsilon_p) \prod_{j \neq i} d\epsilon_j}{\int_{c_2}^{\infty} \cdots \int_{c_p}^{\infty} f(\epsilon_2, \ldots, \epsilon_p) \prod_{j=2}^{p} d\epsilon_j} \right]. \tag{A2.56}$$

For the important special case of two truncation rules ($p = 3$), (A2.56) can be simplified by factoring $f(\epsilon_2, \epsilon_3)$ into conditional and marginal densities and then integrating. This yields, after some manipulation,

$$E(\epsilon_1 | \Xi) = \mu_1 + \frac{\sigma_{12}}{\sigma_{22}^{1/2}} \frac{\phi(c_2^*)}{\Pr(\Xi)} \left\{ 1 - \Phi\left[\frac{c_3^* - \rho c_2^*}{(1-\rho^2)^{1/2}} \right] \right\} + \frac{\sigma_{13}}{\sigma_{33}^{1/2}} \frac{\phi(c_3^*)}{\Pr(\Xi)} \left\{ 1 - \Phi\left[\frac{c_2^* - \rho c_3^*}{(1-\rho^2)^{1/2}} \right] \right\} \tag{A2.57}$$

where $c_i^* = (c_i - \mu_i)/\sigma_{ii}^{1/2}$ and $\rho = \sigma_{23}/(\sigma_{22}\sigma_{33})^{1/2}$.

A2.5 Combined truncation and censoring

Truncation is usually a consequence of the way a sample is selected; censoring is usually more fundamental and is a consequence of the basic nature of the variable that a model attempts to explain. Thus it is very common to have both truncation and censoring present in an applied problem. For instance, the estimation of a labour supply model which respects the non-negativity constraint on hours worked will give rise to such a distribution if the available sample excludes the unemployed.

Consider a bivariate p.d.f. $f(\epsilon_1, \epsilon_2)$ which is to be truncated with respect to ϵ_2 and censored with respect to ϵ_1. Define the censored variable to be $\epsilon_1^c = \max(c_1, \epsilon_1)$. Then the distribution we seek has two components:

$$f(\epsilon_1^c = c_1, \epsilon_2 | \epsilon_2 \geqslant c_2) = \int_{-\infty}^{c_1} \frac{f(\epsilon_1, \epsilon_2)\, d\epsilon_1}{\Pr(\epsilon_2 \geqslant c_2)} \tag{A2.58}$$

which is defined for all $\epsilon_2 \geqslant c_2$, and

$$f(\epsilon_1^c, \epsilon_2 | \epsilon_2 \geqslant c_2) = f(\epsilon_1, \epsilon_2)/\Pr(\epsilon_2 \geqslant c_2) \tag{A2.59}$$

which is defined for $\epsilon_1^c > c_1$ and $\epsilon_2 > c_2$, where

$$\Pr(\epsilon_2 \geqslant c_2) = \int_{-\infty}^{\infty} \int_{c_2}^{\infty} f(\epsilon_1, \epsilon_2)\, d\epsilon_2\, d\epsilon_1. \tag{A2.60}$$

The truncated marginal density of ϵ_1^c alone is of mixed discrete–continuous form:

$$\begin{aligned} \Pr(\epsilon_1^c = c_1 | \epsilon_2 \geqslant c_2) &= 1 - \Pr(\epsilon_1 > c_1 | \epsilon_2 \geqslant c_2) \\ &= 1 - \Pr(\epsilon_1 > c_1, \epsilon_2 \geqslant c_2)/\Pr(\epsilon_2 \geqslant c_2) \\ &= 1 - \int_{c_1}^{\infty} \int_{c_2}^{\infty} f(\epsilon_1, \epsilon_2)\, d\epsilon_2\, d\epsilon_1/\Pr(\epsilon_2 \geqslant c_2) \end{aligned} \tag{A2.61}$$

$$\begin{aligned} f(\epsilon_1^c | \epsilon_2 \geqslant c_2) &= \int_{c_2}^{\infty} \frac{f(\epsilon_1^c, \epsilon_2)\, d\epsilon_2}{\Pr(\epsilon_2 \geqslant c_2)} \\ &= \frac{f(\epsilon_1^c)\Pr(\epsilon_2 \geqslant c_2 | \epsilon_1^c)}{\Pr(\epsilon_2 \geqslant c_2)}. \end{aligned} \tag{A2.62}$$

The expected value of ϵ_1^c in the presence of truncation with respect to ϵ_2 is as follows:

$$E(\epsilon_1^c \mid \epsilon_2 \geqslant c_2) = c_1 \left[\frac{1 - \Pr(\epsilon_1 \geqslant c_1, \epsilon_2 \geqslant c_2)}{\Pr(\epsilon_2 \geqslant c_2)} \right] + \int_{c_1}^{\infty} \frac{\epsilon_1 f(\epsilon_1) \Pr(\epsilon_2 \geqslant c_2 \mid \epsilon_1) \, d\epsilon_1}{\Pr(\epsilon_2 \geqslant c_2)}. \qquad \text{(A2.63)}$$

It is clear from inspection of (A2.61)–(A2.63) that the combination of truncation and censoring gives rise to a considerably greater degree of complexity than does either truncation or censoring alone; in general bivariate rather than univariate integration is now required to characterize the distribution. In the special case of normality, where ϵ_1 and ϵ_2 have a bivariate normal distribution with means μ_1 and μ_2, variances σ_1^2 and σ_2^2 and covariance σ_{12}, these expression simplify somewhat, since the quantities $f(\epsilon_1^c)$, $\Pr(\epsilon_2 \geqslant c_2)$ and $\Pr(\epsilon_2 \geqslant c_2 \mid \epsilon_1^c)$ which appear in (A2.61)–(A2.63) have the special forms

$$f(\epsilon_1^c) = \sigma_1^{-1} \phi(\epsilon_1^*) \qquad \text{(A2.64)}$$

$$\Pr(\epsilon_2 \geqslant c_2) = 1 - \Phi(c_2^*) \qquad \text{(A2.65)}$$

$$\Pr(\epsilon_2 \geqslant c_2 \mid \epsilon_1^c) = 1 - \Phi \left[\frac{c_2^* - \rho \epsilon_1^*}{(1 - \rho^2)^{1/2}} \right] \qquad \text{(A2.66)}$$

where $\epsilon_1^* = (\epsilon_1^c - \mu_1)/\sigma_1$, $c_2^* = (c_2 - \mu_2)/\sigma_2$ and $\rho = \sigma_{12}/\sigma_1\sigma_2$.

Appendix 3

The computation of probability integrals

Many of the likelihood functions derived in the chapters of this book involve probabilities and other quantities that cannot be expressed in closed form but are represented as the integral of a p.d.f. or some other function. This appendix sketches the methods available for the computation of such expressions. Although there is a wide range of possible approaches to this type of approximation problem, most of the common computational techniques are based on polynomial approximations. These usually involve expansions in terms of orthogonal polynomials, which are more convenient and have better convergence properties than simple Taylor series expansions.

A3.1 Orthogonal polynomials

Consider a sequence of polynomials $\{1, P_1(s), P_2(s), P_3(s), \ldots\}$, where s is a real continuously variable quantity and

$$P_k(s) = \alpha_{k0} + \alpha_{k1}s + \ldots + \alpha_{kk}s^k \tag{A3.1}$$

This is said to be a sequence of orthogonal polynomials with respect to an interval $[a, b]$ and a weight function $w(s)$ if each α_{kk} is non-zero and

$$\int_a^b w(s)\, P_j(s)\, P_k(s)\, \mathrm{d}s = 0 \qquad \text{for all } k \neq j. \tag{A3.2}$$

We abbreviate expressions like (A3.2) as follows:

$$\langle P_j P_k \rangle = 0 \tag{A3.3}$$

where the dependence on $w(.)$ and $[a, b]$ is implicit.

Such families of orthogonal polynomials have many convenient properties, for instance the following.

i $\langle P_k\, q \rangle = 0$ for all $q(s)$ that are polynomials of degree less than k.

ii Any polynomial $q(s)$ of order k or less can be expressed in the form

$$q(s) = \sum_{i=0}^{k} c_i\, P_i(s). \tag{A3.4}$$

iii $P_k(s)$ has k real distinct roots, all of which lie in the interval $[a, b]$.

iv The orthogonal polynomials can be generated recursively, starting with $P_0(s) = 0$, from the following recurrence relation:

$$P_{k+1}(s) = \frac{\alpha_{k+1\,k+1}}{\alpha_{kk}} (s - B_k)\, P_k(s) - C_k\, P_{k-1}(s) \tag{A3.5}$$

where

$$B_k = \frac{\langle sP_k(s)\, P_k(s) \rangle}{\langle P_k(s)\, P_k(s) \rangle}$$

and

$$C_k = 0 \qquad \text{for } k = 0$$

$$= \frac{(\alpha_{k+1\,k+1})(\alpha_{k-1\,k-1})\, \langle P_k\, P_k \rangle}{(\alpha_{kk})^2\, \langle P_{k-1}\, P_{k-1} \rangle} \qquad \text{for } k > 0.$$

Orthogonal polynomials are widely used in the approximation of computationally difficult functions, such as probability integrals, although they are also used for other purposes. The choice of a specific family of polynomials usually depends on the nature of the problem at hand; for example, Kiefer (1985) has used an expansion in terms of Laguerre polynomials as a general alternative to the exponential distribution, which has density $\exp(-s)$ and is defined on $[0, \infty]$. Hermite polynomials are often involved in expansions associated with the normal distribution.

The main motivation for orthogonal polynomials is their value in simplifying the problem of least-squares approximation of a function by a polynomial of given order. The least-squares problem for weight function $w(s)$ and interval $[a, b]$ is

$$\min_{q \in Q_k} \langle (g-q)\,(g-q) \rangle \tag{A3.6}$$

where $g(.)$ is the function to be approximated over the interval $[a, b]$ and Q_k is the set of all kth order polynomials. Since $q(s)$ can always be expressed in the form $c_0 P_0(s) + \ldots + c_k P_k(s)$, and since the $P_i(s)$ are orthogonal, we have

$$\min_{c_0 \ldots c_k} \left(\langle g\, g \rangle - 2\sum_{i=0}^{k} c_i\, \langle g\, P_i \rangle + \sum_{i=0}^{k} c_i^2\, \langle P_i\, P_i \rangle \right). \tag{A3.7}$$

Table A3.1 Some common families of orthogonal polynomials

	Chebyshev	Legendre	Hermite	Laguerre
$w(s)$	$(1-s^2)^{-1/2}$	1	$\exp(-s^2)$	$\exp(-s)$
$[a, b]$	$[-1, +1]$	$[-1, +1]$	$[-\infty, +\infty]$	$[0, +\infty]$
$P_k(s)$:				
$k=0$	1	1	1	1
$k=1$	s	s	$2s$	$1-s$
$k=2$	$2s^2-1$	$(3s^2-1)/2$	$4s^2-2$	$(s-4s+2)/2$
$k=3$	$4s^3-3s$	$(5s^3-3s)/2$	$8s^3-12s$	$(-s^3+9s^2-18s+6)/6$
$k=4$	$8s^4-8s^2+1$	$(35s^4-30s^2+3)/8$	$16s^4-48s^2+12$	$(s^4-16s^3+72s^2-96s+24)/24$

Performing this minimization, the least-squares approximating polynomial is a combination of $P_0(s) \ldots P_k(s)$ with coefficients

$$c_i = \frac{\langle g\, P_i \rangle}{\langle P_i\, P_i \rangle} \qquad i=0, \ldots, k \tag{A3.8}$$

It is occasionally possible to evaluate these coefficients by analytical methods; alternatively, the integrals defining the numerator and denominator of (A3.8) can be approximated by numerical quadrature. For many standard functions $g(s)$, tables of coefficients are available (see Abramovitz and Stegun, 1965, and Luke, 1975, for many examples).

A3.2 Numerical quadrature

Most of the difficult computational problems in microeconometrics involve the evaluation of definite integrals. In such cases, numerical integration or quadrature is sometimes used as an alternative to series approximation. Quadrature techniques approximate the integral by a weighted sum, derived from an underlying polynomial approximation to the integrand. Consider the following integral:

$$I = \int_a^b g(s)\, \mathrm{d}s. \tag{A3.9}$$

Now approximate $g(.)$ by a kth order polynomial $q_k(s)$ chosen to coincide with $g(s)$ at each of a set of points $s_0, \ldots, s_k$ in the interval $[a, b]$. This interpolating polynomial can always be written in the Laplace form

$$q_k(s) = g(s_0)\ell_{k0}(s) + \ldots + g(s_k)\ell_{kk}(s) \tag{A3.10}$$

where

$$\ell_{ki}(s) = \prod_{\substack{j=0 \\ j\neq i}}^{k} \frac{s - s_j}{s_i - s_j}. \tag{A3.11}$$

Substituting $q_k(s)$ for the integrand in (A3.9), and using (A3.10)–(A3.11), the resulting approximation is

$$\hat{I} = c_{k0}\, g(s_0) + \ldots + c_{kk}\, g(s_k) \tag{A3.12}$$

where

$$c_{ki} = \int_a^b \ell_{ki}(s)\, \mathrm{d}s \tag{A3.13}$$

is a constant depending on the interval $[a, b]$ and the chosen ordinates $s_0 \ldots s_k$, but not on the function $g(.)$.

Different quadrature rules result from different choices for k and $s_0 \ldots s_k$. Some of the more common are as follows.

midpoint rule:	$k=0,\ s_0=(a+b)/2,\ \hat{I} = (b-a)\, g[(b-a)/2]$
trapezoidal rule:	$k=1,\ s_0 = a,\ s_1 = b,\ \hat{I} = (b-a)[g(a)+g(b)]/2$
Simpson's rule:	$k=2,\ s_0=a,\ s_1 = (a+b)/2,\ s_2 = b,$ $\hat{I} = (b-a)\{g(a)+4g[(a+b)/2]+g(b)\}/6.$

These are extremely crude approximations if applied directly in this form. To improve on them, it is usual to adopt a higher-order polynomial and a finer grid of ordinates or, more commonly, to express I as the sum of a large number of subintegrals:

$$I = \int_a^{d_1} g(s)\, ds + \int_{d_1}^{d_2} g(s)\, ds + \ldots + \int_{d_r}^{b} g(s)\, ds \tag{A3.14}$$

A simple quadrature rule is then applied to each of these subintegrals.

Many different algorithms exist. The choice of subintervals can be very important for the numerical accuracy of these techniques, and adaptive methods are often used. These attempt to determine an optimal choice of subintervals by examining the local behaviour of the integrand. Many of these methods incorporate a stopping rule involving the use of increasingly fine subdivisions until an acceptable level of estimated accuracy is achieved. A full discussion of these and other quadrature techniques can be found in Davis and Rabinowitz (1967).

The main drawback of these general-purpose quadrature algorithms is their computational cost. In cross-sectional econometric problems, a single evaluation of the log-likelihood function may require the calculation of thousands of such integrals, and the computational efficiency of the algorithm is often critically important in determining whether a particular econometric technique is feasible. Unfortunately, quadrature is usually much more costly than formal series approximation, often requiring the evaluation of $g(.)$ at 40 or 50 points for acceptable accuracy.

However, Gaussian quadrature algorithms are available for many integrals, and these often provide the best of both worlds: cost comparable with that of a series approximation, but freedom from the necessity of deriving problem-specific expansions. Gaussian quadrature rules break the integrand up into two parts: $g(s) = w(s)h(s)$, where $w(s)$ is a weight function chosen so that $h(s)$ is smooth and well approximated by a low-order polynomial. If we make this approximation

$$I = \int_a^b w(s)h(s)\,\mathrm{d}s \approx \int_a^b w(s)q_k(s)\,\mathrm{d}s \tag{A3.15}$$

where $q_k(s)$ can again be written in the Laplace form (A3.10)–(A3.11). Thus

$$\hat{I} = c_{k0}h(s_0) + \ldots + c_{kk}h(s_k) \tag{A3.16}$$

where $s_0, \ldots, s_k$ are arbitrary points in $[a, b]$, and $c_{k0}, \ldots, c_{kk}$ are constants given by

$$c_{ki} = \int_a^b w(s)\ell_{ki}(s)\,\mathrm{d}s. \tag{A3.17}$$

The value of this approach lies in the following result, which guides the choice of $s_0, \ldots, s_k$ (see Conte and de Boor, 1972, chapter 5).

Theorem If $s_0, \ldots, s_k$ are chosen as the roots of the $(k+1)$th member $P_{k+1}(s)$ of the family of polynomials orthogonal with respect to $w(.)$ and $[a, b]$, the the Gaussian approximation (A3.16) is exact for any $h(s)$ that is polynomial of order $2k+1$ or less.

Tables of the coefficients c_{ki} and roots $s_0, \ldots, s_k$ are available for many of the combinations of weight function and integration interval that are encountered in practice. Waldman (1985), for example, demonstrates the superiority of Gaussian quadrature in the evaluation of a likelihood function for a duration model with unobserved heterogeneity. For his model, which involves the normal distribution, Waldman uses Gauss–Hermite quadrature based on $w(s) = \exp(-s^2)$ and $[a, b] = [-\infty, +\infty]$ and finds it approximately 20 times faster than either conventional quadrature or series expansion algorithms.

A3.3 The univariate normal cumulative distribution function

The c.d.f. of the standard normal distribution takes the form

$$\Phi(s) = \int_{-\infty}^{s} \varphi(t)\,\mathrm{d}t = (2\pi)^{-1/2} \int_{-\infty}^{s} \exp\left(-\frac{t^2}{2}\right) \mathrm{d}t \tag{A3.18}$$

This is not expressible in closed form, and cannot be evaluated directly within most computer programming languages. However, efficient algorithms for the evaluation of $\Phi(s)$ are now implemented in many statistical packages, and consequently problems which can be posed in terms of $\Phi(.)$ are not considered difficult from the computational viewpoint. Usually, the evaluation of $\Phi(.)$ requires only two to three times as much computer time as the evaluation of a logarithm or exponential.

Abramowitz and Stegun (1965) and Luke (1975) survey the older literature on the approximation of $\Phi(s)$ and the related error functions erf(s) and erfc(s); notable recent additions to this include papers by Kerridge and Cook (1976) and Divgi (1979). Many implementations are based on Chebyshev polynomials, usually in two parts: an approximation over the central part of the range (say $[-3, +3]$) in terms of $s/3$, and an approximation in terms of $3/s$ in the tails of the distribution. Global series approximations are also available, but the majority of these are either slowly convergent or are not convergent uniformly in s. This renders them dangerous to use for problems in which $\Phi(.)$ appears as part of a function that itself has to be integrated over an infinite range. Divgi (1979), however, gives a rapidly convergent series expansion that possesses a uniform error bound and is therefore suitable for such problems. This is based on a least-squares approximation to the Mills ratio $[1-\Phi(s)]/\varphi(s)$ over the interval $[0, +\infty]$, giving an expansion in terms of polynomials orthogonal with respect to a weight function $w(s) = \exp(-s^2)$ and an interval $[a, b] = [0, +\infty]$.

A3.4 Multivariate normal probabilities

Many econometric models, particularly models of discrete choice, involve probabilities of events that are defined in terms of two or more correlated random variables. Except for very special distributional assumptions, this leads to likelihood components that are expressible only as the multiple integral of a joint p.d.f. Such expressions raise formidable computational problems, even for well-known distributions such as the normal.

The c.d.f. of the standard multivariate normal distribution is

$$\Phi(a_1, \ldots, a_q; \mu, \Sigma) = \Pr(y_1 \leqslant a_1, \ldots, y_q \leqslant a_q)$$

$$= \int_{-\infty}^{a_1} \cdots \int_{-\infty}^{a_q} \varphi(y_1, \ldots, y_q; \mu, \Sigma)\, \mathrm{d}y_q \ldots \mathrm{d}y_1 \tag{A3.19}$$

where

$$\varphi(y_1, \ldots, y_q; \mu, \Sigma) = (2\pi)^{-1/2}\, |\Sigma|^{-1/2} \exp[-\tfrac{1}{2}(\mathbf{y}-\mu)'\Sigma^{-1}(\mathbf{y}-\mu)] \tag{A3.20}$$

where $\mathbf{y}' = (y_1 \ldots y_q)$. After standardization, μ is the zero vector and Σ is the correlation matrix. The general normal distribution can be converted to this form by standardizing $a_1, \ldots, a_q$ and transforming the covariance matrix into correlation form. The symmetry of the normal distribution implies that any inequalities of the form $y_i \geqslant a_i$ can be converted to the form of those in

(A3.19) by changing the sign of a_i and the non-diagonal elements of the ith row and column of Σ.

Although multivariate extensions of numerical quadrature are straightforward, their computational cost increases geometrically with the number of dimensions of integration. Thus quadrature is computationally expensive, and the integral (A3.19) is usually evaluated by series approximation for low-dimensional cases. There is, as yet, no really satisfactory algorithm available for normal probabilities defined in more than three or four dimensions.

A3.4.1 The bivariate normal

For the case of $q=2$, the p.d.f. (A3.20) is

$$\varphi(y_1, y_2; \rho) = (2\pi)^{-1} (1-\rho^2)^{-\frac{1}{2}} \exp - \tfrac{1}{2} \left[\frac{y_1^2 + y_2^2 - 2\rho y_1 y_2}{1 - \rho^2} \right] \qquad \text{(A3.21)}$$

where $\rho = \text{corr}(y_1, y_2)$. The corresponding c.d.f. is defined as

$$\Phi(a_1, a_2; \rho) = \int_{-\infty}^{a_1} \int_{-\infty}^{a_2} \varphi(y_1, y_2; \rho)\, \mathrm{d}y_2\, \mathrm{d}y_1. \qquad \text{(A3.22)}$$

The most successful algorithms for the evaluation of (A3.22) are based on series approximations. Such approximations proceed in two stages. Since the integrand (A3.21) is difficult to handle, (A3.22) is first transformed into a more convenient expression defined as a univariate integral. The integrand is then approximated by a simple series expansion and integrated term by term.

There are several algorithms in widespread use. The best known of these is due to Owen (1956), who shows that the c.d.f. can be written in the form

$$\Phi(a_1, a_2; \rho) = \tfrac{1}{2}[\Phi(a_1) + \Phi(a_2) - \delta] - T(a_1, b_1) - T(a_2, b_2) \qquad \text{(A3.23)}$$

where $\delta = 0$ if $a_1 a_2 \geqslant 0$ and $a_1 + a_2 \geqslant 0$ and $\delta = 1$ otherwise, $b_i = (a_i^2/a_1 a_2 - \rho)(1-\rho^2)^{-\frac{1}{2}}$ and

$$T(a, b) = (2\pi)^{-1} \int_0^b \frac{\exp[-a^2(1+t^2)/2]}{1+t^2}\, \mathrm{d}t \qquad \text{(A3.24)}$$

If the exponential function in (A3.24) is expanded in a power series and the resulting terms are integrated, (A3.24) becomes

$$T(a, b) = (2\pi)^{-1} \left(\arctan b - \sum_{i=0}^{\infty} c_i\, b^{2i+1} \right) \qquad \text{(A3.25)}$$

where

$$c_i = \frac{(-1)^i}{2i+1}\left[1 - \exp\left[\frac{-a^2}{2}\right]\sum_{j=0}^{i}\frac{a^{2j}}{j!\,2^j}\right]. \tag{A3.26}$$

This expansion converges rather slowly for large a_1 and a_2, and several workers have modified Owen's algorithm in various ways to improve its numerical efficiency. Divgi (1979) gives references to these, and also describes a superior algorithm based on a decomposition different from (A3.23). Most implementations of this type of algorithm achieve reasonable efficiency, with computing times of five to ten times that of the univariate normal c.d.f. being necessary for acceptable accuracy. Thus, estimation problems involving the bivariate normal c.d.f. are usually feasible on modern computers.

An important determinant of the cost of a non-linear estimation problem is the method used to calculate the gradient of the log-likelihood function. It is possible to avoid the necessity of deriving and programming the likelihood derivatives by employing an optimization algorithm that uses a difference approximation to the gradient vector. However, when the likelihood function involves the bivariate normal c.d.f., this raises two problems: firstly, the computer time required to compute the approximate gradient is very large, since it involves repeated evaluation of the likelihood function. Secondly, most algorithms achieve only a moderate degree of accuracy for the computed c.d.f. (usually only six to seven decimal places), and the resulting approximation errors can cause the differencing procedure to generate an approximate gradient of very low accuracy. Errors of this kind can severely affect the performance of the optimization algorithm.

Thus, it is usually wise to employ optimization methods that require knowledge of the analytical form of the likelihood gradient. For this, one requires the partial derivatives of the c.d.f. $\Phi(a_1, a_2; \rho)$ with respect to a_1, a_2 and ρ, since ρ is usually a parameter to be estimated and a_1 and a_2 are usually dependent on the other model parameters. These derivatives are as follows:

$$\frac{\partial\Phi(a_1, a_2; \rho)}{\partial\rho} = \frac{\rho}{1-\rho^2}\,[\Phi(a_1, a_2; \rho) - 1] \tag{A3.27}$$

$$\frac{\partial\Phi(a_1, a_2; \rho)}{\partial a_1} = \Phi\left[\frac{a_2 - \rho a_1}{(1-\rho^2)^{1/2}}\right]\varphi(a_1) \tag{A3.28}$$

$$\frac{\partial\Phi(a_1, a_2; \rho)}{\partial a_2} = \Phi\left[\frac{a_1 - \rho a_2}{(1-\rho^2)^{1/2}}\right]\varphi(a_2). \tag{A3.29}$$

A3.4.2 Higher-dimensional normal probabilities

Algorithms for the evaluation of normal probabilities in three or more dimensions are much less widely available. Three main approaches are used.

Series approximation For the three-dimensional case, series approximations are usually computationally feasible provided that one is prepared to accept only moderate numerical accuracy (see, for instance, Steck, 1958). Such algorithms can be expected to be five to ten times slower than a comparable bivariate algorithm. For higher-dimensional cases, series methods are usually not feasible.

Simulation At first sight, simulation of normal probabilities appears to have much to recommend it. A crude Monte Carlo algorithm proceeds as follows: (a) generate a vector of q pseudo-random variates; (b) perform the linear transformation required to convert this into an $N(\mu, \Sigma)$ vector; (c) determine whether or not this vector satisfies the inequalities ($y_1 \leqslant a_1$, . . ., $y_q \leqslant a_q$). These steps are repeated a large number of times, and the frequency with which the inequalities are satisfied is used as the estimate of the c.d.f.

The advantages of this algorithm are that its computational cost increases only quadratically with q; it can be used to evaluate probabilities over quite general regions in y space; it can easily be modified to many non-normal cases; and sampling theory gives a good indication of its likely accuracy. Unfortunately, despite these theoretical advantages, simulation methods are usually far too expensive for routine use. If R is the number of replication and P is the probability to be estimated, then elementary sampling theory implies that the variance of the simulated probability is $P(1-P)/R$. Thus, to achieve an accuracy of order ϵ, one must perform $R = P(1-P)/\epsilon^2$ replications. For a small probability, $P = 0.01$, and only moderate accuracy, $\epsilon = 0.0001$, the required number of replications is nearly a million, and for $p = 0.5$ it is 25 million. Although this enormous cost can be reduced by variance reduction techniques, simulation algorithms remain unsuitable for problems in which probabilities must be re-evaluated many times. The study by Lerman and Manski (1981) is a good illustration of the practical limitations of this approach.

However, recent work by McFadden (1987) has established an alternative simulation-based approach which integrates simulation into a non-ML estimation procedure rather than using it as a method of computing the probability components of a likelihood function. This is discussed in chapter 3.

Clark's approximation Many discrete choice models require the evaluation of probabilities of the form $\Pr(u_0 > \max\{u_1, \ldots, u_q\})$, where the u_i are interpreted as random utilities (see chapter 3). If we define y_i to be $u_i - u_0$, then this probability is the c.d.f. of $y_1, \ldots, y_q$ evaluated at the origin. If the original utilities are normal (in other words, if we are dealing with the multinomial probit model), then $y_1, \ldots, y_q$ are also jointly normal. Clark's (1961) approximation proceeds by expressing the maximum of $u_1, \ldots, u_q$ as the result of a sequence of nested binary maximizations: $\max\{u_1, \max\{u_2, \ldots \max\{u_{q-1}, u_q\} \ldots\}\}$. The inner part of the probability involves the random variable $u^*_{q-1} = \max\{u_{q-1}, u_q\}$. Clark gives expressions for the first and second moments of the $(q-1)$-dimensional random vector $(u_1 \ldots u^*_{q-1})$ and approximates their joint distribution by a multivariate normal distribution with those moments. This reduces the dimensionality of the problem by one, and the process is repeated until we reach a probability $\Pr(u_1 > u^*_2)$ which can be evaluated in terms of the univariate normal c.d.f.

Daganzo (1980) presents the details of this approximation, and advocates its use in applications. However, the approximation is known to be rather poor, particularly in the tails of the distribution and for negatively correlated utilities. Moreover, little is known about its performance in more than three dimensions. Its other drawback is that it is not useful for evaluating an arbitrary normal c.d.f. Although one can always express a q-dimensional c.d.f. in the form of a probability of the probit type, simply by constructing an appropriate set of $q+1$ dummy random variables $u_0, \ldots u_q$, it is possible to do this in an infinite number of ways, and each one results in a different arbitrary approximation.

A3.5 Partially integrated normal densities

When a multivariate econometric problem involves both continuous and discrete variables, the likelihood function is composed of terms that are probability densities with respect to some variables and integrated probability functions with respect to others. Under normality, the general term is the following:

$$I = \int_{-\infty}^{a_1} \ldots \int_{-\infty}^{a_p} \varphi(y_1, \ldots, y_p, y_{p+1}, \ldots, y_q; \mu, \Sigma)\, \mathrm{d}y_p \ldots \mathrm{d}y_1. \quad \text{(A3.30)}$$

In the special case of normality, such expressions can be decomposed multiplicatively into simple p.d.f. and c.d.f. components by exploiting the following result.

Theorem Let $(\mathbf{y}^{1\prime} \mid \mathbf{y}^{2\prime}) = (y_1 \ldots y_p\, y_{p+1} \ldots y_q)$ and define $\mu^1 = E(\mathbf{y}^1)$, $\mu^2 = E(\mathbf{y}^2)$, $\Sigma^{11} = \text{cov}(\mathbf{y}^1)$, $\Sigma^{22} = \text{cov}(\mathbf{y}^2)$ and $\Sigma^{12} = \text{cov}(\mathbf{y}^1, \mathbf{y}^2)$. Then $\mathbf{y}^1 | \mathbf{y}^2 \sim N(\mu^*(\mathbf{y}^2), \Sigma^*)$, where $\mu^*(\mathbf{y}^2) = \mu^1 + \Sigma^{12}(\Sigma^{22})^{-1}(\mathbf{y}^2 - \mu^2)$ and $\Sigma^* = \Sigma^{11} - \Sigma^{12}(\Sigma^{22})^{-1}\Sigma^{21}$. Thus, by Bayes' theorem,

$$\varphi(\mathbf{y}^1, \mathbf{y}^2; \mu, \Sigma) = \varphi(\mathbf{y}^1; \mu^*(\mathbf{y}^2), \Sigma^*)\, \varphi(\mathbf{y}^2; \mu^2, \Sigma^{22}) \quad \text{(A3.31)}$$

Using this result, (A3.30) becomes

$$I = \varphi(\mathbf{y}^2; \boldsymbol{\mu}^2, \Sigma^{22}) \int_{-\infty}^{a_1} \cdots \int_{-\infty}^{a_p} \varphi(\mathbf{y}^1; \boldsymbol{\mu}^*(\mathbf{y}^2), \Sigma^*)\, \mathrm{d}y_p \ldots \mathrm{d}y_1 \qquad \text{(A3.32)}$$

The first part of (A3.32) is merely a $(q-p)$-dimensional normal p.d.f., and the second is a p-dimensional c.d.f. which can be evaluated by the methods discussed above.

In the important special case of the bivariate normal density integrated with respect to one of its arguments, this result is

$$I = \Phi\left[\frac{a_1 - \mu_1 - \sigma_{12}(y_2 - \mu_2)/\sigma_{22}}{(\sigma_{11} - \sigma_{12}^2/\sigma_{22})^{½}}\right]\sigma_{22}^{-½}\,\varphi\left(\frac{y_2 - \mu_2}{\sigma_{22}}\right) \qquad \text{(A3.33)}$$

$$= \Phi\left\{\frac{a_1 - \mu_1}{[\sigma_{11}(1-\rho^2)]^{½}} - \frac{\rho(y_2 - \mu_2)}{[\sigma_{22}(1-\rho^2)]^{½}}\right\}\sigma_{22}^{-½}\,\varphi\left(\frac{y_2 - \mu_2}{\sigma_{22}^{½}}\right) \qquad \text{(A3.34)}$$

where $\rho = \mathrm{corr}(y_1, y_2) = \sigma_{12}(\sigma_{11}\sigma_{22})^{-½}$ and $\Phi(.)$ and $\varphi(.)$ here represent the c.d.f. and p.d.f. of the univariate $N(0, 1)$ distribution.

References

Abramowitz, M. and Stegun, I. A. (eds) (1965), *Handbook of Mathematical Functions*, Washington, DC: US Government Printing Office.

Aitchison, J. and Silvey, S. (1957), 'The generalisation of probit analysis to the case of multiple response', *Biometrika*, 44, 131–40.

Aigner, D. J. (1985), 'The residential electricity time-of-use pricing experiments: what have we learned?'. In J. A. Hausman and D. A. Wise (eds), *Social Experimentation*, Chicago, IL: Chicago University Press.

Allen, G. E., Fitts, J. A. and Glatt, E. S. (1981). 'The experimental housing allowance program'. In K. L. Bradbury and A. Downs (eds), *Do Housing Allowances Work?*, Washington, DC: Brookings Institution.

Amemiya, T. (1973), 'Regression analysis when the dependent variable is truncated normal', *Econometrica*, 45, 919–38.

Amemiya, T. (1974), 'Multivariate regression and simultaneous equation models when the dependent variables are truncated normal', *Econometrica*, 42, 999–1012.

Amemiya, T. (1978), 'On a two-step estimation of a multivariate logit model', *Journal of Econometrics*, 8, 13–21.

Amemiya, T. (1981), 'Qualitative response models: a survey', *Journal of Economic Literature*, 19, 483–536.

Amemiya, T. (1984), 'Tobit models: a survey', *Journal of Econometrics*, 24, 3–61.

Amemiya, T. (1986), *Advanced Econometrics*, Oxford: Basil Blackwell.

Amemiya, T. and Boskin, M. (1974), 'Regression analysis when the dependent variable is truncated lognormal, with an application to the determinants of the duration of welfare dependency', *International Economic Review*, 15, 485–96.

Amemiya, T. and Sen, G. (1977), 'The consistency of the maximum likelihood estimator in a disequilibrium model', *Technical Report 238*, Institute for Mathematical Studies in the Social Sciences, Stanford University.

Anderson, T. W. (1958), *An Introduction to Multivariate Statistical Analysis*, New York: Wiley.

Arabmazar, A. and Schmidt, P. (1981), 'Further evidence of the robustness of the Tobit estimator to heteroscedasticity', *Journal of Econometrics*, 17, 253–8.

Arabmazar, A. and Schmidt, P. (1982), 'An investigation of the robustness of Tobit estimator to non-normality', *Econometrica*, 50, 1055–63.

Arellano, M. and Meghir, C. (1987), 'Labour supply and hours constraints', Discussion paper, University College London.

Arrow, K. J. (1951), *Social Choice and Individual Values*, New York: Wiley.

Arrow, K. J. and Enthoven, A. C. (1961), 'Quasi-concave programming', *Econometrica*, 29, 779–800.

Atkinson, A. B. and Mickelwright, J. (1983), 'On the reliability of income data in the Family Expenditure Survey 1970–1977', *Journal of the Royal Statistical Society, Series A*, 146, 33–61.

Atkinson, A. B., Gomulka, J. and Stern, N. H. (1984a), 'Household expenditure on tobacco 1970–1980: evidence from the Family Expenditure Survey', Discussion paper no. 57, ESRC Programme on Taxation, Incentives and the Distribution of Income, London School of Economics.

Atkinson, A. B., Gomulka, J. and Stern, N. H. (1984b), 'Expenditure on alcoholic drink by households: evidence from the Family Expenditure Survey 1970–1980', Discussion paper no. 60, ESRC Programme on Taxation, Incentives and the Distribution of Income, London School of Economics.

Atkinson, A. B., Gomulka, J., Micklewright, J. and Rau, N. (1984), 'Unemployment benefit, duration and incentives in Britain: how robust is the evidence?', *Journal of Public Economics*, 23, 3–26.

Barro, R. and Grossman, H. (1976), *Money, Employment and Inflation*, Cambridge: Cambridge University Press.

Becker, G. S. (1960), 'An economic analysis of fertility'. In *Demographic and Economic Change in Developed Countries*, Princeton, NJ: Princeton University Press.

Becker, G. S. and Tomes, N. (1976), 'Child endowments and the quantity and quality of children', *Journal of Political Economy*, 84 (supplement), S143–62.

Beggs, S., Cardell, S. and Hausman, J. A. (1981), 'Assessing the potential demand for electric cars', *Journal of Econometrics*, 17, 1–20.

Bera, A. K., Jarque, C. M. and Lee, L.-F. (1984), 'Testing the normality assumption in limited dependent variable models', *International Economic Review*, 25, 563–78.

Blackorby, C., Primont, D. and Russell, R. R. (1978), *Duality, Separability and Functional Structure*, Amsterdam: North-Holland.

Block, H. D. and Marschak, J. (1960), 'Random orderings and stochastic theories of responses'. In I. Olgin (ed.), *Contributions to Probability and Statistics*, Stanford, CA: Stanford University Press.

Blomquist, S. (1983), 'The effect of income taxation on male labour supply in Sweden', *Journal of Public Economics*, 24, 169–97.

Blundell, R. W. and Meghir, C. (1987), 'Bivariate alternatives to the Tobit model', *Journal of Econometrics*, *Annals 1987-1*, 34, 179–200.

Blundell, R. W. and Walker, I. (1982), 'Modelling the joint determination of household labour supplies and commodity demands', *Economic Journal*, 92, 351–64.

Blundell, R. W., Ham, J. and Meghir, C. (1987), 'Unemployment and female labour supply', *Economic Journal* (conference papers), 97, 44–64.

Boskin, M. J. (1974), 'A conditional logit model of occupational choice', *Journal of Political Economy*, 82, 389–98.

Bradley, R. A. and Gart, J. J. (1962), 'The asymptotic properties of ML estimators when sampling from associated populations', *Biometrika*, 49, 205–14.

Brown, C. V. (ed.) (1981), *Taxation and Labour Supply*, London: George Allen and Unwin.

Buckley, J. and James, I. (1979), 'Linear regression with censored data', *Biometrika*, 66, 429–36.

Burdett, K., Kiefer, N. M. and Sharma, S. (1985), 'Layoffs and duration dependence in a model of turnover', *Journal of Econometrics, Annals 1985 1*, 28, 51–70.

Burtless, G. and Greenberg, D. (1982), 'Inferences concerning labour supply behaviour based on limited-duration experiments', *American Economic Review*, 72, 488–97.

Burtless, G. and Hausman, J. A. (1978), 'The effect of taxation on labour supply', *Journal of Political Economy*, 86, 1103–30.

Butler, J. S. and Moffitt, R. (1982), 'A computationally efficient quadrature procedure for the one-factor multinomial probit model', *Econometrica*, 50, 761–4.

Chipman, J. S., Hurwicz, L., Richter, M. K. and Sonnenschein, H. F. (eds) (1971), *Preferences, Utility and Demand*, New York: Harcourt Brace.

Chow, G. S. (1983), *Econometrics*, New York: McGraw-Hill.

Christensen, L. R., Jorgenson, D.W. and Lau, L. J. (1975), 'Transcendental logarithmic utility functions', *American Economic Review*, 65, 367–82.

Clark, C. (1961), 'The greatest of a finite set of random variables', *Operations Research*, 9, 145–62.

Cochran, W. G. (1963), *Sampling Techniques*, New York: Wiley.

Cogan, J. F. (1981), 'Fixed costs and labour supply', *Econometrica*, 49, 945–64.

Cohen, R. and Lakhani, B. (1986), *National Welfare Benefits Handbook* (15th edn), London: Child Poverty Action Group.

Conte, S. D. and de Boor, C. (1972), *Elementary Numerical Analysis*, New York: McGraw-Hill.

Cosslett, S. R. (1981), 'Maximum likelihood estimator for choice-based samples', *Econometrica*, 49, 1289–316.

Cox, D. R. (1972), 'Regression models and life tables', *Journal of the Royal Statistical Society, Series A*, 148, 82–117.

Cox, D. R. (1975), 'Partial likelihood', *Biometrika*, 62, 269–76.

Cox, D. R. and Hinkley, D. V. (1974), *Theoretical Statistics*, London: Chapman and Hall.

Cox, D. R. and Isham, V. (1980), *Point Processes*, London: Chapman and Hall.

Cox, D. R. and Oakes, D. (1984), *Analysis of Survival Data*, London: Chapman and Hall.

Cox, D. R. and Snell, E. J. (1968), 'A general definition of residuals', *Journal of the Royal Statistical Society, Series B*, 30, 248–75.

Cragg, J. G. (1971), 'Some statistical models for limited dependent variables with application to the demand for durable goods', *Econometrica*, 39, 829–44.

Cragg, J. G. and Uhler, R. (1970), 'The demand for automobiles', *Canadian Journal of Economics*, 3, 386–406.

Cramer, J. S. (1962), *A Statistical Model of the Ownership of Major Consumer Durables*, Cambridge: Cambridge University Press.

Daganzo, C. (1980), *Multinomial Probit*, New York: Academic Press.

Davis, P. J. and Rabinowitz, P. (1967), *Numerical Integration*, New York: Blaisdell.

Deaton, A. S. (1979), 'The distance function in consumer behaviour with applications to index numbers and optimal taxation', *Review of Economic Studies*, 46, 391–405.

Deaton, A. S. (1981), 'Theoretical and empirical approaches to consumer demand under rationing'. In A. S. Deaton (ed.), *Essays in the Theory and Measurement of Consumer Behaviour*, Cambridge: Cambridge University Press.

Deaton, A. S. (1986), 'Demand analysis'. In Z. Griliches and M. D. Intriligator (eds), *Handbook of Econometrics*, New York, Elsevier, vol. III, ch. 30.

Deaton, A. S. and Irish, M. (1984), 'A statistical model for zero expenditures in household budgets', *Journal of Public Economics*, 23, 59–80.

Deaton, A. S. and Muellbauer, J. (1980a), *Economics and Consumer Behaviour*, Cambridge: Cambridge University Press.

Deaton, A. S. and Muellbauer, J. (1980b), 'An almost ideal demand system', *American Economic Review*, 70, 312–26.

Deaton, A. S. and Muellbauer, J. (1981), 'Functional forms for labour supply and commodity demands with and without quantity rationing', *Econometrica*, 49, 1521–32.

Debreu, G. (1951), 'The coefficient of resource utilisation', *Econometrica*, 19, 273–92.

Debreu, G. (1954), 'Representation of a preference ordering by a numerical function'. In R. M. Thrall, C. H. Coombs and R. L. Davis (eds), *Decision Processes*, New York: Wiley.

Dempster, A. P., Laird, N. M. and Rubin, D. B. (1977), 'Maximum likelihood from incomplete data via the EM algorithm', *Journal of the Royal Statistical Society, Series B*, 39, 1–38.

Desai, M., Keil, M. and Wadhwani, S. (1984), 'Incomes policy in a political business cycle environment: a structural model for the UK economy 1961–1980'. In A. J. Hughes-Hallett (ed.), *Applied Decision Analysis and Economic Behaviour*, Dordrecht: Martinus Nijhoff.

Diamond, P. A. and Hausman, J. A. (1984), 'The retirement and unemployment behaviour of older men'. In H. Aaron and G. Burtless (eds), *Retirement and Economic Behaviour*, Washington, DC: Brookings Institute.

Dickens, W. T. and Lundberg, S. J. (1985), 'Hours restrictions and labour supply', *Working paper no. 1638*, National Bureau of Economic Research.

Diewert, E. (1974), 'Applications of duality theory'. In M. D. Intriligator and D. A. Kendrick (eds), *Frontiers of Quantitative Economics II*, Amsterdam: North-Holland.

Divgi, D. R. (1979), 'Calculation of univariate and bivariate normal probability functions', *Annals of Mathematical Statistics*, 50, 903–10.

Domencich, T. and McFadden, D. (1975), *Urban Travel Demand: A Behavioural Analysis*, Amsterdam: North-Holland.

Dubin, J. and McFadden, D. (1984), 'An econometric analysis of residential electric appliance holdings and consumption', *Econometrica*, 52, 345–62.

Duncan, G. (1980), 'Formulation and statistical analysis of the mixed continuous/discrete model in classical production theory', *Econometrica*, 48, 839–52.

Duncan, G. J. (ed.) (1984), *Years of Poverty, Years of Plenty*, Michigan: Institute for Social Research.

Duncan, G. M. (1986), 'A semi-parametric censored regression estimator', *Journal of Econometrics, Annals 1986-1*, 32, 5-34.

Efron, B. (1978), 'Regression and ANOVA with zero-one data: measures of residual variation', *Journal of the American Statistical Association*, 73, 113-21.

Elbers, C. and Ridder, G. (1982), 'True and spurious duration dependence: the identifiability of the proportional hazards model', *Review of Economic Studies*, 49, 402-11.

Fair, R. C. and Jaffee, D. M. (1972), 'Methods of estimation for markets in disequilibrium', *Econometrica*, 40, 497-514.

Farrell, M. J. (1954), 'The demand for motor cars in the United States', *Journal of the Royal Statistical Society, Series A*, 117, 171-201.

Fernandez, L. (1986), 'Non-parametric maximum likelihood estimation of censored regression models', *Journal of Econometrics, Annals 1986-1*, 32, 35-58.

Fields, G. S. and Mitchell, O. S. (1984), 'The effects of social security reforms on retirement ages and retirement incomes', *Journal of Public Economics*, 25, 143-59.

Flinn, C. and Heckman, J. (1982a), 'Models for the analysis of labour force dynamics'. In R. Basmann and G. Rhodes (eds), *Advances in Econometrics*, Greenwich, CT: JAI Press, vol. 1.

Flinn, C. and Heckman, J. (1982b), 'New methods for analysing structural models of labour force dynamics', *Journal of Econometrics*, 18, 115-68.

Goldberger, A. S. (1983), 'Abnormal selection bias'. In S. Karlin, T. Amemiya and L. A. Goodman (eds), *Studies in Econometrics, Time Series and Multivariate Statistics*, New York: Academic Press.

Goldfeld, S. M. and Quandt, R. E. (1975), 'Estimation in a disequilibrium model and the value of information', *Journal of Econometrics*, 3, 325-48.

Gorman, W. M. (1956), 'A possible procedure for analysing quality differentials in the egg market', reprinted in *Review of Economic Studies*, 47, 843-56.

Gorman, W. M. (1961), 'On a class of preference fields', *Metroeconomica*, 13, 53-6.

Gorman, W. M. (1976), 'Tricks with utility functions'. In M. Artis and R. Nobay (eds), *Essays in Economic Analysis*, Cambridge: Cambridge University Press.

Green, H. A. J. (1961), *Aggregation in Economic Analysis*, Princeton: Princeton University Press.

Griliches, Z. (1977), 'Estimating the returns to schooling: some econometric problems', *Econometrica*, 45, 1-22.

Gronau, R. (1974), 'Wage comparisons - a selectivity bias', *Journal of Political Economy*, 82, 1119-43.

Gumbel, E. J. (1961), 'Bivariate logistic distributions', *Journal of the American Statistical Association*, 56, 335-49.

Gustman, A. L. and Steinmeier, T. L. (1986), 'A structural retirement model', *Econometrica*, 54, 555-84.

Ham, J. (1982), 'Estimation of a labour supply model with censoring due to unemployment and underemployment', *Review of Economic Studies*, 49, 335-54.

Hanemann, W. M. (1984), 'Discrete/continuous models of consumer demand', *Econometrica*, 52, 541-61.

Harrison, A. and Stewart, M. (1987), 'Cyclical variation in strike-settlement probabilities', University of Warwick: mimeo.

Hausman, J. A. (1978), 'Specification tests in econometrics', *Econometrica*, 46, 1251-71.

Hausman, J. A. (1979a), 'Individual discount rates and the purchase and utilisation of energy-using durables', *Bell Journal of Economics*, 10, 33–54.
Hausman, J. A. (1979b), 'The econometrics of labour supply on convex budget sets', *Economics Letters*, 3, 171–4.
Hausman, J. A. (1980), 'The effect of wages, taxes and fixed costs on women's labour force participation', *Journal of Public Economics*, 14, 161–94.
Hausman, J. A. (1985), 'The econometrics of nonlinear budget sets', *Econometrica*, 53, 1255–82.
Hausman, J. A. and McFadden, D. (1984), 'A specification test for the multinomial logit model', *Econometrica*, 52, 1219–40.
Hausman, J. A. and Ruud, P. (1984), 'Family labour supply with taxes', *American Economic Review*, 74, 242–53.
Hausman, J. A. and Wise, D. A. (1976), 'Evaluation of results from truncated samples: the New Jersey Income Maintenance Experiment', *Annals of Economic and Social Measurement*, 6, 421–45.
Hausman, J. A. and Wise, D. A. (1977), 'Social experimentation, truncated distributions and efficient estimation', *Econometrica*, 45, 919–38.
Hausman, J. A. and Wise, D. A. (1978), 'A conditional probit model for qualitative choice: discrete decisions recognising interdependence and heterogeneous preferences', *Econometrica*, 46, 403–26.
Hausman, J. A. and Wise, D. A. (1979), 'Attrition bias in experimental and panel data: the Gary income maintenance experiment', *Econometrica*, 47, 455–73.
Hausman, J. A. and Wise, D. A. (1980), 'Discontinuous budget constraints and estimation: the demand for housing', *Review of Economic Studies*, 49, 75–96.
Hausman, J. A. and Wise, D. A. (1982), 'Stratification on endogenous variables and estimation: the Gary income maintenance experiment'. In C. Manski and D. McFadden (eds), *Structural analysis of discrete data: with econometric applications*, Cambridge, MA: MIT Press.
Hausman, J. A. and Wise, D. A. (eds) (1985), *Social Experimentation*, Chicago, IL: University of Chicago Press.
Hausman, J. A., Kinnucan and McFadden, D. (1979), 'A two-level electricity demand model: evaluation of the Connecticut time-of-day pricing test'. In D. J. Aigner (ed.), *Modelling and Analysis of Electricity Demand by Time-of-day*, Report EA-1304, Electric Power Research Institute, Palo Alto, CA.
Heckman, J. J. (1974), 'Shadow prices, market wages and labour supply', *Econometrica*, 42, 679–94.
Heckman, J. J. (1976), 'The common structure of statistical models of truncation, sample selection and limited dependent variables and a simple estimator for such models', *Annals of Economic and Social Measurement*, 5, 475–92.
Heckman, J. J. (1978), 'Dummy endogenous variables in a simultaneous equation system', *Econometrica*, 46, 931–60.
Heckman, J. J. (1979), 'Sample selection bias as a specification error', *Econometrica*, 47, 153–61.
Heckman, J. and Borjas, G. (1980), 'Does unemployment cause future unemployment? Definitions, questions and answers from a continuous time model of heterogeneity and state dependence', *Economica*, 47, 247–83.
Heckman, J. and Singer, B. (1982), 'The identification problem in econometric models for duration data'. In W. Hildenbrand (ed.), *Advances in Econometrics:*

Proceedings of World Meetings of the Econometric Society, Cambridge: Cambridge University Press.

Heckman, J. and Singer, B. (1984), 'A method for minimising the impact of distributional assumptions in econometric models for duration data, *Econometrica*, 52, 271–320.

Heckman, J. and Willis, R. J. (1977), 'A beta-logistic model for the analysis of sequential labour force participation by married women', *Journal of Political Economy*, 85, 27–58.

Hoadley, B. (1971), 'Asymptotic properties of maximum likelihood estimators for the independent not identically distributed case', *Annals of Mathematical Statistics*, 21, 182–97.

Horvath, W. J. (1968), 'A statistical model for the duration of wars and strikes', *Behavioural Science*, 13, 18–28.

Hsiao, C. (1986), *Analysis of Panel Data*, Cambridge: Cambridge University Press.

Hyman, H. H. (1954), *Interviewing in Social Research*, Chicago, IL: University of Chicago Press.

Ilmakunnas, S. and Pudney, S. E. (1987), 'A model of labour supply in the presence of hours restrictions', Discussion paper, Centre for Labour Economics, London School of Economics.

Jarque, C. M. (1981), 'A test for heteroscedasticity in a limited dependent variable model', *Australian Journal of Statistics*, 23, 159–63.

JICNARS (1971), *National Readership Survey*, London: Joint Industry Committee for National Readership Surveys.

Johnson, N. L. and Kotz, S. (1970), *Continuous Univariate Distributions - 1*, New York: Wiley.

Jovanovic, B. (1979), 'Job matching and the theory of turnover', *Journal of Political Economy*, 87, 972–90.

Kagel, J. H., Battalio, R. C., Rachlin, H., Green, L., Basmann, R. L. and Klein, W. R. (1975), 'Experimental studies of consumer demand behaviour using laboratory animals', *Economic Inquiry*, 13, 22–38.

Kalbfleisch, J. D. and Prentice, R. L. (1980), *Statistical Analysis of Failure Time Data*, New York: Wiley.

Kaplan, E. and Meier, P. (1958), 'Nonparametric estimation from incomplete observations', *Journal of the American Statistical Association*, 53, 467–81.

Karlin, S. and Taylor, H. M. (1975), *A First Course in Stochastic Processes*, New York: Academic Press.

Kay, J. A. and King, M. A. (1986), *The British Tax System* (4th edn), Oxford: Oxford University Press.

Kay, J. A., Keen, M. J. and Morris, C. N. (1984), 'Estimating consumption from expenditure data', *Journal of Public Economics*, 23, 169–81.

Keen, M. (1986), 'Zero expenditures and the estimation of Engel curves', *Journal of Applied Econometrics*, 1, 277–86.

Kemsley, W. F. F. (1975), 'Family Expenditure Survey. A study of differential response based on a comparison of the 1971 sample with the Census', *Statistical News*, November, London: HMSO.

Kemsley, W. F. F., Redpath, R. U. and Holmes, M. (1980), *Family Expenditure Survey Handbook*, London: HMSO.

Kennan, J. (1985), 'The duration of contract strikes in US manufacturing', *Journal of Econometrics, Annals 1985-1*, 28, 1-24.

Kerridge, D. F. and Cook, G. W. (1976), 'Yet another series for the normal integral', *Biometrika*, 66, 401-3.

Kiefer, N. (1978), 'Discrete parameter variation: efficient estimation of a switching model', *Econometrica*, 46, 427-34.

Kiefer, N. (1979), 'On the value of sample separation information', *Econometrica*, 47, 997-1003.

Kiefer, N. M. (1984), 'A simple test for heterogeneity in exponential models of duration', *Journal of Labour Economics*, 2, 539-49.

Kiefer, N. M. (1985), 'Specification diagnostics based on Laguerre alternatives for econometric models of duration', *Journal of Econometrics, Annals 1985-1*, 28, 135-54.

Kiefer, N. M. and Neumann, G. R. (1979), 'An empirical job-search model, with a test of the constant reservation wage hypothesis', *Journal of Political Economy*, 87, 89-107.

Kiefer, N. M. and Neumann, G. R. (1981), 'Individual effects in a non-linear model: explicit treatment of heterogeneity in the empirical job-search model', *Econometrica*, 49, 965-80.

King, M. (1980), 'An econometric model of tenure choice and demand for housing as a joint decision', *Journal of Public Economics*, 14, 137-59.

Kish, L. (1965), *Survey Sampling*, New York: Wiley.

Kohn, M., Manski, C. and Mundel, D. (1976), 'An empirical investigation of factors influencing college going behaviour', *Annals of Economic and Social Measurement*, 5, 391-419.

Kuhn, H. W. and Tucker, A. W. (1951), 'Nonlinear programming'. In J. Neyman (ed.), *Proceedings of the Second Berkeley Symposium on Mathematical Statistics and Probability*, Berkeley, CA: University of California Press.

Lancaster, K. J. (1971), *Consumer Demand: A New Approach*, New York: Columbia University Press.

Lancaster, T. (1972), 'A stochastic model for the duration of a strike', *Journal of the Royal Statistical Society, Series A*, 135, 257-71.

Lancaster, T. (1979), 'Econometric methods for the duration of unemployment', *Econometrica*, 47, 939-56.

Lancaster, T. (1985), 'Generalised residuals and heterogeneous duration models: with applications to the Weibull model', *Journal of Econometrics, Annals 1985-1*, 28, 155-69.

Lancaster, T. and Chesher, A. (1983), 'An econometric analysis of reservation wages', *Econometrica*, 51, 1661-76.

Lancaster, T. and Nickell, S. J. (1980), 'The analysis of re-employment probabilities for the unemployed', *Journal of the Royal Statistical Society, Series A*, 143, 141-65.

Lave, C. (1970), 'The demand for urban mass transit', *Review of Economics and Statistics*, 52, 320-3.

Layard, P. R. G., Barton, M. and Zabalza, A. (1980), 'Married women's participation and hours of work', *Econometrica*, 47, 51-72.

Le Cam, L. (1953), 'On some asymptotic properties of maximum likelihood estimates and related Bayes estimates', *University of California Publications in Statistics*, 1, 277–330.

Lee, L.-F. (1978), 'Unionism and wage rates: a simultaneous equations model with qualitative and limited dependent variables', *International Economic Review*, 19, 415–33.

Lee, L.-F. (1984), 'Tests for the bivariate normal distribution in econometric models with selectivity', *Econometrica*, 52, 843–63.

Lee, L.-F. and Maddala, G. S. (1985), 'The common structure of tests for selectivity bias, serial correlation, heteroscedasticity and non-normality in the Tobit model', *International Economic Review*, 26, 1–20.

Lee, L.-F. and Pitt, M. M. (1984), 'Microeconomic models of consumer and producer demand with limited dependent variables', Discussion paper, University of Minnesota.

Lerman, S. R. (1977), 'Location, housing, automobile ownership and mode to work: a joint choice model', *Transportation Research Board Record*, number 610.

Lerman, S. R. and Manski, C. (1981), 'On the use of simulated frequencies to approximate choice probabilities'. In C. Manski and D. McFadden (eds), *Structural Analysis of Discrete Data with Econometric Applications*, Cambridge, MA: MIT Press.

Lippmann, S. and McCall, J. (1976), 'The economics of job search: a survey', *Economic Inquiry*, 14, 155–89; 347–68.

Liviatan, N. (1961), 'Errors-in-variables and Engel curve analysis', *Econometrica*, 29, 336–62.

Luenberger, D. G. (1972), *Introduction to Linear and Nonlinear Programming*, Reading, MA: Addison-Wesley.

Luke, Y. L. (1975), *Mathematical Functions and their Approximations*, New York: Academic Press.

MaCurdy, T. E. (1981), 'An empirical model of labour supply in a life cycle setting', *Journal of Political Economy*, 89, 1059–85.

Maddala, G. S. (1983), *Limited-dependent and Qualitative Variables in Econometrics*, Cambridge: Cambridge University Press.

Maddala, G. S. and Nelson, F. D. (1975), 'Switching regression models with exogenous and endogenous switching', *Proceedings of the American Statistical Association* (Business and Economics section), 423–6.

Malinvaud, E. (1977), *The Theory of Unemployment Reconsidered*, Oxford: Basil Blackwell.

Manski, C. and Lerman, S. (1977), 'The estimation of choice probabilities from choice-based samples', *Econometrica*, 45, 1977–88.

Manski, C. and McFadden, D. (1981), 'Alternative estimates and sample designs for discrete choice analysis'. In C. Manski and D. McFadden (eds), *Structural Analysis of Discrete Data*, Cambridge, MA: MIT Press.

Marschak, J. (1960), 'Binary choice constraints and random utility indicators'. In K. J. Arrow, S. Karlin and P. Suppes (eds), *Mathematical Methods in the Social Sciences*, Stanford, CA: Stanford University Press.

McFadden, D. (1973), 'Conditional logit analysis of qualitative choice behaviour'. In P. Zarembka (ed.), *Frontiers in Econometrics*, New York: Academic Press.

McFadden, D. (1974), 'The measurement of urban travel demand', *Journal of Public Economics*, 3, 303–28.

McFadden, D. (1975), 'The revealed preferences of a public bureaucracy: theory', *Bell Journal of Economics*, 6, 401–16.

McFadden, D. (1976a), 'Quantal choice analysis: a survey', *Annals of Economic and Social Measurement*, 5, 363–90.

McFadden, D. (1976b), 'The revealed preferences of a public bureaucracy: empirical evidence', *Bell Journal of Economics*, 7, 55–72.

McFadden, D. (1978), 'Modelling the choice of residential location'. In A. Karlquist *et al.* (eds), *Spatial Interaction Theory and Residential Location*, Amsterdam: North-Holland.

McFadden, D. (1982), 'Econometric models of probabilistic choice'. In C. Manski and D. McFadden (eds), *Structural Analysis of Discrete Data: With Econometric Applications*, Cambridge, MA: MIT Press.

McFadden, D. (1984), 'Econometric analysis of qualitative response models'. In Z. Griliches and M. D. Intriligator (eds), *Handbook of Econometrics*, New York: Elsevier, vol. II, ch. 24.

McFadden, D. (1988), 'A method of simulated moments for the estimation of discrete response models without numerical integration', *Econometrica*, 56, forthcoming.

McFadden, D. and Richter, M. K. (1971), 'Revealed stochastic preference', Unpublished: MIT.

McKelvey, R. and Zavoina, W. (1975), 'A statistical model for the analysis of ordinal level dependent variables', *Journal of Mathematical Sociology*, 4, 103–20.

Mills, J. F. (1926), 'Table of the ratio: area to bounding ordinate for any portion of normal curve', *Biometrika*, 18, 395–400.

Mincer, J. (1974), *Schooling, Experience and Earnings*, New York: National Bureau of Economic Research.

Moffitt, R. (1982), 'The Tobit model, hours of work and institutional constraints', *Review of Economics and Statistics*, 64, 510–15.

Muthén, B. and Jöreskog, K. G. (1981), 'Selectivity problems in quasi-experimental studies', Unpublished: University of Uppsala.

Narendranathan, W. and Nickell, S. J. (1985), 'Modelling the process of job search', *Journal of Econometrics, Annals 1985-1*, 28, 29–50.

Neary, J. P. and Roberts, K. W. S. (1980), 'The theory of household behaviour under rationing', *European Economic Review*, 13, 25–42.

Nelson, F. D. (1977), 'Censored regression models with unobserved, stochastic censoring thresholds', *Journal of Econometrics*, 6, 309–27.

Nelson, F. D. (1981), 'A test for misspecification in the censored normal model', *Econometrica*, 49, 131–29.

Newey, W. K. (1987), 'Specification tests for distributional assumptions in the Tobit model', *Journal of Econometrics, Annals 1987-1*, 34, 125–46.

Nickell, S. J. (1979), 'Estimating the probability of leaving unemployment', *Econometrica*, 47, 1249–66.

Olsen, R. J. (1978), 'A note on the uniqueness of the maximum likelihood estimator for the Tobit model', *Econometrica*, 46, 1211–15.

Olsen, R. J. and Farkas, G. (1985), 'Conception intervals and the substitution of fertility over time', *Journal of Econometrics, Annals 1985-1*, 28, 103–12.

Olsen, R. J. and Wolpin, K. I. (1983), 'The impact of exogenous child mortality on fertility: a waiting time regression with dynamic regressors', *Econometrica*, 51, 731–49.

Owen, D. B. (1956), 'Tables for computing bivariate normal probabilities', *Annals of Mathematical Statistics*, 27, 1075–90.

Payne, S. L. (1951), *The Art of Asking Questions*, Princeton: Princeton University Press.

Pitt, M. M. and Lee, L.-F. (1983), 'The income distributional implications of energy price policy in Indonesia', Discussion paper, University of Minnesota.

Pollak, R. A. and Wales, T. J. (1981), 'Demographic variables in demand analysis', *Econometrica*, 49, 1533–51.

Portes, R. D. and Winter, D. (1980), 'Disequilibrium estimates for consumption goods markets in centrally-planned economies', *Review of Economic Studies*, 47, 137–59.

Powell, J. L. (1984), 'Least absolute deviations estimation for the censored regression models', *Journal of Econometrics*, 25, 303–25.

Powell, J. L. (1986), 'Symmetrically trimmed least squares estimation for Tobit models', *Econometrica*, 54, 1435–60.

Prais, S. J. and Houthakker, H. S. (1955), *The Analysis of Family Budgets*, Cambridge: Cambridge University Press.

Pudney, S. E. (1981), 'Instrumental variable estimation of a characteristics model of demand', *Review of Economic Studies*, 48, 417–33.

Pudney, S. E. (1985), 'Frequency of purchase and Engel curve estimation', Discussion paper A56, London School of Economics Econometrics Programme.

Pudney, S. E. (1987), 'A simple specification test for discrete response models', London School of Economics: mimeo.

Pudney, S. E. (1988a), 'A test of stochastic specification for models of choice in the presence of a nonlinear budget frontier', London School of Economics: mimeo.

Pudney, S. E. (1988b), 'Estimating Engel curves: a generalization of the P-Tobit model', *Finnish Economic Papers*, 1, forthcoming.

Quandt, R. E. (1956), 'Probabilistic theory of consumer behaviour', *Quarterly Journal of Economics*, 70, 507–36.

Quandt, R. E. (1968), 'Estimation of modal splits', *Transportation Research*, 2, 41–50.

Quigley, J. M. (1976), 'Housing demand in the short-run: an analysis of polychotomous choice', *Explorations in Economic Research*, 3, 76–102.

Ransom, M. R. (1987), 'A comment on consumer demand systems with binding non-negativity constraints', *Journal of Econometrics*, 34, 355–60.

Redpath, R. U. (1986), 'A second study of differential response comparing Census characteristics of FES respondents and non-respondents', *Statistical News*, February, London: HMSO.

Robinson, P. M. (1986a), 'Nonparametric methods in specification', *Economic Journal* (supplement), 96, 134–41.

Robinson, P. M. (1986b), 'Semiparametric econometrics: a survey', Discussion paper, London School of Economics.

Rosen, H. S. (1976), 'Taxes in a labour supply model with joint wage-hours determination', *Econometrica*, 44, 485–507.

Rosen, H. S. (1979), 'Housing decisions and the US income tax: an econometric analysis', *Journal of Public Economics*, 11, 1-23.

Rosen, H. S. and Quandt, R. E. (1978), 'Estimation of a disequilibrium aggregate labour market', *Review of Economics and Statistics*, 60, 371–9.

Rosett, R. N. and Nelson F. D. (1976), 'Estimation of a two-limit probit regression model', *Econometrica*, 43, 141–6.

Rothbarth, E. (1941), 'The measurement of changes in real income under conditions of rationing', *Review of Economic Studies*, 8, 100–7.

Schmidt, P. (1981), 'Constraints on the parameters of simultaneous Tobit and probit models'. In C. Manski and D. McFadden (eds), *Structural Analysis of Discrete Data with Econometric Applications*, Cambridge, MA: MIT Press.

Schultz, T. (1969), 'An economic model of family planning and fertility', *Journal of Political Economy*, 77, 153–80.

Sealey, C. W. (1979), 'Credit rationing in the commercial loan market: estimates of a structural model under conditions of disequilibrium', *Journal of Finance*, 34, 689–702.

Simmons, P. J. (1974), *Choice and Demand*, London: Macmillan.

Small, K. A. (1987), 'A discrete choice model for ordered alternatives', *Econometrica*, 55, 409–24.

Smith, R. and Rowland, M. (1986), *Rights Guide to Non-means-tested Social Security Benefits* (8th edn), London: Child Poverty Action Group.

Smith, R. J. and Blundell, R. W. (1986), 'An exogeneity test for a simultaneous equation Tobit model with an application to labour supply', *Econometrica*, 54, 679–85.

Spiegelman, R. G. and Yaeger, K. E. (1980), 'Overview: the Seattle and Denver income maintenance experiments', *Journal of Human Resources*, 15, 463–79.

Steck, G. P. (1958), 'A table for computing trivariate normal probabilities', *Annals of Mathematical Statistics*, 29, 780–800.

Stern, N. (1986), 'On the specification of labour supply functions'. In R. Blundell and I. Walker (eds), *Unemployment, Search and Labour Supply*, Cambridge: Cambridge University Press.

Stone, R. (1954), 'Linear expenditure systems and demand analysis: an application to the pattern of British demand', *Economic Journal*, 64, 511–27.

Theil, H. (1971), *Principles of Econometrics*, New York: Wiley.

Tobin, J. (1958), 'Estimation of relationships for limited dependent variables', *Econometrica*, 26, 24–36.

Townsend, P. (1979), *Poverty in the United Kingdom*, Harmondsworth: Penguin.

Tsiatis, A. A. (1981), 'A large sample study of Cox's regression model', *The Annals of Statistics*, 9, 93–108.

Tuma, N. B., Hannan, M. T. and Groenwald, L. P. (1979), 'Dynamic analysis of event histories', *American Journal of Sociology*, 84, 820–54.

Tversky, A. (1972a), 'Choice by elimination', *Journal of Mathematical Psychology*, 9, 341–67.

Tversky, A. (1972b), 'Elimination by aspects: a theory of choice', *Psychological Review*, 79, 281–99.

Tversky, A. and Sattath, S. (1979), 'Preference trees', *Psychology Review*, 86, 542–73.

Venti, S. and Wise, D. (1983), 'Individual attributes and self-selection of higher education', *Journal of Public Economics*, 21, 1-32.

Venti, S. and Wise, D. A. (1984), 'Moving and housing expenditure', *Journal of Public Economics*, 16, 207-43.

Waldman, D. M. (1985), 'Computation in duration models with heterogeneity', *Journal of Econometrics, Annals 1985-1*, 28, 127-34.

Wales, T. J. and Woodland, A. D. (1979), 'Labour supply and progressive taxes', *Review of Economic Studies*, 46, 83-95.

Wales, T. J. and Woodland, A. D. (1980), 'Sample selectivity and the estimation of labour supply functions', *International Economic Review*, 21, 437-68.

Wales, T. J. and Woodland, A. D. (1983), 'Estimation of consumer demand systems with binding non-negativity constraints', *Journal of Econometrics*, 21, 437-68.

Watts, H. W. and Rees, A. (eds) (1974), *Final Report of the New Jersey Graduated Work Incentive Experiment*, Institute for Research on Poverty, University of Wisconsin (Madison).

White, H. (1980), 'Nonlinear regression on cross section data', *Econometrica*, 48, 721-46.

White, H. (1982a), 'Maximum likelihood estimation of misspecified models', *Econometrica*, 50, 1-26.

White, H. (1982b), 'Instrumental variables regression with independent observations', *Econometrica*, 50, 483-500.

Willis, R. J. (1973), 'A new approach to the economic theory of fertility', *Journal of Political Economy*, 81 (supplement), S14-64.

Willis, H. R. (1987), 'A note on specification tests for the multinomial logit model', *Journal of Econometrics, Annals 1987-1*, 34, 263-74.

Yatchew, A. J. (1985), 'Labour supply in the presence of taxes: an alternative specification', *Review of Economics and Statistics*, 67, 27-33.

Zabalza, A. (1983), 'The CES utility function, non-linear budget constraints and labour supply. Results on female participation and hours', *Economic Journal*, 93, 312-30.

Zabalza, A., Pissarides, C. and Barton, M. (1980), 'Social security and the choice between full-time work, part-time work and retirement', *Journal of Public Economics*, 14, 245-76.

Index